AF661591

Alternative Dispute Resolution

Along with the Gram Nyayalayas Act 2008

'Justice delayed is justice denied' is the verdict of our apex court which is a milestone of our justice delivery system. But unfortunately a huge number of cases are pending in different courts of our country. There is an urgent need to devise and evolve a new system to provide speedy justice to each person to attain our Constitutional goal. This system is known as the Alternative Dispute Resolution as it provides for settlement of disputes outside the court.

Arbitration and Conciliation is one of the vital limbs of Alternative Dispute Resolution. The Arbitration and Conciliation Act has been amended in 2015 & 2019 and those have received proper treatment in this edition. Besides Arbitration, Negotiation, Minitrial, Lok Adalat, Lokpal, etc. are dealt with in an erudite manner. A separate chapter on 'Plea Bargaining' is included and it discusses its importance, limitation and future. An in-depth study of the Gram Nyayalayas Act has been made in the light of the judgments of the apex court and different High Courts.

The Arbitration and Conciliation Act 1996 has recently got amended through the Arbitration and Conciliation (Amendment) Act 2019 which completely overhauled the provisions relating to 'Appointment of Arbitrator'. The Arbitration Council of India is being introduced having a lead role in the matter. Qualification & experience of an arbitrator and general norms applicable to Arbitrator are also included by this amendment. All such developments are aptly treated in this edition.

Law is not static. It develops as and when the society demands. To meet the requirements of the legal fraternity, a separate chapter on 'Online Alternative Dispute Resolution' has been incorporated. Dar-ul-Qaza (Sharia Courts) as an Alternative Dispute Redressal Forum is newly included, which opens a new window to this subject. Another inclusion in this edition is 'Early Neutral Evaluation', which makes the work comprehensive and indispensable to the Bench and the Bar.

All the important topics relating to ADR like the appointment of arbitrator, power and duties of an arbitrator, cyber arbitration, fast track arbitration, family court, fast track court, fast track procedure, injunction, maintenance and welfare of parents and senior citizens, mediator and Nyaya Panchayat are discussed at length. The book will be a faithful companion to lawyers, students and other stakeholders as well.

Kolkata
Eastern Law House Private Ltd.
54 Ganesh Chunder Avenue
Kolkata 700 013

New Delhi
Eastern Law House Private Ltd.
36 Netaji Subhash Marg, Daryaganj
New Delhi 110 002

Alternative Dispute Resolution

Along with the Gram Nyayalayas Act 2008

by

Sukumar Ray LLM
District & Sessions Judge

SECOND EDITION

KOLKATA NEW DELHI
EASTERN LAW HOUSE

Published and processed by
EASTERN LAW HOUSE PRIVATE LTD.
54 Ganesh Chunder Avenue
Kolkata 700 013
Tel: (033) 2215-1989
Email: mail@elh.co.in
www.elh.co.in

First Edition 2012
Second Edition 2020

© SUKUMAR RAY AND EASTERN LAW HOUSE PRIVATE LTD. 2020

Whilst all reasonable care has been taken to ensure accuracy of the contents of this book, no person associated with the creation or publishing of this book shall have responsibility for any loss or damages that may be caused to any person due to errors or omissions which may have crept in inadvertently in this publication. Disputes, if any, are subject to Kolkata jurisdiction.

ISBN 978-81-7177-352-7

Printed at
Dey's Offset, Kolkata

"A Principle is a principle and in no case
Can it be watered down
Because of our incapacity to live it in practice.
We have to strive to achieve it,
And the striving should be
Conscious, deliberate and hard."

—Mahatma Gandhi

Preface to the Second Edition

Article 39A of the Constitution of India enjoins that the State shall secure that the operation of the legal system promotes justice on a basis of equal opportunity. For the purposes of understanding the present day law, specially, the laws relating to Alternative Dispute Resolution, it is the duty of every law-abiding citizen to realise the law as a social institution to protect and promote the societal interest. True, the past decade has seen more ferment than any previous decade. It is, therefore, time to ponder where we stand and what we are about in the dispute resolution system.

Almost all the chapters of this edition have been reorganized, re-edited and brought up-to-date. Three new chapters, namely, Online Alternative Dispute Resolution, Early Neutral Evaluation and Dar-ul-Qaza (Sharia Courts) as Alternative Dispute Redressal methods have been incorporated. The latest amendment of the Arbitration and Conciliation Act (Act 33 of 2019 dated 9th August 2019) revamping the original Act of 1996 as amended in 2015, has been taken care of at appropriate places. In the second part of the work, section-wise discussion of the Gram Nyayalayas Act 2008 has been made for the members of the legal fraternity to understand the new concepts brought about by the Act. Besides incorporating available case laws, I have given my own views on many important aspects of the topics covered in the book.

I owe a large debt to my colleagues and well wishers who so kindly went out of their way, busy as they are, to express their ideas and stimulate my thinking in some areas.

Hope, this revised edition will receive appreciation of the legal luminaries and other stakeholders who are associated with this kind of Justice Delivery System. The author will be highly inspired if the readers communicate their considered views and suggestions for improvement of the next edition.

Kolkata
4th October 2019

SUKUMAR RAY

Preface to the First Edition

From the time immemorial members of the society are facing lot of difficulties to resolve their dispute and differences. Various foras are constituted to deal with the feud between the disputants. The existence of Panchayat Court is not unknown to us. More than three cores of cases are pending in our country. In order to get rid of this problem and to reduce the huge pendency of cases legal luminaries are thinking and evolving a new technique and new method. This method is popularly known as Alternative Dispute Resolution Mechanism. The greatest sensation of life is the presentation of a new and growing subject in a lucid manner so that the persons interested in the subject can acquire knowledge or quest or search for some thing. The book primarily attempts to explain the various statutory provisions which deal with the techniques of resolving dispute out of Court. Many intricate aspects of the subject have been explained briefly.

This book is divided in seventeen chapters. From chapter one to fifteen, I have explained the different types of ADR techniques and tools, their historical retrospective, procedure followed in the said forum and their advantages. In chapter sixteen of the book, I have set out in detail with analytical approach the Gram Nyayalayas Act 2008 to present a through knowledge on the said statute. In Chapter seventeen of the book, I have briefly explained and summarized the future and prospects of the Alternative Dispute Resolution System. In order to make the book useful and helpful, method of appointment of arbitrator(s), procedure of reference of dispute under section 89, Civil Procedure Code, powers of family court, plea bargaining, compounding of offences, disposal of cases through Lok Adalat, recall of order by Lok Adalat etc. have been discussed with the help of the cases decided by the Supreme Court and different High Courts.

I express my deep gratitude to my father Madan Gopal Ray and my mother Smt. Seba Ray for their inspiration in the preparation of the book. I convey my thanks to my wife Nita Ray and my sweet son Master Sayak Ray for their help and assistance in writing this book.

I also pay deep regard and gratitude to Mr. B.S. Saluja, Secretary-General of the International Centre for Alternative Dispute Resolution, New Delhi to provide me the ICADR Rules on Arbitration, Conciliation and Minitrial and accord me necessary permission to use the same in my book.

I am also grateful to Shri Somnath Chakraborty of Eastern Law House Private Ltd. for rendering valuable suggestions from time to time to give a proper shape to this book.

I am obliged to Shri Asok De, Director of Eastern Law House Private Ltd. who has taken special initiative to bring out this book.

I hope and believe that this book will serve the purpose for which it is meant.

Any suggestions for improvement of this book will be respectfully acknowledged by me.

Kolkata
16th January 2012

SUKUMAR RAY

Contents

PART TWO PAGE

The Gram Nyayalayas Act 2008—*continued*

PART TWO PAGE

The Gram Nyayalayas Act 2008—*continued*

Appendices

Table of Cases

Introduction

India is a Sovereign Socialist Secular Democratic Republic. The constitutional goal is to set up an egalitarian society and to secure to all its citizens—Justice, social, economic and political. The creation of new forum for determination of dispute and differences in an easy, simple, uncomplicated manner with people's participation in the dispensation of Justice is a constitutional mandate. The object of justice is mainly two-fold: first, to determine the rights of the parties and secondly to provide remedy. Procedural justice has now acquired new dimensions and new look. The modern slogan is: Justice must be effective, speedy, less costly and non-cumbersome. It is true that justice should not be done in a manner which would have the effect of doing away with of justice. Our justice delivery system suffers from the following ailments: (1) Procedural delay in disposal of cases; (2) Complicated procedure; (3) High cost of litigation; (4) Limited number of judges. There is a crude Bengali saying, "Be thee encumbered with litigations" so that others may rope the benefit unjustly. In our society it has become a growing menace on the part of unscrupulous persons to rope in innocent citizens by using the weapon of litigation by falsely making frivolous complaint by misusing the provision of law to foster a new legal terrorism with personal vendetta, the oblique object being to unleash harassment and to soil the unsoiled image and integrity of the innocuous human being in the eye of the people of the society. It is preferable to refer the advice of Abraham Lincon: "Discourage litigation. Persuade your neighbours, make composition whenever you can. As a peace-maker one should encourage being a good human being, to refrain from resorting to lies. There will, still, be business enough." The Apex Court by making in-depth studies of the state of affairs prevailing over the flood gates of litigation in our country whether litigious or non-litigious legal works, has evolved a fair theory of composition of cases and suits for effective and speedy redressal of legal proliferation nowadays, the solemn object being to generate healthy and harmonious co-existence of the people in the society from any bickerings and that lawyers of legal profession have got an important role to play to give a true, transparent, meaningful shape of the said thoughts in reality in the context of the present social scenario and to make the wheel in the justice delivery system in our country less burdensome form the pangs of frivolous litigation consuming unnecessary time; social awareness should be propagated in every stage of the society so that unjustified legal actions are not allowed to continue for years together causing unnecessary misery and sufferings to others in the present day democratic system.

To overcome the delay and to provide effective justice to the consumer of justice, it has become imperative that resort should be had to Alternative Dispute Resolution Mechanism with a view to bringing an end to litigation between the parties at an early date. The Supreme Court in *Salem Advocate Bar Association, Tamil Nadu* v *Union of India*[1] observed: "In certain countries of the world where ADR has been successful to the extent that over 90 per cent of the cases are settled out of court, there is a requirement that the parties to the suit must indicate the form of ADR which they would like to resort to during the pendency of the trial of the suit."

Justification for ADR In the words of John Rawls,[2] "Justice is the first virtue of social institution, as truth is of systems of thought." It is one of the basic principles of justice system is that everyone knows and accepts the same principles of justice—social or

1 AIR 2003 SC 189; 2002 AIR SCW 4627; (2003)1 SCC 49.
2 A *Theory of Justice*, 3rd Indian Reprint, 2008, p. 3.

natural. In order to establish a bond of friendship and to fulfil the 'fundamental character of a well-ordered human association' easy justice and less costly justice is the need and cry of the day. Different authors justify the introduction of ADR system to get rid of the workload of the court from different view-points. Professor Riskin and Westbrook[3] sketched five points of justification. They are as under:

> "Five motives, often intermingled, five most of the current interest in alternatives to traditional litigation: (1) Saving time and money, and possibly rescuing the judicial system from an overload; (2) Having 'better' processes—more open, flexible and responsive to the unique needs of the participants... (3) Achieving 'better' results-outcomes that serve the real needs of the participants or society; (4) Enhancing community involvement in the dispute resolution process; and (5) Broadening access to 'justice'."

Stephen B. Goldberg et. al. in the book *Dispute Resolution: Negotiation, Meditation and other Processes*[4] classically explained the justification of expansion of ADR mechanism. The said author mentions the following nine causes for the growth of ADR system: (*i*) To lower court caseloads and expenses; (*ii*) To reduce the parties' expenses and time; (*iii*) To provide speedy settlement of those disputes that were disruptive of the community or the lives of the parties' families; (*iv*) To improve public satisfaction with the justice system; (*v*) To encourage resolutions that were suited to the parties' needs; (*vi*) To increase voluntary compliance with resolutions; (*vii*) To restore the influence of neighbourhood and community values and cohesiveness of communities; (*viii*) To provide accessible forums to people with disputes, and (*ix*) To teach the public to try more effective processes than violence or litigation for settling disputes.

Object The object of the alternative dispute resolution process of arbitration is to have expeditious and effective disposal of the disputes through a private forum of the parties' choice.

3 *Dispute Resolution and Lawyers*, 2nd Ed. 1998, p. 31.
4 3rd Ed. 1999, pp. 6-9.

Advantages of ADR To give a quick, effective relief alternative dispute resolution for disposal of cases expeditiously is the urgent need of the day.

- It will render speedy relief to the parties.
- It can be used at any stage of the proceedings.
- It is a more time-saving process to resolve the dispute compared with traditional court-practice and procedure.
- It will reduce the burden of the court.
- Presence of lawyer is not necessary. The lawyer can assist the court and help the parties to understand the complicated questions of law or issues involved in the process.
- It can provide better solution to the litigants as expeditiously as possible. The parties can settle their dispute by a day or by few days.
- Parties have every right to approach the regular court when they fail to arrive at a settlement.
- Statement of the parties cannot be used as an admission in court proceedings if the parties fail to arrive at a settlement.
- Parties to the litigations are the best judge to resolve the dispute in a congenial manner.
- The efficacy involving in composition-oriented justice by holding free and frank deliberation and confabulation across the table would get both the parties satisfied from their respective own stand point because the parties become themselves being the spokesman and can have full-fledged right and liberty to express their own grievance and, upon settlement or composition, both the parties would leave the arena with joyous satisfaction without leaving anything unexplored.
- The procedures are flexible. Procedures are not affected with rigors of strict rules and procedures.

- Technicalities of law and procedures, rules of evidence have no place in ADR mechanism.
- Parties can take the help of a neutral person specialized in the field of the subject which is the subject-matter of dispute.

Goals S. Goldberg, E.R. Green and F.A. Sandar, on book titled as *Dispute Resolution*[5] mentioned four important goals of ADR:

- To relieve court congestion as well as undue cost and delay;
- To enhance community involvement in the dispute resolution process;
- To facilitate access to justice; and
- To provide more effective dispute resolution.

Themes of ADR movement The main themes of ADR movement are First, people involved in disputes at all levels of society are looking for quick, simple, confidential, and inexpensive methods to resolve their differences.

Secondly, the legal community made up of attorney, judges, law scholars and lawmakers, has become increasingly concerned about the need to conserve scarce court services for the resolution of complex business and commercial disputes, and to find more appropriate fora for resolving less complex matters such as consumer complaints and some family issues.

Thirdly, those concerned with social and civil rights desire to make justice more accessible to disadvantaged members of society who cannot afford the costs and delays of traditional litigation.

Fourthly, there is the widespread desire to develop higher quality techniques for resolving disputes that will focus on the underlying needs of the disputing parties, empower them to mutually resolve their differences, and result in more satisfactory outcomes.[6]

5 Little Brown, Boston, 1985, p. 6.

6 Susan Patterson & Grant Seabolt, *Essentials of Alternative Dispute Resolution*, p. 3; J. Murry, A. Ran and E. Sherman, *Process of Dispute Resolution—The Role of the Lawyers*, Notes for Teachers, I-13 (1990).

Meaning of Alternative Dispute Resolution The term refers to procedure for settling disputes by means other than litigation, *e.g.* by arbitration, mediation, mini trials. Such procedures, which are usually less costly and more expeditious an increasingly being used in commercial and labour disputes, divorce actions, in resolving motor vehicle and medical malpractice, tax-claims and in other disputes that would likely otherwise involve court litigation.

Alternative Dispute Resolution also mean and include arbitration, conciliation and mediation, negotiation, as well as variety of hybrid procedures, including mediation, last offer arbitration (MEDOLA), mini trial, and neutral evaluation. It is a term for describing the processes of resolving disputes in place of litigation and includes mediation, conciliation, expert determination and early neutral evaluation. Alternative Dispute Resolution is defined as any procedure for setting a dispute by means other than litigation, as by arbitration or mediation.[7]

According to *Halsbury's Laws of England*,[8] Alternative Dispute Resolution (ADR) is a term for describing the processes of resolving disputes in place of litigation and includes mediation, conciliation, expert determination, and early neutral evaluation. It is not unusual for arbitration to be classed as a form of ADR, but this is potentially misleading. In many important respects arbitration has more in common with court-based litigation than with the forms of ADR listed above. Unlike arbitration, none of these forms of ADR have a statutory basis.

Characteristics of ADR system ADR is the "creation of incentives or pressures that force litigants to settle". It has immense comparative value. The features of ADR system are as follows:

- Access is limited to the person who has some interest or claims under the dispute.
- The parties to the dispute have the power to choose their own judge.

7 *Black's Law Dictionary*, 10th Ed. 2014.

8 *Halsbury's Laws of England*, 4th Ed. Reissue, vol. 2(3), para 4, p. 5.

- To commence proceeding and terminate the action consent of the court is immaterial.
- Proceedings are held in public.
- Arbitrator/mediator/conciliator/umpire can resolve the dispute by invoking the own procedure suited in the case.
- The parties may directly participate in the proceedings.
- The disputants bear the cost of the proceedings.
- Modes of proof and argument are competitive and partisan.
- The techniques of ADR are extra-judicial in nature.

Importance of Alternative Dispute Resolution

(1) *Choice of mediator* A mediator can be chosen who has expertise in negotiation, effective dispute resolution and in the particular areas of dispute. Such expertise may be of assistance to the parties in resolving the dispute.

(2) *Problem centered* The mediation process focuses on the interests and underlying concerns of the parties as opposed to their legal rights and remedies in searching for a resolution.

(3) *Control* Each of the parties maintain control of the dispute and its resolution because they design the settlement and agree to live by it that is acceptable to them.

(4) *Privacy* Mediation takes place in private and therefore the details of the dispute and its resolution need not be publicly disclosed.

(5) *Freedom to negotiate* Because the process is confidential and takes place on a without prejudice basis the parties have the freedom to develop and consider innovative settlement idea.

(6) *Enhanced negotiations* The focus of a mediator on the negotiation process can help keep the negotiations on track and moving forward.

(7) *Informal atmosphere* The informal setting and atmosphere of mediation is conducive to effective communication between the parties about what each needs in the agreement.

(8) *Improved relationship* Mediation can preserve or enhance the relationship between the parties.

(9) *Day in court* In mediation, the parties have a full opportunity to be heard and to vent the emotional side of the dispute. This process allows them to move towards considering settlement much more quickly than through indirect negotiations.

(10) *Voluntary* The mediation process is entirely voluntary and accordingly, either party can leave the process at any moment should they feel that it is no longer progressing or that they are somehow being prejudiced by the process.

PART ONE

Chapter 1

Arbitration

Arbitration—meaning The word arbitration is a noun. *Oxford Advanced Learner's Dictionary,*[1] defines arbitration as official process of settling an argument or a disagreement by somebody who is not involved.

According to the *New Encyclopaedia Britannica,*[2] arbitration is a legal method of settling disputes between parties outside ordinary court procedures by deferring to a mutually agreed upon third party who has the authority to determine an "award", a legally binding decision.

Arbitration is most commonly resorted to in cases involving commercial disputes, but it is also practiced in resolving disputes between labour unions and management and in international controversies between sovereign States where diplomatic channels are not sufficient.

According to *Halsbury's Laws of England,*[3] arbitration is a process used by the agreement of the parties to resolve disputes. In arbitrations, disputes are resolved, with binding effect, by a person or persons acting in a judicial manner in private, rather than by a national court of law that would have jurisdiction but for the agreement of the parties to exclude it. The decision of the arbitral tribunal is usually called an award.

1 *Oxford Advanced Learner's Dictionary,* 9th Ed., p. 65.
2 *New Encyclopaedia Britannica,* 15th Ed., vol. I., p. 521.
3 *Halsbury's Laws of England,* 4th Ed. Reissue, vol. 2(3), p. 2.

According to *Black's Law Dictionary*,[4] arbitration is a dispute resolution process in which the disputing parties choose one or more neutral third parties to make a final and binding decision resolving the dispute.

In *Collins* v *Collins*,[5] the court defined 'arbitration' as "an arbitration is a reference to the decision of one or more person, either with or without an umpire, of a particular matter in difference between the parties".

According to *Chambers 21st Century Dictionary*,[6] arbitration is the settling of a dispute, especially an industrial one, between two or more groups by some neutral person who is acceptable to all concerned.

According to *K.J. Aiyar's Judicial Dictionary*,[7] arbitration connotes the adjudication of a dispute by judge appointed by or with the agreement of the parties, such adjudication to be in accordance with the agreement, to the extent permitted by the law.

According to the *New International Webster's Comprehensive Dictionary*,[8] arbitration is the hearing and settlement of a dispute between two parties by the decision of a third party or court to which the matter is referred by the contestants as a means of avoiding war, a strike, a lawsuit, etc.

An arbitration is an extra judicial determination of a controversy by one or more unofficial persons chosen by the parties as a domestic tribunal for the purpose of settling the disputed matter submitted to it for decision and award. It provides a summary and inexpensive method of settling disputes and is encouraged by the courts because of its economy, freedom from technicalities and business-like method of resolving differences. Every arbitration agreement must be liberally construed so as to

4 *Black's Law Dictionary*, 10th Ed. 2014.

5 [1858]26 Beav 306; 28 LJ Ch 186; 53 ER 916; see also *Stroud's Judicial Dictionary*, 5th Ed., vol. 1, p. 169.

6 *Chambers 21st Century Distionary*, p. 64.

7 *Aiyar's Judicial Dictionary*, 13th Ed., p. 96.

8 *New International Webster's Comprehensive Dictionary*, Encyclopedic Ed. 2003, p. 74.

give effect to the intention of the parties and every award must be considered regular, if on the face of it, it is unimpeachable.[9]

History of arbitration In India, there is a long history of arbitration. Arbitration is a mode of settlement of disputes evolved by the society for adjudication and settlement of the disputes and the differences between the parties apart from the courts of law. Arbitration has a tradition, it has a purpose. Arbitration that is a reference of any particular dispute by consent of the parties, to one or more persons chosen by the parties with or without an umpire and an award enforceable by the sovereign power were generally unknown to ancient India. Hindus recognized decisions of Panchayats or bodies consisting of wealthy, influential and elderly men of the community and entrusted them with the power of management of their religions and social functions. The sanction against disobedience to their decision was excommunication, or ostracism and exclusion from all religions and social functions of the community.

We find no specific name of courts or judicial institutions during Vedic age. But village headman or elders resolve the dispute through the process of discussion and deliberation in the *Sabha.* So, there was in existence of *Sabha* in the *Rig Vedic* period[10] which consist of men of high social status and distinction. It is headed by *Sabhapati*, who has the control over the functions of the society and community. Village people also settle their issues through *Samiti* which exercises regular control over king or king's function. Yajnavalkya[11] mentioned three types of institutions to resolve or decide disputes as Puga (*sabha* or assemblies of influential and aged men of the community), Sreni (corporations) and Kula (Council). Brishaspati refers another type of Arbitrator namely *Apratisthita*. It has no fixed place to seat. It is a mobile court like institution to provide justice at the door. Narada provides two types of authorities, i.e. *Kulani* (village council) and *Gana* (assemblies). Kautilya in his master work

9 *Damodar Pershad Gupta* v *Saxena & Co., Delhi* AIR 1958 Punj 476; 1958(60) Pun LR 638.

10 Gautama: *Dharma Sutra*, s-1, p. 1-4.

11 S.N. Bhattacharjee, *Administration of Law and Justice in India*, pp. 93-95.

'Arthasastra' refers *'gramavriddha'* chairman of the village assembly and resolving of dispute by mahattara of the village with the help of five men of the locality (village panch). Arbitration or mediation without the intervention of the court ought undoubtedly to be permitted in India. It is indeed a striking feature of ordinary Indian life and it prevails in all ranks of life to a much greater extent than is the case in England. To refer matters to a panch is one of the natural ways of deciding many a dispute in India.[12] It may be that in some cases the panch more resembles a judicial court because the panch may intervene on the complaint of one party and not necessarily on the agreement of both, e.g. in a caste matter. But there are many cases where the decision is given by agreement between the parties. In the Sanchi inscription of Chandra Gupta-I, there was existence of panchamandali. In the words of great jurist Dr. P. V. Kane all the judicial institutions referred by Yajnavalkya and Narada were actually arbitration tribunals similar with modern day Nyaya Panchayats. In the Great Epic Mahabharata we find the concept of Arbitrator or mediator. Lord Krishna acts as a role of a mediator between Pandava and Kaurava to avoid the war between the two. Sometimes he also acts as an Arbitrator to request the Kauravas to provide at least five villages to Pandavas and to pursued the Kauravas to accent his proposal. Law Commission of India in its 76th Report[13] discussed the arbitration system or village judicial system in ancient India in the following manner:

> ".......... the villagers had a judicial system of their own, which was familiar and respected by them; the various traders and guilds has a similar system.
>
> "The *puga* courts were comprised of persons dwelling in the same place, irrespective of their caste or employment, and were competent to decide cases in which the local public were interested.
>
> "The *srenis* (guilds) were associations of persons engaged. In similar pursuits, of which the merchant's guilds were

12 *Chanbasappa* v *Baslingayya* AIR 1927 Bom 565.

13 November 1978, p. 5.

the most important. They were competent to decide matters relating to their special calling for traders.

"Social matters concerning the members of a particular community could be investigated and decided at the level of the Kulas.

"The three arbitration courts (Kula, Sreni and Puga or Gana), were private tribunals, in the sense that they were not constituted by a royal authority and they resembled Arbitrators to that extent."

Dr. Priyanath Sen in his Tagore Law Lectures on *The General Principles of Hindu Jurisprudence*[14] classically explained the structure and procedure of arbitration courts during ancient period and their role to decide the disputes which came up before them and observed: "families, corporations, and communities may also be charged with the decision of judicial proceedings. It must, however, be understood that these could only decide disputes which came within their special province, being disputes relating to matters which, from their very nature, fell within their special knowledge, for instance, disputes regarding trade and other local concerns. These local courts had a sort of delegated authority within their limited spheres, but their decisions were subject to appeal in the following order; a case having been decided by a family, an appeal, lay to the corporation, by a corporation to the community, and by a community to the officers appointed by the king, or in other words, to the court properly constituted to try all disputes. Narada adds that a decision arrived at by the king's court from which the king is absent is appealable to the king himself."

In brief, in the age of Smriti Sastras there were provisions for delivery of justice through assemblies of men or assessors (Pugah Srenaya). In the age of Katyayana family members are also authorised to settle family dispute by way of family gatherings. Brihaspati also empowered the elatives to try the lesses offences committed by their kingsman. Vyas in his Smriti Sastra provides that kind some times took the assistance of experts or neutral

14 Priyanath Sen, *The General Principles of Hindu Jurisprudence*, p. 363.

person to adjudicate the disputes between merchants and artisans, artisans and actors *Sukranitisara* refers families, associations or corporations as subordinate courts aside the court of king. In the early of civilization there was a popular saying that *panch parameswara*, i.e. decision of five is supreme and it is as good as the decision of Almighty. It has some divine character.

Arbitration during British period The function of Panchayat system prevails in India since the time immemorial. During British rule Panchayat is out of the means of settlement of dispute. Bengal Regulations 1772 and 1781 made a provision that parties can refer the dispute to the Arbitrator and such Arbitrator must be appointed by mutual agreement of the parties and the award shall tentamounts to a decree of a civil court. The award of the Arbitrator may be set aside by the evidence of two credible witness on the ground that; (*i*) the Arbitrator or Arbitrators has or have been guilty of gross corruption; or (*ii*) he or they has/have been partially to the cause in which he/they had made his/their awards. The Regulation of 1781 limited the scope of appeal or review against the order of the Arbitrators because they are appointed by the parties themselves out of their own will or the parties have free choice to select the Arbitrator or third umpire according to their own choice. In 1787 Lord Cornwallis made Regulation. This Regulation empowered the court to refer the dispute for arbitration with the consent of the parties. One of the demerits of the said Regulation is that there is no provision in the Regulation that what is the consequence if the award is not made in time. In the year 1793 Regulation XVI of 1793 was enacted to encourage settlement of dispute through arbitration. The main features of the Regulation are as follows:

- It empowered the court to refer dispute to Arbitrator with the consent of the parties.
- The suits must be related to suits for accounts, partnership debts and breach of contract.
- Valuation of the suit does not exceed 200 sicca rupees.

The Regulations of 1795 and 1803 extended the territorial operation regarding arbitration proceedings to Banarus also. Regulations of the year 1814, 1822 and 1833 extended the scope and jurisdiction of arbitration proceedings in different manner to provide it more effective and meaningful.

Regulation 6 of 1813 provides that arbitration proceedings are applicable to disputes relating to land.

Madras Regulation IV of 1816, Madras Regulation V of 1816 formulated a scheme for working of the Panchayat system in villages and to encourage the village people to workout their problems. Bombay Regulation IV of 1827 and Regulation VII of 1827 created an unique provision for arbitration. It provided for arbitration through their intervention of the court with one rider that suit must not be pending. In the year 1859 the Act VII of 1859 was passed and it codified the procedure of civil courts. Provision of arbitration were incorporated in Chapter VI of the Act.

Arbitration was provided in ss. 312 to 315 of the Act VIII of 1859. In the year 1862 the scope of the Act VIII of 1859 was extended to courts in the presidency towns. The provisions of the VIII of 1859 were repealed by Act X of 1877. The Code of Civil Procedure was thoroughly revised in the year 1882 and Act XIV of 1882 was passed by the British Parliament and it made no change regarding provisions of arbitrations contained in the ss. 506 to 526 of the earlier Act. Before 1899 there was no exclusive enactment dealing with the arbitration. In the year 1899 (Act IX of 1899) was passed. It is applicable to three presidency towns-namely Calcutta, Bombay and Madras. It is also provided for arbitration by agreement without the intervention of the court. This Act resembles the English Arbitration Act of 1889. In the year 1908 the Code of Civil Procedure was enacted and it repealed the earlier Code of 1859. Section 89 and Second Schedule of the Code contained detailed provisions of arbitration in respect of the subject matter of the suit or settlement of dispute through arbitration without the intervention of the court. The Act of 1899 and to make a comprehensive law of arbitration a committee under the Chairmanship of Sir Erle Richards was constituted and it submitted its report on 1927. To review the law of arbitration Shri Ratan Mohan Chatterjee was appointed as special officer and after consideration of the report of Shri Chatterjee, Arbitration Act 1940 was passed. It was a consolidated Act.

Background of the new Act The procedure laid down in the Act of 1940 is technical and it failed to fulfill the demands of the litigants. The Legislature felt that Law of Arbitration must be simple and it should not be hyper technical. In *Food Corporation of India* v *Joginderpal Mohinderpal*[15] the Apex Court observed: "the function of courts of law to oversee that the Arbitrators act within the norms of justice. Once they do so and the award is clear, just and fair, the courts should, as far as possible, give effect to the award of the parties and make the parties compel to adhere to and obey the decision of their chosen adjudicator. It is in this perspective that one should view the scope and limit of correction by the court of an award made by the Arbitrator. We should make the law of arbitration simple, less technical and more responsible to the actual realities of the situations but must be responsive to the canons of justice and fair play and make the Arbitrator adhere to such process and norms which will create confidence, not only by doing justice between the parties, but by creating sense that justice appears to have been done". Again the court observed:[16]

> "Arbitration is a mode of settlement of disputes evolved by the society for adjudication and settlement of the disputes and the differences between the parties apart from the courts of law. Arbitration has a tradition, it has a purpose. Arbitration, that is a reference of any particular dispute by consent of the parties to one or more person chosen by the parties with or without an umpire and an award enforceable by the sovereign power were generally unknown to ancient India. Hindus recognised decisions of Panchayats or bodies consisting of wealthy, influential and elderly men of the community and entrusted them with the power of management of their religions and social functions. The sanction against disobedience to their decision was excommunication, or ostracism and exclusion from all religions and social functions of the community."

15 *Food Corporation of India* v *Joginderpal Mohinderpal* AIR 1989 SC 1263; JT 1989(2) SC 89; (1989)2 SCC 347.

16 *Ibid.*

"It has a social purpose to fulfill today. It has a great urgency today when there has been an explosion of litigations in the courts of law established by the sovereign power. New rights created, or awareness of these rights, the erosion of faith in the intrinsic sense of fairness of men, intolerant and uncompromising attitudes are all the factors which block our courts. The courts are full of litigations, which are pending for long time. Therefore, it should be the endeavour of those who are interested in the administration of justice to help settlement by arbitration, if possible. It has also a social efficacy being the decision by the consent of the parties. It has greater scope of acceptance today when there is a certain erosion of faith in view of the failure to appreciating the functions of the courts of law. It has also the advantage of not quickness of decision but of simplicity of procedure. But in proceedings of arbitration there must be adherence to justice, equity, law and fair play in actions. However, the proceedings of arbitration must adhere to the principles of natural justice and must be in consonance with such practice and procedure which will lead to a proper resolution of the dispute and create confidence of the people for whose benefit these processes are resorted to."

Different kinds of arbitration Arbitration may be (*i*) voluntary, i.e. under an arbitration agreement entered into between the parties, or (*ii*) statutory, i.e. under the provisions of a statute which specifically provides for arbitration.

Statutory arbitration The provisions of s. 2(4) of the Arbitration and Conciliation Act are divided into three parts. First, there is a deeming clause that the statute concerned shall be deemed to be an arbitration agreement and arbitration under that statute shall be deemed to be pursuant to that arbitration agreement. Secondly, there is a clause extending the provisions of Part I of the Arbitration and Conciliation Act 1996, to statutory arbitrations except certain specified sections; namely ss. 40(1), 41 and 43. Thirdly, there is an exception clause providing that provisions of Part I of the Act in so far as they are inconsistent with the enactment and rules of another statutory arbitration shall not apply to that arbitration.[17]

Arbitration agreement "Arbitration agreement" means an agreement by the parties to submit to arbitration all or certain disputes which have arisen or which may arise between them in respect of a defined legal relationship, whether contractual or not.[18]

An arbitration agreement may be in the form of an arbitration clause in a contract of in the form of a separate agreement.[19] An arbitration agreement shall be in writing.[20] An arbitration agreement is in writing if it is contained in—

(*a*) a document signed by the parties;

(*b*) an exchange of letters, telex, telegrams or other means of telecommunication including communication through electronic means which provide a record of the agreement; or

(*c*) an exchange of statements of claim and defence in which the existence of the agreement is alleged by one party and not denied by the other.[1]

The reference in a contract to a document containing an arbitration clause constitutes an arbitration agreement if the contract is in writing and the reference is such as to make that arbitration clause part of the contract.[2]

Russell states "Normally, it will only be appropriate to commence arbitral proceedings once a dispute has arisen between the parties. This is reflected in the fact that most arbitration agreement refer specifically to 'disputes' or 'differences' being submitted to arbitration, and in such cases a tribunal will not have jurisdiction to deal with the matter until a dispute or difference has arisen which has been referred to them for determination."[3]

17 S.K. Chawla, *Law of Arbitration & Conciliation including other ADRs*, 3rd Ed., p. 184.
18 Section 7(1), the Arbitration and Conciliations Act 1996.
19 Section 7(2).
20 Section 7(3).
1 Section 7(4).
2 Section 7(5).
3 Russell on *Arbitration*, 23rd Ed., pp. 182-183.

Essentials Among the attributes which must be present for an agreement to be considered as an arbitration agreement are:[4]

(1) The arbitration agreement must contemplate that the decision of the tribunal will be binding on the parties to the agreement.

(2) That the jurisdiction of the tribunals to decide the rights of parties must derive either from the consent of the parties or from an order of the court or from a statute, the terms of which make it clear that the process is to be an arbitration.

(3) The agreement must contemplate that substantive rights of parties will be determined by the agreed tribunal.

(4) That the tribunal will determine the rights of the parties in an impartial and judicial manner with the tribunal owing an equal obligation of fairness towards both sides.

(5) That the agreement of the parties to refer their disputes to the decision of the tribunal must be intended to be enforceable in law and lastly.

(6) The agreement must contemplate that the tribunal will make a decision upon a dispute which is already formulated at the time when a reference is made to the tribunal.

Section 7 of the Arbitration and Conciliation Act 1996 requires an arbitration agreement to be in writing and sub-sec. (4) describes the kind of that writing. There is nothing in s. 7 to indicate the requirement of the numbers of Arbitrators as a part of the arbitration agreement. The validity of an arbitration agreement does not depend on the number of Arbitrators specified therein. An arbitration agreement specifying an even number of Arbitrators cannot be a ground to render the arbitration agreement invalid.[5]

4 *K.K. Modi* v *K.N. Modi* AIR 1998 SC 1297; JT 1998(1) SC 407; (1998)3 SCC 573.

5 *M.M.T.C. Limited* v *Sterlite Industries (India) Ltd.* (1996)6 SCC 716.

Test A clause in a contract can be construed as an "arbitration agreement" only if an agreement to refer disputes or differences to arbitration is expressly or impliedly spelt out from the clause. The well-settled principles in regard to what constitutes an arbitration agreement are.[6]

(*i*) The intention of the parties to enter into an arbitration agreement shall have to be gathered from the terms of the agreement. If the terms of the agreement clearly indicate an intention on the part of the parties to the agreement to refer their disputes to a private tribunal for adjudication and a willingness to be bound by the decision of such tribunal on such disputes, it is arbitration agreement. While there is no specific form of an arbitration agreement, the words used should disclose a determination and obligation to go to arbitration and not merely contemplate the possibility of going for arbitration. Where there is merely possibility of the parties agreeing to arbitration in future, as contrasted from an obligation to refer disputes to arbitration, there is no valid and binding arbitration agreement.

(*ii*) Even if the words "arbitration" and "Arbitral Tribunal" (or "Arbitrator") are not used with reference to the process of settlement or with reference to the private tribunal which has to adjudicate upon the disputes, in a clause relating to settlement of disputes, it does not detract from the clause being an arbitration agreement if it has the attributes or elements of an arbitration agreement. They are: (*a*) The agreement should be in writing. (*b*) The parties should have agreed to refer any disputes (present or future) between them to the decision of a private tribunal. (*c*) The private tribunal should be empowered to adjudicate upon the disputes in an impartial manner, giving due opportunity to the parties to put forth their case before it. (*d*) The parties should have agreed that the decision of the private tribunal in respect of the disputes will be binding on them.

(*iii*) Where the clause provides that in the event of disputes arising between the parties, the disputes shall be referred to arbitration, it is an arbitration agreement. Where there is a specific and direct expression of intent to have the disputes

6 *Jagdish Chander* v *Ramesh Chander* (2007)5 SCC 719.

settled by arbitration, it is not necessary to set out the attributes of an arbitration agreement to make it an arbitration agreement. But here the clause relating to settlement of disputes, contains words which specifically exclude any of the attributes of an arbitration agreement or contains anything that detracts from an arbitration agreement, it will not be an arbitration agreement. For example, where an agreement requires or permits an authority to act in the interests of only one of the parties, or provides that the decision of the authority will not be final and binding on the parties, or that if either party is not satisfied with the decision of the authority, he may file a civil suit seeking relief, it cannot be termed as an arbitration agreement.

(*iv*) But mere use of the word "arbitration" or "Arbitrator" in a clause will not make it an arbitration agreement, if it requires or contemplates a further or fresh consent of the parties for reference to arbitration. For example, use of words such as "parties can, if they so desire, refer their disputes to arbitration" or "in the event of any dispute, the parties may also agree to refer the same to arbitration" or "if any disputes arise between the parties, they should consider settlement by arbitration" in a clause relating to settlement of disputes, indicate that the clause is not intended to be an arbitration agreement. Similarly, a clause which states that "if the parties so decide, the disputes shall be referred to arbitration" or "any disputes between parties, if they so agree, shall be referred to arbitration" is not an arbitration agreement. Such clauses merely indicate a desire or hope to have the disputes settled by arbitration, or a tentative arrangement to explore arbitration as mode of settlement if and when a dispute arises. Such clauses require the parties to arrive at a further agreement to go to arbitration, as and when the disputes arise. Any agreement or clause in an agreement requiring or contemplating a further consent or consensus before a reference to arbitration, is not an arbitration agreement, but an agreement to enter into an arbitration agreement in future.

Where existence of an arbitration agreement can be found, apart from the existence of the original agreement, the court would construe the agreement in such a manner so as to uphold the arbitration agreement. However, when a question of fraud is raised, the same has to be considered differently. Fraud, as is well known vitiates all solemn acts. A contract would mean a valid contract; an arbitration agreement would mean an agreement which is enforceable in law.[7]

Existence of dispute—pre-requisite for assumption of jurisdiction The existence of a dispute covered by the relevant arbitration clause in question is an essential condition and pre-requisite for assumption of jurisdiction by an Arbitrator. A dispute implies an assertion of a right by one party and repudiation thereof by another.[8]

Arbitral award—must be certain An award ought to be certian, so that no reasonable doubt can arise upon the face of it as to the Arbitrator's meaning, or as to the nature and extent of the duties imposed by it on the parties.[9]

Mere signature—not a waiver Mere signature by a party to an award does not necessarily in all cases estop of him from disputing the correctness of the award.[10]

Attributes of arbitration clause The main attributes of arbitration clause are[11]—(1) An arbitration clause is a collateral term of a contract as distinguished from its substantive terms; but none the less it is an integral part of it; (2) however comprehensive the terms of an arbitration clause may be, the existence of the contract is a necessary condition for its operation, it perishes with the contract; (3) the contract may be *non est* in the sense that it never came legally into existence or it was void *ab initio*; (4) though the contract was validly executed, the parties may put an end to it as if it had never existed and substitute a new contract for it solely governing their rights and liabilities thereunder; (5) in the former case, if the original contract has no legal existence, the arbitration clause also cannot operate,

7 *India Household and Health Care Ltd.* v *LG Household and Health Care Ltd.* AIR 2007 SC 1376; (2007)5 SCC 510; (2007)4 Scale 150.

8 *Nanalal M. Varma & Co. Ltd.* v *Alexandra Jute Mills Ltd.* AIR 1989 Cal 6.

9 *Lal Jagroop Singh* v *B.R. Bahadurpal Singh* AIR 1916 Oudh 160.

10 *Gunnu Meah* v *A. Rahaman* AIR 1929 Rang 166.

11 *Union of India* v *Kishorilal* AIR 1959 SC 1362; (1960)1 SCR 493.

for along with the original contract, it is also void; in the latter case, as the original contract is extinguished by the substituted one, the arbitration clause of the original contract perishes with it; and (6) between the two falls many categories of disputes in connection with a contract, such as the question of repudiation, frustration, breach etc.

Repudiation by one party—effect A contract is the creature of an agreement between the parties and where the parties under the terms of the contract agree to incorporate an arbitration clause, that clause stands apart from the rights and obligations under that contract, as it has been incorporated with the object of providing a machinery for the settlement of disputes arising in relation to or in connection with that contract. The questions of unilateral repudiation of the rights and obligations under the contract or of a full and final settlement of the contract relate to the performance or discharge of the contract. Far from putting an end to the arbitration clause, they fall within the purview of it. A repudiation by one party alone does not terminate the contract. It takes two to end it, and hence it follows that as the contract subsists for the determination of the rights and obligations of the parties, the arbitration clause also survives.[12]

Repudiation and breach of contract—effect In case of repudiation, frustration and breach of contract, the performance of the contract that has come to an end, but the contract is still in existence for certain purposes in respect of disputes arising under it or in connection with it. As the contract subsists for certain purposes, the arbitration clause operates in respect of these purposes.[13]

Limitation Act—applicability The Limitation Act applies to arbitration proceedings and the period visualised by different provisions of the Limitation Act would decide the question of limitation in an arbitration proceeding.[14]

12 *Damodar Valley Corporation* v *K.K. Kar* AIR 1974 SC 158; (1974)1 SCC 141.

13 *Union of India* v *Kishorilal* AIR 1959 SC 1362; (1960)1 SCR 493.

14 *Panchu Gopal Bose* v *Board of Trustees for Port of Calcutta* (1993)4 SCC 338; 1994 AIR SCW 1335.

Powers of court and powers of tribunal—distinction An Arbitrator cannot be equated with a court of law. First, the powers of the court are not restricted to only making directions for protection of the subject-matter of the dispute but the power of the arbitral tribunal is restricted. Secondly, the powers of the court are not subject to any limitation about there being any agreement to the contrary while the power of the arbitral tribunal are subject to any agreement to the contrary. Thirdly, the court has an inherent power whereas an Arbitrator does not have. It is a tribunal of limited jurisdiction. Its jurisdiction is circumscribed by the terms and reference. An Arbitrator can act only within the four corners of the agreement and not beyond thereto. Fourthly, the court can exercise the power only upon an application by a party made to it; while the arbitral tribunal can exercise the powers only when on request by a party. Fifthly, the arbitral tribunal cannot direct measures affecting the rights of third parties but there is no such limitation on the powers of the court when directing interim measures. Lastly, the arbitral tribunal has no power to execute its own order but the court has power to execute its own order.

Contract prevail over principles of natural justice An Arbitrator must ordinarily follow the principles of natural justice but where the parties agree that the proceedings may be conducted in any particular way the contract prevails over what are called the principles of natural justice.[15]

Arbitration agreement not duly stamped—effect Having regard to s. 35 of the Stamp Act, unless the stamp duty and penalty due in respect of the instrument is paid, the court cannot act upon the instrument, which means that it cannot act upon the arbitration agreement also which is part of the instrument.[16]

Arbitration clause—an independent contract When a contract contains an arbitration agreement, it is a collateral term relating to the resolution of disputes, unrelated to the performance of

15 *Mathulla Mathulla* v *Thomas George* AIR 1962 Ker 320; ILR (1962)1 Ker 486.

16 *SMS Tea Estates Pvt. Ltd.* v *Chandmari Tea Co. Pvt. Ltd.* (2011)14 SCC 66; AIR 2011 SC 1972; JT 2011(8) SC 455.

the contract. It is as if two contracts—one in regard to the substantive terms of the main contract and the other relating to resolution of disputes — had been rolled into one, for purposes of convenience. An arbitration clause is therefore an agreement independent of the other terms of the contract or the instrument. Resultantly, even if the contract or its performance is terminated or comes to an end on account of repudiation, frustration or breach of contract, the arbitration agreement would survive for the purpose of resolution of disputes arising under or in connection with the contract.[17]

Unregistered arbitration agreement—can be acted upon An arbitration agreement does not require registration under the Registration Act. Even if it is found as one of the clauses in a contract or instrument, it is an independent agreement to refer the disputes to arbitration, which is independent of the main contract or instrument. Therefore having regard to the proviso to s. 49 of the Registration Act read with s. 16(1)(*a*) of the Arbitration and Conciliation Act, an arbitration agreement in an unregistered but compulsorily registrable document can be acted upon and enforced for the purpose of dispute resolution by arbitration.[18]

Not to decide question lack of jurisdiction as preliminary issue Arbitrator is not bound to decide the question of lack of his jurisdiction as a preliminary issue and may decide it along with other issues on merits to avoid unnecessary duplication of events.[19]

Decide plea of jurisdiction in first instance The arbitral tribunal under sub-sec. (5) of s. 16 is required to decide a plea of lack of jurisdiction in the first instance. This requirement is very much implied under the provisions of sub-sec. (5). Thus, s. 16 empowers the arbitral tribunal to rule on its own jurisdiction as well as on objections with reference to the existence or validity of the arbitration agreement. Empowerment of such power on the arbitral tribunal under s. 16 indicates the intention of the

17 *SMS Tea Estates Pvt. Ltd.* v *Chandmari Tea Co. Pvt. Ltd.* (2011)14 SCC 66; AIR 2011 SC 1972; JT 2011(8) SC 455.

18 *Ibid.*

19 *Scan Organics Ltd.* v *Mukesh Babu Financial Services Ltd.* (1998)3 Raj 240 (Bom); 1998(1) Arb LR 685.

Parliament and its anxiety to see that the arbitral proceeding is set in motion without allowing any hurdle in future.[20]

Conduct of arbitral proceedings (1) Parties shall be given a full opportunity to present their case [s. 18].

(2) Tribunal is not bound by the Code of Civil Procedure 1908 or the Indian Evidence Act 1872 [s. 19(1)].

(3) The arbitral tribunal may conduct the proceedings in the manner it considers appropriate [s. 19(3)].

(4) The parties are free to agree on the procedure to be followed by the arbitral tribunal in conducting its proceedings [Art. 19(1), UNCITRAL Model Law].

(5) The parties are free to agree on the place of arbitration [s. 20(1)].

(6) The place of arbitration shall be determined by the arbitral tribunal having regard to the (*i*) circumstances of the case, and (*ii*) the convenience of the parties [s. 20(2)].

(7) Parties are free to agree upon the language or languages to be used in the arbitral proceedings [s. 22(1)].

The failure of an Arbitrator to give to a party, a proper opportunity to set matters right has been held to be a serious error in law.[1]

Ad hoc arbitration An *ad hoc* arbitration is an arbitration conducted by the parties without recourse to an arbitral institution. In other words, an *ad hoc* arbitration is one which is conducted pursuant to rules agreed by the parties themselves or laid down by the arbitral tribunal. In case of *ad hoc* arbitration if the parties are not able to appoint Arbitrator by way of consensus among them the other party will have to take the benefit of s. 11 of the Arbitration and Conciliation Act 1996. In case of *ad hoc* arbitration the fee of the Arbitrator will have to be agreed by the parties and the Arbitrator.

20 *Karnataka State Road Transport Corporation* v *M. Keshava Raju* AIR 2004 Kant 109; 2003 AIR Kar R 3061; 2004(1) Arb LR 507.

1 *Fairclough Building Ltd.* v *Vale of Belvoir Superstore* [1990]56 BLR 74.

Advantages It has many advantages. They are—

(*i*) It may be used to met the wishes of the parties and the facts of the particular dispute.

(*ii*) It can resolve the dispute efficiently and effectively.

(*iii*) In cases where huge amount are involved it is possible for an experienced tribunal and counsel to devise a procedure, to settle the dispute in an easy manner.

"The object of arbitration is to obtain the fair resolution of disputes by an impartial tribunal without unnecessary delay or expenses."[2]

Institutional arbitration According to Henry Brown and Arthur Marriott,[3] institutional arbitration is arbitration conducted according to the rules of a specific institutions which may, to a greater or lesser extent, exercise a supervisory and supportive role over an arbitration conducted pursuant to its rules. In other words, it is an arbitration administered by an arbitral institution. The well known arbitration institutions are Indian Council of Arbitration, the International Centre for Arbitration and Dispute Resolution, International Chamber of Commerce, American Arbitration Association and London Court of International Arbitration.

The important arbitration institutions are—

- Indian Council of Arbitration;
- Indian Chamber of Commerce;
- International Centre for Alternative Dispute Resolution;
- FICCI Arbitration and Conciliation Tribunal;
- Bank for International Settlements, Switzerland;
- OSCE Court of Conciliation and Arbitration, Geneva;
- Arab British Chambers of Commerce, London;
- Hong Kong International Arbitration Centre;
- Dublin International Arbitration Centre, Ireland (Dublin Dispute Resolution Centre);

2 Russell on *Arbitration*, 23rd Ed., p. 4.
3 *ADR: Principles and Practice*, 2nd Ed., p. 74.

- International Centre for Dispute Resolution, Ireland;
- International Centre for Settlement of Investment Disputes (ICSID), Washington;
- International Arbitral Centre of the Austrian Federal Economic Chamber;
- Permanent Court of Arbitration, Netherlands;
- United Nations Commission on International Trade Land (UNCITRAL), Austria;
- Singapore International Arbitration Centre;
- London Court of International Arbitration;
- Abu Dhabi Chamber of Commerce & Industry;
- ADR Institute of Canada Inc;
- AIDA Reinsurance and Insurance Arbitration Society;
- Arbitration Association of the Republic of China;
- Arbitration Centre of Mexico;
- Arbitration Foundation of Southern Africa (AFSA);
- Arbitration Institute of the Central Chamber of Commerce, Finland;
- Arbitrators' and Mediators' Institute of New Zealand Inc;
- Australian Centre for International Commercial Arbitration;
- Brussels Chamber of Commerce and Industry;
- Cairo Regional Centre for International Commercial Arbitration;
- Arbitration Centre of the Chamber of Commerce and Industry of Geneva;
- Chartered Institute of Arbitrators;
- Conciliation and Arbitration Centre of Panama;
- Court of Arbitration at the Polish Chamber of Commerce;
- Danish Institute of Arbitration;
- German Arbitration Institute (DIS);
- Indonesian National Board of Arbitration (BANI);

- Institute of Arbitrators & Mediators of Australia;
- Japan Commercial Arbitration Association (JCAA);
- Korean Commercial Arbitration Board (KCAB);
- Paris Mediation and Arbitration Centre;
- Swiss Arbitration Association;
- Swiss Chambers' Arbitration Institution;
- Thai Arbitration Institute (TAI);
- UNCITRAL World Intellectual Property Organisation.

Advantages of institutional arbitration The advantages of institutional arbitration are—

(*i*) The rules framed by the institution are framed by the experienced personals and it normally proves to work well in practice.

(*ii*) Most of the institutions provide trained staff to administer the arbitration.

(*iii*) Institution itself reviews the draft form of award before it handed over to the parties concerned.

(*iv*) During the course of arbitral proceeding, the parties get the help and assistance of experienced lawyers and legal experts.

Russell states,[4] "The main advantages of having the arbitration administered by an institution are that: (*a*) it provides a procedural framework for the case; (*b*) it may be able to provide specialist services or Arbitrators with particular expertise; (*c*) it may serve to relieve the parties and the tribunal of some of the administrative burden of conducting the reference; (*d*) the institution can deal with challenges to and replacement of Arbitrators without the need to involve the courts."

Deepto Roy and Madhukeshwar Desai in "*Institutional Arbitration in India–the Way Forward*" has classically explained the advantages of institutional arbitration in the words manner:[5]

4 Russell on *Arbitration*, 23rd Ed., p. 228.

5 *Alternative Dispute Resolution: The Indian Perspective,* edited by Shashank Garg, Oxford University Press, pp. 96-98.

"Compared to ad hoc arbitration, institutional arbitration is more transparent and accountable, and the arbitral institution contributes significant procedural know hows. Tried and tested arbitral rules, which are primarily designed to maximize the efficiency of the arbitration process, are mechanically incorporated in the arbitration agreement. This ensures that even if a situation arises wherein the parties have not contemplated or wherein one of the parties decide to be non-cooperative, the rules usually have fall backs, allowing resolution of issues with the intervention of the institution and permitting the arbitral process to move forward.

"Another inherent advantage of institutional arbitration is the reputation of the institution. This impacts any future challenges to an award of the institution. Awards issued by a well known institution are easier to enforce. Challenges from a procedural perspective are limited, if the procedures of the institution have been followed.

"The institution performs a number of roles including determining whether there is a *prima facie* arbitration agreement, the number of Arbitrators, appointment of Arbitrators, rejection of the Arbitrators, ensure that the arbitrations are conducted in compliance with the rules and replace them if necessary, determine the place of arbitration, fix and extend time limits, determine the fees and expenses of Arbitrators and scrutinize awards. This eliminates any procedural arbitrariness and also reduces any perception of bias.

"Most arbitral institutions have trained staff and case management teams to administer the arbitration. Parties do not have to worry about the logistics of administering the arbitration, collection of fees, recovery of expenses, arbitration venue, and so on.

"Most institutions also have physical facilities and support services, which allow the parties and the Arbitrators to focus on resolving the dispute rather than be concerned with logistical aspects. The institution is ready to assist, especially in the selection of the Arbitrators. Some institutions are also tech savvy to use modern technological tools, for example, e-filing of documents and petitions and video conferencing to resolve disputes.

"In institutional arbitrations, Arbitrators are typically appointed by the institution based on pre specified criteria. This ensures a first level of scrutiny because only Arbitrators who meet the qualification criteria of the institution would qualify for a panel. Institutions maintain extensive database of Arbitrators in order to assist parties in appointment stage.

"Institutions ensure certainty of costs through the use of expedited timelines and specified cost guidelines. The remuneration of Arbitrators is also set out by the institution. Since Arbitrator fee is one of the largest contributors to the costs of arbitration, this (along with clear timelines) is a key advantage for disputing parties.

"The institution will have a prescribed code of conduct or rules of professional ethics, which all the Arbitrators have to comply with, under the supervision of the secretariat of the institution.

"Institutions also set behavioural norms in terms of consistency of procedure and conduct of proceedings, reducing the chances of any procedural capriciousness originating from the tribunal. Institutions ensure that the appointment of Arbitrators is confirmed only if their independence and impartiality is established."

Supreme Court on institutional arbitration In *Union of India* v *Singh Builders Syndicate*,[6] the Supreme Court of India classically examined the importance of institutional arbitration in the following words: "When the arbitration is by a Tribunal consisting of serving officers, the cost of arbitration is very low. On the other hand, the cost of arbitration can be high if the Arbitral Tribunal consists of retired Judge/s. When a retired Judge is appointed as Arbitrator in place of service officers, the Government is forced to bear the high cost of Arbitration by way of private Arbitrator's fee even though it had not consented for the appointment of such non-technical non-serving persons as

6 (2009)4 Scale 49; (2009)4 SCC 523.

Arbitrator/s. There is no doubt a prevalent opinion that the cost of arbitration becomes very high in many cases where retired Judge/s are Arbitrators. The large number of sittings and charging of very high fees per sitting, with several add-ons, without any ceiling, have many a time resulted in the cost of arbitration approaching or eve exceeding the amount involved in the dispute or the amount of the award. When an Arbitrator is appointed by a court without indicating fees, either both parties or at least one party is at a disadvantage. Firstly, the parties feel constrained to agree to whatever fees is suggested by the Arbitrator, even if it is high or beyond their capacity. Secondly, if a high fee is claimed by the Arbitrator and one party agrees to pay such fee, the other party, who is enable to afford such fee or reluctant to pay such high fee, is put to an embarrassing position. He will not be in a position to express his reservation or objection to the high fee, owing to an apprehension that refusal by him to agree for the fee suggested by the Arbitrator, may prejudice his case or create a bias in favour of the other party who readily agreed to pay the high fee. It is necessary to find an urgent solution for this problem to save arbitration from the arbitration cost. Institutional arbitration has provided a solution as the Arbitrators' fees is not fixed by the Arbitrators themselves on case to case basis, but is governed by a uniform rate prescribed by the institution under whose aegis the Arbitration is held. Another solution is for the court to fix the fees at the time of appointing the Arbitrator, with the consent of parties, if necessary in consultation with the Arbitrator concerned. Third is for the retired Judges offering to serve as Arbitrators, to indicate their fee structure to the Registry of the respective High Court so that the parties will have the choice of selecting an Arbitrator whose fees are in their 'range' having regard to the stakes involved. What is found to be objectionable is parties being forced to an Arbitrator appointed by the court and then being forced to agree for a fee fixed by such Arbitrator. It is unfortunate that delays, high cost, frequent and sometimes unwarranted judicial interruptions at different stages are seriously hampering the growth of arbitration as an effective dispute resolution process. Delay and high cost are two areas where the Arbitrators by self regulation can bring about marked improvement."

Distinction between ad hoc arbitration and institutional arbitration

Ad hoc Arbitration	Institutional Arbitration
1. In *ad hoc* arbitration, procedures are made adopted by the parties and the Arbitrator by way of mutual agreement.	1. In case of institutional arbitration there is no need to formulate the rules because rules are already there.
2. Costs of arbitration are high.	2. Costs of arbitration are cheaper.
3. In case of *ad hoc* arbitration there is no panel of specialized Arbitrators.	3. The institution will maintain a panel of specialized Arbitrators along with their profiles.
4. In case of *ad hoc* arbitration there is no committee to scrutinize arbitral awards.	4. In case of institutional arbitration, they can scrutinize awards before the award is finalized.
5. Arbitrator's fees is fixed by way of negotiation.	5. Arbitrator's fees is fixed by the institution.
6. In case of *ad hoc* arbitration, there is no fixed rule to follow or observe.	6. In case of institutional arbitration they are governed by the rules framed by the institution.
7. In case of *ad hoc* arbitration, it is very difficult to expect professionalism from the staffs attached to the process of arbitration.	7. In case of institutional arbitration, the administrative staff and other staffs are under the control of particular institution. So it is very easy to maintain confidentiality of the proceedings.

Procedure

The arbitral proceedings in respect of a particular dispute commence on the date on which a request for that dispute to be referred to arbitration is received by the respondent [s. 21].

↓

The claimant shall state the facts supporting his claim, the points at the issue and the relief or remedy sought [s. 23(1)].

↓

The respondent shall state his defence in respect of the claim of the claimant [s. 23(1)].

↓

Either party may amend or supplement his claim/defence if required so [s. 23(3)].

↓

The statement of claim and defence shall be completed within a period of six months from the date the arbitrator or all the arbitrators, as the case may be, received notice, in writing, of their appointment [s. 23(4)].

↓

Oral hearing for the presentation of evidence or for oral argument [s. 24(1)].

↓

Parties shall be given sufficient advance notice of any hearing and of any meeting of the arbitral tribunal for the purposes of inspection of documents, goods or other property [s. 24(2)].

↓

All the statements, documents or other information supplied to, or applications made shall be communicated to the other party [s. 24(3)].

↓

Expert report or evidentiary document on which the arbitral tribunal may rely in making its decision shall be communicated to the parties [s. 24(3)].

↓

If the claimant fails to communicate his statement of claim the tribunal shall terminate the proceedings [s. 25(*a*)].

↓

When the respondent fails to communicate his statement of defence or a party fails to appear at an oral hearing or to produce documentary evidence the arbitral tribunal may continue the proceedings [s. 25(*b*) & s. 25(*c*)].

↓

The tribunal may appoint one or more experts to determine certain specific issues [s. 26(1)(*a*)].

↓

Tribunal or a party with the approval of the arbitral tribunal may take the assistance of the court in recording evidence [s. 27(1)].

↓

The court may while taking evidence issue the same processes to witnesses as it may issue in suits tried before it [s. 27(4)].

↓

The tribunal shall decide *ex aequo et bono* or as *amiable compositeur* only if the parties have expressly authorized it to do so [s. 28(2)].

↓

The arbitral tribunal shall take into account the terms of the contract and trade usages applicable to the transaction [s. 28(3)].

↓

In arbitral proceedings with more than one Arbitrator, any decision of the arbitral tribunal shall be made by a majority of all its members [s. 29(1)].

↓

Questions of procedure may be decided by tne presiding Arbitrator, if authorized by the parties or all the members of the arbitral tribunal [s. 29(2)].

↓

The arbitral tribunal may use mediation, conciliation or other procedures at any stage of the proceedings to encourage settlement [s. 30(1)].

↓

When the parties settle the dispute during proceedings it shall record the settlement in the form of an arbitral award on agreed terms [s. 30(2)].

↓

An award on agreed terms shall have the same status and effect an any other arbitral award on the substance of the dispute [s. 30(3)].

↓

Award should be in writing and signed by the members of the tribunal but when there is more than one Arbitrator, signature of majority of all the members of a tribunal is sufficient so long as the reason for any omitted signature is stated [s. 31(1) and s. 31(2)].

↓

The award shall state its date and place of arbitration [s. 31(4)].

↓

After the award is made, a signed copy shall be delivered to each party [s. 31(5)].

↓

The arbitral tribunal may, at any time during the arbitral proceedings, make an interim arbitral award on any matter with respect to which it may make final award [s. 31(6)].

↓

A sum directed to be paid by an arbitral award shall, unless the award otherwise directs, carry interest at the rate of two per cent higher than the current rate of interest prevalent on the date of award, from the date of award to the date of payment [s. 31(7)(*b*)].

Fixing of venue Failing an agreement between the parties, the arbitral tribunal, keeping in view the circumstances of the case, including convenience of parties, may fix the venue. But at least for consultation among its members, for hearing witnesses, experts or the parties, or inspection of documents, goods or other property, the arbitral tribunal may meet at any place it considers appropriate, unless otherwise agreed by the parties.[7] According to Russell on *Arbitration*, "In fixing the place of trial the arbitrator should take all the circumstances into consideration and decide according to the balance of convenience. The chief circumstances to be taken into consideration are the place where most of the witnesses reside, the situation of the subject-matter of the dispute, and the balance of convenience and expense".[8]

Waiver of forum selection clause Every clause in an agreement between the parties is binding on the parties, but any covenant is also capable of being waived. If the parties have agreed to go to a particular court, but one party commits breach of such agreement and goes to another court, unless an objection in

7 S.K. Chawla, *Law of Arbitration & Conciliation,* 3rd Ed., p. 571.
8 Russell on *Arbitration*, 19th Ed., p. 264.

such regard is raised at the earliest opportunity by the other party, the court cannot *suo motu* enforce the forum selection clause on the parties to the contract. A forum selection clause, just like most other clauses contained in an agreement between two parties, is capable of being waived.[9]

Seat of arbitration Under the Law of Arbitration, unlike the Code of Civil Procedure which applies to suits filed in courts, a reference to "seat" is a concept by which a neutral venue can be chosen by the parties to an arbitration clause. The neutral venue may not in the classical sense have jurisdiction—that is, no part of the cause of action may have arisen at the neutral venue and neither would any of the provisions of ss. 16 to 21 of the Code of Civil Procedure be attracted.[10]

If the parties do not agree upon venue of arbitration, the arbitral tribunal is required to determine the same taking into consideration the convenience of the parties. It is also incumbent on the arbitral tribunal that the determination shall be clearly stated in the 'form and contents of award'.[11]

The seat of arbitration, as fixed by the agreement, can be changed only by amending the agreement. Arbitrator held proceedings at a different place with consent of parties could not change the seat of arbitration. It only amounted to physical change of venue of arbitration.[12]

Preliminary meeting An arbitral tribunal generally calls a preliminary meeting to have a dialogue with the parties and may also resolve in the preliminary meeting the manner in which it will receive—(*i*) pleadings of the parties; (*ii*) production of documents; (*iii*) written or oral evidence from parties; (*iv*) oral argument presented on behalf of the parties and (*v*) submission of written argument, if any. According to Russell, "There will often be a preliminary meeting held between the tribunal and

9 *Hirok Chowdhury* v *Khagendra Nath Mandal* AIR 2018 Cal 272.

10 *Indus Mobile Distribution Pvt. Ltd.* v *Datawind Innovation Pvt. Ltd.* AIR 2017 SC 2105.

11 *Union of India* v *Hardy Exploration and Production (India) INC* AIR 2018 SC 4871.

12 *Videocon Industries Ltd.* v *Union of India* (2011)6 SCC 161.

the parties at a relatively early stage of the reference. There is no legal requirement for a preliminary meeting, but it is often useful in giving the participants an opportunity to meet and obtain directions from the tribunal for the future conduct of the reference. The need for a meeting will depend upon the extent to which the procedure and any directions to be sought from the tribunal can be agreed between the parties. The costs involved may also be an important consideration, particularly if the arbitration involves parties and their representatives from different jurisdictions. It is becoming relatively commonplace in these circumstances for the preliminary meeting to take the form of a video-conference or a telephone conference call rather than a meeting in person".[13] In preliminary meeting the tribunal may generally dealt with the following points—

(*a*) For delivery of points of claim and defence;

(*b*) For particulars of his opponent's claim or counterclaim, as the case may be;

(*c*) For discovery and inspection of documents;

(*d*) For inspection of property and things—(*i*) by parties and (*ii*) by the Arbitrator;

(*e*) For the arrangement of other matters to shorten or facilitate the hearing;

(*f*) For fixing of a time and place of hearing.

Power to allow amendment The Arbitrator has a discretion to refuse or allow amendments during the proceedings in the claim or defence, if the application is made to him for that purpose. In *Cropper* v *Smith*[14] the Justice Bowen observed: "In dealing with amendments generally, the arbitrator should follow the principles adopted by the courts. The main principle is that amendments should be allowed when they can be made without manifest and grave injustice. Generally speaking, any injustice which might otherwise be done can be cured by an order that the party asking for the amendment shall pay costs occasioned thereby".

13 Russell on *Arbitration*, 23rd Ed., p. 232.
14 [1884]26 Ch D 700.

Prayer to produce document Where the original agreement or a certified copy thereof is not available with the party applying for reference to arbitration and the said agreement or certified copy is retained by the other party to that agreement, then, the party so applying shall file such application along with a copy of the arbitration agreement and a petition praying the court to call upon the other party to produce the original arbitration agreement to its duly certified copy before that court.

Commencement of arbitral proceeding—when Where, before, the commencement of the arbitral proceedings, a court passes an order for any interim measure of protection under s. 9(1), the arbitral proceedings shall commenced within a period of ninety days from the date of such order or within such further time as the court may determine.[15] Russell observed: "The procedures for commencing an arbitration and constituting the tribunal will depend upon what the parties have agreed (or not agreed) as the first step or steps to be taken...... Identification of the date of commencement may be of critical importance to the parties in view of contractual or statutory time limits for commencement of the arbitration. Once arbitration is commenced time stops running and there can be no question of the time limit subsequently expiring as regards causes of action included in the reference".[16]

Russell again states, "a contractual time limit, whether contained in an arbitration agreement or some other provision of the contract, or indeed in arbitration rules referred to in the arbitration agreement, may (1) impose a time limit for commencing arbitration proceedings, and/or (2) provide that a claim shall be barred or extinguished if arbitration is not commenced within the time limit".[17]

Court when entertain application after constitution of arbitral tribunal Once the arbitral tribunal has been constituted, the court shall not entertain an application under s. 9(1), unless the court finds

15 Section 9(2) of the Arbitration and Conciliation Act 1996.
16 Russell on *Arbitration*, 23rd Ed., p. 184.
17 *Ibid.*

that circumstances exist which may not render the remedy provided under s. 17 efficacious.[18]

Matter considered by Supreme Court or High Court before appointment of Arbitrator The Supreme Court or the High Court or the person or institution designated by such court, before appointing an Arbitrator, shall seek a disclosure in writing from the prospective Arbitrator and have due regard to: (*a*) any qualifications required for the Arbitrator by the agreement of the parties; and (*b*) the contents of the disclosure and other considerations as are likely to secure the appointment of an independent and impartial Arbitrator.[19]

Where the appointed Arbitrator was more experienced and qualified than what was required under the arbitration clause, there was no need for interference in the appointment.[20]

Application for appointment of Arbitrator—time limit An application for appointment of an Arbitrator or Arbitrators shall be disposed of by the Supreme Court or the High Court or the person or institution designated by such court, as the case may be, as expeditiously as possible and an endeavour shall be made to dispose of the matter within a period of sixty days from the date of service of notice on the opposite party.[1]

Facts to be disclosed by prospective Arbitrator before his appointment When a person is approached in connection with his possible appointment as an Arbitrator, he shall disclose in writing any circumstances—(*a*) such as the existence either direct or indirect, of any past or present relationship with or interest in any of the parties or in relation to the subject matter in dispute, whether financial, business, professional or other kind, which is likely to give rise to justifiable doubts as to his independence or impartiality; and (*b*) which are likely to affect his ability to devote sufficient time to the arbitration and in particular his ability to complete the entire arbitration within a period of twelve months [see s. 12(1)].

18 Section 9(3) of the Arbitration and Conciliation Act 1996.
19 Section 11(8) of the Arbitration and Conciliation Act 1996.
20 *National Heavy Engg. Coop. Ltd.* v *King Builders* AIR 2001 SC 285; (2001)1 SCC 33.
1 Section 11(13) of the Arbitration and Conciliation Act 1996.

Party when apply for interim measures A party may, during the arbitral proceedings or at any time after the making of the arbitral award but before it is enforced in accordance with s. 36 apply to the arbitral tribunal for interim measures.

Matters for which application made The application for interim measures shall be made for the following matters: (1) for the appointment of a guardian for a minor or person of unsound mind for the purposes of arbitral proceedings; or (2) for interim measure of protection in respect of any of the following matters, namely—(*a*) The preservation, interim custody or sale of any goods which are the subject-matter of the arbitration agreement; (*b*) Securing the amount in dispute in the arbitration; (*c*) The detention, preservation or inspection of any property or thing which is the subject-matter of the dispute in arbitration, or as to which any question may arise therein and authorising for any of the aforesaid purposes any person to enter upon any land or building in the possession of any party, or authorising any samples to be taken, or any observation to be made, or experiment to be tried, which may be necessary or expedient for the purpose of obtaining full information or evidence; (*d*) Interim injunction or the appointment of a receiver; (*e*) Such other interim measure of protection as may appear to the arbitral tribunal to be just and convenient, and the arbitral tribunal shall have the same power for making orders, as the court has for the purpose of, and in relation to, any proceedings before it.

Recording of oral evidence The arbitral tribunal shall, as far as possible, hold oral hearings for the presentation of evidence or for oral argument on day-to-day basis, and not grant any adjournments unless sufficient cause is made out, and may impose costs including exemplary costs on the party seeking adjournment without any sufficient cause.[2] Unless otherwise agreed by the parties, the arbitral tribunal shall decide whether to hold oral hearings for the presentation of evidence or for oral argument, or whether the proceedings shall be conducted on the basis of documents an other materials: Provided that the

2 Second proviso to s. 24(1) of the Arbitration and Conciliation Act which was inserted by the Arbitration and Conciliation (Amendment) Act 2015 (w.e.f. 23.10.2015).

arbitral tribunal shall hold oral hearings, at an appropriate stage of the proceedings, on a request by a party, unless the parties have agreed that no oral hearing shall be held. Secondly, the parties shall be given sufficient advance notice of any hearing and of any meeting of the arbitral tribunal for the purposes of inspection of documents, goods or other property. Thirdly, all statements, documents or other information supplied to, or applications made to, the arbitral tribunal by one party shall be communicated to the other party, and any expert report or evidentiary document on which the arbitral tribunal may rely in making its decision shall be communicated to the parties.

Time limit for arbitral award The award shall be made within a period of twelve months from the date the arbitral tribunal enters upon the reference. An arbitral tribunal shall be deemed to have entered upon the reference on the date on which the Arbitrator or all the Arbitrators, as the case may be, have received notice, in writing, of their appointment. If the award is made within a period of six months from the date the arbitral tribunal enters upon the reference, the arbitral tribunal shall be entitled to receive such amount of additional fees as the parties may agree [see s. 29A].

Extension of time limit

(a) ***By consent*** The parties may, by consent, extend the period specified in sub-sec. (1) for making award for a further period not exceeding six months.

(b) ***By court*** If the award is not made within the period specified in sub-sec. (1) or the extended period specified under sub-sec. (3), the mandate of the Arbitrator(s) shall terminate unless the court has, either prior to or after the expiry of the period so specified, extended the period. But while extending the period under this sub-section, if the court finds that the proceedings have been delayed for the reasons attributable to the arbitral tribunal, then, it may order reduction of fees of Arbitrator(s) by not exceeding five per cent. for each month of such delay.

(c) ***By application*** The extension of period referred to in sub-sec. (4) may be on the application of any of the parties and may be granted only for sufficient cause and on such terms and conditions as may be imposed by the court [see sub-secs. (2), (3) of s. 29A].

Power of court While extending the period referred to in sub-sec. (4), it shall be open to the court to substitute one or all of the Arbitrators and if one or all of the Arbitrators are substituted, the arbitral proceedings shall continue from the stage already reached and on the basis of the evidence and material already on record, and the Arbitrator(s) appointed under this section shall be deemed to have received the said evidence and material. Secondly, in the event of Arbitrator(s) being appointed under this section, the arbitral tribunal thus reconstituted shall be deemed to be in continuation of the previously appointed arbitral tribunal [see sub-secs. (6) and (7) of s. 29A].

Award of cost It shall be open to the court to impose actual or exemplary costs upon any of the parties [s. 29A(8)].

Disposal of application of extension of period—mode and manner An application filed under sub-sec. (5) shall be disposed of by the court as expeditiously as possible and endeavour shall be made to dispose of the matter within a period of sixty days from the date of service of notice on the opposite party [s. 29A(9)].

Procedure before Arbitrator The procedure before Arbitrators may be regulated either by the statute or by agreement or submission. Where the procedure is prescribed by the agreement of submission and where such procedure is not contrary to the laws of the land, that procedure must prevail.[3] When a contract or agreement for arbitration itself does not lay down any particular procedure for the conduct of the arbitration, the courts have said that the Arbitrators must follow the principles of natural justice which are no other than common sense standards of fairness and impartiality such as no party should be condemned unheard or without representation. It was necessary to do that because the Arbitrators are not strict courts of law guided by the

3 *Emperor* v *Angad* AIR 1929 All 69; *Mt. Aftab Begam* v *Haji Abdul Majid Khan* AIR 1924 All 800 (1); *Debi Das* v *Keshava Deo* AIR 1945 All 423; *Durga Prasad* v *Sew Kishen Das* AIR 1949 PC 334; *Baijnath* v *Baj-ranglal Kamalia* AIR 1938 Cal 166; *D.L. Miller and Co. Ltd.* v *Daluram Gogunmull* AIR 1956 Cal 361.

Code of Civil Procedure and Evidence Act laying down massive details of procedure. In the absence of any procedure, prescribed either by statute or by contract, the arbitrators must follow the principles of natural justice, or else there is nothing for the Arbitrators to fall back upon to ensure fair adjudication.[4]

Consideration The following matters may require consideration:

> "Any terms in the arbitration agreement as to how and by whom the reference is to be conducted;
>
> The law or rules to be applied to the merits of the dispute and, if a foreign law is to apply, how it is to be presented;
>
> Any mandatory laws of the seat of the arbitration or other place where hearings or meetings are to be held, insofar as they might affect the conduct of the reference or the award;
>
> Any mandatory laws of the place where enforcement of an award will be sought, insofar as they might affect the conduct of the reference or the award;
>
> The tribunal's jurisdiction;
>
> The procedural or evidential rules incorporated into the arbitration agreement or which the parties or the tribunal otherwise wish to adopt;
>
> Whether (and if so what) interim measures are appropriate;
>
> Whether provisional relief can and should be granted;
>
> How the issues are to be defined;
>
> Whether there should be a determination of particular issues before others;
>
> What documents (if any) to be provided;
>
> Whether (and if so how) the evidence of witnesses of fact is to be adduced;
>
> Whether (and if so how) expert evidence is to be adduced by the parties;
>
> Whether the tribunal wishes to appoint any expert(s), legal adviser or assessor;

4 *Mathulla Mathulla* v *Thomas George* AIR 1962 Ker 320; ILR (1962)1 Ker 486.

Administration of the reference;

Arrangements for the hearing(s);

The place or places at which hearings are to be conducted;

Language(s) to be used in the reference;

Fees and deposits;

Any other issues arising, e.g. confidentiality restrictions, arrangements specific to multiparty or consolidated arbitrations, etc.".[5]

Consider evidence of one party—effect The Arbitrator misconceives his duty if he listens to the evidence of one party behind the back of the other who might be interested either in controverting or is legally entitled to controvert it. Though the Evidence Act is not applicable to proceedings before an Arbitrator but he is bound by the rules of evidence that have been prescribed by the Act and the Code of Civil Procedure which are attracted in the arbitration proceedings. It is true that even in spite of the notice if one of the parties does not voluntarily appear nor it shows the desire to contest the dispute or the claim of the other as the case may be, an *ex parte* award may be justified. If the parties are not given proper notice either of the venue and the date of sitting by the Arbitrator and the award is passed behind his back, it would clearly amount misconduct on the part of the Arbitrator. If the Arbitrator behind the back of the party receives evidence against him the evil is not cured by the Arbitrator even informing him about it. The person who is to be breached by the evidence ought to be present to hear it so that he would be able to meet and answer it. Therefore, it is incumbent on the part of the Arbitrator to follow the procedure at the time of enquiry. It is no doubt true that the Arbitrator is ordinarily free from fetters of adjective law, but that does not make him free from the fundamental principles of justice. Though the Arbitrator may not be strictly bound by the rules and procedures observed in court it does not mean that his procedure should be opposed to natural justice. The basic principle seems to be that where there has been an opportunity afforded to one side to get an advantage

5 Russell on *Arbitration*, 23rd Ed., pp. 233-234.

with the Arbitrator over the other, either by lack of notice or by the absence of the other side and there is even a remote possibility that the advantage so obtained may have unconsciously influenced the mind of the Arbitrator, the proceedings are vitiated by the breach of the principles of natural justice.[6]

Arbitrator should follow principles of natural justice No doubt Arbitrator is not bound by technical rules of procedure but he cannot ignore rules of natural justice. Thread of natural justice should run through the entire arbitration proceedings and the principles of natural justice require that the person who is to be prejudiced by the evidence ought to be present to hear it taken to suggest cross-examination or himself to cross-examine and to be able to find evidence, if he can, that shall meet and answer it, in short to deal with in an ordinary course of legal proceedings. Except in a few cases where exceptions are unavoidable, both sides must be heard each in the presence of the other. If the Arbitrator departs from this rule and hears one party in the absence of the other he is guilty of misconduct. Position of Arbitrator is like Caeser's wife who should be above suspicion. In order to exclude the application of the rules of natural justice two things must co-exist: one is an express exclusion of the principle by a specific rule or term of the contract and the other is that dispute referred to arbitration is of a kind as is capable of being decided by the Arbitrator fairly and honestly without the due observance of rule of natural justice.

In short, Arbitrator is bound by rules of natural justice including the principle incorporated in the maxim *Audi Alteram Partem*. It may be mentioned here that action of Arbitrator cannot be defended on the plea that the evidence was inconsequential or did not affect his mind or was of trifling nature. The Arbitrator cannot take it upon himself that this evidence improperly admitted had no effect on his mind. The Arbitrator must observe principles of natural justice under which both parties are entitled to make representations on their own case and the case of his opponent. The courts will not permit slightest deviation from

6 *Naginder Singh* v *Commander, 44 Border Road Task Force* AIR 1989 Gau 53; 1989(2) Arb LR 233.

principles of natural justice even if such deviation relates to a trifling matter. In fact, it is impossible to gauge the influence which *ex parte* statement/document had upon the mind of Arbitrator.[7]

Judge of choice of parties The Arbitrator is a judge of the choice of the parties. He is not bound by the provisions of the Evidence Act. He can decide matters as best as he thinks fit. Parties are bound by his award. The only limitations on the powers of an Arbitrator are that he should not violate the principles of natural justice; he should give a fair hearing to the parties and should give a reasonable time and opportunity to them to substantiate their respective claims.[8]

Chief rules of natural justice The chief rules of natural justice are to act fairly, in good faith, without bias, and in a judicial temper; to give each party the opportunity of adequately stating his case, and correcting or contradicting any relevant statement prejudicial to his case, and not to hear one side behind the back of the other.[9]

Not shut out one of the parties Though it would always be open to the parties concerned to show by clear evidence that there has been a serious violation of the basic canons of justice and fairplay, it would be one thing to say that the Arbitrator has completely shut out one of the parties and has not permitted it either to file a statement or to examine his witnesses or to support, his case by argument; it is quite another thing to say that he has refused permission to make this or that amendment, or adduce this or that piece of evidence or to emphasise this or that ground in argument. In the former event, there is a violation of the basic principles of fair justice. In the latter, the refusal to afford opportunity to amend or to lead a particular piece of evidence is not denial of hearing, but only the denial of a particular detail, at the discretion of the Arbitrator. Even when it is a court, the refusal of permission to amend or to admit a particular piece of

7 *Wazir Chand Karan Chand* v *Union of India* AIR 1989 Del 175; 1989(37) DLT 164; 1989(1) Arb LR 187.

8 *President of India* v *Kesar Singh* AIR 1966 J&K 113.

9 *Maulabux* v *State of West Bengal* AIR 1990 Cal 318.

evidence does not by itself justify interference by a superior court in revision. The Arbitrator's position is even stronger; after all he has got discretion, he has to exercise only in accordance with the broad canons of fair play and natural justice without being bound by other formalities.[10]

Equal opportunity be given to each parties In the absence of specific provisions to the contrary in the statute or the contract of agreement, the parties to an arbitration proceeding are entitled to a reasonable notice of the time and place of the hearing and have an absolute right to be heard and to present their evidence before the arbitrators. If they are deprived of this right, the court will not hesitate to set aside the award on the ground of misconduct even though there may have been no improper intention.[11]

Fast track procedure

Appointment by agreement The parties to an arbitration agreement, may, at any stage either before or at the time of appointment of the arbitral tribunal, agree in writing to have their dispute resolved by fast track procedure specified in s. 29B(3) [see s. 29B(1)].

Sole arbitrator chosen by parties The parties to the arbitration agreement, while agreeing for resolution of dispute by fast track procedure, may agree that the arbitral tribunal shall consist of a sole arbitrator who shall be chosen by the parties [see s. 29B(2)].

Procedure The arbitral tribunal shall follow the following procedure while conducting arbitration proceedings:

(*a*) The arbitral tribunal shall decide the dispute on the basis of written pleadings, documents and submissions filed by the parties without any oral hearing;

(*b*) The arbitral tribunal shall have power to call for any further information or clarification from the parties in addition to the pleadings and documents filed by them;

(*c*) An oral hearing may be held only, if, all the parties make a request or if the arbitral tribunal considers it

10 *Mathulla* v *Thomas George* AIR 1962 Ker 320; ILR (1962)1 Ker 486.

11 *Damodar Pershad Gupta* v *Saxena & Co., Delhi* AIR 1959 Punj 476; 1958(60) Pun LR 638; *Kamala Saha* v *Jogeshwar Prasad Saha* AIR 1992 Ori 23.

necessary to have oral hearing for clarifying certain issues;

(*d*) The arbitral tribunal may dispense with any technical formalities, if an oral hearing is held, and adopt such procedure as deemed appropriate for expeditious disposal of the case.[12]

Time limit The award under s. 29B shall be made within a period of six months from the date the arbitral tribunal enters upon the reference. If the award is not made within the period specified in sub-sec. (4), the provisions of sub-secs. (3) to (9) of s. 29A shall apply to the proceedings [see sub-secs. (4) and (5) of s. 29B].

Mode of payment of fees The fees payable to the Arbitrator and the manner of payment of the fees shall be such as may be agreed between the Arbitrator and the parties [see s. 29B(6)].

Rate of interest A sum directed to be paid by an arbitral award shall, unless the award otherwise directs, carry interest at the rate of two per cent. higher than the current rate of interest prevalent on the date of award, from the date of award to the date of payment [see s. 31(7)(*b*)].

Regime for costs

Award of cost—Fora In relation to any arbitration proceeding or a proceeding under any of the provisions of this Act pertaining to the arbitration, the court or arbitral tribunal, notwithstanding anything contained in the Code of Civil Procedure 1908 (5 of 1908), shall have the discretion to determine: (*a*) whether costs are payable by one party to another; (*b*) the amount of such costs; and (*c*) when such costs are to be paid [see s. 31A(1)].

Cost—meaning "Costs" means reasonable costs relating to: (*i*) the fees and expenses of the Arbitrators, courts and witnesses; (*ii*) legal fees and expenses; (*iii*) any administration fees of the institution supervising the arbitration; and (*iv*) any other expenses incurred in connection with the arbitral or court proceedings and the arbitral award.[13]

12 See s. 29B(3) of the Arbitration and Conciliation Act.

13 *Explanation* to s. 31A(1) of the Arbitration and Conciliation Act.

Rule regarding payment of cost If the court or arbitral tribunal decides to make an order as to payment of costs, (*a*) the general rule is that the unsuccessful party shall be ordered to pay the costs of the successful party; or (*b*) the court or arbitral tribunal may make a different order for reasons to be recorded in writing.[14]

Factors to be considered In determining the costs, the court or arbitral tribunal shall have regard to all the circumstances, including: (*a*) the conduct of all the parties; (*b*) whether a party has succeeded partly in the case; (*c*) whether the party had made a frivolous counter-claim leading to delay in the disposal of the arbitral proceedings; and (*d*) whether any reasonable offer to settle the dispute is made by a party and refused by the other party.[15]

Order(s) passed by court or arbitral tribunal The court or arbitral tribunal may make any order under s. 31A including the order that a party shall pay: (*a*) a proportion of another party's costs; (*b*) a stated amount in respect of another party's costs; (*c*) costs from or until a certain date only; (*d*) costs incurred before proceedings have begun; (*e*) costs relating to particular steps taken in the proceedings; (*f*) costs relating only to a distinct part of the proceedings; and (*g*) interest on costs from or until a certain date.[16]

Agreement regarding payment of cost of arbitration—validity An agreement which has the effect that a party is to pay the whole or part of the costs of the arbitration in any event shall be only valid if such agreement is made after the dispute in question has arisen.

Termination of proceedings Section 14 of the Arbitration and Conciliation Act specifies the grounds for terminating the mandate of an Arbitrator and substituting by another Arbitrator and methods of doing so. The grounds for terminating the mandate are: (*i*) the arbitrator becomes *de jure* or *de facto* unable to perform his functions; or (*ii*) for some other reasons fails to act without undue delay; or (*iii*) the Arbitrator withdraws from

14 Section 31A(2) of the Arbitration and Conciliation Act.
15 Section 31A(3) of the Arbitration and Conciliation Act.
16 Section 31A(4) of the Arbitration and Conciliation Act.

his office; or (*iv*) the parties agree to the termination of his authority as an Arbitrator; whereas three methods can be employed for terminating the mandate of the Arbitrator. They are—(*a*) by withdrawal of the Arbitrator from his office, (*b*) by agreement of parties and (*c*) by decision by the court.

Section 15 provides for additional grounds for termination of the mandate and for appointment of substitute Arbitrator. The additional grounds provided are (*a*) where the Arbitrator withdraws from office for any reason; or (*b*) by or pursuant to the agreement of the parties. Though sub-sec. (1) purports to state additional grounds for termination of authority of an Arbitrator but one of the grounds mentioned therein is covered by the grounds set out in cl. (*b*) of sub-sec. (1) of s. 14. On the authority of the arbitrator being terminated, a substitute arbitrator in place of arbitrator whose authority is terminated has to be appointed and such appointment, as per sub-sec. (2) is required to be made by following the same procedure as followed while appointing the arbitrator who is being substituted. The arbitral proceedings shall be terminated in the following situations:

(*a*) *By the final award.* It shall be terminated by the final award.[17]

(*b*) *By the order of the arbitral tribunal.* The arbitral tribunal shall issue an order for the termination of the arbitral proceedings where—

(*i*) the claimant withdraws his claim, unless the respondent objects to the order and the arbitral tribunal recognizes a legitimate interest on his part in obtaining a final settlement of the dispute;

(*ii*) the parties agree on the termination of the proceedings; or

(*iii*) the arbitral tribunal finds that the continuation of the proceedings has for any other reason become unnecessary or impossible.[18]

17 Section 32(1).
18 Section 32(2).

(*c*) *By default of the claimant.* Where without showing sufficient cause the claimant fails to communicate his statement of claim the arbitral tribunal shall terminate the proceedings.[19]

(*d*) *By settlement during arbitral proceedings.* If during arbitral proceedings, the parties settle the dispute, the arbitral tribunal shall terminate the proceedings.[20]

Parties agree to termination of mandate Consent order is nothing but an agreement between the parties with super imposed seal of the court. It is open for the parties to provide for termination of the mandate of the Arbitrator while agreeing for arbitration or to reach an agreement in this behalf during the pendency of the arbitration proceedings. In other words, the mandate given to the Arbitrator can be subject to the agreement between the parties.[1]

Withdrawal versus refusal The word 'refuse' denotes a situation before acceptance of an invitation, offer, office, position, privilege and the like, the word 'withdraw' means to retract, retire or retreat from a place, position or situation after acceptance thereof. Therefore, s. 15(2) of the Act does not *per se* apply to a case where an Arbitrator appointed by a party to the agreement declines to accept the appointment or refuses to arbitrate in the matter.[2]

Correction of award and interpretation of award[3] The arbitral tribunal may correct the computation error, any clerical or typographical errors or any other errors of a similar nature either on its own motion or on the application of the party. The tribunal may correct error on its own initiative within 30 days from the date of the arbitral award.[4] Within thirty days from the receipt of the

19 Section 38(3).
20 Section 32(3).
1 *Kifayatullah Haji Gulam Rasool* v *Smt. Bilkish Ismail Mehsania* AIR 2000 Bom 424; 2001(1) Civ LJ 826.
2 *S.B.P. and Company* v *Patel Engineering Ltd.* (2000)10 SCC 293; AIR 2009 SC 450; (2009)13 Scale 335; 2010(1) AIR Kar R 41.
3 Section 33, the Arbitration and Conciliation Act 1996.
4 Section 33(3).

arbitral award, unless another period of time has been agreed upon by the parties[5]—

(*a*) a party, with notice to the other party, may request the arbitral tribunal to correct an computation errors, any clerical or typographical errors or any other errors of a similar nature occurring in the award;

(*b*) if so agreed by the parties, a party, with notice to the other party, may request the arbitral tribunal to give an interpretation of a specific point or part of the award.

If the arbitral tribunal considers the request made is justified it shall make the correction or give the interpretation within thirty days from the receipt of the request and the interpretation shall form part of the arbitral award.[6]

This provision is similar to s. 152, CPC.

Additional award A party with notice to the other party may apply to the arbitral tribunal to make an additional arbitral award as to claims presented in the arbitral proceedings but omitted from the arbitral award.[7] Such application must be filed within thirty days from the receipt of the arbitral award.[8] If the arbitral tribunal considers that the ground of request is justified, it shall make the additional arbitral award within sixty days from the receipt of such request.[9] Provisions of s. 31 is also equally applicable to an additional award made under s. 33.[10]

Award—final "There are three senses in which an award may be said to be "final". First, an award may be final in that it determines all the issues in the arbitration, or determines all the issues which remain outstanding following earlier awards dealing with only some of the issues in the arbitration. Secondly, an award must be final in the sense of being a complete decision

5 Section 33(1).
6 Section 33(2).
7 Section 33(4).
8 Section 33(4).
9 Section 33(5).
10 Section 33(7).

on the particular issues considered without leaving aspects of those issues to be dealt with subsequently or by a third party. Thirdly, an award is final under s. 35 of the Arbitration and Conciliation Act 1996 in that it is final and binding on the parties".[11]

Setting aside of arbitral award by court An application for setting aside arbitral award may be made to a court within three months from the date on which the party making that application had received the arbitral award, or if a request had been made under s. 33 from the date on which that request had been disposed of by the arbitral tribunal. But if the court is satisfied that the applicant was prevented by sufficient cause from making the application within the said period of three months it may entertain the application within a further period of thirty days, but not thereafter.[12]

Time consumed due to *bona fide* prosecution of the application in a wrong forum is a sufficient cause and said delay shall be condoned by the principal civil court of original jurisdiction as contemplated under s. 2(*e*)(*i*) of the Act.

An award when challenged under s. 34 within the time stipulated therein becomes unexecutable. There is no discretion left with the court to pass any interlocutory order in regard to the said award except to adjudicate on the correctness of the claim made by the applicant.

The court does not possess any power to condone delay after the lapse of thirty days from the expiry of three months from date of the delivery of a copy of the award on the parties. Service of the award on one party would be legally efficacious on the opposite contestant. Precedents exhorting a liberal approach especially where the State is concerned do not apply to the Arbitration and Conciliation Act which has not only taken care to generally restrict interference by a civil court, but after laying down a period of 30 days in the proviso to s. 34(3) has taken pains to state that thereafter no scope of enlargement is possible. Section 34(5) of the Arbitration and Conciliation Act must be

11 Russell on *Arbitration*, 23rd Ed., pp. 272-273.
12 Section 34(3).

strictly complied with and the award must actually be served on the officer concerned by the Arbitrator.[13]

Condonation of delay In *Union of India* v *Ogilvy & Mather Ltd.*[14] the Delhi High Court observed:

> The delay of 258 days is exorbitant and said delay cannot be condoned as it would amount to delaying the very object and purpose of prescribing the limitation for challenging the award under s. 34 of the Act and frustrating the scheme of the Act. The circumstances of condonation of delay in re-filling therein have to be in consonance with the aims and objects of the Act. The period of 258 days delay is too excessive to be condoned on the ground pleaded by the petitioner. The re-filling circumstance gives the court power to condone the delay in special circumstances, but the said aspect cannot give any party a leverage period of limitation for filing the objections against the award.

The court in the issue of re-filling also looked into the question of sufficient cause and good grounds for condoning the delay. The illness of the counsel can be a good ground to condone reasonable delay but cannot be overstretched to condone the excessive delay of 258 days, especially where the defects in objections are not vital in character and can be easily handled by the associate counsel having *vakalatnama* in their favour.

Grounds An arbitral award may be set aside by the court only if—

(*a*) the party making the application furnishes proof that—

- (*i*) a party was under some incapacity, or
- (*ii*) the arbitration agreement is not valid under the law to which the parties have subjected it or, failing any indication thereon, under the law for the time being in force; or
- (*iii*) the party making the application was not given proper notice of the appointment of an Arbitrator

13 *National Projects Constructions Corporation Ltd.* v *Bundela Bandhu Construction Company* AIR 2007 Del 202 (DB); 2007(139) DLT 676.

14 AIR 2009 Del 179; 2009(158) DLT 275.

or of the arbitral proceedings or was otherwise unable to present his case; or

(*iv*) the arbitral award deals with a dispute not contemplated by or not falling within the terms of the submission to arbitration, or it contains decisions on matters beyond the scope of the submission to arbitration:

Provided that, if the decisions on matters submitted to arbitration can be separated from those not so submitted, only that part of the arbitral award which contains decisions on matters not submitted to arbitration may be set aside; or

(*v*) the composition of the arbitral tribunal or the arbitral procedure was not in accordance with the agreement of the parties, unless such agreement was in conflict with a provision of this Part from which the parties cannot derogate, or, failing such agreement, was not in accordance with this Part; or

(*b*) the court finds that—

(*i*) the subject-matter of the dispute is not capable of settlement by arbitration under the law for the time being in force; or

(*ii*) the arbitral award is in conflict with the public policy of India.[15]

The court may set aside the award:[16]

(1) If the composition of the arbitral tribunal was not in accordance with the agreement of the parties:

(*a*) failing such agreement, the composition of the arbitral tribunal was not in accordance with Part I of the Act.

(2) If the arbitral procedure was not in accordance with:

(*a*) the agreement of the parties; or

15 Section 34(2) of the Arbitration and Conciliation Act 1996.

16 *Oil and Natural Gas Corpn. Ltd.* v *SAW Pipes Ltd.* AIR 2003 SC 2629; JT 2003(4) SC 171; (2003)5 SCC 705.

(*b*) failing such agreement, the arbitral procedure was not in accordance with Part-I of the Act;

(*c*) If the award passed by the arbitral tribunal is in contravention of provisions of the Act or any other substantive law governing the parties or is against the terms of the contract.

(3) The award could be set aside if it is against the public policy of India, that is to say, if it is contrary to:

(*a*) fundamental policy of Indian law;

(*b*) the interest of India; or

(*c*) justice or morality; or

(*d*) if it is patently illegal.

(4) It could be challenged:

(*a*) as provided under s. 13(5); and

(*b*) Section 16(6) of the Act.

Public policy—meaning 'Public policy' means the collective rules, principles, or approaches to problems that affect the commonwealth or especially promote the general good.[17] The phrase 'Public Policy of India' is required to be given a wider meaning. It can be stated that the concept of public policy connotes some matter which concerns public good and the public interest. What is for public good or in public interest or what would be injurious or harmful to the public good or public interest has varied from time to time.[18]

An award is in conflict with the public policy of India An award is in conflict with the public policy of India, only if, (*i*) the making of the award was induced or affected by fraud or corruption or was in violation of s. 75 or s. 81; or (*ii*) it is in contravention with the fundamental policy of Indian law; or (*iii*) it is in conflict with the most basic notions of morality or justice.[19]

17 *Black's Law Dictionary*, 10th Ed. 2014.

18 *Oil and Natural Gas Corp. Ltd.* v *SAW Pipes Ltd.* AIR 2003 SC 2629; (2003)5 SCC 705.

19 *Explanation* 1 to s. 34(2)(*b*)(*ii*).

Set aside of award An arbitral award arising out of arbitrations other than international commercial arbitrations, may also be set aside by the court, if the court finds that the award is vitiated by patent illegality appearing on the face of the award. But an award shall not be set aside merely on the ground of an erroneous application of the law or by re-appreciation of evidence.[20]

Issuance of prior notice An application under s. 34 shall be filed by a party only after issuing a prior notice to the other party and such application shall be accompanied by an affidavit by the applicant endorsing compliance with the said requirement.[1]

Time limit of disposal of application An application under s. 34 shall be disposed of expeditiously, and in any event, within a period of one year from the date on which the notice under s. 34(5) is served upon the other party.[2]

Prejudice—not required to be proved The principles of natural justice know of no exclusionary rule dependent on whether it would have made any difference if natural justice had been observed. The non-observance of natural justice is itself prejudice to any man and proof of prejudice independently of proof of denial of natural justice is unnecessary. It will come from a person who has denied justice that the person who has been denied justice is not prejudiced.[3]

Award not challenged on the ground of inadequacy An award cannot be challenged on the basis of inadequacy or inadmissibility or impropriety of evidence, particularly when both the parties had the full opportunity to argue their respective cases and adduce evidence. Total absence of evidence or Arbitrator's failure to take into consideration a very material document on record or admission of the parties in arriving at the finding are however good grounds for challenging the proceeding.[4]

20 Section 34(2A).
1 Section 34(5).
2 Section 34(6).
3 *S.L. Kapoor* v *Jagmohan* AIR 1981 SC 136; (1980)4 SCC 379.
4 *West Bengal Industrial Infrastructre Development Corporation* v *Star Engineering Corporation* AIR 1987 Cal 126.

Procedure On receipt of an application for setting aside arbitral award the court may, where it is appropriate and it is so requested by a party, adjourn the proceedings for a period of time determined by it in order to give the arbitral tribunal an opportunity to resume the arbitral proceedings or to take such other action as in the opinion of arbitral tribunal will eliminate the grounds for setting aside the arbitral award.[5]

Enforcement of arbitral award An arbitral award is final and binding on the parties and persons claiming under them.[6] The award shall be enforced under the Code of Civil Procedure 1908 in the same manner as if it were a decree of the court.[7]

Statutory interpretation is an exercise which requires the court to identify the meaning borne by the words in question in the particular context. The purpose of the Act or section has to be inferred from the language used, read in its statutory context and having regard to any aid to interpretation which assists in the particular case.[8] An enforcing court under s. 36 cannot go behind the award of the Arbitrator.[9]

Filing of application does not ipso facto render the award unenforceable Where an application to set aside the arbitral award has been filed in the court under s. 34, the filing of such an application shall not by itself render that award unenforceable, unless the court grants an order of stay of the operation of the said arbitral award in accordance with the provisions of s. 36(3), on a separate application made for that purpose.[10]

Stay of operation of arbitral award Upon filing of an application under s. 36(2) for stay of the operation of the arbitral award, the court may, subject to such conditions as it may deem fit, grant stay of the operation of such award for reasons to be recorded in writing.[11]

5 Section 34(4).
6 Section 35.
7 Section 36.
8 *Union of India* v *Elphinstone Spinning and Weaving Co. Ltd.* AIR 2001 SC 724 (740).
9 *Gaffar Khan* v *Magma Shrachi Finance Ltd.* AIR 2012 Jhar 53.
10 Section 36(2).
11 Section 36(3).

Stay of arbitral award for payment of money and principle to be followed The court shall, while considering the application for grant of stay in the case of an arbitral award for payment of money, have due regard to the provisions for grant of stay of a money decree under the provisions of the Code of Civil Procedure 1908.[12]

Preamble The main purpose of the statement of objects and reasons of the Bill is to explain what reasons induced the mover to introduce the Bill in the House and what objects be sought to achieve.

Rules of construction of a statute Language used in the Act is to be liberally construed so as to give effect to the governing principles embodied in the legislation. Whenever a statute comes up for consideration, it must be remembered that it is not within human powers to foresee the manifold sets of facts which may arise, and, even if it were, it is not possible to provide for them in terms free from all ambiguity.[13] The words of a statute must *prima facie* be given their ordinary meaning.[14]

Power to refer parties to arbitration where there is an arbitration agreement A judicial authority before which an action is brought in a matter which is the subject of an arbitration agreement shall, if a party so applies not later than when submitting his first statement on the substance of the dispute, refer the parties to arbitration.[15] The application shall not be entertained unless it is accompanied by the original arbitration agreement or a duly certified copy thereof.[16] But when an application has been made under s. 8(1) and that the issue is pending before the judicial authority, an arbitration may be commenced or continued and an arbitral award made.[17]

It is beyond the scope of enquiry to examine as to whether a suit is maintanable or barred under the substantive contract

12 Proviso to s. 36(3).

13 *Union of India* v *Elphinstone Spinning and Weaving Co. Ltd.* AIR 2001 SC 724.

14 *Seaford Court Estate Ltd.* v *Asher* [1949]3 All ER 549.

15 Section 8(1).

16 Section 8(2).

17 Section 8(3).

while adjudicating on the validity of the arbitration agreement under s. 8.[18]

The language of s. 8 is peremptory.[19] It is, therefore, obligatory for the court to refer the parties to arbitration in terms of their arbitration agreement. But the court is not empowered to refer parties to arbitration if procedural requirement in s. 8(2) is not compiled with.[20]

Section 8 confers a power on the judicial authority. He must refer the dispute which is the subject matter of an arbitration agreement if an action is pending before him, subject to the fulfillment of the conditions precedent. The said power, however, shall be exercised if a party so applies not later than when submitting his first statement on the substance of the dispute.

The answer to the question whether a dispute falls within an arbitration clause in a contract must depend on (*a*) what is the dispute, and (*b*) what disputes the arbitration clause covers. To take (*b*) first, the language of the arbitration clause in this agreement is as broad as can well be imagined. It embraces any dispute between the parties 'in respect of' the agreement or in respect of any provision in the agreement or in respect of anything arising out of it. If the parties are one on the point that they did enter into a binding agreement in terms which are not in dispute, and the difference that has arisen between them is as to their respective rights under the admitted agreement in the events that have happened, *e.g.* as to whether the agreement has been broken by either of them; or as to the damage resulting from such breach; or as to whether the breach by one of them goes to the foot of the contract and entitles the other party to claim to be discharged from further performance; or as to whether events supervening since the agreement was made have brought the contract to an end so that neither party is required to perform further—in all such cases it seems to me that the difference is within such an arbitration clause as this. In view, however, of

18 *Saso Power Ltd.* v *North America Coal Corp. Pvt. Ltd.* (2016)10 SCC 813.

19 *P. Anand Gajapathi Raju* v *P.V.G. Raju* (2000)4 SCC 539; AIR 2000 SC 1886; JT 2000(4) SC 590.

20 *N. Radhakrishnan* v *Maestro Engineers* (2010)1 SCC 72.

phrases to be found in the report of some earlier decisions, the availability of the arbitration clause when 'frustration' is alleged to have occurred will require closer consideration.[1]

Original arbitration agreement if not available Where the original arbitration agreement or a certified copy thereof is not available with the party applying for reference to arbitration under s. 8(1) and the said agreement or certified copy is retained by the other party to that agreement, then, the party so applying shall file such application alongwith a copy of the arbitration agreement and a petition praying the court to call upon the other party to produce the original arbitration agreement or its duly certified copy before that court.[2]

Conditions The conditions which are required to be satisfied before the court can exercise its powers are:

(1) there is an arbitration agreement;

(2) a party to the agreement brings an action in the court against the other party;

(3) subject matter of the action is the same as the subject-matter of the arbitration agreement;

(4) the other party moves the court for referring the parties to arbitration before it submits his first statement on the substance of the dispute.

Submission of first statement defence—impact The provision creates a right in the person bringing the action to have the dispute adjudicated by the court, once the other party has submitted his first statement of defence. But if the party, who wants the matter to be referred to arbitration applies to the court after submission of his statement and the party who has brought the action does not object, there is no bar on the court referring the parties to arbitration.

First statement on the substance of the dispute The expression 'first statement on the substance of the dispute' contained in s. 8(1) of the 1996 Act must be contra—distinguished with the

1 *Heyman* v *Darwins Ltd.* [1942]1 All ER 337; [1942] AC 356; 111 LJ KB 241.

2 See proviso to s. 8(2).

expression 'written statement'. It employs submission of the party to the jurisdiction of the judicial authority. What is, therefore, is needed is a finding on the part of the judicial authority that the party has waived his right invoke the arbitration clause. If an application is filed before actually filing the first statement on the substance of the dispute, in our opinion, the party cannot be said to have waived his right or acquiesced himself to the jurisdiction of the court. What is, therefore, material is as to whether the petitioner has filed his first statement on the substance of the dispute or not. If not, his application under s. 8 of the 1996 Act, may not be held wholly unmaintainable.[3]

Section 8 of 1996 Act and section 34 of 1940 Act—comparison Section 8 of the 1996 Act contemplates some departure from s. 34 of the 1940 Act. Section 34 of the 1940 Act contemplated stay of the suit; s. 8 of the 1996 Act mandates a reference. Exercise of discretion by the judicial authority, which was the hallmark of s. 34 of the 1940 Act, has been taken away under the 1996 Act. The direction to make reference is not only mandatory, but the arbitration proceedings to be commenced or continued and conclusion thereof by an arbitral award remain unhampered by such pendency.[4]

Section 34 of the 1940 Act runs as follows:

> "34. *Power to stay legal proceedings where there is an arbitration agreement.* Where any party to an arbitration agreement or any person claiming under him commences any legal proceedings against any other party to the agreement or any person claiming under him in respect of any matter agreed to be referred, any party to such legal proceedings may, at any time before filing a written statement or taking any other steps in the proceedings, apply to the judicial authority before which the proceedings are pending to stay the proceedings; and if satisfied that there is no sufficient reason why the matter should not be referred in accordance with the arbitration agreement and that the applicant was, at the time when the proceedings were commenced, and still remains, ready and willing to do all things necessary to the

3 *Rashtriya Ispat Nigam Ltd.* v *Verma Transport Co.* AIR 2006 SC 2800; (2006)7 SCC 275; (2006)8 SCJ 40; (2006)7 Scale 565.

4 *Rashtriya Ispat Nigam Ltd.* v *Verma Transport Co.* (supra).

proper conduct of the arbitration, such authority may make an order staying the proceedings."

Interim measures by court[5] A party may, before or during arbitral proceedings or at any time after the making of the arbitral award but before it is enforced in accordance with s. 36, apply to a court—

(*i*) for the appointment of a guardian for a minor or a person of unsound mind for the purposes of arbitral proceedings; or

(*ii*) for an interim measure of protection in respect of any of the following matters, namely:

(*a*) the preservation, interim custody or sale of any goods which are the subject-matter of the arbitration agreement;

(*b*) securing the amount in dispute in the arbitration;

(*c*) the detention, preservation or inspection of any property or thing which is the subject-matter of the dispute in arbitration, or as to which any question may arise therein and authorizing for any of the aforesaid purposes any person to enter upon any land or building in the possession of any party, or authorising any samples to be taken or any observation to be made, or experiment to be tried, which may be necessary or expedient for the purpose of obtaining full information or evidence;

(*d*) interim injunction or the appointment of a receiver;

(*e*) such other interim measure of protection as may appear to the court to be just and convenient,

and the court shall have the same power for making orders as it has for the purpose of, and in relation to, any proceedings before it.

How application made A party could apply to the court (*a*) before, (*b*) during arbitral proceedings, or (*c*) after the making of the

5 Section 9(1) of the Arbitration and Conciliation Act 1996.

arbitral award but before it is enforced. An application for interim measure can be made to court in India, whether or not the arbitration takes place in India, before or during arbitral proceedings. Once an award is passed then that award itself can be executed.[6] An enforcement of a domestic award is to take place after the time to make an application to set aside the award has expired or such an application has been refused. The term "arbitral award" includes an interim award. There is a difference between an "interim award" and an "interim order". An interim order or directions passed by the arbitral tribunal would not be enforceable in India. If a party cannot secure, before or during the pendency of the arbitral proceedings, an interim order the arbitration proceedings may get frustrated, *e.g.* by non-appointment of a guardian for a minor or person of unsound mind or the subject matter of the arbitration agreement not being preserved. Where such arbitration is held in India the provisions of Part I would compulsorily apply and parties are free to deviate only to the extent permitted by the derogable provisions of Part I. In case of international commercial arbitrations held out of India provisions of Part I would apply unless the parties by agreement, express or implied, exclude all or any of its provisions.[7]

Stay under inherent power by court The court has an inherent jurisdiction to stay proceedings brought in breach of an agreement to decide disputes by arbitration. The inherent jurisdiction can be invoked where:[8]

1. The court cannot be certain that an arbitration agreement exists as is required for a stay but there is an issue whether the parties entered into a binding agreement to arbitrate or whether the subject-matter of the action is within the scope of the arbitration.

2. It is alleged that the arbitration agreement itself (rather than the matrix agreement) was induced by a misrepresentation, whether fraudulent or otherwise.

6 *Bhatia International* v *Bulk Trading* S.A. AIR 2002 SC 1432; JT 2002(3) SC 150; (2002)4 SCC 105.

7 *Ibid.*

8 Russell on *Arbitration*, 23rd Ed., pp. 373-374.

3. Related claims extending beyond the parties to an arbitration but involving parties closely connected to those parties are brought and it would be wasteful of costs and risk conflicting outcomes to allow the closely related legal proceedings to proceed in tandem with the arbitration.
4. For some other reason the application falls short of the requirements for a stay under the Arbitration Act 1996.

Interim injunction Russell states, "parties often seek interim measures in the form of an interim injunction directed at the other party to the reference requiring them to do or refrain from doing something in relation to the dispute. The interim injunction continues according to its terms during the course of the reference until the award is made, when it may or may not be replaced by a final injunction".[9]

Injunction to restrain arbitration An injunction to restrain the continuation of arbitral proceedings can arise in the following cases:[10]

1. Where one party commences an action before the court and successfully opposes a stay on the ground that the arbitration agreement is invalid and the arbitral proceedings based on the invalid agreement continue in defiance of the court's findings.
2. Where a party does not wish to take part in the arbitral proceedings but disputes the substantive jurisdiction of the tribunal and wants to prevent that tribunal determining claims against him. It is virtually impossible to obtain an injunction on this basis absent truly exceptional circumstances; and
3. Where all parties to an arbitration agreement apply to the court under s. 32 of the Arbitration Act 1996 and despite their request for a suspension of the arbitral proceedings the tribunal proceeds with a view to making an award.

9 Russell on *Arbitration*, 23rd Ed., p. 217.
10 Russell on *Arbitration*, 23rd Ed., pp. 376-377.

Enforcement of award of interest—statement of interest to be stated Russell states, "where an applicant seeks to enforce an award of interest, and the whole or any part of the interest claimed relates to a period after the date of the award, he must file a statement giving the following particulars—

(*a*) Whether simple or compound interest was awarded;

(*b*) the date from which interest was awarded;

(*c*) whether rests were provided for, specifying them;

(*d*) the rate of interest awarded; and

(*e*) a calculation showing the total amount claimed up to the date of the certificate and any sum which will become due on a daily basis."[11]

Limitation Once an award is made an application for interim measure can only be made if the award is a "domestic award".[12]

An application under s. 9 of the Act can be entertained by a principal civil court of original jurisdiction (including High Courts) which would have the jurisdiction to decide the question forming the subject matter if the same had been the subject matter of a suit.[13]

Comparison between Arbitration Act 1940 and Arbitration and Conciliation Act 1996 (1) Prior to the Arbitration and Conciliation Act 1996, the Arbitration Act 1940, which was in force in India, provided for domestic arbitration and no provision was there to deal with the foreign awards. So far as the foreign awards are concerned, the same were being dealt with by the Arbitration (Protocol and Convention) Act 1973 and the Foreign Awards (Recognition and Enforcement) Act 1961. The increasing growth of global trade and the delay in disposal of cases in courts under the normal system in several countries made it imperative to have the perception of an alternative dispute resolution system, more particularly, in the matter of commercial disputes. When the

11 Russell on *Arbitration*, 23rd Ed., pp. 543-544.

12 *Bhatia International* v *Bulk Trading S.A.* AIR 2002 SC 1432; JT 2002(3) SC 150; (2002)4 SCC 105.

13 *Union of India* v *Oglivy & Mather Ltd.* AIR 2009 Del 179; 2009(158) DLT 275.

entire world was moving in favour of a speedy resolution of commercial disputes, the United Nations Commission on International Trade Law way back in 1985 adopted the UNCITRAL Model Law of International Commercial Arbitration and since then a number of countries have given recognition to that Model in their respective legislative systems. With the said UNCITRAL Model Law in view the present Arbitration and Conciliation Act 1996 has been enacted in India replacing the Arbitration Act 1940 which was the principal legislation on arbitration in the country that had been enacted during the British rule. The Arbitration and Conciliation Act of 1996 provides not only for domestic arbitration but spreads its sweep to international commercial arbitration too. The Indian law relating to the enforcement of foreign arbitration awards provides for greater autonomy in the arbitral process and limits judicial intervention to a narrower circumference than under the previous law. To attract the confidence of the international mercantile community and the growing volume of India's trade and commercial relationship with the rest of the world after the new liberalization policy of the Government, Indian Parliament was persuaded to enact the Arbitration and Conciliation Act of 1996 on the basis of the UNCITRAL Model Law and, therefore, in interpreting any provisions of the 1996 Act, courts must not ignore the objects and purpose of the enactment of the 1996 Act.[14]

(2) The 1996 Act limits intervention of court with an arbitral process to the minimum and it is certainly not the legislative intent that each and every order passed by an authority under the Act would be a subject-matter of judicial scrutiny of a court of law. Under the present Act the grounds on which an award of an arbitrator could be challenged before the court have been severely cut down and such challenge is now permitted on the basis of invalidity of the agreement, want of jurisdiction on the part of the arbitrator or want of proper notice to a party of the appointment of the arbitrator or of arbitral proceedings. The powers of the arbitrator have been amplified by insertion of specific provisions of several matters.[15]

14 *Konkan Railway Corporation Ltd.* v *Mehul Construction Co.* (2000)7 SCC 201; AIR 2000 SC 2821; JT 2000(9) SC 362.

15 *Konkan Railway Corporation Ltd.* v *Mehul Construction Co.* (supra).

(3) Obstructive tactics adopted by the parties in arbitration proceedings are sought to be thwarted by an express provision in as much as if a party knowingly keeps silent and then suddenly raises a procedural objection, it will not be allowed to do so.[16]

(4) The role of institutions in promoting and organizing arbitration has been recognized. The power to nominate arbitrators has been given to the Chief Justice or to an institution or person designated by him.[17]

(5) The time limit for making awards has been deleted. The existing provisions in the 1940 Act relating to arbitration through intervention of court, when there is no suit pending or by order of the court when there is suit pending, have been removed.[18]

(6) The importance of transnational commercial arbitration has been recognized and it has been specifically provided that even where the arbitration is held in India, the parties to the contract would be free to designate the law applicable to the substance of the dispute.[19]

(7) Under the new law unless the agreement provides otherwise, the arbitrators are required to give reasons for the award. The award itself has now been vested with the status of a decree, inasmuch as the award itself is made executable as a decree and it will no longer be necessary to apply to the court for a decree in terms of the award. All these aim at achieving the sole object to resolve the dispute as expeditiously as possible with the minimum intervention of a court of law so that the trade and commerce is not affected on account of litigations before a court.[20]

(8) The main objective of the legislation was to minimise the supervisory role of courts in the arbitral process. If a comparison is made between the language of s. 11 of the Act and Art. 11 of the Model Law it would be apparent that the Act has designated

16 *Konkan Railway Corporation Ltd.* v *Mehul Construction Co.* (2000)7 SCC 201; AIR 2000 SC 2821; JT 2000(9) SC 362.

17 *Ibid.*

18 *Ibid.*

19 *Ibid.*

20 *Ibid.*

the Chief Justice of a High Court in cases of domestic arbitration and the Chief Justice of India in cases of international commercial arbitration, to be the authority to perform the function of appointment of arbitrator whereas under the Model Law the said power has been vested with the court.[1]

(9) The another objective of the Arbitration Act is to make provision for an arbitral procedure which is fair, efficient and capable of meeting the needs of the specific arbitration and to minimise the supervisory role of courts in the arbitral process and to permit an arbitral tribunal to use mediation, conciliation or other procedures during the arbitral proceedings in settlement of disputes.[2]

Advantages of arbitration

(1) ***No complex procedure*** Arbitrator is not bound to follow the rule of procedure which is complex and time consuming. He has to observe those rules which are necessary and reasonable to resolve the dispute fairly.

(2) ***Choose expert decision maker*** The parties are free to select their own decision maker which is an expert in the field in which the dispute has arisen.

(3) ***Quick disposal*** Arbitrator can resolve the dispute immediately after reference of the same to him. It can take much less time in comparison to time taken by the court.

(4) ***Settle dispute privately*** The parties to an arbitration can keep the proceedings privileged and the same shall be kept beyond public domain.

(5) ***Cost is minimum*** Procedure is simple in comparison with advisoral system of justice. Scope of appeal is very limited. So, it reduces the cost of litigation.

(6) ***Final and binding*** Decision is arrived at by the arbitrator with the consent of the parties. It is final and binding.

(7) ***Innovative*** The Arbitrator can innovate new ideas to resolve the dispute or provide remedy to the parties.

1 *Konkan Railway Corporation Ltd.* v *Mehul Construction Co.* (2000)7 SCC 201; AIR 2000 SC 2821; JT 2000(9) SC 362.

2 *SBP & Co.* v *Patel Engineering Ltd.* (2005)8 SCC 618.

(8) *Convenient* The sitting can be held according to the convenience of the parties.

(9) *Award is as good as decree* Award of the Arbitrator is enforceable and executable like a decree of a civil court.

(10) *Arbitrator assists the parties* The Arbitrator can assist the parties to come to a settlement over the disputed questions.

(11) *Any body represent the disputants* Any competent person even non-lawyer or legal practitioners can present/place the dispute of the disputants to the Arbitrator.

Duties of Arbitrator

To act independently It is the first duty of the Arbitrator to act independently without any shred of lack of independence, because it creates a doubt about his impartiality. An Arbitrator may be 'independent' in the sense that he may have no relationship with any of the parties and yet may not be 'impartial' as suffering from predilections or bias in favour of or against any of the parties. Conversely, an Arbitrator may not be in 'independent' in relation to any of the parties and yet may be capable of taking an impartial view on the matter and thus be 'impartial'. The law expects that the Arbitrator should be 'independent' and 'impartial' both. He exposes himself to legal challenge if he is either not 'independent' or not 'impartial'. The words 'independence' or 'impartiality' have been used disjunctively because justifiable doubts as to either of them disqualifies a person from acting as an Arbitrator.[3]

To act fairly The Arbitrator must act fairly to both the parties. He must not favour one party during the course of proceedings. The Tribunal must act fairly and impartially as between the parties, giving each party a reasonable opportunity of putting his case and dealing with that of his opponent. According to Russell, "it must act fairly as well as impartially as between the parties, in conducting the arbitral proceedings, in its decisions on matters of procedure and evidence and in the exercise of other powers conferred on it".[4]

3 S.K. Chawla, *Law of Arbitration & Conciliation including other ADRs*, 3rd Ed., p. 454.

4 Russell on *Arbitration*, 23rd Ed., p. 156.

To act judicially and to adopt suitable procedure The tribunal must adopt suitable procedures for resolution of the matter which is referred for determination. It is the duty of the Arbitrator to adopt just and suitable procedure regarding submission of claim, written argument and counter-claim. The Arbitrator is duty bound to provide sufficient opportunity to the parties to the proceedings to adduce evidence and cross-examine the witnesses of the adversary.

Act confidentially An arbitral tribunal is subject to a duty to keep the subject matter of the arbitration confidential except when required by law to disclose it".[5]

To avoid delay and unnecessary expenses Another duty cast upon the Arbitrator is to conclude the proceedings with promptitude in order to avoid unnecessary delay and expense.

Act within jurisdiction and Strictly comply with the terms of submission It must act within its jurisdiction. Otherwise the award will be unenforceable. If the submission limits or provides the power and duties of the Arbitrator he must confine himself within the power.

Not to exceed power The arbitral tribunal should not exceed its power in conducting the arbitration. If the Arbitrator exceeds his power, it would result in serious irregularity in the award.

Must not delegate its power Tribunal cannot delegate its function to decide the dispute and difference between parties.

Decide according to law Russell states "The Tribunal must decide a dispute: (*a*) in accordance with the law chosen by the parties as applicable to the substance of the dispute, or (*b*) if the parties so agree, in accordance with such other considerations as are agreed by them or determined by the Tribunal".[6]

Decide dispute in terms of argument following the law An Arbitrator is the creature of an agreement. It is open to the parties to confer upon him such powers and prescribe such procedure for him to follow, as they think fit, so long as they are not opposed to law.

5 Russell on *Arbitration*, 23rd Ed., p. 169.
6 Russell on *Arbitration*, 23rd Ed., p. 169.

All the same, the agreement must be in conformity with law. The Arbitrator must also act and make his award inaccordance with the general law of the land and the agreement.

Duty to disclose The Arbitrator is under oblilgation to disclose information received from one side to the other. In other words, he is not empowered to receive any secret information from one side. Disclosure is imperative to the process of constitution of arbitral tribunal. Disclosure(s) are *sine qua non* to the parties or appointing institutions by prospective Arbitrator(s) of their relationship or other circumstances which might raise justifiable grounds regarding their impartiality and independence. Timely and complete performance of disclosure obligation is vital to the integrity of the arbitral process. The importance of the duty of disclosure becomes quite clear as it is the backbone that holds together the foundation of the arbitration, that is the arbitral tribunal. The disclosure requirement mandates the Arbitrator to make disclosures, both prior to accepting the appointment and in the event of the new development, during the course of arbitration.[7]

Must possess required qualification According to Russell, "an Arbitrator must possess the qualifications required by the arbitration agreement, otherwise he can be removed and /or his award may be set aside".[8]

Power

Power to make order of inspection or discovery of document The Arbitrator has the power to make order for the inspection or discovery of documents on which the parties bank upon in the proceedings. In this respect, the power of the Arbitrator is similar to the power of the court.

Power to award interest The Arbitrator is competent to award interest—

(*a*) from the stage of accrual of cause of action till filing of the arbitration proceeding, i.e. for the pre-reference period;

7 *Alternative Dispute Resolution the Indian Perspective* edited by Shashank Garg, pp. 33-34 (Oxford University Press).

8 Russell on *Arbitration*, 23rd Ed., p. 169.

(*b*) during pendency of proceedings before him, i.e. interest *pendente lite*;

(*c*) future interest arising between the date of award and the date of the decree; and

(*d*) interest arising from the date of decree till realization of the award, i.e. post award interest.

In short, "every Arbitrator, whether nominated by a party or appointed independently, must carry out his duty independently, honestly, and with integrity. Indeed, it is essential to the success of any arbitration that both parties are able to have confidence and trust in the tribunal ability to act with independence and impartiality, both 'independence and impartiality' are interrelated concepts. An Arbitrator may fail to act impartially by favouring one of the parties or by having preconceived prejudices about the issues in dispute. An Arbitrator may fail to be independent because of a relationship with one of the parties, be it financial, professional, or social, which gives the appearance of a personal interest or bias in the result or process of the arbitration. An Arbitrator must not only act impartially but he must also be completely independent of any relationship with any of the parties, else it may case a doubt, at least a reasonable doubt as to his independence and impartiality. Thus, 'Justice should not only be done but seem to be done' applies to arbitral justice too".[9]

According to Russell, "An arbitral tribunal, in discharging its duty to determine the dispute has the following powers[10]—

"To rule on jurisdiction;

To decide all procedural and evidential matters, including;

Location and timing of proceedings;

Language and the need for translations;

The form, timing and possible amendment of any statement of claim or defence;

9 *Alternative Dispute Resolution the Indian Perspective* edited by Shashank Garg, pp. 33-34 (Oxford University Press).

10 Russell on *Arbitration*, 23rd Ed., pp. 143-145.

Disclosure of documents;

Parties questions to each other;

Rules, weight, time, manner and form of evidence;

Whether the tribunal should take the initiative in ascertaining facts and law;

Whether there should be oral or written evidence or submissions;

To appoint experts, legal advisers and assessors;

To order security for costs,

To give directions about property the subject of proceedings,

To direct that a witness be examined on oath or affirmation,

To make provisional orders,

To act in case of a party's default,

To apply to the court for a peremptory order,

To make awards on different issues at different times on different aspects,

To make a declaration,

To order payment of a sum of money in any currency,

To order a party to refrain from doing something,

To order specific performance of a contract other than land,

To order rectification, setting aside or cancellation of a deed or other document,

To award interest,

To terminate arbitral proceedings if the dispute is settled by the parties,

To decide the date of the award,

To correct an award,

To make an additional award on matters in issue but not covered by the award,

To allocate costs between the parties,

To determine the costs recoverable,

To limit recoverable costs to a specific amount."

Russell again states, the specific duties of an arbitral tribunal are as follows:

"To act fairly and impartially between the parties,

To possess the qualifications required by the arbitration agreement,

To be physically and mentally capable of conducting the proceedings,

To conduct the proceedings properly,

To use all reasonable despatch in conducting the proceedings or making an award,

To give each party a reasonable opportunity of putting his case and dealing with that of his opponent,

To adopt procedures suitable to the circumstances of the particular case,

To avoid unnecessary delay or expense,

To provide a fair means for the resolution of the matters falling to be determined,

To attend hearings and participate in deliberations of the tribunal,

Not to exceed its substantive jurisdiction,

Not to exceed its powers,

To conduct the proceedings in accordance with the procedure agreed by the parties,

To deal with all the issues put,

To ensure that any award is neither uncertain nor ambiguous,

To ensure that any award is not obtained by fraud or procured in a way contrary to public policy,

To ensure that any award complies with requirements as to its form,

To act judicially,

To keep the subject matter of the arbitration confidential,

To make its own decision,

To decide according to the law or, if agreed, according to other considerations".[11]

11 Russell on *Arbitration*, 23rd Ed., pp.154-156.

Breach of duties—consequence The breach of duties has the following consequences[12]—(*a*) Breach of duties leads to an Arbitrator's removal and repayment of fees; (*b*) it justifies intervention by the court during a reference; (*c*) it leads to an award being remitted or set aside or declared to be of no effect and; (*d*) it result in a claim for damages in the event of bad faith.

Instance of deliberate breach of duties The instances of serious and deliberate breaches of an Arbitrator's duties are[13]—

(*a*) Deliberately obstructing the proceedings by, for instance, failing to appear at hearings without a reasonable excuse,

(*b*) refusing to participate in the tribunal's deliberations, and

(*c*) leaking details of the tribunal's deliberations before the publication of the award.

Supreme Court on award of interest In *State of Orissa* v *B.N. Agarwalla*,[14] the Supreme Court observes: (*i*) A person deprived of the use of money to which he is legitimately entitled has a right to be compensated for the deprivation, call it by any name. It may be called interest, compensation or damages. This basic consideration is as valid for the period the disputes is pending before the Arbitrator as it is for the period prior to the Arbitrator entering upon the reference. This is the principle of s. 34, CPC and there is no reason or principle to hold otherwise in the case of Arbitrator.

(*ii*) An Arbitrator is an alternative from (*sic* forum) for resolution of disputes arising between the parties. If so, he must have the power to decide all the disputes or differences arising between the parties. If the Arbitrator has no power to award interest *pendente lite*, the party claiming it could have to approach the court for that purpose, even though he may have obtained satisfaction in respect of other claims from the Arbitrator. This would lead to multiplicity of proceedings.

12 Russell on *Arbitration*, 23rd Ed., p. 156.

13 Russell on *Arbitration*, 23rd Ed., p. 176.

14 AIR 1997 SC 925; JT 1997(2) SC 51; (1997)2 SCC 469.

(iii) Interest *pendente lite* is not a matter of substantive law, like interest for the period anterior to reference (pre-reference period). For doing complete justice between the parties, such power has always been inferred.

In an international commercial arbitration, in the absence of an agreement between the parties on interest, the rate of interest awarded would be governed by the law of the seat of the arbitration. The rate of interest awarded must correspond to the currency in which the award is given, and must be in conformity with the laws in force in the *lex fori*. The discretion of the Arbitrator to award interest must be exercised reasonably. An arbitral tribunal while making an award for interest must take into consideration a host of factors, such as: (*i*) the 'loss of use' of the principal sum; (*ii*) the types of sums to which the interest must apply; (*iii*) the time period over which interest should be awarded; (*iv*) the internationally prevailing rates of interest; (*v*) whether simple or compound rate of interest is to be applied; (*vi*) whether the rate of interest awarded is commercially prudent from an economic standpoint; (*vii*) the rates of inflation, (*viii*) proportionality of the count awarded as interest to the principal sums awarded.

On the one hand, the rate of interest must be compensatory as it is a form of reparation granted to the award-holder, while on the other it must not be punitive, unconscionable or usurious in nature. Courts may reduce the interest rate awarded by an arbitral tribunal where such interest rate does not reflect the prevailing economic conditions or where it is nor found reasonable, or it promotes the interests of justice.[15]

Appointment of Arbitrators[16] (1) A person of any nationality may be an Arbitrator, unless otherwise agreed by the parties.

(2) Subject to sub-sec. (6), the parties are free to agree on a procedure for appointing the Arbitrator or Arbitrators.

(3) Failing any agreement referred to in sub-sec. (2), in an arbitration with three Arbitrators, each party shall appoint one

15 *Vedanta Ltd.* v *Shenzen Shandong Nuclear Power Construction Co. Ltd.* AIR 2018 SC 4773.

16 Section 11, the Arbitration and Conciliation Act 1996.

Arbitrator, and the two appointed Arbitrators shall appoint the third Arbitrator who shall act as the presiding Arbitrator.

*[(3*A*) The Supreme Court and the High Court shall have the power to designate, arbitral institutions, from time to time, which have been graded by the Council under s. 43-I, for the purposes of this Act:

Provided that in respect of those High Court jurisdictions, where no graded arbitral institutions are available, then, the Chief Justice of the concerned High Court may maintain a panel of arbitrators for discharging the functions and duties of arbitral institution and any reference to the arbitrator shall be deemed to be an arbitral institution for the purposes of this section and the arbitrator appointed by a party shall be entitled to such fee at the rate as specified in the Fourth Schedule:

Provided further that the Chief Justice of the concerned High Court may, from time to time, review the panel of arbitrators].

(4) If the appointment procedure in sub-sec. (3) applies and—

(*a*) a party fails to appoint an Arbitrator within thirty days from the receipt of a request to do so from the other party; or

(*b*) the two appointed Arbitrators fail to agree on the third Arbitrator within thirty days from the date of their appointment,

**[the appointment shall be made, on an application of the party, by the arbitral institution designated by the Supreme Court, in case of international commercial arbitration, or by the High Court, in case of arbitrations other than international commercial arbitration, as the case may be].

(5) Failing any agreement referred to in sub-sec. (2), in an arbitration with a sole Arbitrator, if the parties fail to agree on the Arbitrator within thirty days from receipt of a request by one

* *Inserted* by the Arbitration and Conciliation (Amendment) Act 2019 (Act 33 of 2019).

** *Substituted* for "the appointment shall be made, upon request of a party, by the Supreme Court or, as the case may be, the High Court or any person or institution designated by such court" by the Arbitration and Conciliation (Amendment) Act 2019 (Act 33 of 2019).

party from the other party to so agree *[the appointment shall be made on an application of the party in accordance with the provisions contained in sub-sec. (4)].

(6) Where, under an appointment procedure agreed upon by the parties,—

(*a*) a party fails to act as required under that procedure; or

(*b*) the parties, or the two appointed Arbitrators, fail to reach an agreement expected of them under that procedure; or

(*c*) a person, including an institution, fails to perform any function entrusted to him or it under that procedure,

**[the appointment shall be made, on an application of the party, by the arbitral institution designated by the Supreme Court, in case of international commercial arbitration, or by the High Court, in case of arbitrations other than international commercial arbitration, as the case may be] to take the necessary measure, unless the agreement on the appointment procedure provides other means for securing the appointment.

***[(6A) ....].

(6B) The designation of any person or institution by the Supreme Court or, as the case may be, the High Court, for the

* *Substituted* for "the appointment shall be made, upon request of a party, by the Supreme Court or, as the case may be, the High Court or any person or institution designated by such court" by the Arbitration and Conciliation (Amendment) Act 2019 (Act 33 of 2019).

** *Substituted* for "a party may request the Supreme Court or, as the case may be, the High Court or any person or institution designated by such court" by the Arbitration and Conciliation (Amendment) Act 2019 (Act 33 of 2019).

*** Sub-section (6A) has been *omitted* by the Arbitration and Conciliation (Amendment) Act 2019 (Act 33 of 2019). Prior to its omission, it was as under:

"(6A). The Supreme Court or, as the case may be, the High Court, while considering any application under sub-sec. (4) or sub-sec. (5) or sub-sec. (6), shall, notwithstanding any judgment, decree or order of any court, confine to the examination of the existence of an arbitration agreement."

purposes of this section shall not be regarded as a delegation of judicial power by the Supreme Court or the High Court.

*[(7) ....].

(8) **[The arbitral institution referred to in sub-secs. (4), (5) and (6)] before appointing an Arbitrator, shall seek a disclosure in writing from the prospective Arbitrator in terms of sub-sec. (1) of s. 12, and have due regard to—

(*a*) any qualifications required for the Arbitrator by the agreement of the parties; and

(*b*) the contents of the disclosure and other considerations as are likely to secure the appointment of an independent and impartial Arbitrator.

(9) In the case of appointment of sole or third Arbitrator in an international commercial arbitration, ***[the arbitral institution designated by the Supreme Court] may appoint an Arbitrator of a nationality other than the nationalities of the parties where the parties belong to different nationalities.

†[(10) ....].

* Sub-section (7) has been *omitted* by the Arbitration and Conciliation (Amendment) Act 2019 (Act 33 of 2019). Prior to its omission, it was as under:

"(7). A decision on a matter entrusted by sub-sec. (4) or sub-sec. (5) or sub-sec. (6) to the Supreme Court, or as the case may be, the High Court or the person or institution designated by such court is final and no appeal including Letters Patent Appeal shall lie against such decision."

** *Substituted* for "The Supreme Court or, as the case may be, the High Court or the person or institution designated by such court " by the Arbitration and Conciliation (Amendment) Act 2019 (Act 33 of 2019).

*** *Substituted* for "the Supreme Court or the person or institution designated by that court" by the Arbitration and Conciliation (Amendment) Act 2019 (Act 33 of 2019).

† Sub-section (10) has been *omitted* by the Arbitration and Conciliation (Amendment) Act 2019 (Act 33 of 2019). Prior to its omission, it was as under:

"(10) The Supreme Court or, as the case may be, the High Court, may make such scheme as the said court may deem appropriate for dealing with matters entrusted by sub-sec. (4) or sub-sec. (5) or sub-sec. (6) to it."

*[(11) Where more than one request has been made under sub-sec. (4) or sub-sec. (5) or sub-sec. (6) to different arbitral institutions, the arbitral institution to which the request has been first made under the relevant sub-section shall be competent to appoint.

* Sub-sections (11) to (14) have been *substituted* by the Arbitration and Conciliation (Amendment) Act 2019 (Act 33 of 2019). Prior to their substitution, they were as under:

"(11) Where more than one request has been made under sub-sec. (4) or sub-sec. (5) or sub-sec. (6) to different High Courts or their designates, the High Court or its designate to whom the request has been first made under the relevant sub-section shall alone be competent to decide on the request.

(12) (*a*) Where the matters referred to in sub-secs. (4), (5), (6), (7), (8) and (10) arise in an international commercial arbitration, the reference to the Supreme Court or as the case may be the High Court in those sub-sections shall be construed as a reference to the Supreme Court.

(*b*) Where the matters referred to in sub-secs. (4), (5), (6), (7), (8) and (10) arise in any other arbitration, the reference to the Supreme Court or, as the case may be, the High Court in those sub-sections shall be construed as a reference to the High Court within whose local limits the principal civil court referred to in cl. (*e*) of sub-sec. (1) of s. 2 is situate and where the High Court itself is the court referred to in that clause, to that High Court.

(13) An application made under this section for appointment of an Arbitrator or Arbitrators shall be disposed of by the Supreme Court or the High Court or the person or institution designated by such court, as the case may, as expeditiously as possible and an endeavour shall be made to dispose of the matter within a period of sixty days from the date of service of notice on the opposite party.

(14) For the purpose of determination of the fees of the arbitral tribunal and the manner of its payment to the arbitral tribunal, the High Court may frame such rules as may be necessary, after taking into consideration the rates specified in the Fourth Schedule.

Explanation. For the removal of doubts, it is hereby clarified that this sub-section shall not apply to international commercial arbitration and in arbitrations (other than international commercial arbitration) in case where parties have agreed for determination of fees as per the rules of an arbitral institution."

(12) Where the matter referred to in sub-secs. (4), (5), (6) and (8) arise in an international commercial arbitration or any other arbitration, the reference to the arbitral institution in those sub-sections shall be construed as a reference to the arbitral institution designated under sub-sec. (3A).

(13) An application made under this section for appointment of an arbitrator or arbitrators shall be disposed of by the arbitral institution within a period of thirty days from the date of service of notice on the opposite party.

(14) The arbitral institution shall determine the fees of the arbitral tribunal and the manner of its payment to the arbitral tribunal subject to the rates specified in the Fourth Schedule.

Explanation. For the removal of doubts, it is hereby clarified that this sub-section shall not apply to international commercial arbitration and in arbitrations (other than international commercial arbitration) where parties have agreed for determination of fees as per the rules of an arbitral institution.]

Where the procedure for appointment has been agreed upon between the parties, the court's function is only to implement the agreed procedure.[17] The court cannot appoint an independent Arbitrator at the first instane.[18]

Mode of appointment If a party fails to appoint an Arbitrator within 30 days from the date of receipt of a request to do so from the other party or if two appointed Arbitrators failed to agree on the third Arbitrator within 30 days from the date of their appointment, the appointment shall be made by the Supreme Court or High Court, as the case may be, instead of the Chief Justice of India or the Chief Justice of the High Court. An application for

17 *BSNL* v *Subash Chandra Kanchan* (2006)8 SCC 279; AIR 2006 SC 3335.

18 *Bell House Ass. (P) Ltd.* v *Southern Railway* AIR 2001 Ker 163; *Indian Engg. Works* v *Coal India Ltd.* AIR 2003 Jhar 15; *Subhash Projects & Mkg. Ltd.* v *South Eastern Coalfields Ltd.* AIR 1998 MP 276.

appointment of Arbitrator shall be disposed of as expeditiously as possible. An endeavour shall be made to dispose of the said application within a period of 60 days from the date of service of notice on the opposite party.

An appointment of an Arbitrator by a party is not complete without communication thereof to the other party. Acceptance of the office by the Arbitrator appears to be necessary to perfect his appointment. It has been so decided in the case of an umpire, and it would seem to be only reasonable that an appointment should not be considered effective until the person appointed has agreed either expressly or tacitly to exercise the function of the office. A mere nomination, unknown to the appointee is not an 'appointment' of him. It does not become an "appointment" merely by being communicated to the other side. It becomes an "appointment" of him as Arbitrator only when he is effectively in the position of an Arbitrator, clothed with the duties and authority of such. The stage of effective appointment is not reached before he has been told that it is desired to appoint him in a particular manner and he has indicated his willingness to act in that matter.[19]

Section 11(5)—when invoked Sub-section (5) of s. 11 of the Arbitration and Conciliation Act 1996 can be invoked by a party if the parties failed to agree on the Arbitrator within 30 days from the receipt of a request by one party from the other party to do so, agree to appointment. Such appointment shall be made upon request of a party by the Supreme Court or High Court, as the case may be, or any other person or institution designated either by Supreme Court or by High Court.

Application under s. 11(6)—when filed An application under sub-sec. (6) of s. 11 can be filed when there is a failure of the procedure for appointment of an Arbitrator. This failure of procedure can arise under different circumstances. It can be a case where a party who is bound to appoint an Arbitrator refuses to appoint the Arbitrator or where two appointed Arbitrators

19 Russell on *Arbitration*, 23rd Ed., pp. 124-127.

fail to appoint the third Arbitrator. If the appointment of an Arbitrator or any function connected with such appointment is entrusted to any person or institution and such person or institution fails to discharge such function, the aggrieved party can approach the Chief Justice (now Supreme Court or the High Court or any person or institution designated by such court) for appointment of an Arbitrator.[20] The nature of order of appointment differs in the case where there is no procedure agreed upon between the parties and when the procedure had been agreed upon between the parties for the appointment of an Arbitrator, if an agreement is entered into between the parties provides the procedure for appointment of Arbitrator, the court has to implement the said procedure, but not to venture upon to pass an order otherwise.[1]

Appointment of serving officer as Arbitrator

Before Amendment Act 2015 Arbitration is a binding voluntary alternative dispute resolution process by a private forum chosen by the parties. It is quite common for Governments, statutory corporations and public sector undertakings while entering into contracts, to provide for settlement of disputes by arbitration, and further provide that the Arbitrator will be one of its senior officers. If a party, with open eyes and full knowledge and comprehension of the said provision enters into a contract with a Government/statutory corporation/public sector undertaking containing an arbitration agreement providing that one of its Secretaries/Directors shall be the Arbitrator, he cannot subsequently turn around and contend that he is agreeable for settlement of disputes by arbitration, but not by the named Arbitrator who is an employee of the other party. No party can say he will be bound by only one part of the agreement and not the other part, unless such other part is impossible of performance or is void being contrary to the provisions of the Act, and such part is severable from the remaining part of the

20 *Datar Switch Gears Ltd.* v *Tata Finance Ltd.* (2000)8 SCC 151.

1 *Kamala Solvent* v *Manipal Finance Corporation Ltd.* AIR 2001 Mad 440.

agreement. The arbitration clause is a package which may provide for what disputes are arbitrable, at what stage the disputes are arbitrable, who should be the Arbitrator, what should be the venue, what law would govern the parties etc. A party to the contract cannot claim the benefit of arbitration under the arbitration clause, but ignore the appointment procedure relating to the named Arbitrator contained in the arbitration clause. So, arbitration agreements in government contracts providing that an employee of the department (usually a high official unconnected with the work or the contract) will be the Arbitrator, are neither void nor unenforceable.[2]

After Amendment Act 2015 After Arbitration and Conciliation (Amendment) Act 2015 the Arbitrator cannot be an employee, consultant, advisor or has any other past or present business relationship with a party. Thus, the serving officer cannot function as Arbitrator even if he is unconnected with work in dispute of the department. But there is an exception. Proviso to sub-sec. (5) of s. 12 provides that "parties may, subsequent to disputes having arisen between them, waive the applicability of this sub-section by an express agreement in writing". Thus, the parties to the dispute subsequent to disputes having arisen between them may by an express agreement in writing appoint serving officer as an Arbitrator.

Condition of neutrality and appointment of Arbitrator Independence and impartiality of the Arbitrator are the hallmarks of any arbitration proceedings. Rule against bias is one of the fundamental principles of natural justice which applied to all judicial and quasi judicial proceedings. It is for this reason that notwithstanding the fact that relationship between the parties to the arbitration and the Arbitrators themselves are contractual in nature and the source of an Arbitrator's appointment is deduced from the agreement entered into between the parties, notwithstanding the same non-independence and non-impartiality of such Arbitrator (though contractually agreed upon) would

2 *Indian Oil Corporation Ltd.* v *Raja Transport (P) Ltd.* AIR 2009 SC 2145; (2009)8 SCC 520; 2010(1) ICC 27; 2009(3) Arb LR 354.

render him ineligible to conduct the arbitration. The genes behind this rational is that even when an Arbitrator is appointed in terms of contract and by the parties to the contract, he is independent of the parties. Functions and duties require him to rise above the partisan interest of the parties and not to act in, or so as to further, the particular interest of either parties. After all, the Arbitrator has adjudicatory role to perform and, therefore, he must be independent of parties as well as impartial.[3] The United Kingdom Supreme Court has beautifully highlighted this aspect in *Jivraj* v *Hashwani*[4] in the following words:

> "the dominant purpose of appointing an Arbitrator is the impartial resolution of dispute between the parties in accordance with the terms of the agreement and, although the contract between the parties and the Arbitrators would be a contract for the provision of personal services, they were not personal services under the discretion of the parties."

Ground raises doubt about independence or impartiality of Arbitrators

The following grounds give rise to justifiable doubts as to the independence or impartiality of Arbitrators—

Arbitrator's relationship with the parties or counsel

1. The Arbitrator is an employee, consultant, advisor or has any other past or present business relationship with a party.

2. The Arbitrator currently represents or advises one of the parties or an affiliate of one of the parties.

3. The Arbitrator currently represents the lawyer or law firm acting as counsel for one of the parties.

4. The Arbitrator is a lawyer in the same law firm which is representing one of the parties.

5. The Arbitrator is a manager, director or part of the management, or has a similar controlling influence, in an affiliate of one of the parties if the affiliate is directly involved in the matters in dispute in the arbitration.

3 *Voestalpine Schienen GMBH* v *Delhi Metro Rail Corporation Ltd.* AIR 2017 SC 939.

4 (2011) UKSC 40.

6. The Arbitrator's law firm had a previous but terminated involvement in the case without the Arbitrator being involved himself or herself.

7. The Arbitrator's law firm currently has a significant commercial relationship with one of the parties or an affiliate of one of the parties.

8. The Arbitrator regularly advises the appointing party or an affiliate of the appointing party even though neither the Arbitrator nor his or her firm derives a significant financial income there from.

9. The Arbitrator has a close family relationship with one of the parties and in the case of companies with the persons in the management and controlling the company.

10. A close family member of the Arbitrator has a significant financial interest in none of the parties or an affiliate of one of the parties.

11. The Arbitrator is a legal representative of an entity that is a party in the arbitration.

12. The Arbitrator is a manager, director or part of the management, or has a similar controlling influence in one of the parties.

13. The Arbitrator has a significant financial interest in one of the parties or the outcome of the case.

14. The Arbitrator regularly advises the appointing party or an affiliate of the appointing party, and the Arbitrator or his or her firm derives a significant financial income therefrom.

Relationship of the Arbitrator to the dispute

15. The Arbitrator has given legal advice or provided an expert opinion on the dispute to a party or an affiliate of one of the parties.

16. The Arbitrator has previous involvement in the case.

Arbitrator's direct or indirect interest in the dispute

17. The Arbitrator holds shares, either directly or indirectly, on one of the parties or an affiliate of one of the parties that is privately held.

18. A close family member of the Arbitrator has a significant financial interest in the outcome of the dispute.

19. The Arbitrator or a close family member of the Arbitrator has a close relationship with a third party who may be liable to recourse on the part of the unsuccessful party in the dispute.

Previous services for one of the parties or other involvement in the case

20. The Arbitrator has within the past three years served as counsel for one of the parties or an affiliate of one of the parties or has previously advised or been consulted by the party or an affiliate of the party making the appointment in an unrelated matter, but the Arbitrator and the party or the affiliate of the party has no ongoing relationship.

21. The Arbitrator has within the past three years served as counsel against one of the parties or an affiliate of one of the parties in an unrelated matter.

22. The Arbitrator has within the past three years been appointed as Arbitrator on two or more occasions by one of the parties or an affiliate of one of the parties.

23. The Arbitrator's law firm has within the past three years acted for one of the parties or an affiliate of one of the parties in an unrelated matter without the involvement of the Arbitrator.

24. The Arbitrator currently serves, or has served within the past three years, as Arbitrator in another arbitration on a related issue involving one of the parties or an affiliate of one of the parties.

Relationship between Arbitrator and another Arbitrator or Counsel

25. The Arbitrator and another Arbitrator are lawyers in the same law firm.

26. The Arbitrator was within the past three years a partner of, or otherwise affiliated with, another Arbitrator or any of the counsel in the same arbitration.

27. A lawyer in the Arbitrator's law firm is an Arbitrator in another dispute involving the same party or parties or an affiliate of one of the parties.

28. A close family member of the Arbitrator is a partner or employee of the law firm representing one of the parties, but is not assisting with the dispute.

29. The Arbitrator has within the past three years received more than three appointments by the same counsel or the same law firm.

Relationship between Arbitrator and party and other involved in the arbitration

30. The Arbitrator's law firm is currently acting adverse to one of the parties or an affiliate of one of the parties.

31. The Arbitrator had been associated within the past three years with a party or an affiliate of one of the parties in a professional capacity, such as a former employee or partner.

Other circumstances

32. The Arbitrator holds shares, either directly or indirectly, which by reason of number or denomination constitute a material holding in one of the parties or an affiliate of one of the parties that is publicly listed.

33. The Arbitrator holds a position in an arbitration institution with appointing authority over the dispute.

34. The Arbitrator is a manager, director or part of the management, or has a similar controlling influence, in an affiliate of one of the parties, where the affiliate is not directly involved in the matters in dispute in the arbitration.

Appointment of Presiding Arbitrator—procedure In an arbitration with three Arbitrators, each party shall appoint one Arbitrator, and the two appointed Arbitrators shall appoint the third Arbitrator who shall act as the presiding Arbitrator. The law nowhere contemplates such appointment being necessarily in writing. The requirement of the law is that there should be an appointment and the appointment should be by the two appointed Arbitrators. It is not necessary within the meaning of s. 11(3) that the presiding Arbitrator must be appointed by the two appointed Arbitrators in writing nor it is necessary that the two appointed Arbitrators must necessarily sit at one place, deliberate jointly and take a decision in the presence of each other in regard to the appointment of the presiding Arbitrator. It is enough if they have actually consulted or conferred with each other and if both or any of them communicates to the parties the appointment of the presiding Arbitrator as having taken place by the joint deliberation of the two. When an effective consultation can be achieved by resort to electronic media and remote conferencing it is not necessary that the two persons required to act in consultation with each other must necessarily sit together at one place unless it is the requirement of law or of the ruling contract between the parties. The appointment need not necessarily be by a writing signed by the two Arbitrators; it satisfies the requirement of law if the appointment (*i*) has been actually made, (*ii*) is preceded by such consultation as to amount to appointment by the two, and (*iii*) is communicated. It is not essential to the validity of the appointment that the parties should be consulted, or involved in the process of appointment or given a previous notice of the proposed appointment. In short, the appointment by Arbitrators of an umpire should be the act of the will and judgment of the two. Such an appointment is to be one of choice and not of chance.[5]

Arbitrator cannot go beyond agreement The Arbitrator is a creature of the agreement itself and therefore he is duty bound to enforce the terms of the agreement and cannot adjudicate a matter beyond the agreement itself. If the Arbitrator adjudicates a claim of a contractor with reference to the clauses of the agreement itself whereby the agreement gets engrafted into the award, it will be open to the court to examine those clauses of the agreement and find out the correctness of the conclusions of the Arbitrator with reference to those clauses.[6] The Arbitrator cannot act arbitrarily irrationally, capriciously or independently of the contract. His sole function is to arbitrate in terms of the contract. He has no power apart from what the parties have given him under the contract. If he has travelled outside the bounds of the contract, he has acted without jurisdiction. But

5 *Grid Corporation of Orissa Ltd.* v *AES Corporation* (2002)7 SCC 736; AIR 2002 SC 3435; 2003(2) AIC 169; 2002(3) Arb LR 486.

6 *State of U.P.* v *Ram Nath International Construction Pvt. Ltd.* AIR 1996 SC 782; (1995)6 Scale 321; (1996)1 SCC 18.

if he has remained inside the parameters of the contract and has construed the provisions of the contract, his award cannot be interfered with unless he has given reasons for the award disclosing an error apparent on the face of it. An Arbitrator who acts in manifest disregard of the contract acts without jurisdiction. His authority is derived from the contract and is governed by the Arbitration Act which embodies principles derived from a specialised branch of the law of agency.[7] He commits misconduct if by his award he decides matters excluded by the agreements.[8] A deliberate departure from contract amounts to not only manifest disregard of his authority or a misconduct on his part, but it may tantamount to a *mala fide* action. A conscious disregard of the law or the provisions of the contract from which he has derived his authority vitiates the award.[9]

Whether arbitration agreement is condition precedent The nature of an arbitration agreement is a condition precedent for exercise of power to appoint an Arbitrator/Arbitral Tribunal, under s. 11 of the Act by the Chief Justice or his designate. It is not permissible to appoint an Arbitrator to adjudicate the disputes between the parties, in the absence of an arbitration agreement or mutual consent.[10]

Principles In *SBP & Co.* v *Patel Engineering Ltd.*[11] the Apex Court observed:

(1) The power exercised by the Chief Justice of the High Court or the Chief Justice of India under s. 11(6) of the Act is not an administrative power. It is a judicial power.

(2) The power under s. 11(6) of the Act, in its entirety, could be delegated, by the Chief Justice of the High Court only to another Judge of that court and by the Chief Justice of India to another Judge of the Supreme Court.

7 Mustill and Boyd's, *Commercial Arbitration*, 2nd Ed., p. 641.

8 *Halsbury's Laws of England*, 4th Ed., vol. II, para 622.

9 *Associated Engineering Company* v *Government of* A.P. AIR 1992 SC 232; (1991)4 SCC 93; 1991(2) Arb LR 180; JT 1991(3) SC 123.

10 *Jagdish Chander* v *Ramesh Chander* (2007)5 SCC 719.

11 (2005)8 SCC 618.

(3) In case of designation of a Judge of the High Court or of the Supreme Court, the power that is exercised by the designated Judge would be that of the Chief Justice as conferred by the statute.

(4) The Chief Justice or the designated Judge will have the right to decide the preliminary aspects as indicated in the earlier part of this judgment. These will be his own jurisdiction to entertain the request, the existence of a valid arbitration agreement, the existence or otherwise of a live claim, the existence of the condition for the exercise of his power and on the qualifications of the Arbitrator or Arbitrators. The Chief Justice or the designated Judge would be entitled to seek the opinion of an institution in the matter of nominating an Arbitrator qualified in terms of s. 11(8) of the Act if the need arises but the order appointing the Arbitrator could only be that of the Chief Justice or the designated Judge.

(5) Designation of a District Judge as the authority under s. 11(6) of the Act by the Chief Justice of the High Court is not warranted on the scheme of the Act.

(6) Once the matter reaches the Arbitral Tribunal or the sole Arbitrator, the High Court would not interfere with the orders passed by the Arbitrator or the Arbitral Tribunal during the course of the arbitration proceedings and the parties could approach the court only in terms of s. 37 of the Act or in terms of s. 34 of the Act.

(7) Since an order passed by the Chief Justice of the High Court or by the designated Judge of that court is a judicial order. an appeal will lie against that order only under Art. 136 of the Constitution to the Supreme Court.

(8) There can be no appeal against an order of the Chief Justice of India or a Judge of the Supreme Court designated by him while entertaining an application under s. 11(6) of the Act.

(9) In a case where an Arbitral Tribunal has been constituted by the parties without having resource to s. 11(6) of the Act, the Arbitral Tribunal will have the jurisdiction to decide all matters as contemplated by s. 16 of the Act.

(10) Where District Judges had been designated by the Chief Justice of the High Court under s. 11(6) of the Act, the appointment orders thus far made by them will be treated as valid; but applications if any pending before him as on this date will stand transferred, to be dealt with by the Chief Justice of the High Court concerned or a Judge of that court designated by the Chief Justice.

(11) All objections relating to appointments of Arbitrators are to be decided under s. 16.

Hon'ble Justice C.K. Thakkar took a dissenting view and stated as under:

(*a*) The function performed by the Chief Justice of the High Court or the Chief Justice of India under sub-sec. (6) of s. 11 of the Act (*i.e.* the Arbitration and Conciliation Act 1996) is administrative, pure and simple, and neither judicial nor quasi-judicial.

(*b*) The function to be performed by the Chief Justice under sub-sec. (6) of s. 11 of the Act may be performed by him or by "any person or institution designated by him".

(*c*) While performing the function under sub-sec. (6) of s. 11 of the Act, the Chief Justice should be *prima facie* satisfied that the conditions laid down in s. 11 are satisfied.

(*d*) The Arbitral Tribunal has power and jurisdiction to rule "on its own jurisdiction" under sub-sec. (1) of s. 16 of the Act.

(*e*) Where the Arbitral Tribunal holds that it has jurisdiction, it shall continue with the arbitral proceedings and make an arbitral award.

(*f*) A remedy available to the party aggrieved is to challenge the award in accordance with s. 34 or s. 37 of the Act.

(*g*) Since the order passed by the Chief Justice under sub-sec. (6) of s. 11 of the Act is administrative, a writ petition under Art. 226 of the Constitution in maintainable. A letters patent appeal/intra-court appeal is competent. A special leave petition under Art. 136 of the Constitution also lies to this court.

(*h*) While exercising extraordinary jurisdiction under Art. 226 of the Constitution, however, the High Court will be conscious and mindful of the relevant provisions of the Act, including ss. 5, 16, 34 to 37 as also the object of the legislation and exercise its power with utmost care, caution and circumspection.

(*i*) The decision of the Constitution Bench in *Konkan Rly. Corpn. Ltd.* v *Rani Construction Pvt. Ltd.*[12] to the extent that it held the function of the Chief Justice under sub-sec. (6) of s. 11 of the Act as administrative is in consonance with settled legal position and lays down correct law on the point.

(*j*) The decision of the Constitution Bench in *Konkan Rly. Corpn. Ltd.* (supra)[12] to the extent that it held cl. (7) of "The Appointment of the Arbitrators by the Chief Justice of India Scheme, 1996" providing for issuance of notice to affected parties as "beyond the term of s. 11" and bad on that ground is not in accordance with law and does not State the legal position correctly.

(*k*) Since the Chief Justice is performing administrative function in appointing an Arbitral Tribunal, there is no "duty to act judicially" on his part. The doctrine of "duty to act fairly", however, applies and the Chief Justice must issue notice to the person or persons likely to be affected by the decision under sub-sec. (6) of s. 11 of the Act.

(*l*) All appointments of Arbitral Tribunals so far made without issuing notice to the parties affected are held legal and valid. Henceforth, however, every appointment will be made after issuing notice to such person or persons.

The similar view was also expressed by the Apex Court in another case[13] held that the Chief Justice or his designate under s. 11(6) acts in an administrative capacity and he does not exercise any judicial function.

Time limit Section 11(6) has not prescribed any period of time. If the opposite party has not made appointment within 30 days of demand, the right to make appointment is not forfeited but

12 (2002)2 SCC 388.

13 *Ador Samia Pvt. Ltd.* v *Peekay Holdings Ltd.* (1999)8 SCC 572; AIR 1999 SC 3246; JT 1999(6) SC 194.

continues. In other words, if the appointment is not made within 30 days of demand, the right to appoint an Arbitrator is not forfeited.[14]

Dispute under Copyright Act—may refer to arbitration There is no provision in the Copyright Act by which adjudication of the disputes arising therein by arbitration is barred either expressly or by implication. Disputes under the Copyright Act do not fall in the category of non-arbitrable dispute. Copyright is not a right *in rem*. So, dispute involving infringement of copyright can be referred to arbitration.[15]

Relation between Arbitration and Conciliation Act and SARFAESI Act SARFAESI Proceedings are in the nature of enforcement proceedings, while arbitration is an adjudicatory process. So, SARFAESI proceedings and arbitration proceedings can go hand in hand. The process of SARFAESI Act is a remedy in addition to the provisions of the Arbitration and Conciliation Act. Thus, application of both Acts is complementary to each other.[16]

Death of a party—effect An arbitration agreement remains alive even after the death of signatories thereto. Death of a party does not discharge it either as repect the deceased or any party thereto. It is enforceable in that event by or against the legal representatives of the deceased; provided however the right to sue or be sued survives.

Government as party An agreement for arbitration or an agreement contained an arbitration clause must fulfill the requirements of Art. 299(1) of the Constitution. The provisions of Art. 299 of the Constitution which are mandatory in character require that a contract made in the exercise of the executive power of the Union or of a State must satisfy three conditions viz. (*i*) it must be expressed to be made by the President or by the Governor of the State, as the case may be; (*ii*) it must be executed on behalf of the President or the Governor, as the case

14 *Datar Switch Gears Ltd.* v *Tata Finance Ltd.* (2000)8 SCC 151.

15 *Impact Metals Ltd., Bollaram* v *MSR India Ltd., Hyderabad* AIR 2017 Hyd 12.

16 *M.D. Frozen Foods Exports Pvt. Ltd.* v *Hero Fin. Corp. Ltd.* AIR 2017 SC 4481.

may be; and (*iii*) its execution must be by such person and in such manner as the President or Governor may direct or authorise.[17]

Extent of judicial intervention An intervention at the pre-arbitral award stage in permissible in the following situations:[18]

(*i*) For appointment of a guardian for a minor or a person of unsound mind for the purposes of arbitral proceedings.

(*ii*) For interim measures on the subject of preservation of the subject matter of the arbitration agreement, detention, preservation or inspection of the property being subject matter of the dispute in arbitration.

(*iii*) A request may be made by a party for appointment of Arbitrator to the Chief Justice or any person or institution designated by him.

(*iv*) To resolve a controversy from the court to decide whether the mandate of an Arbitrator stood terminated because he became *de jure* or *de facto* unable to perform his functions or for other reasons failed to act without undue delay.

(*v*) Court's assistance may be sought in taking evidence.

(*vi*) Where the arbitral tribunal accepts the plea about lack of jurisdiction or that it exceeded the scope of its authority, in such a situation, appeal may be heard by the court from the order of the arbitral tribunal.

Appeal A decision on a matter entrusted by sub-sec. (4) or sub-sec. (5) or sub-sec. (6) to the Chief Justice or his designate is final. No appeal shall lie against such decision.The district Judge and other judicial officers acting as "designated authority" of the Chief Justice under s. 11 are 'persona designata'. They do not come within the ambit of " court subordinate to High Court".[19]

17 *Bihar Eastern Gangetic Fisherman Co-operative Society* v *Sipahi Singh* AIR 1977 SC 2149; (1977)4 SCC 145.

18 S.K. Chawla, *Law of Arbitration & Conciliation including other ADRs*, 3rd Ed., pp. 215-216.

19 *Union of India* v *Girdharilal* AIR 1998 Raj 240.

Arbitration Council of India A new Part IA on Arbitration Council of India was introduced in the Arbitration and Conciliation Act 1996 by the Arbitration and Conciliation (Amendment) Act 2019. It contains ss. 43A to 43M. With a view to strengthen institutional arbitration in the country the High Level Committee under the Chairmanship of Justice B.N. Srikrishna, Former Judge of the Supreme Court vide its report dated 30th July 2017 has recommended for the establishment of an independent body for grading of arbitral institutions and accreditation of arbitrators. The Central Government by notification in the Official Gazette shall establish Arbitration Council of India.[1] It is a body corporate. It shall consist of a Chairman who is either (*a*) a judge of the Supreme Court of India; or (*b*) Chief Justice of a High Court; or (*c*) Judge of a High Court; or (*d*) an eminent person having special knowledge and experience in the conduct or administration of arbitration. The other members are—(1) eminent arbitration practitioner having substantial knowledge and experience in institutional arbitration, both in domestic and international; (2) an eminent academician having experience in research and teaching in the field of arbitration and alternative dispute resolution laws; (3) Secretary to the Government of India in the Department of Legal Affairs, Ministry of law and Justice or his representative; (4) Secretary to the Government of India in the Department of Expenditure, Ministry of Finance or his representative; (5) one representative of a recognised body of commerce and industry, chosen on rotational basis; and (6) Chief Executive Officer.[2] They shall hold office for a term of three years from the date on which they enter upon their office. But no Chairperson shall hold office after attaining the age of 70 years and member shall not hold office after attaining age of 67 years.

It shall be the duty of the Council to take all such measures as may be necessary to promote and encourage arbitration,

1 Section 43B, *inserted* by the Arbitration and Conciliation (Amendment) Act 2019 (Act 33 of 2019).

2 Section 43C, *inserted* by the Arbitration and Conciliation (Amendment) Act 2019 (Act 33 of 2019).

mediation, conciliation or other alternative dispute resolution mechanism and for that purpose to frame policy and guidelines for the establishment, operation and maintenance of uniform professional standards in respect of all matters relating to arbitration. Its other functions include: (*i*) frame policies governing the grading of arbitral institutions and accreditation of arbitrators; (*ii*) review the grading of arbitral institutions and arbitrators; (*iii*) hold training, workshops and courses in the area of arbitration in collaboration of law firms, law universities and arbitral institutions; (*iv*) frame, review and update norms to ensure satisfactory level of arbitration and conciliation; (*v*) act as a forum for exchange of views and techniques to be adopted for creating a platform to make India a robust centre for domestic and international arbitration and conciliation; (*vi*) make recommendations to the Central Government on various measures to be adopted to make provision for easy resolution of commercial disputes; (*vii*) promote institutional arbitration by strengthening arbitral institutions; (*viii*) establish and maintain depository of arbitral awards made in India; (*ix*) make recommendations regarding personnel, training and infrastructure of arbitral institutions; and (*x*) such other functions as may be decided by the Central Government.[3] The Chief Executive Officer of the Council is responsible for day-to-day administration of the council.[4]

The Central Government may remove a member from his office if he—(*a*) is an undischarged insolvent; or (*b*) has engaged at any time (except part-time member), during his term of office, in any paid employment; or (*c*) has been convicted of an offence which, in the opinion of the Central Government, involves moral turpitude; or (*d*) has acquired such financial or other interest as is likely to affect prejudicially his functions as a member; or (*e*) has so abused his position as to render his continuance in

3 Section 43D, *inserted* by the Arbitration and Conciliation (Amendment) Act 2019 (Act 33 of 2019).

4 Section 43M(1), *inserted* by the Arbitration and Conciliation (Amendment) Act 2019 (Act 33 of 2019).

office prejudicial to the public interest; or (*f*) has become physically or mentally incapable of acting as a member.[5]

The council shall maintain an electronic depository of arbitral awards made in India and such other records related thereto in such manner as may be specified by the regulation.[6]

Qualification and Experience of Arbitrator[7] A person shall not be qualified to be an arbitrator unless he—(*i*) is an advocate within the meaning of the Advocates Act 1961 having ten years practice experience as an advocate; or (*ii*) is a chartered accountant within the meaning of the Chartered Accountants Act 1949 having ten years of practice experience as a chartered accountant; or (*iii*) is a cost accountant within the meaning of the Cost and Works Accountants Act 1959 having ten years of practice experience as a cost accountant; or (*iv*) is a company secretary within the meaning of the Company Secretaries Act 1980 having ten years of practice experience as a company secretary; or (*v*) has been an officer of the Indian Legal Service; or (*vi*) has been an officer with law degree having ten years of experience in the legal matters in the Government, Autonomous Body, Public Sector Undertaking or at a senior level managerial position in private sector; or (*vii*) has been an officer with engineering degree having ten years of experience as an engineer in the Government, Autonomous Body. Public Sector Undertaking or at a senior level managerial position in private sector or self-employed; or (*viii*) has been an officer having senior level experience of administration in the Central Government or State Government or having experience of senior level management of a Public Sector Undertaking or a Government company or a private company of repute; (*ix*) is a person, in any other case, having

5 Section 43G, *inserted* by the Arbitration and Conciliation (Amendment) Act 2019 (Act 33 of 2019).

6 Section 43K, *inserted* by the Arbitration and Conciliation (Amendment) Act 2019 (Act 33 of 2019).

7 8th Schedule, *inserted* by the Arbitration and Conciliation (Amendment) Act 2019 (Act 33 of 2019).

educational qualification at degree level with ten years of experience in scientific or technical stream in the fields of telecom, information technology, Intellectual Property Rights or other specialised areas in the Government, Autonomous Body, Public Sector Undertaking or at a senior level managerial position in private sector, as the case may be.

General norms applicable to Arbitrators The arbitrator shall be a person of general reputation of fairness, integrity and capable to apply objectivity in arriving at settlement of disputes;

The arbitrator must be impartial and neutral and avoid entering into any financial business or other relationship that is likely to affect impartiality or might reasonably create an appearance of partiality or bias amongst the parties;

The arbitrator should not involve in any legal proceeding and avoid any potential conflict connected with any dispute to be arbitrated by him;

The arbitrator should not have been convicted of an offence involving moral turpitude or economic offence;

The arbitrator shall be conversant with the Constitution of India, principles of natural justice, equity, common and customary laws, commercial laws, labour laws, law of torts, making and enforcing the arbitral awards;

The arbitrator should possess robust understanding of domestic and international legal system on arbitration and international best practices in regard thereto;

The arbitrator should be able to understand key elements of contractual obligations in civil and commercial disputes and be able to apply legal principles to a situation under dispute and also to apply judicial decisions on a given matter relating to arbitration; and

The arbitrator should be capable of suggesting, recommending or writing a reasoned and enforceable arbitral award in any dispute which comes before him for adjudication.

UNCITRAL Model Law and Arbitration and Conciliation Act 1996 The United Nations Commission on International Trade Law (UNCITRAL) adopted a Model Law in 1985 on International Commercial Arbitration. The General Assembly of the United Nations recommended member-states to give due consideration to the Model Law to have uniformity in arbitration procedure which resulted in passing of the Arbitration and Conciliation Act 1996. The Act is a complete code in itself and consolidates and amends the law relating to domestic arbitration, international commercial arbitration and enforcement of foreign arbitral awards. The preamble expressly refers to UNCITRAL Model Law on International Commercial Arbitration and UNCITRAL Conciliation Rules.

Comparison between UNCITRAL Arbitration Rules 1976, Arbitration and Conciliation Act 1996 and UNCITRAL Model Law on Arbitration Law 1985 and English Arbitration Act 1996

Subject matter	UNCITRAL Arbitration Rules 1976	Arbitration and Conciliation Act 1996	UNCITRAL Model Law on Arbitration Law 1985	English Arbitration Act 1996
Number of Arbitrators	Art. 5	s. 10	Art. 10	s. 15
Appointment of Arbitrator	Arts. 6 to 8	s. 11	Art. 11	s. 16
Challenge of Arbitrators	Arts. 9 to 12	ss. 12-13	Arts. 12-13	s. 24 and s. 24(3)
Commencement of arbitral proceedings	Art. 3	s. 21	Art. 21	s. 12 and s. 14
Place of arbitration	Art. 16	s. 20	Art. 20	s. 3
Language	Art. 17	s. 22	Art. 22	s. 34(2) and s. 37
Statement of claim and defence	Arts. 18-19	s. 23	Art. 23	s. 24

Subject matter	UNCITRAL Arbitration Rules 1976	Arbitration and Conciliation Act 1996	UNCITRAL Model Law on Arbitration Law 1985	English Arbitration Act 1996
Power in case of default of a party	Art. 28	s. 25	Art. 25	s. 41
Procedural and evidential matter	Arts. 24 and 25	s. 24 and s. 27	Arts. 18-19 and Arts. 24 and 27	s. 34
Appointment of experts	Art. 27	s. 26	Art. 26	s. 37
Settlement	Art. 34	s. 30	Art. 30	s. 51
Grounds of termination	Art. 34	s. 32	Art. 32	s. 68(3), s. 69(7) and s. 70(4)
Interpretation of award	Art. 35	s. 33	Art. 33	
Correction of the award	Art. 36	s. 33	Art. 33	s. 57
Additional award	Art. 37	s. 33	Art. 33(3)	s. 57
Costs	Arts. 38 to 40	ss. 38-39	Art. 17G	ss. 59 to 63
Setting aside the award	Art. 12	s. 34	Art. 34	ss. 67-68
Enforcement of the award		s. 36	Art. 35	s. 66
Provisional awards/interim measures	Art. 26	s. 9	Arts. 17-18	s. 39

Arbitration in U.K. The English Arbitration Act 1899 is the first enactment on arbitration. Prior to 1899 arbitrations are regulated by Common Law Procedure Act 1854, the Supreme Court of Judicature Act 1873 and the Supreme Court of Judicature Act 1884. This Act empowered the Arbitrator to remit award or to set aside award. In any cause or matter (other than a criminal proceedings by the crown) if the parties interested, who are not under disability consent may refer the dispute to arbitration. In order to expand the scope of arbitration the Parliament passed the English Arbitration Act 1934. This statute provides that arbitration agreement shall not be discharged by the death of the party to the proceedings. It also gives power to the court to provide relief where the Arbitrator is not impartial or dispute referred involves question of fraud. In the year 1950 the British Parliament enacted the English Arbitration Act 1950 to consolidate the Arbitration Acts 1899 and 1934. This Act makes the following provisions which are not provided in the former Acts—

(*a*) Conduct of proceedings and witnesses.

(*b*) Interim Awards.

(*c*) Power of Arbitrator to award interest.

(*d*) Power of the court where Arbitrator is revoked or authority of Arbitrator is revoked.

(*e*) Enforcement of award.

(*f*) Enforcement of certain foreign awards.

The modern British approach to the arbitration is depicted by the following objecting formulated by British Parliament by enacting English Arbitration Act 1996: "the object of arbitration is to obtain the fair resolution of disputes by an impartial tribunal without unnecessary delay or expense." It was enacted to improve the law relating to arbitration pursuant to an arbitration agreement. It came into force on 31st January 1997.

The salient features of the said Act are as follows:

(*i*) The court is empowered to grant stay of legal proceedings unless satisfied that the arbitration agreement is null and void [s. 9(4)].

(*ii*) The court is authorized to extend time for beginning arbitral proceedings [s. 12].

(*iii*) The Limitation Act is also applicable to arbitral proceedings [s. 13(1)].

(*iv*) The parties are free to agree on the procedure for appointing the Arbitrator or Arbitrators [s. 16(1)].

(*v*) This Act also authorizes the court to remove Arbitrator on the following grounds:

(*a*) that circumstances exist the give rise to justifiable doubts as to his impartiality;

(*b*) that he does not posses the qualifications required by the arbitration agreement;

(*c*) that he is physically or mentally incapable of conducting the proceedings or there are justifiable doubts as to his capacity to do so;

(*d*) that he has refused or failed;

(*i*) property to conduct the proceedings; or

(*ii*) to use all reasonable dispatch in conducting the proceedings or making an award,

and that substantial injustice has been or will be caused to the applicant [s. 24(1)].

(*vi*) A party to arbitral proceedings may be represented in the proceeding by a lawyer or other person chosen by him [s. 36].

(*vii*) Arbitral Tribunal may award simple or compound interest [s. 49(3)].

(*viii*) Arbitral award may be enforced in the same manner as a judgment or order of the court [s. 66(1)].

(*ix*) The court's power to interfere with the arbitral proceeding is very limited [ss. 67 and 71].

(*x*) It widens the powers of the Arbitrator [ss. 38-39, s. 41, s. 45].

Arbitration in Australia Arbitration law of Australia has a long history. In Australia the arbitral institution was established under the Conciliation and Arbitration Act 1904. The Conciliation and Arbitration Act 1904 was passed for the prevention and settlement of industrial disputes extending beyond the limits of one State. Arbitral Tribunal of Australia plays an important and pivotal role to resolve the dispute and differences between labour and capital and working conditions of the workers for more than hundred years. From 1980 onwards the traditional role of the arbitral Tribunal has been considerably changed and its ambit has been expanded. Its powers have also been enhanced and increased.

But after the enactment of the Workplace Relation Act 1996 its functions and jurisdiction have been reduced to a great extent. Nowadays, the Workplace Relation Act plays a key role to maintain the relations between the employer and employees and workmen.

Arbitration in Canada After unconvention on the recognition and enforcement of foreign arbitral awards, Canada enacted commercial Arbitration Act in the year 1986 in pursuant with UNCITRAL model law on arbitration. Before 1886 they conducted arbitral following the English legislation on arbitration.

Arbitration in Sri Lanka Sri Lanka enacted Arbitration Act 1995 following the UNCITRAL model law on arbitration. This Act empowers the Arbitrators to award interest (s. 28).

Arbitration in USA The arbitration in USA has a long history dating back to 1632, when Massachusetts colony accepted arbitration as one of the methods of resolving dispute between the disputants. In 1768 the New York Chamber or Commerce, in 1871 New Orleans Cotton Exchange accepted arbitration as an important means of settlement of dispute. In the year 1888 first law on arbitration was enacted. In the year 1913, U.S. Conciliation service was established to provide speedy and less costly justice to the people. In the year 1925, Federal Arbitration was passed by the Congress. Upto 1930 the arbitration was mainly used to negotiate dispute between the working class people or labour dispute. Its modern development begins with the rapid growth of industries in the United States. The National Labour Relations Act 1935 is the pointer. In the year 1970 and 1990 the scope of the Arbitration Act was expanded for peaceful settlement of dispute in view of UNCITRAL model law on arbitration.

Chapter 2

Conciliation

Conciliation—meaning According to *Black's Law Dictionary*,[1] Conciliation is a settlement of a dispute in an agreeable manner. A process in which a neutral person meets with the parties to a dispute and explores how the dispute might be resolved; especially, a relatively unstructured method of dispute resolution in which a third party facilitates communication between parties in an attempt to help them settle their difference.

According to *Chambers 21st Century Dictionary*,[2] conciliation is to win over some one; to overcome the hostility of someone, to reconcile (people in dispute, etc).

According to *Oxford Advanced Learner's Dictionary*,[3] conciliation is used to make somebody less angry or more friendly, especially by being kind and pleasant or by giving them something. A conciliation service helps to settle disputes between employers and workers.

According to the *New International Webster's Comprehensive Dictionary*,[4] conciliation is the act of bringing into agreement; the settlement or attempt to settle a labour dispute by the proposal of measures acceptable to the disputants.

1 *Black's Law Dictionary*, 10th Ed.
2 *Chambers 21st Century Dictionary*, p. 285.
3 *Oxford Advanced Learner's Dictionary*, 9th Ed.
4 *New International Webster's Comprehensive Dictionary*, Encyclopedic Edition, 2003, p. 271.

In short, conciliation is a peaceful means to settle disputes arising between the parties which prevents the bitterness of their relationship. It mainly depends on the party's desire.

Arbitration and Conciliation—distinction

Arbitration	Conciliation
1. Arbitration is a legal method of settling disputes between the parties by a fair-minded third party (s) who is/ are named by the parties to concentrate on dispute to reach at a decision after hearing parties and considering documents on record.	1. Conciliation is a method of settlement of dispute wherein a neutral third party assists the parties to reach a settlement in an agreeable manner.
2. Arbitration is an independent legal proceeding.	2. Conciliation is an endeavour by a third party to settle the dispute with or without intervention of the court. It is not a legal proceeding.
3. Existence of an agreement is necessary. Such arbitral agreement must be in writing.	3. In order to invoke conciliation no agreement is necessary.
4. An Arbitrator has power to enforce its award.	4. Conciliator has no such power to enforce its decision.
5. Award is binding upon the parties.	5. Resolution proposed by the Conciliator is not binding.
6. In arbitral proceeding the Arbitrator(s) hears both sides, records evidence of both sides and after hearing arguments passes an award.	6. In conciliation the Conciliator holds separate meeting with the parties and transfers messages forward and backward between the parties and helps the parties to come to a solution.
7. The object of arbitration is to "obtain the fair resolution of disputes by an impartial tribunal without unnecessary delay or expense."	7. The object of conciliation is to overcome hostility of the parties.
8. Award must be passed purely on the application of law.	8. Recommendations of the Conciliator need not be based purely on the application of law.

Conciliation and reconciliation—distinction Conciliation is a peaceful means of settlement of disputes arising between the parties through the intervention of a third party. Reconciliation is a means of restoring peace between the parties who were once in cordial relationship but moved to a status of conflict. *Secondly,* conciliation is used in any kind of dispute. Reconciliation is mainly adopted in matrimonial disputes. *Thirdly,* any body can act as a Conciliator. In matrimonial cases, the reconciliation process is done by the Judge of the concerned court. *Lastly,* in reconciliation, the disputants must have once been good relation between them but in conciliation it is not required.

Conciliation and mediation—distinction

Conciliation	Mediation
1. Conciliation is a process of dispute resolution in which a neutral person meets the parties to the dispute and explores how the dispute will be resolved.	1. Mediation is a method of non-binding dispute resolution involving a neutral third party who attempts to resolve the dispute by enabling communications between the disputants.
2. Conciliation is governed by the Arbitration and Conciliation Act 1996 and the Code of Civil Procedure.	2. Mediation is governed by the Code of Civil Procedure.
3. Law determines the extent of confidentiality.	3. Confidentiality relies on trust.
4. Third party acts as facilitator, evaluator as well as intervener.	4. Third party only acts as facilitator.
5. Settlement agreement is the end product of conciliation.	5. Mediation ends when the parties enter into an agreement in regard to the dispute in question.
6. Settlement agreement is executable as decree of a civil court.	6. Agreement is enforceable by law.

History of conciliation The concept of conciliation is as old as hills and it is changing with every needs of the society. It demands a new outlook, a new technique and a new procedure. There are various types of reconciliation which are slowly recognised. Conciliation is playing larger part in modern jurisprudence. The new function of the legal system is not merely juridical but broadly sociological. In developing the concept of reconciliation and giving it legal forms, legal thinkers are adopting various legal devices and wiles. To my mind, conciliation gives a kind of breathing time by holding social balance and to preserve an aura for a workable solution of dissension and hostility.

The method of settling a dispute between the parties adopting conciliation procedure is not unknown in our judicial system. Since the dawn of civilization when practically there were no established and recognized judicial system the village heads panchas headed by a *Sarpanch* or *Mukhia* used to settle disputes amongst the parties which were binding upon them.

With the growth of the civilization the total justice system formulated different procedures of rendering justice and of which Alternative Dispute Resolution (ADR) is comparatively latter conception and it arose out of another concept of settling disputes by arbitration proceedings.

The arbitration proceeding is one of the most common mode of alternative dispute resolution. Though an arbitration is very common, less expensive and speedy than a litigation before a court of law yet it is loosing its popularity fact due to complicacies in its procedure, so the experts was on constant search for an alternative to the method of arbitration. The legal experts have found conciliations as an alternative to arbitration.

A Conciliator is no less important and respectable than an Arbitrator. If one looks back to the Code of Civil Procedure ref: s. 89, Or. 10, rr. 1A, 1B, 1C find a reference having no statutory recognition. But conciliation proceeding are recognized in the Industrial Disputes Act 1947, the Hindu Marriage Act 1955 and the Family Courts Act 1984. The law makers have not yet find any suitable definition of the concept of conciliation but it is well appreciated by the courts, the lawyers and the litigants. Section 62 of the Arbitration and Conciliation Act 1996 deals with procedure for conciliation.

In ancient time there was the existence of Panchayat at village level and they can decide and determine the grievance of the villager over the land dispute and other related matters or small types of offences by imposing fines upon the wrongdoers. During the Mughal period an attempt was made for centralization of judicial system. In 1907, the Royal Commission recommended for creation of village Panchayat having power to deal with the administrative as well as judicial matters. In primordial age the main function of Panchayat was only to alight the dispute through conciliation. The Madras Village Courts Act 1888 is a *magna carta* in the history of settlement of disputes through conciliation. In the Karnataka Land Revenue Act 1964 there was also a provision for settlement of disputes through a sole Arbitrator or through an Arbitration Committee (s. 141). The Code of Civil Procedure 1908 also provides for settlement of disputes by way of compromise [Or. XXIII, r. 3]. The Arbitration and Conciliation Act 1996 was enacted to consolidate and amend the law relating to domestic and international commercial arbitration.

In the Code of Criminal Procedure 1973 there is also a provision for compounding of offences with the permission of the court or without the permission of the court (s. 320).

Salient features The Arbitration and Conciliation Act 1996 laid down the following features of conciliation:

(1) The party initiating conciliation shall send a written invitation to conciliate to his/her adversary briefly identifying the subject of dispute.[5]

(2) The conciliation proceedings shall commence from the date of written acceptance of the invitation to conciliate. There will be no conciliation if there is a refusal of the invitation by the other party of written acceptance of the invitation to conciliate. There will be no conciliation if there is a refusal of the invitation by the other party.[6]

(3) If the offering party does not receive reply of the invitation within 30 days from the date on which he sends the invitation he may treat it as cancelled.[7]

(4) The parties may appoint Conciliator on the agreed terms. There shall be one Conciliator unless the parties agreed that there shall be two or more Conciliator.[8]

5 Section 62(1), the Arbitration and Conciliation Act 1996.
6 Section 62(2) and 62(3).
7 Section 62(4).
8 Section 63(1).

(5) The Conciliator may request the parties to submit their written statements in brief stating the general nature of the dispute and the points at issue. Each party shall submit copy of the statement to other party.[9]

(6) The Conciliator may request the other parties to submit documents and other evidence which they may think necessary and appropriate.[10]

(7) Each party is under obligation to supply copy of the statement, documents and other evidence to the other party.[11]

(8) At any stage of the conciliation proceedings, the Conciliator may request the parties to furnish before him such additional information as he/she deems appropriate.[12]

(9) The Conciliator is not governed by the principles of the Code of Civil Procedure or the Indian Evidence Act.[13]

(10) The Conciliator is under obligation to assist the parties in an independent and impartial manner to gain confidence of the parties and to reach an amicable settlement of their disputes.[14]

(11) The Conciliator must be guided by the principles of objectivity, fairness and justice.[15]

(12) The Conciliator attempted to reach an acceptable settlement giving due consideration of (*a*) rights and obligations of the parties, (*b*) the usages of the trade concerns, (*c*) circumstances surrounding the dispute, and (*d*) previous business practices between the parties, if any.[16]

(13) The Conciliator may at any stage of the proceedings make proposals for settlement of the dispute. It need not be in writing. It need not be accompanied by any reasons.[17]

9 Section 65(1).
10 Section 65(2).
11 Section 65(2).
12 Section 65(3).
13 Section 66.
14 Section 67(1).
15 Section 67(2).
16 Section 67(2).
17 Section 67(4).

(14) The Conciliator in order to facilitate the conduct of the proceedings may arrange for administrative assistance by a suitable institution or person.[18]

(15) The Conciliator may ask the parties either to meet with him or to communicate with them over the dispute in question. Such communication may be oral or in writing. He may meet or communicate with the parties together or with each of them separately.[19]

(16) After receipt of the information the Conciliator shall disclose the substance of the said information to the other party, so that he can submit any explanation over the said information.[1]

(17) When any party furnishes any information to the Conciliator with a specific condition that it should be kept confidential the Conciliator shall not disclose the same.[2]

(18) The parties will cooperate with the Conciliator in good faith. They will make every endeavour to comply with the request of the Conciliator.[3]

(19) The parties to the proceedings on his own initiative submit to the Conciliator suggestions for the settlement of the issues.[4]

(20) After submission of suggestions the Conciliator shall formulate the terms of a possible settlements if he is of the view that there exists elements of a settlement and to submit the same to the parties for their consideration.[5]

(21) After receipt of the observation of the parties he may reformulate the terms of settlement if the factual information so demands.[6]

18 Section 68.
19 Section 69(1).
1 Section 70.
2 Proviso to section 70.
3 Section 71.
4 Section 72.
5 Section 73(1).
6 Section 73(1).

(22) The settlement agreement shall be final and binding on the parties.[7]

(23) The settlement agreement is effectual as an arbitral award.[8]

(24) The Conciliator and parties shall keep confidential all matters relating to the conciliation proceedings. It may extend to the settlement agreement also.[9]

(25) The parties shall not initiate any arbitral or judicial proceedings in respect of the dispute in question during the continuance of the conciliation proceedings.[10]

(26) Conciliation proceedings shall be terminated in the following cases:[11]

(*a*) by signing of the settlement agreement by the parties. It came into force from the date of the agreement;

(*b*) by a written declaration of the Conciliator to the effect that further efforts at conciliation are no longer justified. It is operative from the date of the declaration;

(*c*) by a written declaration by the parties stating that conciliation proceedings are terminated. It is effective from the date of declaration;

(*d*) by a written declaration of a party that conciliation not necessary to other party and Conciliator. It is effective from the date of declaration;

(*e*) when the parties failed to deposit the cost as asked to deposit by the Conciliator within 30 days from the date of order, the Conciliator may suspend the proceedings or declare the conciliation as terminated. The date of termination would be the date of declaration [s. 79(3)].

(27) The Conciliator should not act as an Arbitrator or council of a party in any arbitral or judicial proceedings.[12]

7 Section 73(3).
8 Section 74.
9 Section 75.
10 Section 77.
11 Section 76.
12 Section 80(*a*).

(28) The Conciliator cannot be cited as witness by the parties many arbitral or judicial proceedings.[13]

(29) Views expressed by the parties in conciliation proceedings, admission by the parties, proposals made by the Conciliator, terms of settlement or suggestions regarding proposal for settlement are not admissible in evidence in other proceedings.[14]

Role of the Conciliator The Conciliator act as a liaison officer between the applicant and other party. Its role is quite different from the role of the judge of a traditional law court. He is to help the parties to understand the disputes involved between them. He is a neutral person. Impartiality, integrity, honesty, equality and patience are the five attributes of a Conciliator. The conciliation proceedings will succeed if he convince the parties in a healthy and congenial atmosphere. He shall perform its duties and obligations objectively and impartially to earn the trust and confidence of the parties. The essence of conciliation is to focuses the main issues or points of dispute, protection of privacy, free discussions and confidentiality. He controls the entire conciliation proceedings, dialogues between the parties, communication between the parties. Section 67 and s. 80 of the Arbitration and Conciliation Act 1996 explains the role of the Conciliators. They are as under:

(1) The Conciliator shall assist the parties in an independent and impartial manner in their attempt to reach an amicable settlement of their dispute.[15]

(2) The Conciliator shall be guided by principles of objectivity, fairness and justice, giving consideration to, among other things, the rights and obligations of the parties, the usages of the trade concerned and the circumstances surrounding the dispute, including any previous business practices between the parties.[16]

13 Section 80(*b*).
14 Section 81.
15 Section 67(1).
16 Section 67(2).

(3) The Conciliator may conduct the conciliation proceedings in such a manner as he considers appropriate, taking into account the circumstances of the case, the wishes the parties may express, including any request by a party that the Conciliator hear oral statements, and the need for a speedy settlement of the dispute.[17]

(4) The Conciliator may, at any stage of the conciliation proceedings, make proposals for a settlement of the dispute. Such proposals need not be in writing and need not be accompanied by a statement of the reasons therefore.[18]

(5) The Conciliator shall not act as an Arbitrator or as a representative or counsel of a party in any arbitral or judicial proceedings in respect of a dispute that is the subject of the conciliation proceedings.[19]

(6) The Conciliator shall not be presented by the parties as a witness in any arbitral or judicial proceedings.[20]

Kinds of Conciliation Conciliation is divided into—(*a*) Facilitative Conciliation; (*b*) Evaluative Conciliation; (*c*) Voluntary Conciliation; (*d*) Compulsory Conciliation ; (*e*) Court referred Conciliation; and (*f*) Institutional Conciliation. In facilitative evaluation the Conciliator merely helps the parties to understand their problems and how to resolve the same by clarifying their interests and priorities. In evaluative settlement the Conciliator gives his views on the merits of the respective case of the parties which help the parties to come to an agreeable solution. Some time parties out of their own will and volition settle the dispute with the help of a neutral third party. Such type of conciliation is called voluntary conciliation. When parties are unwilling to meet each other for direct negotiation, then compulsory negotiation can be resorted to. It is normally applicable in labour cases. In India in terms of s. 89 of the Code of Civil Procedure the court may refer the matter to conciliation for settlement.

17 Section 67(3).
18 Section 67(4).
19 Section 80(*a*).
20 Section 80(*b*).

Institutional conciliation is a means of conciliation which is adopted and steered by a certain institution. Such institutions formulate the procedure for conciliation, keep a list of conciliators and frame rules to guide the parties and the Conciliator to settle the dispute. *Ad hoc* conciliation is free conciliation which takes place without the supervision of any institution. Such type of conciliation does not follow any rules and procedure of any institution.

Advantages The advantages of conciliation are as follows—

Maintenance of confidentiality The Conciliator hears in private and the parties are the only persons allowed to participate in the proceedings and as a result confidentiality is maintained.

Cost-effective justice The cost of the proceeding is low in comparison with other ADR mechanisms. It allows the parties to get cost-effective justice in a short span of time.

No delay The main purpose of conciliation is to avoid delay and to obtain fair resolution of dispute as early as possible and consequently, unnecessary delay to resolve the dispute can easily be averted.

Simple procedure The procedure adopted by the Conciliator is informal as well as simple. The procedures of the Code of Civil Procedure and the Evidence Act are not applicable. So, the parties feel comfortable in the process of deliberations.

Flexibility The Conciliator can be much more flexible both in time and procedure and parties are free to fix a date of proceedings according to their choice.

Save time and money The procedure are not lengthy. Therefore, time and money both are saved. It also helps the parties to a great extent in the matter of setting rights and satisfying the parties.

Expert determination Most of the occasions the Conciliator is an expert in the relevant field and therefore, such determination has expanded into the area of general dispute resolution.

Binding nature of settlement agreement When the parties enter into an agreement by consent, then such settlement is final and enforceable.

Maintain peaceful relationship The solution is not imposed upon the parties. They settle the matter according to their satisfaction and persuasion. So, the relationship between the parties is not affected. In short, the main purpose of the conciliation is not only to repair the damages resulting from the contractual relationships but also at finding a kind of balance or equality between the parties' obligations.

Disadvantages It has some disadvantages. They are as under:

No binding nature The process adopted by the Conciliator is not legally binding.

Not legally qualified The Conciliator may not be a legally qualified person. So, there is every chance of omission to consider the vital part of the dispute having bearings on the legal aspects.

Simple procedure The Conciliator adopts a simple procedure to resolve the dispute and therefore, it is highly probable that injustice be delivered to either of the parties.

Result not guaranted Even after consideration of length and breadth of the disputed questions, the parties may not come to a consensus over the decision.

Parties not serious As the process is informal there is high probability that the parties may not take it seriously.

No legal service Parties are not entitled to get legal service.

Stages of Conciliation

CONCILIATION STAGE I

Beginning with the statement of the Conciliator explaining the nitty gritty of the procedure and confidentiality of the procedure.

STAGE II

Request by the Conciliator to the parties to submit brief written statement, nature of the dispute and points are issue.

STAGE III

Request by the Conciliator to the parties to submit additional information if necessary.

Stage IV

Formulation of issues. Issues are the backbone of the dispute. It may arise from the averment made by the applicant in the application and denied by the other.

Stage V

Necessary arrangement for administrative assistance with the consent of the parties.

Stage VI

Communication or meeting between the communicator and the parties.

Stage VII

Disclosure of substance of information by the Conciliator to the other party.

Stage VIII

Submission of proposed terms of settlement to the Conciliator by the party.

Stage IX

Formation of terms of possible settlement and to supply the same to the parties for their observations and opinion.

Stage X

Reformulation of the terms of settlement in the light of observations of the parties, if necessary.

Stage XI

Drawing up of the settlement agreement and authentication of the same by the Conciliator.

Stage XII

Supply of copy of the signed settlement agreement to each of the parties.

Conciliation in Japan The Supreme Court of Japan, in a publication titled as 'Outline of Civil Trial in Japan' explains the procedure adopted in conciliation cases in the following manner:[21]

"Conciliation is a system peculiar to Japan. Its special characteristics is to settle disputes not by means of a formal

21 Quoted by Law Commission of India in its 77th Report, Chapter VIII.

court decision but by mutual concession of the parties concerned through the good office of the Conciliation Committee, composed of either one Judge or one Judge and two Conciliation Commissioners, appointed from among the people in general.

"Since the proceedings are simple and inexpensive, the extent of utilization is very great. So, in one sense, it may be said that it fulfils a part of function of legal aid in our country. In 1968, cases newly received for conciliation numbered 54,323 while the total number of cases received by the courts of the first instance was 1,84,808. The ratio between the two is roughly 1:3. Judging from this fact, we can easily tell what an important part the process of conciliation plays in settling civil disputes. It may also be interesting to note that the number of cases involving domestic disputes newly received for conciliation in 1965 of the Domestic Relations Division of the Family Court amounted to 60,015.

"Historically this system was originally adopted in 1922 for the purpose of settling disputes involving land and house lease as indicated in the Law for Conciliation concerning Lease of Land or House, but since then its scope has been expanded and now it is made available to settle all types of civil disputes.

"The proceedings in conciliation cases are commenced, as a rule, on the application of the parties concerned, but the courts on their own motion, occasionally refer cases pending before them for conciliation. Determination as to whether a case should be disposed of by the Conciliation Committee or by the judge is a matter within the discretion of the court. On the date of conciliation, the Committee or the judge in charge as the case may be, summons the parties concerned and endeavours to settle the disputes either by persuading them to make concessions, or by suggesting proper conditions of settlement.

"When conciliation is successfully accomplished, the terms of conciliation are entered in a protocol. Such a protocol has the same force and effect as a finally binding

> judgment. On the other hand, if the conciliation has not been successful, the proceedings come to an end with the disputes still remaining, unsettled. In that event, if the court deems it necessary, it may resort to the judicial process and adjudicate the case by entering a judgment in place of an agreement, taking every, circumstance into consideration, regardless of the failure of conciliation."

The Code of Civil Procedure does not contemplate such proceedings but such a procedure exits in Japan, France and Norway. In Japan it is the duty of the court either on the application of the parties or *suo motu* to send all civil proceedings either to a body consisting of two laymen and a judge or to judicial Commissioners for a negotiated settlement. If the conciliation court succeeds in persuading the parties to arrive at a settlement, its terms are recoded by the court and the order become binding a judgment. In the event of a failure, the proceeding is dealt with in the ordinary manner. In France, all cases go to a Cantonal Court presided over by a layman for conciliation and an agreed settlement. Failing a settlement, the case goes for disposal to the court. In Norway, such proceedings are an essential preliminary to a proceeding in a civil court. The proceedings first go before a conciliation council, composed of three Mediators, designated by the local authority. The council can record an agreement. If any of the parties fail to appear, the council can in petty cases settle the proceedings. If the conciliation proceedings fail, the parties may approach the court for the redress of their grievances.

Under the procedure, the plaintiff has to summon the defendant on a date to be called "the first settlement day" to attend before the settlement judge by means of a: "Notice of Complaint" in the prescribed form obtainable form a post office. On that day the settlement judge would hear both sides appearing in person without lawyers in a completely informal manner and briefly record the case of each party as stated before him orally and as supplemented or supported by documents produced before him. The statements of the parties would be read over to and signed by them. Having heard parties and read the documents produced, the settlement judge would there and then try to bring the parties to an amicable settlement in regard to the matter in dispute. He would not pronounce his opinion before the parties on the validity or strength of their respective cases but he may act on his views of the strength of the case in his endeavour to promote a settlement. If his effort succeed, the terms agreed to would be signed by the parties and recorded by the judge. The rules would provide that the compromise shall be binding upon the parties and their assigns and, if necessary, a decree may be drawn up. If however, the attempt fails, the matter would be adjourned for a period not exceeding two months to a date to be called the "Second Settlement Day". On that day the settlement Judge would again make a similar attempt to bring the parties to a settlement in an informal manner and without the assistance of lawyers. If he fails again, the settlement Judge would give directions for a trial after which the suit would go for disposal to the trial judge. To ensure the attendance of the defendant in response to a summons to attend on the first settlement day or the attendance of parties on the second settlement day pursuant to the Courts' direction, it would be made a statutory offence punishable with imprisonment of fine for a defendant or a party to refuse or neglect without just cause to attend the court in answer to such summons or directions. Unless this is done, the litigant may be persuaded by lawyers or interested persons to refuse to co-operate in settlement proceedings. The services of ex-judges of all categories or lawyers of not less than ten years experience may be enlisted to relieve the regular judges from the burden of settlement proceedings.

Conciliation in Norway Settlement of dispute by way of conciliation played a very significant role in the Norway legal system. First, Conciliation Board was established in the Norway in the year 1775. The existence of Conciliation Board was also found in the Court of Justice Act 1980, Civil Procedure Act. The Conciliation Board shall consist of three members and their tenure is 4 years. The jurisdiction of the board is limited. Divorce cases, disputes between spouses and parents are outside the purview of the board.

Comparison between UNCITRAL Conciliation Rules 1980 and the Arbitration and Conciliation Act 1996

Subject matter	UNCITRAL Conciliation Rules 1980	Arbitration and Conciliation Act 1996	UNCITRAL Model Law on Conciliation 2001
Commencement of Conciliation Proceedings	Art. 2	s. 62	Art. 4
Number of Conciliators	Art. 3	s. 63	Art. 5
Appointment of Conciliators	Art. 4	s. 64	Art. 6
Submission of statement to Conciliator	Art. 5	s. 65	
Administrative assistance	Art. 8	s. 68	
Role of Conciliator	Art. 7	s. 67	
Communication between Conciliator and parties	Art. 9	s. 69	Art. 8
Disclosure of information	Art. 10	s. 70	Art. 9
Co-operation of parties with Conciliator	Art. 11	s. 71	
Suggestions by parties for settlement of dispute	Art. 12	s. 72	
Settlement agreement	Art. 13	s. 73	
Confidentiality	Art. 14	s. 75	
Termination of conciliation proceedings	Art. 15	s. 76	Art. 10
Resorts to arbitral or judicial proceedings	Art. 16	s. 77	Art. 14
Costs	Art. 17	s. 78	
Deposits	Art. 18	s. 79	
Role of Conciliator in other proceedings	Art. 19	s. 80	Art. 13
Admissibility of evidence in other proceedings	Art. 20	s. 81	Art. 12

Chapter 3

Mediation

Mediation—meaning According to *Black's Law Dictionary*,[1] mediation is a method of non-binding dispute resolution involving a neutral third party who tries to help the disputing parties reach a mutually agreeable solution.

The distinction between mediation and conciliation is widely debated among those interested in ADR, arbitration, and international diplomacy. Some suggest that conciliation is 'a non-binding arbitration', whereas mediation is merely 'assisted negotiation'. Others put it this way: "conciliation involves a third party's trying to bring together disputing parties to help them reconcile their differences, whereas mediation goes further by allowing the third party to suggest terms on which the dispute might be resolved. Still others reject these attempts at differentiation and contend that there is no consensus about what the two words mean—that they are generally interchangeable. Though a distinction would be convenient, those who argue that usage indicates a broad synonymy are most accurate."[2]

According to *Oxford Advanced Learner's Dictionary*,[3] mediation is used as to try to end a disagreement between two or more people or groups by talking to them and trying to find things

1 10th Ed., p. 1130.

2 Bryan A. Garner, *A Dictionary of Modern Legal Usage*, 2nd Ed. 1995.

3 *Oxford Advanced Learner's Dictionary*, 9th Ed.

that everyone can agree on; to mediate differences/disputes/ problems; to succeed in finding a solution to a disagreement between people or groups.

According to *Chambers 21st Century Dictionary*,[4] mediation is the act or process of mediating.

According to the *New International Webster's Comprehensive Dictionary*,[5] mediation is the act of mediating; intercession; interposition. A friendly intervention in the disputes of others, with their consent, for the purpose of adjusting difference. ICADR defines[6] it as a non-binding procedure in which an impartial third party, the Mediator, assists the parties to a dispute in reaching a mutually satisfactory, agreed settlement of the dispute.

In short, "mediation is flexible, cost-effective, confidential process which can be arranged relatively speedily, in which a neutral third party (the Mediator) facilitates discussions and negotiations between the parties in dispute within a relatively structured but flexible process, in a formal setting, during a defined period of time, all of which helps to create an impetus for settlement".[7]

Mediation undoubtedly provides an efficient, effective, speedy, convenient and inexpensive process to resolve disputes with dignity, mutuality, respect and civility where parties participate in arriving at a negotiated settlement rather than being confronted with a third party adjudication of their disputes. The very fact that it enables warring parties to sit across the table and negotiate, even if unsuccessful in dispute resolution, undergoing the process creates an atmosphere of harmony and peace in which parties learn to 'agree to disagree'.[8]

Nature of mediation proceeding Mediation proceedings are totally confidential proceedings. This is unlike proceedings in court

4 *Chambers 21st Century Dictionary*, p. 852.

5 *New International Webster's Comprehensive Dictionary*, Encyclopedic Ed. 2003, p. 791.

6 *Brochure of the International Centre for Alternative Dispute Resolution*, p. 18.

7 Jackson, *ADR Handbook*, 2nd Ed., p. 144.

8 *Dayawati* v *Yogesh Kumar Gosain* 2017(243) DLT 117.

which are conducted openly in the public gaze. If the mediation succeeds, then the Mediator should send the agreement signed by both the parties to the court without mentioning what transpired during the mediation proceedings. If the mediation is unsuccessful, then the Mediator should only write one sentence in his report and send it to the court stating that the "mediation has been unsuccessful". Beyond that, the Mediator should not write anything which was discussed, proposed or done during the mediation proceedings. This is because in mediation, very often, offers, counter offers and proposals are made by the parties but until and unless the parties reach to an agreement signed by them, it will not amount to any concluded contract. If the happenings in the mediation proceedings are disclosed, it will destroy the confidentiality of the mediation process.[9]

Mediation and negotiation—distinction

Mediation	Negotiation
1. The parties to the dispute are the main participants.	1. It normally takes place among the representatives of the parties to the dispute.
2. The purpose of mediation is to provide a forum through which the parties can resolve their disputes and differences.	2. The main purpose of negotiation is to reach or arrive at a compromise or settlement.
3. Mediation is presided over by a neutral person or a person who has no prior involvement in the dispute.	3. In the negotiation process normally parties or their advocates are the key actors.
4. In the context of litigation, mediation is generally an extra-legal procedure that is inserted into the process in an attempt to achieve a better and/or earlier resolution.	4. Negotiation is an integral part of litigation along with pleadings, discovery and other procedural aspects of litigation.
5. During the mediation process an expert may be invited.	5. The expert has no role.
6. Mediation must be planned, scheduled and well structured.	6. Negotiation is informal.

9 *Moti Ram* v *Ashok Kumar* (2011)1 SCC 466; (2010)13 Scale 190.

Mediation	Negotiation
7. It does not occur through mail, telephone, fax or other devices.	7. It may occur through mail, telephone, fax, e-mail or other devices as well as face to face.
8. Mediation generally occurs well before trial.	8. Negotiations can be concurrent with trial.
9. It limits the range of bargaining techniques available to disputants or their advocates.	9. Negotiation provides a wider array of models and techniques for bargaining, and in this respect, may have broader application to a larger variety of disputes and parties.

Arbitration and mediation—distinction

Arbitration	Mediation
1. Decision is made by a neutral third party called Arbitrator who has power to award in the form of monetary relief.	1. Parties themselves are the decision-maker.
2. In order to arrive at a conclusion the Arbitrator may record evidence both oral and documentary and hear arguments of both parties.	2. The Mediator in not concerned with the evidence; he evolves a creative thinking to help and assist the parties to resolve their problem by themselves.
3. Arbitrator is the key actor and both parties try to convince him/her about the merits of their case.	3. In mediation the parties are the key factor and the Mediator is an active participant who devises tactics, often on the spot, to move the parties toward reconciliation.
4. Arbitration is adversarial in nature.	4. Mediation is collaborative in nature.
5. Arbitration is akin to court proceeding, i.e., it is formal in nature.	5. Mediation procedure is informal in nature.
6. The Arbitrator plays the role of a judge to deliver judgment.	6. The third party act as a facilitator.
7. There may be more than one Arbitrator.	7. In the mediation, there is only one Mediator.

Arbitration	Mediation
8. The Arbitrator should not hear the parties in a private meeting and he must be neutral.	8. The Arbitrator should not hear the parties in a private meeting and he must be neutral. The mediation may hear the parties in a private meeting.
9. Arbitrator at the conclusion of hearing passes an award.	9. Mediator may or may not arrive at a solution at the end of the process.
10. Decision of the Arbitrator is final and binding.	10. Mediator has no power to pass any judgment.
11. To pass judgment/award agreement of the parties is not at all necessary because the role of Arbitrator is that of an adjudicator.	11. When both parties agree, then only the dispute is resolved.
12. Arbitration is concluded when the award is passed or handed down.	12. It ends when an agreement is reached or the parties decline to arrive at a concensus.

Essence of mediation The essence of mediation are as follows:[10]

(1) The entire proceedings are confidential. It enables the parties to arrive at a settlement though a proceeding which is not adjudicatory in nature.

(2) It involves the third party as a Mediator or negotiator to resolve the dispute.

(3) It provides an opportunity to the parties to settle the dispute by way of deliberation and discussion.

(4) Proceedings are flexible and parties are not bound to follow the nitty-gritty of the procedural aspects of law.

(5) The parties focuses on their own needs and interests. It is less complicated and less costly.

(6) It enables the parties to disclose their disposition and conflicting interests.

Mediator how assists negotiation process Mediation is an effective process because the presence of a Mediator can assist

10 Henry Brown and Arthur Marriott, *ADR Principles and Practice*, 2nd Ed., p. 583.

the negotiation process between the parties in the following ways:[11]

(*a*) The Mediator adds a new dynamic to and creates a balance between the different negotiating styles and personalities of the parties and their lawyers;

(*b*) By following the rules of principled negotiation the Mediator can lead the parties to work through the deadlock that can be created by purely positional more competitive negotiation, not least by reframing and managing the timing of offers and concessions;

(*c*) The Mediator can be skilled at managing and diffusing strong feelings that may be the key barrier to reaching settlement;

(*d*) Mediators will bring their own personal attributes to the table, such as patience, empathy, ability to listen, good judgment, good communication skills, creativity, the ability to think outside the box, impartiality, authority, and the ability to command respect, all of which can help the parties to review and re-evaluate their case and their needs and interests.

When matter referred to mediation In order to determine whether the dispute would be referred to Mediator or not the following elements/factors will be looked into:[12]

(*a*) Whether the order of the court is needed? Where the court order is needed it is not appropriate to refer the matter to mediation.

(*b*) Whether there is any statutory period of limitation to set the law in motion? If the law provides that a particular suit will be filed within a specific time, the Mediator cannot extend the period of limitation. Time barred application or suits are not entertainable either by the Mediator or even by the parties.

11 Jackson, *ADR Handbook*, 2nd Ed., pp. 145-146.

12 Henry Brown and Arthur Marriott, *ADR Principles and Practice*, 2nd Ed., pp. 416-417.

(*c*) Whether the suit was initiated or defended for strategic reason?

(*d*) Whether negotiated settlement is possible or not?

(*e*) Whether there was any relationship between the parties that has already been shaped or broken down, *i.e.* husband and wife, partners, share-holders, doctor and patient, etc.

(*f*) Whether there is any allegation or counter allegation against each other? It is common experience that "where the issues are raw and recent, parties may not be ready to enter into negotiations to resolve them. Where parties want to find a solution quickly and economically, mediation must be a primary option".

Mediation as effective means of settlement—reason Mediation is effective for the following reasons—

(1) Mediation is a flexible process and can be tailored to meet the needs of the case;

(2) It results in a speedier resolution of the dispute than litigation. Mediation can be arranged quickly, often within a matter of days;

(3) It is cost-effective, particularly if the parties select a low cost, time limited, fixed fee mediation;

(4) It is a confidential and private process.

(5) It avoids an adverse precedent being set by the court;

(6) It avoids the emotional stress that some individuals may feel about giving evidence in court;

(7) A settlement that is reached by mutual agreement is more likely to preserve relationships than a court imposed solution;

(8) Mediation enables the parties to be more creative when reaching settlement;

(9) The terms of settlement may provide for matters that could not be achieved within the constraints of the litigation process and may include matters which the court would have no power to order, such as an apology,

a good reference, or the continuation of a business relationship on different terms;

(10) Even if settlement is not reached at the mediation, going through the mediation process may help the parties to understand each other's case, narrow the issues, and, in some cases, settlement may be more easily achieved after the mediation;

(11) The court may direct the parties to consider mediation, thus imposing a requirement on the parties to engage with the process seriously and with the intention of settling the case;

(12) The parties are likely to be paying for the mediation, both in relation to their own legal costs and their contribution towards the expenses of the mediation (such as the venue) and the Mediator's fees.

(13) Mediation puts control into the hands of the parties themselves. It gives them a forum where they can air their grievances in a confidential process, without the risks inherent in litigation".[13]

Basis of mediation Self-determination, impartiality and removal of conflicts of interests are the three pillars on the basis of which entire edifice of mediation rests.

Self-determination[14] A Mediator shall conduct a mediation based on the principle of party self-determination. Self-determination is the act of coming to a voluntary, uncoerced decision in which each party makes free and informed choices as to process and outcome. Parties may exercise self-determination at any stage of a mediation. Although party self-determination for process design is a fundamental principle of mediation practice, a Mediator may need to balance such party self-determination with a Mediator's duty to conduct a quality process in accordance with these standards. A Mediator cannot personally ensure that each

13 Jackson, *ADR Handbook*, 2nd Ed., pp. 146-147.

14 Standard I of Model Standards of Conduct for Mediators adopted by American Bar Association, American Arbitration Association and Association for Conflict Resolutions in 2005.

party has made free and informed choices to reach particular decisions, but, where appropriate, a Mediator should make the parties aware of the importance of consulting other professionals to help them make informed choices.

Impartiality[15] A Mediator shall decline a mediation if the Mediator cannot conduct it in an impartial manner. Impartiality means freedom from favoritism, bias or prejudice. A Mediator should not act with partiality or prejudice based on any participant's personal characteristics, background, values and beliefs, or performance at a mediation, or any other reason. A Mediator should neither give nor accept a gift, favor, loan or other item of value that raises a question as to the Mediator's actual or perceived impartiality. A Mediator may accept or give *de minimis* gifts or incidental items or services that are provided to facilitate a mediation or respect cultural norms so long as such practices do not raise questions as to a Mediator's actual or perceived impartiality.

Conflicts of interest[16] A Mediator shall avoid a conflict of interest or the appearance of a conflict of interest during and after a mediation. A conflict of interest can arise from involvement by a Mediator with the subject matter of the dispute or from any relationship between a Mediator and any mediation participant, whether past or present, personal or professional, that reasonably raises a question of a Mediator's impartiality. A Mediator shall make a reasonable inquiry to determine whether there are any facts that a reasonable individual would consider likely to create a potential or actual conflict of interest for a Mediator. A Mediator shall disclose, as soon as practicable, all actual and potential conflict of interests. If a Mediator learns any fact after accepting a mediation that raises a question with respect to that Mediator's service creating a potential or actual conflicting of interest, the Mediator shall disclose it as quickly as practicable. If a Mediator's conflict of interest might reasonably be viewed as undermining the integrity of the mediation, a Mediator shall withdraw from or decline to proceed with the mediation regardless of the expressed desire or agreement of the parties to the contrary.

15 Standard II.
16 Standard III.

Confidentiality[17] A Mediator shall maintain the confidentially of all information obtained by the Mediator in mediation, unless otherwise agreed to by the parties or required by applicable law. When the parties to a mediation agree that the Mediator may disclose information obtained during the mediation, the Mediator may do so. A Mediator should not communicate to any non-participant information about how the parties acted in the mediation.

Competence[18] A Mediator shall mediate only when the Mediator has the necessary competence to satisfy the reasonable expectations of the parties. If a Mediator's ability to conduct a mediation is impaired by drugs, alcohol, medication or otherwise, the Mediator shall not conduct the mediation.

Quality of the process[19] A Mediator shall conduct a mediation in a manner that promotes diligence, timeliness, safety, presence of the appropriate participants, party participation, procedural fairness party competency and mutual respect among all participants.

Advertising and solicitation[20] A Mediator shall be truthful and not misleading when advertising, soliciting or otherwise communicating the Mediator's qualifications, experience, services and fees.

Fees and other charges[21] A Mediator shall provide each party or each party's representative true and complete information about mediation fees, expenses and any other actual or potential charges that may be incurred in connection with a mediation.

Advancement of mediation practice[1] A Mediator should act in a manner that advances the practice of mediation. He promotes the cause of advancement of mediation by engaging in some or all of the following:

(*a*) Fostering diversity within the field of mediation.

17 Standard IV.
18 Standard IV.
19 Standard VI.
20 Standard VII.
21 Standard VIII.
1 Standard IX.

(*b*) Striving to make mediation accessible to those who elect to use it, including providing services at a reduced rate or on a *pro bono* basis as appropriate.

(*c*) Participating in research when given the opportunity, including obtaining participant feedback when appropriate.

(*d*) Participating in outreach and education efforts to assist the public in developing an improved understanding of, and appreciation for, mediation.

(*e*) Assisting newer Mediators through training, mentoring and networking.

Role of Mediator Mediator is not an adjudicator, but a facilitator. He is a referee, guide as well as communicator. Carrie Menkle Meadow, Lela Poter Love and Andrea Kupfer Schneider in their book titled as, *Mediation, Practice, Policy and Ethics*, classically explained the role of the Mediator in the following words:[2]

> "The Mediator acts as host and chair, convening the parties for discussions; making arrangements for adequate, safe, and comfortable facilities; attending to special needs of disputants (for example, disabilities or language differences); and ensuring that the agenda is constructive, that any obstacles that develop are addressed, and that agreements are memorialized. The Mediator is a guide, coach and educator, steering the parties toward effective negotiation behaviour and away from destructive, self-defeating maneuvers. The Mediator is a referee, offering each party an equal place at the bargaining table, allowing each voice to be heard, and encouraging parties to get additional resources or to withdraw from mediation if it is no longer constructive. The Mediator is a master communicator and translator, gleaning insights from conversations rife with extreme positions, threats and blame to help parties hear one another's interests, issues, proposals, feelings, principles and values."

The role of the Mediator are many and varied. They are:

(1) *To create a healthy, congenial atmosphere*. It is one of the most important duty of a Mediator to create a healthy

2 Page 91.

and congenial atmosphere to resolve the dispute or differences between the parties only on voluntary basis.

(2) *To help the parties to understand their points of dispute.* Another role of Mediator is to understand the parties to identify their points of disputes or key issues involved in the matter under consideration.

(3) *To solve the dispute.* Mediator helps the parties to resolve the dispute keeping in view the respective interests of the parties.

(4) *Help parties to arrive at a mutual agreement.* Mediator is not an adjudicator, or judge but he merely sets his nod on the mutual agreement of the parties which he arrives at by mutual inter-action and discussion.

(5) *Assist the parties to evaluate the own interest.* The Mediator will work with the parties beyond the formal parameters fixed for the dispute and enable the parties to provide their own interest. In the words of Justice Dhananjay Y. Chandrachur, Mediator has to reflect on the percept of BATNA (Best Alternative to Negotiated Agreement), WATNA (Worst Alternative to Negotiated Agreement), MALTNA (Most Likely Alternative to Negotiable Agreement) in enabling parties to move towards a settlement.

(6) *The Mediator acts as a manager.* The Mediator manages the entire mediation proceeding in the following manner:[3]

(*a*) By making the practical arrangements for the initial mediation meeting.

(*b*) By acting as an informal chair of the meetings and ensuring that when the parties meet with him or her there is an orderly and reasonably secure environment in which discussion can take place effectively and constructively.

(*c*) By assuming responsibility for the conduct of the mediation process in accordance with ground rules accepted by the parties.

3 Henry Brown and Arthur Marriott, *ADR Principles and Practice*, 2nd Ed., p. 347.

(*d*) By formulating, implementing and varying as necessary an agenda for the mediation, where appropriate in consultation with the parties.

(*e*) By managing the meetings, regulating the time spent on different aspects under discussion, deciding whether and when to meet parties separately, deterring abusive conduct, allowing or preventing interruptions, and generally assisting the parties in using the time productively.

(7) *Acts as a facilitator*. Mediator as a facilitator performs the following functions:[4]

(*i*) Helping each party to understand the other party's position.

(*ii*) Prioritising the issues and helping to guide the parties through the range of issues brought to the mediation.

(*iii*) Helping the parties to generate, explore and narrow options for resolving the issues.

(*iv*) Acting as a sounding board for a party to test whether possible proposals may be useful.

(*v*) Examining common interests and aspirations, and possibilities for future relationships where appropriate.

(*vi*) Acknowledging the strength of views and feelings held without necessarily agreeing with these.

(*vii*) Using other communication skills and strategies.

(*viii*) Using impasse strategies if the parties are deadlocked.

(*ix*) Exploring the alternatives to negotiated resolution and their implications.

(*x*) Helping parties to consider and prepare for adjudication.

4 Henry Brown and Arthur Marriott, *ADR Principles and Practice*, 2nd Ed., pp. 348-349.

(8) *The Mediator acts as a scribe or pen-man.* The Mediator as a scribe performs the following functions—

(*a*) To take note of the important aspects of the proceedings.

(*b*) To provide/supply the parties outlines of proposed settlement.

(*c*) To prepare note of the terms and conditions of the proposed settlement.

Carrie Menkel Meadow and Andrea Kupfer Schneider in their book, *Mediation, Practice, Policy and Ethics* graphically explained the evaluative role of the Mediator in the following manner:

Role of Mediator Evaluative

Problem Definition Narrow	Problem Definition Broad
Urges/pushes parties to accept narrow (position-based) settlement	**Urges/pushes** parties to accept broad (interest-based) settlement
Proposes narrow (position-based) agreement	**Develops and proposes** broad (interest-based) agreement
Predicts court or other outcomes	**Predicts** impact (on interests) of not settling
Assesses strengths and weaknesses of each side's case	**Educates self** about parties' interests
Helps parties evaluate proposals	**Helps parties** evaluate proposals
Helps parties develop & exchange narrow (position-based) proposals	**Helps parties** develop & exchange broad (interest-based) proposals
Asks about consequences of not settling	**Helps parties** develop options that respond to interests
Asks about likely court or other outcomes	**Helps parties** understand interests
Asks about strengths and weaknesses of each side's case	

In short, the Mediator will act as a facilitator in the following ways[5]—

1. Gather information from the parties both at the pre-mediation stage and during the mediation about the issues in dispute and their needs and interest;
2. Help the parties to identify the legal and factual issues, and their underlying needs and objectives;
3. Encourage the parties to treat the mediation as their day in court and to air their feelings and emotions, particularly in private meetings, so that the matter can move forward;
4. Help the parties to listen to each other and communicate more effectively with each other;
5. Discourage or defuse confrontational or aggressive communications between the parties that will hinder negotiations, and reframe them if necessary;
6. Encourage the parties to analyse the strength and weakness of their own case and the case presented by the other side;
7. Perform the role of reality checker, perhaps by assuming the role of devil's advocate, if the parties are unrealistic in their assessment;
8. Encourage the parties to think about the BATNA (Best Alternative to a Negotiated Agreement) and the WATNA (Worse Alternative to a Negotiated Agreement), and ensure that they have carried out a full risk assessment, including the costs (and irrecoverable costs) of proceeding to trial;
9. Review the negotiations that have already taken place between the parties, and encourage each party to reflect on why they failed and how they can change their position to move the matter forward; will focus primarily

5 Jackson, *ADR Handbook*, 2nd Ed., pp. 154-155.

on the real interests and concerns of the parties rather than the strict legal merits of their position.

Questions put by facilitative Mediator The questions put by the facilitative Mediator are—

(*a*) Ask questions that test the strengths and weaknesses of each side's case;

(*b*) Explore each party's situation and help them to identify what they really need or want to achieve from the dispute;

(*c*) Encourage the parties to think about the likely outcome of litigation and the costs of obtaining that outcome;

(*d*) Focus each party's to think about the likely outcome of litigation and the costs of obtaining that outcome;

(*e*) Focus each party's attention on their underlying objectives and needs (what is important and why this is so), rather than on a strict analysis and evaluation of the merits of their case;

(*f*) Help the parties to work out a creative solution that is in their best interest;

(*g*) Assist the parties to negotiate more effectively by formulating offers in a way that may be more attractive to the other side, and considering the timing and staging of offers and concessions.[6]

Ethics to be followed by Mediator The Mediator shall:

(1) follow and observe these rules strictly and with due diligence;

(2) not carry on any activity or conduct which could reasonably be considered as conduct unbecoming of a Mediator;

(3) uphold the integrity and fairness of the mediation process;

6 Jackson, *ADR Handbook*, 2nd Ed., p. 170.

(4) ensure that the parties involved in the mediation are fairly informed and have an adequate understanding of the procedural aspects of the process;

(5) satisfy himself/herself that he/she is qualified to undertake and complete the assignment in a professional manner;

(6) disclose any interest or relationship likely to affect impartiality or which might seek an appearance of partiality or bias;

(7) avoid, while communicating with the parties, any impropriety or appearance of impropriety;

(8) be faithful to the relationship of trust and confidentiality imposed in the office of Mediator;

(9) conduct all proceedings related to the resolution of a dispute, in accordance with the applicable law;

(10) recognize that mediation is based on principles of self-determination by the parties and that mediation process relies upon the ability of parties to reach a voluntary, undisclosed agreement;

(11) maintain the reasonable expectations of the parties as to confidentiality;

(12) refrain from promises or guarantees of results.

Model standard of practice for Family and Divorce Mediation The model standard of practice for Family and Divorce Mediation are as under—

(1) A family Mediator shall recognize that mediation is based on the principle of self-determination by the participants.

(2) A family Mediator shall be qualified by education and training to undertake the mediation.

(3) A family Mediator shall facilitate the participants' understanding of what mediation is and assess their capacity to mediate before the participants reach an agreement to mediate. Before family mediation begins a Mediator should provide the participants with an overview of the process and its purposes, including:

(*a*) Informing the participants that reaching an agreement in family mediation is consensual in nature, that a Mediator is an impartial facilitator, and that a Mediator may not impose or force any settlement on the parties;

(*b*) Distinguishing family mediation from other processes designed to address family issues and disputes;

(*c*) Informing the participants that any agreements reached will be reviewed by the court when court approval is required;

(*d*) Informing the participants that they may obtain independent advice from attorneys, counsel, advocates, accountants, therapists or other professionals during the mediation process;

(*e*) Advising the participants, in appropriate cases, that they can seek the advice of religious figures, elders or other significant persons in their community whose opinions they value;

(*f*) Discussing, if applicable, the issue of separate sessions with the participants, a description of the circumstances in which the Mediator may meet alone with any of the participants, or with any third party and the conditions of confidentiality concerning these separate sessions;

(*g*) Informing the participants that the presence or absence of other persons at a mediation, including attorneys, counsellors or advocates, depends on the agreement of the participants and the Mediator, unless a statute or regulation other wise requires or the Mediator believes that the presence of another person is required or may be beneficial because of a history or threat of violence or other serious coercive activity by a participant.

(*h*) Describing the obligations of the Mediator to maintain the confidentiality of the mediation process and its results as well as any exceptions to confidentiality;

(*i*) Advising the participants of the circumstances under which the Mediator may suspend or terminate the mediation process and that a participant has a right to suspend or terminate mediation at any time.

(4) A family Mediator shall conduct the mediation process in an impartial manner. A family Mediator shall disclose all actual and potential grounds of bias and conflicts of interest reasonably known to the Mediator. The participants shall be free to retain the Mediator by an informed, written waiver of the conflict of interest. However, if a bias or conflict of interest clearly impairs a Mediator's impartiality, the Mediator shall withdraw regardless of the express agreement of the participants. The duties of family Mediator are as follows—

(*a*) A family Mediator should not accept a dispute for mediation if the family Mediator can not be impartial.

(*b*) A family Mediator should identify and disclose potential grounds of bias or conflict of interest upon which a Mediator's impartiality might reasonably be question.

(*c*) A family Mediator should resolve all doubts in favour of disclosure. All disclosures should be made as soon as practical after the Mediator becomes aware of the bias or potential conflict of interest. The duty to disclose is a continuing duty.

(*d*) A family Mediator should guard against bias or partiality based on the participants' personal characteristics, background or performance at the mediation.

(*e*) A family Mediator should avoid conflicts of interest in recommending the services of other professionals.

(*f*) A family Mediator should not use information about participants obtained in a mediation for personal gain or advantage.

(5) A family Mediator shall fully disclose and explain the basis of any compensation, fees and charges to the participants.

(6) A family Mediator shall structure the mediation process so that the participants make decisions based on sufficient information and knowledge.

(7) A family Mediator shall maintain the confidentiality of all information acquired in the mediation process, unless the Mediator is permitted or required to reveal the information by law or agreement of the participants.

(8) A family Mediator shall assist participants in determining how to promote the best interests of children.The Mediator should encourage the participants to explore the range of options available for separation or post divorce parenting arrangements and their respective cots and benefits.

(9) A family Mediator shall recognize a family situation involving child abuse or neglect and take appropriate steps to shape the mediation process accordingly.

(10) A family Mediator shall recognize a family situation involving domestic abuse and take appropriate steps to shape the mediation process accordingly.

(11) A family Mediator shall suspend or terminate the mediation process when the Mediator reasonably believes that a participants is unable to effectively participate or for other compelling reason.

(12) A family Mediator shall be truthful in the advertisement and solicitation for mediation.

(13) A family Mediator shall acquire and maintain professional competence in mediation.

Termination of mediation (1) When one of the parties withdraw himself from the mediation proceeding.

(2) When the settlement of the dispute is impossible or parties are unwilling to arrive at a mutual settlement.

(3) When the Mediator is of opinion that continuation of proceeding will not yield any fruitful result, then he can terminate the proceeding.

(4) When the parties arrives at a mutually satisfactory written settlement.

(5) When the Mediator retires from the proceeding.

Litigation versus Mediation

Litigation	Mediation
1. The parties can delegate their powers to their advocates.	1. The parties personally take part in the proceedings.
2. Procedures are rigid and not flexible as mediation.	2. Procedures are flexible.
3. It is a "public process."	3. It is private and confidential.
4. Adjudicator(s) is /are legally trained in law.	4. Mediator may or may not be trained in law.
5. Cost is more than mediation.	5. It is less costly.
6. It "necessarily invokes elements of delay."	6. Its main object is to resolve the dispute as expeditiously as possible.
7. It "deals with power in balances between parties by providing an impartial forum."	7. It is based on the "skill, training and integrity of the Mediator."
8. Institution of the suit is the only resort when the suit is filed solely on legal issues.	8. Mediation is not possible where the suit is filed solely on legal issues.
9. It is helpful where the litigation is filed or defended purely on tactical reasons.	9. It is not helpful "where the litigation is instituted or defended purely for tactical reasons".

Advantage of mediation Joanne Goss[7] has pointed out the following advantages of mediation:

(*a*) *Effective process* Mediation generally enjoys an 80 to 85 per cent success rate.

(*b*) *Better results* The resolution is created by the parties and is therefore tailored to their specific needs. This tends to result in a lower incidence of breach of the agreement reached.

(*c*) *Speed* A mediation can be arranged in a relatively short period of time and has the effect of bringing settlement negotiations "to a head" much more quickly than negotiations directly between parties, resulting in a faster disposition.

(*d*) *Privacy* It takes place in private.

(*e*) *Cost* Time, money and emotion can be saved through early resolution of the dispute. Furthermore, the cost of mediation

7 *An Introduction to Alternative Dispute Resolution*, Alberta Law Review, vol. XXXIV, 1995, pp. 8-9.

can be included with taxable costs and disbursements payable to the successful party.

(f) *Informal atmosphere* "Atmosphere is conducive to effective communication between the parties" about the proposed settlement.

Stages in preparation for Mediation[8]

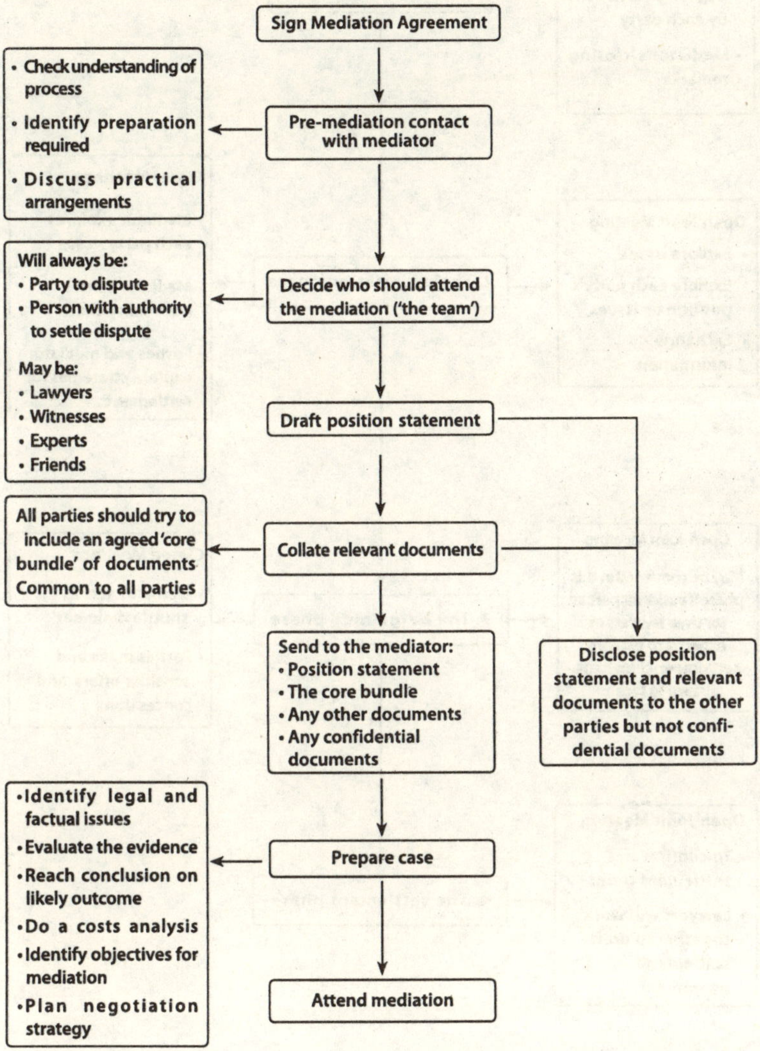

8 Jackson, *ADR Handbook*, 2nd Ed., p. 192.

Mediation Process[9]

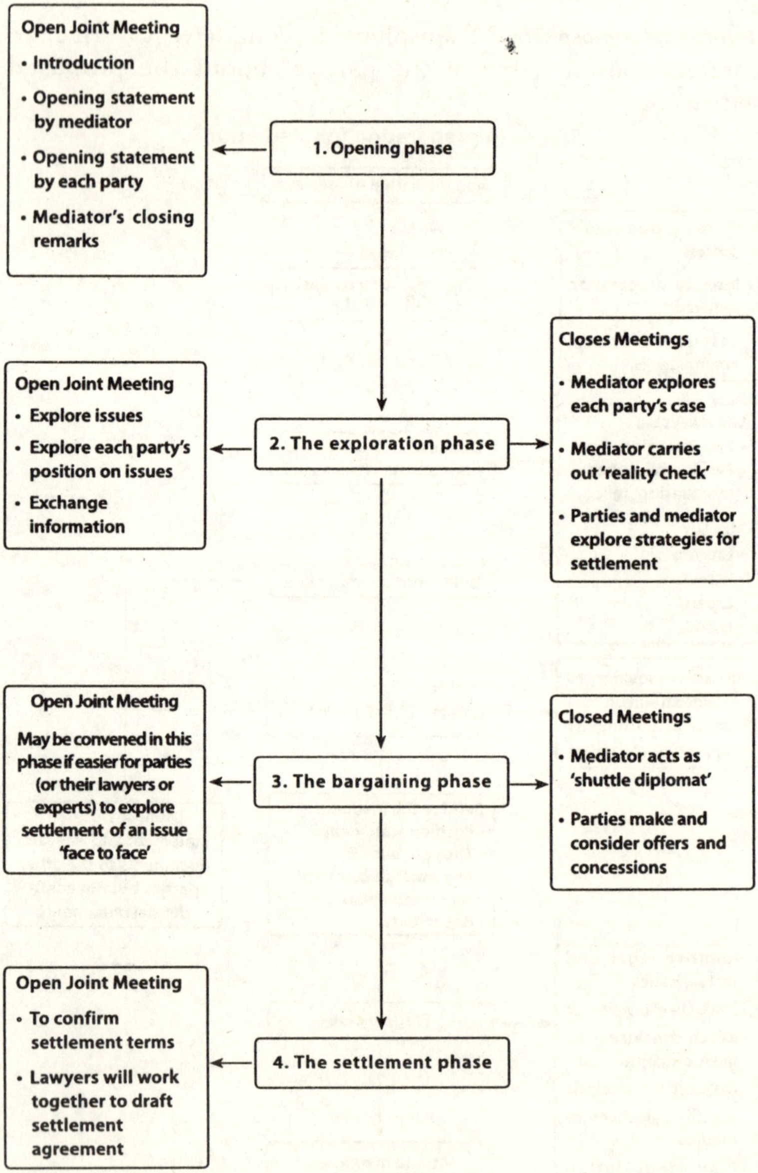

9 Jackson, *ADR Handbook*, 2nd Ed., p. 197.

Stages of Mediation

STAGE I

The Mediator explains the procedure to be adopted by him in order to resolve the dispute and if they may make any statement it will not be used against them and the proceedings are confidential.

STAGE II

Creation of congenial atmosphere for settlement of the dispute by way of free discussion between the Mediator and the parties.

STAGE III

Mediator convince the parties that he is independent and impartial.

STAGE IV

Discussion between the parties regarding the crux of the dispute and their individual views and counter views.

STAGE V

Preparation of the averment of the parties point wise.

STAGE VI

Settlement of the issues by the Mediator on the basis of averment made by the parties.

STAGE VII

Mediator assist the parties to focus their issues to arrive at an amicable settlement of their dispute.

STAGE VIII

Fixation of the place of meeting after consultation with the parties.

STAGE IX

Confidential sitting between the parties and the Mediator separately. The Mediator first held separate meeting with the parties applicant and opponent in order to understand their problem and to assess the interest of the each party.

Stage X

Mediator conduct a joint meeting with the parties and place before each of them their individual problems and their individual views.

Stage XI

Mediator will pursued the parties to arrive at a settlement and he took active part to encourage the parties to participate by speaking freely between them in course of mediation.

Stage XII

When the parties came in an acceptable terms of settlement they may write the same as settlement and each party and Mediator put their signature on it to authenticate the terms of settlement.

Benefits of online mediation The system of mediation has something that is very common throughout the ancient and medieval systems. Having a dispute is common, but the problem lies when the dispute continues over a long period of time. In most cases issues often arise from trivial matters but the solution never arrives. Hence, the concept of mediation is always ideal.

Many often fail to realise that the result of the litigation may not always be in one's favour but the result of a mediation ensures that no one is absolutely at loss. If *Duryadhana* would have agreed to the demand of the five villages then certainly he would not have had to lose his life as well as his kingdom.

When we forward the story to the modern era, the concept of mediation has reached online, the idea of mediation gets strengthened much further. The benefits of online mediation are:

1. *Pocket Pinch* When one does not have to travel it certainly saves a lot of money. The best part is that even the Mediator remains at ease and can afford to reduce his fees in the absence of travelling long distance.

2. *Time* Time is priceless, when one does not have to travel and remain at his place, it can save a lot of problem and difficulties.

This also ensures that some of the best Mediators who stay at far distances can attend the said procedings. Thus, online mediation has the prospective aptitude for intensification and escalation of scope of access to justice for many disputants.

3. *Technological improvement* It is always recommended that the best technology should be adopted. Once people tend to rely on such technology it would be an automatic stimulus to technological growth.

4. *Transparency* In case of online mediation the same is capable of being recorded and thus it would ensure fair proceedings.

5. *User-friendly* It has both psychological and technological advantage. Often it is less intimidating to see a renowned Mediator online and it also encourages the use of better technology.

Limitations of online mediation

1. *Not suitable in all cases* Some matters may require a far more personal approach and a far greater degree of sensitivity. For instance, in a matrimonial dispute, personal care is important. The parties would be in a greater position to relate.

2. *Cost* In case of minor disputes it may not be possible to make use of a good and highly advanced technology, thus it may not be cost effective.

3. *No appeal* It is an inherent difficulty of mediation that the Mediator may often try to tilt the balance of convenience from one party to another and more often than not there is no scope of either reviewing the matter or taking it to appeal.

4. *Uniformed technology* The users of the service may not have similar technological instruments and thus the users may not be able to have a smooth and uniform technology. Thus the mediation may be affected.

5. *Not following legal and procedural norms* The Mediators often are unable to follow the legal and procedural legal intricacies. Thus the principle may end up being violated.

6. *Lack of confidentiality* The service provider too becomes a major player in online mediation and they would have access to the contents therein. Hence, it would be a potential disaster.

7. ***Cyber threats*** The proceedings often can fall prey to hacking or other online threats. The cyber world is certainly a world of risk and uncertainty.

Duty of court to provide mediation to the unwilling party

Following things can be done by the court to make a reluctant or unwilling party consider mediation:[10]

(*i*) The court can offer strong judicial encouragement to the parties to Mediate their dispute. However, the court will not compel parties to mediate if they are unwilling to do so.

(*ii*) The court can make an ADR order directing the parties to consider ADR, in particular mediation.

(*iii*) Although the courts will not mandate parties to use mediation against their will, in some cases, the courts can direct the parties to make contact with a Mediator to consider mediation. This should be regarded as mandatory consideration of mediation, rather than mandatory mediation.

(*iv*) The court can stay proceedings (assuming that proceedings have been issued) and direct the parties to attempt to resolve the dispute by ADR.

(*v*) The court may be able to assist the parties to resolve their dispute by mediation by making appropriate orders for advance disclosure of information or documents relating to one or more issues in the case on the application of one or both parties;

(*vi*) If both parties consent, judicial mediation can be undertaken;

(*vii*) If one or both parties have acted unreasonably in refusing to use mediation to resolve the dispute, the court may mark its disapproval in the form of adverse orders.

10 Jackson, *ADR Handbook*, 2nd Ed., p. 151.

Legality of referral of a case under section 138 of the Negotiable Instruments Act 1881 and its procedure

It is legal to refer a criminal compoundable case as one under s. 138 of the Negotiable Instruments Act 1881 to mediation. In the context of reference of the parties, in a case arising under s. 138 of the Negotiable Instruments Act 1881, to mediation is concerned; the following procedure is required to be followed:[11]

(*i*) When the respondent first enters appearance in à complaint under s. 138 of the Negotiable Instruments Act 1881, before proceeding further with the case, the Magistrate may proceed to record admission and denial of documents in accordance with s. 294 of the Code of Criminal Procedure and if satisfied, at any stage before the complaint is taken up for hearing, there exist elements of settlement, the Magistrate shall inquire from the parties if they are open to exploring possibility of an amicable resolution of the disputes.

(*ii*) If the parties are so inclined, they should be informed by the court of the various mechanisms available to them by which they can arrive at such settlement including out of court settlement; referral to Lok Adalat under the Legal Services Authorities Act 1987; referral to the court annexed mediation centre; as well as conciliation under the Arbitration and Conciliation Act 1996.

(*iii*) Once the parties have chosen the appropriate mechanism which they would be willing to use to resolve their disputes, the court should refer the parties to such forum while stipulating the prescribed time period, within which the matter should be negotiated (ideally a period of six weeks) and the next date of hearing when the case should be again placed before the concerned court to enable it to monitor the progress and outcome of such negotiations.

(*iv*) In the event that the parties seek reference to mediation, the court should list the matter before the concerned

11 *Dayawati* v *Yogesh Kumar Gosain* 2017(243) DLT 117.

mediation centre/mediator on a fixed date directing the presence of the parties/authorized representatives before the Mediator on the said date.

(*v*) If referred to mediation, the courts, as well as the Mediators, should encourage parties to resolve their overall disputes, not confined to the case in which the reference is made or the subject matter of the criminal complaint which relates only to dishonouring of a particular cheque.

(*vi*) The parties should endeavour to interact/discuss their individual resolutions/proposals with each other as well and facilitate as many interactions necessary for efficient resolution within the period granted by the court. The parties shall be directed to appear before the Mediator in a time bound manner keeping in view the time period fixed by the Magistrate.

(*vii*) In the event that all parties seek extension of time beyond the initial six week period, the Magistrate may, after considering the progress of the mediation proceedings, in the interest of justice, grant extension of time to the parties for facilitating the settlement. For the purposes of such extension, the Magistrate may call for an interim report from the Mediator, however keeping in mind the confidentiality attached to the mediation process. Upon being satisfied that *bona fide* and sincere efforts for settlement were being made by the parties, the Magistrate may fix a reasonable time period for the parties to appear before the Mediator appointing a next date of hearing for a report on the progress in the mediation. Such time period would depend on the facts and circumstances and is best left to the discretion of the Magistrate who would appoint the same keeping in view the best interest of both parties.

(*viii*) *Contents of the settlement.* If a settlement is reached during the mediation, the settlement agreement which is drawn-up must incorporate:

(*a*) a clear stipulation as to the amount which is agreed to be paid by the party;

(*b*) a clear and simple mechanism/method of payment and the manner and mode of payment;

(*c*) Undertakings of all parties to abide and be bound by the terms of the settlement must be contained in the agreement to ensure that the parties comply with the terms agreed upon;

(*d*) a clear stipulation, if agreed upon, of the penalty which would ensure to the party if a default of the agreed terms is committed in addition to the consequences of the breach of the terms of the settlement;

(*e*) an unequivocal declaration that both parties have executed the agreement after understanding the terms of the settlement agreement as well as of the consequences of its breach;

(*f*) a stipulation regarding the voluntariness of the settlement and declaration that the executors of the settlement agreement were executing and signing the same without any kind of force, pressure and undue influence.

(*ix*) The Mediator should forward a carefully executed settlement agreement duly signed by both parties along with his report to the court on the date fixed, when the parties or their authorized representatives would appear before the court.

Proceeding before the court

(*x*) The Magistrate would adopt a procedure akin to that followed by the civil court under Order XXIII of the CPC.

(*xi*) The Magistrate should record a statement on oath of the parties affirming the terms of the settlement; that it was entered into voluntarily, of the free will of the parties, after fully understanding the contents and implications thereof, affirming the contents of the agreement placed before the court; confirming their signatures thereon. A clear undertaking to abide by the terms of the settlement should also be recorded as a matter of abundant caution.

(*xii*) A statement to the above effect may be obtained on affidavit. However, the Magistrate must record a statement of the parties proving the affidavit and the settlement agreement on court record.

(*xiii*) The magistrate should independently apply his judicial mind and satisfy himself that the settlement agreement is genuine, equitable, lawful, not opposed to public policy, voluntary and that there is no legal impediment in accepting the same.

(*xiv*) Pursuant to recording of the statement of the parties, the magistrate should specifically accept the statement of the parties as well as their undertakings and hold them bound by the terms of the settlement terms entered into by and between them. This order should clearly stipulate that in the event of default by either party, the amount agreed to be paid in the settlement agreement will be recoverable in terms of s. 431 read with s. 421 of the Code of Criminal Procedure.

(*xv*) Upon receiving a request from the complainant, that on account of the compromise vide the settlement agreement, it is withdrawing himself from prosecution; the matter has to be compounded. Such prayer of the complainant has to be accepted in keeping with the scheme of s. 147 of the Negotiable Instruments Act 188l.[12] At this point, the trial court should discharge/ acquit the accused person, depending on the stage of the case. This procedure should be followed even where the settlement terms require implementation of the terms and payment over a period of time.

(*xvi*) In the event that after various rounds of mediation, the parties conclude that the matter cannot be amicably resolved or settled, information to this effect should be placed before the Magistrate who should proceed in

12 *Rameshbhai Somabhai Patel* v *Dineshbhai Achalanand Rathi* 2005 CrLJ 431.

that complaint on merits, as per the procedure prescribed by law.

(*xvii*) The Magistrate should ensure strict compliance with the guidelines and principles laid down by the Supreme Court in *Damodar S. Prabhu* v *Sayed Babalal*[13] and *Madhya Pradesh State Legal Services Authority* v *Prateek Jain.*[14]

(*xvii*) Criminal case may also be referred wherein there is an underlying civil dispute. While the parties may not be either permitted in law to compound the criminal case or may not be willing to compound the criminal case, they may be willing to explore the possibility of a negotiated settlement of their civil disputes. There is no legal prohibition to the parties seeking mediation so far as the underlying civil dispute is concerned. In case a settlement is reached, the principles laid down by us would apply to settlement of such underlying civil disputes as well.

In case reference in a criminal case is restricted to only an underlying civil dispute and a settlement is reached in mediation, the referring court could require the Mediator to place such settlement in the civil litigation between the parties which would proceed in the matter in accordance with prescribed procedure.

Non-compliance of mediation settlement—procedure to be followed In case the mediation settlement accepted by the court is not complied with, the following procedure is required to be followed:

(*i*) In the event of default or non-compliance or breach of the settlement agreement by the accused person, the magistrate would pass an order under s. 431 read with s. 421 of the Code of Criminal Procedure to recover the amount agreed to be paid by the accused in the same manner as a fine would be recovered.

13 (2010)5 SCC 663.
14 (2014)10 SCC 690.

(*ii*) Additionally, for breach of the undertaking given to the magistrate/court, the court would take appropriate action permissible in law to enforce compliance with the undertaking as well as the orders of the court based thereon, including proceeding under s. 2(*b*) of the Contempt of Courts Act 1971 for violation thereof.

Mediated Settlement Agreement—not a decree The settlement reached in mediation arising out of a criminal case does not tantamount to a decree by a civil court and cannot be executed in a civil court. However, a settlement in mediation arising out of referral in a civil case by a civil court can result in a decree upon compliance with the procedure under Or. XXIII of the CPC. This can never be so in a mediation settlement arising out of a criminal case.

Guidelines for Referral Judges Judges who refer the cases for settlement through any of the ADR methods are known as Referral Judges. So, Referral Judges have played a very significant role in Court Referred Mediation. The guidelines for Referral Judges in regard to sending of cases for settlement of disputes through Mediation are as follows:[15]

(1) As per s. 89 and r. lA of Or. 10, the court should explore the possibility of referral to ADR processes after the pleadings are complete and before framing the issues when the case is taken up for preliminary hearing for examination of parties under Or. 10 of the Code. If for any reason, the court could not considered and referred the matter to ADR processes before framing issues, the case can be refer even after framing of the issues.

In family disputes or matrimonial cases, the ideal stage for mediation would be immediately after service of respondent and before filing of objections/written statements. In such cases the relationship between concerned parties becomes hostile on account of the various allegations in the petition. The hostility

15 Mediation Training Manual for Referral Judges, Mediation and Conciliation Project Committee, Supreme Court of India, pp. 27-29.

would be further aggravated by the counter-allegations made in written statement or objections.

(2) After completion of the pleadings and before framing of the issues, the court shall fix a preliminary hearing for appearance of parties to acquaint itself with the fads of the case and the nature of the dispute between the parties.

(3) The court should first consider whether the case is not fit to be referred to any ADR processes. If the case is not suitable for any ADR process then court should record a brief order referring to the nature of the case and why it is not fit for reference to ADR processes: If case can be referred to ADR processes, the court should explain the choice of five ADR processes to the parties to enable them to exercise their option.

(4) The court should first ascertain regarding choice of parties for arbitration and should inform the parties that arbitration is an adjudicatory process and reference to arbitration will permanently take the suit outside the ambit of the court.

(5) If the parties are not agreeable for arbitration; the court should ascertain whether the parties are agreeable for reference to conciliation which will be governed by the provisions of the Arbitration and Conciliation Act. If all the parties agree for reference to conciliation and agree upon the conciliator/s, the court can refer the matter to conciliation in accordance with s. 64 of the Arbitration and Conciliation Act.

(6) If parties are not agreeable for arbitration and conciliation, the court after taking into consideration the preferences/options of parties, refer the matter to any one of the other three other ADR processes:

(*a*) Lok Adalat

(*b*) Mediation by a neutral third party facilitator or Mediator; and

(*c*) A judicial settlement, where a Judge assists the parties to arrive at a settlement.

(7) If the case is simple or relating to a matter where the legal principles are dearly settled and there is no personal animosity between the parties, the court may refer the matter to Lok Adalat.

(8) If the case is complicated and requires negotiations, the court should refer the case to mediation. If the facility of mediation is not available or where the parties opt for the guidance of a Judge to arrive at a settlement, the case can be refer to another Judge for attempting settlement.

(9) If ADR process is not successful, then court shall proceed with hearing of the case. If case is settled, then court shall examine the settlement and shall make a decree in terms of it keeping in view the legal principles of Or. 23, r. 3 of the Code.

(10) If the settlement includes, terms and conditions which are not the subject matter of the suit, the settlement shall be governed by s. 74 of the Arbitration and Conciliation Act (if it is a Conciliation Settlement) or s. 21 of the Legal Services Authority Act 1987 (if it is a settlement by a Lok Adalat or by mediation which is a deemed Lok Adalat).

(11) If any term of the settlement is *ex facie* illegal or unforceable, the court should draw the attention of parties thereto to avoid further litigations and disputes about executability.

(12) The court shall record the mutual consent of the parties if the case is referred to arbitration or conciliation. If the reference is to any other ADR process, the court should briefly record that having regard 10 the nature of dispute, the case deserves to be referred to Lok Adalat, or mediation or judicial settlement, as the case may be. The Referral Order should not be an elaborate order.

(13) The requirement in s. 89(1) that the court should formulate or reformulate the terms of settlement would only mean that court has to briefly refer to the nature of dispute and decide upon the appropriate ADR process.

(14) If the Presiding Judge of the case assists the parties and if settlement negotiations fail, he should not deal with the adjudication of the matter, to avoid apprehensions of *bias* and prejudice. It is, therefore, advisable to refer cases proposed for Judicial Settlement to another Judge.

(15) If the court refers the case to an ADR process (other than Arbitration), it should keep track of the case by fixing a

hearing date for the ADR Report. The period allotted for the ADR process should not exceed from the period as permitted under applicable Mediation Rules.

The court should take precaution that under no circumstances the ADR process shall be used as a tool in the hands of an unscrupulous litigant to delay the trial of the case.

(16) The court should not send the original judicial record of the case at the time of referring the case for an ADR forum, however only copies of relevant papers of the judicial record should be annexed with referral order. If the case is referred to a court annexed Mediation Centre which is under the exclusive control and supervision of a Judicial Officer, the original file may be made available wherever necessary.

Chapter 4

Lok Adalat

Lok Adalat—meaning The 'Lok Adalat' is an old form of adjudicating system prevailed in ancient India and its validity has not been taken away even in the modern days too. The words 'Lok Adalat' mean 'People's Court'. This system is based on Gandhian principles. It is one of the components of ADR system. As the Indian courts are over-burdened with the backlog of cases and the regular court are to decide the cases involve a lengthy, expensive and tedious procedure. The court takes years together to settle even petty cases. LokAdalat, therefore, provides alternative resolution or devise for expedious and inexpensive justice. In Lok Adalat proceedings there are no victors and vanquished and, thus, no rancour. Experiment of 'Lok Adalat' as an alternate mode of dispute settlement has come to be accepted in India, as a viable, economic, efficient and informal one.

Strategy—present day Lok Adalat is another alternative to Judicial Justice. This is a recent strategy for delivering informal, cheap and expeditious justice to the common man by way of settling disputes, which are pending in courts and also those, which have not yet reached courts by negotiation, conciliation and by adopting persuasive, common sense and human approach to the problem of the disputants, with the assistants of specially trained and experienced members of a team of Conciliators.[1]

1 *P.T. Thomas* v *Thomas Jab* AIR 2005 SC 3575; 2005 AIR SCW 4593; (2005)6 SCC 478; (2005)6 Scale 85; (2005)5 Supreme 374.

Nature Lok Adalats are ambulatory in nature and can supplement the efforts of the court to resolve disputes.

Goals of Justice The natural target of a democratic country is the creation and protection of an unbiased and unprejudiced social and economic order in life, and preservation of equality in every sphere of our society irrespective of status high or low, rich or poor for the establishment of the rule of law in all aspects. If we consider the existing situation, it will be found that most of the Indians having to live in a backward social and economic environment in effect debarred from procuring legal help though the facilities exist in the infrastructure of the rule of law. The present judicial system is too very slow and expensive in the dispensation of justice and on the other it is counter-productive in many cases. As a result of this, it is beyond the easy reach of many poor men. And of course, until and unless the rule of justice reaches the downtrodden its objective will remain unfulfilled. In order to attain this objective it is directed accordingly under Art. 39A of our Constitution that the State Government bear the responsibility of administering justice through a competent judicial machinery. It is a democratic responsibility to secure legal facilities for the rule of law and social justice for people in every stratum of our society.

With this aim in view in the conference of the all India Law Ministers, which took place for the first time in independent India, in the year 1980, it was decided that legal help should be provided freely to the poor with the expense of the State. After that there was a committee established during the tenure of the then Prime Minister Mrs. Indira Gandhi for exploring the easy way to get justice and to preserve the right of the people. Besides this the point was also discussed in some committees formed by the Central and State and even in the Parliament.

Lok Adalat and Legal Services Authorities Act The Legal Services Authorities Act 1987 is the outcome and the rule about Lok Adalat is included as a part of it.

The objects of rule of this Act are described in the preface. These objects are to frame a working committee playing the role of a servant to offer free legal aid to the weaker section of the society, to ensure that no citizen is deprived of enjoying the protection of justice owing to poverty to ensure the improved dispensation of rule and justice through the legal procedure by the formation of Lok Adalat on the basis of equal opportunity.

This Act is applicable at all places in the territory of India except the State of Jammu and Kashmir.

In sub-sec. (1)(*d*) of s. 2 of this Act the Lok Adalat is defined as an Adalat which is formed in accordance with the description of Chapter VI.

Features of Chapter VI The salient features of Chapter VI of the Legal Services Authorities Act 1987 can be summed up as follows:—

(1) Lok Adalat(s) can be constituted of: (*a*) serving or retired judicial officers, and (*b*) other persons.

(2) Except matters relating to offences which are not compoundable, a Lok Adalat has jurisdiction to deal with all matters whether pending or at pre-trial stage provided a reference is made to it by a court in the case of a pending matter, or a reference is made to it by the concerned Authority or Committee when the dispute is at a pre-trial stage and not before a court of law.

(3) A Lok Adalat is required to determine the matter by compromise or settlement between the parties. In doing so it is to be guided by the principles of justice, equity, fair play and other legal principles.

(4) Lok Adalat can be constituted for different areas. At the same time different Lok Adalats can be constituted for exercising distinct and separate jurisdictions over an area.

(5) The award passed by the Lok Adalat is deemed to be a decree of a civil court and therefore enforceable as a decree.

(6) Every award made by the Lok Adalat is final and binding on the parties to the dispute and no appeal is provided therefrom.

(7) In the event of a matter determined by compromise or settlement by a Lok Adalat in a case referred to it by a court, the court fee is to be refunded in the manner laid down in the Court Fees Act 1870.

Brief Scheme The formation, procedure and activities of the District and State Working Committee as a legal servant are elaborately described in the third chapter of the Legal Services Authorities Act 1987. And the same of National Working Committee in the second chapter. In the fourth chapter the persons who are entitled to get the opportunity of this Act have been specified along with and what have to be done by these persons to be considered as eligible to get service of this Act. The rule of Lok Adalat is elaborately described in the chapter six.

Creation of Lok Adalat—reason The judicial system of India is procrastinatory and dilatory. Sometimes in the court the hearing of cases is adjourned without any cause or sometimes on some insufficient grounds. It will not be an exaggeration if it is said that the provisions of the sections of the Civil and Criminal Procedure Code are not applied properly. Though it is not clearly stated how many times the adjournment can be prayed and granted. It is expected from the court that it must ascertain the justification of adjournment before giving order granting it. Though in certain Acts adjudication is stipulated within a particular period, practically it is seen that those cases are also confined in files for a long time without adjudication. For example, in "The Consumer Protection Act" it is clearly directed that the cases must be adjudicated within three months. But it is found that three years have already elapsed yet to the unfortunate clients the adjudication is still a dream. Often owing to various dilatory process and practices the weaker section of the society can no longer depend on this judicial system. The economically solvent persons harass the weaker section in various ways exploring the dilatory tactics of character. Perhaps it is this malady that prompted once Bankim Chandra to comment, "Law is a joke of the rich", Rabindranath also said, in an aggrieved voice "the message of Justice weeps in solitude". The mountain of pending litigations is the result of this dilatory character tactics, and it is seen in everywhere from lower court to the Supreme Court. As a consequence frequently the person who is praying for justice leaves this mundane world before getting justice. This malady of slothfulness and tardiness, vitiating the process of dispensation of justice, is not endemic to our land, nor is it a modern feature. Centuries ago, we find, "laws delay" as one of the agonizing urging that prompted Hamlet to contemplate suicide. This reference to the exasperating dilatoriness of the judicial process forced itself into the soliloquy of the great Shakespearean hero only because it was a serious ailment weakening the legal machinery of the England of Shakespeare. Though in order to accelerate the judicial system the Government often prescribes various remedies, the matter remains where it was. In order to eradicate the problem Lok Adalat is formed.

The object of the Lok Adalat is to accelerate the dispensation of justice and bring about a compromise between the litigant parties as best as possible. The primary object of the Lok Adalat is to make justice reach out to the general public. The programme of the Lok Adalat is arranged in different districts on the basis of that object. The retired judges as well as sitting judges are operating the system of the Lok Adalat. The various types of family and matrimonial litigation and the litigations connected with transport and Motor Accident are being adjudicated by means of Lok Adalat. Of course with full reverence to the court we can say that sufficient interest is not yet being generated among the people regarding this subject. Until and unless the consciousness of general public grows it is impossible for Lok Adalat to play an effective role. Perhaps many people are thinking still now that this very court may also be a victim of the dilatory tactics. Perhaps for this reason they are not praying for justice from Lok Adalat. Of course, the hostile attitude of some classes of lawyers is specially responsible for this. They are more interested in this business than the welfare of the society. These men are apprehensive of their professional loss through this court. None should doubt the capacity of the Lok Adalat to bring welfare to the society. It will unnecessary wastage of time and money to considerable. For this reason it is said that mass campaign should be organized regarding the Lok Adalat in order to raise its social acceptance. The lawyers also attending less to their personal interest should welcome the activity of the Lok Adalat for the welfare of the greater society. Lastly, it must be said that the Lok Adalat is expected to commence in accordance with a particular schedule. Otherwise all efforts will end in smoke.

Organisation of Lok Adalats[2] (1) Every State Authority or District Authority or the Supreme Court Legal Services Committee or every High Court Legal Services Committee or, as the case may be, Taluk Legal Services Committee may organise Lok Adalats at such intervals and places and for exercising such jurisdiction and for such areas as it thinks fit.

(2) Every Lok Adalat organized for an area shall consist of such number of—

(*a*) serving or retired judicial officers; and

(*b*) other persons,

of the area as may be specified by the State Authority or the District Authority or the Supreme Court Legal Services Committee or the High Court Legal Services Committee, or as the case may be, the Taluk Legal Services Committee, organizing such Lok Adalat.

(3) The experience and qualifications of other persons referred to in cl. (*b*) of sub-sec. (2) for Lok Adalats organized by the Supreme Court Legal Services Committee shall be such as may be prescribed by the Central Government in consultation with the Chief Justice of India.

(4) The experience and qualifications of other persons referred to in cl. (*b*) of sub-sec. (2) for Lok Adalats other than referred to in sub-sec. (3) shall be such as may be prescribed by the State Government in consultation with the Chief Justice of the High Court.

(5) A Lok Adalat shall have jurisdiction to determine and to arrive at a compromise or settlement between the parties to a dispute in respect of —

(*i*) any case pending before; or

(*ii*) any matter which is falling within the jurisdiction of, and is not brought before,

any court for which the Lok Adalat is organized:

Provided that the Lok Adalat shall have no jurisdiction in respect of any case or matter relating to an offence not compoundable under any law.

2 Section 19, the Legal Services Authorities Act 1987.

Analysis

Jurisdiction The Lok Adalat has no jurisdiction in respect of any case or matter regarding an offence not compoundable under any law. In short, it is impermissible for the Lok Adalat to enter into any determination or to arrive at a compromise or settlement in relation to a case or matter regarding an offence which is a non-compoundable one, *i.e.* offence punishable under ss. 326, 397, 302, 307 of the Indian Penal Code. The Lok Adalat is not empowered to issue direction upon an investigating officer to do a particular thing in a particular manner to file refer report on the basis that the complaint was made on a misunderstanding or mistake of fact.[3]

Scope The Lok Adalat has jurisdiction to determine and to arrive at a compromise or settlement between the parties to a dispute in respect of two types of cases:[4]

(1) In cases pending before any court for which the Lok Adalat is organised.

(2) Any matter which is falling within the jurisdiction of and is not brought before any court.

Cognizance by Permanent Lok Adalat Section 20(1) refers to the Lok Adalat taking cognizance of cases referred to by the courts and the sub-sec. (2) refers to the Lok Adalat taking cognizance of matters and the pre-litigation stage.[5]

Adjudicatory function and Lok Adalat Lok Adalats have no adjudicatory functions and they are not meant for pressurising the people and bringing pressure on the public officials. The Lok Adalat has no jurisdiction to award less than contractual rate of interest affecting the interest of the Bank (Creditor) as well as the interest of the society by adopting the approach of "flexible and pragmatism" keeping their eyes revetted on the disposal figures of the cases and on the encomiums to be received

3 *State of Kerala* v *Eruakulam District Legal Service Authority* AIR 2008 Ker 70.

4 *Bajaj Allianz Insurance Co. Ltd.* v *Madhava Nair* AIR 2011 Kant 15.

5 *Panna Lal Prasad* v *Manoj Kumar Gupta* AIR 2012 Pat 115.

in print media and from other interest groups.[6] Lok Adalat has no adjudicatory or judicial functions. Its function purely relates to conciliation.[7]

Reference A Lok Adalat determines reference on the basis of a compromise or settlement between the parties at its instance, and puts its seal of confirmation by making an award in terms of the compromise or settlement. When the Lok Adalat is not able to arrive at a settlement or compromise, no award is made and the case record is returned to the court from which the reference was received, for disposal in accordance with law. No Lok Adalat has the power to "hear" parties to adjudicate cases as a court does. It discuses the subject-matter with the parties and persuades them to arrive at a just settlement. In their conciliatory role, the Lok Adalats, are guided by the principles of justice, equity and fair play.[8]

Award of Lok Adalat The Act does not contemplate nor require an adjudicatory judicial determination, but non-adjudicatory determination based on a compromise or settlement, arrived at by the parties, with guidance and assistance from the Lok Adalat. The "award" of the Lok Adalat does not mean any independent verdict or opinion arrived at by any decision-making process. The making of the award is merely an administrative act of incorporating the terms of settlement or compromise agreed by parties in the presence of the Lok Adalat, in the form of an executable order under the signature and seal of the Lok Adalat.

Where no compromise or settlement is signed by the parties and the order of the Lok Adalat does not refer to any settlement, but directs the respondent to either make payment if it agrees to the order, or approach the High Court for disposal of appeal on merits, if it does not agree, is not an award of the Lok Adalat.

6 *Union Bank of India, Bhavnagar* v *Narendra Plastics, Bhavnagar* AIR 1992 Guj 67.

7 *Durgam Rayalingu* v *Chairman, Mandal Legal Services Committee, Mancherial* AIR 2019 Hyd 46.

8 *State of Punjab* v *Jalour Singh* AIR 2008 SC 1209; (2008)2 SCC 660; (2008)2 Scale 52.

Existence of dispute For reference of dispute to Lok Adalat existence of dispute is necessary.[9]

Claim for damages Permanent Lok Adalat has jurisdiction to pass an award for damages when death is caused by drowning in unfenced drain on account of negligence on the part of municipal corporation.[10]

No power to try issue of fraud Permanent Lok Adalat has no inherent jurisdiction to decide the issue of fraud.[11]

Appeal Where an award is made by the Lok Adalat in terms of a settlement arrived at between the parties, it becomes final and binding on the parties to the settlement and becomes executable like a decree of a civil court. No appeal lies against it to any court.

Award—when can challenged If any party wants to challenge the award based on settlement, it can be done only by filing a petition under Art. 226 and/or Art. 227 of the Constitution. But this can be done on very limited grounds.[12]

High Court—when can interfere The High Court may interfere the award of the Lok Adalat in the following:

(*i*) Where a totally arbitrary and unreasonable order has been passed by the Lok Adalat.[13]

(*ii*) The court can go into the legality of the order/orders passed by the Lok Adalat or the permanent Lok Adalat if they are against the letter and spirit of the Legal Services Authorities Act 1987.[14]

(*iii*) Where the Lok Adalat has decided the matter without jurisdiction and in violation of the principles of justice, equity and fairplay.

9 *Basamma* v *Taluka Legal Services Committee* AIR 2003 Kant 242; see also *State Bank of Indore* v *Balaji Traders* AIR 2003 MP 252.

10 *P. Ramanaiah* v *Greater Hyderabad Municipal Corporation at Tank Bund, Hyderabad* AIR 2012 AP 89.

11 *Kanti Devi* v *State* AIR 2012 Pat 86.

12 *State of Punjab* v *Jalour Singh* AIR 2008 SC 1209; (2008)2 SCC 660.

13 *Paras Holidays Pvt. Ltd.* v *State of Haryana* AIR 2009 P&H 9.

14 *Dinesh Kumar* v *Balbir Singh* AIR 2008 HP 59.

Cognizance of cases by Lok Adalats[15] (1) Where in any case referred to in cl. (*i*) of sub-sec. (5) of s. 19—

(*i*) (*a*) the parties thereof agree; or

(*b*) one of the parties thereof makes an application to the court,

for referring the case to the Lok Adalat for settlement and if such court is *prima facie* satisfied that there are chances of such settlement; or

(*ii*) the court is satisfied that the matter is an appropriate one to be taken cognizance of by the Lok Adalat,

the court shall refer the case to the Lok Adalat:

Provided that no case shall be referred to the Lok Adalat under sub-cl. (*b*) of cl. (*i*) or cl. (*ii*) by such court except after giving a reasonable opportunity of being heard to the parties.

(2) Notwithstanding anything contained in any other law for the time being in force, the Authority or Committee organizing the Lok Adalat under sub-sec. (1) of s. 19 may, on receipt of an application from any one of the parties to any matter referred to in cl. (*ii*) of sub-sec. (5) of s. 19 that such matter needs to be determined by a Lok Adalat, refer such matter to the Lok Adalat, for determination:

Provided that no matter shall be referred to the Lok Adalat except after giving a reasonable opportunity of being heard to the other party.

(3) Where any case is referred to a Lok Adalat under sub-sec. (1) or where a reference has been made to it under sub-sec. (2), the Lok Adalat shall proceed to dispose of the case or matter and arrive at a compromise or settlement between the parties.

(4) Every Lok Adalat shall, while determining any reference before it under this Act, act with utmost expedition to arrive at a compromise or settlement between the parties and shall be guided by the principles of justice, equity, fair play and other legal principles.

15 Section 20, Legal Services Authorities Act 1987.

(5) Where no award is made by the Lok Adalat on the ground that no compromise or settlement could be arrived at between the parties, the record of the case shall be returned by it to the court, from which the reference has been received under sub-sec. (1) for disposal in accordance with law.

(6) Where no award is made by the Lok Adalat on the ground that no compromise or settlement could be arrived at between the parties, in a matter referred to in sub-sec. (2), that Lok Adalat shall advice the parties to seek remedy in a court.

(7) Where the record of the case is returned under sub-sec. (5) to the court, such court shall proceed to deal with such case from the stage which was reached before such reference under sub-sec. (1).

Analysis A Lok Adalat is empowered to dispose of the case or the matter placed before it, on the basis of compromise entered into or settlement reached between the parties concerned. An award passed by a Lok Adalat must be based on the consensus arrived at by the parties concerned and not on the basis of adjudication of relative merit of the cases set-up by the contesting or rival parties. An award can be made by the Lok Adalat when both the parties to the proceeding reach a compromise or settlement. When a Lok Adalat passes any order or orders *ex parte* or without a compromise or settlement between the parties as regards the dispute or controversy involved in the suit or case placed before it, such order is *ex facie* against the provisions of the Act. In short, when no compromise or settlement has been reached by the concerned parties, *i.e.* claimant and Insurance Company, the Lok Adalat has no authority to take cognizance of the case under s. 166 of the Motor Vehicles Act directing payment of compensation to the claimant.[16]

Function of Lok Adalat Lok Adalats have no adjudicatory or judicial functions. Their functions relate purely to conciliation. A Lok Adalat determines a reference on the basis of a compromise or settlement between the parties at its instance, and put its seal

16 *New India Assurance Co. Ltd.* v *Lohit District Legal Service Authority* AIR 2008 Gau 166.

of confirmation by making an award in terms of the compromise or settlement.[17]

Procedure When a case is referred to the Lok Adalat for settlement, two courses are open to it:

(*a*) if a compromise or a settlement is arrived at between the parties, to make an award, incorporating such compromise or settlement (which when signed by the parties and counter-signed by the members of the Lok Adalat, has the force of a decree); or

(*b*) if there is no compromise or settlement, to return the record with a failure report to the court.[18]

Lok Adalat—not a court Lok Adalat has no adjudicatory function. The proceeding before a Lok Adalat is not a proceeding before a court.[19]

Settlement and compromise The Lok Adalat can dispose of a matter by way of a compromise or settlement between the parties. If no compromise or settlement is or could not be arrived at, the Lok Adalat is not empowered to pass an order. The expression "Compromise" is not synonymous with the term "Settlement." The word 'compromise' means settlement of differences by mutual concessions. It is an agreement reached by adjustment of confiliting or opposing claims by reciprocal modification of demands. As per Terms Dela Ley, "Compromise is a mutual promise of two or more parties that are at controversy." In the words of Bouvier, compromise is "an agreement between two or more persons who, to avoid a law suit, amicably settle their differences, on such terms as they can agree upon". The word compromise implies some element of accommodation on each side. It is not apt to describe total surrender. It is always bilateral and means mutual adjustment. Settlement is termination of legal proceedings by mutual consent.[20]

17 *State of Punjab* v *Jalour Singh* AIR 2008 SC 1209.

18 *B.P. Moideen Sevamandir* v *A.M. Kutty Hassan* AIR 2008 SC (Supp) 1123; *Kishan Rao, Petitioners* v *Bidar District Legal Services Authority* AIR 2001 Kant 407.

19 *Govardhana* v *Appi* AIR 2015 Kar 188.

20 *Union of India* v *Ananto* AIR 2007 SC 1561.

Counsel cannot arrive compromise on behalf of the party If the parties do not affix the signatures to the compromise petition or the settlement, the counsel representing the parties before the court, though participated in the Lok Adalat and assisted the parties in arriving at a settlement, has no authority to enter into a compromise so as to bind his party.[21]

Execution of gift deed Order passed by the Lok Adalat directing the husband to execute a deed of gift in favour of his wife is proper.[1]

Award passed violating regulations The award is not valid if such award is passed without following the procedure prescribed under regulations.[2]

Award of Permanent Lok Adalat The Permanent Lok Adalat can pass award only on the basis of agreement between the parties, i.e. compromise.[3]

Dispute concerning pension Petition claiming pension does not involve compromise or settlement. Therefore it could not have been disposed of by the Lok Adalat.[4]

Dispute regarding succession certificate The Lok Adalat has no power to issue succession certificate in the absence of other party and when there was no joint application.[5]

Award of Lok Adalat[6] (1) Every award of the Lok Adalat shall be deemed to be a decree of a civil court, or, as the case may be, an order of any other court and where a compromise or settlement has been arrived at, by a Lok Adalat in a case referred to it under sub-sec. (1) of s. 20, the court-fee paid in such case shall be refunded in the manner provided under the Court Fees Act 1870 (7 of 1870).

(2) Every award made by a Lok Adalat shall be final and binding on all the parties to the dispute, and no appeal shall lie to any court against the award.

21 *Govardhana* v *Appi* AIR 2015 Kar 188.
1 *Venugopalan A.K.* v *Pushpavally* AIR 2014 Ker 203.
2 *Srinivash Rai* v *Mahendra Rai* AIR 2014 Pat 53.
3 *Panna Lal Prasad* v *Manoj Kumar Gupta* AIR 2012 Pat 115.
4 *State of Punjab* v *Phulan Rani* AIR 2004 SC 4105.
5 *Jai Devi Hans (Smt.)* v *Beena Singh (Smt.)* AIR 2005 All 349.
6 Section 21, Legal Services Authorities Act 1987.

Analysis Where the compromise was recorded by the court and it was sent to the Lok Adalat for the purpose of drawing up a decree, it cannot be said that the suit was compromised by the Lok Adalat followed by a decree.[7]

Enlargement of time The Lok Adalat has no power to extend the time fixed in the award by invoking s. 148 of the CPC.[8]

Execution The award of the Lok Adalat is fictionally deemed to be decrees of court and therefore, it can be executed like decrees of a civil court.[9] An award passed by the Lok Adalat on reference of a criminal case by the criminal court can only be construed as an order by the criminal court and it is not a decree passed by a civil court. Therefore, it cannot be executed as a decree of a civil court.[10]

Award executed by court if exceeds pecuniary limits Award passed by Lok Adalat is executable by court even if decretal amount exceeds its pecuniary jurisdiction.[11]

Compromise not signed by the parties Award on the basis of compromise which is not signed by the parties is not proper.[12]

No pecuniary limit The compromise duly entered and signed by the parties before the Lok Adalat cannot be set aside on the ground of lack of pecuniary jurisdiction.[13]

Executing Court cannot vary the terms of the decree The civil court gets no jurisdiction to vary the terms of the award or extend the time agreed to between the parties to such an award.[14]

7 *Debasis Jana* v *Rajendra Kumar Das* AIR 2008 Ori 49.
8 *Nimma Venkateswarlu* v *Devireddy Krishnayya alias Venkata Krishnayya* AIR 2007 AP 300.
9 *P.T. Thomas, Appellant* v *Thomas Job* AIR 2005 SC 3575; *K.N. Govindan Kutty Menon* v *C.D. Shaji* AIR 2012 SC 719.
10 *K.N. Govindan Kutty Menon* v *C.D. Shaji* AIR 2010 Ker 97; *M.I. Ibrahim Kutty* v *Indian Overseas Bank* AIR 2005 Mad 335.
11 *Thomas Anthony* v *Florance George* AIR 2007 Ker 31.
12 *Madhu Bala (Smt.)* v *H.P. Singh* AIR 2013 All 55.
13 *Shambhoo Nath* v *State* AIR 2013 Pat 46.
14 *Thomas Job* v *P.T. Thomas* AIR 2004 Ker 47.

Award passed by Lok Adalat in a case under s. 138, N.I. Act The award passed by the Lok Adalat in a proceeding under s. 138 of the N.I. Act is executable like a decree of a civil court.[15]

No distinction between reference by Civil Court and Criminal Court The Act does not make out any distinction between the reference made by a civil court and criminal court had that the award passed by the Lok Adalat based on a compromise has to be treated as a decree capable of execution by a civil court. Even though the award was passed pursuant to a reference of a criminal case made by a criminal court, the award being a decree of a civil court can be executed by civil court.[16]

Award of compensation without following mandatory Procedure—effect If against the desire of the parties, a dispute is decided on merits under sub-sec. (8) of s. 22C of the Legal Services Authorities Act 1987, where neither the provisions of the Code of Civil Procedure are applicable, nor the provisions of Indian Evidence Act are applicable, nor the order is appealable (as per ss. 22D and 22E of the Act of 1987), then no party will come for settlement of the dispute at a pre-litigation stage. If there is consent by all the parties, then only Permanent Lok Adalat can decide the dispute on merits and that too, after making the parties to the dispute fully aware of non-applicability of the provisions of Code of Civil Procedure and the provisions of Indian Evidence Act and after making aware the parties to the dispute that there shall be no appeal against the award, passed by the Permanent Lok Adalat. Thus, the award of compensation passed by Lok Adalat without following mandatory procedure is not valid.[17]

Prayer to reopen award—not permissible An award by the Lok Adalat with the consent of the land owner is a decree in terms of s. 21 of the Legal Services Authorities Act. So, after nearly 3 years and 7 months, prayer to reopen a decree which has reached finality is not maintainable.[18]

15 *Valarmathi Oil Industries* v *Saradhi Ginning Factory* AIR 2009 Mad 180.
16 *Talluri Satish Chandra* v *Thoram Venkateswara Rao* AIR 2017 Hyd 120.
17 *National Insurance Co. Ltd., Ranchi* v *Tulsi Bannerjee* AIR 2017 Jhar 168.
18 *P. Murthy* v *Collector of Cuddalore District* AIR 2017 Mad 191.

Powers of Lok Adalat or Permanent Lok Adalat[19] (1) The Lok Adalat or Permanent Lok Adalat shall, for the purposes of holding any determination under this Act, have the same powers as are vested in a civil court under the Code of Civil Procedure 1908 (5 of 1908) while trying a suit in respect of the following matters, namely:

(*a*) the summoning and enforcing the attendance of any witness and examining him on oath;

(*b*) the discovery and production of any document;

(*c*) the reception of evidence of affidavits;

(*d*) the requisitioning of any public record or document or copy of such record or document from any court or office; and

(*e*) such other matters as may be prescribed.

(2) Without prejudice to the generality of the powers contained in sub-sec. (1), every Lok Adalat or Permanent Lok Adalat shall have the requisite powers to specify its own procedure for the determination of any dispute coming before it.

(3) All proceedings before a Lok Adalat or Permanent Lok Adalat shall be deemed to be judicial proceedings within the meaning of ss. 193, 219 and 228 of the Indian Penal Code (45 of 1860) and every Lok Adalat or Permanent Lok Adalat shall be deemed to be a civil court for the purpose of s. 195 and Chapter XXVI of the Code of Criminal Procedure 1973 (2 of 1974).

Analysis Order passed by Lok Adalat tentamounts to a decree of a civil court. Drawing up of a formal decree by the court where the suit was originally filed is not necessary. Order passed by the Lok Adalat cannot be modified or revised by another Lok Adalat or by any court. Insurance company who is a party to the compromise before Lok Adalat is under obligation to honour the award passed by the Lok Adalat.[20]

'X' husband of the petitioner filed a money suit against 'Y' for recovery of the amount mentioned in the plaint and the suit was

19 Section 22, Legal Services Authorities Act 1987.

20 *Divisional Manager, representing the United India Insurance Co. Ltd.* v *Muktamani Prem* AIR 2008 NOC 2616 (Ori).

decreed in favour of 'X'. After the decree of the suit 'X' died and his legal representatives filed an execution proceeding for realization of the amount. The court asked the legal representatives of 'X' to file succession certificate. The wife of 'X' projected herself as the successor of 'X' on the basis of a will executed by the decree holder. Lok Adalat passed an award declaring that the wife of 'X' is the sole legal heir under the will. Wife of 'X' (petitioner) produced the award of Lok Adalat instead of succession certificate. The court held that production of succession certificate is mandatory and the award of the Lok Adalat cannot be a substitute for succession certificate.[1]

Need of Permanent Lok Adalat In *Abdul Hassan* v *Delhi Vidyut Board*[2] the Delhi High Court classically explained the need of Permanent Lok Adalat in the following words:

> There is a very huge pendency of cases in various courts. The staggering pendency is disturbing. It must be noted that in this country there are only 10.5 Judges per million population. The situation is compounded by lack of adequate number of supporting staff and equipment. In the present scenario there is not only an imminent requirement of increasing the number of courts commensurate with the growing population and ever is increasing litigation, there is also a paramount need to appoint Permanent Lok Adalats where the expertise of the retired Judges and judicial officers and other suitable persons could be utilized in resolution of matters by reconciliation.

Again, the court observed: It is the interest of the citizen of India that Permanent Lok Adalats are established and held continuously so that the purpose for which Act was enacted could be achieved. It appears to me that unless permanent and continuous Lok Adalats are set up, it may not be possible to reduce the pendency in courts. Besides, a solitary appearance of parties before a Lok Adalat which is organized for a day or two may not be adequate for arriving at a compromise or settlement. The need of the hour is frantically beckoning for setting up Lok Adalats or permanent and continuous basis. What we do today will shape our tomorrow. The choice is between an overburdened

1 *Sreemanthula Kesavchari* v *Yayyavuru Vallamma* AIR 2008 AP 74.
2 AIR 1999 Del 88.

court system being crushed under its own weight, and alternative dispute resolution machinery including an inexpensive and quick dispensation of justice by Lok Adalats. For facilitating expeditious disposal of all kinds of cases permanent Lok Adalats must be set up in DVB, MCD, NDMC, DDA, MTNL, GIC and various departments of the Government. It also seems to me that the accumulation of cases in courts can be reduced or prevented if Permanent Lok Adalats are established for the Union Territory of Delhi. There should also be one or more Permanent Lok Adalats, depending upon the magnitude of the work, for resolving the disputes between (1) the citizens and the Government of India, and (2) the Government of India and its employees.

Pre-litigation Conciliation and Settlement[3]

Definitions[4] In this chapter (Ch. VIA) and for the purposes of ss. 22 and 23, unless the context otherwise requires,—

(*a*) "Permanent Lok Adalat" means a Permanent Lok Adalat established under sub-sec. (1) of s. 22B.

(*b*) "Public utility service" means any—

(*i*) transport service for the carriage of passengers or goods by air, road or water; or

(*ii*) postal, telegraph or telephone service; or

(*iii*) supply of power, light or water to the public by any establishment; or

(*iv*) system of public conservancy or sanitation; or

(*v*) service in hospital or dispensary; or

(*vi*) insurance service,

and includes any service which the Central Government or the State Government, as the case may be, may, in the public interest, by notification, declare to be a public utility service for the purposes of this chapter.

Analysis A Lok Adalat is empowered to settle dispute only when the parties agree for such settlement. In other words power of

3 Chapter VIA, Legal Services Authorities Act 1987.
4 Section 22A.

adjudication is not contemplated in so far as the Lok Adalats constituted under Chapter VI of the Act. But Permanent Lok Adalat is competent to decide contentious issues as well. Permanent Lok Adalat has power to adjudicate the dispute subject to condition that the dispute is not related to any offence. The jurisdiction of Permanent Lok Adalat is much more wider than Lok Adalat constituted under Chapter VI of the Act. Permanent Lok Adalats are entitled to deal with disputes touching upon public utility services and other disputes as well. It has jurisdiction to decide dispute related to life insurance service. Life insurance service is treated as a part of the public utility service. The public utility service touching upon the insurance business is a dispute arising out of the insurance business carried on by the insurance company. There are several disputes which arise between the insured and the insurer, for example dispute arising on account of deficiency in service rendered by the insurance company. Such dispute obviously come within the purview of s. 22A(*b*)(*vi*).[5]

Motor accident claim and Permanent Lok Adalat The dispute raise by injured or for that matter a legal heir of deceased person claiming compensation arising out of a motor accident cannot be treated as insurance service rendered by the insurance company. A claim by the injured in a motor accident is only a claim for compensation filed by the injured who has suffered from a tortious act of another persons. A tortious act gives rise to claim for damages, by a person who has suffered from the act. When the accident occurred on account of the negligence of the driver of the vehicle, then the claimant is entitled to compensation. This is a matter for adjudication by a court on an aspect which essentially involves a claim by an injured person against a tortfeasor. A dispute which comes into existence from a claim petition filed by the injured in a motor accident is not a dispute touching upon insurance service. So Permanent Lok Adalat has no jurisdiction to decide a claim petition filed by a claimant arising out of a motor accident.[6]

5 *New India Assurance Company Limited* v *Sabharathanam* alias *Sabha Rathinam* AIR 2009 Ker 71.

6 *New India Assurance Company Limited* v *Sabharathanam* alias *Sabha Rathinam* AIR 2009 Ker 71.

Permanent Lok Adalat—whether a real court Permanent Lok Adalats are not courts in the real sense. They are created to provide quick and cheap relief to the litigants against in action wrongful action of authorities dealing with public utility service in day to day life. It would be bereft of jurisdiction to adjudicate the dispute as to title.[7] When the parties failed to arrive at an amicable settlement or agreement even after reconciliation the Permanent Lok Adalat is empowered to decide the dispute.[8] Permanent Lok Adalat cannot directly invoke the provisions of s. 22C(8) for an award of compensation to the consumer of BSNL without resorting to settle the dispute between the parties regarding deficiency in service of BSNL.[9]

Order passed by the Permanent Lok Adalat without affording an opportunity to the petitioner to represent his version is violative of statutory mandate contemplated in s. 20(3) of the Act and is liable to be set aside.[10]

Lok Adalat has no power to grant pensionery benefit to the petitioner if the parties failed to reach a settlement or compromise in terms of the Act.[11]

Service—concept of The concept of service is very wide and it depends in the context in which it has been used in an enactment.[12]

Basis of settlement The Lok Adalat constituted under Chapter VI of the Act, can settle disputes only on the basis of compromise or settlement between the parties. If the parties do not arrive at a settlement or compromise, the case is either returned to the court of law or the parties are advised to seek remedy in a court of law. This causes unnecessary delay in dispensation of justice.

7 *Union Territory Chandigarh* v *Permanent Lok Adalat* AIR 2009 NOC 496 (P&H).

8 *PU Lalkanglova Sailo* v *Pi Ngurthantluangi Sailo* AIR 2009 Gau 39.

9 *Bharat Sanchar Nigam Limited* v *State of Jharkhand* AIR 2009 NOC 806 (Jhar).

10 *Oriented Insurance Company* v *State of Bihar* AIR 2009 NOC 495 (Pat).

11 *Divisional Social Welfare Office, Nagpur* v *Narayan Dindar Gokhale* AIR 2009 NOC 805 (Bom).

12 *Bajaj Allianz Insurance Co. Ltd.* v *Madhava Naire* AIR 2011 Kant 15.

The framers of law, therefore, decided to amend the Act by inserting a new Chapter VI-A to set up Permanent Lok Adalats to provide compulsory pre-litigative mechanism for conciliation and settlement of cases relating to "Public Utility Service". Under the new scheme, the Permanent Lok Adalat will in the first instance, try to bring about conciliation between the parties and in case the parties are not able to arrive at settlement the Permanent Lok Adalat shall proceed to dispose of the matter on merits.

Special features The special feature of the amendments to the Legal Services Authorities (Amendment) Act 2002 are—

(*i*) It seeks to provide compulsory pre-litigative mechanism for conciliation and settlement of cases relating to public utility services.

(*ii*) The public utility services like transport of passengers or goods by air, road or water, postal, telegraph or telephonic service, supply of power and water to the public, public conservancy or sanitation, hospitals and insurance have been brought within the purview of the Permanent Lok Adalats.

(*iii*) After an application is filed by any party before the Permanent Lok Adalat for settlement, no party shall invoke jurisdiction of any court or Tribunal.

(*iv*) The Permanent Lok Adalat conduct the conciliation proceedings in such a manner as it considers appropriate taking into account the circumstances of the case, the wishes of the parties including any request for oral hearing. The Lok Adalat shall assist the parties in an independent and impartial manner in their attempt to reach an amicable settlement of their dispute. Where it appears to Lok Adalat that there exists an element of settlement which may be acceptable to the parties. It shall formulate the terms of a possible settlement and submit them to the parties for their observations. After receiving observations from the parties, it may formulate the terms of a possible settlement in the light of such observations.

(*v*) In case the parties are not able to arrive at any compromise or settlement, the Lok Adalat shall proceed to dispose of the case on merits if it does not relate to an offence. The Lok Adalat while determining the case on merits shall be guided by the principles of justice, objectively, fair play, equity and other principles.

(*vi*) The Lok Adalat shall have the requisite powers to specify its own procedure for determination of any dispute coming before it.

(*vii*) Award made by Permanent Lok Adalats shall be final, binding and shall not be questioned in any original suit, application, or adjudication proceedings.

(*viii*) The award shall be deemed to be a decree of civil court.

(*ix*) Monetary jurisdiction of Permanent Lok Adalats fixed at ₹10 lakhs with power conferred on the Government to revise it from time to time.

(*x*) Permanent Lok Adalat will comprise a chairperson with judicial experience and two other persons having adequate experience in public utility services.

Establishment of Permanent Lok Adalats[13] (1) Notwithstanding anything contained in s. 19, the Central Authority or, as the case may be, every State Authority shall, by notification, establish Permanent Lok Adalats at such places and for exercising such jurisdiction in respect of one or more public utility services and for such areas as may be specified in the notification.

(2) Every Permanent Lok Adalat established for an area notified under sub-sec. (1) shall consist of—

(*a*) a person who is, or has been, a District Judge or Additional District Judge or has held judicial office Higher in rank than that of a District Judge, shall be the Chairman of the Permanent Lok Adalat; and

(*b*) two other persons having adequate experience in public utility service to be nominated by the Central Government or, as the case may be, the State

13 Section 22B of the Legal Services Authorities Act 1987.

Government on the recommendation of the Central Authority or, as the case may be, the State Authority,

appointed by the Central Authority or, as the case may be, the State Authority, establishing such Permanent Lok Adalat and the other terms and conditions of the appointment of the Chairman and other persons referred to in cl. (*b*) shall be such as may be prescribed by the Central Government.

Jurisdiction of Permanent Lok Adalat Although the jurisdiction of Permanent Lok Adalat is limited but they are of wide amplitude. The Permanent Lok Adalat does not simply adopt the role of an Arbitrator but the role of an adjudicator. The award of Arbitrator is subject matter of challenge but the award of Permanent Lok Adalat is not. The Permanent Lok Adalat has an authority to decide the matter. It has an adjudicating role to play.[14]

The Permanent Lok Adalats cannot perform their adjudicatory function and proceed to decide the claim based on tortuous liability merely because the petitioners are operating a public utility service under s. 22A(*b*) of the Act of 1987. Therefore, the award passed by the Lok Adalat is not valid.[15] The authority to decide a dispute available to Permanent Lok Adalat only when there is an element of settlement referable to the pre-existing rights and obligations. The scope of settlement would arise only when the parties admit their rights and obligations. In the event the rights and obligations itself are in dispute, the Permanent Lok Adalat cannot shift its role as an adjudicator from the beginning itself to decide the dispute.[16]

Limitation (*i*) The Permanent Lok Adalat has no authority to decide a case which involves complicated questions of fact and law.

(*ii*) It has no jurisdiction in relation to the question whether the burglary has been committed or not being pending before the criminal court.

14 *United India Insurance Co. Ltd.* v *Ajay Sinha* AIR 2008 SC 2398; 2008 AIR SCW 3970; (2008)8 Scale 509; (2008)7 SCC 454.

15 *Divisional Railway Manager, Bilaspur* v *P.U.P. Lok Adalat, Bilaspur* AIR 2017 Chh 41.

16 *New India Assurance Co. Ltd. Thiruvananthapuram* v *Jebby M. Aliyar* AIR 2018 Ker 181.

(*iii*) It has no jurisdiction in regard to the dispute in question where the value of the suit property exceeds ten lakh rupees.

(*iv*) It has no jurisdiction in respect of any matter relating to an offence not compoundable under any law.

Matrimonial dispute and Permanent Lok Adalat The Permanent Lok Adalat in a pre-litigation conciliation and settlement proceeding has no jurisdiction to entertain and pass an award of mutual divorce under s. 13B of the Hindu Marriage Act 1955. The jurisdiction of Permanent Lok Adalat is confined only to public utility service as prescribed in the notifications and not to any other matter. Matrimonial dispute is not a public utility service. So, the Permanent Lok Adalat is not empowered or authorized to entertain and dispose of the dispute by passing the order of mutual divorce.[17] In order to attract the jurisdiction of Permanent Lok Adalat it must be established that the service must have some relation with public utility.[18] When the plaintiff is permitted to bring a suit as *informa pauperis* (as a poor person) the concerned Legal Services Authority is under statutory obligations to resort necessary financial assistance or help to the plaintiff for payment of process fee and to bear all the expenses for the production of the witness.[19]

Comparison between Lok Adalat and Permanent Lok Adalat The procedure for Permanent Lok Adalat is different from Lok Adalat organized under s. 19 of the Legal Services Authorities Act 1987.

Procedure followed in Lok Adalat (1) After receipt of the record from the concerned court it has to act with utmost expedition to arrive at a compromise or settlement between the parties.

(2) Where no award is made by the Lok Adalat on the ground that no compromise or settlement is arrived at between the parties the case record shall be returned by Lok Adalat to the court from which the reference has been received.

(3) Thereafter, the court to whom the record has been returned has to proceed to deal with the said case from the stage

17 *Rita Kumari Shahu* alias *Saha* v *Shyam Sundar Shahu* 2007(2) ICC 648.

18 *United India Insurance Co. Ltd.* v *Ajay Sinha* AIR 2008 SC 2398; 2008 AIR SCW 3970; (2008)7 SCC 454.

19 *T.A. Rama Swami* v *Pappammal* AIR 2009 NOC 90 (Mad).

which was reached before such reference was made to the Lok Adalat.

Procedure followed by Permanent Lok Adalat (1) Permanent Lok Adalat after the receipt of the application direct the party to file written statement mentioning the facts and nature of the dispute and the points or issues involved in the suit.

(2) The applicant can supplement such statement with any document and other evidence.

(3) The other parties are required to be permitted to file written reply to the statements of claim submitted by the applicant.

(4) The Permanent Lok Adalat has to conduct conciliation proceedings between the parties.

(5) It is the duty of the opposite parties/respondents to cooperate in good faith with the Permanent Lok Adalat in conciliation of the dispute referred to the Permanent Lok Adalat.

(6) If the Permanent Lok Adalat is of the view that there exists element of settlement it may formulate the terms of possible settlement of the dispute and give to the parties concerned for their observation and in case the parties reach at an agreement on the settlement of dispute, they shall sign the settlement agreement and the Permanent Lok Adalat shall pass on award in terms of the said settlement.

(7) If during the course of proceeding the parties failed to reach a workable settlement the dispute is to be adjudicated upon by the Permanent Lok Adalat, if the said dispute does not relate to any offence.

(8) Permanent Lok Adalat has an adjudicatory role to play. Lok Adalat has no adjudicatory or judicial functions.[20]

(9) Award passed by Lok Adalat or Permanent Lok Adalat is not appealable.

(10) Jurisdiction of Lok Adalat is much wider than that of Permanent Lok Adalat.

20 *Dinesh Kumar* v *Balbir Singh* AIR 2008 HP 59.

Cognizance of cases by Permanent Lok Adalat[1] (1) Any party to a dispute may, before the dispute is brought before any court, make an application to the Permanent Lok Adalat for the settlement of dispute:

Provided that the Parmanent Lok Adalat shall not have jurisdiction in respect of any matter relating to an offence not compoundable under any law:

Provided further that the Permanent Lok Adalat shall also not have jurisdiction in the matter where the value of the property in dispute exceeds ten lakh rupees.

Provided also that the Central Government, may, by notification, increase the limit of ten lakh rupees specified in the second proviso in consultation with the Central Authority.

(2) After an application is made under sub-sec. (1) to the Permanent Lok Adalat, no party to that application shall invoke jurisdiction of any court in the same dispute.

(3) Where an application is made to a Permanent Lok Adalat under sub-sec. (1), it—

(*a*) shall direct each party to the application to file before it a written statement, stating therein the facts and nature of dispute under the application points or issues in such dispute and grounds relied in support of, or in opposition to, such point or issues, as the case may be, and such party may supplement such statement with any document and other evidence which such party deems appropriate in proof of such facts and grounds and shall send a copy of such statement together with a copy of such document and other evidence, if any, to each of the parties to the application;

(*b*) may require any party to the application to file additional statement before it at any stage of the conciliation proceedings;

(*c*) shall communicate any document or statement received by it from any party to the application to the other party, to enable such other party to present reply thereto.

1 Section 22C of the Legal Services Authorities Act 1987.

(4) When statement, additional statement and reply, if any, have been filed under sub-sec. (3), to the satisfaction of the Permanent Lok Adalat, it shall conduct conciliation proceedings between the parties to the application in such manner as it thinks appropriate taking into account the circumstances of the dispute.

(5) The Permanent Lok Adalat shall, during conduct of conciliation proceedings under sub-sec. (4), assist the parties in their attempt to reach an amicable settlement of the dispute in an adequate and impartial manner.

(6) It shall be the duty of every party to the application to cooperate in good faith with the Permanent Lok Adalat in conciliation of the dispute relating to the application and to comply with the direction of the Permanent Lok Adalat to produce evidence and other related document before it.

(7) When a Permanent Lok Adalat, in the aforesaid conciliation proceedings, is of opinion that there exist elements of settlement in such proceedings which may be acceptable to the parties, it may formulate the terms of a possible settlement of the dispute and give to the parties concerned for their observations and in case the parties reach at an agreement on the settlement of the dispute, they shall sign the settlement agreement and the Permanent Lok Adalat shall pass an award in terms thereof and furnish a copy of the same to each of the parties concerned.

(8) Where the parties fail to reach at an agreement under sub-sec. (7), the Permanent Lok Adalat shall, if the dispute does not relate to any offence, decide the dispute.

Analysis Section 22C(1) provides the provision for settlement of disputes. The authority has to take recourse to conciliation mechanism one of the important attributes of the conciliation proceedings is that nobody shall be forced to take part therein. Secondly, it is voluntary in nature.

The proceedings are akin to alternative dispute resolution mechanism. It may be treated at par with conciliation and arbitration. There is a basic distinction between the arbitration proceedings and procedure adopted under s. 22C of the Act.

The arbitration is a binding procedure whereas the proceedings adopted under s. 22C of the Legal Services Authorities Act are not binding ones. Secondly, award of Permanent Lok Adalat is not appealable. The award of an Arbitrator is subject matter of challenge. Lastly, the role of Permanent Lok Adalat is much more wider than Arbitrator. Permanent Lok Adalat has also an adjudicatory role. But it must not give an impression to any of the disputants that it from the very beginning has an adjudicatory role to play in relation to its jurisdiction without going into the statutory provisions and restrictions imposed by the statute.[2]

Exclusion of jurisdiction of civil court Section 22C and s. 22E exclude the jurisdiction of civil court when an application is made by either party to the Permanent Lok Adalat to settle a dispute at the pre-litigation stage, the Permanent Lok Adalat shall do so, and the other party is precluded from approaching the civil court. The provisos which limit the jurisdiction of Permanent Lok Adalat must be interpreted in an expansive manner because provision seeking to bar jurisdiction of a civil court requires strict interpretation. Section 22C(8) deals with determination of dispute. It creates another adjudicatory authority. The decision of Permanent Lok Adalat by legal fiction is a decision of a civil court. It has the right to 'decide' a case. The expression 'decide' means to determine or to form definite opinion or to render judgment. The main object behind the enactment of this section is that most of the petty cases which ought not to go in the regular courts would be settled in the pre-litigation stage itself.[3]

Scope The jurisdiction of Permanent Lok Adalat is confined to public utility services only whereas Lok Adalats under s. 19 has jurisdiction over all the matters in respect of case pending before any court or any matter which is falling within the jurisdiction of and is not brought before any court.[4]

Conditions First, the parties should give consent for their dispute to be decided by the Permanent Lok Adalat and secondly, before

2 *United India Insurance Co. Ltd.* v *Ajay Sinha* AIR 2008 SC 2398; 2008 AIR SCW 3970; (2008)7 SCC 454; (2008)8 Scale 509.

3 *Ibid.*

4 *Bajaj Allianz Insurance Co. Ltd.* v *Madhava Naire* AIR 2011 Kant 15.

deciding the dispute on merits, the Permanent Lok Adalat should first formulate and offer the terms of settlement to the disputing parties and make an endeavour to resolve the dispute through conciliation.[5]

Not to determine nature of offence For the purpose of determination of the issue and claim regarding Burglary and House Breaking Policy the Permanent Lok Adalat is not required to determine whether offence committed by any accused is 'compoundable' or not.[6]

Role of Judges of Permanent Lok Adalat The Permanent Lok Adalat has no power, jurisdiction or authority to decide the dispute, on merits without there being any consent by the petitioner. The pre-dominant role of the Permanent Lok Adalat is of a Conciliator and not of an adjudicator.[7] It cannot decide dispute on merits between parties in absence of written consent.[8]

Constitutional validity of s. 22C(8) In *SDO Electricity OP Sub-Division No. 9, Chandigarh* v *Union of India*[9] the constitutional validity of this section was challenged and the petitioner prayed for striking down the said provisions *ultra vires*. The court observed that States or Union Territory have no right to assail their own Acts and Laws in court as unconstitutional and invalid. The Calcutta High Court in *State* v *Keshab Chandra Naskar*[10] observed: the State cannot denounce its own Acts and Laws. It cannot ask the court to declare its own statutes void and unconstitutional.

Dispute relating to release of electricity connection by consumer can be decided by Permanent Lok Adalat because it

5 *Divisional Manager, New India Assurance Co. Ltd.* v *Urmila Devi* AIR 2010 Jhar 133; *Dr. Amika Kumary* v *State of Kerala* AIR 2012 Ker 16.

6 *Ajay Sinha* v *Br. Manager, United India Insurance Co. Ltd.* AIR 2006 Jhar 113.

7 *Sandip Ekka* v *Selesta Kerketa* AIR 2011 Jhar 130; *National Insurance Company* v *Kartik Gorain* AIR 2010 Jhar 59.

8 *Gajanand Prasad Keshri* v *State of Jharkhand* AIR 2010 Jhar 100; *Branch Manager, Tata AIG General Insurance Co. Ltd.* v *Mrs. Bandana Devi* AIR 2010 Jhar 119.

9 AIR 2008 P&H 141.

10 AIR 1962 Cal 338.

is not required to be adjudicated or decided in a regular trial before competent civil court.

Electricity connection cannot be denied merely on the ground that the consumer has failed to obtain the no objection certificate from the appropriate authority.[11]

Procedure of Permanent Lok Adalat[12] The Permanent Lok Adalat shall, while conducting conciliation proceedings or deciding a dispute on merit under this Act, be guided by the principle of natural justice, objectivity, fair play, equity and other principles of justice, and shall not be bound by the Code of Civil Procedure 1908 (5 of 1908) and the Indian Evidence Act 1872 (1 of 1872).

Composition Permanent Lok Adalat comprises of one judicial officer and two other persons having adequate experience in public utility service does not show any abhorrence to the rule of law nor such composition becomes violative of principles of fairness and justice or is contrary to Arts. 14 and 21 of the Constitution of India.[13]

Jurisdiction of Permanent Lok Adalat The procedure prescribed before the Permanent Lok Adalat is principles of natural justice, objectivity, fair play, equity. Once the award is passed by the Permanent Lok Adalat under the Act, it shall be deemed to be a decree of the civil court, it shall be final and shall not be called in question in any original suit.[14]

Award of Permanent Lok Adalat to be final[15] (1) Every award of the Permanent Lok Adalat under this Act made either on merit or in terms of a settlement agreement shall be final and binding on all the parties thereto and on persons claiming under them.

(2) Every award of the Permanent Lok Adalat under this Act shall be deemed to be a decree of a civil court.

11 *Chandigarh Electricity Department Operation Division No. 1* v *Permanent Lok Adalat for Public Utility Services, Chandigarh* AIR 2008 NOC 2088 (P&H).

12 Section 22D of the Legal Services Authorities Act 1987.

13 *Bar Council of India* v *Union of India* AIR 2012 SC 3246.

14 *Bajaj Allianz Insurance Co. Ltd.* v *Madhava Nair* AIR 2011 Kant 15.

15 Section 22E of the Legal Services Authorities Act 1987.

(3) The award made by the Permanent Lok Adalat under this Act shall be by a majority of the persons constituting the Permanent Lok Adalat.

(4) Every award made by the Permanent Lok Adalat under this Act shall be final and shall not be called in question in any original suit, application or execution proceeding.

(5) The Permanent Lok Adalat may transmit any award made by it to a civil court having local jurisdiction and such civil court shall execute the order as if it were a decree made by that court.

Analysis Award of Permanent Lok Adalat is final and binding on all the parties. It would be deemed to be a decree of a civil court. Jurisdiction of the civil court to call in question any award made by the Permanent Lok Adalat is barred. It has the jurisdiction to transfer any award to a civil court and such civil court is mandated to execute the order as if it were the decree by the court. Award made by the Permanent Lok Adalat is executable as a decree. No appeal shall lie against the award passed by the Permanent Lok Adalat.[16]

Where the award was passed by Permanent Lok Adalat on the basis of compromise duly signed by the counsel for the claimant or counsel for the opposite party, such award is valid and binding. It cannot be challenged on the ground that before entering into the compromise, the counsel did not seek instructions from the client.[17]

Ex parte award Permanent Lok Adalat has no power to pass *ex parte* award.[18]

Award not executable When the settlement or compromise does not bear the signature of one of the co-sharers, then such award is not executable.[19]

Not bound by CPC The Permanent Lok Adalat shall not be bound by the provisions of the Code of Civil Procedure and Indian

16 *United India Insurance Co. Ltd.* v *Ajay Sinha* AIR 2008 SC 2398.

17 *Sumer Singh* v *Shaukat Hussain* AIR 2008 Raj 107.

18 *Executive Engineer Electrical (NESCO)* v *Chairperson, Permanent Lok Adalat (P.U.S.)* AIR 2013 Ori 121.

19 *Bal Reddy* v *Taluka Legal Services Committee, Narayanapet* AIR 2012 AP 60.

Evidence Act and all what is required of it is to follow principles of natural justice, objectivity, fair play and equity.[20]

Absence of appeal—not violative of Constitutional provisions No appeal is provided from the award passed by the Permanent Lok Adalat does not render the said provision unconstitutional.[1]

Procedure (1) The court where the case is pending for adjudication can refer the same to the Lok Adalat for adjudication in the following situations:[2]

(*a*) where the party agrees to refer the dispute to the Lok Adalat; or

(*b*) where one of the parties to the suit files an application expressing his intention to settle the matter through Lok Adalat; and

(*c*) on its own motion.

In an appropriate case the court can refer the matter to a Lok Adalat without the consent of the parties. Before sending the matter to the Lok Adalat the court must be satisfied that:

(*i*) there are chances of settlement;

(*ii*) the matter is appropriate one to be taken cognizance by the Lok Adalat.

So, it is the duty of the court to first explore the possibility of settlement. But it is absolutely unnecessary for the court to investigate whether there are chances of settlement.

For a court to refer a case to Lok Adalat on an application by only either party to a case in terms of s. 20(1)(*i*)(*b*) casts an obligation on the court to apply its mind to the facts of the case, nature of the dispute and to get itself satisfied that there are sufficient chances of settlement of the dispute at the Lok Adalat.[3]

Whether the parties to the dispute, either singularly or jointly, agree for reference does not arise, but the quintessence for

20 *Dr. Amika Kumary* v *State of Kerala* AIR 2012 Ker 16.

1 *Bar Council of India* v *Union of India* AIR 2012 SC 3246.

2 Section 20 of the Legal Services Authorities Act 1987.

3 *A. Ahmed Pasha* v *C. Gulnazjabeen* AIR 2001 Kant 412.

invoking this provision is that the matter is an appropriate one to be taken cognizance of by the Lok Adalat.[4]

(2) Before making reference the court shall give reasonable opportunity of being heard to the parties. The purpose of reference is to explore the possibility of conciliation with the mediation of an independent agency which has the expertise in that behalf and statutory backing for its decision.[5]

(3) Both pending and pre-litigative matters can be sent to a Lok Adalat. Pending matters can be sent to the Lok Adalat by the respective courts where such matters are pending. The latter type of cases can be referred to the Lok Adalat by the State Legal Services Authority, District Legal Services Authority or Supreme Court Legal Services Authority or High Court Legal Services Committee or Taluka Legal Services Committee. The reference in such cases is to be made only after providing reasonable opportunity of hearing to the parties by the concerned Authority or Committee.[6]

(4) When the pending cases are referred to the Lok Adalat for settlement, the court should mention the date on which the parties to the suit would appear before the Adalat. In order to avoid future complication or delay the court or authority may issue notice upon the parties mentioning the date of appearance before the Lok Adalat. In case of matters which are at pre-litigative stage, the Authority or Committee also issue or serve notice upon the parties mentioning the date, venue and time of the Lok Adalat.

(5) After appearance of the parties the Lok Adalat will provide a reasonable opportunity of hearing to them and tried to dispose of the matter by arriving at a compromise or settlement between the disputants. The parties must be given sufficient advance notice of any hearing before the Lok Adalat.[7]

4 *Pushpa Suresh Bhutada* v *Subhash Bansilal Maheshwari* AIR 2002 Bom 126.

5 *Supra.*

6 *Abdul Hassan and National Legal Services Authority* v *Delhi Vidyut Board* AIR 1999 Del 88.

7 *Supra.*

(6) Judge(s) of the Lok Adalat help the parties to understand the question of law involved in the suit or case. The purpose of Lok Adalat is only to help the parties to arrive at a settlement. The real settlement must be made by the parties.

(7) Parties are permitted to explain their views over the dispute in question.

(8) Judge(s) of the Lok Adalat plays the role of the Mediator when the parties are in dilemma to arrive at a just decision.

(9) The parties to the suit can take the assistance of their Advocate(s) to present their case to the Lok Adalat.

(10) After hearing of the parties or their concerned Advocate if it appears to the Lok Adalat that the terms of compromise is lawful and reasonable and not opposed to public policy or public interest, the Lok Adalat shall pass an award. In short, the Lok Adalat is required to arrive at a compromise or settlement between the parties by being guided by the principles of justice, fair play and other legal principles.

While deciding the dispute the Lok Adalat is required to examine the question as to whether the parties have in fact entered into compromise or not? If it is found that parties did not entered into compromise or settlement as alleged by the petitioner neither they were present before the Lok Adalat nor signed the compromise alleged to have been entered into by the parties before Lok Adalat, in that eventuality Lok Adalat cannot pass an award and it is obligatory on the part of the Lok Adalat to recall the award. Before passing the award the Lok Adalat must be satisfied that (*a*) real parties are appeared before them, (*b*) the settlement was not arrived at by playing fraud upon the Lok Adalat.[8]

(11) The Lok Adalat is required to note that presence of the parties and satisfy itself that the parties have voluntarily, out of their own accord, with a free will have entered into settlement.[9]

(12) After settlement of the dispute an award shall be made in writing and it shall be signed by the members of the Lok Adalat.

8 *Smt. Shashi Prateek* v *Charan Singh Verma* AIR 2009 All 109.
9 *Basamma* v *Taluka Legal Services Committee* AIR 2003 Kant 242.

(13) A signed copy of the award shall be delivered to each party free of cost.

(14) In case the Lok Adalat fails to make an award—(*a*) when reference is made by court, it is required to return the reference to the court from which it was sent to the Lok Adalat, or (*b*) when reference is made by an authority or committee, the parties are required to advise to seek remedy in a court of law. The court on receipt of the record from the Lok Adalat is required to proceed with the case from the stage reached before such a reference was made.[10]

Conciliatary role of Permanent Lok Adalat Permanent Lok Adalat will first try to conciliate the matter and if any agreement is arrived at between the parties, to pass the order accordingly. In case, no agreement is arrived at then to adjudicate the matter in view of provision of s. 22C(8).[11]

Power of Lok Adalat (1) Lok Adalat can take cognizance of a case (*a*) where the party agrees to refer the same to it, or (*b*) where one of the parties make an application for settlement through Lok Adalat.

(2) Jurisdiction of the Lok Adalat is very wide in amplitude. This Act confers the wide possible jurisdiction on the Lok Adalat. It can deal with any matter irrespective of its legal character and irrespective of the court or Tribunal in which it might be pending and even when it is not so pending and is still at pre-trial or pre-litigation stage.[12]

The jurisdiction of the Lok Adalat is not confined to settle disputes in pending cases but also to matters which are not filed before any court. So, it is not necessary that to confer power on a Lok Adalat, the dispute must be first filed before a court.[13]

(3) Lok Adalat is empowered to dispose of the case or matter referred to it only on the basis of compromise or settlement

10 *Abdul Hassan and National Legal Services Authority* v *Delhi Vidyut Board* AIR 1999 Del 88.

11 *ICICI Prudential Life Insurance Co. Ltd.* v *State of Rajasthan* AIR 2011 Raj 64.

12 *Abdul Hassan and Nation Legal Services Authority* v *Delhi Vidyut Board* AIR 1999 Del 88.

13 *Moni Mathai* v *Federal Bank Ltd., Arakkunnam* AIR 2003 Ker 164.

between the parties alone. If no compromise or settlement is arrived at between the parties, no award can be made by the Lok Adalat.

The expression "to determine and arrive at a compromise or settlement" implies the jurisdiction that could be exercised by the Lok Adalat cannot extend to decide a dispute where one of the parties is not amenable or agreeable to a compromise or settlement. The moment one the parties to the dispute express unwillingness to arrive at a compromise or settlement, the Lok Adalat would stand stripped of its jurisdiction to deal with the dispute in any manner.[14]

(4) The Lok Adalat shall have the same powers as are vested in a civil court under the Code of Civil Procedure.

(5) Every Lok Adalat shall have the requisite powers to specify its own procedure.

(6) The Lok Adalat has also power to settle the dispute in which the interest of a minor is involved. If the next fiend or guardian of a minor applies to the Lok Adalat for leave to enter into any agreement or compromise on behalf of a minor with reference to the subject matter of the reference before the Lok Adalat, the Lok Adalat has every authority and jurisdiction to grant such leave on being satisfied that the agreement or compromise is for the benefit of the minor. In granting leave it has to take note of the entire fact situation and also asked the guardian to file an affidavit to the effect that the proposed agreement or compromise is for the benefit of the minor. In a case where the interest of the minor is involved the compromise between the parties will be acted upon by the Lok Adalat on the fulfillment of the following conditions:

(*a*) the settlement is in the interest of the minor;

(*b*) that settlement does not in any manner impair the interest of the minor;

(*c*) such settlement has not been made to defeat any interest of the minor; and

14 *Commissioner Karnataka State Public Instruction* (*Education*), *Bangalore* v *Nirupadi Virbhadrappa Shiva Simpi* AIR 2001 Kant 504.

(*d*) the person acting on behalf of the minor to arrive at the settlement does not have any interest contrary to that of the minor in the dispute in question.[15]

(7) The Lok Adalat can take up uncontested civil cases where the defendant admitted the claim of the plaintiff and parties are not on issue on any point.[16]

Duties of Lok Adalat (*a*) When the matter is referred to the Lok Adalat, the Lok Adalat is expected to look into the question whether all the parties to the suit are entering into settlement or compromise. Because if all the parties to the suit do not enter into compromise, no award can be made on the basis of any compromise or settlement entered into between some of the parties only to the suit.[17]

(*b*) The Lok Adalat is required to see that it shall with utmost effort on or settlement between the parties.

(*c*) It is required to first examine and see whether all the parties to the litigation have entered into compromise or settlement. If some parties are unwilling for settlement, the Lok Adalat has no jurisdiction to pass an award because the dispute remains uncompromised.[18]

(*d*) It is its duty to see that all parties are present before it.

(*e*) It is also the duty of the Lok Adalat to see that notice was issued to all the parties to the suit or dispute.

(*f*) It has to verify whether the real parties were appear before him.

(*g*) It has to verify whether the compromise or settlement has been arrived at between all parties to the litigation.

(*h*) The Lok Adalats are also bound to follow the principles of justice, equity, fair play and other legal principles.

15 *Merling* alias *Sherly Augustin* v *Yesudas* AIR 2007 Ker 199.

16 *State Bank of India* v *Balaji Traders* AIR 2003 MP 252.

17 *Kishan Rao* v *Bidar District Legal Services Authority* AIR 2001 Kant 407.

18 *Kishan Rao* v *Bidar District Legal Services Authority* AIR 2001 Kant 407.

(*i*) It has to satisfy itself that the compromise or settlement arrived by the parties out of their sweet will, voluntarily and not being influenced by force, fraud, coercion, undue influence or any extraneous influence.

(*j*) The Lok Adalats shall also not forget that their duty is not to dispose of cases somehow but settle cases amicably.[19]

Reference by court—suo motu The court before whom the case is instituted and finding shall refer the case to the Lok Adalat for settlement, if the parties thereto agree to opt for redressal of the dispute before that forum. But when only one of the party to the dispute makes an application to the court for reference of the case to the Lok Adalat for settlement, even in such a situation the court shall refer the dispute to the Lok Adalat for settlement, but the additional requirement is that the court should be *prima facie* satisfied that there are chances of such settlement.The purpose of relegating the parties first to the Lok Adalat is obviously for conciliation.[20]

Reference at pre-litigation case Sections 19 and 20 of the Act of 1987 confer jurisdiction on a Lok Adalat even without reference of the dispute by a court.[1]

Reference of writ petition to Lok Adalat Code of Civil Procedure is applicable to writ proceedings. So, writ proceedings can be referred to Lok Adalat.[2]

Lok Adalat—no power to dispose of suit for non-prosecution Lok Adalat cannot dispose of any civil suit for non-prosecution and is required to return the case to the court from where reference was made.[3]

Right affecting minor In a matter where a minor is involved, a compromise or settlement between the parties may be accepted

19 *Moni Mathai* v *Federal Bank Ltd.* AIR 2003 Ker 164.

20 *Sau. Pushpa Suresh Bhutada* v *Subhash Bansilal Maheshwari* AIR 2002 Bom 126.

1 *Chalunvadi Murali Krishna* v *District Legal Service Authority, Prakasam District, Ongol* AIR 2013 AP 41.

2 *High Court Legal Services Committee* v *ICICI Bank Ltd.* AIR 2016 Cal 88.

3 *Jagdish Buddhuram* v *State of Andhra Pradesh* AIR 2016 Chh 66.

and acted upon by the Lok Adalat, if it is satisfied on basis of materials produced or called for by it, that the settlement is in the interest of the minor also.[4]

Can Lok Adalat recall its own order The nature or functioning of Lok Adalat is of a tribunal of special category. In *Shashi Prateek* v *Charan Singh Verma*[5] the Allahabad High Court observed:

> The remedy to move for recalling the order/award obtained on the basis of playing fraud and misrepresentation upon the petitioner and upon the Lok Adalat, cannot be foreclosed, for simple reason that no court or tribunal can be regarded as powerless to recall its own order if it is convinced that the order was obtained through fraud or misrepresentation of such a high degree or dimension as would affect the very basis of claim.

So, the remedy to recall the order/award passed by the Lok Adalat on the ground of—

(*a*) fraud, or

(*b*) misrepresentation, or

(*c*) mistake of fact cannot be barred. The power to recall its order on the ground of fraud, misrepresentation or mistake is inherent in every court or statutory functionary. Because fraud affects the solemnity, regularity and orderliness of the proceedings of the court or statutory bodies and amounts to abuse of their process.

Order of Lok Adalat is subject matter of judicial review The power of judicial review over legislative action is an essential feature of our Constitution. It is also a part of the basic structure of the Constitution. The power vested in the High Court under Art. 227 to exercise judicial superintendence over the decisions of all courts and tribunals within their respective jurisdiction is also a part of the basic structure of the Constitution and cannot be taken away even by amending the Constitution.[6] But in *Shashi*

4 *Merlin* alias *Sherly Augustin* v *Yesudas* AIR 2007 Ker 199.

5 AIR 2009 All 109.

6 *L. Chandra Kumar* v *Union of India* AIR 1997 SC 1125; 1997 AIR SCW 1345.

Prateek v *Charan Singh Verma*[7] the Allahabad High Court took a contrary view. According to Allahabad High Court:

> "Although the provisions of the Act are intended to make the award of the Lok Adalat arrived at on the basis of compromise or settlement between the parties to dispute as final and the remedies of appeal, review and revision against the award of Lok Adalats are not available under law, but being a tribunal of special nature, the remedy to recall the order/award passed by Lok Adalat on the ground of fraud or misrepresentation or mistake of fact cannot be held to be barred under law, as power to recall its order on the aforesaid grounds is inherent in every court or tribunal or statutory functionary. Similarly, the awards made by the Lok Adalat organized or established under the Act cannot be held to be immune from judicial review as this court under Art. 227 of the Constitution has ample power of superintendence over decisions of all the courts or tribunals throughout the territories in relation to which it exercises jurisdiction, therefore, I have no hesitation to hold that orders passed or awards made by Lok Adalats organised or established under the Act within the territorial limits of this Court, are subject to judicial review on the grounds available under Art. 226/227 of the Constitution of India, otherwise person aggrieved would be left remediless."

To my view, the law laid down by the Allahabad High Court and Karnataka High Court is a correct approach. Law is made for the benefit of the society. When a party obtained an award by practicing fraud upon his adversary or upon the Lok Adalat what will happen in that case? Whether the aggrieved party would be remediless? Obviously, the scope of the judicial review is very limited. But when the decree/award was passed by Lok Adalat due to fraud playing upon the Lok Adalat and the aggrieved party or misrepresentation upon the petitioner and Lok Adalat or when the Lok Adalat passed the decree/award out of mistake, the scope of review is open. Otherwise, unscrupulous litigious public will be encouraged and real consumers of justice will suffer is solitude.

7 AIR 2009 All 109.

Under Art. 227 of the Constitution the High Court has ample power of superintendence over decisions of all courts or tribunals throughout the territories in relation to which it exercises jurisdiction. Lok Adalat is a tribunal of special category. Therefore, orders passed or awards made by Lok Adalats organized or established under the Act within the territorial limits of the respective High Courts are subject to judicial review on the grounds available under Art. 226/227 of the Constitution of India, otherwise the aggrieved person would be remediless.

In *Board of Trustees of the Port of Visakhapatnam* v *Presiding Officer, Lok Adalat cum Secretary*,[8] the Andhra Pradesh High Court observed that "Though the award of Lok Adalat is not a result of a contest on merits just as a regular suit by a court in a regular trial is, however, it is as equal and on a par with a decree on compromise and will have the same binding effect and be conclusive. Just as the decree passed on compromise cannot be challenged in a regular appeal, the award of the Lok Adalat, being akin to the same, cannot be challenged by any of the regular remedies available under the law, including by invoking Art. 226 of the Constitution and challenging the correctness of the award, on any ground. Judicial review cannot be invoked in such awards, especially on the grounds as were raised in the revision petition."

In *Commissioner, Karnataka State Public Instruction (Education), Bangalore* v *Nirupadi Virbhadrappa Shiva Simpi*,[9] the question whether the order of Lok Adalat shall be final or is it open to challenge under Arts. 226 and 227 of the Constitution of India was discussed at length. In the instant case plaintiff (respondent in the writ petition) filed a civil suit seeking a decree of mandatory injunction declaring the plaintiff as belonging to Hindu Simpi Cast and not Hindu Lingayat. Subsequently the case was referred to Lok Adalat for settlement and disposal on the prayer of the counsel for the plaintiff. The Lok Adalat decreed the suit ignoring the objection raised by the additional Government pleader that he had no authority to enter into any settlement. The State challenged the award of the Lok Adalat by

8 (2000)5 ALT 577.
9 AIR 2001 Kant 504.

filing writ petition under Art. 226 of the Constitution. The court observed: "It is apparent and it is a matter of record that the Government is not willing to accede to the claim of the respondent that he belongs to Simpi Cast. In such a situation, it is always desirable that the petitioner-State should be provided with an opportunity to defend its cause. If the State is prevented from doing so, under the guise of finality, it would lead to public injury and denial of a fair trial to the State. It is essential that in the interest of justice such public injury must be prevented, where necessary, by interference under Art. 226 of the Constitution."

The court set aside the award of the Lok Adalat and observed:[10]

The broader concept of justice would always demand adherence to the fundamental principles of judicial procedure. Strict compliance with the provisions of the statute concerned and refraining from exercising the powers not vested in it would have ensured such adherence by the Lok Adalat. In the case on hand the order having been passed in violation of the fundamental principles of judicial procedure and in addition, the order passed being not within the competence of the Lok Adalat to the impugned order craves for the interference of this court under Art. 226 of the Constitution.

Merits of Lok Adalat (1) It can be used at any time, even in the pending cases.

(2) The parties to the dispute can directly interact with the Judge through their counsel which is not permissible in regular courts of law.

(3) Presence of advocate is not necessary. The parties to the dispute can also place its case and explain its views directly to the Judge.

(4) Settlement to the dispute can be arrived at more expediously as well as less costly.

10 *Commissioner, Karnataka State Public Instruction (Education), Bangalore* v *Nirupadi Virbhadrappa Shiva Simpi* AIR 2001 Kant 504.

(5) All proceedings before the Lok Adalat shall be deemed to be judicial proceedings.

(6) The State pays the salary of the Judges because one of the aims of the State is to provide access to justice. But other cases the cost of proceedings falls on the parties.

(7) The Lok Adalat can take cognizance of the case even if one of the parties makes an application to the regular court to settle the dispute through Lok Adalat.

(8) The parties to the dispute are required to pay any court fee and if court fee is allowed by paid the amount will be refunded if the dispute is settled at Lok Adalat according to the rules.

(9) The basic features of Lok Adalat are the procedural flexibility and speedy trial of the disputes. There is no strict application of procedural laws like the Code of Civil Procedure and the Evidence Act while assessing the claim by Lok Adalat.

(10) The award of the Lok Adalat is final and binding on the parties.

(11) Award of the Lok Adalat has the status of a decree of a civil court.

(12) Award by the Lok Adalat is non-appealable, which does not cause the delay in settlement of disputes finally.

The Lok Adalat will pass the award with the consent of the parties, therefore there is no need either to reconsider or review the matter again and again, as the award passed by the Lok Adalat shall be final. An appeal shall not lie from the award of the Lok Adalat as under s. 96(3), CPC.[11]

(13) Lok Adalat has the power of a civil court.

(14) Lok Adalat will pass the award with the consent of the parties. Therefore, there is no need either to reconsider or review the matter again and again, as the award passed by the Lok Adalat shall be final.

11 *P.T. Thomas* v *Thomas Job* AIR 2005 SC 3575; see also *Mahila Bhanwari Bai* v *Kashmir Singh* AIR 2009 MP 232; *United India Insurance Co. Ltd.* v *Rajendra Singh* JT 2000(3) SC 151; 2000 All LJ 849.

(15) Lok Adalats are boon to the litigating public that they can get their disputes settled fast and free of cost amicably.

Refund of court fee When a matter is settled through Lok Adalat, court-fee paid on the plaint can be refunded.[12]

Settlement by bank regarding recovery of debt When the bank has agreed to settle the matter through Lok Adalat and filed application before the Debt Recovery Tribunal for referring the matter to the Lok Adalat the Debt Recovery Tribunal cannot stand in the way.[13]

Award of Lok Adalat and Art. 227 of the Constitution Lok Adalat cannot pass any award contrary to the provision of law. But the High Court by invoking its power under Art. 227 of the Constitution can correct an illegality committed by Lok Adalat.[14]

Redetermination of compensation A Lok Adalat shall have jurisdiction to determine and arrive at a compromise or settlement between the parties to a dispute in respect of—(*i*) any case pending before, or (*ii*) any matter which is falling within the jurisdiction of and is not brought before, any court for which the Lok Adalat is organised. The Lok Adalat has no jurisdiction to redetermine the compensation awarded by Land Acquisition Officer under Land Acquisition Act because it is only the collector who is vested with the jurisdiction to redetermine the compensation.[15]

12 *Ambika Rajan* v *Basheera Beevi* AIR 2009 Ker 151; *Vasudevan V.A., Petitioner* v *State of Kerala* AIR 2004 Ker 43; *Smt. Chandrakanti Das* v *State of Orissa* AIR 2010 Ori 23; *S. Manilal Panicker* v *Titto Abraham* AIR 2012 Ker 51; *Smt. Sukhpali Devi* v *Civil Judge (S.D.)* AIR 2016 All 175.

13 *Central Bank of India* v *Debt Recovery Tribunal, Coimbatore* AIR 2012 Mad 108.

14 *Suryakant Naidu* v *Amit Kumar* AIR 2016 Chh 126.

15 *District Collector, Machilipatnam Krishna* v *Chairman, District Legal Services Authority, Krishna District* AIR 2019 Hyd 39.

Chapter 5

Code of Civil Procedure and Settlement of Dispute Outside the Court

Settlement of disputes outside the court[1] (1) Where it appears to the court that there exist elements of a settlement which may be acceptable to the parties, the court shall formulate the terms of settlement and give them to the parties for their observations and after receiving the observations of the parties, the court may reformulate the terms of a possible settlement and refer the same for—

(*a*) arbitration;

(*b*) conciliation;

(*c*) judicial settlement including settlement through Lok Adalat; or

(*d*) mediation.

(2) Where a dispute has been referred—

(*a*) for arbitration or conciliation, the provisions of the Arbitration and Conciliation Act 1996 (26 of 1996) shall apply as if the proceedings for arbitration or conciliation were referred for settlement under the provisions of that Act;

(*b*) to Lok Adalat, the court shall refer the same to the Lok Adalat in accordance with the provisions of

1 Section 89, Code of Civil Procedure 1908.

sub-sec. (1) of s. 20 of the Legal Services Authorities Act 1987 (39 of 1987) and all other provisions of that Act shall apply in respect of the dispute so referred to the Lok Adalat;

(*c*) for judicial settlement, the court shall refer the same to a suitable institution or person and such institution or person shall be deemed to be a Lok Adalat and all the provisions of the Legal Services Authorities Act 1987 (39 of 1987) shall apply as if the dispute were referred to a Lok Adalat under the provisions of that Act;

(*d*) for mediation, the court shall effect a compromise between the parties and shall follow such procedure as may be prescribed.

Reason for enactment This provision has been incorporated in view of the opinion *expressed by the Law Commission* in its 129th Report and endeavour to evolve a fair and just formula, acceptable to both parties for an amicable settlement of the issues in dispute. The intention of the legislature behind enacting s. 89, CPC is that where it appears to the court that there exists an element of a settlement which may be acceptable to the parties, they, at the instance of the court, shall be made to apply their mind so as to opt for one or the other of the four ADR methods mentioned in the section and if the parties do not agree, the court shall refer them to one or the other of the said modes.[2]

The Law Commission of India in its 163th Report opined that proposed s. 89 may be suitably modified to provide as under:

(*a*) After settlement of issues in every suit (when both the parties would have also filed their basic documents as required by the proposed provisions relating to filing of documents along with the pleadings), the suit shall be referred to a board of conciliators to explore whether there existed elements of settlement which were acceptable to the parties and if it appeared to the board that such elements of settlement did exist, they shall

2 *Salem Advocate Bar Association, Tamil Nadu* v *Union of India* (2005)6 SCC 344; AIR 2005 SC 3353; JT 2005(6) SC 486; (2005)6 Scale 26.

refer the suit for arbitration, judicial settlement or settlement through Lok Adalat. Method of conciliation could be tried by the Board itself if found feasible. Such reference could be made either after reformulating the terms of possible settlement if the board found the same feasible and advisable or without such reformulation, as the case may be.

(*b*) The Presiding officer of the principal civil court in every city and town shall constitute, in consultation with his senior colleagues, a Board of conciliators consisting of retired judicial officers and senior lawyers of known integrity and competence.

(*c*) A time limit should be prescribed within which the board of conciliators shall complete its work, i.e. either refer the suit to arbitration/judicial settlement or settlement through Lok Adalat or bring about a settlement through conciliation if it finds that such a course was advisable or report to the court that it could not find any elements of settlement which might be acceptable to the parties and that, therefore, any reference of the suit to arbitration/conciliation/judicial settlement or settlement through Lok Adalat was not warranted or advisable. This period could range between 4 months to one year, as may be specified by each court.

(*d*) To delete the alternative mode of "mediation" mentioned under a cl. (2) of sub-sec. (1) of the proposed s. 39. Mediation by a court could be resorted to at any stage of the proceedings and it should not be stipulated as a matter of law either at the stage of the issues or at any subsequent stage. Such a court is always open to the court and there is no reason to define or codify it. Accordingly, cl. (*d*) in sub-sec. (2) of s. 39 might be deleted.

Purpose In *Salem Advocate Bar Association, Tamil Nadu* v *Union of India*[3] the Supreme Court explain the purpose and ambit of this section in the following words:

3 AIR 2003 SC 189; JT 2002(9) SC 175; (2003)1 SCC 49.

> "...... section 89 has been inserted is to try and see that all the cases which are filed in court need not necessarily be decided by the court itself. Keeping in mind the laws delays and the limited number of Judges which are available. It has now become imperative that resort should be had to Alternative Dispute Resolution Mechanism with a view to bring to and end litigation between the parties at an early date. The Alternative Dispute Resolution (ADR) Mechanism as contemplated by s. 89 is arbitration or conciliation or judicial settlement including settlement through Lok Adalat or mediation... In certain countries of the world where ADR has been successful to the extent that over 90 per cent of the cases are settled out of court, there is a requirement that the parties to the suit must indicate the form of ADR which they would like to resort to during the pendency of the trail of the suit. If the parties agree to arbitration, then the provisions of the Arbitration and Conciliation Act 1996 will apply and that case will go outside the stream of the court but resorting to conciliation or judicial settlement or mediation with a view to settle the dispute would not *ipso facto* take the case outside the judicial system. All that this means is that effort has to be made to bring about an amicable settlement between the parties but if conciliation or mediation or judicial settlement is not possible, despite efforts being made, the case will ultimately go to trial."

Section 89 has been inserted in the Code by way of CPC (Amendment) Act 1999 with a view to implement 129th Reports of the Law Commission of India and to make conciliation scheme effective. By virtue of the said provision, it has now become obligatory for the court to refer the dispute for settlement either by way of arbitration, conciliation, mediation, judicial settlement or through Lok Adalat. It is only after the parties failed to get their disputes settled through anyone of the alternative dispute resolution mechanism, the court shall continue proceeding with the hearing of the suit.[4]

4 *Leishangthem Bidyabati* v *Heigrujam Risao Benson Singh* I(2017) DMC 563; 2017(1) Gau LT 639.

Object The object of s. 89 of the Code is that settlement should be attempted by adopting an appropriate ADR process before the case proceeds to trial. Neither s. 89 nor r. 1A of Or. 10 of the Code is intended to supersede or modify the provisions of the Arbitration and Conciliation Act 1996 or the Legal Services Authorities Act 1987. On the other hand, s. 89 of the Code makes it clear that two of the ADR processes arbitration and conciliation, will be governed by the provisions of the Arbitration and Conciliation Act and the two other ADR processes Lok Adalat settlement and mediation (see amended definition in para 25 above), will be governed by the Legal Services Authorities Act. As for the last of the ADR processes judicial settlement (see amended definition in para 25 above), s. 89, CPC makes it clear that it is not governed by any enactment and the court will follow such procedure as may be prescribed (by appropriate rules).

Foundation of s. 89[5] This section rests on compromise, which needs agreement between the contesting parties. A compromise cannot be one-sided. If a dependant offers to compromise the suit and the plaintiff outright reject the offer, no compromise can be reached; in such a situation if the trial court declines to delay disposal of the suit by resorting to efforts of compromise, it cannot be said to have failed to exercise its jurisdiction under s. 89, CPC.

Duties of the court The Judge is expected to bring to bear on the subject his understanding, narrowing down the area of conflict, persuading the parties to accept a fair settlement and is required to put his concentrated efforts in this behalf.[6] Section 89 makes it obligatory for the court to refer the dispute after the issues re-framed for settlement either by way of arbitration, conciliation, mediation, judicial settlement or through Lok Adalat. But no court can compel any unwilling party to submit to the jurisdiction of the arbitration and to get their dispute settled through arbitration. It is only when all the parties agree to get their dispute settled and express their intention in this regard before

5 *W.B.S.E. Board* v *Shanti Conductors Pvt. Ltd.* AIR 2004 Gau 70.

6 129th Report of the Law Commission of India.

the civil court, the civil court can formulate the terms of settlement and refer the dispute to arbitration.[7]

No negotiation between the parties—effect Where there is no negotiations between the parties and no settlement between the parties but the court rendered a judgment where the decision is not based either on any judicial reasoning or any settlement between the parties but based on what the Judge considered as a just and expeditious solution to the dispute under s. 89 read with s. 151 of the Code, such order is not valid because neither s. 89 or s. 151 of the Code authorizes or enables the court to pass such an order.[8]

Procedure Where a dispute has been referred for arbitration or conciliation—

(*a*) The provision of the Arbitration and Conciliation Act 1996 shall apply as if the proceedings for arbitration or conciliation were referred for settlement under the provisions of the said Act.

(*b*) Provisions of the 1996 Act would apply from the stage after reference and not before the stage of reference when options under s. 89, CPC are given by the court and chosen by the parties.

(*c*) The 1996 Act comes into play only after the stage of reference upto the award.[9]

Stages of the procedure[10]

When the pleadings are complete, before framing issues, the court shall fix a preliminary hearing for appearance of parties. The court should acquaint itself with the facts of the case and the nature of the dispute between the parties.

7 *BOC India Ltd* v *Instant Sales Pvt. Ltd.* AIR 2007 Cal 275; 2007(2) Cal LJ 385.

8 *Shyamalika Das* v *General Manager, GRIDCO* (2010)15 SCC 268; 2010(10) Scale 470.

9 *Salem Advocate Bar Association* v *Union of India* (2005)6 SCC 344; AIR 2005 SC 3353.

10 *Afcons Infrastructure Ltd.* v *Cherian Varkey Construction Company Private Limited* (2010)8 SCC 24; JT 2010(7) SC 616.

↓

The court should first consider whether the case falls under any of the category of the cases which are required to be tried by courts and not fit to be referred to any ADR processes. If it finds that the case falls under any excluded category, it should record a brief order referring to the nature of the case and why it is not fit for reference to ADR processes. It will then proceed with the framing of issues and trial.

↓

In other cases (that is, in cases which can be referred to ADR processes) the court should explain the choice of five ADR processes to the parties to enable them to exercise their option.

↓

The court should first ascertain whether the parties are willing for arbitration. The court should inform the parties that arbitration is an adjudicatory process by a chosen private forum and reference to arbitration will permanently take the suit outside the ambit of the court. The parties should also be informed that the cost of arbitration will have to be borne by them. Only if both parties agree for arbitration, and also agree upon the arbitrator, the matter should be referred to arbitration.

↓

If the parties are not agreeable for arbitration, the court should ascertain whether the parties are agreeable for reference to conciliation which will be governed by the provisions of the Arbitration and Conciliation Act. If all the parties agree for reference to conciliation and agree upon the Conciliator(s), the court can refer the matter to conciliation in accordance with s. 64 of the Arbitration and Conciliation Act.

↓

If the parties are not agreeable for arbitration and conciliation, which is likely to happen in most of the cases for want of consensus, the court should, keeping in view the preference options of parties, refer the matter to

anyone of the other three ADR processes: (*a*) Lok Adalat; (*b*) mediation by a neutral third-party facilitator or Mediator; and (*c*) a judicial settlement, where a Judge assists the parties to arrive at a settlement.

↓

If the case is simple which may be completed in a single sitting, or cases relating to a matter where the legal principles are clearly settled and there is no personal animosity between the parties (as in the case of motor accident claims), the court may refer the matter to Lok Adalat. In case where the questions are complicated or cases which may require several rounds of negotiations, the court may refer the matter to mediation. Where the facility of mediation is not available or where the parties opt for the guidance of a Judge to arrive at a settlement, the court may refer the matter to another Judge for attempting settlement.

↓

If the reference to the ADR process fails, on receipt of the report of the ADR forum, the court shall proceed with hearing of the suit. If there is a settlement, the court shall examine the settlement and make a decree in terms of it, keeping the principles of Or. 23, r. 3 of the Code in mind.

↓

If the settlement includes disputes which are not the subject-matter of the suit, the court may direct that the same will be governed by s. 74 of the Arbitration and Conciliation Act (if it is a conciliation settlement) or s. 21 of the Legal Services Authorities Act 1987 (if it is a settlement by a Lok Adalat or by mediation which is a deemed Lok Adalat). If the settlement is through mediation and it relates not only to disputes which are the subject-matter of the suit, but also other disputes involving persons other than the parties to the suit, the court may adopt the principle underlying Or. 23, r. 3 of the Code. This will be necessary as many settlement agreements deal with not only the disputes which are the subject-matter of the suit or proceeding in which the reference is made, but also other disputes which are not the subject-matter of the suit.

↓

If any term of the settlement is *ex facie* illegal or unenforceable, the court should draw the attention of parties thereto to avoid further litigations and disputes about excitability.

Lok Adalat and Legal Services Authorities Act When a case referred to Lok Adalat or Permanent Lok Adalat for settlement the provision of Legal Services Authorities Act 1987 would apply from the stage after exercise of options and making of reference.

Section 89(2) and mediation When mediation succeeds and parties agree to the terms of settlement, the Mediator will report to the court and the court, after giving notice and hearing to the parties, "effect" the compromise and pass a decree in accordance with the terms of settlement accepted by the parties. The mere reference of the matter to mediation/conciliation does debar the court from hearing the matter where settlement is not arrived at. The Judge who makes the reference only considers the limited question as to whether there are reasonable grounds to expect that there will be settlement, and on that ground he cannot be treated to be disqualified to try the suit afterwards, if not settlement is arrived at between the parties.[11]

Settlement through institutionalized mediation The parties must be encouraged the settlement of disputes through an institutionalized alternative dispute resolution mechanism. "Mediation must stand on its own; its success judged on its own record, un-assisted by Judges".

Duty of family court In order to resolve the dispute between the couple the family court is under an obligation to refer the matter to the mediation and thereafter conclude such proceedings.[12] Family Courts Act casts a duty on the court to assist and persuade the parties to arrive at a settlement by referring them to alternative dispute resolution processes of conciliation and/or mediation. The Family Court Judge must shown a human approach while

11 *Salem Advocate Bar Association* v *Union of India* (2005)6 SCC 344; AIR 2005 SC 3353.

12 *Basanthi* v *Ashok S. Thalange* 2016(6) Kar LJ 507.

dealing with the matrimonial dispute because the marriage is an institution of great social relevance.[13]

Reference of dispute by civil judge—validity After CPC (Amendment) Act 1999, inserting s. 89 in Part V, any civil court can refer the suit or proceeding before it to arbitration if there are elements of settlement acceptable to the parties. When the matter is referred to arbitration as per s. 87(2)(*a*) of CPC, the provisions of Arbitration Act shall apply as if the matter is referred to arbitration under the provisions of Arbitration Act. It is not only the District Court which is empowered under s. 89 of CPC to refer the disputes to arbitration but also all civil courts in the hierarchy including High Court can refer the disputes to arbitration. In a case Civil Judge (Junior Division) may refer the dispute to arbitration and after the award is passed, if the successful party has to enforce the award only before a District Court, it would violate provisions of CPC and Civil Courts Act. As seen from ss. 37 and 38 of CPC, a decree has to be executed by the court, which passed the decree. Therefore, if an arbitral award is made pursuant to reference made by a court within its pecuniary jurisdictional limits, it is only that court, which can execute/enforce such award and not any other court.[14]

SECTION 89 AND ORDER X, RULES 1A, 1B AND 1C OF CPC

Direction of the court to opt for any mode of alternative dispute resolution[15] After recording the admissions and denials, the court shall direct the parties to the suit to opt either mode of the settlement outside the court as specified in sub-sec. (1) of s. 89. On the option of the parties, the court shall fix the date of appearance before such forum or authority as may be opted by the parties.

Appearance before the conciliatory forum or authority[16] Where suit is referred under r. 1A, the parties shall appear before such forum or authority for conciliation of the suit.

13 *Bhavana Ramaprasad* v *Yadunandan Parthasarathy* AIR 2015 Kar 6; *Leishangthem Bidyabati* v *Heigrujam Risao Benson Singh* I(2017) DMC 563: 2017(1) Gau LT 639.

14 *Bhoomatha Para Boiled Rice & Oil Mills* v *Maheshwari Trading Co.* AIR 2011 AP 137.

15 Order X, r. 1A, CPC.

16 Order X, r. 1B, CPC.

Appearance before the court consequent to the failure of efforts of conciliation[17] Where a suit is referred under r. 1A and presiding officer of conciliation forum or authority is satisfied that it would not be proper in the interest of justice to proceed with the matter further, then, it shall refer the matter again to the court and direct the parties to appear before the court on the date fixed by it.

Section 89 uses both the words "shall" and "may" whereas Or. 10, r. 1A uses the word "shall" but on harmonious reading of these provisions it becomes clear that the use of the word "may" in s. 89 only govern the aspect of reformulation of the terms of a possible settlement and its reference to one of ADR methods. There is no conflict. It is evident that what is referred to one of the ADR modes is the dispute which is summarised in the terms of settlement formulated or reformulated in term of s. 89.[18]

Consent of parties and reference of dispute to arbitration An order recording the nomination of Arbitrators by consent and referring the disputes to arbitration, can be made in any suit or other proceedings, even if they do not arise under the arbitration agreement or under the Act. If for example a civil suit is filed by a party against the other and there is no arbitration agreement between them, but during the course of the said suit both parties agree that the matter should be referred to a named Arbitrator for arbitration and the court accordingly refers it to arbitration, is not an appointment of an Arbitrator under s. 8 of the Arbitration and Conciliation Act 1996 but a consent order referring the disputes to the Arbitrators already appointed by the parties.[19]

Mechanical reference may be counter productive In view of s. 89 of Code of Civil Procedure, it is the duty of court to ensure that parties have recourse to the Alternative Dispute Resolution processes and to encourage litigants to settle their disputes in

17 Order X, r, 1C, CPC.

18 *Salem Advocate Bar Association* v *Union of India* AIR 2005 SC 3353; JT 2005(6) SC 486; (2005)6 SCC 344.

19 *Milkfood Pvt. Ltd.* v *GMC Ice Cream Pvt. Ltd.* AIR 2011 SC 2533; (2011)12 SCC 573.

an amicable manner. But there should be no pressure, force, coercion or threat to the litigants to settle disputes against their wishes. Judges also require some training in selecting and referring cases to Lok Adalats or other ADR processes. Mechanical reference to unsuited mode of ADR process may well be counter productive.[20]

Reference of family dispute When the dispute is between the members of one family, it would, therefore, be in the interest of family that efforts should be made to settle the dispute amicably.[21]

Not to refer dispute of unwilling party No court can compel any unwilling party to submit to the jurisdiction of the arbitration and to get their dispute settled through arbitration as per s. 89, CPC. It is only when all the parties agree to get their dispute settled and express their intention in this regard before the civil court, the civil court can formulate the terms of settlement and refer the dispute to arbitration.[22]

Reference of dispute to Arbitrator after matter was decided on merits—not proper The purpose of referring disputes to Arbitrator is that long pending disputes before the courts are avoided. There is no purpose of sending a dispute to arbitrator after trial has been completed in the civil court and the matter decided on merits. Both s. 8 of the Act of 1996 and s. 89, CPC are applicable when the suit or other proceedings before the court are at the initial stage and the courts are of the view that the matters can be decided through the means of an alternative dispute redressal system. So, sending a dispute to arbitrator after trial has been completed in the Civil Court and the matter decided on merits by invoking s. 8 of the Arbitration and Conciliation Act 1996 and s. 89 of the Code of Civil Procedure is impermissible.[23]

20 *B.P. Moideen Sevamandir* v *A.M. Kutty Hassan* (2009)2 SCC 198; (2008)16 Scale 403.

21 *Sk. Bhikan* v *Mehamoodabee* AIR 2017 SC 1243.

22 *BOC India Ltd.* v *Instant Sales Pvt. Ltd.* AIR 2007 Cal 275.

23 *Chanchal Ghosh* v *Tripura Truck Owners Syndicate, Agartala* AIR 2015 Tri 1.

Settlement does not cause further litigation The Mediators of the Mediation Cell, while mediating and drawing up of the Settlement Agreement, ought to take care of the implementation of the settlement arrived at. The attempt of the Mediator should be to bind the parties by providing such default clauses as may discourage further litigation. A Settlement Agreement drawn up by the Mediation Cell should not be allowed to furnish a cause of action for further litigation.[24]

Relation—section 8 of the Arbitration and Conciliation Act 1996 and s. 89, CPC Under s. 8 of the Arbitration and Conciliation Act 1996 the court is required to refer the parties to arbitration in a matter where there is an arbitration agreement. Section 89, CPC cannot be resorted to for interpreting s. 8 of the Act of 1996 as it stands on a different footing and it would be applicable even in cases where there is no arbitration agreement for referring the dispute for arbitration. Further, for that purpose, the court has to apply its mind to the condition contemplated under s. 89, CPC and even if application under s. 8 of the Act is rejected, the court is required to follow the procedure prescribed under the said section.[25]

Dr. Justice Dhananjaya Y. Chandrachud in his article "*Mediation—Realizing the Potential and Designing Implementation Strategies*" nicely explained the limitation of this section in the following manner:[26]

> "The difficulty with the provisions of s. 89 lies in the fact that it mandates that where it appears to the court that there exists an element of settlement which may be acceptable to the parties, the court shall formulate the terms of settlement and after receiving comments of the parties my reformulate the terms of possible settlement after which parties may be referred to arbitration,

24 *Karuna Bhalla* v *Rajeev Bansal* 2017 Law Suit (Del) 1790.

25 *Sukanya Holdings Pvt. Ltd.* v *Jayesh H. Pandy* AIR 2003 SC 2252; 2003 AIR SCW 2209; JT 2003(4) SC 58; (2003)5 SCC 531; (2003)4 Scale 7; (2003)3 Supreme 324; 2004(1) ICC 459; 2003(3) Bom LR 147.

26 National Judicial Workshop on "*Effective Use of ADR and Plea Burgaining for reduction of Delay and Arrears in Courts*", vol. I, p. 15.

conciliation, judicial settlement or mediation. The requirement that the court must formulate the terms of possible settlement places a significant burden on the court even before referring the parties to mediation. The court in such a case may be required to spend a considerable degree of time and effort in imploring parties to settle their dispute and to draw up the terms of a possible settlement. The very object of conciliation or mediation is to place the parties under the facilitative function of a mediator who will then enable them to explore their interests and to consider various options for negotiating settlements. Placing the burden of formulating the term of a possible settlement on the court even before the parties are referred to mediation is thus not appropriate because it is only when parties have taken recourse to mediation that the full range of option can be explored by them."

Chapter 6

Plea Bargaining

Meaning of plea bargaining The comprehensive definition of the term "Plea Bargaining" is very much wanting. It has not been statutorily explained. Various jurists and scholars define it from various view points. In its most traditional and general sense, "plea bargaining" refers to pre-trial negotiations between the defendant, usually conducted by the counsel and the prosecution, during which the defendant agrees to plead guilty in exchange of certain concessions by the prosecutor. "Plea bargaining" falls into two distinct categories depending upon the type of prosecutional concession that is granted. The first category is "charge bargaining" which refers to a promise by the prosecutor to reduce or dismiss some of the charges brought against the defendant in exchange for a guilty plea. The second category, "sentence bargaining" refers to a promise by the prosecutor to recommend a specific sentence or to refrain from making any sentence recommendation in exchange for a guilty plea. Both methods affect the dispositional phase of the criminal proceedings by reducing defendant's ultimate sentence.[1] According to *Black's Law Dictionary*[2] it means "a negotiated agreement between a prosecutor and a criminal defendant whereby the defendant pleads guilty or no contest to a lesser

1 See 142th Report of Law Commission of India.

2 *Black's Law Dictionary*, 10th Ed., p. 1338.

offense or to one of multiple charges in exchange for some concession by the prosecutor, usually a more lenient sentence or a dismissal of the other charges."

In the works of A.W. Alschuler,[3] plea bargaining consists of the exchange of official concessions for a defendant's act of self conviction. Those concessions may relate to the sentence imposed by the court or recommended by the prosecutor, the offence charged, or a variety of other circumstances.

Osborn's Concise Law Dictionary[4] defines plea bargaining as an arrangement by which a defendant to criminal proceedings may agree to plead guilty to one or more charges in return for the prosecution extending some advantage to him, e.g. dropping another charge. Such a bargain will be closely scrutinised by the court and a judge should never indicate what sentence he has in mind to induce a defendant to charge his plea.

In short, plea bargaining is the primary apparatus through which judges, public prosecutors, accused, investigating officer and the victim cooperate and work together toward their individual and collective goals.[5]

Law Commission of Canada—plea bargaining Law Reform Commission of Canada[6] defined the plea bargaining as the "agreement by the accused to plead guilty in return for the promise of some benefit". Plea bargaining is an active negotiation process by which the accused pleads guilty by surrendering or waiving his right to trial in order to get the following concessions or benefits:

(*a*) some lesser punishment;

(*b*) to keep their names away from publicity; and

(*c*) speedy disposal of case.

3 Columbia Law Review, 1979, p. 1.
4 *Osborn's Concise Law Dictionary*, 8th Ed. 1993, p. 251.
5 David Levinson, *Encyclopedia of Crime and Punishment*, vol. 3, p. 1149.
6 Working Paper No. 60, 1989, p. 3.

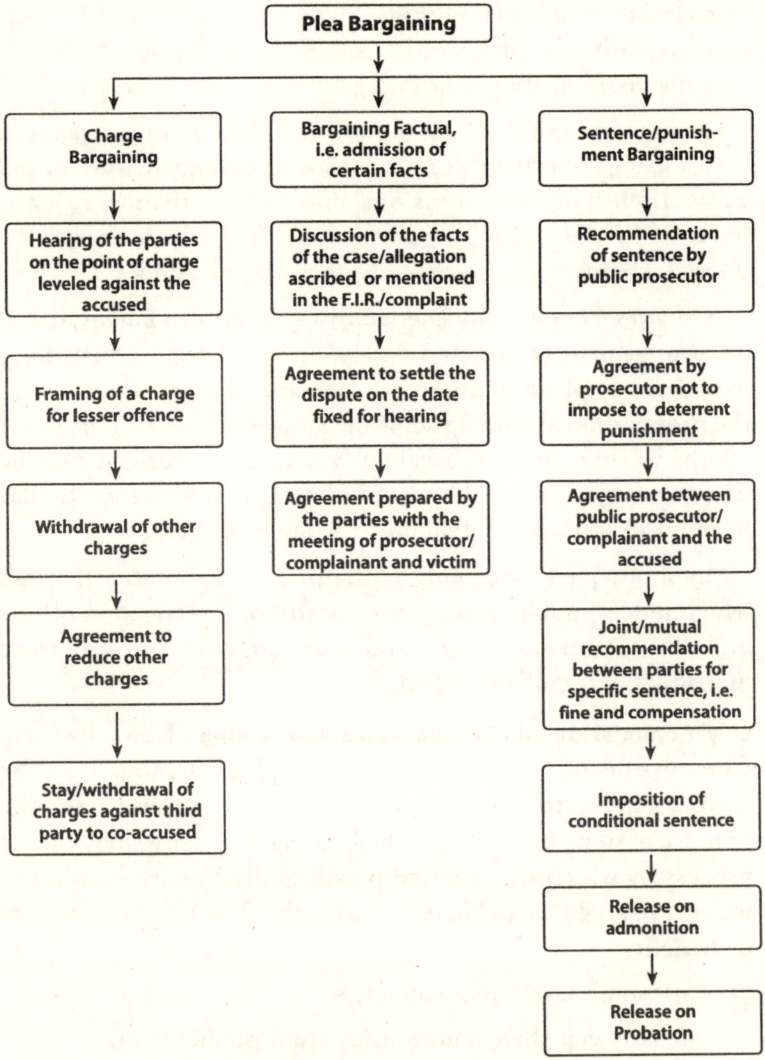
Plea Bargaining
Charge Bargaining
Hearing of the parties on the point of charge leveled against the accused
Framing of a charge for lesser offence
Withdrawal of other charges
Agreement to reduce other charges
Stay/withdrawal of charges against third party to co-accused
Bargaining Factual, i.e. admission of certain facts
Discussion of the facts of the case/allegation ascribed or mentioned in the F.I.R./complaint
Agreement to settle the dispute on the date fixed for hearing
Agreement prepared by the parties with the meeting of prosecutor/ complainant and victim
Sentence/punish-ment Bargaining
Recommendation of sentence by public prosecutor
Agreement by prosecutor not to impose to deterrent punishment
Agreement between public prosecutor/ complainant and the accused
Joint/mutual recommendation between parties for specific sentence, i.e. fine and compensation
Imposition of conditional sentence
Release on admonition
Release on Probation

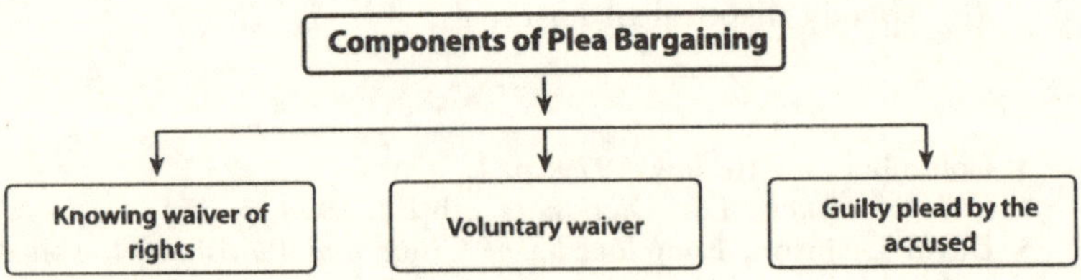
Components of Plea Bargaining
Knowing waiver of rights
Voluntary waiver
Guilty plead by the accused

Advantages of plea bargaining

Save money The cases by way of plea bargaining are disposed of within a very short time. Therefore, it saves money and time.

Participatory process In regular trial there is no scope of mutual dialogue between the complainant/prosecutor and the accused. But in this system they have a chance to talk face to face to workout mutually satisfactory disposition.

Presence of advocate not necessary Presence of advocate is not necessary. The accused even without his advocate or lawyer can workout a mutually satisfactory disposition of the case by exchanging his views amongst themselves.

Provide quick remedy Normally or ordinarily cases are pending in courts for years together for disposal. On the contrary, by way of plea bargaining the cases can be decided even within a month or within few days.

Reduce stress and strain The parties are not willing to hang their litigation for years therefore it reduces their stress and strain.

Important tool to reduce congestion in jail Indian jails are overcrowded. If plea bargaining is successful it will help the jail authorities to manage the congestion/population in jails.

Victim will get compensation Section 265E of the Code of Criminal Procedure 1973 provides that it is obligatory for the court to provide compensation to the victim when bargaining process is complete and the judgment is delivered on the basis of mutually satisfactory disposition.

In other words, "plea bargaining which encourages an early guilty plea, has advantages for each of the main stakeholders. The defendant's remorse is rewarded with a more lenient sentence, the victims saved the ordeal of cross-examination and uncertain outcome of the case and most of the all the public is saved the enormous resources of a full trial".[7] In short, "victim has now moved from being a forgotten actor to become a key player in the criminal justice process".

7 Regina Rauxloh, *Plea Bargaining in National and International Law*, pp. 35-36.

To avoid harassment Where the cases are disposed of quickly, it will save the accused from the harassment when the cases are pending in courts for years together the accused is to attend the court on the date fixed for hearing, engage lawyer, took leave from employer, if is in-service and consequently spent money as lawyer's fees, conveyance charges and other expenses. Therefore, it reduces the mental pressure and harassment of the accused.

To manage case flow management Speedy trail is the integral facet of criminal justice system. Indian courts are overburdened due to variety of factors like judge-population ratio, poor infrastructure, judge pendency, etc. In order to maintain and manage case load to dispose of cases through plea bargaining is an urgent need.

Getting out bail In custody the accused who either do not have the right to bail or cannot afford bail may get out of jail immediately following the judge's acceptance of a plea. Depending on the offence, the accused may get out altogether or on probation, with or without some community service obligation. The accused may have to serve more time, but will get out much sooner than if the case had gone to trial.[8]

Getting the matter over quickly This has the intangible benefit of providing resolution to what is almost always a stressful event. Going to trial usually requires much more time in court than a plea bargain.[9]

Having fewer and/or less serious offences on one's record Pleading guilty or no contest in exchange for a reduction in the number of charges or the seriousness of the offences can look a lot better on a defendant's record than the convictions that might result following trial. This can be particularly important if the defendant is convicted in the future.[10]

8 Attorneys Paul Bergman & Sara J. Berman-Barrett, *The Criminal Law Handbook: Know Your Rights, Survive the System,* 2018, Berkeley, *Nolo Press*, 15th Ed., pp. 430-431.

9 Attorneys Paul Bergman & Sara J. Berman-Barrett, *The Criminal Law Handbook: Know Your Rights, Survive the System,* 2018, Berkeley, *Nolo Press*, 15th Ed., p. 431.

10 Attorneys Paul Bergman & Sara J. Berman-Barrett, *The Criminal Law Handbook: Know Your Rights, Survive the System,* 2018, Berkeley, *Nolo Press*, 15th Ed., p. 431.

Avoiding publicity The persons who depend on their reputation in the community to earn a living and people who don't want to bring further embarrassment to their families all may choose to plead guilty or no contest to get and keep their names out of the limelight as quickly as possible.While news of the plea itself may be public, the news is short-lived compared to news of a trial. And rarely is a defendant's background explored in the course of a plea bargain to the extent it may be done in trial.[11]

Limitations of plea bargaining (1) Offences punishable with death, imprisonment for life are outside the purview of plea bargaining.[12]

(2) Offence punishable with imprisonment for more than seven years are also outside the scope of plea bargaining.[13]

(3) Plea bargaining is not applicable to offences which affects the socio-economic conditions of the country.[14]

The offences under the following statutes shall be affecting the socio-economic conditions of the country:[15]

(*i*) Dowry Prohibition Act 1961.

(*ii*) The Commission of Sati (Prevention) Act 1987.

(*iii*) The Indecent Representation of Women (Prohibition) Act 1986.

(*iv*) The Immoral Traffic (Prevention) Act 1956.

(*v*) The Protection of Women from Domestic Violence Act 2005.

(*vi*) The Infant Milk Substitutes, Feeding Bottles and Infant Foods (Regulation of Production, Supply and Distribution) Act 1992.

11 Attorneys Paul Bergman & Sara J. Berman-Barrett, *The Criminal Law Handbook: Know Your Rights, Survive the System,* 2018, Berkeley, *Nolo Press,* 15th Ed., pp. 431-432.

12 Section 265A(1)(*a*), the Code of Criminal Procedure 1973.

13 Section 265A(1)(*a*), the Code of Criminal Procedure 1973.

14 Section 265A(1)(*b*), the Code of Criminal Procedure 1973.

15 Notification No. S.O. 1042(E), dated 11th July 2006.

(*vii*) Provisions of Fruit Products Order 1955 (issued under the Essential Services Commodities Act 1955).

(*viii*) Provisions of Meat Food Products Orders 1973 (issued under the Essential Commodities Act 1955).

(*ix*) Offences with respect to animals that find place in Schedule-I and Part-II of the Schedule-II as well as offences related to altering of boundaries of protected areas under the Wildlife (Protection) Act 1972.

(*x*) The Scheduled Castes and Scheduled Tribes (Prevention of Atrocities) Act 1989.

(*xi*) Offences mentioned in the Protection of Civil Rights Act 1955.

(*xii*) Offences listed in ss. 23 to 28 of the Juvenile Justice (Care and Protection of Children) Act 2000. [Now it is the Juvenile Justice (Care and Protection of Children) Act 2015].

(*xiii*) The Army Act 1950.

(*xiv*) The Air Force Act 1950.

(*xv*) The Navy Act 1957.

(*xvi*) Offences specified in ss. 59 to 81 and 83 of the Delhi Metro Railway (Operation and Maintenance) Act 2002.

(*xvii*) The Explosives Act 1884.

(*xviii*) Offences specified in ss. 11 to 18 of the Cable Television Networks (Regulation) Act 1995.

(*ix*) The Cinematograph Act 1952.

(4) Offences which have been committing against a woman, i.e. outraging of modesty of woman, rape, kidnapping, dowry, death, cruelty towards married woman, etc. do not come with the scope of plea bargaining.[16]

16 Section 265A(1), the Code of Criminal Procedure 1973.

(5) Plea bargaining is inapplicable to offences committed against a child below the age of 14 years.[17]

(6) Where the accused has been previously convicted, he cannot file an application for plea bargaining.[18]

American system of plea bargaining American system of criminal justice is the pioneer of plea bargaining methodology. Federal Rules of Criminal Procedure codified the plea bargaining agreement. Rule 11(*e*) is the pointer.

In American system, plea bargaining takes place at three different stages—

(*a*) With the prosecuting agency.

(*b*) With the judge conducting the trial.

(*c*) With probation officials in specified cases.

The constitutional validity of the plea bargaining was challenged in *Brody* v *United States*[19] and the American Supreme Court upheld the constitutional validity of the plea bargaining and observed:

> "The issue we deal with is inherent in the criminal law and its administration because guilty pleas are not constitutionally forbidden, because the criminal law characteristically extends to judge or jury a range of choice in setting the sentence in individual cases, and because both the State and the defendant often find it advantageous to preclude the possibility of the maximum penalty authorised by law. For a defendant who sees slight possibility of acquittal, the advantage of pleading guilty and limiting the probable penalty are obvious—his exposure is reduced, the correctional process can begin immediately, and the practical burdens of a trial are eliminated. For the State there are also advantages the more promptly imposed punishment after an admission of guilt may more effectively attain the objectives of punishment; and with the avoidance of trial, scarce resources are conserved for those cases in

17 Section 265A(1), the Code of Criminal Procedure 1973.
18 Section 265B(2), the Code of Criminal Procedure 1973.
19 25 L Ed 2d 747; 297 US 742.

which there is a substantial issue of the defendant's guilt or in which there is substantial doubt that the State can sustain its burden of proof. It is this mutuality of advantage that perhaps explains the fact that at present well over three-fourths of the criminal convictions in this country rest on the pleas of guilty, a great many of them no doubt motivated at least in part by the hope or assurance of a lesser penalty then might be imposed if there were a guilty verdict after a trial to judge or jury".

Utility of plea bargaining The importance of plea bargaining has been explained by U.S. Supreme Court in *Newton* v *Rumery*[20] in the following manner:

> "The net result of every plea bargain is an admission of wrongdoing by the defendant and the imposition of the criminal sanction with its attendant stigma. Although there may be some cases in which an innocent person pleads guilty to a minor offence to avoid risk of conviction of a more serious charge, it is reasonable to presume that such cases are rare and represent the exception rather than the rule.......the plea bargain represents a practical compromise between the prosecutor and the defendant that takes into account the burdens of litigation and its probable outcome as well as society's interest in imposing appropriate punishment upon an admitted wrongdoer. The dependent admits wrongdoing for conduct upon which the guilty plea is based and avoids further prosecution; the prosecutor need not go to trial; and an admitted wrongdoer is punished all under close judicial supervision. By simultaneously establishing and limiting defendant's criminal liability, plea bargains delicately balance individual and social advantage."

U.S. Supreme Court on plea bargaining The U.S. Supreme Court[1] has taken the view that–

(1) the Constitution does not forbid the plea of guilty;

20 369 US 426; 94 L Ed 2d 405.

1 142nd Report of the Law Commission of India.

(2) the constitutional right to trial can be waived provided the waiver is made voluntarily and with sufficient awareness of the relevant circumstances and the likely consequences of such waiver;

(3) well over 75% of the criminal convictions in the U.S.A. rest on the pleas of guilty;

(4) convictions based on guilty plea are not free from hazards for the innocent but experience shows that there is not much likelihood of defendants advised by competent counsel condemning themselves falsely. This view is based on the expectation that courts will satisfy themselves that pleas of guilty are voluntarily and intelligently made by competent defendants with adequate advice of counsel and there is no reason to question the accuracy and reliability of the admission made by the defendants that they committed the crimes with which they are charged. All trial courts are now required to interrogate the defendants who entered guilty plea so that the waiver of these fundamental rights will affirmatively appear in the record;

(5) plea bargaining is an essential component of the administration of justice and, if properly administered, it deserves to be encouraged;

(6) the practice is considered desirable because—

(*a*) otherwise if every criminal charge were subjected to full-scale trial, if would be necessary to multiply by many times the number of judges-court facilities;

(*b*) it leads to prompt and largely final disposition of most of the criminal cases;

(*c*) it avoids much of the corrosive impact of enforced idleness during pre-trial confinement for those who are denied release pending trial;

(*d*) the public is protected from those who are prone to continue criminal conduct even white on pre-trial release;

(*e*) by shortening the time between the charge and the disposition, it enhances the rehabilitative prospects of the guilty when they are ultimately imprisoned;

(*f*) judicial and prosecutorial resources are conserved for those cases in which there is a substantial issue of the defendant's guilt or in which there is substantial doubt whether the State can sustain its burden of proof;

(*g*) a promptly imposed punishment after an admission of guilt may more effectively attain the objectives of punishment whilst avoiding trial;

(7) both the State and the defendant often find it advantageous to preclude the possibility of the maximum penalty authorised by law;

(8) for a defendant who sees slight possibility of acquittal, the advantages of pleading guilty and limiting the probable penalty are obvious, namely—

(*a*) his exposure is reduced;

(*b*) the correctional process can, begin immediately;

(*c*) the practical burdens of a trial are elimination;

(9) the defendant may choose to plead guilty as he may consider a breach of the law as sufficient reason for surrendering himself and accepting the punishment;

(10) the defendant may choose to plead guilty on realizing that it is not worth the agony and expense of a trial to himself and his family in view of the evidence gathered by the prosecution.

Reason for use of plea bargaining The supports of this practice have advanced the following five reasons in support of this method of resolution of the dispute:

(1) Most people arrested, they say, are guilty any way; why bother with a trial?

(2) Why waste public money?

(3) "Plea-bargaining" is a compromise; both sides loss a little and gain a little.

(4) Trials consume time and costs.

(5) It is best (for both sides) to avail it since on the one hand there is always a chance that even if the defendant is guilty and the evidence is adequate there is a chance of a slip up. On the other the defendant saves time and money and earns a concession in the form of a less serious offence or sentence.

Depending upon the crime charged and the sentencing structure of the jurisdiction, defendant seeks one or more of the following concessions:

(1) a charge reduction to some lesser offence with a correspondingly shorter maximum or minimum sentence;

(2) prosecution on only one or two multiple charges with other counts dismissed;

(3) alteration from a charge carrying a particular damaging label which imples depravity on the part of the defendant to a charge with less negative connotations, for example, rape to assault; or

(4) a promise for the prosecutor to recommend probation at the time of sentencing.[2]

Distinction between American system and Indian system

American System	Indian System
1. Power of Plea Bargaining is vested with the prosecuting agency.	1. It rests only on the accused.
2. The prosecuting agency has a responsibility to play.	2. The statute provides a responsibility on the Judge.
3. In U.S.A. most of the cases the role of the Judge is limited and prohibits the active participation of Judges in the plea-negotiation process.	3. Judge is not only act as a participator but also act a monitor and key-player of the negotiation process.

2 Donal J. Newman's *Introduction to Criminal Justice*, 2nd Ed., p. 225.

Recommendation of the Law Commission of Canada on plea bargaining[3]

1. The term "plea agreement" should be defined as meaning any agreement by the accused to plead guilty in return for the prosecutor's agreeing to take or refrain from taking a particular course of action.

2. The term "plea discussion" should be defined as meaning a discussion directed towards the conclusion of a plea agreement.

3. (1) The term "improper inducement" should be defined as meaning any inducement that necessarily renders suspect the genuineness or factual accuracy of the accused's plea, and as including the following conduct when it is engaged in for the purpose of encouraging the accused to plead guilty:

(*a*) the laying of any charge not believed to be supported by provable facts;

(*b*) the laying of any charge that is not usually laid with respect to an act or omission of the type attributed to the accused;

(*c*) a threat to lay charge of the type described in paragraphs (*a*) or (*b*) above;

(*d*) a threat that any not guilty plea entered by the accused will result, upon the accused's conviction, in the prosecutor's asking for a sentence more severe than the sentence that is usually imposed upon a similar accused person who has been convicted, following a not guilty plea, of the offence with which the accused is charged;

(*e*) any offer, threat or promise the fulfilment of which is not a function of the maker's office;

(*f*) any material misrepresentation; and

(*g*) any attempt to persuade the accused to plead guilty notwithstanding his or her continued denial of guilt.

3 142nd Report of the Law Commission of India.

(2) The term "improper inducement" should be defined so as to make it clear that encouraging the accused to enter into a plea agreement, as defined in Recommendation 1, is not in itself an improper inducement.

4. (1) The prosecutor and the accused, or counsel for the accused on his or her behalf, should be permitted to have plea discussions.

(2) No judicial officer before whom proceedings in respect of the accused are or will be held should take part in plea discussions.

(3) Notwithstanding part (2), it should be permissible for the Chief Justice, or a judge whom he or she has designated, to initiate and preside over plea discussions between the prosecutor and the defence, provided it is emphasized that the accused will not be appearing before that judge and is not obliged to conclude any plea agreement.

(4) A judge may in general terms, inform the prosecution and defence as to the potential benefit of plea discussions, and may provide them with an opportunity to have such discussions.

5. A prosecutor, police officer or defence counsel should not offer any improper inducement to an accused.

6. No judicial officer before whom proceedings in respect of the accused are or will be held should offer any inducement for the purpose of encouraging an accused to plead guilty to any offence.

7. (1) A prosecutor should not, when the accused has retained counsel, have plea discussions directly with the accused the absence of the accused's counsel.

(2) A prosecutor with whom an unrepresented accused wishes to have plea discussions should inform the accused that—

(*a*) representation by counsel may be advantageous to the accused; and (*b*) if the accused cannot afford to retain counsel, he or she should ascertain from the provincial legal aid plan whether he or she is eligible for assistance,

and should not thereafter have plea discussions directly with the accused unless the accused has informed the prosecutor unequivocally that he or she will not be retaining counsel.

8. (1) Prosecutor should afford accused persons in similar circumstances the same opportunities for engaging in plea discussions.

(2) A prosecutor should endeavour to ensure, in the course of plea discussions, that accused persons in similar circumstances receive equal treatment.

9. Counsel for an accused person should not conclude on the accused's behalf any plea agreement that requires the accused to plead guilty to an offence of which the accused maintains he or she is innocent.

10. A prosecutor should not suggest, conclude or participate in any plea agreement that:

(*a*) requires the accused to plead guilty to an offence that is not disclosed by the evidence;

(*b*) requires the accused to plead guilty to charges that inadequately reflect the gravity of the accused's provable conduct, unless, in exceptional circumstances, they are justifiable in terms of the benefits that will accrue to the administration of justice, the protection of society, or the protection of the accused;

(*c*) requires the prosecutor to withhold or distort evidence; or

(*d*) contemplates a disposition that departs significantly from that which, in the absence of a plea agreement, would have resulted upon the accused's pleading guilty to the same offence, unless, in exceptional circumstances, it is justifiable in terms of the benefits that will accrue to the administration of justice, the protection of society, or the protection of the accused.

11\. (1) A prosecutor should, unless the circumstances make it impracticable to do so, solicite and weigh carefully the views of any victims before concluding a plea agreement.

(2) A prosecutor who concludes a plea agreement should endeavour to ensure that victims are told the substance of, and reasons for, that agreement, unless compelling reasons, such as a likelihood of serious harm to the accused or to another person, require otherwise.

12\. (1) A prosecutor and an accused who have concluded a plea agreement should, before the accused's plea is entered, disclose to the court—

(*a*) the substance of, and reasons for, that agreement; and

(*b*) whether any previous plea agreement has been disclosed to another judge in connection with the same matter and, if so, the substance of that agreement.

(2) The disclosure and justification contemplated by part (1) of this recommendation should be made in open court unless compelling reasons, such a likelihood of serious harm to the accused or to another person, require otherwise.

13\. Upon being informed that the prosecutor and the accused have concluded a plea agreement, the judge should be able, where he or she considers it necessary to do so, to ascertain by questioning whether the accused understands the substance and consequences of that plea agreement.

14\. No plea agreement or submission should be binding on judge.

15\. In any case in which the judge, having informed of the existence and substance of a plea agreement and of the reasons for that agreement, determines that an accused should not be judicially disposed of in the manner contemplated by the plea agreement, the judge should inform the accused of this fact.

16. Before any guilty plea is accepted from an accused, the judge should be able, where he or she considers it necessary to do so, to ascertain by questioning whether any inducement to plead guilty, other than an inducement disclosed as part of a plea agreement, has been offered to the accused.

17. In any case in which the prosecutor and the accused have concluded a plea agreement, the judge should be able, before any guilty plea is accepted from the accused, to make such inquiry as he or she considers necessary in order to be satisfied that a factual basis for the accused's guilty plea exists.

18. In determining whether to accept an accused's plea of guilty to any offence other than the offence charged, the judge should consider the substance of, and reasoned for, any plea agreement concluded between the accused and the prosecutor.

19. The judge should reject an accused's guilty plea if *inter alia* he or she has reasonable grounds to believe:

(*a*) that the plea was entered as a result of an improper inducement;

(*b*) that the plea was entered as a result of a judicial officer's having offered an inducement for the accused to plead guilty;

(*c*) where the accused, pursuant to what is currently s. 606(4) of the Code of Criminal Procedure is pleading not guilty of the offence charged but guilty of [another] offence arising out of the same transaction that the offence to which the accused is pleading guilty inadequately reflects the gravity of the accused's provable conduct; or

(*d*) that no factual basis for the accused guilty plea exists.

20. An accused who has entered a guilty plea should be entitled to withdraw that plea before sentence, or to appeal against a conviction based thereon:

(*a*) if it was entered as a result of an improper inducement;

(*b*) if it was entered as a result of the judge's having offered an inducement for the accused to plead guilty;

(*c*) if it was entered as a result of a significant misapprehension as to the substance or consequences of a plea agreement concluded between the accused and the prosecutor; or

(*d*) if the prosecutor has breached's a plea agreement concluded with the accused.

21. Where an accused has pleaded guilty to an offence and, upon his or her conviction, has received a sentence that is permitted under the Code of Criminal Procedure in the circumstances and that accords with, or is within the range anticipated by, a plea agreement, the prosecutor should not be permitted to appeal against the sentence received by the accused unless it is shown—

(*a*) that the prosecutor, in the course of plea discussions, was wilfully misled by the accused in some material respect; or

(*b*) that the court, in passing sentence, was wilfully misled in some material respect.

22. In any case in which the accused has pleaded guilty to an offence in accordance with a plea agreement concluded between the accused and the prosecutor, any proceedings taken subsequently against the accused in contravention of that agreement should be prohibited unless the prosecutor:

(*a*) was, in the course of plea discussion, wilfully misled by the accused in some material respect, or

(*b*) was induced to conclude the plea agreement by conduct amounting to an obstruction of justice.

23. Evidence of a guilty plea, later withdrawn, or of an offer to plead guilty to an offence, or of statements made in connection with any such plea or offer, should be inadmissible on the issue of guilt or credibility in any proceeding.

Classification Plea bargaining may be classified into (1) Charge bargain, (2) Sentence bargain, and (3) Fact bargain. In case of charge bargain the accused pleads guilty to reduce charges. In charge discussion the following things may occur—(*a*) reduction of charge to lesser offence; (*b*) withdrawal of other charges; (*c*) agreement to reduce multiple charges into one single charge; (*d*) agreement by the prosecutor not to proceed on a charge. Sentence bargain means assurance of lesser sentence or alternative punishment in lieu of accused's pleading guilty and in course of hearing the following discussions may occur—(*a*) recommendation by the prosecutor for a specific sentence, (*b*) agreement between the prosecutor and the defence counsel with regard to the sentence proposed by the defence counsel; (*c*) agreement by and between public prosecutor and defence counsel not to propose severe punishment; and (*d*) condition to be imposed on a conditional sentence. Fact bargaining is a negotiation process in which admission of certain fact is made in return for an agreement not to introduce certain other facts into evidence.

Plea bargaining in India Originally criminal justice system of India does not recognize plea bargaining. But provisions for guilty plead for petty offences are very much in the Code of Criminal Procedure 1973, i.e. s. 206(1), s. 206(3) and Motor Vehicles Act 1988 [s. 208(1)]. In *State of U.P.* v *Chandrika*[4] the Supreme Court expressed the view that the concept of "plea bargaining" is not recognised and is against public policy under our criminal justice system. Section 320, CrPC provides for compounding of certain offences with the permission of the court and certain others even without permission of the court. Except the above, the concept of negotiated settlement in criminal cases is not permissible. This method of short-circuiting the hearing and deciding the criminal appeals or cases involving serious offences requires no encouragement. Neither the State nor the Public Prosecutor nor even the Judge can bargain that evidence would not be led or appreciated in consideration of getting flea-bite sentence by pleading guilty.

4 AIR 2000 SC 164; (1999)8 SCC 638; 2000 CrLJ 384.

In *Madanlal Ramchandra Daga* v *State of Maharashtra,*[5] the Supreme Court held:

> "In our opinion it is very wrong for a court to enter into a bargain of this character. Offences should be tried and punished according to the guilt of the accused. If the court thinks that leniency can be shown on the facts of the case it may impose a lighter sentence. But the court should never be a party to a bargain by which money is recovered for the complainant through their agency. We do not approve of the action adopted by the High Court...."

In *Murlidhan Meghraj Loya* v *State of Maharashtra,*[6] Supreme Court observed that plea bargaining is unconstitutional and observed:

> "To begin with, we are free to confess to a hunch that the appellants had hastened with their pleas of guilty hopefully, induced by an informal, tripartite understanding of light sentence in lieu of *nolo contendere stance.* Many economic offenders resort to practices the Americans call 'plea bargaining', 'plea negotiation', 'trading out' and 'compromise in criminal cases' and the trial Magistrate drowned by a docket burden nods assent to the sub rosa ante-room settlement. The businessman culprit, confronted by a sure prospect of the agony and ignominy of tenancy of a prison cell, 'trades out' of the situation, the bargain being a plea of guilt, coupled with a promise of 'no jail'. These advance arrangements please everyone except the distant victim, the silent society. The prosecutor is relieved of the long process of proof, legal technicalities and long arguments, punctuated by revisional excursions to higher courts, the court sighs relief that its ordeal, surrounded by a crowd of papers and persons, is avoided by one case less and the accused is happy that even if legalistic battles might have held out some astrological hope of abstract acquittal in the expensive hierarchy of the justice system he is free early in the day to pursue his old profession. It is idle to speculate

5 AIR 1968 SC 1267; 1968 CrLJ 1467; (1968)3 SCR 34.
6 AIR 1976 SC 1929; 1976 CrLJ 1527; (1976)3 SCC 684.

> on the virtue of negotiated settlements of criminal cases, as obtains in the United States but in our jurisdiction, especially in the area of dangerous economic crimes and food offences, this practice intrudes on society's interests by opposing society's decision expressed through predetermined legislative fixation of minimum sentences and by subtly subverting the mandate of the law. The jurists across the Atlantic party condemn the bad odour of purchased pleas of guilt and partly justify it philosophically as a sentence concession to a defendant who has, by his plea 'aided in ensuring the prompt and certain application of correctional measures to him'."

Again Supreme Court strongly disapproved the practice of plea bargaining in *Kasambhati Abdulrehmanbhai Sheikh* v *State of Gujarat*[7] and held that conviction based on the plea of guilty entered by the appellant as a result of plea bargaining cannot be sustained. It is to our mind contrary to public policy to allow a conviction to be recorded against an accused by inducing him to confess to a plea of guilty on an allurement being held out to him that if he enters a plea of guilt, he will be let off very lightly. Such a procedure would be clearly unreasonable, unfair and unjust and would be violative of the new activist dimension of Art. 21 of the Constitution.

It would have the effect of polluting the pure fount of justice, because it might induce an innocent accused to plead guilty to suffer a light and inconsequential punishment rather than go through a long and arduous criminal trail which, having regard to our cumbrous and unsatisfactory system of administration of justice, is not only long drawn out and ruinous in terms of time and money, but also uncertain and unpredictable in its result and the Judge also might be likely to be deflected from the path of duty to do justice and he might either convict an innocent accused by accepting the plea of guilty or let off a guilty accused with a light sentence, thus, subverting the process of law and frustrating the social objective and purpose of anit-adulteration statute. This practice would also tend to encourage corruption

7 AIR 1980 SC 854; 1980 CrLJ 553; (1980)3 SCC 120.

and collusion and as a direct consequence, contribute to the lowering of the standard of justice. There is no doubt in our mind that the conviction of an accused based on a plea of guilty entered by him as a result of plea bargaining with the prosecution and the Magistrate must be held to be unconstitutional and illegal.

To relieve the courts from dockets explosion and amounting of arrears piling in the courts for years together, the Law Commission takes up the matter of feasibility of introducing the concept of plea bargaining for variety factors. They are as under:[8]

(1) The dockets of the courts are over-crowded. The arrears of criminal cases awaiting trial have assumed menacing proportions.

(2) Large number of persons accused of criminal offences who have not been able to secure bail or are unable to furnish bail have to languish in jails as under-trial prisoners for years.

(3) A majority of the cases ultimately end in acquittal and even so the time of the court is pre-empted by the protracted trial stretching over a number of years in respect of such cases.

(4) The accused have to undergo mental torture of an impending trial and potential conviction for a number of years.

(5) The accused have also to spend considerable sums of money by way of legal expenses.

(6) The accused have to remain in a state of uncertainty and are unable to settle down in life for a number of years awaiting the completion of the trial.

(7) The jails are over-crowded and the public exchequer has to bear the resultant economic burden.

(8) During the course of the detention as under-trial prisoners, the accused persons are exposed to the influence of hardened criminals.

The Law Commission of India in its 142nd report discussed in detail about the introduction of plea bargaining in India. The Law

8 142nd Report of the Law Commission of India.

Commission of India favoured the insertion of the plea bargaining in the Code of Criminal Procedure for the following reasons:

(1) It is not just and fair that an accused who feels contrite and wants to make amends or an accused who is honest and candid enough to plead guilty in the hope that the community will enable him to pay the penalty for the crime with a degree of compassion and consideration should be treated on par with an accused who claims to be tried at considerable time-cost and money-cost to the community.

(2) It is desirable to infuse life in the reformative provisions embodied in s. 360 of the Code of Criminal Procedure and in the Probation of Offenders Act which remain practically unutilized as of now.

(3) It will help the accused who have to remain as under-trial prisoners awaiting the trial as also other accused on whom the sword of domiciles of an impending trial remains hanging for years to obtain speedy trial with attendant benefits such as—

  (*a*) end of uncertainty,

  (*b*) saving in litigation-cost,

  (*c*) saving in anxiety-cost,

  (*d*) being able to know his or her fate and to start a fresh life without fear of having to undergo a possible prison sentence at a future date disrupting his life or career,

  (*e*) saving avoidable visits to lawyer's office and to court on every date of adjournment.

(4) It will, without detriment to public interest, reduce the back-breaking burden of the court cases which have already assumed menacing proportions.

(5) It will reduce congestion in jails.

(6) In the U.S.A. nearly 75% of the total convictions are secured as a result of plea-bargaining.

(7) Under the present system 75% to 90% of the criminal cases if not more, result in acquittals.

Scheme formulated by Law Commission for plea bargaining The following scheme is formulated by Law Commission of India for speedy disposal of criminal cases by way of plea bargaining—

(1) The scheme may be invoked only by the offender himself.

(2) There will be no negotiations for plea-bargaining with the prosecuting agency or its advocate none of whom will have any role to play in the matter of moving the Competent Authority for invocation of the scheme.

(3) The Competent Authority will be a 'plea-judge' designated by the Chief Justice of the concerned High Court from amongst the sitting judges competent to try cases punishable with imprisonment upto 7 years. And a Bench of two retired High Court Judges nominated in this behalf by the Chief Justice of the State concerned in respect of offences punishable with imprisonment for 7 years or more.

(4) The application will be entertained only after the Competent Authority is, upon ascertaining in the manner specified in the scheme, is satisfied that it is made voluntarily and knowingly.

(5) The Competent Authority will hear the application in the presence of the aggrieved party and the Public Prosecutor or an assistant Public Prosecutor and after affording a short hearing to them.

(6) The Competent Authority shall have the power to impose a jail term, and/or fine and/or direct the accused applicant to pay compensation to the aggrieved party for compounding the offence in regard to the offences which are compoundable with or without the leave of the court.

(7) The Competent Authority shall award a minimum jail term of say six months or one year in respect of specified offences if the scheme is extended in this behalf in the light of the provisions in the scheme.

(8) The Competent Authority may award a jail term not exceeding one half of the maximum provided by the relevant provision where the Competent Authority is not called upon to exercise the powers to release on probation under the Probation of Offenders Act or under s. 360 of the Code of Criminal Procedure in accordance with the guidelines.

(9) In the first instance, as an experimental measure, the scheme may be made applicable only to offences which are liable for punishment with imprisonment of less than seven years and/ or fine if both the Central and the State Government so resolves by notification issued by such Government and published in Government gazette.

(10) The scheme may be made applicable to offences liable to be punished with imprisonment for 7 years and more after properly evaluating and assessing the results of the application of the scheme to offences liable to be punished with imprisonment for less than 7 years.

STATUTORY PROVISION

Chapter XXIA, Code of Criminal Procedure 1973

Application of the Chapter.[9] (l) This Chapter shall apply in respect of an accused against whom—

(*a*) the report has been forwarded by the officer in charge of the police station under s. 173 alleging therein that an offence appears to have been committed by him other than an offence for which the punishment of death or of imprisonment for life or of imprisonment for a term exceeding seven years has been provided under the law for the time being in force; or

(*b*) a Magistrate has taken cognizance of an offence on complaint, other than an offence for which the punishment of death or of imprisonment for life or of imprisonment for a term exceeding seven years, has been provided under the law for the time being in force, and after examining complainant and witnesses under s. 200, issued the process under s. 204,

but does not apply where such offence affects the socio-economic condition of the country or has been committed against a woman, or a child below the age of fourteen years.

(2) For the purposes of sub-sec. (1), the Central Government shall, by notification, determine the offences under the law for the time being in force which shall be the offences affecting the socio-economic condition of the country.

9 Section 265A, the Code of Criminal Procedure 1973.

Application for plea bargaining[10] (l) A person accused of an offence may file application for plea bargaining in the court in which such offence is pending for trial.

(2) The application under sub-sec. (1) shall contain a brief description of the case relating to which the application is filed including the offence to which the case relates and shall be accompanied by an affidavit sworn by the accused stating therein that he has voluntarily preferred, after understanding the nature and extent of punishment provided under the law for the offence, the plea bargaining in his case and that he has not previously been convicted by a court in a case in which he had been charged with the same offence.

(3) After receiving the application under sub-sec. (1), the court shall issue notice to the Public Prosecutor or the complainant of the case, as the case may be, and to the accused to appear on the date fixed for the case.

(4) When the Public Prosecutor or the complainant of the case, as the case may be, and the accused appear on the date fixed under sub-sec. (3), the court shall examine the accused *in camera*, where the other party in the case shall not be present, to satisfy itself that the accused has filed the application voluntarily and where—

(*a*) the court is satisfied that the application has been filed by the accused voluntarily, it shall provide time to the Public Prosecutor or the complainant of the case, as the case may be, and the accused to work out a mutually satisfactory disposition of the case which may include giving to the victim by the accused the compensation and other expenses during the case and thereafter fix the date for further hearing of the case;

(*b*) the court finds that the application has been filed involuntarily by the accused or he has previously been convicted by a court in a case in which he had been charged with the same offence, it shall proceed further in accordance with the provisions of this Code from the stage such application has been filed under sub-sec. (1).

10 Section 265B, CrPC.

Guidelines for mutually satisfactory disposition[11] In working out a mutually satisfactory disposition under cl. (*a*) of sub-sec. (4) of s. 265B, the court shall follow the following procedure, namely—

(*a*) in a case instituted on a police report, the court shall issue notice to the Public Prosecutor, the police officer who has investigated the case, the accused and the victim of the case to participate in the meeting to work out a satisfactory disposition of the case:

Provided that throughout such process of working out a satisfactory disposition of the case it shall be the duty of the court to ensure that the entire process is completed voluntarily by the parties participating in the meeting:

Provided further that the accused, if he so desires, may participate in such meeting with his pleader, if any, engaged in the case;

(*b*) in a case instituted otherwise than on police report, the court shall issue notice to the accused and the victim of the case to participate in a meeting to work out a satisfactory disposition of the case:

Provided that it shall be the duty of the Court to ensure, throughout such process of working out a satisfactory disposition of the case, that it is completed voluntarily by the parties participating in the meeting:

Provided further that if the victim of the case or the accused, as the case may be, so desires, he may participate in such meeting with his pleader engaged in the case.

Report of the mutually satisfactory disposition to be submitted before the court[12] Where in a meeting under s. 265C, a satisfactory disposition of the case has been worked out, the court shall prepare a report of such disposition which shall be signed by the presiding officer of the court and all other persons who participated in the meeting and if no such disposition has been worked out, the court shall record such observation and proceed further in accordance with the provisions of this Code from the

11 Section 265C, CrPC.
12 Section 265D, CrPC.

stage the application under sub-sec. (1) of s. 265B has been filed in such case.

Disposal of the case[13] Where a satisfactory disposition of the case has been worked out under s. 265D, the court shall dispose of the case in the following manner, namely:—

(*a*) the court shall award the compensation to the victim in accordance with the disposition under s. 265D and hear the parties on the quantum of the punishment, releasing of the accused on probation of good conduct or after admonition under s. 360 or for dealing with the accused under the provisions of the Probation of Offenders Act 1958 (20 of 1958), or any other law for the time being in force and follow the procedure specified in the succeeding clauses for imposing the punishment on the accused;

(*b*) after hearing the parties under cl. (*a*), if the court is of the view that s. 360 or the provisions of the Probation of Offenders Act 1958 (20 of 1958), or any other law for the time being in force are attracted in the case of the accused, it may release the accused on probation or provide the benefit of any such law, as the case may be;

(*c*) after hearing the parties under cl. (*b*), if the court finds that minimum punishment has been provided under the law for the offence committed by the accused, it may sentence the accused to half of such minimum punishment;

(*d*) in case after hearing the parties under cl. (*b*), the Court finds that the offence committed by the accused is not covered under cl. (*b*) or cl. (*c*), then, it may sentence the accused to one-fourth of the punishment provided or extendable, as the case may be, for such offence.

Judgment of the court[14] The court shall deliver its judgment in terms of s. 265E in the open court and the same shall be signed by the presiding officer of the court.

13 Section 265E, CrPC.
14 Section 265F, CrPC.

Finality of the judgment[15] The judgment delivered by the court under s. 265G shall be final and no appeal (except the special leave petition under Art. 136 and writ petition under Arts. 226 and 227 of the Constitution) shall lie in any court against such judgment.

Power of the court in plea bargaining[16] A court shall have, for the purposes of discharging its functions under this Chapter, all the powers vested in respect of bail, trial of offences and other matters relating to the disposal of a case in such court under this Code.

Period of detention undergone by the accused to be set off against the sentence of imprisonment[17] The provisions of s. 428 shall apply, for setting off the period of detention undergone by the accused against the sentence of imprisonment imposed under this Chapter, in the same manner as they apply in respect of the imprisonment under other provisions of this Code.

Savings[18] The provisions of this Chapter shall have effect notwithstanding anything inconsistent therewith contained in any other provisions of this Code and nothing in such other provisions shall be construed to constrain the meaning of any provision of this Chapter.

Explanation. For the purposes of this Chapter, the expression "Public Prosecutor" has the meaning assigned to it under cl. (*u*) of s. 2 and includes an Assistant Public-Prosecutor appointed under s. 25.

Statements of accused not to be used[19] Notwithstanding anything contained in any law for the time being in force, the statements or facts stated by an accused in an application for plea bargaining filed under s. 265B shall not be used for any other purpose except for the purpose of this Chapter.

Non-application of the Chapter[20] Nothing in this Chapter shall apply to any juvenile or child as defined in cl. (*k*) of s. 2 of the Juvenile Justice (Care and Protection of Children) Act 2000 (56 of 2000).

15 Section 265G, CrPC.
16 Section 265H, CrPC.
17 Section 265I, CrPC.
18 Section 265J, CrPC.
19 Section 265K, CrPC.
20 Section 265L, CrPC.

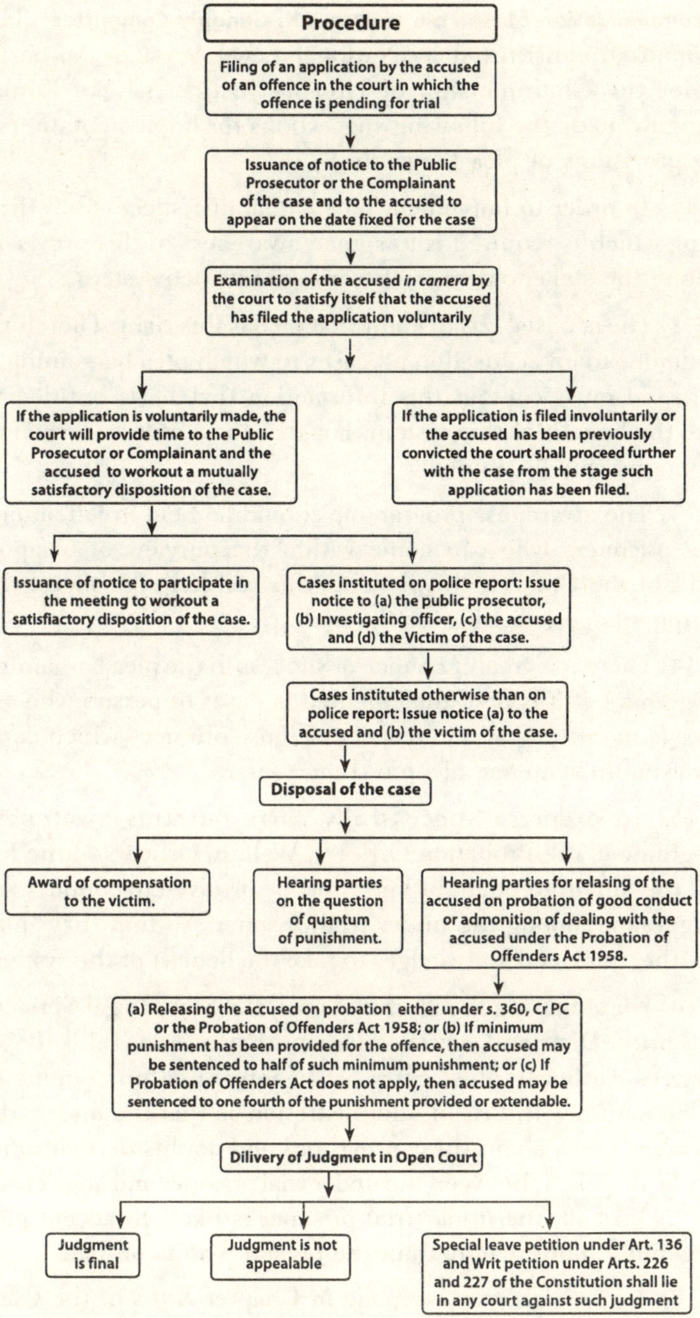
Procedure
Filing of an application by the accused of an offence in the court in which the offence is pending for trial
Issuance of notice to the Public Prosecutor or the Complainant of the case and to the accused to appear on the date fixed for the case
Examination of the accused *in camera* by the court to satisfy itself that the accused has filed the application voluntarily
If the application is voluntarily made, the court will provide time to the Public Prosecutor or Complainant and the accused to workout a mutually satisfactory disposition of the case.
If the application is filed involuntarily or the accused has been previously convicted the court shall proceed further with the case from the stage such application has been filed.
Issuance of notice to participate in the meeting to workout a satisfiactory disposition of the case.
Cases instituted on police report: Issue notice to (a) the public prosecutor, (b) Investigating officer, (c) the accused and (d) the Victim of the case.
Cases instituted otherwise than on police report: Issue notice (a) to the accused and (b) the victim of the case.
Disposal of the case
Award of compensation to the victim.
Hearing parties on the question of quantum of punishment.
Hearing parties for relasing of the accused on probation of good conduct or admonition of dealing with the accused under the Probation of Offenders Act 1958.
(a) Releasing the accused on probation either under s. 360, Cr PC or the Probation of Offenders Act 1958; or (b) If minimum punishment has been provided for the offence, then accused may be sentenced to half of such minimum punishment; or (c) If Probation of Offenders Act does not apply, then accused may be sentenced to one fourth of the punishment provided or extendable.
Dilivery of Judgment in Open Court
Judgment is final
Judgment is not appealable
Special leave petition under Art. 136 and Writ petition under Arts. 226 and 227 of the Constitution shall lie in any court against such judgment

Recommendation of Hon'ble Justice A.K. Ganguly Committee The committee constituted by National Legal Services Authority under the Chairmanship of Hon'ble Justice Ashoke Kumar Ganguly made the following suggestions for implementation of the provisions of plea bargaining—

(1) In order to implement plea bargaining successfully, first thing which is required is to spread awareness of this provision among the stakeholders in the criminal justice system.

(2) The accused has to know that he has this right. Therefore, summons to an accused in all cases to which plea bargaining is attracted must contain this information that he is entitled to take the benefit of this system. For that the statutory format of summons may be altered.

(3) The awareness programme should be held in jail among trial prisoners who can come within the purview of Chapter XXIA of the Code. If this is done, this will help decongest the overpopulated jails all over the country.

(4) There is a greater chance of success in the plea bargaining programme if it is first implemented in cases of person who are already in custody and in respect of those offences which carry a maximum sentence of upto three years.

(5) In order to successfully carry out this awareness programme, the Probation Officers, Welfare Officers of the Jail and the Superintendent of Jails must be involved to conduct the programme among the under trial prisoners so that they may get "the informed knowledge" to take the benefit of the system.

(6) For achieving the aforesaid goal, the State Legal Services Authority, District Legal Services Authority and Taluk Legal Services Authority must carry on an integrated programme in collaboration with Prison Administration so that the under trial prisoners know about these provisions and doubts in their mind may be dispelled. Between the under trial prisoner and an accused who is on bail, the under trial prisoner is likely to accept plea bargaining more readily than the person who is on bail.

(7) A provision may be made in Chapter XXIA of the Code making it mandatory for the court to inform the accused who

appears in connection with trial of an offence, to which Chapter XXIA applies, that it is open to the accused to take the advantage of plea bargaining. Somewhat similar provision has been made, obviously in a different context, in Or. XXXIIA, r. 3 of the Code of Civil Procedure.

(8) Once an application for plea bargaining is filed by an accused, he has no chance of withdrawing the same. If it fails, the matter reverts back to regular trial and the accused does not suffer any prejudice for whatever he has stated in his application. Therefore, a Judge must have a changed mind set to see that such application does not fail. He should also develop negotiating skills.

(9) Therefore, training of judicial officers at State Judicial Academy level and also at the level of National Judicial Academy, Bhopal on this subject is essential. This would certainly improve their capability to achieve the desired results. Moreover, positive change of attitude and concern will be the result of intensive training to the judicial officers.

(10) Chapter XXIA of the Code is a self-contained provision so far as our country is concerned. Judicial Offices must have clear of their role under the various provisions contained in Chapter XXIIA. Unless they master the statutory provisions and understand the object behind it, they may not be able to implement plea bargaining effectively.

(11) Legal Services Authorities have to perform a major role in the propagation of this concept. They must conduct seminars creating awareness among the lawyers about the problems of backlog and the relevance of plea bargaining as an alternative.

(12) Lawyers have a vital role to play in view of their participation in the negotiation process. For this, the Legal Services Authorities with the help of various Bar Associations may conduct classes for lawyers and legal aid counsel. Services of Judges and Jurists can be sought for creating awareness.

(13) Every prosecutor in the country must master the provisions of Chapter XXIA of the Code relating to plea bargaining. Intensive training at the instance of the State Legal Services Authorities for prosecutors is highly essential. Services of eminent judges and jurists can be utilized. Along with the

prosecutors, investigating officers and officer working in correctional agencies also should be sensitized on the importance of these provisions.

(14) Public Prosecutors can coordinate investigating agencies, probation officers; so that the entire class of officers working in various departments of Government can be educated. Each prosecutor can develop a strategy to effectuate the plea bargaining process with the help of the State Legal Services Authorities. Trainings/Seminars can be conducted to disseminate knowledge on this aspect.

Success and failure of plea bargaining in India In order to ensure success, a system of plea bargaining should encompass the following requirement—(1) The accused must be represented by counsel; (2) The hearing must take place in open court; (3) The Judge overseeing the implementation of the scheme must be impartial and in no way involved in the bargaining; (4) The Judge must be satisfied that the accused is pleading guilty knowingly and voluntarily; (5) The Judge must retain a broad discretion as to whether to accept or reject the plea bargaining; and (6) Any court order rejecting a plea bargaining application must be kept confidential to prevent prejudice to the accused.

The following safeguards must be kept in mind by all the stake-holders involved in the process—(*a*) Judicial independence and impartiality; (*b*) complete and timely disclosure of prosecution case; (*c*) complete record of disposition and discussions to be maintained to promote consistency and transparcency; (*d*) to be ensured that the views of victim and investigating agency are solicited and also to ensure their understanding of the agreement; (*e*) plea must be voluntary and there must be awareness of circumstances and likely consequences.

Future of plea bargaining Plea bargaining is criticised mainly for the reason that the accused has to forego their constitutional right of fair trial. Secondly, the avowed object of sentencing policy has been ignored, as a consequence, the societal interest is hampered by reducing the sentence by plea bargaining. An important shortcoming of this system is that "a considerable sentence discount might pressurise an innocent defendant into pleading guilty, while the police investigation against real offender is called off".[21] There is a critical question as to whether a person who is guilty of a serious offence should be let off merely because of the fact that he has admitted his guilt. On the other hand, one cannot but wonder that if a person truly repents his guilt then it would be the best practice to punish him further and keep him with a number of hardened criminals.

The modern scenario is that plea bargaining may be a necessity. In a country where overcrowding of jails and logging of cases are very common, plea bargaining may just offer a solution to a lot of problems.

As yet the concept of plea bargaining has not developed in India as in its model, American system. The concept of plea bargaining is merely present in Chapter XXIA of the Code of Criminal Procedure 1973. Moreover, the concept of plea barganing is not applicable in all cases, for instance where the maximum punishment is with death or where it is a crime against women or against a child below the age of 14 years. However, one cannot rule out the fact that the offender may actually repent his guilt and would want to correct himself but if he were to be sent to jail for a couple of years then it may just have the opposite result.

The concept of plea bargaining can also be linked with that of probation as one may be convicted and punished but may not have to be in jail. Morever, the offender may serve out punishmnt without facing incarcenation.

However, many eminent jurists are still of the opinion that plea bargaining is mostly useful as a tool of reducing burden of the judicial system and ensuring a high rate of conviction. Nevertheless, it is also equally true that if a person would be shown some leniency of having the courage to be honest and to admit his guilt, it would certainly give out a strong message to the society.

The fact is that the there is immense pressure on the judiciary and there is a need of encouraging the offenders to come out

21 Ragina Rauxloh, *Plea Bargaining in National and International Law*, p. 41.

with the truth and having repentence for their actions which would certainly have a positive outcome. Hence, lawyers as well as judges may encourage the method of plea barganing.

There is, however, a chance that plea bargaining may often lead to misuse in many cases. Some social thinkers apprehend that involvement of the Investigating Officer or the police official in the process invites coercion or involvement of the victim brings corruption. There is always a chance that there would be interference by the political or beauracratic levels so as to protect the offenders. It is not unknown that a high ranked navy official was pardoned of murder just a day after his conviction was upheld by the Hon'ble Supreme Court. If plea bargaining was to be made more liberal there is a possibility of great misuse of a good law.

Chapter 7

Compounding of Offences and the Code of Criminal Procedure 1973

Compounding of offences—meaning The meaning of the words "Compounding of offences" is very much wanting in the Code of Criminal Procedure. The word compound means to put together, combine or construct or to settle a matter by payment of money instead of other liability. According to *Black's Law Dictionary*[1] compounding of a crime means the offence of either agreeing not to prosecute a crime that one knows has been committed or agreeing to hamper the prosecution.

Compounding is forbearance from prosecuting a crime. It may be for material consideration, it may be for other considerations. Receipt of money or compensation may be one consideration. Considerations relevant, irrelevant, sublime or coarse may prompt a victim to forbear from prosecution. The court is concerned only with the willingness of the victim to forbear from prosecution. If he is willing and his decision to forbear is genuine and voluntary the composition has to be accepted when the offence is compoundable without permission. The interests of society becomes relevant only in a case where permission of the court is necessary for composition.[2]

Object Settlement of disputes certainly caters to harmony. But the harmony sought to be achieved is not between individuals alone. Law has its ultimate objective of harmony among the

1 *Black's Law Dictionary*, 10th Ed., p. 346.
2 *Navnitbhai Ratibhai Adhyaru* v *State of Gujarat* 2018 CrLJ 2680.

polity. That is why settlement of offences by the individuals—victim and the miscreant—is not permitted by law unless the offences are declared by law to be compoundable.

The act of achieving harmony between the parties at variance can be achieved only by the processes known to law. Different methods are available. Slightly different processes may be there in achieving this objective of harmony. Disputes can be settled, compromises, compounded, consented, etc. to achieve harmony.[3]

Principle No private citizen, even if he be the direct victim of the crime, can settle, compromise or compound any criminal offence. Such a composition is not permitted by law ordinarily. It is against public policy to permit settlement, compromise or composition of felony. But this principle of law admits exceptions. The law declares certain offences to be compoundable. Except those offences which are declared by law to be compoundable, no other offence is compoundable. Litigants resort to the unethical, immoral or amoral course of turning hostile on oath to give effect to such non-permissible compromise, settlement or compounding. But the policy of law is not to accept such composition/settlement unless the office is declared by law to be compoundable.[4] In the words of Roscoepound,[5] "as the social interest in peace and order–the general security in its lowest terms–comes to be secured more effectively by regulation and ultimate putting down of feud as a remedy, payment of composition becomes a duty rather than a privilege".

Guidelines The guidelines in regard to compounding of offences under s. 320 can be summed up as follows are: (1) Composition under s. 320, CrPC is a unilateral act. (2) The victim [person shown in column 3 of ss. 320(1) and 320(2)] can himself make an application for composition. (3) It is not necessary for the court to insist on a joint application for composition. The victim can of course make a joint application along with the accused. (4) It is not necessary for the court to insist on the personal appearance of the accused before court to consider an application for

3 *Y.P. Baiju* v *State of Kerala* 2008 CrLJ 928.
4 *Y.P. Baiju* v *State of Kerala* (*supra*).
5 *An Introduction to the Philosophy of Law*, p. 74.

composition under s. 320, CrPC. (5) The mere fact that the court has already issued a non-bailable warrant against the accused and that is pending is no reason for the court not to proceed further with the case. All steps for which personal presence of the accused is not necessary can be continued even if the non-bailable warrant remains unexecuted and the accused has not personally appeared.[6]

Statutory provision Section 320, CrPC deals with composition of offences. Sub-sections (1) and (2) of s. 320 are identically worded except for the requirement of consent of the court.

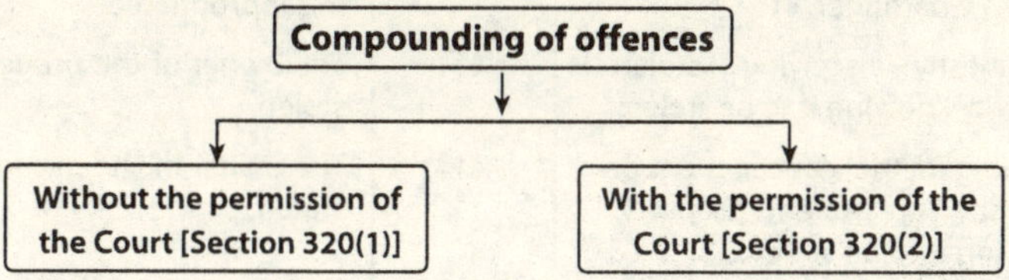

The following offences are compoundable without the permission of the court:[7]

Offence	Section of the Indian Penal Code applicable	Person by whom offence may be compounded
1	2	3
Uttering words, *etc.*, with deliberate intent to wound the religious feelings of any person.	298	The person whose religious feelings are intended to be wounded.
Voluntarily causing hurt.	323	The person to whom the hurt is caused.
Voluntarily causing hurt on provocation.	334	The person to whom the hurt is caused.
Voluntarily causing grievous hurt on grave and sudden provocation.	335	The person to whom the hurt is caused.
Wrongfully restraining or confining any person.	341, 342	The person restrained or confined.
Wrongfully confining a person for three days or more.	343	The person confined.
Wrongfully confining a person for ten days or more.	344	The person confined.

6 *Y.P. Baiju* v *State of Kerala* 2008 CrLJ 928.
7 Section 320(1), CrPC.

1	2	3
Wrongfully confining a person in secret.	346	The person confined.
Assault or use of criminal force.	352, 355, 358	The person assaulted or to whom criminal force is used.
Theft.	379	The owner of the property stolen.
Dishonest misappropriation of property.	403	The owner of the property misappropriated.
Criminal breach of trust by a carrier, wharfinger, etc.	407	The owner of the property misappropriated
Dishonestly receiving stolen property knowing it to be stolen.	411	The owner of the property stolen.
Assisting in the concealment or disposal of stolen property, knowing it to be stolen.	414	The owner of the property stolen.
Cheating.	417	The person cheated.
Cheating by personation.	419	The person cheated.
Fraudulent removal or concealment of property, etc., to prevent distribution among creditors.	421	The creditors who are affected thereby.
Fraudulently preventing from being made available for his creditors a debt or demand due to the offender.	422	The creditors who are affected thereby.
Fraudulent execution of deed of transfer containing false statement of consideration.	423	The person affected thereby.
Fraudulent removal or concealment of property.	424	The person affected thereby.
Mischief, when the only loss or damage caused is loss or damage to a private person.	426, 427	The person to whom the loss or damage is caused.
Mischief by killing or maiming animal.	428	The owner of the animal.
Mischief by killing or maiming cattle, etc.	429	The owner of the cattle or animal.
Mischief by injury to works of irrigation by wrongfully diverting water when the only loss or damage caused is loss or damage to private person.	430	The person to whom the loss or damage is caused.

1	2	3
Criminal trespass.	447	The person in possession of the property trespassed upon.
House trespass.	448	The person in possession of the property trespassed upon.
House trespass to commit an offence (other than theft) punishable with imprisonment.	451	The person in possession of the house trespassed upon.
Using a false trade or property mark.	482	The person to whom loss or injury is caused by such use.
Counterfeiting a trade or property mark used by another.	483	The person to whom loss or injury is caused by such use.
Knowingly selling, or exposing or possessing for sale or for manufacturing purpose, goods marked with a counterfeit property mark.	486	The person to whom loss or injury is caused by such use.
Criminal breach of contract of service.	491	The person with whom the offender has contracted.
Adultery.	497	The husband of the woman.
Enticing or taking away or detaining with criminal intent a married woman.	498	The husband of the woman and the woman.
Defamation, except such cases as are specified against section 500 of the Indian Penal Code (45 of 1860) in column 1 of the Table under sub-section (2).	500	The person defamed.
Printing or engraving matter, knowing it to be defamatory.	501	The person defamed.
Sale of printed or engraved substance containing defamatory matter, knowing it to contain such matter.	502	The person defamed.
Insult intended to provoke a breach of the peace.	504	The person insulted.
Criminal intimidation.	506	The person intimidated.
Inducing person to believe himself an object of divine displeasure.	508	The person induced.

The following offences are compoundable with the permission of the court are runs as follows:[8]

Offence	Section of the Indian Penal Code applicable	Person by whom offence may be compounded
1	2	3
Causing miscarriage.	312	The woman to whom miscarriage is caused.
Voluntarily causing grievous hurt.	325	The person to whom hurt is caused.
Causing hurt by doing an act so rashly and negligently as to endanger human life or the personal safety of others.	337	Ditto.
Causing grievous hurt by doing an act so rashly and negligently as to endanger human life or the personal safety of others.	338	Ditto.
Assault or criminal force in attempting wrongfully to confine a person.	357	The person assaulted or to whom the force was used.
Theft, by clerk or servant of property in possession of master.	381	The owner of the property stolen.
Criminal breach of trust.	406	The owner of the property in respect of which the breach of trust has been committed.
Criminal breach of trust by a clerk or servant.	408	The owner of the property in respect of which the breach of trust has been committed.
Cheating a person whose interest the offender was bound, either by law or by legal contract, to protect.	418	The person cheated.
Cheating and dishonestly inducing delivery of property or the making, alteration or destruction of a valuable security.	420	The person cheated.
Marrying again during the lifetime of a husband or wife.	494	The husband or wife of the person so marrying.

8 Section 320(2), CrPC.

1	2	3
Defamation against the President or the Vice-President or the Governor of a State or the Administrator of a Union territory or a Minister in respect of his public functions when instituted upon a complaint made by the Public Prosecutor.	500	The person defamed.
Uttering words or sounds or making gestures or exhibiting any object intending to insult the modesty of a woman or intruding upon the privacy of a woman.	509	The woman whom it was intended to insult or whose privacy was intruded upon.

Rest of the provisions of s. 320, CrPC reads as:

(3) When an offence is compoundable under this section, the abetment of such offence or an attempt to commit such offence (when such attempt is itself an offence) or where the accused is liable under s. 34 or 149 of the Indian Penal Code (45 of 1860) may be compounded in like manner.

(4)(*a*) When the person who would otherwise be competent to compound an offence under this section is under the age of eighteen years or is an idiot or a lunatic, any person competent to contract on his behalf, may, with the permission of the court compound such offence.

(*b*) When the person who would otherwise be competent to compound an offence under this section is dead, the legal representative, as defined in the Code of Civil Procedure 1908 (5 of 1908) of such person may, with the consent of the court compound such offence.

(5) When the accused has been committed for trial or when he has been convicted and an appeal is pending, no composition for the offence shall be allowed without the leave of the court to which he is committed, or, as the case may be, before which the appeal is to be heard.

(6) A High Court or Court of Session acting in the exercise of its powers of revision under s. 401 may allow any person to

compound any offence which such person is competent to compound under this section.

(7) No offence shall be compounded if the accused is, by reason of a previous conviction, liable either to enhanced punishment or to a punishment of a different kind for such offence.

(8) The composition of an offence under this section shall have the effect of an acquittal of the accused with whom the offence has been compounded.

(9) No offence shall be compounded except as provided by this section.

Duty of the court Duties of the court are as under:

(*a*) Where the offences falls under s. 320(1) of the Code, it is compoundable and the court is bound to record the same.[9]

(*b*) Section 320(2), CrPC specified offences compoundable with the permission of the court and the court may have to apply its mind whether the offence falls under sub-sec. (2) of s. 320 of the Code.[10]

(*c*) Where the permission of the court is required under s. 320(2), CrPC the court will have to exercise its discretion to grant or not to accord permission to the victim for composition.[11]

(*d*) The voluntariness of composition can be verified by the court to satisfy itself that the composition is true, genuine and voluntary.[12]

(*e*) Notice must be given to the prosecution before recording composition in cases where public interest or State interest are involved.[13]

9 *Yesudas* v *Sub-Inspector of Police, Kalamassery* 2008 CrLJ 1290.
10 (*Supra*).
11 *Y.P. Baiju* v *State of Kerala* 2008 CrLJ 928.
12 (*Supra*).
13 *Yesudas* v *Sub-Inspector of Police, Kalamassery* 2008 CrLJ 1290.

Who may apply The victim [person shown in column 3 of s. 320(1) and 320(2)] can himself make an application for composition. It is not necessary for the court to insist on a joint application for composition. The victim of course make a joint application alongwith the accused.[14]

When composition is made permissible The offence can be compounded at any time after the commission of the offence because composition cannot only a post cognizance event. If pending investigation there is composition of parties must certainly have the option of either coming to the court or to the police.[15]

When composition is not permissible No offence shall be compounded if the accused is, by reason of a previous conviction, liable either (*a*) to enhanced punishment, or (*b*) to a punishment of a different kind for such offence.[16]

Effect of composition The composition of an offence shall have the effect of acquittal of the accused with whom the offence has been compounded.[17] If the effect of composition is to amount to an acquittal then no stigma should be attach to the character of the accused.

Withdrawal of a case and compounding of offence—distinction

Withdrawal of case	Compounding of offence
1. Section 321 of the Code of Criminal Procedure 1973 deals with withdrawal from prosecution.	1. Section 320 of the Code of Criminal Procedure, 1973 deals with compounding of offences.
2. The Public Prosecutor or Assistant Public Prosecutor in charge of a case may, with the consent of the Court, at any time before the judgment is pronounced withdraw from the prosecution of any person either generally or in respect of any one or more of the offences for which he is tries.	2. The offence may be compounded by the injured person or any person competent to contract on his/her behalf if he/she is minor, idiot or a lunatic.

14 *Yesudas* v *Sub-Inspector of Police, Kalamassery* 2008 CrLJ 1290.
15 *Yesudas* v *Sub-Inspector of Police, Kalamassery* 2008 CrLJ 1290.
16 Section 320(7), CrPC.
17 Section 320(8), CrPC.

Withdrawal of case	Compounding of offence
3. Withdrawal is a unilateral act.[18]	3. Composition is a bilateral act.[18]
4. Consent of the court is mandatory.	4. Consent/permission of the court is not at all necessary for the offences specified in sub-sec. (1) of s. 320.
5. If withdrawal is made (*a*) before a charge has been framed, the accused shall be discharged or (*b*) after a charge has been framed or when no charge is required, he/she shall be acquitted in respect of such offence(s).	5. The composition of an offence shall have the effect of an acquittal of the accused with whom the offence has been compounded.

No compromise in case of rape In case of a rape or attempt to rape, the conception of compromise under no circumstances can really be thought of. These are crimes against the body of a woman which is her own temple. These are offences which suffocate the breath of life and sully the reputation. And reputation, needless to emphasise, is the richest jewel one can conceive of in life. No one would allow it to be extinguished. When a human frame is defiled, the "purest treasure", is lost. Dignity of a woman is a part of her non-perishable and immortal self and no one should ever think of painting it in clay. There cannot be a compromise or settlement as it would be against her honour which matters the most. It is sacrosanct. Sometimes solace is given that the perpetrator of the crime has acceded to enter into wedlock with her which is nothing but putting pressure in an adroit manner; and we say with emphasis that the courts are to remain absolutely away from this subterfuge to adopt a soft approach to the case, for any kind of liberal approach has to be put in the compartment of spectacular error. Or to put it differently, it would be in the realm of a sanctuary of error.[19]

18 *Y.P. Baiju* v *State of Kerala* 2008 CrLJ 928.
19 *State of M.P.* v *Madan Lal* 2015 CrLJ 3976; (2015)7 SCC 681.

No embargo on power under s. 482, CrPC The compromise, in a modern society, is the *sine qua non* of harmony and orderly behaviour. It is the soul of justice and if the power under s. 482 of the CrPC is used to enhance such a compromise which, in turn, enhances the social amity and reduces friction, then it truly is "finest hour of justice". Disputes which have their genesis in a matrimonial discord, landlord-tenant matters, commercial transactions and other such matters can safely be dealt with by the court by exercising its powers under s. 482 of the CrPC in the event of compromise, but this is not to say that the power is limited to such cases. There can never be any such rigid rule to prescribed the exercise of such power, especially in the absence of any premonitions to forecast and predict eventualities which the cause of justice may throw up during the courses of a litigation.

There is no statutory bar under the CrPC which can effect the inherent power of this court under s. 482. Further, the same cannot be limited to matrimonial cases alone and the court has the wide power to quash the proceedings even in non-compoundable offences notwithstanding the bar under s. 320 of the CrPC, in order to prevent the abuse of law and to secure the ends of justice. The power under s. 482 of the CrPC is to be exercised *Ex Debitio Justitiae* to prevent an abuse of process of court. There can neither be an exhaustive list nor the defined parameters to enable a High Court to invoke or exercise its inherent powers. It will always depend upon the facts and circumstances of each case. The power under s. 482 of the CrPC has no limits. However, the High Court will exercise it sparingly and with utmost case and caution. The exercise of power has to be with circumspection and restraint. The court is a vital and an extraordinary effective instrument to maintain and control social order. The courts play role of paramount importance in achieving peace, harmony and everlasting congeniality in society. Resolution of a dispute by way of a compromise between two warring groups, therefore, should attract the immediate and prompt attention of a court which should endeavour to give full effect to the same unless such compromise is abhorrent to lawful composition of the society or would promote savagery.[20]

Continuance of proceeding after compromise Continuance of the criminal proceedings, after a compromise has been arrived at between the complainant and the accused, would amount to abuse of process of court and an exercise in futility since the trial would be prolonged and ultimately, it may end in a decision which may be of no consequence to any of the parties.[21]

20 *Kulwinder Singh* v *State of Punjab* 2017 CrLJ 2161; *Lukesh Dhaniram Sonkar* v *State of Chhattisgarh* 2016 CrLJ 2848.

21 *CBI* v *Sadhu Ram Singh* 2017 CrLJ 2269; *Amit Chabra* v *State of Uttrakhand* 2015 CrLJ 3846; *Lorina Nongseij* v *State of Meghalaya* 2016 CrLJ 1067; 2016(159) AIC 831.

Chapter 8

Panchayat and Nyaya Panchayat

Panchayat—meaning The word 'Panchayat' means 'a body consists of five' or a 'council of five'. Panchayat system in India has had a long origin. The function of the Panchayat is akin to jury system. But they are different to each other in origin and character.

Distinction—Jury System and Panchayat The jury system "originated as a body of men used in an inquisition or an inquest, required by the king or his Government". The latter was "a people's institution which served local needs, administration of justice and the policing of the village".

History In the Mahabharata, we find the existence of "Gram Sansad" as an institution of self-Government. Ordinarily Panchayats were headed by village elders. Civil cases relating to the parties were decided by the Panchayats according to personal laws of the disputants. Complicated matters were referred to *pandits* for their views and decision.[1] During Mughal period Panchayat consisting of laymen performed judicial functions. They decided cases according to customs and Hindu laws if the parties were Hindus. Some times they applied the principle of justice, equity and fair play with the advent of time "Paura Sabhas' and "Janapada" came into being to maintain order in the society and to check the arbitrary power of the authority.

1 Gled Hill, *The Republic of India*, Vol. VI, pp. 5, 66-67.

Panchayat was the creation of the villagers themselves and was composed of persons who were generally respected and to whose decisions the villagers were accustomed to give unqualified obedience. The Panchayats were called upon to determine the disputes which were simple disputes between one villager and another and which would otherwise have tended to disrupt the rural harmony. Civil Justice Committee of 1924-25 nicely explained the working of the Panchayat in the following manner:[2]

> "The village Panchayat–villagers mediating between contending parties in their own village—has, in some form or other, existed in this country from the earliest times and that without resort to any elaborate or complicated machinery. The judicial work of the Panchayat is part of that village system which in most parts of India and Burma has been the basis of the indigenous administration from time immemorial."

Panchayat system—after Independence During British rule the Britishers felt necessity for decentralization of power. They try to establish "Panchayat raj" or "local or village Government". In the year 1950, our country adopted the new Constitution. Article 40 provides that the State shall take steps to organize village Panchayats and endow them with such powers and authority as may be necessary to enable them to function as units of self- Government. This provision has been introduced in the Constitution to enable the villagers to administer their own affairs. Following this constitutional provision various provinces enacted Gram Panchayat Act, *i.e.* Punjab Gram Pacnchayat Act 1952, Rajasthan Panchayat Act 1953, West Bengal Panchayat Act 1957, Bombay Village Panchayats Act 1954, the Travancore Cochin Village Courts Act 1954, etc. Nearly, 70% of the Indians live in the villages and in order to social and economic development and to provide social justice which is our constitutional goal and mandate, our Legislatures

2 The Civil Justice Committee Report 105-106, 14th Report of the Law Commission of India, 1958.

Amended the Indian Constitution in the year 1992. Part-IX of the Constitution enumerated the provision for Constitution of Panchayats and their powers.

Salient features of the Part-IX of the Constitution Salient features are as follows:

1. There shall be a Panchayat in every village.[3]
2. Panchayat is a Constitutional body.
3. Panchayat at the intermediate level may not be constituted in a State having a population not exceeding twenty lakhs.[4]
4. All seats in a Panchayat shall be filled by persons chosen by direct election from territorial constituencies in the Panchayat area.[5]
5. Each Panchayat area shall be divided into territorial constituencies in such manner that the ratio between the population of each constituency and the number of seats allotted to it shall be the same throughout the Panchayat.[6]
6. Chairman of a Panchayat shall be elected by and from amongst the elected members of the Panchayats.[7]
7. Seats shall be reserved for weaker sections of the society, i.e. the Scheduled Castes and the Scheduled Tribes. Such seats may be reserved by way of rotation to different constituencies in a Panchayat.[8]
8. One-third of the total number of reserved seats have been reserved for women belonging to the Scheduled Castes or the Scheduled Tribes.[9]

3 Article 243B(1), Constitution of India.
4 Article 243B(2), Constitution of India.
5 Article 243C(2).
6 Article 243C(2).
7 Article 243C(4).
8 Article 243D(1).
9 Article 243D(2).

9. One-third of the total number of seats of the Panchayat has been reserved for women which will be allotted by rotation to different constituencies in a Panchayat.[10]
10. Reservation of the offices of the Chairman for the Scheduled Castes, the Schedules Tribes and women has been made obligatory. One-third of the total number of officers of Chairpersons in the Panchayats are reserved for women. Such offices shall be reserved by way of rotation to different Panchayats at each level.[11]
11. The duration of Panchayats is five years.[12] Such period is to be counted from the date appointed for its first meeting.
12. An election to constitute a Panchayat must be completed either before the expiry of its duration of five years or before the expiration of a period of six months from the date of it dissolution.[13]
13. A person cannot be qualified to be appointed as a member of Panchayat unless he/she has completed the age of twenty-one years.[14]
14. The State Government may enact any provision for reservation of seats or offices of Chairperson in the Panchayat at any level in favour of members of backward community.[15]
15. The State Government may, by law, endow the Panchayats with such powers and authority which is necessary to enable them to function as institutions of self-Government and such law may contain provisions for the devolution of powers and responsibilities upon Panchayats with respect to—
    (*a*) the preparation of plans for economic development and social justice.

10 Article 243D(3).
11 Article 243D(4).
12 Article 243E(1).
13 Article 243E(3).
14 Article 243F(1).
15 Article 243D(6).

(*b*) the implementation of schemes for economic development and social justice.[16]

16. The Legislature of a State may by law, authorise the Panchayat to levy and collect taxes, duties, tolls and fees in accordance with appropriate procedure.[17]
17. The Governor of a State shall constitute Finance Commission at the expiration of every fifth year to review the financial position of the Panchayat and to make recommendations to the Governor as to the measures needed to improve the financial position of the Panchayats.[18]
18. The Legislature of a State may by law, make provisions with respect to the maintenance of accounts by the Panchayats and auditing of such accounts.[19]
19. The power of superintendence, direction, and control of the preparation of electoral rolls for the conduct of all elections are vested in State Election Commission who is appointed by the Governor.[20]
20. States of Nagaland, Meghalaya and Mizorum, hill areas in the State of Manipur for which District Councils exist and hill areas of the District of Darjeeling in the State of West Bengal for which Darjeeling Gorkha Hill Council exists are outside the purview of this amended provisions of the Constitution.[21]

Nyaya Panchayat

Nyaya Panchayat—meaning Etymologically, Nyaya means justice and Panchayat means village council or a body of village men regarding village administration. So, in simple terms Nyaya Panchayat means Panchayat court.

16 Article 243G.
17 Article 243H.
18 Article 243I(1).
19 Article 243I(2).
20 Article 243K.
21 Article 243M of the Constitution of India.

Functions The main function of the Nyaya Panchayat is to settle dispute by way of conciliation and mediation. The main purpose of the Nyaya Panchayat is to resolve the dispute through the mutually acceptable settlement.

History The concept of Nyaya Panchayat is not unknown to us. In the early days, even in the days of Aristotle, people also took part in the justice delivery system. In the age of Smriti Sastras, the resolving the dispute between the villagers and villagers were decided by the village headman or Kulo or village assembly. In the early days of our Indian Judicial System State courts were established under the Village Court Act 1888, *i.e.* Madras Village Courts Act. Under the Madras Village Court Acts the Panchas were appointed by way of election and this court exercised jurisdiction in a village or a group of villages where population is not less than five hundred. After Madras Village Court Act, Mysore Village Courts Act 1913, Orissa Gram Panchayat Act 1949, Rajasthan Panchayat Act 1953, United Provinces Village Courts Act 1892, Assam Rural Panchayat Act 1948, Bihar Panchayat Raj Act 1947. The Central Provinces and Berar Panchayats Act 1946, Orissa Gram Panchayat Act 1949 were enacted. Under the above Acts, the Panchayat courts or village courts were established in the villages with a limited jurisdiction to decide the cases. If we go through the Act of the various provinces we find that the mode of all appointment of the members of the Panchayats are divergent and different. Sometimes, they are elected by election or sometimes they are nominated by the Government. It further appears that sometimes they have appointed by villagers or sometimes they are elected through the Panchayat members. Before the enactment of the Government of India Act 1935 almost all the provinces of British India enacted Village Panchayat Act for the creation of village court and they vested limited jurisdiction/power to the village court to resolve the small and petty cases. After enactment of the Government of India Act 1935 various provinces enacted legislation to centralize the power and to make the villagers self-sufficient and to run their administration by the villagers. Subsequently, Government of India appointed a committee under the chairmanship of G.R. Rajagopaul regarding the working of the Panchayat courts.

Recommendations of G.R. Rajagopaul Committee The committee made the following recommendations—

1. The jurisdiction of the Nyaya Panchayat should be exclusive.
2. Such jurisdiction must be limited to money suits and other matters incidental thereto.
3. The pecuniary limits of jurisdiction of the civil matter will be upto ₹500.
4. In criminal cases the offences for which only fine is prescribed as punishment can only be tried by the Nyaya Panchayat. And in order to give effect to the above recommendations the committee draw up the Bill relating to Nyaya Panchayat in the year 1962. The Law Commission of India and the study Team on Nyaya Panchayat through its working paper on alternative Forum for resolution of disputes at grass-roots level explained the history of Nyaya Panchayat in the following manner:[22]

Manner of election "Prior to the Mughal period, village communities created their own Panchayats. There was no element of election. Respectable members of the village community formed the Panchayat and the decisions were generally accepted by the village community. Few disputes landed in courts. They were resolved more or less by a process of conciliation at the village level. Undoubtedly, during the Mughal period, some attempt was made for centralisation of justice system but the Britishers realised that there is a sort of an emotional attachment to Panchayat system and it might provide a reliable basis for decentralisation of administration including judicial administration. The Royal Commission of 1907 upon decentralisation in India recommended the Constitution and development of village Panchayats with certain administrative

22 77th Report of the Law Commission of India.

powers and jurisdiction in petty civil and criminal cases. Panchayats were largely responsible for revenue administration of the village. 'Nyaya Panchayat' so named dealt with resolution of disputes. These Nyaya Panchayats are in vogue in one or the other form, sometimes active, more often dormant. Earliest statutory recognition came in the form of the Village Courts Act 1888 in Madras and the work done by such court with its very limited jurisdiction was appreciated by the High Courts of Madras by expressing the hope that more and more people will resort to the village courts. Number of other provinces adopted legislation similar to the Madras Act."[23]

Panchayat and Nyaya Panchayat—distinction Sometimes the Panchayat and Nyaya Panchayat are used synonymously but there is a gulf of difference and demarcation of function between the Panchayat and Nyaya Panchayat. The Supreme Court in *State of U.P* v *Pradhan Sangh Kshettra Samiti*[24] classically explained the difference between the Panchayat and Nyaya Panchayat in the following manner:

> "Admittedly, the basis of organization of the Nyaya Panchayat under the Act is different from the basis of the organization of the Gram Panchayat and the functions of the two also differed. The Nyaya Panchayat are in addition to the Gram Panchayat. The Constitution does not prohibit the estimation of the Nyaya Panchayat and on the other hand the organization of the Nyaya Panchayat will be in promotion of directive principles content in Art. 39A of the Constitution." With a view to give a proper concept of social justice or Swaraj Indian Constitution incorporated various Articles in Indian Constitution to establish institution of self-Government.

Views of Law Commission on Panchayat Court The Law Commission of India in its 14th report titled as "Reform of Judicial Administration" made the following recommendation regarding Nyaya Panchayat or Panchayat court:

23 77th Report of the Law Commission of India.
24 AIR 1995 SC 1512 (1531).

(1) Panchayat courts are capable of doing a good deal of useful work by relieving the regular courts of petty civil litigation and criminal cases of the simpler type.

(2) The Panchayats are in a position to dispose of simple cases more cheaply and expeditiously and with less inconvenience to all concerned than ordinary courts.

(3) An effort should be made to establish and popularise Panchayat courts in States where they are not firmly established.

(4) Wherever possible, a Panchayat court should be constituted for a group of villages situated in a nearby area.

(5) Nyaya panchas should be nominated by a suitable authority out of those elected panchas who possess certain prescribed qualifications like literacy.

(6) In order to provide continuity the terms of office of Nyaya panchas should be staggered.

(7) Nyaya panchas should be given training before they are allowed to exercise judicial functions.

(8) To get over the difficulty caused by the existence of factions, the panchas deciding a case might be required to belong to a neighbouring village, or each party to a dispute may be allowed to select his Panch.

(9) The jurisdiction of Panchayat courts should be exclusive.

(10) Nature of cases (civil) and the list of offences (criminal) triable by these courts are set out at length in the various State enactments and do not call for any enlargement.

(11) The upper limit of the civil jurisdiction of Panchayats should be ₹200 or ₹250. In special cases with the approval of the High Court their jurisdiction may be increased to ₹500.

(12) The criminal jurisdiction of Panchayat courts should be limited to inflicting a fine of ₹50. They should not have the power to award sentences of imprisonment

either substantively or in default of payment of fine or to bind over parties to keep the peace. Cases in which such action is necessary should be made over to the regular courts.

(13) The court fee, if any, levied by the Panchayat courts should be nominal.

(14) Panchayat courts should not be bound by procedural codes or by the law of evidence.

(15) Panchayat courts should wherever possible seek to effect an amicable settlement between the parties.

(16) Legal practitioners should not be permitted to appear in these courts.

(17) A revision should lie from the decisions of the Panchayat courts in civil and criminal matters to the Munsif or Sub-Divisional Magistrate, who should be empowered to transfer a case from one Panchayat court to another or to the regular court for trial.

(18) The power of revision should not given to the District Judge nor should a right of appeal to a lager Panchayat be allowed.

(19) The District Judge should be empowered to direct the removal of panchas if he is satisfied upon a report that the pancha in question has been guilty of misconduct in the discharge of his judicial functions. There should be a provision for an appeal against such order of removal.

(20) Panchayat courts should be empowered to distrain or seize movable property in execution of their decrees and to send them if necessary to the Collector for execution.

(21) A special officer or special officers should be appointed for the purpose of imparting training to panchas and to supervise the administration of Panchayat courts.

(22) More detailed information should be collected and published regarding the working of the Panchayat courts.

Criminal Jurisdiction

Name of the Act	Nature of Offences triable	Punishment	To whom Complaint be filed	On what basis Nyaya Panchayat take cognizance
1. Andhra Pradesh Mandala Nyaya Panchayat Act 1995.	(*i*) Offences punishable under ss. 160, 277, 278, 283 to 291, 323, 334, 341, 342, 352, 354, 379 (where value of property does not exceed ₹550,00) and s. 426 of the Indian Penal Code (when the amount or loss does not exceed ₹50,000). (*ii*) Offences under Chapter V of the Cattle Trespass Act 1871. (*iii*) Offences punishable under A.P. Panchayat Raj Act 1994. (*iv*) Offences against Women punishable under Indian Penal Code and Triable by Judicial Magistrate of the 1st class. (*v*) Cases under s. 125, Code of Criminal Procedure, 1973.	Impose fine not exceeding the prescribed amount but shall not award any sentence of imprisonment, though prescribed for such offence.	Nyaya Panchayat	Either on a complaint or on a police report.
2. Assam Rural Panchayat Act 1948.	(*i*) Offences punishable under Indian Penal Code which are specified under s. 83 of Act XXVII of 1948. (*ii*) Offences under Cattle Trespass Act 1871.	Fine which may extend to ₹250 No power to impose imprisonment.	Panchayat	Complaint-written or oral.

Name of the Act	Nature of Offences triable	Punishment	To whom Complaint be filed	On what basis Nyaya Panchayat take cognizance
3. Bihar Panchayati Raj Act 1947.	(*i*) Offences punishable under ss. 140, 143, 145, 147, 151, 153, 160, 172, 174, 178, 179, 269, 274, 277, 283, 285, 286, 289, 290, 294, 323, 334, 336, 341, 352, 356, 357, 358, 379 to 381 (where value of the stolen property does not exceed ₹100), ss. 403, 411 (where value of the stolen property does not exceed ₹100), ss. 426, 430, 447, 448, 461, 504, 506 and 510 of IPC. (*ii*) Offences under ss. 24 & 26 of the Cattle Trespass Act 1871. (*iii*) Offences under Bengal Public Gambling Act 1867.	1st class or 2nd class Nyaya Panchayat imposes fine upto ₹ 100 or simple imprisonment upto one month, 3rd class Nyaya Panchayat imposes fine upto ₹ 50 or simple imprisonment upto 7 days.	Gram Cutcherries through Sarpanchas.	Complaint oral or written.
4. Orissa Gram Panchayat Act 1949.	All offences punishable under Indian Penal Code specified in s. 64 of the Act.	Fine upto ₹50. Award imprisonment in case of default of fine.	Gram Panchayat	Complaint oral or written.
5. Madhya Pradesh Act II of 1951.	(*i*) All the offences punishable under India Penal Code & Triable by the Magistrate specified in the schedule of the Act. (*ii*) Offences under Cattle Trespass Act 1871.	Impose fine upto ₹50.	Gram Panchayat	Complaint oral or written.
6. Himachal Pradesh Panchayati Raj Act 1970	(*i*) Offences under ss. 160, 172, 173, 178, 179, 180, 228, 264, 265, 266, 267, 269, 277, 283, 285, 286, 288, 289, 290, 294, 323, 334, 341, 352 & 379 of the IPC (If the value of the property involved does not exceed ₹ 250).	Fine upto ₹100 but cannot impose sentence of imprisonment.	Sarpancha or Upa-Sarpancha or Pancha of Nyaya Panchayat.	Complaint oral or written.

Name of the Act	Nature of Offences triable	Punishment	To whom Complaint be filed	On what basis Nyaya Panchayat take cognizance
	(*ii*) Offences under ss. 24 and 26 of the Cattle Trespass Act 1871. (*iii*) Offences under ss. 3, 4 and 7 of the Public Gambling Act 1876. (*iv*) Offences under Punjab Vaccination Act 1880. (*v*) Offences under Himachal Pradesh Panchayati Raj Act 1968.			
7. Kerala Village Courts Act 1960	Offences under ss. 160, 172, 174, 179, 269, 277, 279, 283, 285, 289, 290, 294, 323, 334, 336, 352, 358, 379 (where value of the stolen Property does not exceed ₹ 50), 426 (when loss or damage does not exceed ₹ 50), 504 & 510 of the Indian Penal Code.	Fine upto ₹ 100 and imprisonment upto one month for default of payment of fine except woman accused.	Village Court.	Complaint oral or written.
8. Uttar Pradesh Panchayati Raj Act 1947.	(*i*) Offences punishable under ss. 140, 160, 172, 174, 179, 269, 277, 283, 285, 289, 290, 294, 323, 334, 341, 352, 357, 358, 374, 379, 403, 411 (if the value of the property involved does not exceed ₹50), 426, 428 430, 431, 447, 448, 504, 506, 509 & 510 of the Indian Penal Code. (*ii*) Offences under Cattle Trespass Act 1871.	Fine may extend to ₹100. But they are not authorised to award imprisonment either substantive or in default of fine.	Sarpancha or Naib Sarpancha of Panchayati Adalat.	Complaint written or oral.

Name of the Act	Nature of Offences triable	Punishment	To whom Complaint be filed	On what basis Nyaya Panchayat take cognizance
	(*iii*) Offences under Public Gambling Act 1887.			
9. Delhi Panchayati Raj Act.	(*i*) Offences punishable under ss. 140, 160, 172, 174, 179, 269, 277, 283, 285, 289, 290, 294, 323, 334, 341, 352, 357, 358, 374, 379, 403, 411 (if the value of the property involved does not exceed ₹ 50), 426, 428, 430, 431, 447, 448, 504, 506, 509 & 510 of the Indian Penal Code. (*ii*) Offences under Cattle Trespass Act 1871. (*iii*) Offences under Delhi Public Gambling Act 1955.	Fine upto ₹ 100.	Panchayati Adalat.	Complaint written or oral.
10. Punjab Gram Panchayat Act 1952.	(*i*) Offences punishable under ss. 140, 160, 172, 174, 179, 269, 277, 283, 285, 289, 290, 294, 323, 334, 341, 352, 357, 358, 374, 379, 403, 411 (if the value of the property involved does not exceed ₹50), 426, 428, 430, 431, 447, 448, 504, 506, 509 & 510 of the Indian Penal Code. (*ii*) Offences under Punjab Vaccination Act. (*iii*) Offences under Punjab Juvenile Smoking Act 1918. (*iv*) Offences under Public Gambling Act 1887. (*v*) Offences	Fine upto ₹100 or may release on admonition.	Sarpancha or Naib Sarpancha of Nyaya Panchayat.	Complaint oral or written.

Name of the Act	Nature of Offences triable	Punishment	To whom Complaint be filed	On what basisNyaya Panchayat take cognizance
	under ss. 26 and 33 of the Indian Forest Act. (*iv*) Offences under Punjab Law Preservation Act 1900.			
11. Rajasthan Panchayati Raj Act 1953	(*i*) Offences punishable under ss. 140, 160, 172, 174, 175, 178, 179, 180, 188, 202, 228, 264, 265, 266, 267, 269, 277, 278, 279, 283, 285, 286, 288, 289, 290, 294, 323, 334, 336, 341, 352, 356, 358, 374, 379 to 381, 403, 411 (if the value of the property does not exceed ₹25), 426, 428, 430, 447, 448, 461, 504, 506, 509 & 510 of the Indian Penal Code. (*ii*) Offences under Cattle Trespass Act 1871. (*iii*) Offences under Prevention of cruelty to Animals Act 1890. (*iv*) Offences punishable under Rajasthan Prevention of Juvenile Smoking Act 1950 etc.	Fine upto ₹ 50 impose imprisonment in default of payment of fine.	Nyaya Panchayat through Sarpancha or Naib Sarpancha.	Complaint oral or written.
12. West Bengal Panchayat Act 1973.	(*i*) Offences under ss. 26 & 27 of the Cattle Trespass Act 1871 (1 of 1871). (*ii*) Offences under enactments (other than the Indian Penal Code (45 of 1860) and this Act) or any Rules or bye-laws made thereunder which are punishable with fine only upto a limit of ₹ 50.	Fine may extend to ₹ 100. But they are not authorised to award or imprisonment either substantive or in default of fine.	Nyaya Panchayat through Sarpancha or Naib Sarpancha.	Complaint oral or written.

Name of the Act	Nature of Offences triable	Punishment	To whom Complaint be filed	On what basis Nyaya Panchayat take cognizance
	(*iii*) Offences under s. 34 of the Police Act 1861 (5 of 1861). (*iv*) Offences under the Bengal Ferries Act 1885 (Ben. Act 1 of 1885), except those under ss. 28 and 30. (*v*) Offences under the following sections of the Indian Penal Code, namely ss. 160, 269, 277, 289, 290, 294, 323, 341, 352, 358, 426, 447, 448, 504 and 510 and when the value of the property in the opinion of the Nyaya Panchayat is over ₹ 200, ss. 379 and 441. (*vi*) Offences under the following section of the Indian Penal Code, namely, ss. 283, 428, 430, 431, 506 and 509; and when the value of the property in the opinion of the Magistrate is not over two hundred rupees, s. 403.			

Basis of Nyaya Panchayat Justice, social, economic and political is our Constitutional goal. To provide justice fundamental rights and directives principle of State policy are incorporated in the Constitution in the hope and expectation that the day the tree of true liberty would bloom in India. In order to ensure equal justice of the people of India a new Article, i.e. Art. 39A was inserted in the Constitution. Article 39A provides that the State shall secure that the operation of the legal system promotes justice, on a basis of equal opportunity, and shall in particular, provide free legal aid, by suitable legislation or schemes or in any other way, to ensure that opportunities for securing justice are not denied to any citizen by reason of economic or other disabilities. In order to provide justice to the downtrodden and downwarded people the legislature need a forum which is a half way between the traditional law court and ancient Panchayat system. To reduce the pendency of huge backlog and to reach justice at the doorstep, we saw the birth of Nyaya Panchayat. It is in conformity with the principles of Directives Principles of State Policy. In way back in 1958, in the course of a discussion in the Rajya Sabha, the then Minister of Law and Justice, Government of India, Mr. Ashoke Kr. Sen observed:

> "There is no doubt the system of justice which obtains today is too expensive for the common man. The small dispute must necessarily be left to be decided by a system of Panchayat justice—call it the People's Court, call it the Popular Court, call it anything—but it would certainly be subject to such safeguards as we may devise—the only means by which for ordinary disputes in the village level the common man can be assured of a system of judicial administration which would not be too expensive for him and which would not be too dilatory for him".

Law Commission of India—its view In 77th Report Law Commission strongly expressed its views regarding creation of Nyaya Panchayat as instruments of justice and held:

> "Changes, modifications and amendments have been made both in the hierarchy of courts as well as in the procedures followed by them, as the society gradually became more and more developed. The present day complications and delays in disposal of cases are not so much on account of the technical and cumbersome nature of our legal system as they are due to other factors operating in and outside the courts. In spite of the fact that we are still heavily dependent on agriculture, we can no longer be regarded as an undeveloped peasant society, in view of the great strides that have been made in the direction of industrialization and urbanization of population, besides expansion of trade and commerce. It will be a retrograde step to revert to the primitive method of administration of justice by taking our disputes to a group of ordinary laymen ignorant of the modern

complexities of life and not conversant with legal concepts and procedures. The real need appears to be to further improve the existing system to meet modern requirements in the context of our national ethos and not to replace it by an inadequate system which was left behind long ago."

The Privy Council also recognize the Panchayat as important means of settlement of dispute. In *Sitanna* v *Marivada Viranna*[25] it has observed:

> "Reference to a villiage Panchayat is the time-honoured method of deciding disputes of this kind, and has these advantage, that it is comparatively easy for the panchayatdars to ascertain the true facts, and that, as in this case, it avoids protracted litigation which, as observed by one of the witnesses, might have proved ruinous to the estate. Looking at the whole their Lordships see no reason for doubting that the award was a fair and honest settlement of a doubtful claim based both and an legal and moral grounds, and are therefore of opinion that there is no grounds for interfering with it."

Great Scholar S.N. Agarwal in his book *Gandhian Constitution of India*,[26] advocated for establishment of Nyaya Panchyat in the following words to provide justice at the door step:

> The Gram Panchayat shall be entrusted with the dispensing of justice; no separate judicial Panchayats are necessary. The poor peasant need not go out of his village, spend hard-earned money and waste weeks and months in towns on litigation. He can get all the necessary witnesses in the village and fight out his own case without being exploited by lawyers. When intricate points of law arise, sub-judge from the Taluka or District could come down to the village and assist the panchyat in deciding difficult cases. The sub-judge shall also act as friend, philosopher and guide, to the ignorant villagers by acquainting them with the laws of the State. Such a judicial system will not only be simple

25 AIR 1934 PC 105.

26 Quoted by K.N. Chandrasekhran Pillai in his Article *Criminal Jurisdiction of Nyaya Panchayats*, Journal of the Indian Law Institute, vol. XIX, pp. 440-481.

and cheap but also 'just' because the details of civil and criminal cases will be, more or less, open secrets in the village and there shall be hardly any scope for fraud and juggleries.

Provision of Appeal

Sl. No.	Name of the Act	Name of Revisional Authority	Period of Limitation
1.	Himachal Pradesh Nyaya Panchayat Act 1994.	Judicial Magistrate/ Civil Judge (Senior Division)/Collector.	30 days from the date of order.
2.	Jammu & Kashmir Panchayat Raj Act 1989.	District and Sessions Judge.	60 days from the date of order.
3.	Bihar Gram Kachahari Conduct Rules 2007.	Full Bench of Gram Kachahari.	30 days from the date of order of judgment of the Bench of the Gram Kachahari.
4.	Kerala Village Courts Act 1960.	Sub-Divisional Magistrate/ District Magistrate.	30 days from the date of order.
5.	Himachal Pradesh Panchayati Raj Act 1970.	Full Bench of Panchas.	30 days from the date of order under appeal.
6.	Chattisgarh Gram Nyayalaya Adhiniyam 1996.	Civil Judge / Judicial Magistrate.	30 days from the date of order/ judgment.
7.	Gram Nyayalayas Act 2008.	District Judge / Sessions Judge.	30 days from the date of order/ judgment.

Provision for Revision

Sl. No.	Name of the Act	Name of Revisional Authority	Period of Limitation
1.	Uttar Pradesh Panchayati Raj Act 1947. (There is no provision for Appeal).	Sub-Divisional Magistrate.	60 days from the date of order.
2	Delhi Panchayati Raj Act 1954.	Additional District Magistrate.	60 days from the date of order.
3.	Himachal Pradesh Panchayati Raj Act 1970. (There is also Provision for Appeal).	Subordinate Judge.	60 days from the date of order.
4.	Rajasthan Panchayat Act 1953.	Magistrate of the first class.	30 days from the date of order.

Evaluation—working of Nyaya Panchayat Critics attacked the appointment of members of presiding officers of the Nyaya Panchayat on the ground that the appointment is guided by the political influences and their appointment is against the principle of separation of power.

Great scholar M.P. Jain while evaluating the working of the Nyaya Panchayat says:[27] "The revival of the ancient institution of Panchayats as an instrument of local self-Government may be justified on the basis of the theory of participatory democracy. But the question has been discussed over and over again whether the Panchayats should be given some judicial powers or not. For the present, the participation of village Panchayats in the administration of justice is still in an experimental stage. Speaking generally, their civil powers are confined to simple matters of small value and minor offences. Also, lawyers are barred from appearing before them. But opinion on the efficacy of Nyaya Panchayats as a judicial institution is divided. Proponents of Nyaya Panchayats argue that they provide a cheap and expeditious mechanism to settle disputes with people's participation and, to the extent these Panchayats dispose of cases, they provide relief to the ordinary courts and help in expediting judicial work. The Nyaya Panchayats are seen as a solution to the problem of mounting arrears of cases before the courts. But, on the other hand, views have been expressed that Panchayats are faction-ridden; all kind of factions based on caste, community, personal or political considerations arise compromising the impartiality of Panchayat members and, thus, the efficacy of Nyaya Panchayats is eroded."

Again he says:[28] "It may be a great desideratum to have a regular system of village courts manned by trained personnel, but this does not seem to be within the realm of possibility in the near future as no State wants to spend large funds on administration of justice. Today, justice is urban based. This situation needs to be corrected by taking justice near to the door

27 M.P. Jain, *Outlines of Indian Legal History*, 5th Ed., Reprint 1996, p. 242.
28 *Ibid*, p. 245.

steps of the people otherwise justice will continue to be denied to large numbers of poor people. Therefore, to provide a semblance of justice, Nyaya Panchayats in some form have to be created on the basis of participation by the people."

However, if the Nyaya Panchayat discharges his function in a proper angle to resolve the small and petty cases the burden of court will be relaxed and the litigants will be seen the fate of his case. For this realization the members of the Nyaya Panchayat will be free from :

(*a*) political influences;

(*b*) other extraneous force;

(*c*) elite approach;

(*d*) procedural nitty gritty;

(*e*) strict rules of evidence;

(*f*) social prejudices etc.

But they must be guided by the rule of law, the principles of natural justice and justice, equity and fair play.

Chapter 9

Fast Track Court

Historical retrospective 13th Finance Commission in its report categorically viewed that improvement of justice delivery system is a critical component of the initiative to ensure better outputs and outcomes. At present 14,000 Districts and subordinate courts in the country are disposing off both important as well as petty cases. The pressure on judicial time on account of petty cases can be relieved by allowing them to morning/evening courts/ courts of special judicial or Metropolitan Magistrates. At present, Indian Courts are over-burdened. In the assessment of L.N. Singhi, Senior Advocate of Supreme Court of India:[1]

> "Increasing institution of cases, mounting arrears, accumulating congestion in courts and inevitable law's delays have given rise not to a body of scientific and rational blueprints in terms of institutional organization and procedural methods or in terms of assessments of judicial manpower requirements, but to a spate of alarm signals and dire shibboleths. If there are more and more cases in courts, that is because we have a population explosion, we have a more complex and friction-prone society, our dispute resolution and conciliation system are bereft of efficacy, we have increasingly greater awareness of rights, and perhaps because we have more injustice and more arbitrariness in our midst. The Government are under an

1 (2004)10 Scale Jour 22.

obligation to provide an adequate machinery for justice, to appoint more judges and to give them better emoluments and facilities, to build more courthouses, to enact better laws, to devise better dispute resolution procedures, and to administer more effectively and equitably, rather than to blame lawyers and judges for the increase and proliferation of litigation. Courts in India cannot apply a mechanical-statistical razorblade or wave a magic wand to wipe out the enormous pendency of arrears. Nor can the court afford to turn a blind eye or a deaf ear to the rank injustices and incongruities of administration merely because they have already too much on their hands. If the courts begin to do that systematically, they might endanger the confidence and credibility they have come to enjoy."

At present, near about 40 lakh cheque bounced cases are pending in various courts in our country. It is our common experience that cheque bounces cases and other criminal cases took average 2-3 years time to get the final result. In the words of Hon'ble Justice A.R. Lakhann, "long delays in courts causes great hardship not only to the accused but even to the victim and the State. The accused, who is not let out on bail, may remain in jail for number of months or even years awaiting conclusion of the trial. Thus, effort is required to be made to improve the management of the prosecution in order to increase the certainty of conviction and punishment for most serious offenders. It is experienced that there is increasing laxity in the court work by the police personnel, empowered to investigate the case." He again says:

"Judiciary today is more deserving of public confidence than ever before. The judiciary has a special role to play in the task of achieving social-economic goals enshrined in the Constitution while maintaining their aloofness and independence; the Judges have to be aware of the social changes in the task of achieving socio-economic justice for the people. The Indian Judicial system is constantly exposed to new challenges, new dimensions and new signals and has to survive in a world in which perhaps the only real certainty is that the circumstances of tomorrow will not be the same as those of today. The need of the hour is to correct misconception about the Judiciary by making it more accessible and more explicit, by utilizing the resources available to improve the service to the public, by reducing delays and making courts more efficient and less daunting."[2]

K.G. Balakrishnan, Hon'ble Former Chief Justice says:[3] "The criminal justice system in the country is designed to protect the citizens of this country from the onslaught of criminal activities of a section of the community which indulges in such acts. The outcome of any criminal justice system must be to inspire confidence and create an attitude of respect for the rule of law. An efficient criminal justice system is one of the cornerstones of good governance. When we think of criminal justice system it consists of the police, prosecuting agency, various courts, the jail and the host of other institutions connected with the system. The State as a guardian of fundamental rights of its citizens is duty-bound to ensure speedy trial and avoid excessively long delays in trial of criminal cases that could result in grave miscarriage of justice. It is in the interest of all concerned that the guilt of innocence of the accused is determined as quickly as possible. But, unfortunately, there are a large number of cases pending in various courts. Various factors contribute to large pendency of criminal cases in the subordinate courts. Speedy trial of criminal cases should be recognized as an urgent need of the present judicial system in order to decide the fate of lakhs of litigants, it will help enhance the faith of genera public in the present judicial system. In order to have a strong socio-economic system, it is important that each and every state of trial of an accused should move at reasonably fast pace..."

Law Commission of India—recommendation The Law Commission of India in its 213th Report advocated for establishment of fast track court for cheque bounce cases, i.e. offence committed under s. 138 of Negotiable Instruments Act, to provide actual fruit or the benefit of this section to the payee of the cheque. The Law Commission recommended that:[4]

2 *Voice of Justice* by Justice A.R. Lakshmanan, Ed. 2006, pp. 245-250.

3 http.#Supreme Cout to in India.nic.in speeches 2007.

4 213th Report, Law Commission of India, p. 21.

(*a*) Fast Track Courts of Magistrate should be created to dispose of the dishonoured cheque cases under s. 138 of the Negotiable Instruments Act 1881;

(*b*) The Central Government and State Governments must provide necessary funds to meet the expenditure involved in the creation of Fast Track Courts, supporting staff and other infrastructure.

Fast Track Court for Sessions' Triable Cases 11th Finance Commission allotted ₹502.90 crores for the purpose of setting up of 1734 courts in various courts to deal with long pendency cases particularly Sessions cases. In *All India Judges' Association* v *Union of India*,[5] the Hon'ble Justice B.N. Kripal observed that an independent and efficient judicial system is one of the basic structure of our Constitution. If sufficient number of judges are not appointed, justice would not be available to the people, thereby undermining the basic structure. It is well known that justice delayed is justice denied. Time and again the inadequacy in the number of judges as adversely being commented upon.

Supreme Court on Fast Track Court The Supreme Court in *Brijmohanlal* v *Union of India*,[6] gives a total parameter regarding manner and mode of appointment of judges and other functionaries for the smooth sailing and functions of the Fast Track Courts in the following manner:

Directions by the court (1) The first preference for appointment of judges of the Fast Track Courts is to be given by *ad hoc* promotions from amongst eligible judicial officers. While giving such promotion, the High Court shall follow the procedures in force in the matter of promotion to such posts in Superior/Higher Judicial Services.

(2) The second preference in appointments to Fast Track Courts shall be given to retired judges who have good service records with no adverse comments in their ACRs, so far as judicial acumen, reputation regarding honesty, integrity and character are concerned. Those who were not given the benefit of two

5 (2002)4 SCC 247; JT 2002(3) SC 503; (2002)3 Scale 291.
6 (2002)5 SCC 1; AIR 2002 SC 2096; JT 2002(4) SC 605.

years' extension of the age of superannuation, shall not be considered for appointment. It should be ensured that they satisfy the conditions laid down in Arts. 233(2) and 309 of the Constitution. The High Court concerned shall take a decision with regard to the minimum-maximum age of eligibility to ensure that they are physically fit for the work in Fast Track Courts.

(3) No judicial officer who was dismissed or removed or compulsorily retired or made to seek retirement shall be considered for appointment under the Scheme. Judicial officers who have sought voluntary retirement after initiation of departmental proceedings/inquiry shall not be considered for appointment.

(4) The third preference shall be given to members of the Bar for direct appointment in these courts. They should be preferably in the age group of 35-45 years, so that they could aspire to continue against the regular posts if the Fast Track Courts ease to function. The question of their continuance in service shall be reviewed periodically by the High Court based on their performance. They may be absorbed in regular vacancies, if subsequent recruitment takes place and their performance in the Fast Track Courts is found satisfactory. For the initial selection, the High Court shall adopt such methods of selection as are normally followed for selection of members of the Bar as direct recruits to the Superior/Higher Judicial Services.

(5) Overall preference for appointment in Fast Track Courts shall be given to eligible officers who are on the verge of retirement subject to they being physically fit.

(6) The recommendation for selection shall be made by a committee of at least three Judges of the High Court, constituted by the Chief Justice of the High Court concerned in this regard. The final decision in the matter shall be taken by the Full Court of the High Court.

(7) After *ad hoc* promotion of judicial officers to the Fast Track Courts, the consequential vacancies shall be filled up immediately by organizing a special recruitment drive. Steps should be taken in advance to initiate process for selection to fill

up these vacancies much before the judicial officers are promoted to the Fast Track Courts, so that vacancies may not be generated at the lower levels of the subordinate judiciary. The High Court and the State Government concerned shall take prompt steps to fill up the consequential as well as existing vacancies in the subordinate courts on priority basis. The State Government concerned shall take necessary decisions within a month from the receipt of the recommendations made by the High Court.

(8) Priority shall be given by the Fast Track Courts for disposal of those sessions cases which are pending for the longest period of time, and/or those involving undertrials. Similar shall be the approach for civil cases, *i.e.* old cases shall given priority.

(9) While the staff of a regular Court of Additional District and Sessions Judge includes a Sessions Clerk and an Office Peon, work in Fast Track Courts is reported to be adversely affected due to shortage of staff as compared to regular courts performing same or similar functions. When single Orderly or Clerk proceeds on leave, work in Fast Track Courts gets held up. The staff earmarked for each such court are a Peshkar/ Superintendent, a Stenographer and an Orderly. If the staff is inadequate, the High Court and the State Government shall take appropriate decision to appoint additional staff who can be accommodated within the savings out of the existing allocation by the Central Government.

(10) Provisions for the appointment of Public Prosecutor and Process Server have not been made under the Fast Track Courts Scheme. A Public Prosecutor is necessary for effective functioning of the Fast Track Courts. Therefore, a Public Prosecutor may be earmarked for each such court and the expenses or the same shall be borne out of the allocation under the head "Fast Track Courts". Process service shall be done through the existing mechanism.

(11) A State Level Empowered Committee headed by the Chief Secretary of the States all monitor the setting up of earmarked number of Fast Track Courts an smooth functioning of such courts in each State, as per the guidelines already issued by the Government of India.

(12) The State Government shall utilize the funds allocated under the Fast Track Courts Scheme promptly and will not withhold any such funds or divert them to other uses. They shall send the utilization certificates from time to time to the Central Government, who shall ensure immediate release of funds to the State Governments on receipt of required utilization certificates.

(13) At least one Administrative Judge shall be nominated in each High Court to monitor the disposal of cases by Fast Track Courts and to resolve the difficulties and shortcomings, if any, with the administrative support and cooperation of the State Government concerned. The State Government shall ensure requisite cooperation to the Administrative Judge.

(14) No right will be conferred on judicial officers in service for claiming any regular promotion on the basis of his/her appointment on *ad hoc* basis under the Scheme. The service rendered in Fast Track Courts will be deemed as service rendered in the parent cadre. In case any judicial officer is promoted to higher grade in the parent cadre during his tenure in Fast Track Courts, the service rendered in Fast Track Courts will be deemed to be service in such higher grade.

(15) The retired judicial officers who are appointed under the Scheme shall be entitled to pay and allowances equivalent to the pay and allowance they were drawing at the time of their retirement, minus total amount of pension drawn/payable as per rules.

(16) Persons appointed under the Scheme shall be governed, for the purpose of leave, reimbursement of medical expenses, TA/DA, conduct rules and such other service benefits, by the rules and regulations which are applicable to the members of the judicial services of the State of equivalent status.

(17) The High Court concerned shall periodically review the functioning of the Fast Track Courts and in case of any deficiencies and/or shortcoming, take immediate remedial measures, taking into account views of the Administrative Judge nominated.

(18) The High Court and the State Government shall ensure that there exists no vacancy so far as the Fast Track Courts are

concerned, and necessary steps in that regard shall be taken within three months from today. In other words, steps should be taken to set up all the Fast Track Courts within the stipulated time.

Views of Dr. Manmohan Singh, the then PM Dr. Manmohan Singh, the then Hon'ble Prime Minister of India on the inauguration ceremony of the conference of Chief Ministers and Chief Justices of High Courts on administration of justice on Fast Track Court on 8.4.2007 categorically viewed that "Fast Track Courts are another answer to dealing with the problem of arrears. Though the initial scheme of Fast Track Courts was to end in the year 2005, our Government has extended it to the year 2010, providing Central support to the States. The Government has provided ₹509 crores for this purpose. I have been, however, informed that receipt of utilisation reports from the States in this regard is not very satisfactory and hence, there are delays in disbursal. I sincerely hope the State Government will take note of this and speed up procedures to ensure smooth flow of Central assistance for this very important purpose."[7]

Views of Hon'ble CJI Justice K.G. Balakrishnan (the then Hon'ble Chief Justice) while addressing at the joint conference of Chief Ministers and Chief Justices at Bigyan Bhawan, New Delhi on 8.4.2010 expressed his view that "So far backlog in subordinate courts is concerned, additional courts must be created and additional judicial officers must be appointed till the backlog is cleared. *Ad hoc* judges under Art. 224A of the Constitution should be appointed to clear the backlog in the High Courts for a period of five years or till the backlog is cleared. All the cases which are pending in the High Court for two years or more can be allotted to these *ad hoc* judges. Since the annual institution in the High Courts as well as in subordinate courts exceeds their respective annual disposal, additional judges in the High Courts as well as in subordinate courts should be appointed on permanent basis to deal with the increase in institution over the disposal."[8]

7 (2007)4 SCC Jour 9 (at 11).
8 (2007)4 SCC Jour 13 (at 18).

Malimath Committee on arrear of cases The Malimath Committee also recommended for working out of an arrear eradication scheme for disposal of cases pending for more than 2 years. The scheme provides identification of the cases are can be summarily disposed off under s. 262 and also petty cases under s. 206 as well as cases which are compoundable under s. 320 of the Code of Criminal Procedure.

In subordinate courts 8465632 number of civil cases are pending and 20230409 criminal cases are pending.[9] In High Courts, 3079708 civil cases and 1164280 criminal cases are pending[10] and 55,588 cases are pending in the Supreme Court.[11] So, a huge number of cases are pending in the subordinate courts. So it is very difficult to dispose off all the cases by the subordinate regular courts. So it is necessary to set up the Fast Track Civil Courts and Criminal Courts both as Civil Judge (Senior Division) and Civil Judge (Junior Division) as well as Magistrate level for disposal of those cases.

9 Court News (October-December, 2017) vol. XII. Issue No. 4, p. 7.
10 Court News (October-December, 2017) vol. XII Issue No. 4, p. 6.
11 Court News (October-December, 2017) vol. XII Issue No. 4, p. 5.

Chapter 10

Fast Track Arbitration

Meaning Fast Track Arbitration is the method of accelerating the disposition or arbitration cases in an effort to settle the matter in a short time as far as practicable. It is a quick way to achieve the disposal of arbitration matter. ICADR[1] defines it as a form of arbitration in which the arbitration award is rendered in particularly short time and at reduced cost.

Features of Fast Track Arbitration

(*i*) The parties to an action is agreed to resolve the matter by Fast Track Arbitration.

(*ii*) Such agreement should be in writing.

(*iii*) Such agreement may be made at any time before or at the time of appointment of the arbitral tribunal.

(*iv*) Fast Track Arbitral Tribunal shall consist of a sole Arbitrator.

(*v*) Such Arbitrator shall be chosen by parties unanimously.

(*vi*) A word must be passed within six months from the date of the Constitution of the Fast Track Arbitral Tribunal.

Procedure[2] (1) Within fifteen days of the constitution of the Fast Track Arbitral Tribunal, the person who raised the dispute

1 Brochure of the International Centre for Alternative Dispute Resolution, p. 18.

2 17th Report of the Law Commission of India.

(hereinafter referred to as the claimant) shall send simultaneously to the tribunal and the opposite parties (hereinafter referred to as the respondents)—

(*a*) a claim statement containing the facts, the points in issue and the relief claimed;

(*b*) documentary evidence, if any, in support of his case;

(*c*) where reliance is placed on the testimony of any witness (including that of a party) a copy of the witness's affidavit in writing;

(*d*) where reliance is placed on the opinion of an expert, the particulars relating to that expert, his qualifications and experience, and a copy of his opinion;

(*e*) list of interrogatories, if any;

(*f*) application for discovery or production of documents, if any, mentioning their relevancy;

(*g*) full address, including e-mail of fax, telephone numbers, if any, of all claimants and of all the parties, for the purpose of expediting communication and correspondence;

(*h*) any other material considered relevant by the applicant.

(2) The respondent shall, within fifteen days after receipt of the claim statement and the documents referred to in sub-para. (1) simultaneously send to the Fast Track Arbitral Tribunal as well as to the claimant, his defence statement, together with documentary evidence, witness testimony by affidavit (including that of a party) and expert opinion, if any, in support thereof, together with counter claims, if any, supported by documents.

(3) The procedure specified in this Schedule shall apply to such counter claims as they apply to a claim.

(4) Within fifteen days of the receipt of the defence statement or of the counter claims, the claimant shall send to the Fast Track Arbitral Tribunal and to the respondents his rejoinder and statement of defence to the counter claim.

(5) Within fifteen days of the receipt of the defence statement the counter claim, the respondent shall simultaneously send his

rejoinder to the said statement, to the Fast Track Arbitral Tribunal as well as to the claimant.

(6) In case of discovery or production of documents is allowed, the parties shall be permitted to submit their supplementary statements, if any, to the Fast Track Arbitral Tribunal within a specified period and to simultaneously send copies therof to each other.

(7) The Fast Track Arbitral Tribunal shall decide the disputes on the basis of the pleadings and documents, affidavits of evidence, expert opinion, if any, and the written submission filled by the parties.

(8) The Fast Track Arbitral Tribunal may permit any witness to be orally questioned and lay down the manner in which evidence shall be recorded or for receiving affidavits in lieu of oral evidence.

(9) The Fast Track Arbitral Tribunal may otherwise permit oral evidence to be adduced, if it considers that any request for oral evidence by any party is justified or where the Fast Track Arbitral Tribunal itself considers that such oral evidence is necessary.

(10) The Fast Track Arbitral Tribunal may, in addition, call for any further information or clarification from the parties in addition to the pleadings, documents and evidence placed before it.

Representation by counsel The Fast Track Arbitral Tribunal shall permit the parties to appear and conduct the case personally or through their counsel or by any person duly authorized by the parties to represent them.

Written notes of arguments or oral arguments After the conclusion of the evidence, the Fast Track Arbitral Tribunal may direct all the parties to file their written notes of argument or may, at its discretion, in addition permit oral arguments and shall fix a time schedule therefore and may also restrict the length of oral arguments.

Conduct of proceedings (1) The Fast Track Arbitral Tribunal shall conduct proceedings in such a manner that the arbitral proceedings are, as far as possible, taken up day after day, at least continuously for three days on each occasion.

(2) The Fast Track Arbitral Tribunal shall ordinarily fix the time schedule in such a manner so that the proceedings may be conducted continuously from 10.30 A.M. to 1 P.M. and 2 P.M. to 4.30 P.M. every day.

Parties to be bound by the procedure and time schedule The time schedule fixed under paragraphs 3 and 5 and the procedure specified under paragraph 6 by Fast Track Arbitral Tribunal, shall be binding on the parties.

Consultation of experts (1) At any time during the course of arbitration and before the passing of the award, the Fast Track Arbitral Tribunal may, at its discretion, if need be, consult any expert or technically qualified person or a qualified accountant for assistance in relation to the subject-matter in dispute, at the expense of the parties, and shall communicate the report of the above said person to the parties to enable them to file their response.

(2) If the Fast Track Arbitral Tribunal considers on its own or on the request of parties that any clarification or examination of the above said persons referred to in sub-paragraph (1) or examination of any other person is necessary, it may call upon the said person to clarify in writing or to call him or such other person as a witness for necessary examination.

In case there is default on the part of any party to adhere to the time limits specified in this Schedule or are fixed by the Fast Track Arbitral Tribunal or there is violation of any interim orders or directions of the Fast Track Arbitral Tribunal issued under s. 17 or under this Schedule, the Fast Track Arbitral Tribunal may pass peremptory orders against the defaulting party giving further time for compliance including peremptory orders to provide appropriate security in connection with an interim order or direction.

In case the Fast Track Arbitral Tribunal is satisfied that a party to the arbitration is unduly or deliberately delaying the arbitral proceedings, or the implementation of the peremptory orders, the Fast Track Arbitral Tribunal may impose such costs as it may deem fit on the defaulting party or may pass an order striking out the pleadings of the party concerned or excluding material or draw adverse inference against the said party and in case security for costs of arbitration is not furnished the claim may be dismissed.

The Fast Track Arbitral Tribunal may dismiss the claim if the claimant does not effectively prosecute the arbitral proceedings or file the papers within the time granted or neglects or refuses to obey the peremptory orders of the tribunal or to pay the dues or deposits as ordered by the Fast Track Arbitral Tribunal.

If the opposite party does not file its defence or does not effectively prosecute its defence or file the paper within the time granted or refuses to obey the peremptory orders of the tribunal, the Fast Track Arbitral Tribunal may make an *ex parte* award.

The Fast Track Arbitral Tribunal shall pass an award within six months from the date of the constitution of the Fast Track Arbitral Tribunal or within such extended periods as specified.

The parties may, by consent, extend the period by a further period not exceeding three months.

If the Fast Track Arbitration Award is not made within the period specified under sub-paragraph (1) and the period agreed to by the parties under sub-paragraph (2), the arbitration proceeding shall, subject to the provisions of sub-paragraph (4), stand suspended until an application for extension is made to the High Court by any party to the Fast Track Arbitration or where none of the parties makes an application as foresaid, until such an application is made by the arbitral tribunal.

Position after Amendment Act 2015 By the Arbitration and Conciliation (Amendment) Act 2015 it was statutorily provided that in case of Fast Track arbitration the Arbitral Tribunal shall as far as possible hold oral hearing for the presentation of evidence and for oral argument on day to day basis and proceedings shall be conducted on the basis of documents and other materials. Such tribunal shall not grant an adjournment unless sufficient cause is made out. The tribunal is also empowered to impose cost including exemplary cost on the party seeking adjournment without any sufficient cause. But there is no time limit for approaching the court for seeking extension of time so it may cause delay. It is provided in the Statute that the award shall be made within a period of 12 months, but in case of complex disputes the resolution or adjudication of disputes may not be possible to address within this time frame.

The parties to an arbitration agreement, may, at any stage either before or at the time of appointment of the arbitral tribunal, agree in writing to have their dispute resolved by fast track procedure.[3] The parties to the arbitration agreement, while agreeing for resolution of dispute by fast track procedure, may agree that the arbitral tribunal shall consist of a sole Arbitrator who shall be chosen by the parties.[4]

Procedure The arbitral tribunal shall follow the following procedure while conducting arbitration proceedings:[5]

(*a*) The arbitral tribunal shall decide the dispute on the basis of written pleadings, documents and submissions filed by the parties without any oral hearing;

(*b*) The arbitral tribunal shall have power to call for any further information or clarification from the parties in addition to the pleadings and documents filed by them;

(*c*) An oral hearing may be held only, if all the parties make a request or if the arbitral tribunal considers it necessary to have oral hearing for clarifying certain issues;

(*d*) The arbitral tribunal may dispense with any technical formalities, if an oral hearing is held, and adopt such procedure as deemed appropriate for expeditious disposal of the case.

Time limit The award shall be made within a period of six months from the date the arbitral tribunal enters upon the reference.[6]

3 Section 29B(1), Arbitration and Conciliation Act 1996.
4 Section 29B(2).
5 Section 29B(3).
6 Section 29B(4).

Extension of time If the award is not made within the specified period, the parties may, by consent, extend the said period for making award for a further period not exceeding six months. But if the award is not made within the said period of six months or the extended period, the mandate of the Arbitrator(s) shall terminate unless the court has, either prior to or after the expiry of the period so specified, extended the period. While extending the period, if the court finds that the proceedings have been delayed for the reasons attributable to the arbitral tribunal, then, it may order reduction of fees of Arbitrator(s) by not exceeding five per cent. for each month of such delay. The extension of period may be on the application of any of the parties and may be granted only for sufficient cause and on such terms and conditions as may be imposed by the court. While extending the period, it shall be open to the court to substitute one or all of the Arbitrators and if one or all of the Arbitrators are substituted, the arbitral proceedings shall continue from the stage already reached and on the basis of the evidence and material already on record, and the Arbitrator(s) appointed under this section shall be deemed to have received the said evidence and material.[7]

An application filed for extension of period shall be disposed of by the court as expeditiously as possible and endeavour shall be made to dispose of the matter within a period of sixty days from the date of service of notice on the opposite party.[8]

7 Section 29B(5) and sub-secs. (3) to (6) of s. 29A.
8 Section 29A(9).

Chapter 11

Lokpal

Lokpal—meaning The concept of lokpal is synonymous with the word ombudsman. Literally it means an agent or a delegate. The new *International Webster's Comprehensive Dictionary*[1] defines ombudsman as a Governmental official appointed to receive and report grievances against the Government. According to *Black's Law Dictionary*,[2] Ombudsman is an official appointed to receive, investigate and report on private citizen's complaints about the Government. Ombudsman serves as an alternative to the adversary system for resolving disputes especially between citizens and Government agencies. An ombudsman is an independent and non-partisan officer of the legislature who supervises the administration or one who deals with specific complaints from the public against administrative injustice and maladministration and one who has the power to investigate, criticize and publicize, but not to reverse administration action.

Historical retrospective The concept of ombudsman is old like a heel. In ancient China, the ombudsman is like an institution, like congressional ombudsman was established in the year 221 B.C. Even in the Muslim world we find the existence of ombudsman. In Sweden ombudsman was established or created in 1809. Subsequently, Finland in the year 1990, Denmark in

1 *International Webster's Comprehensive Dictionary*, Encyclopedic Edition, 2003, p. 881.

2 *Black's Law Dictionary*, 8th Ed., p. 1115.

the year 1952 and Norway in the year 1963 appointed ombudsman for protection of the individual citizen from tyranny and impersonal depotism of administrator or against the administrative abuse and misuse of power of modern bureaucrats. In Sweden, Denmark and Norway the legislature selected him and he is accountable to the legislature. In Sweden and Finland the Ombudsman can also proceed against the wrong decision of a Judge, even though he is not the appellate authority. In Finland, the ombudsman was also empowered to penalize a cabinet minister. The great scholar and legal luminary Justice P.B. Mukharji in his *New Jurisprudence* criticizes the establishment of ombudsman where the ministerial responsibility to parliament or legislature prevailed and he says:[3]

> "The countries which adopted it originally are not countries where ministerial responsibility to Parliament or Legislature prevailed. Because the ministers were not responsible to Parliament therefore the need for that institution was felt in those countries. To introduce such an innovation will be against the principle of Parliamentary supremacy and democracy and responsible Government where ministerial responsibility is to Parliament and to law courts alone. Secondly, it seriously and virtually prejudices the rule of law and equality of law where independent judiciary and independent judicial system operate. To say that the Ombudsman will proceed against ministers or judges is to dethrone the supremacy of Parliament and the supremacy of the court. England therefore did not accept the institution of Ombudsman as such but only created a Parliamentary Commissioner for grievances, the essence of whose duty is only to receive complaints, and put them forward to the representative members of Parliament or the local M.P. to redress such grievances. Lastly, as a type of administrative tribunal, the institution of Ombudsman is bound to fail and cannot succeed in a country of the complexity both in size and administration and of the variety or problems as in India."

3 Mukharjee on the *New Jurisprudence, the Grammar of Modern Law* (Tagore Law Lectures), 1970, p. 296; see also 2nd Ed., pp. 366-367.

In short, the ground against the establishment of the ombudsman are as follows:

The countries where the institutions like ombudsman was introduced; (1) ministers are not answerable to the parliament or legislature; (2) it is against the principles of parliamentary democracy and supremacy; (3) it is virtually prejudices the rules of law and the equality of law; (4) it de-thrones the supremacy of Parliament and supremacy of the court.

Reason for establishment of ombudsman Dr. D.R. Saxena in his Article, *The Principles of Ombudsman and the Lokpal Bill, 1985: Some observations*, classically explained the reasons for establishment of ombudsman like an institution in the following words:

"(*a*) The modern State has assumed an enormous multitude of functions as the result of social and welfare legislations, affecting the lives and property of every one.

(*b*) The activities of public administration have become so comprehensive and the power of the bureaucracy so great that the legal status of the individual needs additional protection.

(*c*) The legislature traditionally concerned with the observance of laws and ruling by public officials, has extensively delegated its powers to the administrative authorities and at the same time it is not proving competent enough to supervise the executive and administrators.

(*d*) The parliamentary debate is inadequate.

(*e*) History of mankind testifies that every democratic Government has to necessarily face the evil of corruption, nepotism and maladministration in whatever state it is practiced and at whatever times. A check against such evils will make democracy function more effectively than ever.

(*f*) Handling of grievances by executive is meaningless. In the present set up of our administration it is a necessity to have an office of ombudsman which will serve the purpose of an additional safeguard on the rights of the subject. Such an office will operate, not only as a check against the acts of the executive but also against the legislature in general.

(*g*) There being innumerable number of cases where the law provides no remedy for an aggrieved party. Administrative agencies may have within their structure, channels for complaint but such a system lacks impartiality.

(*h*) This ombudsman gives the citizen an expert and impartial agent without personal cost to the complaint, without the tension of adversary litigation and without requirement of counsel or the intervention of those highly placed.

(*i*) Presence of the ombudsman has psychological value. His office gives the citizen confidence that there exists a watch dog for them.

(*j*) Appointment of Ombudsman signifies the Government's desire to make sure that the Government official are not guilty of any injustice to any citizen and they refrain from arbitrary acts."

Need for Lokpal—why As the days rolled in, the modern thinkers felt the need for the institution as the system where parliamentary politics is inadequate to cope with the complexities of abuse or misuse of power by the modern bureaucrats.

Gradually, it was introduced in different European, American and Asian countries. In our country, the first Administrative Reforms Commission felt the need of this institution. The establishment of the Lokpal and the Lokayukta was felt in the early 60s. In the year 1970 Orissa, in the year 1971 Maharashtra, in the year 1973 Rajasthan, Bihar and in the year 1974 Uttar Pradesh introduced Lokayukta Bill. Orissa is the first State which introduced Lokayukta Act.

The then Hon'ble President of India Dr. A.P.J. Abdul Kalam at the inauguration of the VIII All India Conference of Lokayukta and Upa-Lokayukta at Dehradun on 27th September 2004 explained the need of this institution in the following manner:

> "The transparency and the goodness of implementation can be made visible either through technology or through an independent body providing an independent adjudicating and speedy settlement mechanism. To promote this visibility in the administration to all the participants of democracy, an independent body outside: the system is essential, since it is not desirable for one to judge his own actions. Lokayukta is expected to fill the need of this independent institution which is essential to maintain the vibrancy of a democracy with inbuilt self-imposed checks and balances. This mechanism will make the people belief that what is wrong, irregular will not be exonerated by Lokayukta who will be able to garner the trust, respect and yearning of the people and make such institution a household name."

The then Hon'ble Prime Minister Dr. Manmohan Singh at 8th Indian Conference Lokayukta and Up-lokayukta categorically says:

The establishment of the institutions of Lokayukta and Uplokayukta is part of an ongoing effort to provide clean, transparent and accountable Government to the people. Our struggle for independence too was also a struggle for good governance. Mahatma Gandhiji had understood the gathering crisis of corruption and prophesied that the public would need to be in the forefront in exposing corrupt practices and taking to task those who were involved in them. He wrote in Young India in 1928:

> "Corruption will be out one day, however much one may try to conceal it; and the public can, as its right and duty, in every case of justifiable suspicion, call its servants to strict account, dismiss them, sue them in a law court or appoint an arbitrator or inspector or scrutinize their conduct, as it likes".

Brief history of Lokpal in India In order to provide transparent Government Administrative Reforms Commission was established under the Chairmanship of Sri Morarji Desai. In view of the report of the said Commission, Lokpal Bill was tabled on the Parliament on May 1968 and the Lok Sabha give 'no' to the Bill on 20th August 1969. Subsequently, the Bill was sent to Rajya Sabha for the approval of the Rajya Sabha but in the meantime 4th Lok Sabha was dissolved. Again the Bill was introduced in the Lok Sabha on 11th April 1971, but the Bill was not passed because the Lok Sabha was dissolved in the year 1977. In the year 1977 Janata Government came into power in the Center and State Government actively considered the re-introduction of the Bill regarding the Lokpal. Again the Bill was re-introduced on 28th July 1977. Then the Bill was sent to Joint Committee of the Parliament, again the Bill was tabled on the Parliament with the report of the Joint Committee on May 1979. But after dissolving the Lok Sabha in the year 1979, Lokpal Bill did not see the light of Act. Again, the Lokpal Bill was introduced in the Lok Sabha by the then Law Minister Asok Kumar Sen on 26th August 1985. The Government felt the necessity for the establishment of the Lokpal on the ground that the responsibility of good and transparent Government of the people of the country lies with the elected representative. It can be made visible either through an individual body or through technology or through an individual body providing an individual and adjudicating and speedy settlement mechanism or both.

In 2002 the Commission to "Review of the Working of the Constitution" under the Chairmanship of M.N. Venkatachiliah has recommended for appointment of Lokpal at the Centre and of Lokayukata for the states to look into the allegations of corruption against administrators including legislators. In 2005 the second Administrative Reforms Commission also strongly recommended for establishment of Lokpal without delay. In 2011 Group of Ministers under the Chairmanship of Pranab Mukherjee suggested various measures to overcome corruption and had a re-look at the proposal for enactment of Lokpal Bill. On 8th April the Government constituted a Joint Drafting Committee. The Government introduced Lokpal Bill 2011 in the Lok Sabha on 4th August 2011 but was subsequently withdrawn. The Bill was referred to the department related Parliamentary Standing Committee on 8th August 2011 for examination and report. There was discussion over the Bill in both Houses of Parliament on 27th August 2011. The Lokpal and Lokayuktas Bill 2011 was introduced on 22nd December 2011 and passed by the Lok Sabha on 27th December 2011. The Bill was tabled in the Rajya Sabha on 29th December 2011 but it was referred to Select Committee of the Rajya Sabha. The Bill was passed by the Rajya Sabha on 17th December after certain amendments of the earlier Bill and it was passed by the Lok Sabha again on 18th December 2013. The Bill received the assent of the President of India on 1st January 2014 and came into force on and from 16th January 2014. The Lokpal and Lokayuktas and other related law (Amendment) Bill 2014 was introduced in the Lok Sabha on — to streamline and harmonise the provisions relating to furnishing of information on assets and liabilities by public servants. The Amendment Bill was referred to the Parliamentary Standing Committee on 25th December 2014 after it was introduced in the Lok Sabha on 18th December 2014. Thereafter, on 7th December 2015, the report of the Parliamentary Standing Committee was submitted and the Standing Committee has given some recommendations. The Lokpal and Lokayuktas (Amendment) Bill 2016 was introduced in Lok Sabha on 27th July 2016 by the Minister for Personnel, Public Grievances and Pensions, Dr. Jitendra Singh. It was passed by the Lok Sabha on 27th July 2016 and by Rajya Sabha on the next day. The Amendment Bill 2016 received the assent of the President of India on 29th July 2016 which was given retrospective effect from 16th January 2016.

The objects and reasons for the Legislation which highlight its unique character and importance in the contemporary world are as follows:

> "The need to have a legislation for Lokpal has been felt for the quite some time. In its interim report on the 'Problems of Redressal of Citizen's Grievances', submitted in 1966, the Administrative Reforms Commission, *inter alia*, recommended the setting up of an institution of Lokpal at the Centre. To give effect to this recommendation of the Administrative Reforms Commission, eight Bills on Lokpal were introduced in the Lok Sabha in the past. However, these Bills had lapsed consequent upon the dissolution of

the respective Lok Sabha; except in the case of 1985 bill, which was subsequently withdrawn after its introduction.

"India is committed to pursue the policy of 'Zero Tolerance against Corruption'. India ratified the United Nations Convention against Corruption by deposit of Instrument of Ratification on the 9th of May 2011. This Convention imposes a number of obligations, some mandatory, some recommendatory and some optional on the Member States. The Convention, *inter alia*, envisages that State Parties ensure measures in the domestic law for criminalization of offences relating to bribery and put in place an effective mechanism for its enforcement. The obligations of the Convention, with reference to India, have come into force with effect from the 8th of June 2011. As a policy of Zero tolerance against Corruption, the Bill seeks to establish in the country, a more effective mechanism to receive complaints relating to allegations of corruption against public servants, including Ministers, Members of Parliament, Chief Ministers, Members of Legislative Assemblies, public servants and to inquire into them and take follow up actions. The bodies, namely, Lokpal and Lokayuktas which are being set up for the purpose will be constitutional bodies. This setting up of these bodies will further strengthen the existing legal and institutional mechanism thereby facilitating a more effective implementation of some of the obligations under the aforesaid Convention."

Salient features of the Lokpal Bill 1985 The main features of the Lokpal Bill 1985 are as follows—

(1) Lokpal shall be appointed by the President of India after consultation with the Chief Justice of India.

(2) He should be qualified to be appointed as a Judge of the Supreme Court.

(3) Tenure of the Lokpal is five years.

(4) He must not be a member of Parliament or any State Legislature or hold any office of profit.

(5) Lokpal is empowered to investigate complaints which are punishable under the Indian Penal Code or Prevention of Corruption Act 1947.

(6) Lokpal's salary and other expenditure shall be meet from the consolidated fund of India.

(7) The removal procedure of the Lokpal is similar to Judges of the Supreme Court of India. He shall be removed only on the ground of proved misbehaviour or incapacity.

(8) Lokpal may enquire conduct of any persons other than the Union Ministers, Minister of State or Deputy Ministers or Parliamentary Secretaries of the Union.

(9) Complaints may be made to the Lokpal only by the citizens of India. Complaint must be supported by an affidavit along with prescribed fee.

(10) Lokpal may impose sentence of imprisonment upto six months or with fine if any persons intentionally insult or causes any obstruction to the functions of the Lokpal.

(11) The Lokpal can also punish a person who made a false complaint. The prescribed punishment is the imprisonment upto three years and fine which may extend to ₹50,000.

(12) The entire proceeding must be held *in camera*.

(13) Members of army, navy, air forces, Central and State Government, local bodies are outside the purview of the Lokpal.

(14) After the completion of the inquiry/investigation the Lokpal shall submit his report to the Prime Minister and Prime Minister will intimate Lokpal within three months from the date of receipt of the report about the action taken by him.

(15) The Lokpal also lay the consolidatory annual report to the President of India and the President of India within 90 days from the date of submission of report to him/her presents the same to the each Houses of the Parliament along with his/her explanatory note.

Features of Lokpal and Lokayuktas Act 2013 The Lokpal and Lokayuktas Act 2013 was enacted for the establishment of a body of Lokpal for the Union and Lokayuktas for States to inquire into allegations of corruption against certain public functionaries and for the matters connected therewith or incidental thereto. The features of the Lokpal and Lokayuktas Act 2013 are as follows:

(1) Lokpal shall be established at the Centre and Lokayuktas in the States.

(2) Lokpal shall consist of a chairperson and eight members. Fifty per cent of the members shall be Judicial members. The chairperson shall be a person who is or has been a Chief Justice of India or is or has been a judge of the Supreme Court or an eminent person.

(3) At least 50% of the members of the Lokpal shall be from amongst the persons belonging to the Scheduled Castes, the Scheduled Tribes, other Backward Classes and women.

(4) The chairperson or a member of the Lokpal shall not be a Member of Parliament or a member of a Legislature of any State or Union territory or shall not be convicted of any offence involving moral turpitude or must have completed the age of forty five years on the date of assuming office or shall not be a member of any Panchayat or Municipality or shall not hold any office of profit or trust or be connected with any political party or carry on own business or practice any profession.

(5) Chairperson and members shall be appointed by the President on the basis of recommendation of a Selection Committee.

(6) The Selection Committee of the Lokpal shall consist of the Prime Minister, Speaker of the House of the People, Leader of the Opposition in the House of the People, Chief Justice of India or a Judge of the Supreme Court nominated by him and an eminent person nominated by the President.

Chairperson and members are appointed for a term of five years from the date on which he enters upon his office or until he attains the age of seventy years, whichever is earlier.

(7) The Lokpal shall inquire or cause an inquiry to be conducted into any matter involved in or arising from or connected with any allegation of corruption made in a complaint in respect of offences under the Prevention of Corruption Act 1988 committed by the Prime Minister, present and former Union Ministers, present and former Member of Parliament, Group A, B, C, D officers, Chairperson or member or officer or employee of a company, society or trust set up by an Act of Parliament or wholly or partly financed by the Central Government or controlled by it, director, manager, secretary or other officer of association of persons that have received funding from the Government and have an annual income above a specified amount or have received public donation and have an annual income above a specified amount or received foreign funding above Rupees ten lakh a year.

(8) The Lokpal shall not inquire into any matter against the Prime Minister if the complaint relates to international relations, external and internal security, public order, atomic energy and space.

(9) An inquiry against the Prime Minister shall be held *in camera* and approved by at least two-thirds of the members of the Full Bench of the Lokpal. But if the Lokpal comes to the conclusion that the complaint deserves to be dismissed, the records of the inquiry shall not be published or made available to anyone.

(10) The Lokpal on receipt of a complaint, if it decides to proceed further, may order the preliminary inquiry by its inquiry wing or any agency including Delhi Special Police Establishment to ascertain whether there exists a *prima facie* case for proceeding in the matter.

(11) The inquiry wing or agency shall conduct a preliminary inquiry and submit report to the Lokpal within sixty days from the date of receipt of the reference. After consideration of the report the Lokpal shall: (*a*) order an investigation; (*b*) initiation of the departmental proceedings or (*c*) closure of the proceedings against the public servant and to proceed against the complainant for making a false and frivolous or vexatious complaint.

(12) Every preliminary inquiry shall ordinarily be completed within a period of ninety days from the date of receipt of the complaint but such period may be extended for a further period of ninety days.

(13) In case the Lokpal decides to proceed to investigate into the complaint, the investigation shall be completed within a period of six months from the date of its order.

(14) Lokpal has the power to grant sanction for prosecution.

(15) Lokpal has all powers of a civil court in certain matters.

(16) Lokpal may for the purpose of conducting any preliminary inquiry or investigation utilise the services of officers of Central or State Government.

(17) The Central Government shall constitute special courts as per recommendation of the Lokpal to hear and decide the cases arising out of the Prevention of Corruption Act 1988. The trial shall be completed within a maximum period of two years.

(18) Lokpal shall not inquire into any complaint made against the Chairman or any Member.

(19) The Chairman or any Member shall be removed from his office by order of the President on grounds of misbehaviour after the Supreme Court, on a reference being made to it by the President on a petition signed by at least one hundred Members of Parliament.

(20) Every public servant shall make a declaration of his assets and liabilities in prescribed form.

(21) No suit, prosecution or other legal proceedings shall lie against any public servant or the Lokpal or any officer, employee, agency in respect of anything done in good faith.

(22) The period of limitation for filing complaint before the Lokpal is seven years from the date of commission of the alleged offence.

(23) No civil court shall have jurisdiction in respect of any matter which the Lokpal is empowered by or under the Lokpal and Lokyakuta Act 2013 to determine.

(24) Legal assistance for defending a case before the Lokpal shall be provided to every person against whom complaint has been made before it, if such assistance is requested for.

(25) Every State shall establish a body to be known as the Lokayukta for the State to deal with complaints relating to corruption against certain public functionaries within a period of one year from the date of commencement of the Act.

Absence of primacy of opinion of Chief Justice of India or his nominee The absence of provisions in the Lokpal and Lokayuktas Act 2013 does not by itself render the Act *ultra vires* the basic structure of the Constitution.[4]

Non-availability of Leader of Opposition Sub-section (2) of s. 4 makes it clear that the appointment of Chairperson or a Member of the Lokpal will not become invalid merely because of the reason of any vacancy in the Selection Committee. If the Leader of Opposition is not available, surely, the Chairperson and the other two Members of the Selection Committee, namely, the Speaker of the Lok Sabha and the Chief Justice of India or his nominee may proceed to appoint an eminent jurist as a Member of the Selection Committee.[5]

Effect of Amendment made to Prevention of Corruption Act The amendment made to the Prevention of Corruption Act 1988 by the Lokpal and Lokayuktas Act 2013 applies to all accused charged with offences under this Act irrespective of the fact whether the action is initiated under the Lokpal and Lokayuktas Act 2013, or any other law.[6]

Workings The Act had been brought into force on 16th January, 2014 by a notification issued in the Official Gazette by the Government of India. Despite efflux of a long period of time the provisions of the Act have not been implemented. At present there is no Lokpal, Lokayukta or Uplokayukta in the States of

4 *Just Society* v *Union of India* AIR 2017 SC 2428.

5 *Common Cause: A Registered Society* v *Union of India* AIR 2017 SC 3084; (2017)7 SCC 158; (2017)5 Scale 333.

6 *Rakesh Kumar Paul* v *State of Assam* 2017(242) DLT 79; 2017(3) RCR (Cri) 996; 2017(3) UC 1756; (2017)9 Scale 24.

Jammu & Kashmir, Manipur, Puducherry, Sikkim, Telangana, Tripura and Arunachal Pradesh. Very recently the Hon'ble Supreme Court Bench consisting of Justice Ranjan Gogei (as his Lordship then was) and Justice Banumathi directed Chief Secretaries of States to file an affidavit explaining the steps taken to appointment of a Lokayukta and also specify the reason for delay or non-appointment. In short, non-implementation of the provisions of this Act sufficiently demonstrates the lack of executive/legislative will to give effect to a salutary enactment en-grafting a vital requirement of democratic functioning of the Government, namely, accountability of the political executive and those in high echelons of public office, to an independent body, i.e. Lokpal/Lokayukta.

Very recently, i.e. on March 2019 Justice Pinaki Chandra Ghose, a Former Supreme Court Judge was appointed as the country's first Lokpal, the anti-corruption ombudsman. Justice Dilip B. Bhosale, Pradip Kumar Mohanty, Abhilasha Kumari and Ajay Kumar Tripathi are the Judicial Members in the Lokpal. The non-judicial members are Dinesh Kumar Jain, Archana Ramasundaram, Mahender Singh and Dr. Indrajeet Prasad Gautam.

Chapter 12

Negotiation

Meaning The word negotiation is a noun and the word negotiate is a verb. In ordinary sense the expression negotiate means to confer or to bargain or to bring about an agreement or arrange a treaty by conferencing.[1] *Oxford Advanced Learner's Dictionary*[2] defines negotiation as a formal discussion between people who are trying to reach an agreement.

The word "negotiate" is a technical word and as used with reference to commercial paper, it is almost a word of art. It may be used in two senses, as meaning to discuss or arrange for a sale or bargain, or the preliminaries of a business transaction, and also to sell or discount negotiable paper, or assign or transfer it by endorsement or delivery. In law and law books, it is sometimes used in both senses. The word "negotiate" used in connection with business transactions ordinarily means to bargain with another respecting a transaction or to conduct communication or conferences with a view to reaching a settlement or agreement.[3] It is that what passes between the parties or their agents in course of or incident to the making of a contract and is also conversation in arranging terms of a contract. It also means "to discuss or arrange a sale or a bargain,

1 *Chambers 21st Century Dictionary*, p. 916.

2 *Oxford Advanced Learner's Dictionary*, p. 1020.

3 *Dev Kubai N. Mankar* v *Rajesh Builders* AIR 1997 Bom 142; 1997(1) Bom CR 664; 1997(1) Civ LJ 905; 1997(1) Mah LJ 403.

to arrange the preliminaries of a business transaction." According to *Black's Law Dictionary*,[4] negotiation is a consensual bargaining process in which the parties attempt to reach agreement on a disputed or potentially disputed matter. Negotiation is process of submission and consideration of offers until acceptable offer is made and accepted. It means the deliberations, discussion or conference upon the terms of a proposed agreement or the act of settlement or arranging the terms of and conditions of a bargain, or sale, or other business transaction. Negotiation is a communication process used to put deals together.

ICADR[5] defines negotiations as a non-binding procedure in which discussions between the parties are initiated without the intervention of any third party with the object of arriving at a negotiated settlement to the dispute.

Climate The climate in which the negotiation takes place should be congenial. The climate is seriously affected in the following situations:

First, the atmosphere in which negotiation of disputes occurs is usually full of tension.

Secondly, the parties involved in negotiating frequently place very different values on the dispute.

Parties to a dispute are likely to misunderstand what is important to their opponents and to assume that the other side is looking only for the highest or lowest possible monetary settlement.

Another phenomenon that contributes to the negotiation climate is the expectation that very little will be accomplished from negotiating and that the best that can be hoped for is to arrive at some "split the baby" compromise that satisfies no one.

Finally, the differences in the experience, values and expectations of the attorneys on the one hand and their clients on the other contribute significantly to the negotiation climate.[6]

4 *Black's Law Dictionary*, 10th Ed., p. 1200.

5 *Brochure of the International Centre for Alternative Dispute Resolution*, p. 18.

6 Susan R. Patterson, Esq. D. Grant Seabolt, Jr., Esq., *Essentials of Alternative Dispute Resolution*, 2nd Ed., pp. 24-25.

Classification Negotiation can be broadly divided into four groups namely, distributive negotiation, interest-based negotiation, competitive negotiation and cooperative negotiation.

Distributive negotiation It may occur when two or more parties are trying to claim the maximum amount of value for themselves. It is assumed that the disputants have a fixed amount of resource which they will divide among themselves. It focuses "on what each party is willing to give or take an order to settle. The goal is to gain the most concessions from the other party".[7]

Interest-based negotiation This type of negotiation is collaborative. Under this type of negotiation two things are to be done—first, beside the issues relating to dispute other interests are to be identified and satisfied, and secondly, to identify other common interests of the parties that they can solve together. It is also known as "integrative negotiating".

Competitive negotiation In this type of negotiation the negotiator treats negotiation as a battle to win or achieve his or her highest gain. "A competitive negotiator views the interests of the parties as antagonistic and does not consider that they may have interests in common".

Cooperative negotiation The negotiator tries to find out several alternative solutions to a dispute which the parties may consider to come to an acceptable solution. The main purpose of the negotiator is to give maximum benefit to his client but at the same time he/she must look into the interest of the other side so that some of his/her object is satisfied. In short, in this type of negotiation the main aim is to find out an agreeable solution which is not only acceptable but fair to the parties. It is also termed as integrative problem—solving or soft bargaining or win-win negotiation. The nicety of this negotiation is that both the parties are committed to fair deal and future negotiation between them which cements the spirit of cooperation and trust.

7 Susan R. Patterson, Esq. D. Grant Seabolt, Jr., Esq., *Essentials of Alternative Dispute Resolution*, 2nd Ed., p. 26.

Distributive negotiation and interest based negotiation—distinction

Distributive Negotiation	Interest based Negotiation
1. Parties try to gain maximum for themselves.	1. The negotiator attempts to settle the dispute between the parties by offering mutually acceptable solution.
2. It is based on win-lose theory.	2. Win-win situation is the basic foundation of this negotiation.
3. This approach to negotiation has been called positional negotiating.	3. It is collaborative.
4. It is ordinarily used when resources are limited.	4. It can be used when resources are in abundance.
5. Self-interest and individual profit motive of the parties are the main goal.	5. Protection of mutual interest and gain are the prime factor.
6. It promotes "shared gain/shared pain" approaches.	6. It unites the parties in a dispute solving mission.
7. It can take up only one issue at a time.	7. It can take up multiple issues to find an acceptable solution.
8. When it is used development of relationship between the parties has no concern.	8. It is used when the parties seek to develop good and healthy long-term relationship between them.

Competitive negotiation and cooperative negotiation—distinction The notable difference between competitive and cooperative negotiation is that the battle to win is the main motto of competitive negotiation whereas the achievement of win-win situation and problem resolution attitude is the main purpose of cooperative negotiation. Secondly, in competitive negotiation the negotiator adopts adversarial approach but in cooperative negotiation the negotiator applies problem-resolution tactics to resolve the dispute and differences between the disputants. Thirdly, in competitive negotiation the negotiator views the interests of the parties as antagonistic but in cooperative negotiation the negotiator views the parties having some interest and values that need to be identified. Fourthly, in competitive negotiation parties "attempts to isolate the opposition" whereas in cooperative negotiation both parties act as joint problem solver.

Fifthly, in competitive negotiation the parties stick to their opening demand and in cooperative negotiation parties are eager for a just solution based on their common agenda or demand. Sixthly, humiliation of opposition is another motto of the winning party but in cooperative negotiation humiliation to opposition is not at all beneficial. Seventhly, in competitive negotiation the negotiator relies on "adversarial tactics" but in cooperative negotiation the negotiator relies on "thorough knowledge of the facts of the case". Lastly, in competitive negotiation the goal is to "make the greatest possible gains for his/her side, to the detriment of the other" whereas cooperative negotiator "hopes to gain most what if important to his or her client, the negotiator realizes that he or she must help the other side to achieve at least some of its objectives".

Stages There are six phases in the negotiation process. They are—(1) Preparation phase; (2) Preliminary phase; (3) Information phase; (4) Competitive phase; (5) Closing/agreement phase and (6) Follow up/Cooperative phase.

(1) *Preparation phase* It is better to be called fact-finding stage. In this phase the negotiator studies the facts of the case and law applicable to the fact situation, develop his course of action and plan for negotiation because the entire negotiation depends upon the solid foundation of the preparation phase. Some of the duties of the negotiator at this phase can be listed as follows:

> "(1) Researching the facts of the case and the applicable law understanding the position(s) of the client in the dispute.
>
> (2) Identifying and thinking through all possible arguments that support the client's position.
>
> (3) Thoroughly probing what the client wants to achieve in the case and prioritizing those goals as essential, important, or merely desirable.
>
> (4) Determining the probable outcome of the case if a negotiated settlement is not achieved.
>
> (5) Developing a strategy and plan for negotiations.

(6) Reviewing the plan with the client and obtaining all necessary approval or authority from the client to negotiate according to the plan."[8]

(2) *Preliminary phase* It is the opening session of the negotiation process. In this stage the parties first introduce themselves and exchange their information—personal as well as professional. It is the first opportunity "to establish the tone of the negotiations as competitive or cooperative, unfriendly or congenial".[9] The main focus of this phase is on the long-term goals and consequences and mutual principles and concerns.

(3) *Information phase* In this phase two things are done—first, to understand the case of the opposite party and its position, and secondly, the needs and desires of the parties to the dispute. The parties normally attempt to collect more and more information as far as possible about each party's case. The main purpose of this phase is to anticipate the questions which the opponent will put and how such will be answered and defended.

(4) *Competitive phase* In this phase the negotiator either tries to adopt competitive or hard bargaining theory or distributive method to arrive at a conclusion. The negotiator makes offers to the parties and justifies the offer placed before the parties by him/her. If the other side acceptes the offer, then the negotiator switches off to the next stage, i.e. settlement stage.

(5) *Closing phase* When the parties think that the settlement which they are likely to enter is suitable to them, then they enter into an agreement for settlement.

(6) *Follow up stage* When all the above stages are over, the parties to the negotiation process enter into the follow-up stage. In this stage the settlement is reduced into writing and parties put their signature and the negotiator also puts his/her signature thereon in presence of the parties.

8 Susan R. Patterson, Esq. D. Grant Seabolt, Jr., Esq., *Essentials of Alternative Dispute Resolution*, 2nd Ed., p. 31.

9 Susan R. Patterson, Esq. D. Grant Seabolt, Jr., Esq., *Essentials of Alternative Dispute Resolution*, 2nd Ed., p. 33.

Characteristics

(*i*) It is a non-binding method by which disputes are determined.

(*ii*) Discussions and deliberations are held between the disputants or their representatives to arrive at or find an acceptable solution to a problem or difficulty.

(*iii*) It is initiated without the interventions of any third party or umpire.

(*iv*) Consensus between the parties is the *sine qua non* of the process. Parties will arrive at a settlement only if all parties agree.

Advantages Joanne Goss listed the advantages of negotiation as follows:[10]

(*a*) "*Satisfaction*. The solution generated is the creation of the parties themselves.

(*b*) *Speed*. Negotiations can be commenced and concluded at any time, allowing for quick resolution of the dispute.

(*c*) *Cost*. Both time and money can be saved if the matter is resolved quickly.

(*d*) *Privacy*. Negotiations usually take place in private, on a without prejudice basis.

(*e*) *Relationship*. Negotiations can lead to an improvement in the business or social relationship of the parties involved in the negotiations, thereby yielding benefits over and above the simple resolution of the conflict of dispute."

Drawbacks First, when the negotiation is not successful it causes delay to resolve the dispute by instituting law suit.

Secondly, sometimes parties are not willing to resolve the dispute seriously so there is very remote change to determine the dispute.

10 *An Introduction to Alternative Dispute Resolution*, Alberta Law Review, vol. XXXIV (1995), p. 4.

Thirdly, if the parties failed to arrive at a consensus it will bring more conflict between the parties.

Fourthly, it is only binding upon the parties.

Fifthly, if the negotiation is unsuccessful it will enhance the cost of litigation.

Lastly, the principle of *stare decisis* does not apply to negotiation.

Chapter 13

Minitrial

Minitrial—meaning The word 'minitrial' is of recent origin. In common parlance it means an informal settlement process of dispute in a summary manner with the help of neutral advisor. According to *Black's Law Dictionary*[1] minitrial is a private, voluntary and informal form of dispute resolution in which each party's attorney presents an abbreviated version of its case to a neutral third party and to the opponent's representatives, who have settlement authority. ICADR[2] defines it as a non-binding procedure in which the disputant parties are presented with summaries of their cases to enable them to assess the strength, weaknesses and prospects of the case and then an opportunity to negotiate a settlement with the assistance of a neutral advisor. It is not a trial in real sense but a "highly structured settlement process".[3]

Minitrial

Negotiation+
Mediation+
Adjudication

Purpose The main purpose of minitrial "is to convert a dispute from a legal problem to a business problem by putting the

1 *Black's Law Dictionary*, 10th Ed., p. 1147.
2 *Brochure of the International Centre for Alternative Dispute Resolution*, p. 18.
3 Joanne Goss, *An Introduction to Alternative Dispute Resolution*, ALBERIA Law Review, vol. 34, No. 1, 1995, p. 22.

resolution of the dispute back into the hands of the disputant directly involved".[4] The idea behind the minitrial is that the parties can resolve a dispute on their own more efficiently if litigant representatives with settling authority are educated about the strengths and weaknesses of each side, giving summary presentations of their best cases under the eye of a jointly selected neutral advisor.[4]

Characteristics According to Liebermann and Henry,[5] the minitrial has the following characteristics:

(1) The parties negotiate a set of procedural ground rule (a protocol) that will govern the non-binding minitrial.

(2) The time for preparation is relative short, because six weeks and three months and the amount of discovery is relatively limited.

(3) The hearing itself is sharply abbreviated–usually no more than two days.

(4) The hearing is often conducted by a third-party neutral, typically called the 'neutral advisor'.

(5) The case is presented to representative of the parties with authority to settle; there is no judge or jury.

(6) The lawyers present their 'best' case; they do not have time to delve into side issues.

(7) Immediately after the hearing, the party representatives meet privately to negotiate a settlement.

(8) The proceedings are confidential "the parties generally commit themselves to refrain from disclosing detail of the proceedings to any outsider".

Matters required to be considered In order to conduct minitrial the following matters required to be looked into:[6]

(*a*) The venue and date.

4 Alfred C. Aman Jr & Willian T. Mayton, *Administrative Law*, 2nd Ed., p. 291.

5 Henry and Liebermann, *The Manager Guide to Resolving Legal Disputes,* Harper & Row, 1985, p. 36.

6 Henry Brown and Arthur Marriott, *ADR Principles and Practice*, 2nd Ed., pp. 364-365.

(*b*) The length of time allowed for the process.

(*c*) The form and time-scale within which each side will provide written submissions before the presentations.

(*d*) What documents will be furnished by way of an agreed bundle or individual bundles to explain and amplify the case.

(*e*) The time to be allowed for the claimant's advocate to present the claimant's case.

(*f*) Whether technical experts will be called.

(*g*) Whether any other witnesses will be called.

(*h*) Whether any further information should be furnished and if so, what and how.

(*i*) What time should be allowed for each of the advocates to make responding statements.

(*j*) Who should attend the minitrial to represent corporate parties.

(*k*) Role of the neutral adviser.

(*l*) Practical arrangements for the settlement negotiations.

(*m*) The non-binding, confidential and privileged nature of.

(*n*) Practical matters need to be clarified, *i.e.* responsibility for costs.

(*o*) Any other matters specifically relevant to the individual case.

Conduct of minitrial

A minitrial may proceed in the following manner:[7]

(1) The neutral adviser welcomes the parties, addresses them about the process and its confidential, privileged and non-binding nature and chairs the proceedings which follow.

7 Brown & Marriott's *ADR Principles and Practice*, 4th Ed., pp. 403-404.

(2) The claimant's lawyer presents the claimant's case, summarizing the evidence, and making submissions. Use may be made of photographs, films, charts and other devices in making this presentation. This may take an agreed period of, say, two or three hours.

(3) As expert then summarises the technical position on behalf of the claimant, similarly using projectors, diagrams and any other devices that may be useful to explain and clarify the technical aspects. This may take an agreed period of, say 90 minutes.

(4) Key witnesses any outline relevant aspects of the claimant's case (Alternatively, the lawyer may instead summarise the proposed evidence in his or her presentation).

(5) The neutral adviser may ask the claimant's lawyer and witnesses any question to clarify the case. This is not generally done by way of cross-examination or to help make good shortcomings, but rather by way of genuine enquiry to assist understanding. Of course, such questions may have a probing effect. The parties may also put questions; and the defendant's lawyer may ask some questions of the claimant's lawyer and in some cases to the witnesses, if this has been agreed.

(6) The defendant's lawyer then presents the defendant's case for the same agreed period, similarly using any useful devices; and the procedures and timetable for experts, witnesses and questions will be reciprocated.

(7) If so agreed, time may be allowed for the experts to have a brief dialogue in from of the tribunal, perhaps responding to questions asked by one another.

(8) Winding up statement may be made, taking an agreed period of, say one hour each.

(9) The neutral adjourns with the parties to discuss the matter.

Matters relevant to non-binding evaluation The following maters are relevant to neutral non-binding evaluation:[8]

(1) Some ADR process are specifically designed with the aim of providing a neutral evaluation independently of any facilitation. Examples of these are the minitrial (Executive Tribunal), the summary jury trial, and neutral evaluation.

(2) Most ADR processes such as mediation place their primary focus on facilitations, and in some cases may introduce an element of evaluation mainly to assist the facilitative process. If the parties can resolve the matter on the basis of their interests, concerns and their own evaluations of the issues and risks, then neutral evaluation is unnecessary.

(3) The main aim of neutral evaluation is to help parties to gain a more objective and realistic view of the position, and where appropriate to shift from unrealistic positions.

(4) If required and agreed, a neutral other than the mediator or ADR practitioner may be asked to undertake the evaluation (for example a barrister or other lawyer jointly instructed by the parties for this purpose). A neutral evaluation as to the likely outcome of the case given to both or all parties may contain inherent potential problems in that it may well entrench or harden the position of the party considered to be likely to succeed. This may make it more difficult rather than easier to arrive at a negotiated resolution.

(5) The value of the evaluation also depends on the level of expertise and experience of the evaluator. As a matter of ethical property, no mediator should undertake any from of evaluation in mediation unless competent to do so, and practiced in facilitation.

(6) There is a substantial responsibility in altering the parties' perceptions by an evaluation that is necessarily personal. It is not to be lightly undertaken and requires a high standard of processional care.

8 Brown & Marriott's *ADR Principles and Practice*, 4th Ed., p. 397.

(7) Any evaluation should be consistent, even if the matter of presentation varies. It is not, however, necessary for a practitioner to discuss the same issues with each party. Indeed, it may well be appropriate for evaluative challenges or observations to be made confidentially to one party without informing the other that this has been done.

(8) If an evaluation is undertaken, it should be done competently and sensitively, at an appropriate time and in a way there is neither determinative nor coercive, and which leave decision-making control squarely with the parties.

Advantages (1) It is confidential. It is also non-binding.

(2) Parties are free to discuss the matter in detail before arriving at a settlement. They can also take the assistance of expert or even their expert counsel. Both parties also have full knowledge about the merits and weaknesses of each parties case.

(3) It saves some time and money. Very short is provided to resolve the dispute naturally it will take few time to adjudicate the dispute and similarly cost of lawyer and other functionaries will be low.

(4) It is held privately. So, the disputants can maintain their privacy.

(5) It is an informal modes of settlement of dispute to effective communication between the parties about their dispute and differences.

(6) The process is voluntary and therefore, either party can leave the process at any time when they feel that they will be prejudiced if they arrive at a settlement.

(7) The parties meet privately in a congenial atmosphere to negotiate the agreement and accordingly, it can improve the relationship between the parties.

(8) It is a flexible devise. Procedure adopted in the minitrial can be tailored, modified according to the needs of the party.

When minitrial is resorted to Minitrial is proper in the following situations[9]—

(1) Disputes where the parties, at least at the executive level, have the will to settle.

(2) Disputes where the outstanding issues involve factual rather than purely legal questions or a mix of the two.

(3) Disputes where the parties have had a long-term business relationship which they hope to continue.

(4) Disputes where the cost of litigation and trial are likely to be very high.

(5) Disputes that involve parties from more than one country.

(6) Disputes where senior decision-makers with authority are available to settle a matter in the best interest of the organization.

(7) Disputes that would benefit from decision-makers who are knowledgeable about the subject-matter of the disagreement and about customs of the industry.

9 Susan R. Patterson, Esq. D. Grant Seabolt, Jr., Esq., *Essentials of Alternative Dispute Resolution*, 2nd Ed., pp. 142-143.

Chapter 14

Family Court under Family Courts Act 1984

Reason for enactment In order to secure speedy disposal of family disputes and disputes relating to marriage our Legislature enacted the Family Courts Act 1984. It received the assent of the President of India on 14th September 1984. The objects of this Act as set out in the Preamble are as follows:

(*i*) Establishment of Family Courts with a view to promote conciliation among the couples.

(*ii*) To secure speedy settlement of disputes relating to marriage and family affairs and for matters connected therewith.

The purpose of enactment was essentially to set up Family Courts for the settlement of family disputes, emphasizing on conciliation and achieving socially desirable results and adherence to rigid rules of procedure and evidence should be eliminated. In other words, the purpose was for early settlement of family disputes.[1]

Nature Section 7 of the Family Courts Act is procedural and does not give any substantive right to any party.[2]

Establishment of Family Court The State Government after consultation with the High Court shall establish a Family Court

1 *Shabana Bano* v *Imran Khan* AIR 2010 SC 305.
2 *Viraf Phiroz Bharucha* v *Manosi Viraf Bharucha* AIR 2015 Bom 42.

for every area of city or a town whose population exceeds one million.[3] The State Government may appoint one or more persons as Judge of the Family Court.[4] The judge of the Family Court must be a person who has for at least seven years held a judicial office in India or has for at least seven years been an advocate of a High Court or possesses such other qualifications as prescribed by the Central Government.[5] Judge of such court shall a person of ability to protect and preserve the institution of marriage and standing with adequate knowledge and experience in dealing with problems relating to marriage and expertise to promote the welfare of the children and to promote the settlement of disputes by conciliation and counselling.[6]

Powers of Family Court The Family Court was set up for settlement of family disputes. The reason for enactment of this Act was to set up a court which would deal with disputes concerning the family by adopting an approach radically different from that adopted in ordinary civil proceedings.[7]

The Family Court is empowered to adjudicate the following suits and proceeding[8]—

(*a*) a suit or proceeding between the parties to a marriage for a decree of nullity of marriage or restitution of conjugal rights or judicial separation or dissolution of marriage;

(*b*) a suit or proceeding for a declaration as to the validity of a marriage or as to the matrimonial status of any person;

(*c*) a suit or proceeding between the parties to a marriage with respect to the property of the parties or of either of them;

3 Section 3(1)(*a*).
4 Section 4(1).
5 Section 4(3).
6 Section 4(4)(*a*).
7 *K.A. Abdul Jaleel* v *T.A. Shahida* 2003 AIR SCW 2710; AIR 2003 SC 2525; (2003)4 SCC 166; (2003)3 Scale 785; 2003(4) Mah LJ 7; 2003(3) East Cri C 36; 1(2003) DMC 765; 2003(2) Hindu LR 295.
8 *Explanation* to s. 7(1), the Family Courts Act 1984.

(*d*) a suit or proceeding for an order or injunction in circumstances arising out of a marital relationship;

(*e*) a suit or proceeding for a declaration as to the legitimacy of any person;

(*f*) a suit or proceeding for maintenance;

(*g*) a suit or proceeding in relation to the guardianship of the person or the custody of, or access to, any minor.

Family Court has exclusive jurisdiction to adjudicate upon the application filed under s. 125 of the Code of Criminal Procedure.[9]

Enhancement of maintenance An application for enhancement of maintenance under the Muslim Women (Protection of Rights on Divorce) Act 1986 can be decided by Family Court.[10]

With respect to the property of the parties—implication The expression "with respect to the property of the parties" refers to parties to marriage and not parties to the proceedings.[11]

Interim relief When the Family Court has no jurisdiction to entertain the petition filed by the husband under the Hindu Marriage Act, it cannot grant interim relief under the Family Courts Act 1984.[12]

Adjournment Family Court judges are expected to decide the matter as expeditiously as possible.[13]

District Court—meaning of District Court includes a High Court which exercising ordinary original civil jurisdiction.[14]

Application of Evidence Act The Family Court though not bound by the sophisticated rules of relevancy or admissibility of evidence but it does not possess unregulated or unbridled power or freedom

9 *Shabana Bano* v *Imran Khan* AIR 2010 SC 305.

10 *Gyasuddin Khan* alias *Gayasuddin Khan* v *Kahkashan Khan* AIR 2015 Ori 66.

11 *Devaki Antharjanam* v *Narayanan Namboodiri* AIR 2007 Ker 38.

12 *Minoti Anand* v *Subhash Anand* AIR 2009 Bom 65.

13 *Bhuwam Mohan Singh* v *Meena* AIR 2014 SC 2875.

14 *Anima Bharatram* v *Sumant Bharatram* AIR 2016 Del 171.

to receive in evidence indiscriminately all matters that are brought before them. The hearsay which is inherently inadmissible cannot be therefore acknowledged as an evidence in any proceeding before a Family Court also. Family Courts are bound to adhere to the fundamental rules of evidence based on logic, fairness and expediency and also principles of natural justice.[15]

Limitations Where a Family Court has been established no District Court or Magistrate shall have jurisdiction to determine the suit or proceeding relating to marriage or maintenance. Every pending proceeding shall stand transferred to such Family Court on the date on which it is established.[16] In short, the function of the court "is not merely technically juridical and legalistic but broadly sociological".

When a Family Court is established under s. 3 of the Act, no suit or proceeding for maintenance can be entertained by any District Court or, as the case may be, by any other subordinate Civil Court in relation to the area, which falls within the territorial jurisdiction of the Family Court. In short, once family court is established the jurisdiction of the civil court is barred.[17]

Clause (*c*) of Explanation to s. 7(1)(*b*) specifically deals with property disputes. The dispute should be relating to "property of the parties" or of "either of them". For the Family Court to exercise its jurisdiction two conditions must be satisfied. First, the said dispute should be between the parties to the marriage only; and secondly, the dispute should be in respect of the property of the parties or either of them. Both these conditions must be satisfied before the Family Court can take cognizance of a suit or proceedings under the Act, in respect of property disputes. Therefore, it is clear that the Family Court has no jurisdiction to entertain and try a suit or proceeding claiming a property by persons other than the parties to the marriage. Further, the property in dispute should belong exclusively to the parties or either of them. If persons other than the parties to the

15 *Pramod E.K.* v *Louna V.C.* AIR 2019 Ker 85.
16 Section 8, Family Courts Act 1984.
17 *Nishamoni Kalita* v *Sarada Kalita* AIR 2009 Gau 62.

marriage have an interest in the said dispute, the Family Court has no jurisdiction to adjudicate the dispute. In other words, the parties to the marriage cannot claim right in a property, in which third parties also have interest, before the Family Court.[18]

Duties of Family Court

(i) *Amicable settlement of dispute* Family Court should make an endeavour to assist and persuade the parties in arriving at a settlement in respect of the subject matter of the suit or proceedings.[19]

It is the mandate of law as also the social obligation of the judge to make an earnest attempt for reconciliation.[20]

When the Family Court had not taken any step to satisfy itself after hearing the parties and after making any enquiry about the soleminization of marriage between the parties and truthfulness of the averments in the petition, nor had taken any effort to satisfy itself that the consent of the parties had not been obtained by force, fraud or undue influence, the decree is liable to be set aside.[21]

(ii) *True balance* It is essentially the function of the court of maintaining true balance between the parties. In the words of Justice P.B. Mukharji, "Jurisprudence is trying to balance the binding sanctity of marriage on one hand and on the other the social condition which makes it contrary to public policy to insist on maintaining a union which has broken down".[1]

Procedure

(*i*) All proceedings except the proceedings under Chapter IX of the Code of Criminal Procedure shall be governed by the provisions of the Code of Civil Procedure.[2]

18 *G. Pentamma* v *G. Anjali* AIR 2010 AP 224; *Muhammed Davood* v *Hafsath* AIR 2010 Ker 21.
19 Section 9, Family Courts Act 1984.
20 *Hina Singh* v *Satya Kumar Singh* AIR 2007 Jhar 34.
21 *Seema Pathak* v *Chotelal Pandey* AIR 2017 Jhar 59.
1 Mukharji on the *New Jurisprudence, the Grammer of Modern Law* (Tagore Law Lectures), 2nd Ed., p. 454.
2 Section 10(1).

(*ii*) Proceedings under Chapter IX of the Code of Criminal Procedure shall be regulated by the provisions of the Code of Criminal Procedure and order passed by the Family Court shall be executed in the manner prescribed by that Code.[3]

(*iii*) The proceedings may be held *in camera* if the court so desires.[4]

(*iv*) Family court may take the services of a medical expert or welfare expert in promoting the welfare of the family.[5]

(*v*) Right to legal representation is barred but if the Family Court considers it necessary in the interest of justice, it may seek the assistance of a legal expert as *amicus curiae*.[6]

(*vi*) The Court will record a memorandum of the substance of what the witness deposes. It shall not be necessary to record the evidence of the witnesses at length. Such memorandum must be signed by the witness and the Judge.[7]

(*vii*) Evidence of a formal character may be given by affidavit.[8]

(*viii*) Decree or order of the Family Court barring order under Chapter IX of the Code of Criminal Procedure must be executed in the manner as prescribed by the Code of Civil Procedure for execution of decrees and orders.[9]

(*ix*) Judgment of a Family Court must consist of concise facts of the case, points for determination, decision and reasons for such decision.[10]

3 Section 10(2), Family Courts Act 1984.
4 Section 11.
5 Section 12.
6 Section 13.
7 Section 15.
8 Section 16(1).
9 Section 18(1).
10 Section 17.

Appointment of Judges The State Government may, with the concurrence of the High Court, appoint one or more persons to be the Judge or Judges of a Family Court.[11] When a Family Court consists of more than one Judge[12]—

(*a*) each of the Judges may exercise all or any of the powers conferred on the court by this Act or any other law for the time being in force;

(*b*) the State Government may, with the concurrence of the High Court, appoint any of the Judges to be the Principal Judge and any other Judge to be the Additional Principal Judge;

(*c*) the Principal Judge may, from time to time, make such arrangements as he may deem fit for the distribution of the business of the court among the various Judges thereof;

(*d*) the Additional Principal Judge may exercise the power of the Principal Judge in the event of any vacancy in the office of the Principal Judge or when the Principal Judge is unable to discharge his functions owing to absence, illness or any other cause.

Qualification for appointment of Judge A person shall not be qualified for appointment as a Judge unless he[13]—

(*a*) has for at least seven years held a judicial office in India or the office of a member of a Tribunal or any post under the Union or a State requiring special knowledge of law; or

(*b*) has for at least seven years been an advocate of a High Court or of two or more such courts in succession; or

(*c*) possesses such other qualifications as the Central Government may, with the concurrence of the Chief Justice of India prescribe.

11 Section 4(1).
12 Section 4(2).
13 Section 4(3).

Selection criteria of appointment of Judges In selecting persons for appointment as Judges[14]—

(*a*) every endeavour shall be made to ensure that persons committed to the need to protect and preserve the institution of marriage and to promote the welfare of children and qualified by reason of their experience and expertise to promote the settlement of disputes by conciliation and counselling are selected; and

(*b*) preference shall be given to women.

Age of retirement No person shall be appointed as, or hold the office of, a Judge of a Family Court after he has attained the age of sixty-two years.[15]

Salary of the Judges The salary or honorarium and other allowances payable to, and the other terms and conditions of service of a Judge shall be such as the State Government may, in consultation with High Court, prescribe.[16]

Jurisdiction A Family Court shall—

(*a*) have and exercise all the jurisdiction exercisable by any District Court or any subordinate civil court under any law for the time being in force in respect of suits and proceedings of the nature referred to in the Explanation; and

(*b*) be deemed, for the purposes of exercising such jurisdiction under such law, to be a District Court or, as the case may be, such subordinate civil court of the area to which the jurisdiction of the Family Court extends;[17]

(*c*) the jurisdiction exercisable by a Magistrate of the first class under Chapter IX (relating to order for maintenance of wife, children and parents) of the Code of Criminal Procedure 1973 (2 of 1974); and

14 Section 4(4).
15 Section 4(5).
16 Section 4(6).
17 Section 7(1).

(*d*) such other jurisdiction as may be conferred on it by any other enactment.[18]

Declaration of illegitimacy of child Dispute between the parties about the illegitimacy or legitimacy of child born during the subsistence of marriage can be adjudicated by Family Court.[19]

Circumstances related to matrimonial relationship—implication Adjudication of matrimonial disputes in a congenial atmosphere is the function of the Family Court. No doubt, a broad and liberal approach is required in determining the jurisdiction of the Family Court. But, it does not meant that, the Family Court has the jurisdiction to adjudicate matters not even remotely connected with marriage and marital relationship. Exclusion of jurisdiction of civil courts cannot be readily inferred. The expression "in circumstances arising out of a marital relationship" in cl. (*d*) of the Explanation to s. 7(1) of the Act, denotes such circumstances surrounding, preceding and closely following a marital relationship, that is, the principal event of marriage and the eventualities surrounding the same. The "circumstances" must have a direct bearing on marriage. Prime consideration should be as to whether the cause of the lis has got any bearing with marital relationship. If the cause of action is emerging out of any circumstances related to matrimonial relationship and the same could not have existed independently, then the suit can be maintained before the Family Court, and it will fall under cl. (*d*) of the Explanation to s. 7(1) of the Act. It is not necessary that, parties to a suit or proceeding under that clause, shall be parties to a marriage.[20]

Dispute relating to adoption Any dispute with regard to the adoption and declaration respecting any aspect touching adoption could be settled only by the competent court of civil jurisdiction, which is certainly not a Family Court.[21]

18 Section 7(2).

19 *Laila* v *Muhammed Ali* AIR 2009 Ker 173; *Davu Gopal Lunani* v *Siva Gopal Lunani* AIR 2014 AP 29.

20 *Vijayalakshmy* v *P.K. Jayashree* AIR 2019 Ker 53.

21 *Udhayabhanu* v *Ranganayaki* AIR 2009 Mad 91.

But Family Court has jurisdiction to entertain application for adoption of abandoned or destitute child.[1]

Marital status The Family Court is competent to declare marital status of the parties.[2]

Custody of children Clause (*g*) to Explanation to sub-sec. (1) of s. 7 provides that the Family Court would have jurisdiction to decide a suit or proceeding in relation to the guardianship of the person or the custody of, or access to any minor. It does not speak about the dispute between the husband and wife (father and mother of the minor). There are no such restriction in cl. (*g*) of Explanation to sub-sec. (1) of s. 7. Under the circumstances, considering cl. (*g*) of Explanation to sub-sec. (1) of s. 7, Family Court would have jurisdiction to decide a suit or proceeding in relation to the guardianship of the person or the custody of, or access to, any minor, even if the same is initiated by the person other than husband and wife (father and mother of the minor).[3]

Suit relating to joint family property Suit relating to joint family property in which there are many co-sharers other than the spouses, it cannot be said that the suit is arising out of marital relation.[4]

Negative declaration Family Court has jurisdiction to decide affirmative or negative declaration regarding marital status of any person.[5]

Irretrievably broken down of marriage—not a ground of divorce No law having been enacted treating irretrievable break down of marriage as a ground for divorce, a Family Court or even a High Court does not have the power to grant a decree of divorce on the ground that a marriage has irretrievably been broken down. However, in exercise of its power under Art. 142 of the

1 *Tarun Kadam* v *State of M.P.* AIR 2015 MP 31.
2 *Asfaq Qureshi* v *Aysha Qureshi* AIR 2010 Chh 58.
3 *Lt. Col Iqbalbahadur Teghbahadur Dutt* v *Ann Saurabh Dutt* AIR 2016 Guj 189.
4 *Manita Khurana* v *Indra Khurana* AIR 2010 Del 69.
5 *Balram Yadav* v *Fulamaniya Yadav* AIR 2016 SC 2161.

Constitution of India, since the Supreme Court has the plenary power "to pass such decree or make such order as is necessary for doing complete justice in any case or order pending before it", it clearly follows that the Supreme Court may, if it deems necessary in order to do complete justice, dissolve a Hindu marriage on the ground that the marriage has irretrievably broken down.[6]

Suits and proceedings The suits and proceedings of the following nature are entertainable by the Family Court[7]—

(*a*) a suit or proceeding between the parties to a marriage for a decree of nullity of marriage (declaring the marriage to be null and void or, as the case may be, annulling the marriage) or restitution of conjugal rights or judicial separation or dissolution of marriage;

(*b*) a suit or proceeding for a declaration as to the validity of a marriage or as to the matrimonial status of any person;

(*c*) a suit or proceeding between the parties to a marriage with respect to the property of the parties or of either of them;

(*d*) a suit or proceeding for an order or injunction in circumstances arising out of a marital relationship;

(*e*) a suit or proceeding for a declaration as to the legitimacy of any person;

(*f*) a suit or proceeding for maintenance;

(*g*) a suit or proceeding in relation to the guardianship of the person or the custody of, or access to, any minor.

Civil court Family Court while exercising powers and jurisdiction relating to matters referred to in the Explanation to s. 7(1) is a civil court and it has all the trappings of a civil court.[8]

6 *Bhavana Ramaprashad* v *Yadunandan Parthasarathi* AIR 2015 Kant 6; *Bhola Kumar* v *Seema Devi* AIR 2015 Pat 119.

7 Explanation to s. 7(1).

8 *P. Sunder Raj* v *P. Sarika Raj* AIR 2015 P&H 83; *S.D. Joshi* v *High of Judicature at Bombay* (2011)1 SCC 252.

Evolve own procedure In the family matters the court is required to evolve its own procedure in bringing about settlement between the parties.[9]

Advantage of Family Court Advantages of Family Courts are many. They are as under—

(*a*) *Proceedings in camera.*[10] All the proceedings before the Family Courts may be held *in camera* (in the court room with all spectators excluded) if it so desires or if either party so desires.

(*b*) *Right to legal representation.*[11] No party to a suit or proceedings before a Family Court shall be entitled, as of right, to be represented by a legal practitioner. If the Family Court considers it necessary in the interest of justice, it may seek the assistance of a legal expert as *amicus curiae*.

In *Komal S. Padukone* v *Principal Judge, Family Court, Bangalore*,[12] the Karnataka High Court has explained the following principles of representation through counsel in Family Courts:

(*i*) A petition to the Family Court may be presented by a petitioner either in person or through an authorised agent. The petition may be presented even by an Advocate as an authorised agent. But, if the petitioner wants 'representation' by a legal practitioner, he should seek and obtain the permission of the Family Court.

(*ii*) A respondent; who is served with notice of the proceedings, may either appear in person or enter appearance through an authorised agent (including a legal practitioner). But, if the respondent wants to be represented by a legal practitioner in the proceedings, he should

9 *Basant Kumar Jha* v *Mithlesh Jha* AIR 2007 Raj 243.
10 Section 11.
11 Section 13.
12 AIR 1992 Kant 427; II(1999) DMC 301; ILR (1999) Kant 1866; 1999(2) Hindu LR 652; 1999(5) Kant LJ 667.

seek and obtain the permission of the Family Court.

(*iii*) In regard to proceedings before the Family Court, 'entering appearance' in response to a notice/ summons through an authorised agent (including a legal practitioner), is different from being represented in the proceedings by a legal practitioner.

(*iv*) While representation through legal practitioner without permission is barred, entering appearance in a case, in response to a noticed summons, through a legal practitioner is not barred, if a legal practitioner, having entered appearance, wants to represent party in the proceedings, permission of the Family Court should be obtained for such representation.

(*v*) When one party has been permitted to be represented by a Legal Practitioner, such permission cannot under any circumstances, be denied to the other party.

(*vi*) The authorised agent (or the legal practitioner permitted to represent a party) can prosecute or defend the proceedings and represent the party unless and until the Family Court makes a specific order to the parties to appear in person, either on a specified date or on further hearing dates, depending on the facts of the case and stage of the case. Once an order for personal appearance has been specifically made, a party will have to seek exemption from his appearance, if he is not able to appear in the matter.

(c) *Right to accept any document.*[13] Family Court may receive any report, statement, documents, information or any matter as evidence to deal effectually even if they are not relevant or admissible under the India

13 Section 14.

Evidence Act 1872. Tape recorded conversation between spouses is admissible in evidence.[14]

(*d*) *Recording of evidence at length not necessary.* In a suit or proceeding before a Family Court recording of evidence at length is not necessary.[15]

(*e*) *Evidence of formal character on affidavit.* Evidence of formal character may be given on affidavit.[16] As a result it reduces the cost of litigation and saves the valuable time of the court.

(*f*) *No appeal in certain cases.*[17] In the following cases appeal is not maintainable:

(*i*) if the order is an interlocutory order;

(*ii*) if the decree or order passed by the Family Court with the consent of the parties;

(*iii*) if the order passed by the Family Court under Chapter IX (sections 125-128) of the Code of Criminal Procedure 1973.

(*g*) *Benefit of privilege communication.* It is not available in family court proceeding.[18]

Manner of recording of evidence Section 14 of the Family Courts Act empowers the Family Court to receive as evidence any report, statement, documents, information or matter that may, in its opinion, assist it to deal effectually with a dispute, whether or not the same would be otherwise relevant or admissible under the Indian Evidence Act 1872. Section 15 of the said Act further provides that in suits or proceedings before a Family Court, it shall not be necessary to record the evidence of witnesses at length, but the Judge, as the examination of each witness proceeds, shall, record or cause to be recorded, a memorandum of the substance of what the witness disposes, and such memorandum shall be signed by the witness and the Judge and

14 *Vishal Kaushik* v *Family Court* AIR 2015 Raj 146.

15 Section 15.

16 Section 16.

17 Section 19.

18 *Preeti Jain* v *Kunal Jain* AIR 2016 Raj 153.

shall form part of the record. Section 16 of the said Act empowers the Family Court to receive evidence by way of affidavit of any person, where such evidence is of a formal character. Such person, however, on the application of any parties to the suit or proceeding can be summoned and examined by the Family Court, as to the facts contained in his affidavit. The manner of recording of the evidence adduced by a witness, as stipulated in s. 15 of the Family Courts Act, cannot in any way take away the right of the other party to cross-examine such witness. In the Family Court, where the parties are normally not allowed to be represented by legally trained persons, the responsibility of the Judge of such court is more, who has to inform the parties to the proceeding about their right to put questions to the witness examined by the other party, by way of cross-examination. Examination of a witness cannot be complete unless that witness is made available for cross-examination by the other party.[19]

Provision of CPC—not strictly applicable The Code of Civil Procedure which provides complete mechanism for decision of a civil suit and passing of the judgment and decree on the issues raised in a suit also makes provisions that the other courts may pass such judgments which shall contain a concise statement of the case, the points for determination, the decision thereon, and the reasons for such decision and same provision has been inserted in the Family Courts Act 1984, and both these provisions do not talk about the 'issues' to be framed by the court and the decisions on the 'issues'. Thus the procedure prescribed in Chapter IV of the Family Courts Act, therefore, is with the view to simplify the proceedings before the Family Court so as to achieve the objects of the Family Courts Act so that the matters are disposed of quickly without complying the strict provisions of the Code of Civil Procedure which of course was made generally applicable and was subject to the other provisions of the Act 1984. Therefore, in the light of the provisions of s. 17 and the other provisions of the Act, it is not mandatory for the Family Court to frame issues; however, its judgment must contain a concise statement of the case, the points for determination, the decision thereon and the reasons for such decision. The provisions of

19 *Saraswati Sarker* v *Lalit Chandra Sarker* AIR 2010 Gau 142.

CPC are not strictly applicable to proceedings before Family Court.[20]

Family Courts Act and Hindu Marriage Act The provision of s. 28 of the Hindu Marriage Act stands superseded by s. 19 of the Family Courts Act.[1]

Temporary stay of couple and jurisdiction A place where the couple had casual or temporary visit, including the place where the couple had resided either for a health check up or business or for a change, cannot be treated to be a place of residence. Thus, the court having territorial jurisdiction over such places cannot be treated to be a competent court of law for the purpose of a proceeding under the provisions of the Act.[2]

Overriding effect Section 20 of the Family Courts Act 1984 provides that the provisions of the Family Courts Act 1984 would have overriding effect on any text, rule or any other law for the time being in force or in any instrument having effect by virtue of any law other than Family Courts Act 1984 in force immediately before the commencement of the Family Courts Act 1984 with respect to any matter for which provision has been made in the Family Courts Act 1984.

Appeal "Appeal", is defined as the transfer of a case from a lower to a higher forum in the hope of reversing or modifying the decision of the former.

In the *Law Dictionary* by Bouvier an appeal is defined as the removal of a case from a court of inferior to one of superior jurisdiction for the purpose of obtaining a review and re-trial, and it is explained that in its technical sense it differs from a writ of error in this, that it subjects both the law and the facts to a review and re-trial, while the latter is a common law process which involves matter of law only for re-examination; it is added, however, that the term "appeal" is used in a comprehensive sense so as to include both what is described technically as an appeal and also the common law writ of error.

20 *Subhash* alias *Prakash* v *Priyanka Subhash Dewanga* AIR 2013 Chh 164.

1 *Ashutosh Kumar* v *Anjali Shrivastav* AIR 2009 All 100.

2 *Priyadarshani Mohapatra* v *Lalmohan Mohapatra* AIR 2018 Ori 31.

An appeal shall lie to the High Court from the every judgment or order of the Family Court on the ground of both question of law and fact.[3] But there is no provision in the Act for appeal against interlocutory order.[4] Such appeal must be preferred within 30 days from the date of judgment or order.[5] It must be heard by a bench consisting of two or more judges.[6]

An appeal against order under s. 13 of the Hindu Marriage Act lies before Family Court.[7]

Nature of appeal Appeal against judgment and order of Family Court shall lie before the High Court as miscellaneous appeal and not as first appeal.[8]

Order under s. 125, CrPC An appeal against order passed under s. 125 of CrPC by the Family Court is not maintainable.[9]

Period of limitation For an appeal filed under s. 19(1) of the Family Courts Act will be governed by the period of limitation prescribed under s. 28(4) of the Hindu Marriage Act.[10]

Computation of period of appeal The appeal period is to be counted from the date of judgment of the Family Court.[11]

Limitation

(1) *Consent decree* No appeal shall lie from a decree or order passed by a Family Court with the consent of the parties.[12]

(2) *Order relating to maintenance* No appeal shall lie against an order passed by a Family Court under Chapter IX of the Code of Criminal Procedure.[13]

3 Section 19(1)
4 Section 19(4).
5 Section 19(3).
6 Section 19(6).
7 *C. Govindaraj* v *Padnimi* AIR 2009 Kant 108.
8 *Sunita Kumari* v *Prem Kumar* AIR 2009 Pat 183.
9 *Geeta Bareth* v *Keshab Prashad Bareth* AIR 2013 Chh 3.
10 *Shivram Dodanna Shetty* v *Sou Sharmila Shivram Shetty* AIR 2017 Bom 1.
11 *Ranjana Rani Panda* v *Sanjay Kumar Panda* AIR 2017 Ori 25.
12 Section 19(2).
13 Section 19(1), s. 19(5).

(3) *Revision* It means "a re-examination or careful review for correction or improvement".[14]

The High Court may *suo motu* or on the application of either of the parties call for and examine the record of any proceeding on the following grounds—

(*i*) for the purpose of satisfying about the correctness of the order;

(*ii*) legality or propriety of the order; and

(*iii*) as to the regularity of such proceeding.

Revision—when not permissible Revision against the interlocutory order of the Family Court is not permissible. It is specifically mentioned in the Act that except as aforesaid, no appeal or revision shall lie to any court from any judgment, order or decree of a Family Court. The statute is silent about the revision or appeal against an interlocutory order.

National Human Rights Commission It is an independent autonomous body. It is created with the purpose of protecting human rights against the State action.

Function The following are the some of the important functions of the National Human Rights Commission—

(1) It can inquire *suo motu* or on a petition presented to it by a victim or any person on his or her behalf regarding violation of human rights and negligence in the prevention of such violation by a public servant.

(2) It can intervene in any proceeding pending before a court involving any allegations of violation of human rights with the approval of such court.

(3) It can visit any jail and study its condition. It may also make recommendations for reformation or protection of the living conditions of the inmates.

(4) It may review the factors including acts of terrorism and recommend appropriate remedial measure.

14 *Black's Law Dictionary*, 10th Ed., p. 1515.

(5) It may make recommendations for the effective implementations of treaties and other International Instruments on human rights.

(6) It may undertake and promote research in the field of human rights.

(7) It can spread human rights literacy among various sections of society through publications, media, seminars and other available means.

(8) The commission has been vested with certain powers of a civil court under the Code of Civil Procedure for enforcing production of documents, attendance of witness or examination of witness. Any proceeding before the commission shall be treated as a judicial proceeding.

Chapter 15

Maintenance Tribunal and the Maintenance and Welfare of Parents and Senior Citizens Act 2007

The Maintenance and Welfare of Parents and Senior Citizens Act 2007 was enacted to provide for appropriate mechanism to be set up to provide need-based maintenance to the parents and senior citizens. It is true the parents can claim maintenance by resorting the provision provided in s. 125, CrPC from their sons or daughters but the said procedure is time consuming and complex. Present day society needs simple, less complex, less expensive and speedy and timely justice.

Scope Recently maintaining and taking care of the aged and elderly persons and the parents has posed as a social challenge with decline and dilution of the joint family system. This Act has been enacted to provide speedy redressal of grievance of parents and senior citizens.[1]

Object The object of the Act is to protect and to provide effective provisions for the maintenance and welfare of parents and senior citizens.[2]

1 *Deepak Sharma* v *State of Rajasthan* AIR 2016 Raj 188.

2 *Reju* v *The Maintenance Tribunal, Thiruvananthpuram* AIR 2016 Ker 97.

Who can claim maintenance Maintenance can be claimed by[3]

(*a*) parent or grant-parent, against one or more of his children not being a minor;

(*b*) childless senior citizen against his relative referred to in s. 2(*g*).

When maintenance is permissible Maintenance is permissible in the following situations.[4]

(*a*) If the senior citizen or parent is unable to maintain himself

  (*i*) from his/her own earning, or

  (*ii*) out of the property owned by him/her.

(*b*) The children must have sufficient means to maintain the applicant (parent).

(*c*) The relative of a senior citizen having sufficient means shall maintain such senior citizen provided.

  (*i*) he is in possession of the property of such senior citizen, or

  (*ii*) he would inherit the property of such senior citizen.

(*d*) The respondent/opponent/opposite party must have refused or neglected to maintained the applicant petitioner.

Maintenance It includes provision for food, clothing, residence, medical attendance and treatment.[5]

Welfare measure The welfare measure can be imposed against any person, based on the accepted relationship between the parties involving mutual obligation for a considerable time though such persons may not have legal obligation to pay the maintenance.[6]

3 Section 4(1).

4 Section 4.

5 Section 2(*b*) and *Rajeshkumar Bansraj Gandhi* v *State of Gujarat* AIR 2016 Guj 129.

6 *Reju* v *The Maintenance Tribunal, Thiruvananthpuram* AIR 2016 Ker 97.

Who can make application A senior citizen or parent is entitled to seek maintenance.[7] An application for maintenance may be made[8]—

(*a*) by a senior citizen or a parent, as the case may be; or

(*b*) if he is incapable, by any other person or organization authorized by him; or

(*c*) the Tribunal may take cognizance *suo motu*.

Obligation of the children or relative The obligation of the children to maintain his parent extends to the needs of such parent either father or mother or both, as the case may be, so that such parent may lead a normal life.[9] Any person being a relative of a senior citizen and having sufficient means shall maintain such senior citizen provided he is in possession of the property of such senior citizen or he would inherit the property of such senior citizen.[10] Where more than one relatives are entitled to inherit the property of a senior citizen, the maintenance shall be payable by such relative in the proportion in which they would inherit his property.[11]

Quantum of maintenance The tribunal considering the financial conditions of the parties and illness of the petitioner/father awarded maintenance at the rate of ₹7500 per month.[12]

Maintenance as monetary relief The maintenance is a monetary relief and such maintenance may be flowing from the earning out of the property.[13]

Direction to hand over possession of property When the son failed to provide maintenance and neglected to look after his father the

7 Section 4.
8 Section 5(1).
9 Section 4(3).
10 Section 4(4).
11 Proviso to s. 4(4); *Rajeshkumar Bansraj Gandhi* v *State of Gujarat* AIR 2016 Guj 129.
12 *Prem Kumar* v *Krishan Kumar Sharma* AIR 2016 P&H 40.
13 *Rajeshkumar Bansraj Gandhi* v *State of Gujarat* AIR 2016 Guj 129.

tribunal has jurisdiction to issue direction upon the son to hand over the possession of the property to the father.[14]

Overriding effect The provisions of the Maintenance and Welfare of Parents and Senior Citizens Act 2007 shall have effect notwithstanding anything inconsistent therewith contained in any enactment other than this Act, or in any instrument having effect by virtue of any enactment other than this Act.[15]

Constitution of Maintenance Tribunal The State Government shall within a period of six months from the date of the commencement of this Act may, by notification in the Official Gazette, constitute for each Sub-Division one or more Tribunals as may be specified in the notification for the purpose of adjudicating and deciding upon the order for maintenance under s. 5.[16]

The Tribunal shall be presided over by an officer not below the rank of Sub-Divisional Officer of a State.[17]

Where two or more Tribunals are constituted for any area, the State Government may, by general or special order, regulate the distribution of business among them.[18]

Forum The proceedings may be taken against any children or relative in any District[19]—

(*a*) where he resides or last resided; or

(*b*) where children or relative resides.

The expression 'is' used in s. 126 of the Code of Criminal Procedure cannot be given the same meaning as the word "reside" or the expression "the last resided". It connotes in the context the presence or the existence of the persons in the district where the proceedings are taken.

14 *Jayantram Vallabhdas Meswania* v *Vallabhdas Govindram Meswani* AIR 2013 Guj 160.
15 Section 3.
16 Section 7(1).
17 Section 7(2).
18 Section 7(3).
19 Section 6(1).

Procedure

Stage 1

Filing of the application for maintenance before the maintenance Tribunal.

Stage 2

On receipt of the application the Tribunal shall issue a process for procuring the presence of children or relative against whom the application is filed [s. 6(2)].

Where the children or relative is residing out of India, the summons shall be served by the Tribunal through such authority, as the Central Government may, by notification specify in this behalf [s. 6(5)].

For securing the attendance of the children or relative the Tribunal shall have the power of a Judicial Magistrate of first class as provided under the Code of Criminal Procedure 1973 [s. 6(3)].

Stage 3

The Tribunal before hearing the application may refer the same to a Conciliation Officer and such Conciliation Officer shall submit his findings within one month and if amicable settlement has been arrived at, the Tribunal shall pass an order to that effect [s. 6(6)].

Stage 4

Where the opponent is willfully avoiding service or willfully neglecting to attend the Tribunal, the Tribunal may proceed to hear and determine the case ex parte [Proviso to s. 6(4)].

Stage 5

On receipt of the application for maintenance, after giving notice of the application to the opposite parties and after giving the parties an opportunity of being heard hold an inquiry for determining the amount of maintenance [s. 5(3)].

STAGE 6

All the evidence to such proceedings shall be taken in the presence of the children or relative against whom an order for payment of maintenance is proposed to be made and shall be recorded in the manner prescribed for summons cases [s. 6(4)].

STAGE 7

Application shall be disposed of within ninety days from the date of the service of notice of the application to such person [s. 5(4)].

STAGE 8

Maintenance allowance and expenses of the proceeding shall be payable from the date of order, or, if so ordered, from the date of the application for maintenance or expenses of proceeding as the case may be [s. 5(7)].

STAGE 9

A copy of the orders of maintenance and expenses of proceedings shall be given free of cost to the senior citizen or to parent [s. 11(1)].

STAGE 10

If the children or relative so ordered fail, without sufficient cause to comply with the order, any such Tribunal may, for every breach of the order, issue a warrant for levying the amount due in the manner provided for levying fines, and may sentence such person for the whole, or any part of each month's allowance for the maintenance and expenses of proceeding, as the case be, remaining unpaid after the execution of the warrant, to imprisonment for a term which may extend to one month or until payment if sooner made whichever is earlier [s. 5(8)].

But no warrant shall be issued for the recovery of any amount due under s. 5 unless application be made to the Tribunal to levy such amount within a period of three months from the date on which it became due [Proviso to s. 5(8)].

Power of the Tribunal The Maintenance Tribunal has the following powers:

(*a*) *Power to award maintenance allowance.*[20] It has the power to award maintenance allowance after hearing both sides or *ex parte*, where the opponent is unwilling to appear before the tribunal or to avoid the process of the tribunal willfully or deliberately.

(*b*) *Powers of a civil court.*[1] The Tribunal shall have all the powers of a civil court for the purpose of taking evidence on oath and of enforcing the attendance of witnesses and of compelling the discovery and production of documents and material objects and for such other purposes as may be prescribed; and the Tribunal shall be deemed to be a civil court for all the purposes of s. 195 and Chapter XXVI of the Code of Criminal Procedure 1973 (2 of 1974).

(*c*) *Power to alteration in allowance.*[2] On proof of misrepresentation or mistake of fact or a change in the circumstances of any person, receiving a monthly allowance under s. 9, for the maintenance ordered under that section to pay a monthly allowance for the maintenance, the Tribunal may make such alteration, as it thinks fit, in the allowance for the maintenance.

(*d*) *Power to award of interest.*[3] Where any Tribunal makes an order for maintenance made under this Act, such Tribunal may direct that in addition to the amount of maintenance, simple interest shall also be paid at such rate and from such date not earlier than the date of making the application as may be determined by the Tribunal which shall not be less than five per cent and not more than eighteen per cent.

The application for maintenance under Chapter IX of the CrPC pending before the commencement of the

20 Section 6.
1 Section 8(2).
2 Section 10(1).
3 Section 14.

Act 2007 is to be withdrawn before there is entitlement to file an application for maintenance under Act 2007.[4]

(*e*) *Enforcement of the order.*[5] Maintenance order may be enforced by any Tribunal in any place where the person against whom it is made.

Appellate Tribunal The State Government may by notification in the Official Gazette, constitute the Appellate Tribunal for each district to hear the appeal against the order of the Tribunal.[6] It shall be presided over by an officer not below the rank of District Magistrate.[7]

Right of appeal An appeal can be filed by any senior citizen or parent or by an aggrieved person.[8]

Right of legal representation Section 17 would not come in the way of legal representation on behalf of the parties.[9]

Application—who can file An application under s. 22 is maintainable against any person. The only right is that the applicant should be a senior citizen and he/she has a property of any kind whether movable or immovable or self-acquired, tangible or intangible and includes and right and interest in such property.[10]

Right of appeal by daughter-in-law She can file appeal when she is an aggrieved party.[11]

Period of limitation Appeal is to be filed within a period of 30 days from the date of order.[12]

4 *Paramjit Kumar Saroya* v *Union of India* AIR 2014 P&H 121.
5 Section 11.
6 Section 15(1).
7 Section 15(2).
8 *Rajeshkumar Bansraj Gandhi* v *State of Gujarat* AIR 2016 Guj 129; *Paramjit Kumar Saroya* v *Union of India* AIR 2014 P&H 121.
9 *Paramjit Kumar Saroya* v *Union of India* AIR 2014 P&H 121.
10 *Balbir Kaur* v *Presiding Officer-cum-S.D.M of the Maintenance and Welfare of Senior Citizen Tribunal, Pehowa, District Kurukshetra* AIR 2016 P&H 4.
11 *Balbir Kaur* v *Presiding Officer-cum-S.D.M of the Maintenance and Welfare of Senior Citizen Tribunal, Pehowa, District Kurukshetra* AIR 2016 P&H 4.
12 *Ibid.*

Procedure

Stage 1

Presentation of appeal

Any senior citizen or a parent who is aggrieved by an order of a Tribunal may prefer an appeal to the Appellate Tribunal within sixty days from the date of order [s. 16(1)].

The Appellate Tribunal may entertain the appeal after the expiry of sixty days if it is satisfied that the appellant was prevented by sufficient cause from preferring the appeal in time [second proviso to s. 16(1)].

Stage 2

Service of notice

On receipt of an appeal, the Appellate Tribunal shall, cause a notice to be served upon the respondent [s. 16(2)].

Stage 3

Call for record

The Appellate Tribunal may call for the record of proceedings from the Tribunal against whose order the appeal is preferred [s. 16(3)].

Stage 4

Hearing of the appeal

The Appellate Tribunal may, after examining the appeal and the records called for either allow or reject the appeal [s. 16(4)].

Stage 5

Decision

The Appellate Tribunal shall adjudicate and decide upon the appeal filed against the order of the Tribunal and the order of the Appellate Tribunal shall be final [s. 16(5)].

No appeal shall be rejected unless an opportunity has been given to both the parties of being heard in person or through a duly authorized representative [proviso to s. 16(5)].

Advantages of the Act The advantages of the Act are:

(1) The senior citizen or parent can file/present the application against any children or relative in any district;[13]

(*a*) where he resides or last resided; or

(*b*) where children or relative resides.

But according to s. 126, CrPC an application by the father or the mother claiming maintenance has to be filed where the person from whom maintenance is claimed lives.[14]

(2) Application must be disposed of within ninety days from the date of service of notice of the application upon the respondent.[15] There is no such time limit in the Code of Criminal Procedure 1973.

(3) No warrant can be issued on account of failure to pay the amount due within a period of three months from the date on which it became due.[16] But according to proviso to s. 125(3), CrPC, no warrant shall be issued for the recovery of any amount due unless application be made to the court to levy such amount within a period of one year from the date on which it became due.

(4) No party to a proceeding before a Tribunal or Appellate Tribunal shall be represented by a legal practitioner.[17]

(5) A copy of the order of maintenance to be supplied without payment at any fee to the senior citizen or to parent.[18]

(6) The maintenance amount must be deposited within thirty days from the date of announcing the order by the Tribunal.[19]

(7) The quantum of maintenance allowance cannot exceed ten thousand rupees per month.[20]

13 Section 6(1).
14 *Vijoy Kumar Prosad* v *State of Bihar* AIR 2004 SC 2123.
15 Section 5(4).
16 Proviso to s. 5(8).
17 Section 17.
18 Section 11(1).
19 Section 13.
20 Section 9(2).

(8) The Tribunal may direct payment of simple interest in addition to the amount of maintenance. Such interest shall not be less than five per cent and not more than eighteen pre cent.[1]

(9) Where any application for maintenance under Chapter IX of the Code of Criminal Procedure 1973 is pending before a court at the commencement of the Act, then the court shall allow the withdrawal of such application on the request of the parent and such parent shall be entitled to file an application for maintenance before the Tribunal.[2]

(10) The Tribunal may also award interim maintenance allowance during pendency of the proceeding.[3]

Father is a pension holder Father who has given his life-long savings to settle the son cannot be denied fruits of earning of the son, merely because he is getting pension.[4]

Will A Will speaks from the date of death of the testator,[5] and it does not involve any transfer, nor effect any transfer *inter-vivos* but is a legal expression of the wishes and intention of a person in regard to his properties which he desires to be carried into effect after his death.[6]

Transferee—meaning The transferee would mean person who is allowed possession and/or occupation of the premises/property or part of the premises/property from which the transferor, *i.e.* the owner of the premises/property can, otherwise, receive income/earning, *i.e* maintenance.[7]

Jurisdiction of civil court barred Civil court has no jurisdiction in respect of any matter to which any provision of the Act applies.[8]

1 Section 14.
2 Proviso to s. 14.
3 Section 5(2).
4 *Deepak Sharma* v *State of Rajasthan* AIR 2016 Raj 188.
5 R.K. Bag & D.P. Dey, *Wills–Law and Practice*, p. 12.
6 *Smt. Rajkanwar* v *Smt. Sita Devi* AIR 2015 Raj 61.
7 *Jayantram Vallabhdas Meswania* v *Vallabhdas Govindram Meswani* AIR 2013 Guj 160.
8 *Deepak Sharma* v *State of Rajasthan* AIR 2016 Raj 188.

Chapter 16

Online Alternative Dispute Resolution

Alternative Dispute Resolution is the buzz word in the present e-commerce world. Perhaps before the concept of arbitration has become a household concept, the next level of Alternative Dispute Resolution is already here. It is Online Alternative Dispute Resolution. This will not only revolutionize the concept of Alternative Dispute Resolution but would also popularize it to a great extent. It is primarily because of the fact that the cyber world is something that is easily accessible to many people who would therefore be aware of such a concept.

Online dispute resolution is a new branch of alternative dispute resolution which uses technology to help dispute resolution between various parties. It primarily tries to include mediation and arbitration along with negotiation, which itself is a form of conciliation or a combination of all three modes. ODR may be instrumental to augment the traditional means of resolving disputes by using innovative techniques and technology in the process. According to American Arbitration Association, "online dispute resolution is a branch of dispute resolution which uses technology to facilitate the resolution of disputes between parties. It primarily involves negotiation, mediation or arbitration, or a combination of all three. In this respect it is often seen as being the online equivalent of alternative dispute resolution. However, ODR can also augment these traditional means of resolving disputes by applying innovative techniques and online technologies to the process".

ODR may be applied to a range of disputes such as interpersonal disputes, consumer to consumer disputes (C2C) or even marital separation, regular court disputes and even the much-hyped interstate conflicts. It is an efficient mechanism in order to resolve disputes and will impact on the development of e-commerce. The application of ODR is not merely limited to the disputes in relation with business to consumer online transactions but it may be apt for all disputes that fall within the ambit of Alternative Dispute Resolution.

Dispute resolution techniques have a range of methods where parties may have full control of the procedure, methods where a third party is in control of the process as well as aware of the outcome. The primary methods of resolving disputes are usually complemented with the Information and Communication Technology.

From a basic approach of the concepts between the regular Dispute resolution and the ODR one would not find any difference in the concept between the two. Both involve a process where the dispute is to be settled by a neutral person and both are to include the process of recording the evidence as well as adjudicating on these issues.

ODR was created from a synergy between ADR and ICT as a method for resolving disputes that were related to traditional or online disputes. With the advent of the ICT it may not be out of place to say that the difference between ODR and the traditional ADR is virtually non-existent. The only and obvious difference between ADR and ODR are that there is the use of technology in one and the other one still follows the traditional system. It is a *sine qua non* that in case of ODR the hindrance of time and place is removed and it not only becomes a quick and easy process but it also becomes cost-effective as well. Generally, in case of traditional ADR one would have to fix a venue and make arrangement for the Arbitrators as well as the parties along with their pleaders to arrive. Moreover, as a usual norm the pleaders or attorneys tend to charge more than their usual fees as they would have to travel to another place. With the advent of online arbitration it would be as simple as a cake-walk for the pleaders as well as an Arbitrator to discuss the matters by way of video-conferencing.

The other revolutionary aspect in ODR is that it has introduced the concept of a fourth party which means that the system by which data is entered is a vital player and it would be capable of maintaining absolute neutrality in recording and transmission of data. The fourth party, i.e. technology also ends up crucially in determining schedules, fixing appointments, trying to enforce deadlines etc. This would reduce the general dilatory practice that is often adopted in other modes. The fourth party is thus also capable of acting as the clerk, attendant, stenographer, personal assistant, etc. Software such as Google Doc, is an example of a software which takes down dictation and it is very simple to use. Thus it is like having a complete setup at the lowest possible cost.

Advantages of cyber arbitration The advantages of cyber arbitration are certainly many. In a world where time is money it is imperative that a quick and easy system of dispute redressal is made. In Technical Notes on Online Dispute Resolution it has been observed that it "can assist the parties in resolving the dispute in a simple, fast, flexible and secure manner, without the need for physical presence at a meeting or hearing. ODR encompasses a broad range of approaches and forms (including but not limited to ombudsmen, complaints boards, negotiation, conciliation, mediation, facilitated settlement, arbitration and others), and the potential for hybrid processes comprising both online and offline elements. As such, ODR represents significant opportunities for access to dispute resolution by buyers and sellers concluding cross-border commercial transactions, both in developed and developing countries".[1] The main advantages of cyber arbitration are:[2]

1. *Cost effective* The cost of transportation of not just the parties but their pleaders along with the Learned Arbitrator tends to become a considerable amount. Moreover, booking a venue is not a cheap deal; along with the venue there has to be other arrangements including making a court set-up. Thus, the chance of having a low-cost dispute resolution becomes almost

1 Resolution adopted by UN General Assembly on 13.12.2016.

2 Pablo Cortes, *Online Dispute Resolution for Consumers in the European Union*, pp. 56-61.

impossible. Once these traditional costs are eliminated, the parties would stand to gain a lot.

2. ***Ensures everyone's availability*** Arbitration usually suffers from the problem of arriving at a mutually convenient date. Usually many Arbitrators and some counsel have to travel to a number of places in order to attend arbitration proceedings. This is mainly because of the fact that a regular lawyer has a number of matters in a day and he manages to attend all of them because the court complex is generally within a confined area and from one courtroom he would be able to rush to the other courtroom. However, in case of arbitration the venues tend to become a bit far. This is because different sets of parties choose different venues based on their preferences as well as their budgets. Moreover, for practitioners who are regularly into arbitration tend to go abroad for international arbitration matters. Thus, with the advent of cyber arbitration as soon as one matter gets over, the practitioner may take switch on his phone and attend the arbitral proceedings. This not only ensures the availability but it also helps in quick disposal of the matters.

3. ***Environment friendly*** The court proceedings generally give one the impression that it involves a lot of paper work. It is perhaps a curse in modern day civilization that till date we are unable to go paperless in court proceedings and thus we are ending up causing irreparable damage to the environment. Only a completely paperless proceeding would help the environment. With the advent of cyber arbitration one would be able to reduce the paper work and show a good gesture towards mother nature.

4. ***Encouraging scientific temperament*** A common idea of the general public are that whenever one enters a courtroom he feels like he is either in a museum or he is transported back in time. The very look of the courtroom makes one feel that perhaps the computer has just come into existence and people are still trying to gather the idea of how to use it. This is mainly because even if one would end up finding a computer with the Judge the pleaders have to rely on the hardcopies. Many are adverse to the idea of the lawyers using their phones or tabs in courtrooms. This is also because the seniors have come up by seeing the conventional methods in the age-old legal profession. Perhaps

the cyber arbitration would change the face of how legal proceedings take place in India.

5. Encouraging foreign investment The global multinationals are often very adverse to the legal systems of the developing countries and they would prefer a quick disposal of any dispute. Moreover, in high-stake matters the top officials of the companies would prefer to attend the proceedings themselves. The world of cyber arbitration would certainly facilitate the top officials of the MNC's to be present and also take important calls.

6. Making India adjust to the international market The law must follow the market if the law is aiming at a greater degree of economic growth. The market situations are often dynamic and complex. Today countries like Saudi Arabia have shown the world how making a nation favorable for trade helps the whole nation to flourish. The world of cyber arbitration undoubtedly will help the countries' legal framework more suitable for international trade and commerce.

7. Quicker disposal of cases Undoubtedly, the very concept of arbitration itself helps in quick disposal of cases but the concept of cyber arbitration goes a step further because of the fact that cyber arbitration would allow a number of proceedings to take place in a day and it would also allow the parties and their pleaders to be available at a mutually convenient time. Hence, one could easily expect that the proceedings may even be held on a day-to-day basis and under such circumstances one may expect the commercial disputes to reach quicker conclusion.

Challenges in cyber arbitration The world of technology is always filled with a number of problems. One could never ignore the fact that the virtual world is susceptible to a number of white collar crimes. Moreover, in a country like India, though the use of mobile phones has become common, but the irony of a large rate of illiteracy still remains. Moreover, India specifically lacks cyber literacy and legal awareness. Thus getting litigations to settle disputes through cyber arbitration is certainly a great challenge ahead. The major challenges that are likely to be faced are:[3]

3 Pablo Cortes, *Online Dispute Resolution for Consumers in the European Union*, pp. 75-83.

1. ***Lack of confidentiality*** It would be impossible to avail the facility of cyber arbitration without the help of service providers like Google, Yahoo, Skype, etc. These players would be instrumental in causing the live streaming of such audio video data. If one were to rely on their own software then the cost of building and operating such a software would be huge, and also it may not provide the quality as being already provided by the major players. Thus it would be apt to hold that the parties as well as the Arbitrator would prefer the cost-effective means by relying on the major players. However, the major problem is that once any data transmission is availed for with the help of major players such as Google, Yahoo, etc., they would end up having access to all the data that is being transmitted. Of course, it would be impractical to think that an institution as big as Google would be able to track all the data. However, the catch is that they rely on finding key words or a string of words. Once they are able to locate such key words or string of words, then they would be able to mark the same and send it up for surveillance. The funny part is that this surveillance process too may be without any human intervention. It is somewhat through artificial intelligence. It is here where the reliability or the importance of a conversation gets marked. Thus, in case of a sensitive matter, one is not completely safe from their data being exposed to the major players.

2. ***Hacking*** Perhaps the greatest threat in the virtual world is hacking. There are two main aspects of hacking that one should be aware of. The first one is of course a genuine instance where a person hacks into your system and ends up finding the data in your system. The second instance is called "*blame the hacker..*". More often than not persons tend to blame the hackers any instance that they are embarrassed to confess. This also means that a person who has the authority to do some thing may often misuse the same and take the plea that his system was hacked. The real problem with hacking is that it is very difficult to trace out instances of hacking, and under such circumstances there would be no means of establishing the truth. In the world of arbitration, there are often high-stake matters and a person who would be able to disclose such confidential information may be able to make a huge profit. Thus, cyber arbitration stands to bear a great degree of risk and chances of hacking.

3. ***Inadequate legal set-up*** It is trite to say that the law is unable to keep up with technology. Each and every day there is a new discovery or development and almost every six months there is a technological revolution. If one were to even observe the middle class they would find that the phones being used by them are mostly of the latest model. The irony is that the Information Technology Act 2000 had its last major amendment on 2008. Thus the law is already a decade behind the present state of affairs. Under such circumstances it would be virtually impossible to settle disputes that may crop up due to such technological non-upgradation.

4. ***Process of recording evidence*** In arbitration the recording of evidence is done in a manner similar to the civil cases with the prime difference that the Code of Civil Procedure or the Evidence Act is not applicable. Moreover, the Arbitrator may not be a person from the law fraternity, and the pleaders themselves may not be advocates but may belong to other fields. Thus, in the absence of a codified legislation there would be huge confusion as to how the evidence would be recorded and whether it would follow a similar fashion to what is usually adopted in courts. This might lead to a great degree of confusion because recording of evidence through video conferencing itself is a tedious process.

5. ***Risk of link failure*** The cyber arbitration process mostly requires a process of online streaming. It would be almost like a news channel where the reporter is directly reporting to the anchor at the news room. In such a situation the net connectivity or the link plays a pivotal role. In situations where the link fails the streaming process is snapped. The risk is even larger when the parties, along with their counsel and the arbitrators may be using different computer systems. Use of different computer systems means that each computer system has the chance of a failing link. The worst part is that even if one link fails the whole process may be affected and halted till the link returns.

6. ***Maintaining records*** Maintaining records would be one of the most difficult processes in any legal proceeding, and without proper maintenance of the records the whole proceedings may be affected. There is no doubt that the virtual world is the best place to store records. The records may be stored in clouds, devices, etc. but the problem is that a mere virus attack or a bug is enough to disrupt the data if not properly protected. Various High Courts have already held that server copies are equivalent to certified copies. However, in case of arbitration a major problem is that there is no uniform site for all Arbitrators. This means that in case of cyber arbitration a new online platform may have to be created.

7. ***No uniform platform*** The courts in India already have found an online platform and the National Informatics Center plays a vital role in that regard. However, the concept of arbitration is basically private and there is a question of creating a new platform for each and every instance of arbitration in the virtual world. Thus in the absence of a uniform platform that would act as a standard platform, implementing the concept of cyber arbitration would be a matter of great difficulty.

8. ***Lack of understanding*** Many people are yet to even understand the concept of arbitration. There are often misconceptions like that as an Arbitrator is paid by the parties, the Arbitrators can be treated like ordinary employees instead of being treated like Judges. The other part is that people often feel that the concept of cyber arbitration is something very expensive and they even feel that they would not be appropriately represented.

9., ***Psychological barriers*** Justice must not only be done but it must also be seen to be done. Often people have accustomed themselves with the idea of a courtroom where the lawyers argue for a long time in front of the judge. Usually the intense atmosphere of the courtrooms is something that people have psychologically adjusted themselves with, anything else may be nothing short of blasphemy. Under such circumstances people may not be able to trust the system of arbitration, let alone cyber arbitration.

Principles In Technical Notes on Online Dispute Resolution it has been observed that "principles that underpin any ODR process include fairness, transparency, due process and accountability. ODR may assist in addressing a situation arising out of cross border e-commerce transactions, namely the fact that traditional judicial mechanisms for legal recourse may not offer an adequate solution for cross border e-commerce disputes. ODR ought to be simple, fast and efficient, in order to be able to be used in a real world setting, including that it should not impose costs, delays and burdens that are disproportionate to the economic value at stage".[4]

Transparency It is desirable to disclose any relationship between the ODR administrator and a particular vendor, so that users of the service are informed of potential conflicts of interest. The ODR administrator may wish to public anonymized data or statistics on outcomes ODR processes, in order to enable parties to assess its overall record, consistent with applicable principles of confidentiality. Pablo Cortes in his book *Online Dispute Resolution for the Consumers in the European Union*[5] has opined: "The principle of transparency sets the information that parties have to be aware of when participating in arbitration, i.e. procedural and substantive provisions. This principle includes transparency with regard to funding systems, which should not create a bias in favour of any of the parties involved".

All relevant information should be available on the ODR administrator's website in a user friendly and accessible manner.

Independence It is desirable for the ODR administrator to adopt a code of ethics for its neutrals, in order to guide neutrals as to conflicts of interest and other rules of conduct. It is useful for the ODR administrator to adopt policies dealing with identifying and handling conflicts of interest. The ODR administrator may wish to implement comprehensive policies governing selection and training of neutrals. An internal oversight/quality assurance process may help the ODR administrator to ensure that a neutral conforms with the standards it has set for itself. Pablo Cortes in his book *Online Dispute Resolution for the Consumers in the European Union*[6] has laid down the following principles regarding Online Dispute Resolution:

1. "The Principle of independence for ODR arbitrators must be equivalent to the standard expected from offline

4 Resolution adopted by UN General Assembly on 13.12.2016.
5 Pages 201-202.
6 Pages 201-202.

neutral third parties; hence, they must not have either an interest in the dispute or a professional or personal connection with one of the parties.

2. "ODR providers must create a fair redress environment, unbiased towards any individual participant in the process.
3. "Software algorithms must similarly be designed to offer no systemic benefit to one party over another.
4. "Online Arbitrator should be immune from legal actions for negligence".

Consent The ODR process should be based on the explicit and informed consent of the parties.[7] Pablo Cortes in his book *Online Dispute Resolution for the Consumers in the European Union* has opined:[8]

"1. The adversarial principle guarantees that the parties can present their arguments fairly in addition to the necessary experts statements. In this regard, the Arbitrator must employ special care so that disputants can use the available ODR technology competently. Another issue that needs to be dealt with is the allocation of the burden of proof. An obvious concern is the vulnerability of electronic documents when used as evidence. Electronic signatures and cryptography may assure authenticity, although often at a high cost. It is necessary to find equilibrium between security, as part of due process, and cost efficiency.

2. "The principle of effectiveness states that dispute resolution processes must be fast and cost effective. Effectiveness must be balanced with the need for maintaining credibility in terms of accuracy of decisions and perceived justice.

3. "The principle of legality implies that adjudicative ODR must comply with the national law of the consumer's habitual residence.

7 Resolution adopted by UN General Assembly on 13.12.2016.
8 Pages 201-202.

4. "The principle of liberty means that the consumer must agree to arbitration freely.
5. "The principle of legal representation states that parties cannot be deprived of their right to be legally assisted, however, parties should not be compelled to use legal representation. There should be a specific mandate for parties in ODR to disclose whether they are legally represented."

Stages of an ODR proceeding An ODR proceeding may consist of stages including negotiation; facilitated settlement; and a third (final) stage. When a claimant submits a notice through the ODR platform to the ODR administrator, the ODR administrator informs the respondent of the existence of the claim and the claimant of the response. The first stage of proceedings–a technology enabled negotiation–commences, in which the claimant and the respondent negotiated directly with one another through the ODR platform. If that negotiation process fails (i.e. does not result in a settlement of the claim), the process may move to a second, "facilitated settlement" stage. At this stage the ODR administrator appoints a neutral, who communicates with the parties in an attempt to reach a settlement. If facilitated settlement fails, a third and final stage of ODR proceedings may commence, in which case the ODR administrator or neutral may inform the parties of the nature of such stage.

Scope of ODR process An ODR process may be particularly useful for disputes arising out of cross border, low value e-commerce transactions. An ODR process may apply to disputes arising out of both a business-to-business as well as business-to-consumer transactions. An ODR process may apply to disputes arising out of both sales and service contracts.[9]

Commencement of ODR proceedings

Preparatory stage In order that an ODR proceeding may begin, it is desirable that the claimant provide to the ODR administrator a notice containing the following information: (*a*) The name

9 Technical Notes on Online Dispute Resolution adopted by General Assembly on 13.12.2016.

and electronic address of the claimant and of the claimant's representative (if any) authorized to act for the claimant in the ODR proceedings; (*b*) The name and electronic address of the respondent and of the respondent's representative (if any) known to the claimant; (*c*) The grounds on which the claim is made; (*d*) Any solutions proposed to resolve the dispute; (*e*) The claimant's preferred language of proceedings; and (*f*) The signature or other means of identification and authentication of the claimant and/or the claimant's representative. The respondent would communicate its response to the ODR administrator within a reasonable time of being notified of the availability of the claimant's notice on the ODR platform, and that the response is to include the following elements: (*a*) The name and electronic address of the respondent and the respondent's representative (if any) authorized to act for the respondent in the ODR proceedings; (*b*) A response to the grounds on which the claim is made; (*c*) Any solutions proposed to resolve the dispute; (*d*) The signature or other means of identification and authentication of the respondent and/or the respondents' representative; and (*e*) Notice of any counterclaim containing the grounds on which the counterclaim is made.

First Stage (Negotiation) The first stage may be a negotiation, conducted between the parties *via* the ODR platform. The first stage of proceedings may commence following the communication of the respondent's response to the ODR platform, and: (*a*) Notification thereof to the claimant; or (*b*) Failing a response, the lapse of a reasonable period of time after the notice has been communicated to the respondent. But if the negotiation does not result in a settlement within a reasonable period of time, the process would proceed to the next stage.[10]

Second Stage (Facilitated settlement) The second stage of ODR proceedings may be facilitated settlement, whereby a neutral is appointed and he communicates with the parties to try to achieve a settlement. It may commence if negotiation *via* the platform

10 Technical Notes on Online Dispute Resolution adopted by General Assembly on 13.12.2016.

fails for any reason (including non-participation or failure to reach a settlement within a reasonable period of time), or where one or both parties to the dispute request to move directly to the next stage of proceedings. Upon commencement of the facilitated settlement stage of proceedings, it is desirable that the ODR administrator appoint a neutral, and notify the parties of that appointment, and provide certain details about the identity of the neutral. If the facilitated settlement cannot be achieved within a reasonable period of time, the process may move to a final stage.[11]

Final stage If the neutral has not succeeded in facilitating the settlement it is desirable that the ODR administrator or neutral informs the parties of the nature of the final stage, and of the form that it may take.[12]

Duties of neutral The duties of neutral are: (*i*) the neutral be enabled to conduct the ODR proceedings in such a manner as he or she considers appropriate; (*ii*) The neutral be required to avoid unnecessary delay or expense in the conduct of the proceedings; (*iii*) The neutral be required to provide a fair and efficient process for resolving disputes; (*iv*) The neutral be required to remain independent, impartial and to treat both parties equally throughout the proceedings; (*v*) The neutral be required to conduct proceedings based on such communications as are before the neutral during the proceedings; (*vi*) The neutral be enabled to allow the parties to additional information in relation to the proceedings; and (*vii*) The neutral be enabled to extend any deadlines set out in any applicable ODR rules for a reasonable time.[13]

Future of cyber arbitration in India Often the legal proceedings are criticized by many due to the huge pendency of cases. The horror of a long-drawn litigation often ends up causing people to forgo their rights and if they are able to draw up a settlement the

11 Technical Notes on Online Dispute Resolution adopted by General Assembly on 13.12.2016.

12 Technical Notes on Online Dispute Resolution adopted by General Assembly on 13.12.2016.

13 Technical Notes on Online Dispute Resolution adopted by General Assembly on 13.12.2016.

parties may stand to benefit. Some people may even find that one party tries to drag the litigation long enough to either frustrate the claim of the opposite party or till one party reaches the end of his life. Civil cases in particular take even a longer time than criminal cases. Thus the litigant often tries to take a rather inappropriate resort to criminal law. However, such cases are either nipped in the bud or else at the time of judgment and the result may not end up being fruitful. The advent of arbitration led to a paradigm shift in such concept of long-drawn litigation. The parties decide for themselves as to what means they shall take to resolve a dispute at the time of entering into contracts and thus at a later stage there is no scope of backing out of such promise. However, there is no bar to entering into arbitration even at a later stage.

The concept of cyber arbitration rather helps to stimulate the concept of arbitration. Today many of the services are either app based or they are online. People even choose digital cash over regular cash or cheque, thus the virtual world is no stranger to the general people. Rather many people are comfortable with the cyber world and refer it to the real world. In such a situation one may hope that people would find it easier to relate to the online arbitration. Even the service providers who are providing their service online would prefer to resolve disputes online. Hence, for them to organize a day solely for the purpose of arbitration, would be a practical as well as a preferable option.

Many of the Non Banking Financial Companies (NBFC) which are not within the purview of the SARFAESI Act tend to rely on the Arbitral awards in order to secure their dues. These NBFC's often give loan to people all over the country but their contract stipulates the venue of arbitration to be where their head office is situated. Here it is practically impossible for the debtor to come down all the way in order to attend the proceedings. Usually the debtor is far more concerned in repaying back the loan instead of attending the proceedings. In such a situation the forum of online arbitration may help in at least to avoid *ex parte* disposal of matters and such debtors may at least have a scope for getting themselves represented. The latest trend is that even the governmental bodies have resorted to arbitration and this may perhaps allow a great deal of private persons having dispute with the government to opt for cyber arbitration instead of taking recourse to the conventional process of arbitration.

The other major player would be the travellers. There are a large number of people who are always on the go. For them to attend a proceeding may require months of planning and the cyber arbitration may just end all their woes. It is almost like watching a live telecast of the proceedings except for the part that the user gets to be a part of the proceedings.

In a country where e-commerce is of such prevalence and now that digital money is in regular use one can expect that the world of cyber arbitration may open up endless possibilities. The best part of it is that it may also result in creating huge employment opportunities. Once litigants end up getting quick reliefs the number of proceedings would go up sky-high. This means that there would be demand of pleaders as well as Arbitrators. On the other hand, the support staves needed would also ensure that people from the IT industry as well as other fields may find more opportunities.

Conclusion Whenever there is anything new it would involve some risks and obstacles. However the real test is whether that idea is here to stay or not. The virtual world has already made its way into the lives of billions of people across the world and the best part is that these are just the initial years of the cyber boom. The number of users would soon multiply. Almost every third person you know would either have an account in social media or at least a mail account. This means that even the virtual world has created a new legacy where people identify themselves with this virtual world. In such a situation turning one's face away from it would be utter foolishness. It would certainly be best to give it a shot and see its fate.

Initially small matters or matters with low monetary involvement shall find its way into this field. This is mainly because the major companies would not feel like taking the risk of their confidential information reaching into the hands of other persons. However, the world of cyber arbitration has the potential of reaching a large number of people at once and this would perhaps be the turning point in the economy of India.

One would also expect a private or a public private partnership in creating a platform for online or cyber arbitration. Once this platform comes into existence it would revolutionize arbitration as a whole and it may be like a major industry. Till such a platform or host arrives it would be difficult for cyber arbitration to reach its peak. Even without the platform one can reasonably expect that the number would not be too little. All it would require is a few business houses to rely on this concept before it takes off.

Chapter 17

Early Neutral Evaluation (ENE)

"If longevity of litigation is made an item in Olympics, no doubt the Gold will come to India."

—NANI PALKHIVALA

Early Neutral Evaluation is a non-binding assessment and evaluation of the facts of the case, evidence of the parties or legal aspect of the case on a particular issue or as a whole. Normally, the parties will appoint a neutral third party to assess and evaluate the facts in issue, evidence and law relating to the dispute in question and after considering all aspects the said evaluator would give his opinion on the merits of the case or a particular issue. It is a process of alternative dispute resolution which has been adopted in the United States of America. In the words of Robert A. Goodin, "Early neutral evaluation is a technique used in American litigation to provide early focus to complex commercial litigation and, based on that focus, to provide a basis for sensible case management or offer resolution of the entire case, in the very early stages". It is merely participative in nature. In *Bawa Masala Company* v *Bawa Masala Company Private Limited*[1] the Delhi High Court adopted this technique to resolve the dispute between the parties as the parties were agreed to settle the same by the process of Early Neutral Evaluation.

When can be resorted to Early Neutral Evaluation can ordinarily be resorted at the early stage of a dispute but there is no legal

1 AIR 2007 Del 284.

bar to utilize this technique at the subsequent stages of the proceedings. But "neutral evaluation employed at the early stages of a case can assist settlement by mediation, and can be carried out before or even during the mediation, and before or at any time during the process of litigation".[2] .

Advantages The advantages are: (1) The evaluation is unbiased.

(2) It will help the parties to settle the dispute or differences between them either by way of negotiation or mediation.

(3) It is very useful paticularly when "one or more of the parties has taken an unrealistic and entrenched view of one or more of the issues, or the case as a whole".[3]

(4) It is very useful when the issues involved in the case require more analytical approach on law, technical or specialist process; and

(5) It can help the parties to appreciate the strength and weakness of the case which paves the way for amicable settlement.

Mode of appointment of evaluator Ordinarily, the parties would appoint the neutral evaluator but they can take the assistance of the ADR provider. In the matter of appointment, law involved in the case, technical or special nature of the case may be considered.

Procedure First, a senior counsel or a panel with expertise and experience in the subject matter of litigation are called upon to conduct ENE. Such persons are referred to as the Evaluator or a neutral person.

Secondly, a written brief is provided by the lawyers to such neutral evaluator, summarising the facts, legal arguments and authorities in support of each party's case. In a nutshell, the process would be same as would be required for making submissions in court.

Thirdly, in the initial session before the evaluator, a decision-maker of each party accompanied by their lawyers would be

2 Jackson, *ADR Handbook*, 2nd Ed., pp 265-266.
3 Jackson, *ADR Handbook*, 2nd Ed., p. 266.

present and a short concise presentation would be made by the counsels for each side referring to the documents and legal propositions. It is open to the evaluator to raise queries on the counsels for the parties and to involve the decision-makers of the parties in the process. The neutral evaluator thereafter retires to prepare what according to the neutral evaluator is the central dispute in the case and what as per the neutral evaluator is the likely outcome on each of the issues/aspects. The evaluator also estimates the costs to each of the parties.

Lastly, the evaluator shares his conclusion with the parties either at joint sessions or at private sessions, called caucuses. Said private caucuses are often useful as they may allow a more frank and free discussion about the strengths and weaknesses of the respective parties. If no settlement is possible the matter is referred back to the court without disclosing the reason for the failure of the process of ENE. Thus, the confidentiality and the principles of mediation are equally applicable to such ENE.

Early Neutral Evaluation and Arbitration—distinction The process of ENE is, however, distinct from arbitration as there is no testimony on oath or examination and such neutral evaluation is not recorded. The process is confidential and cannot be used by any of the parties against the other. There is no award or result filed. It is really a judgment by the neutral evaluator on the basis of material on record without the judgement being binding and in a case of non-acceptance, the matter is referred back to the court without disclosure of reasons as in the case of a mediation.

Early Neutral Evaluation	Arbitration
1. In the process of Early Neutral Evaluation the examination of the parties or recording of their oral testimony is not necessary.	1. Examination of the witnesses on oath is necessary unless dispensed with by the parties.
2. It is private and confidential process.	2. The process is not confidential.
3. No award or formal judgment is required to be passed.	3. There must be an award.
4. It can also "take place outside the litigation process, but parallel with	4. It cannot run parallel with other litigation process.

Early Neutral Evaluation	Arbitration
it, and even before litigation has been commenced at all".[4]	
5. Parties may voluntarily adopt this process.	5. It is a *quasi*-judicial machinery to settle a dispute.
6. It is a non-binding assessment and evaluation of the merits of the case of the parties.	6. Award is binding upon the parties.

Early Neutral Evaluation and Mediation—distinction

Early Neutral Evaluation	Mediation
1. It is an "advisory and Evaluative process".[5]	1. It is not an evaluative process but it is essentially a facilitative process.
2. It is not a process of settlement of disputes by way of discussion towards proposal and counter proposal.	2. Ordinarily terms of settlement come from the parties to the litigation.
3. The duty of the evaluator is to assess the merits and demerits of each party's case.	3. The mediator makes an endeavour to find out the most acceptable solution by bridging the gap between the parties.

Early Neutral Evaluation and section 89, CPC—relation Early Neutral Evaluation is a different form of alternate dispute resolution and so it can be resorted to for a negotiated settlement in pursuance to s. 89, CPC specially when the parties volunteer for the same. The provisions of s. 89, CPC provide for Alternative Dispute Resolution Mechanism, which *inter alia* includes mediation. Early Neutral Evaluation also broadly follows the same process as a mediation, though the concept is not negotiated settlement, but a neutral assessment.

Future in India An early neutral evaluation is a process by which an expert comes to a balanced and unbiased evaluation of the

4 Jackson, *ADR Handbook*, 2nd Ed., p 265.
5 Jackson, *ADR Handbook*, 2nd Ed., p 265.

dispute and identifies the strength or weakness of respective case of the parties. The parties can make a choice for early neutral evaluation by inserting a clause in the contract to that effect. Early neutral evaluation is a form of alternative dispute resolution which has become more popular day by day. In England there is an express provision regarding early neutral evaluation in the Civil Procedure Rules. Early neutral evaluation has great advantage. It conserves and maintains, perpetuates, secures and stock-piles business confidentiality. It can carve and endure acceptable and agreeable litigation manoeuvre and method. It is true it can enhance a scope of communication and interaction between parties about their case and counter case, evidence and counter evidence and give a chance for client and lawyers to assess the real position and pin-point or specify and clarify, explicate, illuminate, simplify the crucial and key issues in dispute in order to throw light on it. It can give the parties and the lawyers the opportunity to diagnose the dispute in question in proper perspective. It can be used in the following situations:

(1) *Deadlock situation* When the parties have reached the situation in which no progress is possible, the independent and impartial evaluator by giving his unbiased opinion would help the parties to arrive at a just settlement.

(2) *Wide disparity between parties* When there is wide disparity between parties ENE can play a great role to remove the gap between the parties.

(3) *Unrealistic view* When one of the parties has an unrealistic view over the dispute in question, the independent evaluator can help him to understand the actual scenario.

ENE has some disadvantages namely: (*a*) The party in whose favour the assessment is made is more reluctant to settle the matter by way of negotiation; (*b*) the loser party will be in disadvantaged position of getting chances of achieving an acceptable settlement or solution; (*c*) it is also disproportionately expensive and time consuming if the parties fail to come to an acceptable solution; and (*d*) ENE procedure is too short and informal to deal with the complex questions involved in the case.

In India more than three crores of cases are pending. In that situation ENE has a significant role to reduce the burden of the court by way of early resolution. Though settlement is not the immediate goal of ENE, the process can flex or tip-off to settlement. In India the cases related to business dispute, dispute between government organisation and service provider, problem regarding construction, i.e. between the promoter and land owner, commercial dispute, dispute between insurer and insured, dispute between landlord and tenant, dispute between shipping and trade, between the couple regarding custody of child, matrimonial dispute, dispute between brothers and sisters regarding the partition or share can effectively be settled through the process of Early Neutral Evaluation and in this way the burden of the court can easily be averted.

The success or failure of Early Neutral Evaluation depends upon the following factors:

1. Party's faith in the fairness and objectivity of the evaluator.
2. Chance of success in the court room dual.
3. Positive attitude of the parties.
4. Advice of the lawyers about the strength or weakness of the case.
5. Family background and social situation.

In India it is our common experience that some lawyers before filing a case categorically and specifically state to the parties about the weakness and plus points of his/her case. This removes the chance of unnecessary litigation. Similarly, Early Neutral Evaluation also helps the parties so that they may not involve themselves in unnecessary litigation. It will save the valuable time and money and restore good relation with his family members, neighbours and service providers. In India if the cases are settled through Early Neutral Evaluation it will save time, money as well as restore mental and social peace. In India there is a great scope to settle matrimonial dispute, custody issues, financial disputes between service provider and contractor and Government organisation and service provider, contractual dispute relating to small business transaction or dispute between partners of a firm can easily be assessed by Early Neutral Evaluation. So in India ENE can be used to analyse and examine any fusion or concurrence and conjunction of legal evidential, factual or technical issue or conundrum. In short, self-confident, self-reliant, unbeholden and untrammelled evaluator can help the parties to apprise and assess the merits of their respective cases. There is great significance of ENE of the present day scenario, where time and money both are the key factors to reduce the burden of the court as well as the financial burden of the individual. If the cases are assessed by way of Early Neutral Evaluation process the parties would be able to specify and identify the issues of controversy and it will demonstrate the limits of the case which will reduce and narrow the gap between the parties which shall ultimately help the parties to restore their mental peace as well as their personal relation.

Chapter 18

Dar-ul-Qaza (Sharia Courts) as Alternative Dispute Redressal Forum

The Arabic word "dar" means "a house" and "*qaza*" denotes a final decision or a binding decree. Etymologically, thus, Dar-ul-Qaza means house of decisions (court). The qazi is the pronouncer of decisions (judge). Down the memory lane of history of Muslim Law we find that Dar-ul-Qazas are empowered to adjudicate civil as well as criminal cases and they even pass an *ex parte* order against parties if they failed to appear before them. *Sadar Nizamat Adalat* was assisted by the chief qazi of the district with two muftis and Islamic law was applicable and fatwas were binding in nature but after 1817 the decisions of qazis and muftis lost their binding character.

Fatwas means opinion given by Dar-ul-Qaza or Kazi on a particular matter of disputed facts or questions. Dar-ul-Qazas and Nizam-e-Qaza are certain types of body who give opinions. The adjudication by a legal authority sanctioned by law is enforceable and binding and meant to be obeyed unless upset by an authority provided by law itself. The power to adjudicate must flow from a validly made law. Person deriving benefit from the adjudication must have the right to enforce it and the person required to make provision in terms of adjudication has to comply with that and on its failure consequences as provided in law are to ensue. These are the fundamentals of any legal judicial system. The decisions of Dar-ul-Qaza or the Fatwa do not satisfy any of the rigors of law. But "about 100 of such courts have been functional for decades. These courts provide speedy and inexpensive justice to poor woman. No one can be forced to go such courts. Their orders are not binding and lack legal sanctity. However, it's perfectly legal if all the parties concerned want to comply with their orders. Unlike the Khap panchayats, these courts do not deal with criminal cases and cannot forcibly enforce their orders".[1]

Dar-ul-Qaza—legal validity Dar-ul-Qaza is neither created nor sanctioned by any law made by the competent legislature. Therefore, the opinion or the Fatwa issued by Dar-ul-Qaza or for that matter anybody is not adjudication of dispute by an authority under a judicial system sanctioned by law. A Qazi or Mufti has no authority or powers to impose his opinion and enforce his Fatwa on any one by any coercive method. In fact, whatever may be the status of Fatwa during Mughal or British Rule, it has no place in independent India under our Constitutional scheme. It has no legal sanction and cannot be enforced by any legal process either by the Dar-ul-Qaza issuing that or the person concerned. The person or the body concerned may ignore it and it will not be necessary for anybody to challenge it before any court of law. It can simply be ignored. In case any person or body tries to impose it, their act would be illegal.

Dar-ul-Qaza as alternative dispute resolution forum The object of establishment of Dar-ul-Qaza or similar type of institution might have been laudable but it has no legal status. It is bereft of any legal pedigree and has no sanction in laws of the land. They are not part of the *corpus juris* of the State. A Fatwa is an opinion only an expert is expected to give. It is not a decree, not binding on the court or the State or the individual. It is not sanctioned under our constitutional scheme. But this does not mean that the existence of Dar-ul-Qaza or for that matter the practice of issuing Fatwas is by itself illegal. It is an informal justice delivery system with the objective of bringing about amicable settlement between the parties. It is within the discretion of the persons concerned either to accept, ignore or reject it. However, as the

1 Faizen Mustafa and Mahendra Shukla, *Justice More Accessible,* The Indian Express, 16th July 2018, p. 7.

Fatwa gets strength from the religious community; it causes serious psychological impact on the person intending not to abide by that. Smt. Monika Arora, criticized the nomenclature of Sharia Court as arbitration centre by putting the question, "if they are mere arbitration/mediation centres, why not call them Sharia counselling or mediation centres?". She also made a excellent line of demarcation between functioning of Sharia Councils in the UK and of Sharia Court in India in the following words: "In the UK, for example, Sharia Councils and not Sharia courts are operated which provide advice to those Muslims who voluntarily choose to use them to resolve civil and family disputes. Therefore, even if both the parties agree to settle their disputes outside the court, these bodies can be called Sharia Councils or arbitration centres but under no circumstances can they be called Sharia Courts."[2]

Social impact Sociologist Anindita Chakraborty made an in-depth study on working of Dar-ul-Qaza in Kanpur and Lucknow and found that Muslim women resolved their family conflicts by approaching (sometimes simultaneously) civil courts, Dar-ul-Qaza as well as local, neighbourhood fora for redressal and help. She also noticed that 95% cases were brought by women either to seek maintenance and /or divorce if the husband was unwilling or unable to provide maintenance. She also pointed out that at times, the Dar-ul-Qaza adjudicated on property redistribution as women preferred it over civil court for its inexpensive and expedient nature.[3] State-sponsored system of codified law and civil and criminal courts co-exists with a whole range of other less formal and unofficial community or religious dispute-settlement bodies. For Muslims, these include qazis' offices, Shariat courts, caste, qaum, or sect panchayats, and Jamaat committees or councils of elders associated with local mosques. Men and women who are experiencing family difficulties normally approach such bodies before, or instead of, turning to

2 Monika Arora, *A Parallel Injustice System*, Indian Express, 27th July 2018, p. 9.

3 Anindita Chakraborty, Suchandra Ghosh, *Judicial Reform versus Adjudication of Personal Law,* Economic & Political Weekly, vol. LII, Issue No. 49, 9th December 2017.

the civil courts. The family court is a place of last resort; only a minuscule percentage of those who experience marital difficulties ever use it. Most still prefer to resolve family disputes by more familiar, informal, local means.[4]

A person cannot raise any question as to issuance of Fatwa on a religious issue or any other issue so long it does not impinge upon the rights of individuals guaranteed under law. Fatwa may be issued in respect of issues concerning the community at large at the instance of a stranger but if a Fatwa is sought by a complete stranger on an issue not concerning the community at large but merely an individual, then the Dar-ul-Qaza or for that matter any body may consider the desirability of giving any response and while considering it should not be completely unmindful of the motivation behind the Fatwa. Thus, Dar-ul-Qaza is not to give any response or issue Fatwa concerning an individual, unless asked for by the person involved or the person having direct interest in the matter. However, in case of the person involved or the person directly interested or likely to be affected being incapacitated, by any person having some interest in the matter, issuance of Fatwa on rights, status and obligation of individual Muslim would not be permissible, unless asked for by the person concerned or in case of incapacity, by the person interested. Fatwas touching upon the rights of an individual at the instance of rank strangers may cause irreparable damage and therefore would be absolutely uncalled for. It shall be in violation of basic human rights. It cannot be used to punish the innocent. No religion including Islam punishes the innocent. Religion cannot be allowed to be merciless to the victim. Faith cannot be used as dehumanising force.[5]

Opinion not enforceable No Dar-ul-Qaza or any body or institution by any name, shall give verdict or issue Fatwa touching upon the rights, status and obligation, of an individual unless such an individual has asked for it. In the case of incapacity of such an individual, any person interested in the welfare of such person may be permitted to represent the cause of concerned individual.

4 Sylvia Vatuk, *Marriage and its Discontents*, pp. 8-9.
5 *Vishwa Lochan Madan* v *Union of India* AIR 2014 SC 2957.

In any event, the decision or the Fatwa issued by whatever body being not emanating from any judicial system recognised by law, it is not binding on anyone including the person who had asked for it. Further, such an adjudication or Fatwa does not have the force of law and, therefore, cannot be enforced by any process using coercive method. Any person trying to enforce that by any method shall be illegal and has to be dealt with in accordance with law.[6] Javed Anand in his article has expressed his great concern about the working of the Sharia Court to the tune of Constitutional principles of India in the following words: "Justice from India's courts of law is a long-drawn and costly process, making justice beyond the reach of India's poor. An alternative dispute redress mechanism may be a great idea. But what fidelity to the constitutional principles of equality (Article 14), non-discrimination (Article 15) and right to life with dignity (Article 21) can we expect from a Sharia court–by whatever name called—headed by clerics who believe and preach that Islam means discriminatory, unjust, inhuman and demeaning anti-women practices such as triple talaq, nikah, halala and polygamy?"[7]

Rename of Fatwa court—an argument Though it has no legal sanctity, it can act as a conciliatory forum or mediation centre to resolve the dispute and differences between the couple, custody issue, family matters or business transaction between the parties if they agree to resolve the same by amicable means or by way of persuasion because the persons who give their opinion on a particular issue is an expert in the said field. Great scholar and academicians Faizen Mustafa and Mahendra Shukla have classically explained the position of Dar-ul-Qaza (Sharia Courts) in the following words, "Dar-ul-Qaza (Sharia Courts) are not courts in the strict sense of the term but counselling or arbitration centres. They are accessible, useful, informal and voluntary institutions that provide speedy and inexpensive justice to the poor."[8] The mediatory role of Sharia Courts and non-binding

6 *Vishwa Lochan Madan* v *Union of India* AIR 2014 SC 2957; (2014)7 SCC 707; (2014)8 Scale 330.

7 *Courts of Injustice*, The Indian Express, 30th July 2018, p. 7.

8 *Justice More Accessible*, The Indian Express, 16th July 2018, p. 7.

nature of fatwas is a reflection and recognition of changing social realities in India which is necessary for prevention and protection of docket explosion in traditional courts. "For it marks, in the Indian context, a change in Islamic legal semantics where a fatwa is no more a judicial verdict and Dar-ul-Qaza is not a court that delivers justice to adversarial litigants but an ADR mechanism to resolve disputes of consenting parties. In which case, the *ulama* may consider re-naming Dar-ul-Qaza as Daral Sulah (Arbitration Centre) and Daral Ifta, the department of fatwa, as Darul Ra'y (Department of Opinions)".[9] In reality, the Apex Court in *Vishwa Lochan Madan's* case gave recognition of these fora as Alternative Dispute Resolution Fora in the legal panorama of family law in India but in order to avoid confusion it is prudent to rename the Sharia Court as Sharia Counselling centres or Sharia Mediation Centre because the word "court" always implies an adjudicatory body created by law and in the name of court no one can violate or undermine the constitutional principles and ethos of rule of law particularly when the Supreme Court has specifically held that adjudication or Fatwa does not have the force of law.

9 A. Faizur Rahman, *New Semantics of Sharia*, The Hindu, 27th July 2014.

Chapter 19

Future and Prospects of the Alternative Dispute Resolution System

> **"A System of Justice which a very substantial section of its own citizens cannot afford is a system which contains a fundamental flaw and leaves them vulnerable to exploitation."**
>
> **—LORD WOOLF**

With the advancement of awareness in general the people are increasingly coming forward to establish their rights through courts. The judicial infrastructure which was grossly inadequate to cope with the existing pressure is now on the verge of being collapsed and it has now become imperative to innovate a mechanism to meet the increasing demand of the people at large. That apart, the conventional justice delivery system is very expensive and it is not possible on the part of the ordinary people to reach the court for getting access to justice. We also experienced that the process of delivering justice is so slow that people often do not expect to get result even during his lifetime. It is mainly on account of inadequate infrastructure and procedural complexities. In adversarial process of delivering justice lawyers play a very important role in shaping the case. Only the rich people can engage the really competent lawyer to represent his case. The poor people come to court ill equipped just to be lost in procedural niceties before agitating the substantive right or denying the liability.

Keeping these aspects in view, we should address the unique system of ADR, an innovation for the society of the future. India is a land of unity in diversity. As a consequence there is diversity of needs as well as interests of the members of the society and their goals are different and therefore, conflict and cross-conflict is an inevitable part of our lives. Some are resolved by way of communication and cooperation and some require assistance of some expert or neutral third party to come to a consensual opinion. In the words of Thomes F. Crum, "Our lives are not dependent on whether or not we have we have conflict. It is what we do with conflict that makes the difference".[1] "Conflict is natural; neither positive nor negative, it just is. Conflict is just an interference pattern of energies. Winning and losing are goals for games, not for conflicts. Learning, growing, and co-operating are goals for resolving conflicts. Conflict can be seen as a gift of energy, in which neither sides loses and a new dance is created. Resolving conflict is rarely about who is right. It is about acknowledgement and appreciation of differences. Conflict begins within, As we unhitch the burden of belief systems and heighten out perceptions, we love more fully and freely".[2]

Alternate Dispute Resolution (ADR) system, as the name suggests, is a system supplementary to the existing justice delivery system we have now. Is the name appropriate? Is it supplementary or supplant to the existing system?

In ancient India we had a beautiful heritage of getting the dispute settled through the village elders. People were trained by habit to accept the verdict even if it went against them. They did not take their disputes to courts ordinarily. But there was no effective force of legal sanction behind those decisions. It is true that sometimes village communities used to enforce its dictates by social boycott. But that had the tendency of being tyrannical and is obviously not suitable for the present social system and structure. Our judicial system is remodeled by introducing ADR to meet the pressing needs. It must be clearly understood that ADR is not something unconnected with the existing judicial system, rather it is an integral part of it.

1 Thomas F. Crum, *The Magic of Conflict—Turning a Life of Work into a Work of Art*, p. 21.

2 Thomas F. Crum, *The Magic of Conflict—Turning a Life of Work into a Work of Art*, p. 49.

Modes of resorting to ADR ADR may be resorted to during the pendency of litigation or even before that. Whenever a dispute arises the parties may, instead of rushing towards courts, get the dispute settled through alternate dispute resolution methods of arbitration, conciliation, mediation or through Lok Adalat . Even the parties involved in a litigation may choose to adopt ADR.

Great virtue of ADR is that unlike adversarial system of justice dispensation, their is no winner or loser in this system. Parties after great deal of deliberation arrive at a decision agreed to by both of them. So the psychological trauma of being defeated or humiliated is totally absent. The ordeal of reaping the fruits of litigation through execution is substantially reduced.

As a part of judicial process The existing judicial system encourages ADR. It has now become the duty of the court to ascertain in pending litigations if there is scope for settling disputes amicably particularly in disputes relating to family matters courts must take initiatives to settle through mediation.

The system, however, is discussed in the backdrop of legal services and legal awareness.

People are now-a-days made aware of their right to get free legal services through institutions set up for that purpose. People may approach the Legal Service Authority instead of approaching the court when any of his rights is adversely affected. The authority then takes necessary initiatives to identify the bone of contention and to arrive at a settlement and for that purpose may summon the other party to take part in a deliberation. When the other party appears, the authority mediates to help them to get their differences resolved. The authority sometimes engages persons having necessary expertise in mediation. If the endeavour succeeds, the matter is directly referred to Lok Adalat, another unique institution innovated for effective ADR system. Though the name contains the word 'adalat', it is not really a court in the traditional sense as we understand. Amongst the judges who constitute such adalat one must be a man having experience in social service. The Lok Adalat does not decide the matter in dispute by applying legal provisions rather its award is based on consensus of the parties to the dispute. But the award can be enforced in a manner as if it were a decree of a civil court. Even the courts may send the parties to the Lok Adalat besides adopting other modes of ADR provided therein, under certain specified circumstances laid down in s. 89 of the CPC and under s. 20 of the Legal Services Authorities Act. In Lok Adalat the approach is more humane than legal. But we must not take ADR as panacea for all evils as it has its own shortcomings too.

The main criticism is that there is every possibility of uncared for problems or the wrongs suffered by the poor, downtrodden or underprivileged sections of the society. Secondly, informal, inexpensive and speedy justice may not always be synonymous with fair justice or adjudication. Thirdly, the decision of the ADR forum may be ill informed due to deficiencies in the decision making process or lack of procedural protection. Fourthly, in reality ADR slows down the development of law because there is no scope for interpretation of law with reference to the dispute in question. Fifthly, by way of legislation new rights have been created to protect women, children and weaker sections of the society. Indeed these new rights would become simply a mirage, if matrimonial disputes or family disputes for enforcement of these rights are referred to mediation. Lastly aims and objectives of the laws relating to woman, child and their rights are inconsistent with mediation, which in India is only a facilitative process, requiring the Mediator to use certain procedures, techniques and skills to help the disputing parties to negotiate agreed resolutions of a dispute without adjudication.

The laws in India give to the Mediator no status higher than a facilitator, and consequently, equal to a Conciliator who can play a proactive and interventionist role. Therefore, the use of the word Mediators may be re-considered. It may also be kept in mind that in USA a Mediator has been given a pro-active role.

Conciliation is a non-adjudicatory ADR process. It is governed by the provisions of the Arbitration and Conciliation Act 1996. There can be a valid reference to conciliation only if both parties to the dispute agree to have negotiation with the help of third party or parties either by an agreement or by the process of invitation and acceptance followed by appointment of conciliator. If both parties do not agree for conciliation, there can be no conciliation.

Apart from conciliation there are other three ADR processes, i.e. Lok Adalat, Mediation and Judicial Settlement. If the parties are not agreeable for either arbitration or conciliation, both of which require consent of all parties, the court has to consider which of the other three ADR processes which do not require the consent of parties for reference, is suitable and appropriate and may as well refer the parties to such ADR processes. If the mediation process is not available the court will have to choose between reference to Lok Adalat or Judicial Settlement.

Mediation has a very important role when the public values are at stake. If the suit is complicated and lengthy, Mediation will be the appropriate choice. In my view divorce proceedings, matrimonial disputes relating to custody and maintenance, domestic violence, labour dispute must be sought to be settled through mediation in lieu of traditional court system. Arbitration is one of the means through which various disputes can be settled. The award of the Arbitrator is binding on the parties and is executable as if a decree of a court. When a matter is settled through Lok Adalat the award is deemed to be a decree of a civil court.

In case of labour dispute arbitration is the most useful instrument or means to resolve the same dispute due to a variety of factors. They are—

(*a*) The parties can select their own Arbitrators;

(*b*) Selected persons are experts in their own field;

(*c*) Experts are neutrals;

(*d*) Procedural nitty-gritty need not be followed;

(*e*) Parties can evolve their own procedure to resolve the dispute;

(*f*) Limited scope of judicial review.

Cases suitable for ADR Process[3] The following categories of cases can be settled through ADR process:

3 *Afcons Infrastructure Limited* v *Cherian Varkey Construction Company Private Limited* (2010)8 SCC 24; JT 2010(7) SC 616; 2010 AIR SCW 4983; (2010)8 SCR 1053.

(1) All cases relating to trade, commerce and contracts, including—

- disputes arising out of contracts (including all money claims);
- disputes relating to specific performance;
- disputes between suppliers and customers;
- disputes between bankers and customers;
- disputes between developers builders and customers;
- disputes between landlords and tenants/licensor and licensees;
- disputes between insurer and insured;

(2) All cases arising from strained or soured relationships, including—

- disputes relating to matrimonial causes, maintenance, custody of children;
- disputes relating to partition/division of property among family members/coparceners/co-owners; and
- disputes relating to partnership among partners.

(3) All cases where there is a need for continuation of the pre-existing relationship in spite of the disputes, including—

- disputes between neighbours (relating to easement rights, encroachments, nuisance, etc.);
- disputes between employers and employees;
- disputes among members of societies/associations/ apartment owners' associations;

(4) All cases relating to tortious liability, including—

- claims for compensation in motor accidents/other accidents.

(5) All consumer disputes, including—

- disputes where a trader/supplier/manufacturer/service provider is keen to maintain his business/professional reputation and credibility or product popularity.

(6) All offences which are compoundable.

Cases outside the scope of ADR Process[4] Certain categories of cases are not suitable for reference for settlement through ADR Process. They are:

(1) Representative suits under Or. 1, r. 8, CPC which involve public interest or interest of numerous persons who are not parties before the court.

(2) Disputes relating to election to public offices (as contrasted from disputes between two groups trying to get control over the management of societies, clubs, association, etc.).

(3) Cases involving grant of authority by the court after enquiry, as for example, suits for grant of probate or letters of administration.

(4) Cases involving serious and specific allegations of fraud, fabrication of documents, forgery, impersonation, coercion, etc.

(5) Cases requiring protection of courts, as for example, claims against minors, deities and mentally challenged and suits for declaration of title against the Government.

(6) Cases involving prosecution for criminal offences.

Law Commission of India—view The Law Commission of India in its 222nd report has enunciated the role of the ADR and its future in the following words:

> There is lot of flexibility in the use of ADR methods. The flexibility is available in the procedure as well as the way solutions are found to the dispute. The solutions can be problem-specific. The rigidity of precedent as used in adversarial method of dispute-resolution will not come in the way of finding solutions to the disputes in a creative way. If ADR method is successful it brings about a satisfactory solution to the dispute and parties will not only be satisfied, the ill-well that would have existed between them will also and ADR methods, especially

4 *Afcons Infrastructure Limited* v *Cherian Varkey Construction Company Private Limited* (2010)8 SCC 24; JT 2010(7) SC 616; 2010 AIR SCW 4983; (2010)8 SCR 1053.

mediation and conciliation not only address the dispute, they also address the emotions underlying the dispute. In fact, ADR to be successful, first the emotions and ego existing between the parties will have to be addressed. Once the emotions and ego are effectively addressed, resolving the dispute becomes easy. This requires wisdom and skill of counselling on the part of the Mediator or Conciliator. The ADR method is participatory and there is scope for the parties to the dispute to participate in the solution-finding process. As a result they honour the solution with commitment. Above all, the ADR methods are cheaper and affordable by the poor also. As of now, there are some aberrations when it comes to the expenses incurred in arbitration. In course of time, when there is good number of quality arbitrators, the expenses of arbitration will also decrease. The promotion of institutional arbitration will go a long way in improving the quality of ADR services and making them really cheaper. The development of ADR methods will provide access to many litigants. It helps in reducing the enormous workload that is put on the judiciary. This will go a long way in improving not only the access to justice but also even the quality of justice.

Relation—ADR System and Court System There is no conflict between traditional law courts and ADR mechanism. Section 89 of the Code of Civil Procedure and r. 1A of Or. 10 provides the stage at which the court should explore whether the matter should be referred to ADR processes, is after the pleadings are complete, and before framing the issues, when the matter is taken up for preliminary hearing for examination of parties under Or. 10. The courts are made to resolve the public or constitutional issues. ADR movement is limited to determine the disputes or resolve the issues only related to private rights, dispute between the parents and school authorities, dispute between landlords and tenant, etc. It is better to say ADR movement is restricted to issues where public laws and constitutional laws are inapplicable. It is true where the settlement agreement in a conciliation or mediation or a settlement award of a Lok Adalat may not require a seal of approval of a court for its enforcement when they are made in a direct reference by the parties without intervention of the court. Whenever settlement is reached before non-adjudicatory ADR forum are placed before the court, the court should apply the principles of Or. 23, r. 3 of the Code.

ADR movement—evaluation ADR movement is in its nascent or formative stage. Some actively criticise ADR as the privatization of justice. Automatically various questions crop up in our mind. They are—

(*a*) what is the impact of ADR upon our traditional court system?

(*b*) who will bear the cost of arbitration, conciliation and mediation?

(*c*) can the scope of s. 12 of the Legal Services Authorities Act 1987 be extended to the ADR mechanism where one of the parties is a pauper or unable to bear the cost of litigation?

(*d*) whether private parties use the ADR in lieu of or in addition to suits?

(*e*) whether ADR is able to resolve to the question of general public importance?

(*f*) whether there is any programme to make ADR mechanism more effective or meaningful in the long run?

(*g*) whether there is any qualification for experts/Conciliators/Mediators?

In India Lok Adalat movement has got a momentum. In our country 9,68,01,825 cases have been settled through Lok Adalat as on 31.03.2017 and compensation awarded in Motor Accident Claim Cases was ₹208, 608, 882, 450 as on 31.03.2017. As on 31.03.2017 total 1,719,168 numbers of Lok Adalats have been organized in the country since its inception.[5] In our country from April 2017 to March 2018 the number of cases settled through mediation is 1,07,587. From April 2017 to March 2018 2297 Judicial officers Mediators, 4875 Lawyers Mediators and

5 *Nyaya Deep*, Volume XVIII, Issue 1&II, January 2017 & April 2017.

815 other Mediators were deployed.[6] In USA the success rate of voluntary ADR proceeding was in the year 2017 was 75%, in the year 2016 was 75%, in the year 2015 is 71%, in the year 2014 was 69% and in the year 2013 was 82% and court ordered proceedings was in the year 2017 is 55%, in the year 2016 was 52%, in the year 2015 was 58%, in the year 2014 was 56 % and in the year 2013 was 62%.[7] In UK reference of family dispute to mediation is mandatory before knocking the door of the court to give them relief. In UK at present settlement rate of dispute by way of mediation is ranging from 86 % to 90%. So, we have miles to go to provide justice at the door step. Snadra Day O' Connor, a former US Supreme Court Judge said "the courts of this country should not be the places where the resolution of disputes begins. They should be the places where the disputes end after alternatives methods of resolving disputes have been considered and tried".

It is high time to consider the role of the ADR functionaries. Problem is that mushroom rise of self-proclaimed ADR experts who claim that they are able to resolve any kind of dispute in any manner whatsoever. This tendency is not only dangerous for the consumers of justice but also the society at large. Sometimes people are misguided and misled by the self-proclaimed experts and their colourful advertisement in the reputed newspapers. The people who are tired due to prolonged litigations, it is very easy to exploit them by offering them to resolve the dispute within a few days or months. People must be aware of this. We believe that ADR movement will be successful in our country to resolve the dispute and differences between the parties in an easy, simple and un-complicated manner. Dedicated experts and Mediators are necessary to resolve the dispute in its right direction. Research, further study and analytical approach by the legal functionaries are necessary to achieve the desired result. Massive awareness must be created about the ADR, so the people can use the ADR mechanism to settle the disputes. We hope and believe that one day the tree of true liberty would bloom in India and everybody will get social justice in the tune of

6 *News Letter*, 2018.

7 Report of Department of Justice, U.S.

constitutional mandate. We are waiting for better tomorrow and best day thereafter.

It is important to remember that ADR is basically a system which is complementary to the prevailing dispute decision system. Those two together may make a whole, the whole being the totality of the judicial system. That explains why they may and should co-exist together in any judicial system prevailing anywhere. It is needless to say, therefore, that ADR does not supplement the prevailing judicial system ordinarily in vogue. The point, therefore, is that the prevailing judicial system and ADR together constitute the whole of the judicial system.

Our Summit Court has encourged the parties and conducting lawyers to settle the disputes amicably out of court. Settlement of cases relating to family dispute, contract related dispute, commercial dispute, dispute between intra-department of Government and contractual dispute between Government and private parties should be encouraged to be settled either by way of arbitration or mediation and for this purpose more and more participation of lawyer is necessary so that the courts can give more time and attention to important legal issues in which the adjudication by the court is urgently required. Out Legislators have great concern with the success of the ADR movement to give a fresh breath to the consumers of justice. In 2015 the Arbitration and Conciliation Act 1996 was amended to make certain provisions for completion of arbitration within a specific time frame and make provision for fast track procedure. In the recent past certain amendments are made in the Specific Relief Act for efficient process of dispute resolution with minimum court interference and also restricting the power of the court to grant injunction in cases if it would impede or delay the progress or completion of any infrastructure project or interfere with the continued provision of relevant facility related thereto or for services being the subject matter of such project. In the words of Great jurist and Judge of the Supreme Court of India, Justice D.Y. Chandrachud, "In a country such as India where dispute resolution mechanisms are dynamic and will continue to develop to meet India's rapidly changing needs, there are myraid opportunities for practitioners of ADR. The extent to which ADR will be successful in India will depend largely on the fostering of an ADR culture within the bar, bench, law schools and society". Thus, in order to give real fruits of settlement of dispute through ADR massive awareness among the litigants, lawyers and each and every stake-holder of the justice delivery system is necessary and to make them aware that this system would develop not to win the case but to maintain peace and harmony in the society. It is the best way to avoid future trouble. In short, the main ideology of this ADR mechanism is not victory of one side but progress of the society. Thus, the co-relation, cooperation and active participation of judges, lawyers, litigants and other stake-holders is mandatory to make it successful and make it a complete institution.

PART TWO

The Gram Nyayalayas Act 2008

Historical perspective The system of justice in India is as old as possibly the World is. The expression "Nyayalaya" has been used in the UPONISHAD itself.

King with the minister used to administer justice to individuals. The system obviously had its own merits and demerits. The limitation of the ancient system was when one had to get justice in a system where the State or the King was also of the parties. Obviously, no litigant could dream of any remedy against the State or the King.

When the Hindu era came to an end, the Indian litigants were treated by the Nawab or the Sultan or the Muslim ruler. In various names it was called. Dewaniam and Dewanikhas are the prominent institutions of the Royal remedies to the Indian litigants.

Again, this system was under challenge of two threats. First, dispensing justice in a system where the ruler or the State was the party. As such any remedy against the State or the ruler was an absurdity. Secondly, in dispensing justice there was a natural tendency to give precedence to the Muslim litigants in preference to the Hindu litigants where the two litigant-parties represented the two classes.

In course of time the doctrine of separation of powers was introduced in Europe. It led to division of powers between the Legislature, the Executive, and the Judiciary.

The ancient system of dispensing justice gave way to introduction of the British Judicial System in course of time during the colonial era. But the British were more interested in commerce first and next in politics. The British wanted to create a middle-class intelligentsia. That is why, the British introduced the Code of Civil Procedure. A litigant seeking for justice has to take recourse to complex and lengthy procedure to obtain remedy in a civil court.

Again, the British also introduced the Code of Criminal Procedure. The finality of decision under the Code of Criminal Procedure is also much time-consuming because of lengthy procedure of the Code of Criminal Procedure. In all probability one of the purposes of the Code of Civil Procedure and the Code of Criminal Procedure lay in benefiting the middle-class intelligentsia who are members of the legal profession.

Presently the litigants have become tired because of long pendency of cases because of redtapism inherent in the Code of Civil Procedure and the Code of Criminal Procedure.

This process of thesis and anti-thesis from dispensing "NYAYA" in the Hindu Era, dispensing justice in the Muslim Era and redtapism of the two Codes has led to synthesization.

The present Act is the said synthesization.

Advantages The following are the advantages flowing from different provisions of the Act:

(*a*) The litigants are benefited most because they get justice speedily. The lengthy procedure has been cut short. Thus time, energy and money of the litigants are saved.

(*b*) The members of the legal profession are benefited next. The roll-strength of the bar is increasing day by day. The filing both on Civil and Criminal side are diminishing. As more or less 10% of each bar association are active legal practitioners, the remaining 90% are dependant directly or indirectly on the 10% active legal practitioner. There is no denial of the fact that frustration and sharp practice are independent provision to carry on independent profession at the doorsteps will nurture fresh oxygen and help to the beginners and at least those who are not high aspirants.

(*c*) It will benefit the society. An ever vigilant judiciary at hand with its eyes and ears open renders much more service to the Sub-Divisional Judicial system lying far away from the remote villages as well as from district headquarters.

Indeed, if the short-comings are obviated, then the rule of law and an environment of peace can be restored in all corners of India.

Criticism of the Act—powers Section 6 postulates that a person shall not be qualified to be appointed as a Nyayadhikari unless he is eligible to be appointed as a Judicial Magistrate of the First Class. Section 5 has vested the power of appointment of Nyayadhikari with State Government. Consequently, State Government or in other words, executive shall be the appointing authority of the judicial system. It is doubtful if a Nyayadhikari shall have the courage to pass any judgment against the State Government. It is suggested that the power of appointment subject to test or interview is to be vested with the Judiciary, *i.e.* the High Court.

There is marked disparity between the schedules and the qualification of a Nyayadhikari appointed under s. 6. It cannot ever be dreamt of that Judicial Magistrate of the First Class or a Munsif has the qualification trying a suit concerning specific performance of contract of unlimited pecuniary jurisdiction (Second Schedule, Part (*i*)(*a*) right to purchase of property).

Recovery of possession (Second Schedule (*ii*)(*a*) village and farm house possession).

Item (*iii*) (*a*) claims under the Payment of Wages Act 1936.

(*b*) Claims under the Minimum Wages Act 1948.

(*c*) Money suits (obviously of unlimited jurisdiction).

(*d*) Disputes arising out of partnership of unlimited pecuniary jurisdiction.

(*e*) Disputes as to use of forest produce.

It is submitted that while some of the items mentioned in the schedule are now triable by the Senior Judges, such as Civil Judges (Senior Division) and even District Judges and Additional District Judges.

The vesting of power of trying civil suits of the nature mentioned above is never expected at the hands of a junior officer and that too appointed by the State Government. It is sure to frustrate the very policy for execution of which it has been enacted.

Reasons for enactment Gram Nyayalayas Act was enacted for the following reasons.[1]

1. Access to justice by the poor and the disadvantaged remains a worldwide problem. Article 39A of the Constitution directs the State to secure that the operation of the legal system promotes justice, on the basis of equal opportunity, and shall, in particular provide free legal aid, by suitable legislation or schemes or in any other way, to ensure that opportunities for securing justice are not denied to any citizen by reason of economic or other disabilities.

2. To give effect to the said mandate the Government has taken various measures to strengthen the judicial system by simplifying the procedural laws; incorporating various alternative dispute resolution mechanisms such as arbitration, conciliation and mediation, conducting of Lok Adalats, etc., establishing Fast Track Courts, Special Courts and Tribunals and providing free legal aid to the poor, women and children.

3. To provide access to justice at the grass root level, the Law Commission of India in its 114th Report on Gram Nyayalaya recommended establishment of Gram Nyayalyas so that speedy, inexpensive and substantial justice could be provided to the common man. Accordingly, the Government introduced the Gram Nyayalayas Bill 2007 in Rajya Sabha on 15th May 2007 to give effect to the said recommendations of the Law Commission. The bill was referred to the Department Related Standing Committee on Personnel, Public Grievances, Law and Justice. The said Standing Committee presented its twenty-second Report on the 6th September 2007. The recommendations made by the said standing Committee are substantive in nature and the Government has accepted most of its recommendations. Further the Government on 1st February 2008 had organised a conference of State Law Ministers, Law Secretaries and Registrar Generals of High Courts to seek their views on the various

1 Statement of Objects and Reasons, the Gram Nyayalayas Bill 2008.

provisions of the said Bill. The suggestions made at the said conference were also considered by the Government. Since giving effect to the recommendations of the Department Related Standing Committee and also the suggestions made at the conference required amendments to almost all the clauses of the Bill, it is considered appropriate by the Government to withdraw the said Bill and to introduce a fresh Bill on the lines recommended by the said Standing Committee.

Features of Gram Nyayalayas Bill The main features of the Gram Nyayalayas Bill are as follows:

(*a*) The Gram Nyayalaya shall be court of Judicial Magistrate of the First Class and its presiding officer (Nyayadhikari) shall be appointed by the State Government in consultation with the High Court. The qualifications, salary, terms and conditions of service of the Nyayadhikari shall be the same as that of the Judicial Magistrate of the First Class;

(*b*) the Gram Nyayalaya shall be established for every Panchayat at intermediate level or a group of contiguous Panchayats at intermediate level in a district or where there is no Panchayat at intermediate level in any State, for a group of contiguous Panchayats;

(*c*) the Gram Nyayalaya shall be a mobile court and shall exercise the powers of both Criminal and Civil Courts. The pecuniary jurisdiction of the civil suits, etc. shall be notified by the concerned High Court;

(*d*) the Gram Nyayalaya shall try criminal cases, civil suits, claims or disputes which are specified in the First Schedule and the Second Schedule to the proposed Bill;

(*e*) the Central Government as well as the State Governments have been given power to amend the First Schedule and the Second Schedule of the proposed Bill as per their respective legislative competence;

(*f*) the Gram Nyayalaya shall follow summary procedure in criminal trial as provided under sub-sec. (1) of s. 262 and ss. 262, 264 and 265 of the Code of Criminal Procedure 1973 with certain modifications and as regards other matters which are not provided in the Bill, the provisions of the Code of Criminal Procedure shall be applicable;

(*g*) the Gram Nyayalaya shall exercise the powers of a Civil Court with certain modifications and shall follow the special procedure as provided in the Bill; as regards other matters which are not provided in the Bill, the provisions of the Code of Civil Procedure 1908 shall be applicable;

(*h*) the Gram Nyayalaya shall try to settle the disputes as far as possible by bringing about conciliation between the parties and for this purpose, it shall make use of the Conciliators to be appointed;

(*i*) the judgment and order passed by the Gram Nyayalaya shall be deemed to be a decree and to avoid delay in its execution, the Gram Nyayalaya shall follow summary procedure for its execution;

(*j*) the Gram Nyayalaya shall not be bound by the rules of evidence provided in the Indian Evidence Act 1872 but shall be guided by the principles of natural justice and subject to any rule made by the High Court;

(*k*) an appeal from the judgment, sentence or order of the Gram Nyayalaya in criminal cases, to the extent provided in the Code of Criminal Procedure 1973 shall lie to the Court of Session, which shall be heard and disposed of within a period of six months from the date of filing of such appeal;

(*l*) an appeal from the judgment and order of the Gram Nyayalaya in civil cases, to the extent provided in the Code of Civil Procedure 1908 shall lie to the District Court, which shall be heard and disposed of within a period of six months from the date of filing of the appeal;

(*m*) a person accused of an offence may file an application for plea bargaining in Gram Nyayalaya in which such offence is pending trial and the same will be disposed of by that Gram Nyayalaya in accordance with the provisions of Chapter XXIA of the Code of Criminal Procedure 1973.

The Gram Nyayalayas Act 2008

An Act to provide for the establishment of Gram Nyayalayas at the grass roots level for the purposes of providing access to justice to the citizens at their doorsteps and to ensure that opportunities for securing justice are not denied to any citizen by reason of social, economic or other disabilities and for matters connected therewith or incidental thereto.

BE it enacted by Parliament in the Fifty-ninth year of Republic of India as follows:

CHAPTER I

Preliminary

1. Short title, extent and commencement. (1) This Act may be called the Gram Nyayalayas Act 2008.

(2) It extends to the whole of India except the State of Jammu and Kashmir, the State of Nagaland, the State of Arunachal Pradesh, the State of Sikkim and to the tribal areas.

Explanation. In this sub-section, the expression 'tribal areas' means the areas specified in Parts I, II, IIA and III of the Table below paragraph 20 of the Sixth Schedule to the Constitution within the State of Assam, the State of Meghalaya, the State of Tripura and the State of Mizoram, respectively.

(3) It shall come into force[2] on such date as the Central Government may, by notification published in the Official Gazette, appoint; and different dates may be appointed for different States.

Object of statement and reasons The main purpose of the statement of objects and reasons of the Bill is to explain what reasons induced the mover to introduce the Bill in the House and what object be sought to achieve.[3]

Rules of construction of a statute A cardinal principle of construction of statute that the true or legal meaning of an enactment is derived by considering the meaning of the words used in the enactment in the light of any discernible purpose or object which

2 Came into force on 02.10.2009 *vide* Notification No. S.O. 2313(E) dated 11.9.2009, Gazette of India, Extra., Part II–section 3(*ii*).

3 *Union of India* v *Elphinstone Spinning and Weaving Co. Ltd.* AIR 2001 SC 724.

comprehends the mischief and its remedy to which the enactment is directed.[4]

Language used in the Act is to be liberally construed so as to give effect to the governing principles embodies in the legislation. Whenever a statute comes up for consideration it must be remembered that it is not within human powers to foresee the manifold sets of facts which may arise, and, even if it were, it is not possible to provide for them in terms free from all ambiguity.[5] The words of a statute must *prima facie* be given their ordinary meaning.[6] Statutory interpretation is an exercise which requires the court to identify the meaning borne by the words in question in the particular context. The purpose of the Act of section has to be inferred from the language used, read in its statutory content and having regard to any aid to interpretation which assists in the particular case.[7]

Rules of interpretation The principle of rule of interpretation requires two things—

(*a*) first, while interpreting two inconsistent, or, obviously repugnant provisions of an Act, the courts should make an effort to interpret the provisions as to harmonise them so that the purpose of the Act may be given effect to and both the provisions may be allowed to operate without rendering either of them otiose, and

(*b*) secondly, the statute has to be read as a whole to find out the real intention of the legislature.[8]

The important principles of interpretation are as follows:

(1) It is the duty of the courts to avoid a head-on clash between two sections of the Act and to construe the provisions which appear to be in conflict with each other in such manner as to harmonize them.

4 *Union of India* v *Elphinstone Spinning and Weaving Co. Ltd.* AIR 2001 SC 724.

5 *Seaford Court Estates Ltd.* v *Asher* [1949]2 All ER 155.

6 *Noke* v *Doncasster Collieries* [1940]3 All ER 549.

7 *R* v *Secretary of State* [2001]1 All ER 195.

8 *Sultana Begum* v *Prem Chand Jain* (1997)1 SCC 373.

(2) The provisions of one section of a statute cannot be used to defeat the other provision unless the court, in spite of its efforts, finds it impossible to effect reconciliation between them.

(3) It has to be borne in mind by all the courts all the time that when there are two conflicting provisions in the Act, which cannot be reconciled with each other, they should be so interpreted that, if possible, effect should be given to both. This is the essence of the rule of "harmonious construction."

(4) The courts have also to keep in mind that an interpretation which reduces one of the provisions as a "dead letter" or "useless lumber" is not harmonious construction.

(5) To harmonize is not to destroy any statutory provision or to render it otiose.

Intention of Legislature The Legislature's intention is relevant only when the language used by it is ambiguous, capable of two interpretations, and the court is required to adopt that interpretation which is in accordance with the legislature's intention. If the language is simple or plain, having only one interpretation, the court's duty is to adopt that interpretation and it would not be justified in embarking upon any inquiry into the Legislature' intention. Moreover, even when a court has to ascertain the Legislature's intention, it has to do from the words used by itself; it cannot speculate about the Legislature's intention or assume it without any data.[9]

2. Definitions. In this Act, unless the context otherwise requires,—

(*a*) 'Gram Nyayalaya' means a court established under sub-section (1) of section 3;

(*b*) 'Gram Panchayat' means an institution (by whatever name called) of self-government constituted, at the village level, under Article 243B of the Constitution, for the rural areas;

(*c*) 'High Court' means,—

(*i*) in relation to any State, the High Court for that State;

(*ii*) in relation to a Union territory to which the jurisdiction of the High Court for a State has been extended by law, that High Court;

---

9 *Bansraj* v *State* AIR 1956 All 27.

(*iii*) in relation to any other Union territory, the highest court of criminal appeal for that territory other than the Supreme Court of India;

(*d*) 'notification' means a notification published in the Official Gazette and the expression 'notified' shall be construed accordingly;

(*e*) 'Nyayadhikari' means the presiding officer of a Gram Nyayalaya appointed under section 5.

(*f*) 'Panchayat at intermediate level' means an institution (by whatever name called) of self-government constituted, at the intermediate level, under Article 243B of the Constitution, for the rural areas in accordance with the provisions of Part IX of the Constitution;

(*g*) 'prescribed' means prescribed by rules made under this Act;

(*h*) 'Schedule' means the Schedule appended to this Act;

(*i*) 'State Government', in relation to a Union territory, means the administrator thereof appointed under Article 239 of the Constitution;

(*j*) words and expressions used herein and not defined but defined in the Code of Civil Procedure, 1908 (5 of 1908) or the Code of Criminal Procedure, 1973 (2 of 1974) shall have the meaning respectively assigned to them in those Codes.

Proviso "The proper function of a proviso is to except and to deal with a case which would otherwise fall within the general language of the main enactment, and its effect is confined to that case."[10] A proviso is "added to an enactment to quality or create an exception to what is in the enactment, and ordinarily, a proviso is not interpreted as stating a general rule."[11]

Purpose A proviso may serve five different purposes:

(1) qualifying or excepting certain provisions from the main enactment;

(2) it may entirely change the very concept of the intendment of the enactment by insisting on certain mandatory conditions to be fulfilled in order to make the enactment workable;

10 *M. & S.M. Railway Co. Ltd.* v *Bezwada Municipality* AIR 1944 PC 71.

11 *Ishverlal Thakorelal Almaula* v *Motibhai Nagjibhai* (1966)1 SCR 367; AIR 1966 SC 459.

(3) it may be so embedded in the Act itself as to become an integral part of the enactment and thus acquire the tenor and colour of the substantive enactment itself; and

(4) it may used merely to act as an optional addenda to the enactment with the sole object of explaining the real intendment of the statutory provision.[12]

(5) Where the proviso consists of two parts, one part may be declaratory but the other part may not be so. Therefore, merely because one part of the proviso has been held to be declaratory it does not follow that the second part of the proviso is also declaratory.[13]

Explanation An explanation added to a statutory provision is not a substantive provision in any sense of the term but as the plain meaning of the word itself shows it is merely meant to explain or clarify certain ambiguities which may have crept in the statutory provision.[14]

Object The object of an explanation to statutory provision is:[15]

(*a*) to explain the meaning and intendment of the Act itself,

(*b*) where there is any obscurity or vagueness in the main enactment, to clarify the same so as to make it consistent with the dominant object which it seems to subserve,

(*c*) to provide an additional support to the dominant object of the Act in order to make if meaningful and purposeful,

(*d*) an explanation cannot in any way interfere with or change the enactment or any part thereof but where some gap is left which is relevant for the purpose of the explanation, in order to suppress the mischief and

12 *Shah Bhojraj Kuverji Oil Mills & Ginning Factory* v *Subhash Chandra Yograj Sinha* (1962)2 SCR 159; AIR 1961 SC 1596; *S. Sundaram* v *V.R. Pattabiraman* AIR 1985 SC 582; (1985)1 SCC 591; (1985)1 Cur CC 904; (1985)1 Rent LR 414.

13 *Commissioner of Income-Tax, Bhopal* v *M/s. Shelly Products* AIR 2003 SC 2532.

14 *S. Sundaram Pillai* v *V.R. Pattabiraman* AIR 1985 SC 582; (1985)1 SCC 591; 1985(1) Cur CC 904; 1985(1) Rent LR 414.

15 *S. Sundaram Pillai* v *V.R. Pattabiraman* AIR 1985 SC 582; (1985))1 SCC 591; 1985(1) Cur CC 904; 1985(1) Rent LR 414.

advance the object of the Act if can help or assist the court in interpreting the true purport and intendment of the enactment, and

(*e*) if cannot, take away a statutory right with which any person under a statute has been clothed or set at naught the working of an Act by becoming an hindrance in the interpretation of the same.

According to *Bindra's Interpretation of Statutes*,[16] "an explanation does not enlarge the scope of the original section that it is supposed to explain. It is axiomatic that an explanation only explains and does not expand or add to the scope of the original section. The purpose of an explanation is, however, not to limit the scope of the main provision. The construction of the explanation must depend upon its terms, and no theory of its purpose can be entertained unless it is to be inferred from the language used. An 'explanation' must be interpreted according to its on tenor".

Preamble Preamble is the introductory part of a statute. It should be read along with other provisions of the Act to find out the meaning of the words in enacting provisions to decide whether they are clear or ambiguous but the preamble in itself not being an enacting provision is not of the same weight as an aid to construction of a section of the Act as are other relevant enacting words to be found elsewhere in the Act. The utility of the preamble diminishes on a conclusion as to clarity of enacting provisions. It is therefore said that the preamble is not to influence the meaning otherwise ascribable to the enacting parts unless there is a compelling reason for it. If in an Act the preamble is general or brief statement of the main purpose, it may well be of little value. Where the language of an Act is clear, the preamble must be disregarded though, where the object meaning of an enactment is not clear the preamble may be resorted to explain it. Where very general language is used in an enactment which, it is clear must be intended to have a limited application, the preamble may be used to indicate to what particular instances, the enactment is intended to apply. The preamble cannot control

16 *Bindra's Interpretation of Statutes*, 5th Ed., p. 67.

the enacting part of a statute, which is expressed in clear and unambiguous terms. But if any doubt arise on the words of the enacting part, the preamble may be resorted to, to explain it.[17]

A definitional clause A definitional clause is a small dictionary. The meaning which it gives to the words is always subject to context.[18]

Impact or use of definition clause When a word has been defined in the interpretation clause, *prima facie* that definition governs wherever that word is used in the body of the statute unless the context requires otherwise. According to the context, Cross-Statutory Interpretation "is both internal and external". The internal context requires the interpreter to situate the disputed words within the section of which they are part in relation to the rest of the Act. The external context involves determining the meaning from ordinary linguistic usage (including any special technical meanings), from the purpose for which the provision was passed, and from the place of the provisions within the general scheme of statutory and common law rules and principles.

Even where the definition is exhaustive inasmuch as the word defined is said to mean a certain things, it is possible for the word to have a somewhat different meaning in different sections of the Act depending upon the subject or context.[19]

Character An interpretation clause of a comprehensive character is "not to be taken as strictly defining what the meaning of a work must be under all circumstances but merely as declaring what things may be comprehended within the term, here the circumstances require that they should".[20]

Include and definition clause Where in a definition clause the word 'include' is used, it is so done in order to enlarge the meaning of the works or phrases occurring in the body of the statute when it is so used, these words or phrases must be construed as comprehending not only such things which they signify according to their natural import, but also those things which the interpretation clause declares that they shall include.

17 *Attorney-General* v *H.R.H. Prince Ernest Augustus of Hanover* [1957] AC 436; [1957]1 All ER 49.

18 *Sunkara Laxman Rao* v *D China Papaiah Raju* AIR 1980 AP 191.

19 *Pushpa Devi* v *Milkhi Ram* (1990)2 SCC 134.

20 *S.I. Bank* v *Pichuthayappan* AIR 1954 Mad 377.

Where in a definition section of a statute, a word is defined to mean a certain thing, wherever that word is used in that statute, it shall mean what is stated in the definition unless the context otherwise requires. But where the definition is an inclusive definition, the word not only bears its ordinary, popular and natural sense whenever that would be applicable but it also bears its extended statutory meaning. At any rate, such expansive definition should be so construed as not cutting down the enacting provisions of an Act unless the phrase is absolutely clear in having opposite effect.[21]

How interprete All statutory definitions have to be read subject to the qualification variously expressed in the definition clauses which created them and it may be that even where the definition is exhaustive inasmuch as the word defined is said to mean a certain thing, it is possible for the word to have a somewhat different meaning in different sections of the Act depending upon the subject or context. That is why all definitions in statutes generally begin with the qualifying words, similar to the words used in the present case, namely "unless there is anything repugnant in the subject or context". Thus there may be sections in the Act where the meaning may have to be departed from on account of the subject or context in which the word had been used and that will be giving effect to the opening sentence in the definition section, namely "unless there is anything repugnant in the subject or context". In view of this qualification, the court has not only to look at the words but also to look at the context, the collocation and the object of such words relating to such matter and interpret the meaning intended to be conveyed by the use of the words "under those circumstances".[22]

CHAPTER II

Gram Nyayalaya

3. Establishment of Gram Nyayalayas. (1) For the purpose of exercising the jurisdiction and powers conferred on a Gram Nyayalaya by this Act, the State Government, after consultation with the High

21 *S.K. Gupta* v *K.P. Jain* AIR 1979 SC 734; (1979)3 SCC 54; 1979 Tax LR 2053.

22 *Whirlpool Corpn.* v *Registrar of Trade Marks* (1998)8 SCC 1.

Court, may, by notification, establish one or more Gram Nyayalayas for every Panchayat at intermediate level or a group of contiguous Panchayats at intermediate level in a district or where there is no Panchayat at intermediate level in any State, for a group of contiguous Gram Panchayats.

(2) The State Government shall, after consultation with the High Court, specify, by notification, the local limits of the area to which the jurisdiction of a Gram Nyayalaya shall extend and may, at any time, increase, reduce or alter such limits.

(3) The Gram Nyayalayas established under sub-sec. (1) shall be in addition to the courts established under any other law for the time being in force.

Appointment after consultation The State Government after consultation with the High Court may by notification establish one or more Gram Nyayalayas for every Panchayat or a group of contiguous Panchayats at intermediate level in a District. The consultation with the High Court is mandatory and its infraction renders the appointment illegal.

Object of consultation The object of consultation is to render consultation meaningful to serve or achieve the intended purpose of the Act. Prior consultation is obligatory. The Apex Court in *Indian Administrative Service (SCS) Association, U.P.* v *Union of India*[1] observed that when the object of the consultation is only to apprise of the proposed action and when the opinion or advice is not binding on the authorities or person and is not bound to be accepted, the prior consultation is only directory. The State Government after consultation with the High Court may at any time extend, increase or reduce or alter the local limits of the jurisdiction of the Gram Nyayalaya. The Gram Nyayalayas are established in addition to courts established under any other law for the time being in force to reach the justice at the doorsteps of the litigants.

4. Headquarters of Gram Nyayalaya. The headquarters of every Gram Nyayalaya shall be located at the headquarters of the intermediate Panchayat in which the Gram Nyayalaya is established or such other place as may be notified by the State Government.

1 1993 AIR SCW 1135.

Scope of s. 4 Sitting of the Gram Nyayalaya must be held at the headquarters of the intermediate Panchayat. The State Government may also notify any place as headquarters of the Gram Nyayalaya.

> **5. Appointment of Nyayadhikari.** The State Government shall, in consultation with the High Court, appoint a Nyayadhikari for every Gram Nyayalaya.

Scope of s. 5 The State Government shall appoint Nyayadhikari for Gram Nyayalaya after consultation with the High Court. Consultation implies meeting of minds between the State Government (proposer) and the High Court (the persons to be consulted) on the subject of consultation.

> **6. Qualification for appointment of Nyayadhikari.** (1) A person shall not be qualified to be appointed as a Nyayadhikri unless he is eligible to be appointed as a Judicial Magistrate of the First Class.
>
> (2) While appointing a Nyayadhikari, representation shall be given to the members of the Scheduled Castes, the Scheduled Tribes, women and such other classes or communities as may be specified by notification, by the State Government from time to time.

Qualification A person shall be appointed as Nyayadhikari if he is qualified or eligible to be appointed as a Judicial Magistrate of the First Class.

Code of Criminal Procedure and Gram Nyayalayas Act—comparison Section 11(3) of the Code of Criminal Procedure provides that the High Court may, whenever it appears to it to be expedient or necessary, confer the powers of a Judicial Magistrate of the first class or of the second class on any member of the Judicial Service of the State, functioning as a Judge in a civil court. If we reconcile the provisions of s. 6 of the Act and s. 11(3) of the Code of Criminal Procedure, it appears that Nyayadhikari would be a Law Graduates with other qualifications which is necessary to qualify for the State Judicial Service. At the time of appointment of Nyayadhikari it must be considered that the members of the Scheduled Caste, the Scheduled Tribes, women and such other classes or communities should be properly or adequately represented. Section 6(2) is incorporated in the Act to establish that members of all the sections of the society are properly represented or involved in the Justice Delivery System.

7. **Salary, allowances and other terms and conditions of service of Nyayadhikari.** The salary and other allowances payable to, and the other terms and conditions of service of, a Nyayadhikari shall be such as may be applicable to the Judicial Magistrate of the first class.

Scope of s. 7 Nyayadhikari shall receive such salary and other allowance as may be provided for the Judicial Magistrate of the first class.

8. **Nyayadhikari not to preside over proceedings in which he is interested.** The Nyayadhikari shall not preside over the proceedings of a Gram Nyayalaya in which he has any interest or is otherwise involved in the subject matter of the dispute or is related to any party to such proceedings and in such a case, the Nyayadhikari shall refer the matter to the District Court or the Court of Session, as the case may be, for transferring it to any other Nyayadhikari.

Scope of s. 8 Nyayadhikari is not empowered to preside over the proceedings of a Gram Nyayalaya in the following situations:

(*a*) when he has any interest in the subject matter of the dispute;

(*b*) when he is otherwise involved in the subject matter of the dispute;

(*c*) when he is related to any party to the proceedings.

If the petitioner or the respondent is a relative of Nyayadhikari either by blood or adoption, then he is not authorized to preside over the proceedings.

Object The main object behind the enactment of this section is to provide fair or unbiased justice to the consumers of justice.

Procedure During the pendency of the proceedings if it appears to the Nyayadhikari that he has some interest in the proceedings directly or indirectly or one of the parties to the proceedings is his relative, he shall refer the matter to the District Judge or the Court of Session for transferring it to any other Nyayadhikari. Such Nyayadhikari shall have all the power of the previous Nyayadhikari as if the said matter in dispute was initiated or filed before him.

9. **Nyayadhikari to hold mobile courts and conduct proceedings in villages.** (1) The Nyayadhikari shall periodically visit the villages

> falling under his jurisdiction and conduct trial or proceedings at any place which he considers is in close proximity to the place where the parties ordinarily reside or where the whole or part of the cause of action had arisen:
>
> Provided that where the Gram Nyayalaya decides to hold mobile court outside its headquarters, it shall give wide publicity as to the date and place where it proposes to hold mobile court.
>
> (2) The State Government shall extend all facilities to the Gram Nyayalaya including the provision of vehicles for holding mobile court by the Nyayadhikari while conducting trial or proceedings outside its headquarters.

Scope of s. 9 The Nyayadhikari must visit the villages within its jurisdiction periodically to conduct trial or proceedings. He shall conduct trial at any place which he considers is in close proximity to the place where the parties ordinarily reside or where the cause of action wholly or partly arises. Causes of action means bundle of essential facts which are necessary for the suitor to establish his case. The Gram Nyayalaya may also hold mobile court outside its headquarters after giving wide publicity of the time, schedule, date or venue of the mobile court. The State Government is under obligation to extend cooperation to the Gram Nyayalaya to facilitate the works for holding court by the Nyayadhikari.

Object The main object of the Constitution is to provide 'Justice social, economic and political' to the people of India particularly downtrodden masses who are still afraid to visit the Court due to financial constraints or other social factors. Article 38(1) of the Constitution provides that the State shall strive to promote the welfare of the people by securing and protecting as effectively as it may a social order in which justice social, economic and political shall inform all the institutions of the national life. People's participation in the Justice Delivery System or to provide justice at the doorsteps are the Constitutional goal. This section is enacted by the Legislature keeping in view the real or underlying object of the Directive Principles of the State Policy which are inserted in the Constitution of India "in the hope and expectation that one day the tree of true liberty would bloom in India". Secondly, to provide participatory forum in the light of social justice. Thirdly, to involve the villagers and to create their confidence in the Justice Delivery System. Lastly, to give relief to the rural masses who are subjected to various crude forms of injustice and exploitation in the line of Gandhi's dream 'Sarvodaya'. Because 70% of Indians are in the villages, unless and until it is possible to provide fruits to the rural community the real Constitutional goal of "Social Justice" will be a myth.

> **10. Seal of Gram Nyayalaya.** Every Gram Nyayalaya established under this Act shall use a seal of the court in such form and dimensions as may be prescribed by the High Court with the approval of the State Government.

Scope of s. 10 Gram Nyayalaya shall use the seal of the court in the form and dimensions as prescribed by the High Court. Such seal so prescribed must be made with the approval of the State Government. Approval of the State Government is mandatory. Gram Nyayalaya is not authorised to use the seal which is not prescribed by the High Court or approved by the State Government. Gram Nyayalaya cannot use the seal according to its own will or desire.

CHAPTER III

Jurisdiction, Powers and Authority of Gram Nyayalaya

> **11. Jurisdiction of Gram Nyayalaya.** Notwithstanding anything contained in the Code of Criminal Procedure, 1973 (2 of 1974) or the Code of Civil Procedure, 1908 (5 of 1908) or any other law for the time being in force, the Gram Nyayalaya shall exercise both civil and criminal jurisdiction in the manner and to the extent provided under this Act.

Scope of s. 11 The jurisdiction of Gram Nyayalaya is very wide. Gram Nyayalaya has both civil and criminal jurisdictions. There is no conflict between the jurisdiction of Gram Nyayalaya and the jurisdiction of the court provided either in the Code of Criminal Procedure 1973 or the Code of Civil Procedure 1908 or any other law for the time being in force. The Gram Nyayalaya may exercise its jurisdiction only in respect of the matter mentioned in the schedules of the Act.

> **12. Criminal jurisdiction.** (1) Notwithstanding anything contained in the Code of Criminal Procedure, 1973 (2 of 1974) or any other

law for the time being in force, the Gram Nyayalaya may take cognizance of an offence on a complaint or on a police report and shall—

(*a*) try all offences specified in Part I of the First Schedule; and

(*b*) try all offence and grant relief, if any, specified under the enactments included in Part II of that Schedule.

(2) Without prejudice to the provisions of sub-section (1) the Gram Nyayalaya shall also try all such offences or grant such relief under the State Acts which may be notified by the State Government under sub-section (3) of section 14.

How take cognizance The Gram Nyayalaya may take cognizance of an offence on the basis of complaint or on a police report. It shall try all offences specified in Part I and Part II of the First Schedule.

Presentation of complaint It shall also try the other offences under the State Acts which may be notified by the State Government. The manner and process of presentation or filing of complaint before the Gram Nyayalaya has not been provided in the Act. In that case, the Gram Nyayalaya must follow the procedure provided in s. 200 of the Code of Criminal Procedure.

13. Civil Jurisdiction. (1) Notwithstanding anything contained in the Code of Civil Procedure, 1908 (5 of 1908) or any other law for the time being in force, and subject to sub-section (2), the Gram Nyayalaya shall have jurisdiction to—

(*a*) try all suits or proceedings of a civil nature falling under the classes of disputes specified in Part I of the Second Schedule;

(*b*) try all classes of claims and disputes which may notified by the Central Government under sub-section (1) of section 14 and by the State Government under sub-section (3) of the said section.

(2) The pecuniary limits of the Gram Nyayalaya shall be such as may be specified by the High Court, in consultation with the State Government, by notification, from time to time.

Jurisdiction to try civil suits The Gram Nyayalaya is empowered to try all suits or proceedings of a civil nature specified in Part I of the Second Schedule or try all classes of claims and disputes which may be notified by the Central Government. In order to determine the disputes under s. 13 of the Act the Gram Nyayalaya must be satisfied that:

(*a*) the dispute must be of a civil nature;

(*b*) such classes of disputes must be either (*i*) specified in Part I of the Second Schedule; or (*ii*) notified by the Central Government. "Suit of a civil nature" means a suit in which the right to property or to an office is contested (Explanation I of s. 9, Code of Civil Procedure).

Jurisdiction in regard to specific performance of contract The Gram Nyayalaya has the jurisdiction to entertain and decide the civil suit relating to "right of purchase of property" and consequently the Gram Nyayalaya can entertain and decide the civil suit praying for decree for specific performance of the contract in respect of the property which is situated within its jurisdiction.[2]

Pecuniary jurisdiction The High Court may from time to time in consultation with the State Government fix the pecuniary limits of the Gram Nyayalaya.

Manner of institution of suits The manner of filing of civil cases/disputes before the Gram Nyayalaya has not been sketched in the Act. In that case the Gram Nyayalaya may be governed by the rules and procedure provided in the Code of Civil Procedure or according to the principle of natural justice and fairplay which is compatible with the object of the Act for which it was enacted.

Dispute pertaining to use of way—not under jurisdiction of Gram Nyayalaya The jurisdiction vested with the Gram Nyayalaya under s. 13(l)(*a*) is not for trying all suits or proceedings of a civil nature but confined only to those classes of disputes specified in Part-I of the Second Schedule. Three classes of cases are brought under the head 'civil disputes': (*a*) right to purchase of property, (*b*) use of common pasture, and (*c*) regulation and timing of

2 *Shobha Janardhan Masram* v *Ganpat Gulabrao Thakre* 2015(5) Mh LJ 271.

taking water from irrigation channel. Three other sets of disputes are brought under the category 'property disputes'—(*a*) village and farm houses (possession); (*b*) water channels; and (*c*) right to draw water from a well or tube well. In the third category, certain other disputes are included under the head 'other disputes'. A dispute with respect to user of way either public or private cannot be brought under Part-I of Second Schedule. The nature of jurisdiction vested with the Gram Nyayalayas is governed by s. 13 of the Act. The civil disputes included in Part-I of Second Schedule alone can be tried by the Gram Nyayalayas constituted under the Act. In short, in order to invoke the jurisdiction vested with Gram Nyayalayas it should satisfy the pecuniary limits of jurisdiction and also the requirement under s. 13 of the Act. Only those matters which would come under the purview of s. 13 having the value upto pecuniary limits alone can be tried by Gram Nyayalayas. The words "use of common pasture" would stand for a right to use a common grass land. So, the dispute pertaining to user of way cannot be brought under the purview of "common pasture" even by giving an exhaustive meaning.[3]

> **14. Power to amend Schedules.** (1) Where the Central Government is satisfied that it is necessary or expedient so to do, it may, by notification, add to or omit any item in Part I or Part II of the First Schedule or Part II of the Second Schedule, as the case may be, and it shall be deemed to have been amended accordingly.
>
> (2) Every notification issued under sub-section (1) shall be laid before each House of Parliament.
>
> (3) If the State Government is satisfied that it is necessary or expedient so to do, it may, in consultation with the High Court, by notification, add to any item in Part III of the First Schedule or Part III of the Second Schedule or omit from it any item in respect of which the State Legislature is competent to make laws and thereupon the First Schedule or the Second Schedule, as the case may be, shall be deemed to have been amended accordingly.
>
> (4) Every notification issued under sub-section (3) shall be laid before the State Legislature.

---

3 *Binil Thomas* alias *Joseph* v *Shibu Vijayan* AIR 2019 Ker 42.

Scope of s. 14 The Central Government may add to or omit any item in Part I or Part II of the First Schedule or Part II of the Second Schedule if it is necessary or expedient to provide justice to the masses or according to the needs of the people. Because law is not static, it must be altered or changed according to the need of the society, demands of the society or problem or complexity of the society. Such change must be made by notification in the Official Gazette. Notification must be laid before each House of Parliament. The State Government may also add any item in Part III of the Second Schedule or omit any item in respect of which the State Legislature is competent to make laws. But amendment shall be made by the State Government subject to fulfilment of the following conditions:

(*i*) State Government must be satisfied that it is necessary or expedient to add or delete the item from the array of the First Schedule;

(*ii*) it must be made in consultation with the High Court;

(*iii*) it must be made by notification in the Official Gazette;

(*iv*) Notification must be laid before the State Legislature.

15. Limitation. (1) The provisions of the Limitation Act 1963 (36 of 1963) shall be applicable to the suits triable by the Gram Nyayalaya.

(2) The provisions of Chapter XXXVI of the Code of Criminal Procedure, 1973 (2 of 1974) shall be applicable in respect of the offences triable by the Gram Nyayalaya.

Applicability of Limitation Act The provisions of the Limitation Act 1963 are applicable to the suits triable by the Gram Nyayalaya. Gram Nyayalaya is governed by the rules of limitation relating to bar of limitation, legal disability, expiry of the prescribed period when the court is closed, continuous running of time, suit against trustees, exclusion of time in legal proceedings, exclusion of time in cases where leave to sue is applied for, effect of fraud or mistake, acknowledgement in writing, continuing breaches and torts etc. The suit before the Gram Nyayalaya must be filed within the time specified in the Limitation Act 1963. When the suit is filed after expiry of the period of limitation prescribed in the Limitation Act 1963 the suit is barred by limitation. The

Gram Nyayalaya has no power to condone the delay even on the ground of sufficient cause. Section 5 of the Limitation Act 1963 is applicable in case of appeal, or any application, other than application under any of the provisions of Or. 21 of the Code of Civil Procedure. Section 5 of the Limitation Act is applicable to suits. If we consider the provision of s. 5 of the Limitation Act and s. 15(1) of the Act side by side it is clear that s. 5 is applicable to proceedings before the Gram Nyayalaya.

Gram Nyayalaya and Code of Criminal Procedure 1973 The provisions of Chapter XXXVI (s. 467 to s. 473) of the Code of Criminal Procedure are applicable in respect of offences triable by the Gram Nyayalaya. The Gram Nyayalaya is not empowered to take cognizance of an offence specified in the schedule after expiry of the period of limitation; such period of limitation shall be—

(*a*) six months, if the offence is punishable with fine only;

(*b*) one year, if the offence is punishable with imprisonment for a term not exceeding one year;

(*c*) three years, if the offence is punishable with imprisonment for a term exceeding one year, but not exceeding three years.

The period limitation, in relation to an offender, shall commence:

(*a*) on the date of the offence; or

(*b*) where the commission of the offence was not known to the person aggrieved by the offence or to any police officer, the first day on which such offence comes to the knowledge of such person or to any police officer, whichever is earlier; or

(*c*) where it is not known by whom the offence was committed, the first day on which the identity of the offender is known to the person aggrieved by the offence or to the police officer making investigation into the offence, whichever is earlier. In computing the said period, the day from which such period is to be continued shall be excluded.

16. Transfer of pending proceedings. (1) The District Court or the Court of Session, as the case may be, with effect from such date as may be notified by the High Court, may transfer all the civil or criminal cases, pending before the courts subordinate to it, to the Gram Nyayalaya competent to try or dispose of such cases.

(2) The Gram Nyayalaya may, in its discretion, either retry the cases or proceed from the stage at which it was transferred to it.

Scope of s. 16 After constitution of Gram Nyayalaya the District Court or the Court of Session may transfer all civil or criminal cases pending before the court subordinate to it, to the Gram Nyayalaya for disposal for the said cases. The expression "competent to try" means having jurisdiction or authority to try or dispose of such cases.

Object Section 16 is enacted in order to reduce the workload of the traditional law courts by entrusting the Gram Nyayalaya with certain types of cases. In other words, the object of this section is quick disposal of cases which are pending in the courts for years together for final adjudication.

Conditions Before transferring the cases to Gram Nyayalaya the District Court or the Court of Session may consider the following factors:

(*a*) the case is pending before the courts subordinate to it;

(*b*) such Gram Nyayalaya has already been in force or come into existence from the date as mentioned in the notification;

(*c*) such Gram Nyayalaya is competent to try or dispose of such cases as specified in the First and Second Schedules of the Act;

(*d*) the court must look into the convenience of the parties before transferring the case to the Gram Nyayalaya;

(*e*) the court must also promote or advance the cause of justice.

Procedure After receipt of the record from the District Court or the Court of Session the Gram Nyayalaya may either (*i*) retry the cases, or (*ii*) proceed from the stage at which it was transferred to it.

To my view, the first option is not healthy, because the Act was framed or passed only to give speedy and easy justice to the ignorant masses and if the first option is followed, it will unquestionably consume more time. The cases which are pending in the court for years together will not see the light of judgment easily. If the Gram Nyayalaya will follow or accept the second option it will be easy to provide much quicker justice in comparison with first option. It is true the Gram Nyayalaya may in its discretion retry the cases. But the said discretion must be reasonable, and acceptable, not arbitrary or painful. This Act is enacted to achieve Social Justice, one of our Constitutional goals. Keeping in view the Constitutional goal, it is more healthy, congenial or acceptable for the Gram Nyayalaya to opt for the second option to try the pending cases from the stage at which it was transferred to it to give quick, easy and less costly relief.

> **17. Duties of ministerial officers.** (1) The State Government shall determine the nature and categories of the officers and other employees required to assist a Gram Nyayalaya in the discharge of its functions and provide the Gram Nyayalaya with such officers and other employees as it may think fit.
>
> (2) The salaries and allowances payable to, and other conditions of service of, the officers and other employees of the Gram Nyayalaya shall be such as may be prescribed by the State Government.
>
> (3) The officers and other employees of a Gram Nyayalaya shall perform such duties as may, from time to time, be assigned to them by the Nyayadhikari.

Scope of s. 17 The State Government shall appoint from time to time officers and other employees which are required to discharge the functions of the Gram Nyayalaya. The State Government shall determine the nature and categories of the officers and staff. The officers and staff are entitled to salaries and other allowances which are applicable to the employees and officers of the concerned State Government and they are under the obligation to perform duties which are assigned to them by the Nyayadhikari from time to time.

CHAPTER IV

Procedure in Criminal Cases

18. Overriding effect of Act in criminal trial. The provisions of this Act shall have effect notwithstanding anything contained in the Code of Criminal Procedure, 1973 (2 of 1974) or any other law, but save as expressly provided in this Act, the provisions of the Code shall, in so far as they are not inconsistent with the provisions of this Act, apply to the proceedings before a Gram Nyayalaya, and for the purpose of the said provisions of the Code, the Gram Nyayalaya shall be deemed to be a Court of Judicial Magistrate of the first class.

Applicability Provisions of the Code of Criminal Procedure are applicable to the proceedings before a Gram Nyayalaya provided they are not in consistent with the provisions of this Act.

Non-obstante clause This section opines with a *non-obstante* clause. *Non-obstante* clause[4] is a legislative device which is usually employed to give overriding effect to certain provisions over some contrary provisions that may be found either in the same enactment or some other enactment, that is to say, to avoid the operation and effect of all contrary provisions. "Notwithstanding anything contained in the Code of Criminal Procedure 1973 or any other law" must mean notwithstanding anything to the contrary contained in that Code or any Act and as such it must refer to the exempting provisions which would be contrary to the general applicability of the Code or the Act. It need not be co-extensive with the operative part of the section.[5] Proceedings before Gram Nyayalaya are deemed to be judicial proceedings and it deemed to be a court of Judicial Magistrate of the first class.

Powers of the Judicial Magistrate of the first class under the Code of Criminal Procedure

(1) The court of a Magistrate of the first class may pass a sentence of imprisonment for a term not exceeding three years, or of fine not exceeding ten thousand rupees or of both [s. 29(2), CrPC].

4 *Union of India* v *G.M. Kokil* AIR 1984 SC 1022; 1984 SCC (Lab) 631.
5 *Aswini Kumar Ghose* v *Arabindo Bose* AIR 1952 SC 369.

(2) Where any person dies or disappears, or rape is alleged to have been committed on any woman, while such person or woman is in the custody of the police or in any other custody authorized by the Magistrate or the Court, in addition to the inquiry or investigation held by the police, an inquiry shall be held by the Judicial Magistrate or the Metropolitan Magistrate within whose local jurisdiction the offence has been committed [s. 176(1A), CrPC].

(3) Any Metropolitan Magistrate or Judicial Magistrate may record any confession or statement made to him in the course of an investigation. [s. 164(1), CrPC].

(4) Judicial Magistrate of the first class may make compensation for accusation without reasonable cause [s. 250, CrPC].

(5) Judicial Magistrate of the first class may award compensation upto one thousand rupees to persons groundlessly arrested [s. 358, CrPC].

(6) The Court or Judicial Magistrate of the first class may award compensation [s. 357, CrPC].

Importance of s. 18 of the Act Consistent with the principle of achievement of justice, social, economic as enshrined in the Preamble to the Constitution of India, Part III thereof, and more particularly the Art. 39A of the Constitution, the Gram Nyayayalas Act 2008 (Act 4 of 2009) which received the assent of the President on 7th of January 2009 has been enacted to make justice delivery system accessible to the citizen of the rural areas, who by reason of economic and social incapacitation are found enable to approach the regular courts of law for redressal of their legal grievance. The object of the Act is to provide speedy and less expensive justice according to the procedure provided in the Act itself, shown by complex and complicated details as are ordinarily found and prescribed in the procedural laws and different jurisdictions.

An officer eligible to be appointed as Judicial Magistrate of the 1st class has been vested with both civil and criminal jurisdictions to try civil and criminal cases as specified in

Part I and Part II of the First Schedule and Part I of the Second Schedule of the Act.

Section 18 in Chapter IV and s. 23 in Chapter V of the Gram Nyayalayas Act gives out two *non-obstante* clauses, both in identical words, so as to override the provisions of the Code of Criminal Procedure 1973 and the Code of Civil Procedure 1908, or any other laws in the matters connected therewith. The object being to avoid the complicated procedural mechanism so as to render the justice delivery system easy, simple, speedy and less expensive.

With respect to the civil proceeding the language employed in s. 23 is identical with the former.

These are *non-obstante* clauses introduced on the presumption of the possible existence of conflict between the provisions of this Act and the procedural laws as are established in the Code of Criminal Procedure 1973 and the Code of Civil Procedure 1908, as amended. It is generally known that a *non-obstante* clause is a legislative device usually employed to give overriding effect to certain provisions over some contrary provisions that may be found either in the same enactment or some other enactments dealing with almost the same matter. In other words, more often than not, though *non-obstante* clause conflict is rather invited so as to give effect to the scheme and object of the enactment creating such *non-obstante* clause.

Anatomy of s. 18 or s. 23 Anatomy of s. 18 (or s. 23) thus boils down to the following legal situations:

(*a*) The provisions of Act 4 of 2009 so far as they relate to the matters of procedure will prevail over the procedural laws in extent of other laws in force. Thus in case of conflict between the two the former shall prevail over the latter.

(*b*) Save the areas of conflict expressly provided in which case remedial measure has been provided in (*a*) above, ordinary laws of procedure in so far as they are not inconsistent with the Act, will apply to the proceedings before a Gram Nyayalaya.

Where *non-obstante* clause is intended to override certain other provisions of the same enactment the enacting start by the statute, where it is clear and ambiguous, be taken to control the *non-obstante* clause were both cannot be real harmoniously; but where, as in the instant case the Act in question, two or more different enactments operate in the same field, problems of interpretation will arise. The law is fairly well settled such statutory interpretation has no fixed conventional modality cases of such conflict have to be decided with reference to the object and the purpose of the laws under consideration.

It may, however, be seen in the first time that the citizens in the rural arrears have not been absolutely denied the right to approach the regular courts even in respect of the matter covered in the Schedule I and Schedule II inasmuch as sub-sec. (3) of s. 3 provides that the Gram Nyayalaya shall be in addition to the Courts established under other laws in force. There is no express provision prohibiting approach to the regular courts by the inhabitants under Gram Panchayat in respect of the matter specified in the statute.

Section 30 of the Act has allowed evidence of the brief nature otherwise not admissible and not relevant, as achievement of substantial justice or truly speaking, substantive equality has been the motto behind discarding the rigors of the rules of evidence, so that miscarriage of justice may be not occur.

However, militant might it seen, offences triable through warrant procedure, either in the complaint case or in the police case, have been allowed to be tried by the Nyayadhikari through summary procedure, ordinarily power to try summarily is vested with the Judge/Magistrate of sufficient understanding and maturity. Given the enormous power vested with the Nyayadhikari it is only to be expected that only the Senior Magistrate should be appreciated to discharge the functions under Act. Having read ss. 6 and 7 of the Act, the Judicial Magistrate of the first class intended to be appointed for running regular courts and those for the Gram Nyayalayas stand on the same footstep, for the standard of selection in the two has not been discriminated against (unless the Government of the High Court prescribes a different procedure of selection). The Nyayadhikari have been given the choice to invent procedure as they may deem fit. There may be likelihood or the inexperienced Magistrates being misguided resulting in the abuse of the process of law.

One who is not familiar with the scheme of the new Act may be prove to reason that a citizen of the Gram Panchayat approaching a regular court and the one resorting to the Nyayalaya over identical matter covering the same value of prosperity have been differentiated. The same differentiation may be noticeable amongst the persons sued differently.

The object of the Act is doubtlessly laudable given the hard reality of life of a rural citizen. So far, the Act has not been implemented in West Bengal. It is the High Court that may clear the doubt that may arise in course of working with the Act of the Gram Nyayalayas. It is only when by the use of *non-obstante* clause inequality springs for the ultimate effect of such *non-obstante* clause may fall for consideration.

19. Gram Nyayalaya to follow summary trial procedure. (1) Notwithstanding anything contained in sub-section (1) of section 260 or sub-section (2) of section 262 of the Code of Criminal Procedure, 1973 (2 of 1974), the Gram Nyayalaya shall try the offences in a summary way in accordance with the procedure specified in Chapter XXI of the said Code and the provisions of sub-section (1) of section 262 and sections 263 to 265 of the said Code, shall, so far as may be, apply to such trial.

(2) When, in the course of a summary trial, it appears to the Nyayadhikari that the nature of the case is such that it is undesirable to try it summarily, the Nyayadhikari shall recall any witness who may have been examined and proceed to re-hear the case in the manner provided under the Code of Criminal Procedure, 1973 (2 of 1974).

Scope of s. 10 This section empowers the Gram Nyayalaya to try the offences in a summary way in accordance with the procedure specified in Chapter XXI of the Code of Criminal Procedure. The provisions of sub-sec. (1) of s. 262 and sections 263 to 265 of the Code of Criminal Procedure are applicable in such trial.

Procedure

(1) The procedure specified in the Code of Criminal Procedure for the trial of summons case shall be followed.

(2) The Gram Nyayalaya shall maintain a register containing the following particulars, namely:

(*a*) the serial number of the case;

(*b*) the date of the commission of the offence;

(*c*) the date of the report or complaint;

(*d*) the name of the complainant (if any);

(*e*) the name, parentage and residence of the accused;

(*f*) the offence complained of and the offence (if any) proved, and in cases coming under cl. (*ii*), cl. (*iii*) or cl. (*iv*) of sub-sec. (1) of s. 260, the value of the property in respect of which the offence has been committed;

(*g*) the plea of the accused and his examination (if any);

(*h*) the finding;

(*i*) the sentence or other final order;

(*j*) the date on which proceedings terminated.

(3) Substance of accusation, *i.e.* the particulars of the offence of which he is accused, shall be stated and explained to him.

(4) When the accused does not plead guilty, the Gram Nyayalaya shall record the substance of evidence and judgment containing a brief statement of the reasons for the findings.

(5) Judgment must be written in the language of the court.

(6) If in the course of summary trial it appears that it was undesirable to try it summarily, the Nyayadhikari shall (*a*) recall the witnesses who have been examined, and (*b*) proceed to rehear the case in the manner provided under the Code of Criminal Procedure 1973.

(7) Nyayadhikari is authorised to pass a sentence of imprisonment upto three months.

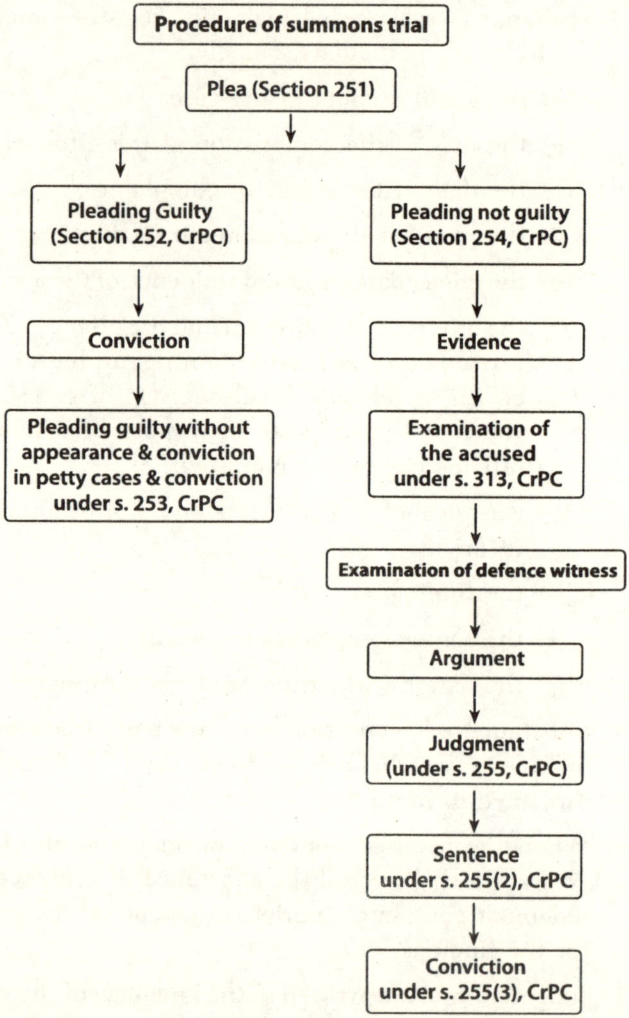

Comparison between the Code of Criminal Procedure and the Gram Nyayalayas Act 2008 (*a*) Under the Code of Criminal Procedure any Chief Judicial Magistrate, any Metropoliton Magistrate or any Magistrate of the first class specially empowered in this behalf by the High Court is empowered to try offence summarily.[6] Gram Nyayalaya is also empowered to try the offences summarily.

6 Section 260, Code of Criminal Procedure 1973.

(*b*) The following offences shall be tried summarily:[7]

(*i*) offences not punishable with death, imprisonment for life or for imprisonment for a term exceeding two years;

(*ii*) theft, under s. 379, s. 380 or s. 381 of the Indian Penal Code (45 of 1860), where the value of the property stolen does not exceed two thousand rupees;

(*iii*) receiving or retaining stolen property, under s. 411 of the Indian Penal Code (45 of 1860), where the value of the property does not exceed two thousand rupees;

(*iv*) assisting in the concealment or disposal of stolen property, under s. 414 of the Indian Penal Code (45 of 1860), where the value of such property does not exceed two thousand rupees;

(*v*) offences under ss. 454 and 456 of the Indian Penal Code (45 of 1860);

(*vi*) insult with intent to provoke a breach of the peace, under s. 504 and criminal intimidation punishable with imprisonment for a term which may extend to two years, or with fine, or with both, under s. 506 of the Indian Penal Code (45 of 1860);

(*vii*) abetment of any of the foregoing offences;

(*viii*) an attempt to commit any of the foregoing offences, when such attempt is an offence;

(*ix*) any offence constituted by an act in respect of which a complaint may be made under s. 20 of the Cattle-trespass Act 1871 (1 of 1871).

The Gram Nyayalaya shall try all the offences summarily which he is empowered to try or dispose of.

(*c*) The powers of Gram Nyayalaya and those of the Magistrate under the Code of Criminal Procedure in regard to summary trial are the same.

7 Section 260, Code of Criminal Procedure 1973.

(*d*) Section 19(2) of the Gram Nyayalayas Act 2008 is similar to s. 260(2) of the Code of Criminal Procedure.

> **20. Plea bargaining before Gram Nyayalaya.** A person accused of an offence may file an application for plea bargaining in Gram Nyayalaya in which such offence is pending trial and the Gram Nyayalaya shall dispose of the case in accordance with the provisions of Chapter XXIA of the Code of Criminal Procedure, 1973 (2 of 1974).

Plea bargaining—meaning This section makes a provision for plea bargaining. The concept of plea bargaining has gained statutory recognition in the Code of Criminal Procedure (Amendment) Act 2006. But it has a long history. If we go through the pages of history we find that the concept of plea bargaining was in existence in some other form. The expression, 'plea bargaining', has not been defined either in the Code of Criminal Procedure or the Gram Nyayalayas Act. In common parlance it means bargain between the complainant and the victim. In legal parlance it means an agreement between the accused of an offence and the prosecutor in view of the prosecutors agreeing to follow a particular course of action or abstain from taking into particular course of action on the basis of acceptance of the accusations leveled against him by the prosecution. In the *New International Webster's Comprehensive Dictionary of the English Language*, plea bargaining has been defined as follows:

> "a process in which a defendant in law case arranges, as with a distinct attorney, to plead guilty to a lesser charge in order to avoid standing trial for a more serious one and the risk of severer punishment". Albert W. Alschulur in his article titled as "*Plea-bargaining and its History*" defines it thus : "plea-bargaining consists of the exchange of official concessions for a defendant's act of self-conviction. Those concessions may relate to the sentence imposed by the Court or recommended by the prosecutor, the offence charged, or a variety of other circumstances." *Oxford Advanced Learner's Dictionary of Current English* gives the following meaning of the word, 'plea-bargaining',: "an arrangement in Court by which a person admits to being guilty of a smaller crime in the hope of receiving less severe

punishment for more serious crime". *Black's Law Dictionary* defines the word plea-bargaining as indicating "a negotiated agreement between a prosecutor and a criminal defendant whereby the defendant pleads guilty to a lesser offence or to one of multiple charge in exchange for some concession by the prosecutor, usually a more lenient sentence or a dismissal of the other charges". The committee constituted by National Legal Services Authority under the Chairmanship of Justice Ashoke Kumar Ganguly classically explained introduction of plea bargaining in the legal scenario of Indian soil in the following manner: Criminal cases in India have assumed alarming proportions and the petty cases also form a bulk of such pendency. As a result, petty criminal cases and the cases in which punishment upto seven years has been prescribed have clogged the system so much that grave offences which have the effect of tearing the social fabric are not tried promptly. Under the present criminal justice system a criminal, even if booked, can defer punishment to such an extent that the people at large have a feeling that the punishment, if at all is imposed, actually becomes illusory and evasive. In most of the cases, the purpose of punishment as a deterrence is diluted by such inordinate delay. In view of large pendency of the criminal cases there is a great deal of pressure on the police machinery, which often results in perfunctory investigation, and leading to acquittals. The rate of conviction in Indian courts is abysmally poor.

Law Commission's view—plea bargaining The Law Commission of India in its 142nd report classically explained the justification for introduction of the scheme of plea bargaining in the Indian Criminal Justice system in the following words:

(1) "It is not just and fair that an accused who feels contrite and wants to make amends or an accused who is honest and candid enough to plead guilty in the hope that the community will enable him to pay the penalty for the crime with a degree of compassion and consideration should be treated on part with an accused who claims to be tried at considerable time-cost and money-cost to the community.

(2) It is desirable to infuse life in the reformative provisions embodied in s. 360 of the Code of Criminal Procedure and in the Probation of Offenders Act which remain practically unutilized now.

(3) It will help the accused who have to remain as under-trial prisoners awaiting the trial as also other accused on whom the sword of Democles of an impending trial remains hanging for years to obtain speedy trial with attendant benefits such as—

(*a*) end of uncertainty;

(*b*) saving in litigation cost;

(*c*) saving in anxiety cost;

(*d*) being able to know his or her fate and to start a fresh life without fear of having to undergo a possible prison sentence at a future date disrupting his life or career;

(*e*) saving avoidable visits to lawyer's office and to court on every date of adjournment.

(4) It will, without detriment to public interest, reduce the back-breaking burden of the court cases which have already assumed menacing proportions.

(5) It will reduce congestion in jails.

(6) In the U.S.A. nearly 75% of the total convictions are secured as a result of plea bargaining.

(7) Under the present system 75% to 90% of the criminal cases if not more, result in acquittals".

Procedure (1) Any accused person not being a juvenile in conflict with law covered under s. 2(*k*) of the Juvenile Justice (Care and Protection of Children) Act 2000 and against whom trial is pending may file an application for plea bargaining.

(2) Such application for plea bargaining must be filed in Gram Nyayalaya where the offence is pending for trial.

(3) The application shall contain—

(*a*) a brief description of the case relating to which the application is filed including the offence to which the case relates;

(*b*) it shall be accompanied by an affidavit sworn by the accused stating that he has preferred this application voluntarily and after understanding the nature and extent of punishment prescribed for the offence;

(*c*) it shall also contain a statement that he has not previously been convicted by a court in a case in which he had been charged with the same offence;

(*d*) after receipt of the application the Gram Nyayalaya shall issue a notice to the Public Prosecutor or the complainant and fix up a date for appearance of the accused;

(*e*) after appearance of the accused the Gram Nyayalaya shall examine the accused *in camera* and ascertain the voluntariness of the application submitted by the accused;

(*f*) when the Gram Nyayalaya is satisfied that the accused has submitted the application voluntarily, it shall provide time to the public prosecutor or the complainant of the case and ask the accused to workout a mutually satisfactory disposition of the case;

(*g*) if the Gram Nyayalaya finds that the application has been filed involuntarily by the accused or he has been previously convicted in a case in which he has been charged with the same offence, the case shall revert back to trial from the stage where such application has been filed;

(*h*) when the case has been instituted on a police report, the Gram Nyayalaya shall issue notice to the Public Prosecutor, the Investigating Officer, the accused and the victim to participate in the meeting to work out a satisfactory disposition of the case;

(*i*) in a case instituted otherwise than on police report, Gram Nyayalaya shall issue notice to the accused and the victim to participate in the meeting to workout a satisfactory disposition of the case. Both the victim and the accused may take the assistance of their pleaders;

(*j*) after meeting, if a satisfactory disposition of the case has been worked out, the Gram Nyayalaya shall prepare a report and such report shall be signed by the Gram Nyayalaya and all other persons who participated in the meeting. When no workable disposition has been worked out, the Gram Nyayalaya shall dispose of the case by following the procedure prescribed in the Gram Nyayalayas Act for the trial of such cases;

(*k*) where a satisfactory disposition has been worked out, the Gram Nyayalaya may follow the following options:

(1) it may award compensation to the victim in accordance with the disposition; or

(2) he may hear the parties on the quantum of sentence; or

(3) he may hear the parties on the question of release of the accused on probation of good conduct or after admonition under s. 360 of the CrPC or under the provisions of Probation of Offenders Act 1958;

(*l*) after hearing the parties, if the Gram Nyayalaya is of the view that s. 360, CrPC or the Probation of Offenders Act attracted it may release the accused on probation;

(*m*) after hearing the parties, if the Gram Nyayalaya finds that minimum punishment has been provided under the law for the offence committed by the accused it may sentence the accused to half of such minimum punishment;

(*n*) after hearing the parties if the Gram Nyayalaya finds that the accused should not be released on probation, or no minimum punishment has been provided, it may sentence the accused to one-fourth of the punishment provided or extendable;

(*o*) the period of detention undergone by the accused shall be set off against the sentence of imprisonment.

Limitations of plea bargaining The plea bargaining does not apply relating to offence affecting the socio-economic condition of the country or where the offence has been committed against women or a child below the age of 14 years. The Central Government vide Notification No. S.O. 104(E), dated 11th July 2006 notified the offences under the following Acts outside the ambit of plea bargaining:

1. Dowry Prohibition Act 1961.
2. The Commission of Sati Prevention Act 1987.
3. The Indecent Representation of Women (Prohibition) Act 1986.
4. The Immoral Traffic (Prevention) Act 1956.
5. The Protection of Women from Domestic Violence Act 2005.
6. The Infant Milk Substitutes, Feeding Bottles and Infant Foods (Regulation of Production, Supply and Distribution) Act 1992.
7. Provisions of Fruit Products Order 1955 (issued under the Essential Services Commodities Act 1955).
8. Provision of Meat Food Products Orders 1973 (issued under the Essential Services Commodities Act 1955).
9. Offences with respect to animals that find place in Schedule I and Part II of the Schedule II as well as offences related to altering of boundaries of protected areas under the Wildlife (Protection) Act 1972.
10. The Scheduled Castes and Scheduled Tribes (Prevention of Atrocities) Act 1989.
11. Offences mentioned in the protection of Civil Rights Act 1955.
12. Offences listed in ss. 23 to 28 of the Juvenile Justice (Care and Protection of Children) Act 2000.
13. The Army Act 1950.
14. The Air Force Act 1950.
15. The Navy Act 1957.

16. Offences specified in ss. 59 to 81 of the Delhi Metro Railway (Operation and Maintenance) Act 2002.
17. The Explosives Act 1884.
18. Offences specified in ss. 11 to 18 of the Cable Television Networks (Regulation) Act 1995.

21. **Conduct of cases in Gram Nyayalaya and legal aid to parties.** (1) For the purpose of conducting criminal cases in the Gram Nyayalaya on behalf of the Government, the provisions of section 25 of the Code of Criminal Procedure, 1973 (2 of 1974) shall apply.

(2) Notwithstanding anything contained in sub-section (1), in a criminal proceeding before the Gram Nyayalaya, the complainant may engage an advocate of his choice at his expense to present the case of prosecution with the leave of the Gram Nyayalaya.

(3) The State Legal Services Authority, constituted under section 6 of the Legal Services Authorities Act 1987 (39 of 1987), shall prepare a panel of advocates and assign at least two of them to be attached to each Gram Nyayalaya so that their services may be provided by the Gram Nyayalaya to the accused unable to engage an advocate.

Scope of s. 21 The provisions of s. 25 of the CrPC are applicable for the purpose of conducting criminal cases before the Gram Nyayalaya on behalf of the Government. Assistant Public Prosecutor appointed by the State Government shall conduct the cases on behalf of the Government. Police officer should not ordinarily be appointed as Assistant Public Prosecutor. The complaint may engage an advocate of his choice with the permission of the Gram Nyayalaya and he shall bear all the expenses of the advocate to present the case of the prosecution. Section 21(2) of the Act is similar to the proviso to s. 24(8), CrPC. The State Legal Services Authority shall prepare a panel of advocates and shall assign at least two of them to be attached to each Gram Nyayalaya to render legal services to the accused who are unable to engage an advocate to defend their case due to financial constraint or hardship.

22. **Pronouncement of judgment.** (1) The judgment in every trial shall be pronounced by the Nyayadhikari in open court immediately after the termination of the trial or at any subsequent time, not exceeding fifteen days, of which notice shall be given to the parties.

(2) The Gram Nyayalaya shall deliver a copy of its judgment immediately to both the parties free of cost.

Scope of s. 22 After conclusion of the trial the Nyayadhikari shall pronounce judgment in open court. Judgment shall be pronounced within 15 days from the date of conclusion of trial. When the judgment is delivered at any subsequent date, notice should be given to the parties in respect of pronouncement of judgment. Section 22(1) of the Act is similar to s. 353(1) of the CrPC. No review of an order or judgment is contemplated under the Act.

Review and powers of Gram Nyayalaya There is no provision in the Act authorizing the Gram Nyayalaya to entertain the review application against the judgment. Once a judgment has been pronounced by the Gram Nyayalaya, no review can be entertained against that judgment. It is a statutory principle of law that once a matter is finally disposed of by a court, the said court (or Forum), in the absence of a specific statutory provision, becomes *functus officio* and disentitled to entertain a fresh prayer for the same relief unless the former order of final disposal is set aside by a court of competent jurisdiction in a manner prescribed by law.[8]

Section 22(2) and judgment The Gram Nyayalaya shall deliver copy of judgment free of cost to both the parties. Sub-section (2) of s. 22 is similar to s. 23(4) of the Hindu Marriage Act 1955 and s. 24 of the Protection of Women from Domestic Violence Act 2005. In the Code of Criminal Procedure, there is no provision to supply copy of the judgment to both the parties free of cost. Section 128 of the Code of Criminal Procedure contemplates supply of copy of order of maintenance or interim maintenance without payment to the person in whose favour it is made or to his guardian or to the person to whom the allowance for the maintenance or the allowance for the interim maintenance and expresses of proceedings is to be paid. In view of s. 363 of the CrPC when the accused is sentenced to imprisonment or where the judgment is appealable by the accused, a copy of the judgment shall be given to him free of cost.

8 *U.J.S. Chopra* v *State of Bombay* AIR 1955 SC 633; 1955 CrLJ 1410.

CHAPTER V

Procedure in Civil Cases

23. Overriding effect of the Act in civil proceedings. The provisions of this Act shall have effect notwithstanding anything contained in the Code of Civil Procedure, 1908 (5 of 1908) or any other law, but save as expressly provided in this Act, the provisions of the Code shall, in so far as they are not inconsistent with the provisions of this Act, apply to the proceedings before a Gram Nyayalaya; and for the purpose of the said provisions of the Code, the Gram Nyayalaya shall be deemed to be a Civil Court.

Scope of s. 23 This section is a *non-obstante* clause. Where there is any inconsistency or departure between a *non-obstante* clause and other provisions, one of the objects of such a clause is to indicate that it is the *non-obstante* clause which would prevail over the other clauses. The expression 'notwithstanding' implies that other provisions shall now prevail over the main provision. The provision of the Code of Civil Procedure shall apply to the proceeding before a Gram Nyayalaya if they are not inconsistent with the provisions of the Gram Nyayalayas Act 2008. The Gram Nyayalaya shall be deemed to be a civil court. This section has an overriding effect over the other statutory provisions prevailing in India. The Hon'ble Apex Court in *Aswini Kumar Ghose* v *Arbinda Bose*[9] classically explained the effect of *non-obstante* provision in the following words. 'It should first be ascertained what the enacting part of the section provides on fair construction of the words used according to their natural and ordinary meaning, and *non-obstante* clause is to be understood as operating to set aside as no longer valid anything contained in relevant existing laws which is inconsistent with the new enactment.'

24. Special procedure in civil disputes. (1) Notwithstanding anything contained in any other law for the time being in force, every suit, claim or dispute under this Act shall be instituted by making an application to the Gram Nyayalaya in such form, in such manner, and accompanied by such fee, not exceeding rupees one hundred, as may be prescribed by the High Court, from time to time, in consultation with the State Government.

9 AIR 1952 SC 369.

(2) Where a suit, claim or dispute has been duly instituted, a summons shall be issued by the Gram Nyayalaya, accompanied by a copy of the application made under sub-section (1), to the opposite party to appear and answer the claim by such date as may be specified therein and the same shall be served in such manner as may be prescribed by the High Court.

(3) After the opposite party files his written statement, the Gram Nyayalaya shall fix a date for hearing and inform all the parties to be present in person or through their advocates.

(4) On the date fixed for hearing, the Gram Nyayalaya shall hear both the parties in regard to their respective contentions and where the dispute does not require recording of any evidence, pronounce the judgment; and in case where it requires recording of evidence, the Gram Nyayalaya shall proceed further.

(5) The Gram Nyayalaya shall also have the power,—

(*a*) to dismiss any case for default or to proceed *ex parte*; and

(*b*) to set aside any such order of dismissal for default or any order passed by it for hearing the case *ex parte*.

(6) In regard to any incidental matter that may arise during the course of the proceedings, the Gram Nyayalaya shall adopt such procedure as it may deem just and reasonable in the interest of justice.

(7) The proceedings shall, as far as practicable, be consistent with the interests of justice and the hearing shall be continued on a day-to-day basis until its conclusion, unless the Gram Nyayalaya finds the adjournment of the hearing beyond the following day to be necessary for reasons to be recorded in writing.

(8) The Gram Nyayalaya shall dispose of the application made under sub-section (1) within a period of six months form the date of its institution.

(9) The judgment in every suit, claim or dispute shall be pronounced in open court by the Gram Nyayalaya immediately after conclusion of hearing or at any subsequent time, not exceeding fifteen days, of which notice shall be given to the parties.

(10) The judgment shall contain a concise statement of the case, the point for determination, the decision thereon and the reasons for such decision.

(11) A copy of the judgment shall be delivered free of cost to both the parties within three days from the date of pronouncement of the judgment.

Scope of s. 24 This section laid down the special provisions relating to institution, service of summons, recording of evidence and hearing of the proceeding in civil disputes. The provisions laid down in the Act are quite different from the nitty gritty of the procedure provided in the Code of Civil Procedure. Every civil suit, claim or dispute must be filed before the Gram Nyayalaya by making an application in the form and manner prescribed by the High Court along with prescribed fee which shall not exceed rupees one hundred. The said application must be disposed of within six months from the date of its institution. It also empowered the Gram Nyayalaya to decide the case *ex parte* (in the absence of one party).

The provisions of the Code of Civil Procedure which are not inconsistent with the provisions of the Gram Nyayalayas Act 2008, are only applicable to the proceedings before the Gram Nyayalaya and the civil suits or proceedings are required to be disposed by the Gram Nyayalaya by following the procedure as laid down in s. 24 of the Gram Nyayalayas Act 2008.

Object The main object of this section is to provide justice in a summary way. Another purpose of the Act is to provide justice to the parties so that they can enjoy the fruits of the decree/ order. It is our common experience that civil suits, particularly partition suits, are pending for generation after generation which results in frustration and tension to the litigants. If suits are pending for years after years, it may give birth to various off-shoots and even criminal cases. This section is also a part of semi-final legislation. Section 24(11) of the Act in its nature is unique. It provides that a copy of the judgment shall be given to both the parties free of cost within three days from the date of pronouncement of judgment. It is mandatory in nature. It is enacted in order to reduce the harassment of the litigants. It is a common saying that the real trouble of the decree holder begins after getting the decree. Keeping in view the trouble and tyranny of the litigants, the legislature incorporated this provision so that he/she can enjoy or avail the fruits of the judgment. Section 24(11) of the Act is similar to s. 23(4) of the Hindu Marriage Act and s. 24 of the Protection of Women from Domestic Violence Act 2005.

Payment of court fees This section enacts that the court fee shall not exceed 100 rupees, if the decision which is appealed against the decision of the Gram Nyayalaya. The court fee that become payable at the time of appeal shall only be the court fee as shall becomes payable before the Gram Nyayalaya if the suit were to be filed at the same time, no matter the institution was earlier in point of time when the plaintiff had paid a higher court fee under the schedule of the court fees payable under the Court Fee Act.[10]

Gram Nyayalayas Act 2008 and Code of Civil Procedure—distinction

Gram Nyayalayas Act 2008	Code of Civil Procedure
1. Every suit, claim or dispute be instituted by making an application to the Gram Nyayalaya [s. 24(1)].	1. Every suit shall be instituted shall by presentation of plaint [s. 26(1)].
2. It shall be filed in such form or manner prescribed by the High Court [s. 24(1)].	2. In every plaint, facts shall be proved by affidavit [s. 25(2)].
3. Application must be accompanied by fee not exceeding rupees one hundred [s. 24(1)].	3. Court fees must be paid in terms of Court Fees and Suits Valuation Act 1970.
4. Where a suit, claim or dispute has been duly instituted a summons shall be issued by the Gram Nyayalaya to the opposite party to appear and answer the claim by such date as may be specified therein [s. 24(2)].	4. Where a suit has been duly instituted, a summons may be issued to the defendant to appear and answer the claim and may be served in manner prescribed on such day not beyond 30 days from the date of the institution of the suit [s. 27 and Or. V, r. 6].
5. Every summons shall be accompanied by a copy of the application [s. 24(2)].	5. Every summons shall be accompanied by a copy of the plaint [Or. V, r. 2].
6. The summons shall be served upon the opposite party in such manner as may be prescribed by the High Court [s. 24(2)].	6. Summons shall be served in the manner prescribed in the Or. V of the CPC.

10 *Surinder Singh* v *State Bank of Patiala* 2015(2) Pun LJ 521; 2015(7) RCR (Civ) 642.

Gram Nyayalayas Act 2008	Code of Civil Procedure
7. Application need not be filed in duplicate.	7. The plaint must be filed in duplicate [Or. IV, r. 1].
8. There is no time fixed for filing statement.	8. The defendant must submit, written statement within 30 days from the date of service of summons on him but the Court may extend the period upto 90 days [Or. VII, r. 1].
9. After submission of written statement the Gram Nyayalaya a date for hearing [s. 24(3)].	9. After submission of written statement the Court shall shall fix frame issues under Or. XIV and fix the date for hearing.
10. After hearing the parties if the Gram Nyayalaya is of the view that the dispute does require recording of any evidence, it shall pronounce judgment [s. 24(4)].	10. There is no provision to pronounce judgment only on the contentions of the parties. But the Court may pronounce judgment on the basis of admi-ssions made in the pleadings or otherwise—orally or in writing [Or. XII, r. 6].
11. Where the dispute requires recording of evidence, the Gram Nyayalaya shall decide the case after recording of evidence and hearing the contentions of respective parties [s. 24(4)].	11. The court shall record evidence in terms of Or. XVIII, r. 3 to r. 17A.
12. The Gram Nyayalaya may also dismiss any case for default or to proceed any case *ex parte* [s. 24(5)].	12. The court may dismiss the suit under Or. IX, r. 2 or r. 3 or r. 5 or r. 8 and to proceed with any case *ex parte* under Or. IX, r. 6(1)(*a*).
13. Gram Nyayalaya is also empowerd to set aside the order of dismissal for dafault or any order passed *ex parte* [s. 24(5)].	13. The court may restore the suit to original file and number under Or. IX, r. 4 or r. 9. The court may also set aside the *ex parte* order against defendant under Or. IX, r. 13.

Gram Nyayalayas Act 2008	Code of Civil Procedure
14. In regard to any incidental matter arising out of the proceeding, the Gram Nyayalaya shall adopt the procedure which is just and reasonable in the interest of justice [s. 24(6)].	14. Incidental matters are decided according to the procedure provided in the Code, *i.e.* under Or. VI, r. 17, Or. 22, rr. 1 to 10, Or. 39, rr. 1 and 2, 2A, Or. 40 etc. If no provision is contemplated in the Code they are guided by s. 151.
15. The proceeding must be held on a day-to-day basis until its conclusion [s. 24(7)].	15. There is no provision for day-to-day hearing.
16. The Gram Nyayalaya may grant adjournment of the hearing beyond the following day necessary for reasons to be recorded in writing [s. 24(7)].	16. The court may grant adjournment at any stage of suit if sufficient cause is shown view of Or. XVII, r. 1.
17. The application must be disposed of within six months from the date of its institution [s. 24(8)].	17. There is no time limit.
18. The judgment must be delivered in open court immediately after conclusion of hearing or within 15 days from the date of conclusion of hearing after due notice to the parties [s. 24(9)].	18. The court, after the case has been heard shall pronounce judgment in open court either at once or within days of which due notice shall be given to the parties or their pleaders [Or. XX, r. 1].
19. The judgment must contain (*a*) precise statement of the case, (*b*) the points for determination, (*c*) decision, (*d*) the reasons for the decision [s. 24(10)].	19. The judgment shall contain a concise statement of the case, the points for determination, the decision thereon and the reasons for such decision [Or. XX, r. 4].
20. A copy of the judgment must be delivered to the parties free of cost within three days from the date of pronouncement of the judgment [s. 24(11)].	20. There is no provision in the Code of Civil Procedure in regard to supply of copy to the parties free of cost.

25. Execution of decrees and orders of Gram Nyayalaya. (1) Notwithstanding anything contained in the Code of Civil Procedure, 1908 (5 of 1908), the judgment passed by a Gram Nyayalaya shall be deemed to be a decree and it shall be executed by a Gram Nyayalaya as a decree of the civil court and for this purpose, the Gram Nyayalaya shall have all the powers of a civil court.

(2) The Gram Nyayalaya shall not be bound by the procedure in respect of execution of a decree as provided in the Code of Civil Procedure, 1908 (5 of 1908) and it shall be guided by the principles of natural justice.

(3) A decree may be executed either by the Gram Nyayalaya which passed it or by the other Gram Nyayalaya to which it is sent for execution.

Scope of s. 25 The judgment pronounced by the Gram Nyayalaya is tantamount to a decree of a civil court. It is executable by a Gram Nyayalaya like a decree of a civil court. It has the power of a civil court regarding execution of the decree. The Gram Nyayalaya is not bound to observe the nitty-gritty of the rules of procedure provided in the Code of Civil Procedure 1908.

Guiding principles The Gram Nyayalaya must be guided by the principles of natural justice. This section is enacted to make an endeavour to reach the benefits of the decree to the litigant or decree-holder as expeditiously as practicable. Code of Civil Procedure provides various rules and procedures (Or. 21) for execution of decree. Order 21 is practically engrafted as the procedure of mini trial after conclusion of full trial. Some cases took more time for execution than the time taken for conclusion of case/suit. In order to shorten the time of execution, the present legislation enacted this provision and provided that "it shall be guided by the principles of natural justice". The use of the expression 'shall' is ordinarily indicative of the mandatory nature of the provision, but having regard to the context in which it is used or having regard to the intention of the legislation, the same can be construed as directory.[11]

11 *Salem Advocate Bar Association* v *Union of India* AIR 2005 SC 3353.

Factors to consider provision mandatory or directory In order to determine whether a particular provision is mandatory or directory, the following factors shall be taken into consideration:

(*a*) the purpose for which the provision has been made and its nature;

(*b*) the intention of the legislature in making the provision, the serious inconvenience or injustice to persons resulting from whether the provisions is read one way or the other;

(*c*) the relation of the particular provision to other provisions dealing with the same subject, and other considerations which may arise on the facts of a particular case including the language of the provision.[12]

Execution One Gram Nyayalaya also transfer the case to another Gram Nyayalaya for execution. It means that the decree passed by Gram Nyayalaya is either executed by the Gram Nyayalaya which has passed the decree or other Gram Nyayalaya to which it is sent for execution. Section 25(2) is akin to s. 39 of the Code of Civil Procedure.

> **26. Duty of Gram Nyayalaya to make efforts for conciliation and settlement of civil disputes.** (1) In every suit or proceeding, endeavour shall be made by the Gram Nyayalaya in the first instance, where it is possible to do so, consistent with the nature and circumstances of the case, to assist, persuade and conciliate the parties in arriving at a settlement in respect of the subject matter of the suit, claim or dispute and for this purpose, a Gram Nyayalaya shall follow such procedure as may be prescribed by the High Court.
>
> (2) Where in any suit or proceeding, it appears to the Gram Nyayalaya at any stage that there is a reasonable possibility of a settlement between the parties, the Gram Nyayalaya may adjourn the proceeding for such period as it thinks fit to enable them to make attempts to effect such a settlement.
>
> (3) Where any proceeding is adjourned under sub-section (2), the Gram Nyayalaya may, in its discretion, refer the matter to one or more Conciliators for effecting a settlement between the parties.

12 *Raza Buland Sugar Co. Ltd., Rampur* v *The Municipal Board, Rampur* AIR 1965 SC 895.

(4) The power conferred by sub-section (2) shall be in addition to, and not in derogation of, any other power of the Gram Nyayalaya to adjourn the proceeding.

Duty In every suit or proceeding an endeavour shall be made by the Gram Nyayalaya to arrive at a settlement through conciliation according to the procedure framed by the High Court. The Gram Nyayalaya may at any stage of the proceeding adjourn the case if there is a reasonable possibility of a settlement between the parties, and it may, in its discretion, refer the matter to one or more conciliators for effecting a settlement between the parties.

Computation of Limitation The Act is silent whether the time spent for settlement of dispute through conciliator shall be excluded in computing the period of six months, the maximum time fixed for disposal of the application.

Purpose The main purpose of this section is to encourage settlement of dispute through conciliation, one of the modes of alternative dispute resolution.

27. Appointment of Conciliators. (1) For the purpose of section 26, the District Court shall, in consultation with the District Magistrate, prepare a panel consisting of the names of social workers at the village level having integrity for appointment as Conciliators who possess such qualifications and experience as may be prescribed by the High Court.

(2) The sitting fee and other allowances payable to, and the other terms and conditions for engagement of, Conciliators shall be such as may be prescribed by the State Government.

Scope of s. 27 The District Court in consultation with the District Magistrate shall prepare a panel of conciliators which should include names of social workers having integrity at the village level for appointment. The qualification and experience for appointment as conciliator may be prescribed by the High Court. The fees, allowances and terms and conditions for engagement of conciliators shall be fixed by the State Government.

28. Transfer of civil disputes. The District Court having jurisdiction may, on an application made by any party or when there is considerable pendency of cases in one Gram Nyayalaya or whenever it considers necessary in the interests of justice, transfer any case pending before a Gram Nyayalaya to any other Gram Nyayalaya within its jurisdiction.

Scope of s. 28 The District Court may transfer any case pending before a Gram Nyayalaya to any other Gram Nyayalaya within its jurisdiction either:

(*a*) *suo motu, i.e.* on its own motion;

(*b*) on an application made by any party.

Ground The District Court may transfer the case:

(*i*) when there is considerable pendency of cases in one Gram Nyayalaya; or

(*ii*) whenever it considers necessary in the interest of justice.

The expression 'case' used in s. 28 has not been defined in the Act. It includes all matters coming up before the Gram Nyayalaya for judicial adjudication or determination. It also includes execution or other incidental matters or off-shoots or miscellaneous proceedings. This section is similar to s. 24 of the Code of Civil Procedure.

Procedure After transfer of the case to the Gram Nyayalaya the Gram Nyayalaya may either retry it or proceed from the stage at which it was transferred.

CHAPTER VI

Procedure Generally

29. Proceedings to be in the official language of the State. The proceedings before the Gram Nyayalaya and its judgment shall, as far as practicable, be in one of the official languages of the State other than the English language.

Scope of s. 29 The proceedings before the Gram Nyayalaya and its judgment shall as far as practicable be conducted in the official language of the State other than English language.

30. Application of Indian Evidence Act, 1872. A Gram Nyayalaya may receive as evidence any report, statement, document, information or matter that may, in its opinion, assist it to deal effectually with a dispute, whether or not the same would be otherwise relevant or admissible under the Indian Evidence Act 1872 (1 of 1872).

Admission of evidence The Gram Nyayałaya may receive any report, statement, document, information or matter as evidence even if they are not relevant or admissible in terms of Indian Evidence Act but the Gram Nyayalaya must be of the view that those evidence are necessary to deal effectually with a dispute. The Gram Nyayalaya recognize both oral and documentary evidence. But it is not guided by the rules of evidence in the strict sense. The section is enacted to simplify the rules of procedure and admissibility of documents or facts in issue.

Facts to be considered to admit evidence In order to admit any fact or matter or document as evidence, the Gram Nyayalaya must satisfy itself that:

(*a*) the fact or matter is connected or co-related with the fact in issue or dispute in question; and

(*b*) such matter, statement, report or document is necessary to adjudicate the dispute effectively.

31. Record of oral evidence. In suits or proceedings before a Gram Nyayalaya, it shall not be necessary to record the evidence of witnesses at length, but the Nyayadhikari, as the examination of each witness proceeds, shall, record or cause to be recorded, a memorandum of substance of what the witness deposes, and such memorandum shall be signed by the witness and the Nyayadhikari and it shall from part of the record.

ANALYSIS

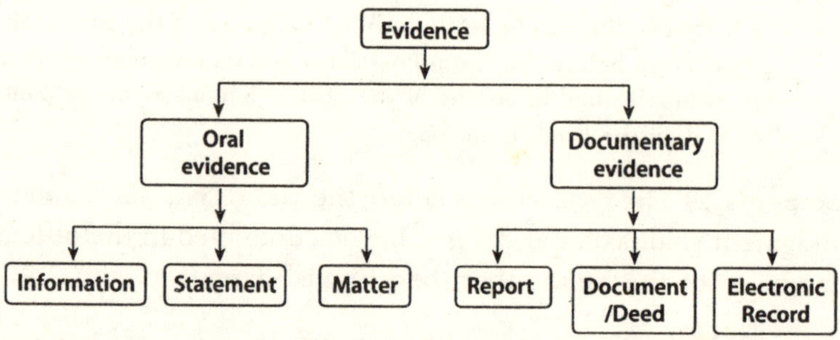

Scope of s. 31 Oral evidence means the statements which the courts permits or requires to be made before it by witness in relation to matters of fact under inquiry (s. 3 of the Indian

Evidence Act 1872). All facts except the contents of documents or electronic records may be proved by oral evidence (s. 59 of the Indian Evidence Act 1872). The contents of documents may be proved either by primary or by secondary evidence (s. 61 of the Indian Evidence Act 1872). In suits or proceedings before the Gram Nyayalaya, the recording of the evidence of witnesses at length is not necessary. Only the memorandum of substance of what the witness deposes shall be recorded and such memorandum shall be signed by the witness and the Nyayadhikari. Such memorandum shall form part of the record.

Nature The proceedings before the Gram Nyayalaya are to be disposed summarily.

Essentials of oral evidence

(1) It must be direct;

(2) It must be the evidence of a witness who says he saw it;

(3) It must be the evidence of a witness who says he heard it;

(4) It must be the evidence of a witness who says he perceived it by that sense or in that manner;

(5) It must be the evidence of the person who holds that opinion on the grounds where it refers to an opinion.

32. Evidence of formal character on affidavit. (1) The evidence of any person where such evidence is of a formal character, may be given by affidavit and may, subject to all just exceptions, be read in evidence in any suit or proceeding before a Gram Nyayalaya.

(2) The Gram Nyayalaya may, if it thinks fit, and shall, on the application of any of the parties to the suit or proceeding, summon and examine any such person as to the facts contained in his affidavit.

Evidence by affidavit Where the evidence is of a formal character it may be given by affidavit. This section is similar to s. 296 of the Code of Criminal Procedure. The provision engrafted in s. 32 is a departure from the usual mode of giving evidence is by examining the witness in open court and it involves spending of time of the witness, the trouble to teach the court and wait till he is called by the Court. It also involves costs which on many occasions are not small.

Object The object of enacting this provision is to help the court to gain the time and cost, besides relieving the witness of his troubles, when all that the said witness has to say in court relates only to some formal points. What is evidence of a formal character depends upon the facts of the case. Evidence, if necessary relates to formalities prescribed by law, should normally be tendered by affidavits and not by examining the witnesses in court. If any party to a lis wishes to examine the deponent of the affidavit it is open to him to make an application before the Gram Nyayalaya that he requires the deponent to be examined or cross-examined. This is enumerated in sub-sec. (2) of s. 32 of the Act. When any such application is made it is the duty of the Gram Nyayalaya to call such person to the Gram Nyayalaya for the purpose of being examined.[13]

CHAPTER VII

Appeals

33. Appeal in criminal cases. (1) Notwithstanding anything contained in the Code of Criminal Procedure, 1973 (2 of 1974) or any other law, no appeal shall lie from any judgment, sentence or order of a Gram Nyayalaya except as provided hereunder.

(2) No appeal shall lie where—

(*a*) an accused person had pleaded guilty and has been convicted on such plea;

(*b*) the Gram Nyayalaya has passed only a sentence of fine not exceeding one thousand rupees.

(3) Subject to sub-section (2), an appeal shall lie from any other judgment, sentence or order of a Gram Nyayalaya to the Court of Session.

(4) Every appeal under this section shall be preferred within a period of thirty days from the date of judgment, sentence or order of a Gram Nyayalaya:

Provided that the Court of the Session may entertain an appeal after the expiry of the said period of thirty days if it is satisfied that

13 *State of Punjab* v *Naibudin* 2002 SCC (Cri) 33.

the appellant had sufficient cause for not preferring the appeal within the said period.

(5) An appeal preferred under sub-section (3) shall be heard and disposed of by the Court of Session within six months from the date of filing of such appeal.

(6) The Court of Session may, pending disposal of the appeal, direct the suspension of the sentence or order appealed against.

(7) The decision of the Court of Session under sub-section (5) shall be final and no appeal or revision shall lie from the decision of the Court of Session:

Provided that nothing in this sub-section shall preclude any person from availing of the judicial remedies available under Articles 32 and 226 of the Constitution.

Scope of s. 33 The scope of appeal is not very wide. There is only provision for appeal to the Court of Session or the District Court. The legislature is against the three-tier system of appeal so far as the present Act is concerned. The main object of this Act is to provide justice at the door steps. This Act is a part of the ADR system which is oppressed to lengthy complicated procedural law. The provision of appeal or revision does not always ensure just decision. High Courts may also commit an error. The provision of appeal may create a peculiar impression in the mind of the litigant who lost in the legal battle. If there were any higher court of appeal to review the decision of the Supreme Court, there is also a chance to reverse the order of the Supreme Court.

Requisite of appeal The requisites of a valid appeal are, first, that no one can appeal from a judgment or decree unless he was a party to the action or was treated as such or is the legal representative of a party or has privity of estate, title or interest, apparent on the face of the record; secondly, that the appellant has an interest in the subject matter of the suit, and thirdly that the appellant is prejudicially affected by the decree complained of.

Law Commission of India—its view Many aspect of appeal were discussed by the Law Commission in its 114th report and it was observed as follows:

"A provision of an appeal by itself is not guarantee of a just decision. It has some supervisory flavour. An assumption that an appeal to the higher court ensures justice is wholly misleading. Numerous cases can be cited in which the plaintiff won in the trial court, lost in first appeal before the District Court, won in second appeal in the High Court and lost in the appeal by his opponent in the Supreme Court. Which of the four is a just decision? And it is a trite saying in the corridor of courts that if a higher forum for appeal against the decision of the Supreme Court is devised, the judgment of the Supreme Court there is ever likely of it being revered. After all it said and done, a total eradication of a subjective point of view in decision-making process is wholly impossible. Coupled with that is the fact that while interpreting socially beneficial legislation, the social philosophy and value-system of the Judge at various levels in the hierarchy of courts plays an important part in the decision-making process. How can one explain the reversal of numerous decisions of the High Court by the Supreme Court, and how can one explain the reversal of the decision of the Supreme Court by its larger Bench? This proves, if proof was needed, that there is an element of subjectivism in all decision-making processes. It has to be curtailed, restrained and as far as possible eliminated. Having said that, it must be confessed that it looms large for whatever worth it is. It is equally fallacious to assume that the errors are not committed at higher level. Number of decisions of the Supreme Court can be cited to substantiate the proposition that the decision of the trial court which was set aside by the High Court was restored by the Supreme Court. It can, therefore, be said with confidence that a provision for appeal is not a guarantee of justice nor a bulwark against arbitrary or biased decision.

"**Restriction** It is equally true that no one is infallible. The Court of appeal accordingly has been described as a court of error. Therefore, its jurisdiction has been held to be coextensive with the trial court. It was said that at least there must be one forum which must have power to correct the errors of newly created forum of Gram Nyayalaya."

Gram Nyayalayas Act and Code of Criminal Procedure—comparison

Gram Nyayalayas Act	Code of Criminal Procedure
1. No appeal shall lie from any judgment, sentence or order of a Gram Nyayalaya except as provided in the Act [s. 33(1)].	1. No appeal shall lie from any judgment or order of a criminal court exccept as provided for by the Code of Criminal Procedure or by any other law for the time being in force [s. 372].
2. There is no provision for appeal by the victim against any order passed by Gram Nyayalaya acquitting the accused or convicting for a lesser offence or imposing inadequate compensation.	2. The victim has a right of appeal against any order passed by the court acquitting the accused or convicting for a lesser offence or imposing inadequate compensation (Proviso to s. 372).
3. There shall be no appeal if the accused as pleaded guilty and has been convicted on such plea [s. 33(2)(*a*)].	3. There shall be no appeal where an accused has pleaded guilty and convicted on such plea— (*a*) if the conviction is by a High Court; or (*b*) if the conviction is by a Court of Session, Metropolitan Magistrate or Magistrate of the first or second class, except as to the extent or legality of the sentence (s. 373).
4. There shall be no appeal where the Gram Nyayalaya has passed only a sentence of fine not exceeding one thousand rupees [s. 32(2)(*b*)].	4. There shall be no appeal by a convicted person in any of the following cases, namely:– (*a*) where a High Court passes only a sentence of imprisonment for a term not exceeding six months or of fine not exceeding one thousand rupees, or of both such imprisonment and fine; (*b*) where a Court of Session or a Metropolitan Magistrate passes only a sentence of imprisonment for a term not exceeding three months or of fine not

Gram Nyayalayas Act	Code of Criminal Procedure
	exceeding two hundred rupees, or of both such imprisonment and fine; (*c*) where a Magistrate of the first class passes only a sentence of fine not exceeding one hundred rupees; or (*d*) where, in a case tried summarily, a Magistrate empowered to act under s. 260 passes only a sentence of fine not exceeding two hundred rupees.
5. An appeal shall lie from any judgment, sentence or order of the Gram Nyayalaya to the Court of Session except those orders/ judgments no provision of appeal has been provided in the Act. [s. 33(3)].	5. An appeal against the sentence on the ground of it inadequacy or an order of acquittal shall lie to the— (*a*) to the Court of Session, if the sentence is passed by a Magistrate. In case of acquittal offence must, cognisable and non-bailable (*b*) to the High Court, if the sentence or the order of acquittal passed by a Court other than a High Court or an order of acquittal passed by the Court of Session in revision (ss. 377 & 378).
6. Appeal shall be made within thirty days from the date of judgment, sentence or order of Gram Nyayalaya [s. 33(4)].	6. Period of limitation is governed by Arts. 114 and 115 of the Limitation Act 1963.
7. There is no provision for appeal to the High Court.	7. No appeal shall be entertained by the High Court except with the leave of the High Court [s. 378(3)].
8. The appeal preferred shall be disposed of within six months from the date of filing of such appeal [s. 33(5)].	8. There is no time-frame in the Code regarding disposal of appeal.

Gram Nyayalaya Act	Code of Criminal Procedure
9. The Court of Session shall during the pendency of the appeal, suspended the sentence or order against the appeal has been preferred [s. 33(6)].	9. The Appellate Court may, for reasons to be recorded in wirting, order that the execution of the sentence or order appealed against be suspended and also, if the is in confinement, that he be released on bail, or on his own bound [s. 389(1)].
10. There is no provision for recording further evidence by the Appellate Court or directing it to be taken by Gram Nyayalaya.	10. The Appellate Court, if it thinks additional evidence to be necessary, shall record its reasons and may either take such evidence itself, or direct it to be taken by a Court of Session or a Magistrate [s. 391].
11. There is no provision for summary disposal of appeal.	11. Where the Appellate Court considers that there is no sufficient ground for interfering, it may dismiss the appeal summarily [s. 384].
12. The decision of the Court of Session is final [s. 33(7)].	12. Judgments and orders passed by an Appellate Court upon an appeal is final (Section 393).
13. No appeal or revision shall lie from the decision of the Court of Session [s. 33(7)].	13. An appeal shall lie to the Supreme Court under Art. 134 of the Constitution of India.
14. Section 33 does not preclude the aggrieved person to resort to the remedies available under Arts. 32 and 226 of the Constitution of India.	14. There is no provision in the Code.

34. Appeal in civil cases. (1) Notwithstanding anything contained in the Code of Civil Procedure, 1908 (5 of 1908) or any other law, and subject to sub-section (2), an appeal shall lie from every judgment or order, not being an interlocutory order, of a Gram Nyayalaya to the District Court.

(2) No appeal shall lie from any judgment or order passed by the Gram Nyayalaya—

(*a*) with the consent of the parties;

(*b*) where the amount or value of the subject matter of a suit, claim or dispute does not exceed rupees one thousand;

(*c*) except on a question of law, where the amount or value of the subject matter of such suit, claim or dispute does not exceed rupees five thousand.

(3) Every appeal under this section shall be preferred within a period of thirty days from the date of the judgment or order of a Gram Nyaylaya:

Provided that the District Court may entertain an appeal after the expiry of the said period of thirty days if it is satisfied that the appellant had sufficient cause for not preferring the appeal within the said period.

(4) An appeal preferred under sub-section (1) shall be heard and disposed of by the District Court within six months from the date of filing of the appeal.

(5) The District Court may, pending disposal of the appeal, stay execution of the judgment or order appealed against.

(6) The decision of the District Court under sub-section (4) shall be final and no appeal or revision shall lie from the decision of the District Court:

Provided that nothing in this sub-section shall preclude any person from availing of the judicial remedies available under Articles 32 and 226 of the Constitution.

Appeal—meaning An appeal is removal of the cause from a lower to one of higher forum for the purposes of obtaining a review or retrial. An appeal, generally speaking, is a rehearing by a superior court on both law and fact.[14]

As to appeal the following principles are pertinent,[15] viz.

(1) That the legal pursuit of a remedy, suit appeal and second appeal are really but steps in a series of proceedings all connected by an intrinsic unity and are to be regarded as one legal proceeding.

14 *Deep Chand* v *Land Acquisition Officer* AIR 1994 SC 1901.
15 *Garikapatti* v *Subbiah Choudhury* AIR 1957 SC 540.

(2) The institution of the suit carries with it the implication that all rights of appeal then in force are preserved to the parties thereto till the rest of the career of the suit.

Nature The right of appeal is not a mere matter of procedure but is a substantive right.

Scope—appeal The right of appeal is a vested right and such a right to enter the superior court accrues to the litigant and exists as on from the date the lis commences and although it may be actually exercised when the adverse judgment is pronounced such rights is to be governed by the law prevailing at the date of the institution of the suit or proceeding and not by the law that prevails at the date of its decision or at the date of the filing of the appeal.

Right of appeal—when taken away This vested right of appeal can be taken away only be a subsequent enactment, if it so provides expressly or by necessary intendment and not otherwise.

Second appeal Only one appeal is provided against the judgment and decree passed by the Gram Nyayalaya and the judgment and decree passed by the District Court in appeal under s. 34(4) of the Gram Nyayalayas Act 2008 is not appellable or revisable. The second appeal is not maintainable because the civil suit and the counterclaim are decided by the Gram Nyayalaya.

Essentials of appeal Right of appeal is a right of entering a superior court and invoking its aid and interposition to redress the error of the court below. Two things which were required to constitute appellate jurisdiction were the existence of the relation of superior and inferior court and the power of the part of the former to review decisions of the latter. In the words of Story, the essential criterion of appellate jurisdiction is that it revises and corrects the proceedings in a cause already instituted and does not create that cause. The appellate jurisdiction may be exercised in a variety of forms and, indeed, in any form in which the legislature may choose to prescribe.

Comparison—Gram Nyayalayas Act and Code of Civil Procedure

Gram Nyayalayas Act	Code of Civil Procedure
1. An appeal shall lie from every judgment or order, not being an interlocutory order, of a Gram Nyayalaya to the District Court [s. 34(1)].	1. An appeal shall lie from every decree passed by any court exercising original jurisdiction to the Court authorised to hear appeals from the decisions of such Court [s. 96(1)].
2. There is no express provision of appeal from decree passed *ex parte*.	2. An appeal may lie from an original decree passed *ex parte* [s. 96(2)].
3. No appeal shall lie from any judgment or order passed by the Gram Nyayalaya with the consent of the parties [s. 34(2)(*a*)]	3. No appeal shall lie from a decree passed by the Court with the consent of the parties [s. 96(3)].
4. No appeal shall lie from any judgment or order passed by the Gram Nyayalaya where the amount or value of the subject matter of a suit, claim or dispute does not exceed rupees one thousand [s. 34(2)(*b*)] or except on a question of law, where the amount or value of the subject matter of such suit, claim or dispute does not exceed rupees five thousand [s. 34(2)(*c*)].	4. No appeal shall lie except on question of law, from a decree in any suit of the nature cognisable by Court of Small Causes, when the amount or value of the subject matter of the original suit does not exceed ten thousand rupees [s. 96(4)].
5. Appeal shall be filed within 30 days from the date of the judgment or order of a Gram Nyayalayas [s. 34(3)].	5. Period of limitation is 90 days for appeal to the High Court and 30 days to any other Court [Art. 116 and Art. 117, Limitation Act 1963].
6. There is no provision of second appeal.	6. An appeal shall lie to the High Court from every decree passed in appeal by any Court subordinate to the High Court, if the High Court is satisfied that the case involves a substantial question of law [s. 100(1)].

Gram Nyayalayas Act	Code of Civil Procedure
7. There is no provision of appeal to the Supreme Court.	7. An appeal shall lie to the Supreme Court from any judgment, decree or final order in a civil proceedings of a High Court, if the High Court certifies—(*a*) that the case involves a substantial question of law of general importance; and (*b*) that in the opinion of the High Court the said question needs to be decided by the Supreme Court [s. 109].
8. There is no provision for dismissal of appeal.	8. If on the day fixed for hearing the appellant does not appear the Court may dismiss the appeal [Or. XLI, r. 11(2)].
9. There is no provision for readmission of appeal dismissed for default.	9. The Appellate Court may readmit the appeal if it is proved that the appellant was prevented by any sufficient cause from appearing when the appeal was called on for hearing [Or. XLI, r. 19].
10. The District Court may entertain an appeal after the expiry of the period of thirty days if it is satisfied that the appellant has sufficient cause for not preferring the appeal within the said period [s. 34(3), proviso].	10. When an appeal is presented after the expiry of the period of limitation, it shall be accompanied by an application supported by affidavit setting forth the facts on which the appellant relies to satisfy the court that he had sufficient cause for not preferring the appeal within such period [Or. XLI, r. 3A(1)].
11. The District Court may, pending disposal of the appeal, stay execution of the judgment or order appealed against [s. 34(5)].	11. Appellate Court may for sufficient cause order stay of execution of decree appealed against [Or. XLI, r. 5].
12. An appeal shall be disposed of within six months from the date of filing of the appeal [s. 34(4)].	12. Every appeal shall be heard as expeditiously as possible and endeavour shall be made to conclude such hearing within sixty days from the date on which the memorandum of appeal is filed [Or. XLI, r. 11A].

Gram Nyayalayas Act	Code of Civil Procedure
13. There is no provision for remand of case by Appellate Court.	13. When the Court from whose decree an appeal is preferred has disposed of the suit upon a preliminary point and the decree is reversed in appeal, the Appellate Court may, if it thinks fit, by order remand the case [Or. XLI, r. 23].
14. There is no provision for production of additional evidence in Appellate Court.	14. The Appellate Court may take additional evidence if—(*i*) the Court from whose decree the appeal is preferred has refused to admit evidence which ought to have been admitted, or (*ii*) the party seeking to produce additional evidence, establishes that notwithstanding the exercise of due diligence, such evidence was not within his knowledge or could not, after the exercise of due diligence, be produced by him at the time when the decree appealed against was passed, or (*iii*) the Appellate Court requires any document to be produced or any witness to be examined to enable it to pronounce judgment, or for any other substantial cause [Or. XLI, r. 27].
15. The decision of the District Court is final [s. 34(6)].	15. District Court is not the highest court of appeal.
16. No appeal or revision shall lie from the decision of the District Court [s. 34(6)].	16. An appeal shall lie to the High Court or the Supreme Court on the ground of substantial question of law [ss. 100 & 109].
17. Section 34 does not stand in the way to invoke the judicial remedies available under Arts. 32 and 226 of the Constitution [s. 34(6), proviso].	17. There is no such provision in the Code.

Chapter VIII

Miscellaneous

35. Assistance of police to Gram Nyayalaya. (1) Every police officer functioning within the local limits of jurisdiction of a Gram Nyayalaya shall be bound to assist the Gram Nyayalaya in the exercise of its lawful authority.

(2) Whenever the Gram Nyayalaya, in the discharge of its functions, directs a revenue officer or police officer or Government servant to provide assistance to the Gram Nyayalaya, he shall be bound to provide such assistance.

Scope of s. 35 The police officer is bound to assist the Gram Nyayalaya in the exercise of its lawful authority. It means that the police officer functioning within the local limits of jurisdiction of Gram Nyayalaya is under statutory obligation to assist the Gram Nyayalaya in the discharge of its lawful authority or function. The legislative import of this section is to give proper assistance of police force to the Gram Nyayalaya whenever necessary to perform its function. Because Gram Nyayalaya has no separate agency to enforce its order. The expression "police officer" has not been defined in this Act.

To whom directions issued The Gram Nyayalaya may also issue directions upon (*i*) revenue officer, (*ii*) police officer, or (*iii*) Government servant, to provide assistance to the Gram Nyayalaya to perform its functions smoothly and they are also bound to provide assistance to Gram Nyayalaya as and when required so. The expression 'revenue officer', 'police officer' and 'Government servant' have not been defined in the Act.

Public servant and Government servant—distinction There is a difference between public servant and Government servant. The expression public servant is much wider than Government servant. Section 14 of the Indian Penal Code defines the expression 'Servant of Government' in the following words: "The words 'servant of Government' denote any officer or servant continued, appointed or employed in India by or under the authority of Government." In a wide sense, a Government servant must be a servant and secondly, he is appointed or employed by the Government. Public servant may or may not receive salary or remuneration for the performance of his duty. Government servant must be in the pay of the Government or receive remuneration from the Government Exchequer. Government servant is a species whereas public servant is a genus.

> **36. Nyayadhikaris and employees, etc. to be public servants.** The Nyayadhikaris and the officers and other employees of the Gram Nyayalayas shall be deemed, when acting or purporting to act in pursuance of any of the provisions of this Act, to be public servants within the meaning of section 21 of the Indian Penal Code (45 of 1860).

Scope of s. 36 The Nyayadhikaris and the officers and other employees of the Gram Nyayalaya are public servants when they are acting or purporting to act in pursuance of any of the provisions of the Act. The expression 'public servant' bear the same meaning which is used and defined in s. 21 of the Indian Penal Code.

Prosecution of Judges and public servants[16] (1) When any person who is or was a Judge or Magistrate or a public servant not removable from his office save by or with the sanction of the Government is accused of any offence alleged to have been committed by him while acting or purporting to act in the discharge of his official duty, no court shall take cognizance of such offence except with the previous sanction save as otherwise provided in the Lokpal and Lokayuktas Act 2013—

(*a*) in the case of a person who is employed or, as the case may be, was at the time commission of the alleged offence employed, in connection with the affairs of the Union, of the Central Government;

(*b*) in the case of a person who is employed or, as the case may be, was at the time of commission of the alleged offence employed, in connection with the affairs of a State, of the State Government:

Provided that where the alleged offence was committed by a person referred to in cl. (*b*) during the period while a Proclamation issued under cl. (1) of Art. 356 of the Constitution was in force in a State, cl. (*b*) will apply as if for the expression

16 Section 197, the Code of Criminal Procedure 1973.

'State Government' occurring therein, the expression 'Central Government' were substituted.

Explanation. For the removal of doubts it is hereby declared that no sanction shall be required in case of a public servant accused of any offence alleged to have been committed under ss. 166A, 166B, 354, 354A, 354B, 354C, 354D, 370, 375, 376, 376A, 376AB, 376C, 376D, 376DA, 376DB or s. 509, IPC.

(2) No court shall take cognizance of any offence alleged to have been committed by any member of the Armed Forces of the Union while acting or purporting to act in the discharge of his official duty, except with the previous sanction of the Central Government.

(3) The State Government may, by notification, direct that the provisions of sub-sec. (2) shall apply to such class or category of the members of the Forces charged with the maintenance of public order as may be specified therein, wherever they may be serving, and thereupon the provisions of that sub-section will apply as if for the expression "Central Government" occurring therein, the expression "State Government" were substituted.

(3A) Notwithstanding anything contained in sub-sec. (3), no court shall take cognizance of any offence, alleged to have been committed by any member of the Forces charged with the maintenance of public order in a State while acting or purporting to act in the discharge of his official duty during the period while a Proclamation issued under cl. (1) of Art. 356 of the Constitution was in force therein, except with the previous sanction of the Central Government.

(3B) Notwithstanding anything to the contrary contained in this Code or any other law, it is hereby declared that any sanction accorded by the State Government or any cognizance taken by a court upon such sanction, during the period commencing on the 20th day of August 1991 and ending with the date immediately preceding the date on which the Code of Criminal Procedure (Amendment) Act 1991, receives the assent of the President, with respect to an offence alleged to have been committed during the period while a Proclamation issued under cl. (1) of Art. 356 of the Constitution was in force in the State, shall be invalid and it shall be competent for the Central Government in such matter to accord sanction and for the court to take cognizance thereon.

(4) The Central Government or the State Government, as the case may be, may determine the person by whom, the manner in which, and the offence or offences for which, the prosecution of such Judge, Magistrate or public servant is to be conducted, and may specify the court before which the trial is to be held.

Public servant—meaning "The word 'Public Servant'[17] denote a person falling under any of the descriptions hereinafter following; namely:–

Every Commissioned Officer in the Military, Naval or Air Forces of India;

Every Judge including any person empowered by law to discharge, whether by himself or as a member of any body of persons, any adjudicatory functions;

Every officer of a Court of Justice (including a liquidator, receiver or commissioner) whose duty it is, as such officer, to investigate or report on any matter of law or fact, or to make, authenticate, or keep any document, or to take charge or dispose of any property, or to execute any judicial process, or to administer any oath, or to interpret, or to preserve order in the court, and every person specially authorized by a Court of Justice to perform any of such duties;

Every juryman, assessor, or member of a Panchayat assisting a Court of Justice or public servant;

Every arbitrator or other person to whom any cause or matter has been referred for decision or report by any Court of Justice, or by any other competent public authority;

Every person who holds any office by virtue of which he is empowered to place or keep any person in confinement;

Every officer of the Government whose duty it is, as such officer, to prevent offences, to give information of offences, to bring offenders to justice, or to protect the public health, safety or convenience;

Every officer whose duty it is, as such officer, to take, receive, keep or expend any property on behalf of the Government, or

17 Section 21, the Indian Penal Code.

to make any survey, assessment or contract on behalf of the Government, or to execute any revenue process, or to investigate, or to report, on any matter affecting the pecuniary interests of the Government, or to make, authenticate or keep any document relating to the pecuniary interests of the Government, or to prevent the infraction of any law for the protection of the pecuniary interests of the Government;

Every officer whose duty it is, as such officer, to take, receive, keep or expend any property, to make any survey or assessment or to levy any rate or tax for any secular common purpose of any village, town or district, or to make, authenticate or keep any document for the ascertaining of the rights of the people of any village, town or district;

Every person who holds any office in virtue of which he is empowered to prepare, publish, maintain or revise an electoral roll or to conduct an election or part of an election;

Every person—

(*a*) in the service or pay of the Government or remunerated by fees or commission for the performance of any public duty by the Government;

(*b*) in the service or pay of a local authority, a corporation established by or under a Central, Provincial or State Act or a Government company as defined in s. 617 of the Companies Act 1956 (1 of 1956)."

Judges—whether public servant Judges are not the employees. As members of judiciary, they exercise the sovereign judicial power of the State. They are the holders of the public office in the same way as the members of the Council of Ministers and members of the Legislature.[18]

Applicability—s. 197, CrPC The protection given under s. 197 is to protect responsible public servants against the institution of possibly vexatious criminal proceedings for offences alleged to have been committed by them while they are acting or purporting to act as public servants. The policy of the legislature is to afford adequate protection to public servants to ensure that they are

18 *All India Judges Association* v *Union of India* AIR 1993 SC 2493.

not prosecuted for anything done by them in the discharge of their official duties without reasonable cause, and if sanction is granted, to confer on the Government, if they choose to exercise it, complete control of the prosecution.[19]

This protection has certain limits and is available only when the alleged act done by the public servant is reasonably connected with the discharge of his official duty and is not merely a cloak for doing the objectionable act. If in doing his official duty, he acted in excess of his duty, but there is a reasonable connection between the act and the performance of the official duty, the excess will not be a sufficient ground to deprive the public servant from the protection. The question is not as to the nature of the offence such as whether it was committed by a public servant acting or purporting to act as such in the discharge of his official duty. Before s. 197 can be invoked.[20]

It must be shown that the official concerned was accused of an offence alleged to have been committed by him while acting or purporting to act in the discharge of his official duties. It is not the duty which requires examination so much as the act, because the official act can be performed both in the discharge of the official duty as well as in dereliction of it. The act must fall within the scope and range of the official duties of the public servant concerned. It is the quality of the act which is important and the protection of this section is available if the act falls within the scope and range of his official duty. There cannot be any universal rule to determine whether there is a reasonable connection between the act done and the official duty, nor is it possible to lay down any such rule. One of the safe and sure test in this regard would be to consider if the omission or neglect on the part of the public servant to commit the act complained of could have made him answerable for a charge of dereliction of his official duty. If the answer to this question is in the affirmative, it may be said that such act was committed by the public servant while acting in the discharge of his official duty and there was

19 *State of UP* v *Paresh Nath Singh* 2009 CrLJ 3069 (SC); 2009 AIR SCW 3712; (2009)6 SCC 372; (2009)8 Scale 553.

20 *State of UP* v *Paresh Nath Singh* 2009 CrLJ 3069 (SC); 2009 AIR SCW 3712; (2009)6 SCC 372; (2009)8 Scale 553.

every connection with the act complained of and the official duty of the public servant. This aspect makes it clear that the concept of s. 197 does not get immediately attracted on institution of the complaint case.

Protection—when available The protection given under s. 197 is to protect responsible public servants against the institution of possibly vexatious criminal proceedings for offences alleged to have been committed by them while they are acting or purporting to act as public servants. The policy of the legislature is to afford adequate protection to public servants to ensure that they are not prosecuted for anything done by them in the discharge of their official duties without reasonable cause, and if sanction is granted, to confer on the Government, if they choose to exercise it, complete control of the prosecution. This prosecution has certain limits and is available only when the alleged act done by the public servant is reasonably connected with the discharge of his official duty and is not merely a cloak for doing the objectionable act. If in doing his official duty, he acted in excess of his duty, but there is a reasonable connection between the act and the performance of the official duty, the excess will not be a sufficient ground to deprive the public servant from the protection.

Official duty—meaning Use of the expression 'official duty' implies that the act or omission must have been done by the public servant in the course of his service and that it should have been in discharge of his duty. The section does not extend its protective cover to every act or omission done by a public servant in service but restricts its scope of operation to only those act or omissions which are done by a public servant in discharge of official duty.[21]

Official duty implies[22] that the act or omission must have been done by the public servant in course of his service and such act or omission must have been performed as part of duty which further must have been official in nature. The section

21 *State of UP* v *Paresh Nath Singh* 2009 CrLJ 3069 (SC); 2009 AIR SCW 3712; (2009)6 SCC 372; (2009)8 Scale 553.

22 *State of UP* v *Paresh Nath Singh* 2009 CrLJ 3069 (SC); 2009 AIR SCW 3712; (2009)6 SCC 372; (2009)8 Scale 553.

has, thus, to be construed strictly, while determining its applicability to any act or omission in course of service. Its operation has to be limited to those duties which are discharged in course of duty. But once any act or omission has been found to have been committed by a public servant in discharge of his duty then it must be given liberal and wide construction so far its official nature is concerned. For instance a public servant is not entitled to indulge in criminal activities. To that extent the section has to be construed narrowly and in a restricted manner. But once it is established that act or omission was done by the public servant while discharging his duty then the scope of its being official should be construed so as to advance the objective of the section in favour of the public servant. Otherwise the entire purpose of affording protection to a public servant without sanction shall stand frustrated.

> **37. Inspection of Gram Nyayalayas.** The High Court may authorize any judicial officer superior in rank to the Nyayadhikari to inspect the Gram Nyayalayas within his jurisdiction once in every six months or such other period as the High Court may prescribe and issue such instructions, as he considers necessary and submit a report to the High Court.

Scope of s. 37 The section empowers the High Court to authorize any judicial officer superior in rank to the Nyayadhikari to inspect the Gram Nyayalaya (*i*) once in every six month (*ii*) or such other period as may be prescribed by the High Court. After completion of inspection he shall report to the High Court. This section is part of supervisory jurisdiction of High Court. It was enacted to maintain transparency in the works of the Gram Nyayalaya or to control the arbitrary or caprious function of the Gram Nyayalaya. If there is no check and balance in the function of the Gram Nyayalaya their is every chance of misuse of its powers.

> **38. Power to remove difficulties.** (1) If any difficulty arises in giving effect to the provisions of this Act, the Central Government may, by order published in the Official Gazette, make such provisions not inconsistent with the provisions of this Act, as may appear to it to be necessary or expedient for removing the difficulty:

Provided that no order shall be made under this section after the expiry of a period of three years from the date of commencement of this Act.

(2) Every order made under this section shall be laid, as soon as may be after it is made, before each House of Parliament.

39. Power of High Court to make rules. (1) The High Court may, by notification, makes rules for carrying out the provisions of this Act.

(2) In particular, and without prejudice to the generality of the foregoing power, such rules may provide for all or any of the following matters, namely :–

(*a*) the form and dimensions of the seal of the Gram Nyayalayas under section 10;

(*b*) the form, the manner and the fee for institution of suit, claim or proceeding under sub-section (1) of section 24;

(*c*) manner of service on opposite party under sub-section (2) of section 24;

(*d*) procedure for conciliation under sub-section (1) of section 26;

(*e*) qualifications and experience of Conciliators under sub-section (1) of section 27;

(*f*) the period for inspection of Gram Nyayalayas under section 37;

(3) Every notification issued by the High Court shall be published in the Official Gazette.

Scope of s. 39 This section authorises the High Court to make rules to provide the form and dimensions of the seal of the Gram Nyayalaya, fee for institution of the suit, claim or proceeding, manner of service on opposite party, procedure for conciliation, qualification and experience of conciliators and the period for inspection of Gram Nyayalaya for carrying out the provisions of the Act. This section is similar to s. 477 of the CrPC and ss. 122, 125, 128 and 129 of the CPC. Every notification issued by the High Court must be published in the Official Gazette. Broadly speaking rule making power of the High Court has three attributes:

(*i*) It must be made by way of notification;

(*ii*) Such rules are necessary for carrying out the provisions of the Act; and

(*iii*) Such notification must be published in the Official Gazette. It is akin to s. 477(2) of the CrPC.

Power of High Court to make rules (1) Every High Court may, with the previous approval of the State Government, make rules—

(*a*) as to the persons who may be permitted to act as petition-writers in the criminal courts subordinate to it;

(*b*) regulating the issue of licences to such persons, the conduct of business by them, and the scale of fees to be charged by them;

(*c*) providing a penalty for a contravention of any of the rules so made and determining the authority by which such contravention may be investigated and the penalties imposed;

(*d*) any other matter which is required to be, may be, prescribed.

(2) All rules made under this section shall be published in the Official Gazette.

Code of Civil Procedure 1908

Power of certain High Courts to make rules[23] High Courts not being the court of a Judicial Commissioner may, from time to time after previous publication, make rules regulating their own procedure and the procedure of the civil courts subject to their superintendence, and may be such rules annul, alter or add to all or any of the rules in the First Schedule.

Power of other High Courts to make rules[1] High Courts, other than the Courts specified in s. 122, may exercise the powers conferred by that section in such manner and subject to such conditions as the State Government may determine:

Provided that any such High Court may, after previous publication, make a rule extending within the local limits of its

23 Section122 of the Code of Civil Procedure 1908.

1 Section 125 of the Code of Civil Procedure 1908.

jurisdiction any rules which have been made by any other High Court.

Rules to be subject to approval[2] Rules made under the foregoing provisions shall be subject to the previous approval of the Government of the State in which the court whose procedure the rules regulate is situate or, if that court is not situate in any State, to the previous approval of Central Government.

Matters for which rules may provide[3] (1) Such rules shall be not inconsistent with the provisions in the body of this Code, but, subject thereto, may provide for any matters relating to the procedure of civil courts.

(2) In particular, and without prejudice to the generality of the powers conferred by sub-sec. (1), such rules may provide for all or any of the following matters, namely—

(*a*) the service of summonses, notices and other processes by post or in any other manner either generally or in any specified areas, and the proof of such service;

(*b*) the maintenance and custody, while under attachment, of live-stock and other movable property, the fees payable for such maintenance and custody, the sale of such live-stock and property, and the proceeds of such sale;

(*c*) procedure in suits by way of counter-claim, and the valuation of such suits for the purposes of jurisdiction;

(*d*) procedure in garnishee and charging orders either in addition to, or in substitution for, the attachment and sale of debts;

(*e*) procedure where the defendant claims to be entitled to contribution or indemnity over against any person whether a party to the suit or not;

(*f*) summary procedure—

(*i*) in suits in which the plaintiff seeks only to recover a debt or liquidated demand in money payable

2 Section 126 of the Code of Civil Procedure 1908.
3 Section 128 of the Code of Civil Procedure 1908.

by the defendant, with or without interest, arising—

on a contract express or implied; or

on an enactment where the sum sought to be recovered is a fixed sum of money or in the nature of a debt other than a penalty; or

on a guarantee, where the claim against the principal is in respect of a debt or a liquidated demand only;

or on a trust; or

(*ii*) in suits for the recovery of immovable property, with or without a claim for rent or *mesne profits*, by a landlord against a tenant whose term has expired or has been duly determined by notice to quit, or has become liable to forefeiture for non-payment of rent, or against persons claiming under such tenant;

(*g*) procedure by way of originating summons;

(*h*) consolidation of suits, appeals and other proceedings;

(*i*) delegation to any Registrar, Prothonotary or Master or other official of the court of any judicial, *quasi-judicial* and non-judicial duties; and

(*j*) all forms, registers, books, entries and accounts which may be necessary or desirable for the transaction of the business of civil courts.

Power of High Courts to make rules as to their original civil procedure
Notwithstanding anything in this Code, any High Court not being the Court of a Judicial Commissioner may make such rules not inconsistent with the Letters Patent or order or other law establishing it to regulate its own procedure in the exercise of its original civil jurisdiction as it shall think fit, and nothing herein contained shall affect the validity of any such rules in force at the commencement of this Code.

40. Power of State Government to make rules. (1) The State Government may, by notification, make rules for carrying out the provisions of this Act.

(2) In particular, and without prejudice to the generality of the foregoing power, such rules may provided for all or any of the following matters, namely:–

(*a*) the salaries and allowances payable to, and the other terms and conditions of service of, the officers and other employees of the Gram Nyayalayas under sub-section (2) of section 17;

(*b*) the sitting fee and other allowances payable to, and the other terms and conditions for engagement of, Conciliators under sub-section (2) of section 27.

(3) Every rule made by the State Government under this Act shall be laid as soon as may be after it is made, before the State Legislature.

Scope of s. 40 This section deals with the rule making power of the State Government. The rule making power of the State Government has the following features:

(*i*) It is made by notification.

(*ii*) It may make rules for carrying out the provisions of the Act.

(*iii*) Such rule must be laid before the State Legislature.

The First Schedule

(*See* sections 12 and 14)

Part I

Offences under the Indian Penal Code (45 of 1860), etc.

(*i*) offences not punishable with death, imprisonment for life or imprisonment a term exceeding two years;

(*ii*) theft, under section 379, section 380 or section 381 of the Indian Penal Code (45 of 1860), where the value of the property stolen does not exceed rupees twenty thousand;

(*iii*) receiving or retaining stolen property, under section 411 of the Indian Penal Code (45 of 1860), where the value of the property does not exceed rupees twenty thousand;

(*iv*) assisting in the concealment or disposal of stolen property, under section 414 of the Indian Penal Code (45 of 1860), where the value of such property does not exceed rupees twenty thousand;

(*v*) offences under sections 454 and 456 of the Indian Penal Code (45 of 1860);

(*vi*) insult with intent to provoke a breach of the peace, under section 504, and criminal intimidation, punishable with imprisonment for a term which may extend to two years, or with fine, or with both, under section 506 of the Indian Penal Code (45 of 1860);

(*vii*) abetment of any of the foregoing offences;

(*viii*) an attempt to commit any of the foregoing offences, when such attempt is an offence.

PART II

Offences and Relief under the other Central Acts

(*i*) any offence constituted by an act in respect of which a complaint may be made under section 20 of the Cattle-trespass Act 1871 (1 of 1871);

(*ii*) The Payment of Wages Act 1936 (4 of 1936);

(*iii*) The Minimum Wages Act 1948 (11 of 1948);

(*iv*) The Protection of Civil Rights Act 1955 (22 of 1955);

(*v*) Order for maintenance of wives, children and parents under Chapter IX of the Code of Criminal Procedure 1973 (2 of 1974).

(*vi*) The Bonded Labour System (Abolition) Act 1976 (19 of 1976).

(*vii*) The Equal Remuneration Act 1976 (25 of 1976);

(*viii*) The Protection of Women from Domestic Violence Act 2005 (43 of 2005).

PART III

Offences and Relief under the State Acts

(To be notified by the State Government)

The Second Schedule

(*See* sections 13 and 14)

Part I

Suits of a Civil Nature within the Jurisdiction of Gram Nyayalayas

(*i*) Civil Disputes;

(*a*) right to purchase of property;

(*b*) use of common pasture;

(*c*) regulation and timing of taking water from irrigation channel.

(*ii*) Property Disputes;

(*a*) village and farm houses (possession);

(*b*) water channels;

(*c*) right to draw water from a well or tube well.

(*iii*) Other Disputes;

(*a*) claims under the Payment of Wages Act 1936 (4 of 1936);

(*b*) claims under the Minimum Wages Act 1948 (11 of 1948);

(*c*) money suits either arising from trade transaction or money lending;

(*d*) disputes arising out of the partnership in cultivation of land;

(*e*) disputes as to the use of forest produce by inhabitants of Gram Panchayats.

Part II

Claims and Disputes under the Central Acts Notified under sub-section (1) of section 14 by the Central Government

(To be notified by the Central Government)

Part III

Claims and Disputes under the State Acts Notified under sub-section (3) of section 14 by the State Government

(To be notified by the State Government)

Appendices

Appendix 1

National Litigation Policy 2010

INTRODUCTION

Whereas at the National Consultation for Strengthening the Judiciary toward Reducing Pendency and Delays held on the 24th and 25th October 2009 the Union Minister for Law and Justice, presented resolutions which were adopted by the entire Conference unanimously. And Wherein the said Resolution acknowledged the initiative undertaken by the Government of India to frame a National Litigation Policy with a view to ensure conduct of responsible litigation by the Central Government and urges every State Government to evolve similar policies. The National Litigation Policy is as follows:

I. The Vision/Mission

1. The National Litigation Policy is based on the recognition that Government and its various agencies are the pre-dominant litigants in courts and Tribunals in the country. Its aim is to transform Government into an Efficient and Responsible litigant. This policy is also based on the recognition that it is the responsibility of the Government to protect the rights of citizens, to respect fundamental rights and those in charge of the conduct of Government litigation should never forget this basic principle.

"Efficient Litigant" Means

- Focusing on the core issues involved in the litigation and addressing them squarely.
- Managing and conducting litigation in a cohesive, coordinated and time-bound manner.
- Ensuring that good cases are won and bad cases are not needlessly persevered with.

- A litigant who is represented by competent and sensitive legal persons: competent in their skills and sensitive to the facts that Government is not an ordinary litigant and that a litigation does not have to be won at any cost.

"Responsible Litigant" Means

- That litigation will not be resorted to for the sake of litigating.
- That false pleas and technical points will not be taken and shall be discouraged.
- Ensuring that the correct facts and all relevant documents will be placed before the court.
- That nothing will be suppressed from the court and there will be no attempt to mislead any court or Tribunal.

2. Government must cease to be a compulsive litigant. The philosophy that matters should be left to the courts for ultimate decision has to be discarded. The easy approach, "Let the court decide," must be eschewed and condemned.

3. The purpose underlying this policy is also to reduce Government litigation in courts so that valuable court time would be spent in resolving other pending cases so as to achieve the Goal in the National Legal Mission to reduce average pendency time from 15 years to 3 years. Litigators on behalf of Government have to keep in mind the principles incorporated in the National mission for judicial reforms which includes identifying bottlenecks which the Government and its agencies may be concerned with and also removing unnecessary Government cases. Prioritisation in litigation has to be achieved with particular emphasis on welfare legislation, social reform, weaker sections and senior citizens and other categories requiring assistance must be given utmost priority.

4. The Stakeholders:

(A) In ensuring the success of this policy, all stake-holders will have to play their part–the Ministry of Law & Justice, Heads of various Departments, Law Officers and Government Counsel, and individual officers all connected with the concerned litigation. The success of this policy will depend on its strict implementation. Nodal Officers will be appointed by Heads of Department.

"Head of Department" means the administrative person ultimately responsible for the working of the Department or Agency, as the case may be.

(B) The appointment of Nodal Officers must be done carefully. The Nodal Officer has a crucial and important role to play in the overall and specific implementation of this Policy, including but not limited to the references made hereinafter. Every

Ministry must be mindful of the responsibility to appoint proper Nodal Officers who have legal background and expertise. They must be in a position to pro-actively manage litigation. Whilst making such appointments, care must be taken to see that there is continuity in the incumbents holding office. Frequent changes in persons holding the position must be avoided. Nodal Officers must also be subjected to training so that they are in a position to understand what is expected of them under the National Litigation Policy.

(C) Accountability is the touch-stone of this Policy. Accountability will be at various levels; at the level of officers in charge of litigation, those responsible for defending cases, all the lawyers concerned and Nodal Officers. As part of accountability, there must be critical appreciation on the conduct of cases. Good cases which have been lost must be reviewed and subjected to detailed scrutiny to ascertain responsibility. Upon ascertainment of responsibility, suitable action will have to be taken. Complacency must be eliminated and replaced by commitment.

(D) There will be Empowered Committees to monitor the implementation of this Policy and accountability. The Nodal Officers and the Heads of Department will ensure that all relevant data is sent to the Empowered Committees. The Empowered Committee at the National level shall be chaired by the Attorney General for India and such other members not exceeding six in number as may be nominated by the Ministry of Law with an Additional Secretary to be the Member Secretary. There will be four Regional Empowered Committees to be chaired by an Additional Solicitor General nominated by the Ministry of Law. It shall include all the Assistant Solicitors General of the Region and such other members including a Member Secretary nominated by the Ministry of Law. The Regional Committees shall submit monthly reports to the National Empowered Committee which shall in turn submit Comprehensive Reports to the Ministry of Law. It shall be the responsibility of the Empowered Committee to receive and deal with suggestions and complaints including from litigants and Government Departments and take appropriate measures in connection therewith.

II. Government Representation

(A) While it is recognized that Government Panels are a broad based opportunity for a cross section of lawyers, Government Panels cannot be vehicles for sustaining incompetent and inefficient persons. Persons who recommend names for inclusion on the Panel are requested to be careful in making such recommendations and to take care to check the credentials of those recommended with particular reference to legal knowledge and integrity.

(B) Screening Committees for constitution of Panels will be introduced at every level to assess the skills and capabilities of people who are desirous of being on Government Panels before their inclusion on the Panel. The Ministry of Law shall ensure that the constitution of Screening Committees will include representatives of the Department concerned. The Screening Committees will make their recommendations to the Ministry of Law. Emphasis will be on identifying areas of core competence, domain expertise and areas of specialisation. It cannot be assumed that all lawyers are capable of conducting every form of litigation.

(C) Government advocates must be well equipped and provided with adequate infrastructure. Efforts will be made to provide the agencies which conduct Government litigation with modern technology such as computers, internet links, etc. Common research facilities must be made available for Government lawyers as well as equipment for producing compilations of cases.

(D) Training programs, seminars, workshops and refresher courses for Government advocates must be encouraged. There must be continuing legal education for Government lawyers with particular emphasis on identifying and improving areas of specialization. Law schools will be associated in preparing special courses for training of Government lawyers with particular emphasis on identifying and improving areas of specialization. Most importantly, there must be an effort to cultivate and in still values required for effective Government representation.

(E) National and regional conferences of Government advocates will be organized so that matters of mutual interest can be discussed and problems analysed.

(F) Advocates on Record must play a meaningful role in Government litigations. They cannot continue to be merely responsible for filing appearances in Court. A system of motivation has to be worked out for Government advocates under which initiative and hard work will be recognised and extraordinary work will be rewarded. This could be in the form of promotions or out of turn increments.

(G) It will be the responsibility of all Law Officers to train Panel lawyers and to explain to them what is expected of them in the discharge of their functions.

(H) Panels will be drawn up of willing, energetic and competent lawyers to develop special skills in drafting pleadings on behalf of Government. Such Panels shall be flexible. More and more advocates must be encouraged to get on to such Panels by demonstrating keenness, knowledge and interest.

(I) Nodal Officers will be responsible for active case management. This will involve constant monitoring of cases particularly to examine whether cases have gone "off track" or have been unnecessarily delayed.

(J) Incomplete briefs are frequently given to Government Counsel. This must be discontinued. The Advocates-on-Record will be held responsible if incomplete briefs are given. It is the responsibility of the person in charge of the Central Agency concerned, to ensure that proper records are kept of cases filed and that copies retained by the Department are complete and tally with what has been filed in Court. If any Department or Agency has a complaint in this regard it can complain to the Empowered Committee.

(K) There should be equitable distribution of briefs so that there will be broad based representation of Government. Additional Solicitors General will be associated with regard to distribution of briefs in the High Court. Complaints that certain Panel advocates are being preferred in the matter of briefing will be inquired into seriously by the Empowered Committee.

(L) Government lawyers are expected to discharge their obligations with a sense of responsibility towards the court as well as to Government. If concessions are made on issues of fact or law, and it is found that such concessions were not justified, the matter will be reported to the Empowered Committee and remedial action would follow.

(M) While Government cannot pay fees which private litigants are in a position to pay, the fees payable to Government lawyers will be suitably revised to make it remunerative. Optimum utilisation of available resources and elimination of wastage will itself provide for adequate resources for revision of fees. It should be ensured that the fees stipulated as per the Schedule of Fees should be paid within a reasonable time. Malpractice in relation to release of payments must be eliminated.

III. Adjournments

(A) Accepting that frequent adjournments are resorted to by Government lawyers, unnecessary and frequent adjournments will be frowned upon and infractions dealt with seriously.

(B) In fresh litigations where the Government is a Defendant or a Respondent in the first instance, a reasonable adjournment may be applied for, for obtaining instructions. However, it must be ensured that such instructions are made available and communicated before the next date of hearing. If instructions are not forthcoming, the matter must be reported to the Nodal Officer and if necessary to the Head of the Department.

(C) In Appellate Courts, if the paper books are complete, then adjournments must not be sought in routine course. The matter must be dealt with at the first hearing itself. In such cases, adjournments should be applied for only if a specific query from the court is required to be answered and for this, instructions have to be obtained.

(D) One of the functions of the Nodal Officers will be to coordinate the conduct of litigation. It will also be their responsibility to monitor the progress of litigation, particularly to identify cases in which repeated adjournments are taken. It will be the responsibility of the Nodal Officer to report cases of repeated and unjustified adjournments to the Head of Department and it shall be open to him to call for reasons for the adjournment. The Head of the Agency shall ensure that the Records of the case reflect reasons for adjournment, if these are repeated adjournments. Serious note will be taken of cases of negligence or default and the matter will be dealt with appropriately by referring such cases to the Empowered Committee. If the advocates are at fault, action against them may entail suspension/removal of their names from Government Panels.

(E) Cases in which costs are awarded against the Government as a condition of grant of adjournment will be viewed very seriously. In all such cases the Head of Department must give a report to the Empowered Committee of the reasons why such costs were awarded. The names of the persons responsible for the default entailing the imposition of costs will be identified. Suitable action must be taken against them.

IV. Pleadings/Counters

(A) Suits or other proceedings initiated by or on behalf of Government have to be drafted with precision and clarity. There should be no repetition either in narration of facts or in the grounds.

(B) Appeals will be drafted with particular attention to the Synopsis and List of Dates which will carefully crystallise the facts in dispute and the issues involved. Slipshod and loose drafting will be taken serious note of. Defaulting advocates may be suspended/removed from the Panels.

(C) Care must be taken to include all necessary and relevant documents in the appeal paper book. If it is found that any such documents are not annexed and this entails an adjournment or if the court adversely comments on this, the matter will be enquired into by the Nodal Officer and reported to the Head of Department for suitable action.

(D) It is noticed that Government documentation in court is untidy, haphazard and incomplete, full of typing errors and blanks. Special formats for Civil Appeals, Special Leave Petitions, Counter Affidavits will be formulated and circulated by way of guidance and instruction as a Government Advocates Manual. This will include not only contents but also the format, design, font size, quality of paper, printing, binding and presentation. It is the joint responsibility of the Drafting Counsel and the Advocate on Record to ensure compliance.

(E) Counter Affidavits in important cases will not be filed unless the same are shown to and vetted by Law Officers. This should, however, not delay the filing of counters.

V. Filing of Appeals

(A) Appeals will not be filed against *ex parte ad interim* orders. Attempt must first be to have the order vacated. An appeal must be filed against an order only if the order is not vacated and the continuation of such order causes prejudice.

(B) Appeals must be filed intra court in the first instance. Direct appeals to the Supreme Court must not be resorted to except in extraordinary cases.

(C) Given that Tribunalisation is meant to remove the loads from Courts, challenge to orders of Tribunals should be an exception and not a matter of routine.

(D) In Service Matters, no appeal will be filed in cases where:

(*a*) the matter pertains to an individual grievance without any major repercussion;

(*b*) the matter pertains to a case of pension or retirement benefits without involving any principle and without setting any precedent or financial implications.

(E) Further, proceedings will not be filed in service matters merely because the order of the Administrative Tribunal affects a number of employees. Appeals will not be filed to espouse the cause of one section of employees against another.

(F) Proceedings will be filed challenging orders of Administrative Tribunals only if:

(*a*) there is a clear error of record and the finding has been entered against the Government;

(*b*) the judgment of the Tribunal is contrary to a service rule or its interpretation by a High Court or the Supreme Court;

(*c*) the judgment would impact the working of the administration in terms of morale of the service, the Government is compelled to file a petition; or

(*d*) if the judgment will have recurring implications upon other cadres or if the judgment involves huge financial claims being made.

(G) Appeals in Revenue matters will not be filed:

(*a*) if the stakes are not high and are less than that amount to be fixed by the Revenue Authorities;

(*b*) if the matter is covered by a series of judgments of the Tribunal or of the High Courts which have held the field and which have not been challenged in the Supreme Court;

(c) where the assessee has acted in accordance with long standing industry practice;

(*d*) merely because of change of opinion on the part of jurisdictional officers.

(H) Appeals will not be filed in the Supreme Court unless:

(*a*) the case involves a question of law;

(*b*) if it is a question of fact, the conclusion of the fact is so perverse that an honest judicial opinion could not have arrived at that conclusion;

(*c*) where public finances are adversely affected;

(*d*) where there is substantial interference with public justice;

(*e*) where there is a question of law arising under the Constitution;

(*f*) where the High Court has exceeded its jurisdiction;

(*g*) where the High Court has struck down a statutory provision as *ultra vires*;

(*h*) where the interpretation of the High Court is plainly erroneous.

(I) In each case, there will be a proper certification of the need to file an appeal. Such certification will contain brief but cogent reasons in support. At the same time, reasons will also be recorded as to why it was not considered fit or proper to file an appeal.

VI. Limitation—Delayed Appeals

(A) It is recognized that good cases are being lost because appeals are filed well beyond the period of limitation and without any proper explanation for the delay or without a proper application for condonation of delay. It is recognized that such delays are not always *bona fide* particularly in cases where high revenue stakes are involved.

(B) Each Head of Department will be required to call for details of cases filed on behalf of the Department and to maintain a record of cases which have been dismissed on the ground of delay. The Nodal Officers must submit a report in every individual case to the Head of Department explaining all the reasons for such delay and identifying the persons/causes responsible. Every such case will be investigated and if it is found that the delay was not *bona fide*, appropriate action must be taken. Action will be such that it operates as a deterrent for unsatisfactory work and malpractices in the conduct of Government litigation. For this purpose, obtaining of the data and fixing of responsibility will play a vital role. Data must be obtained on a regular basis annually, bi-monthly or quarterly.

(C) Applications for condonation of delay are presently drafted in routine terms without application of mind and resorting to word processed "boiler plate." This practice must immediately stop. It is responsibility of the drafting counsel to carefully draft an application for condonation of delay, identifying the areas of delay and identifying the causes with particularity. Drafting advocates who fail to adhere to this may be suspended/removed from the Panel.

(D) Every attempt must be made to reduce delays in filing appeals/applications. It shall be responsibility of each Head of Department to work out an appropriate system for elimination of delays and ensure its implementation.

(E) Belated appeals filed beyond the period of limitation cannot be approached merely from the point of view that courts have different approaches towards condonation of delay. Since some courts liberally grant condonation of delay, a general apathy seems to have taken over. The tendency on the part of Government counsel to expect leniency towards Government for condonation of delay must be discouraged. The question of limitation and delay must be approached on the premise that every court will be strict with regard to condonation of delay.

VII. Alternative Dispute Resolution Arbitration

(A) More and more Government departments and PSUs are resorting to arbitration particularly in matters of drilling contracts, hire of ships, construction of highways, etc. Careful drafting of commercial contracts, including arbitration agreements must be given utmost priority. The Ministry of Law and Justice recognizes that it has a major role to play in this behalf.

(B) The resort to arbitration as an alternative dispute resolution mechanism must be encouraged at every level, but this entails the responsibility that such an arbitration will be cost effective, efficacious, expeditious, and conducted with high rectitude. In most cases arbitration has become a mirror of court litigation. This must be stopped.

(C) It is recognized that the conduct of arbitration at present leaves a lot to be desired. Arbitrations are needlessly dragged on for various reasons. One of them is by repeatedly seeking adjournments. This practice must be deplored and stopped.

(D) The Head of Department will call for the data of pending arbitrations. Copies of the roznama, etc. (record of proceedings) must be obtained to find out why arbitrations are delayed and ascertain who is responsible for adjournments. Advocates found to be conducting arbitrations lethargically and inefficiently must not only be removed from the conduct of such cases but also not briefed in future arbitrations. It shall be the responsibility of the Head of Department to call for regular review meetings to assess the status of pending arbitration cases.

(E) Lack of precision in drafting arbitration agreements is a major cause of delay in arbitration proceedings. This leads to disputes about appointment of arbitrators and arbitrability which results in prolonged litigation even before the start of arbitration. Care must be taken whilst drafting an arbitration agreement. It must correctly and clearly reflect the intention of the parties particularly if certain items are required to be left to the decision of named persons such as engineers are not meant to be referred to arbitration.

(F) Arbitration agreements are loosely and carelessly drafted when it comes to appointment of arbitrators. Arbitration agreements must reflect a well defined procedure for appointment of arbitrators. Sole arbitrator may be preferred over a Panel of three Arbitrators. In technical matters, reference may be made to trained technical persons instead of retired judicial persons.

(G) It is also found that certain persons are "preferred" as arbitrators by certain departments or corporations. The arbitrator must be chosen solely on the basis of knowledge, skill and integrity and not for extraneous reasons. It must be ascertained whether the arbitrator will be in a position to devote time for expeditious disposal of the reference.

(H) It is found that if an arbitration award goes against Government it is almost invariably challenged by way of objections filed in the arbitration. Very often these objections lack merit and the grounds do not fall within the purview of the scope of challenge before the courts. Routine challenge to arbitration awards must be discouraged. A clear formulation of the reasons to challenge Awards must precede the decision to file proceedings to challenge the Awards.

VIII. Specialised Litigation

(A) Proceedings seeking judicial review including in the matter of award of contracts or tenders.

Such matters should be defended keeping in mind Constitutional imperatives and good governance. If the proceedings are founded on an allegation of the breach of natural justice and it is found that there is substance in the allegations, the case shall not be proceeded with and the order may be set aside to provide for a proper hearing in the matter. Cases where projects may be held up have to be defended vigorously keeping in mind public interest. They must be dealt with and disposed off as expeditiously as possible.

(B) Cases involving vires, or statutes or rules and regulations.

In all such cases, proper affidavits should be filed explaining the rationale between the statute or regulation and also making appropriate averments with regard to legislative competence.

(C) Public Interest Litigations (PILs)

Public Interest Litigations must be approached in a balanced manner. On the one hand, PILs should not be taken as matters of convenience to let the courts do what Government finds inconvenient. It is recognized that the increase in PILs stems from a perception that there is governmental inaction. This perception must be changed. It must be recognized that several PILs are filed for collateral reasons including publicity and at the instance of third parties. Such litigation must be exposed as being not *bona fide*.

PILs challenging public contracts must be seriously defended. If interim orders are passed stopping such projects then appropriate conditions must be insisted upon for the Petitioners to pay compensation if the PIL is ultimately rejected.

(D) PSU Litigations

Litigation between Public Sector Undertakings *inter se* between Government Public Sector Undertakings is causing great concern. Every effort must be made to prevent such litigation. Before initiating such litigation, the matter must be placed before the highest authority in the public sector such as the CMD or MD. It will be his responsibility to endeavour to see whether the litigation can be avoided. If litigation cannot be avoided, then alternative dispute resolution methods like mediation must be considered. Section 89 of the Code of Civil Procedure must be resorted to extensively.

IX. Review of Pending Cases

(A) All pending cases involving Government will be reviewed. This Due Diligence process shall involve drawing upon statistics of all pending matters which shall be provided for by all Government departments (including PSUs). The Office of the Attorney General and the Solicitor General shall also be responsible for reviewing all pending cases and filtering frivolous and vexatious matters from the meritorious ones.

(B) Cases will be grouped and categorized. The practice of grouping should be introduced whereby cases should be assigned a particular number of identity according to the subject and statute involved. In fact, further sub-grouping will also be attempted. To facilitate this process, standard forms must be devised which lawyers have to fill up at the time of filing of cases. Panels will be set up to implement categorization, review such cases to identify cases which can be withdrawn. These include cases which are covered by decisions of courts and cases which are found without merit withdrawn. This must be done in a time bound fashion.

Appendix 2

UNCITRAL Model Law on International Commercial Arbitration

Chapter I

General Provisions

Article 1—Scope of application

(1) This Law applies to international commercial* arbitration, subject to any agreement in force between this State and any other State or States.

(2) The provisions of this Law, except Articles 8, 9, 17H, 17I, 17J, 35 and 36 apply only if the place of arbitration is in the territory of this State.

(3) An arbitrations is international if:

(*a*) the parties to an arbitration agreement have, at the time of the conclusion of this agreement, their places of business in different States; or

(*b*) one of the following places is situated outside the State in which the parties have their places of business:

(*i*) the place of arbitration if determined in, or pursuant to, the arbitration agreement;

(*ii*) any place where a substantial part of the obligations of the commercial* relationship is to be performed or the

* The term "commercial" should be given a wide interpretation so as to cover matters arising from all relationships of a commercial nature, whether contractual or not. Relationships of a commercial nature include, but are not limited to the following transactions: any trade transaction for the supply or exchange of goods or services; distribution agreement; commercial representation or agency; factoring; leasing; construction of works; consulting; engineering; licensing; investment; financing; banking; insurance; exploitation agreement or concession; joint venture and other forms of industrial or business co-operation; carriage of goods or passengers by air, sea, rail or road.

place with which the subject-matter of the dispute is most closely connected; or

(*c*) the parties have expressly agreed that the subject-matter of the arbitration agreement relates to more than one country.

(4) For the purposes of paragraph (3) of this Article—

(*a*) if a party has more than one place of business, the place of business is that which has the closest relationship to the arbitration agreement;

(*b*) if a party does not have a place of business, reference is to be made to his habitual residence.

(5) This Law shall not affect any other law of this State by virtue of which certain disputes may not be submitted to arbitration or may be submitted to arbitration only according to provisions other than those of this Law.

Article 2—Definitions and rules of interpretation

For the purpose of this law:

(*a*) "arbitration" means any arbitration whether or not administered by a permanent arbitral institution;

(*b*) "arbitral tribunal" means a sole arbitrator or a panel of arbitrators;

(*c*) "court" means a body or organ of the judicial system of a State;

(*d*) where a provision of this Law, except Article 28, leaves the parties free to determine a certain issue, such freedom includes the right of the parties to authorise a third party, including an institution, to make that determination;

(*e*) where a provision of this Law refers to the fact that the parties have agreed or that they may agree or in any other way refers to an agreement of the parties, such agreement includes any arbitration rules referred to in that agreement;

(*f*) where a provision of this Law, other than in Articles 25(*a*) and 32(2)(*a*), refers to a claim, it also applies to a counter-claim, and where it refers to a defence, it also applies to a defence to such counter-claim.

Article 2A—International origin and general principles

(1) In the interpretation of this Law, regard is to be had to its international origin and to the need to promote uniformity in its application and the observance of good faith.

(2) Questions concerning matters governed by this Law which are not expressly settled in it are to be settled in conformity with the general principles on which this Law is based.

Article 3—Receipt of written communications

(1) Unless otherwise agreed by the parties:

(*a*) any written communication is deemed to have been received if it is delivered to the addressee personally or if it is delivered at his place of business, habitual residence or mailing address; if none of these can be found after making a reasonable inquiry, a written communication is deemed to have been received if it is sent to the addressee's last known place of business, habitual residence or mailing address by registered letter or any other means which provides a record of the attempt to deliver it;

(*b*) the communication is deemed to have been received on the day it is so deliverd.

(2) The provisions of this Article do not apply to communications in court proceedings.

Article 4—Waiver of right to object

A party who knows that any provision of this Law from which the parties may derogate or any requirement under the arbitration agreement has not been complied with and yet proceeds with the arbitration without stating his objection to such non-compliance without undue delay or, if a time-limit is provided therefor, within such period of time, shall be deemed to have waived his right to object.

Article 5—Extent of court intervention

In matters governed by this Law, no court shall intervene except where so provided in this Law.

Article 6—Court or other authority for certain functions of arbitration assistance and supervision

The functions referred to in Articles 11(3), 11(4), 13(3), 14, 16(3) and 34(2) shall be performed by ..... [Each State enacting this Model Law specifies the court, courts or, where referred to therein, other authority competent to perform these functions].

CHAPTER II

Arbitration Agreement

Option I—Article 7—Definition and form of arbitration agreement

(1) "Arbitration agreement" is an agreement by the parties to submit to arbitration all or certain disputes which have arisen or which may arise between them in respect of a defined legal relationship, whether contractual or not. An arbitration agreement may be in the form of an arbitration clause in a contract or in the form of a separate agreement.

(2) The arbitration agreement shall be in writing.

(3) An arbitration agreement is in writing if its content is recorded in any form, whether or not the arbitration agreement or contract has been concluded orally, by conduct, or by other means.

(4) The requirement that an arbitration agreement be in writing is met by an electronic communication if the information contained therein is accessible so as to be useable for subsequent reference; "electronic communication" means any communication that the parties make by means of data messages; "data message" means information generated, sent, received or stored by electronic, magnetic, optical or similar means, including, but not limited to, electronic data interchange (EDI), electronic mail, telegram, telex or telecopy.

(5) Furthermore, an arbitration agreement is in writing if it is contained in an exchange of statements of claim and defence in which the existence of an agreement is alleged by one party and not denied by the other.

(6) The reference in a contract to any document containing an arbitration clause constitutes an arbitration agreement in writing, provided that the reference is such as to make that clause part of the contract.

Option II—Article 7—Definition of arbitration agreement

"Arbitration agreement" is an agreement by the parties to submit to arbitration all or certain disputes which have arisen or which may arise between them in respect of a defined legal relationship, whether contractual or not.

Article 8—Arbitration agreement and substantive claim before court

(1) A court before which an action is brought in a matter which is the subject of an arbitration agreement shall, if a party so requests not later than when submitting his first statement on the substance of the dispute, refer the parties to arbitration unless it finds that the agreement is null and void, inoperative or incapable of being performed.

(2) Where an action referred to in paragraph (1) of this article has been brought, arbitral proceedings may nevertheless be commenced or continued, and an award may be made, while the issue is pending before the court.

Article 9—Arbitration agreement and interim measures by court

It is not incompatible with an arbitration agreement for a party to request, before or during arbitral proceedings, from a court an interim measure of protection and for a court to grant such measure.

CHAPTER III

Composition of Arbitral Tribunal

Article 10—Number of arbitrators

(1) The parties are free to determine the number of arbitrators.

(2) Failing such determination, the number of arbitrators shall be three.

Article 11—Appointment of arbitrators

(1) No person shall be precluded by reason of his nationality from acting as an arbitrator, unless otherwise agreed by the parties.

(2) The parties are free to agree on a procedure of appointing the arbitrator or arbitrators, subject to the provisions of paragraphs (4) and (5) of this Article.

(3) Failing such agreement,

(*a*) in an arbitration with three arbitrators, each party shall appoint one arbitrator, and the two arbitrators thus appointed shall appoint the third arbitrator; if a party fails to appoint the arbitrator within 30 days of receipt of a request to do so from the other party, or if the two arbitrators fail to agree on the third arbitrator within 30 days of their appointment, the appointment shall be made, upon request of a party, by the court or other authority specified in Article 6;

(*b*) in an arbitration with a sole arbitrator, if the parties are unable to agree on the arbitrator, he shall be appointed, upon request of a party, by the court or other authority specified in Article 6.

(4) Where, under an appointment procedure agreed upon by the parties—

(*a*) a party fails to act as required under such procedure, or

(*b*) the parties, or two arbitrators, are unable to reach an agreement expected of them under such procedure, or

(*c*) a third party, including an institution, fails to perform any function entrusted to it under such procedure,

any party may request the court or other authority specified in Article 6 to take the necessary measure, unless the agreement on the appointment procedure provides other means for securing the appointment.

(5) A decision on a matter entrusted by paragraph (3) or (4) of this Article to the court or other authority specified in Article 6 shall be subject to no appeal. The court or other authority, in appointing an arbitrator, shall have due regard to any qualifications required of the arbitrator by the agreement of the parties and to such considerations as are likely to secure the appointment of an independent and impartial arbitrator and, in the case of a sole or third arbitrator, shall take into account as well the advisability of appointing an arbitrator of a nationality other than those of the parties.

Article 12—Grounds for challenge

(1) When a person is approached in connection with his possible appointment as an arbitrator, he shall disclose any circumstances likely to give rise to justifiable doubts as to his impartiality or independence. An arbitrator, from the time of his appointment and throughout the arbitral proceedings, shall without delay disclose any such circumstances to the parties unless they have already been informed of them by him.

(2) An arbitrator may be challenged only if circumstances exist that give rise to justifiable doubts as to his impartiality or independence, or if he does not possess qualifications agreed to by the parties. A party may challenge an arbitrator appointed by him, or in whose appointment he has participated, only for reasons of which he becomes aware after the appointment has been made.

Article 13—Challenge procedure

(1) The parties are free to agree on a procedure for challenging an arbitrator, subject to the provisions of paragraph (3) of this Article.

(2) Failing such agreement, a party who intends to challenge an arbitrator shall, within 15 days after becoming aware of the constitution of the arbitral tribunal or after becoming aware of any circumstances referred to in Article 12(2), send a written statement of the reasons for the challenge to the arbitral tribunal. Unless the challenged arbitrator withdraws from his office or the other party agrees to the challenge, the arbitral tribunal shall decide on the challenge.

(3) If a challenge under any procedure agreed upon by the parties or under the procedure of paragraph (2) of this Article is not successful, the challenging party may request, within 30 days after having received notice of the decision rejecting the challenge, the court or other authority specified in Article 6 to decide on the challenge, which decision shall be subject to no appeal; while such a request is pending, the arbitral tribunal, including the challenged arbitrator, may continue the arbitral proceedings and make an award.

Article 14—Failure or impossibility to Act

(1) If an arbitrator becomes *de jure* or *de facto* unable to perform his functions or for other reasons fails to act without undue delay, his mandate terminates if he withdraws from his office or if the parties agree on the termination. Otherwise, if a controversy remains concerning any of these grounds, any party may request the court or other authority specified in Article 6 to decide on the termination of the mandate, which decision shall be subject to no appeal.

(2) If, under this Article or Article 13(2), an arbitrator withdraws from his office or a party agrees to the termination of the mandate of an arbitrator, this does not imply acceptance of the validity of any ground referred to in this Article or Article 12(2).

Article 15—Appointment of substitute arbitrator

Where the mandate of an arbitrator terminates under Article 13 or 14 or because of his withdrawal from office for any other reason or because of the revocation of his mandate by agreement of the parties or in any other case of termination of his mandate, a substitute arbitrator shall be appointed according to the rules that were applicable to the appointment of the arbitrator being replaced.

CHAPTER IV

Jurisdiction of Arbitral Tribunal

Article 16— Competence of arbitral tribunal to rule on its jurisdiction

(1) The arbitral tribunal may rule on its own jurisdiction, including any objections with respect to the existence or validity of the arbitration agreement. For that purpose, an arbitration clause which forms part of a contract shall be treated as an agreement independent of the other terms of the contract. A decision by the arbitral tribunal that the contract is null and void shall not entail *ipso jure* the invalidity of the arbitration clause.

(2) A plea that the arbitral tribunal does not have jurisdiction shall be raised not later than the submission of the statement of defence. A party is not precluded from raising such a plea by the fact that he has appointed, or participated in the appointment of, an arbitrator. A plea that the arbitral tribunal is exceeding the scope of its authority shall be raised as soon as the matter alleged to be beyond the scope of its authority is raised during the arbitral proceedings. The arbitral tribunal may, in either case, admit a later plea if it considers the delay justified.

(3) The arbitral tribunal may rule on a plea referred to in paragraph (2) of this Article either as a preliminary question or in an award on the merits. If the arbitral tribunal rules as a preliminary question that it has jurisdiction, any party may request, within thirty days after having received notice of that ruling, the court specified in Article 6 to decide the matter, which decision shall be subject to no appeal; while such a request is pending, the arbitral tribunal may continue the arbitral proceedings and make an award.

CHAPTER IVA

Interim Measures and Preliminary Orders

Section 1 – Interim Measures

Article 17—Power of the Arbitral Tribunal to Order Interim Measures

(1) Unless otherwise agreed by the parties, the arbitral tribunal may, at the request of a party, grant interim measures.

(2) An interim measure is any temporary measure, whether in the form of an award or in another form, by which, at any time prior to the

issuance of the award by which the dispute is finally decided, the arbitral tribunal orders a party to:

(*a*) Maintain or restore the *status quo* pending determination of the dispute;

(*b*) Take action that would prevent, or refrain from taking action that is likely to cause, current or imminent harm or prejudice to the arbitral process itself;

(*c*) Provide a means of preserving assets out of which a subsequent award may be satisfied; or

(*d*) Preserve evidence that may be relevant and material to the resolution of the dispute.

Article 17A—Conditions for granting interim measures

(1) The party requesting an interim measure under Article 17(2)(*a*), (*b*) and (*c*) shall satisfy the arbitral tribunal that:

(*a*) Harm not adequately reparable by an award of damages is likely to result if the measure is not ordered, and such harm substantially out-weighs the harm that is likely to result to the party against whom the measure is directed if the measure is granted; and

(*b*) There is a reasonable possibility that the requesting party will succeed on the merits of the claim. The determination on this possibility shall not affect the discretion of the arbitral tribunal in making any subsequent determination.

(2) With regard to a request for an interim measure under Article 17(2)(*d*), the requirements in paragraphs (1)(*a*) and (*b*) of this Article shall apply only to the extent the arbitral tribunal considers appropriate.

Section 2 – Preliminary Orders

Article 17B—Applications for preliminary orders and conditions for granting preliminary orders

(1) Unless otherwise agreed by the parties, a party may, without notice to any other party, make a request for an interim measure together with an application for a preliminary order directing a party not to frustrate the purpose of the interim measure requested.

(2) The arbitral tribunal may grant a preliminary order provided it considers that prior disclosure of the request for the interim measure to the party against whom it is directed risks frustrating the purpose of the measure.

(3) The conditions defined under Article 17A apply to any preliminary order, provided that the harm to be assessed under Article 17A(1)(*a*), is the harm likely to result from the order being granted or not.

Article 17C—Specific regime for preliminary orders

(1) Immediately after the arbitral tribunal has made a determination in respect of an application for a preliminary order, the arbitral tribunal shall give notice to all parties of the request for the interim measure, the application for the preliminary order, the preliminary order, if any, and all other communication, including by indicating the content of any oral communication, between any party and the arbitral tribunal in relation thereto.

(2) At the same time, the arbitral tribunal shall give an opportunity to any party against whom a preliminary order is directed to present its case at the earliest practicable time.

(3) The arbitral tribunal shall decide promptly on any objection to the preliminary order.

(4) A preliminary order shall expire after twenty days from the date on which it was issued by the arbitral tribunal. However, the arbitral tribunal may issue an interim measure adopting or modifying the preliminary order, after the party against whom the preliminary order is directed has been given notice and an opportunity to present its case.

(5) A preliminary order shall be binding on the parties but shall not be subject to enforcement by a court. Such a preliminary order does not constitute an award.

Section 3 – Provisions Applicable to Interim Measures and Preliminary Orders

Article 17D— Modification, suspension termination

The arbitral tribunal may modify, suspend or terminate an interim measure or a preliminary order it has granted, upon application of any party or, in exceptional circumstances and upon prior notice to the parties, on the arbitral tribunal's own initiative.

Article 17E—Provision of security

(1) The arbitral tribunal may require the party requesting an interim measure to provide appropriate security in connection with the measure.

(2) The arbitral tribunal shall require the party applying for a preliminary order to provide security in connection with the order unless the arbitral tribunal considers it inappropriate or unnecessary to do so.

Article 17F—Disclosure

(1) The arbitral tribunal may require any party promptly to disclose any material change in the circumstances on the basis of which the measure was requested or granted.

(2) The party applying for a preliminary order shall disclose to the arbitral tribunal all circumstances that are likely to be relevant to the

arbitral tribunal's determination whether to grant or maintain the order, and such obligation shall continue until the party against whom the order has been requested has had an opportunity to present its case. Thereafter, paragraph (1) of this Article shall apply.

Article 17G—Costs and damages

The party requesting an interim measure or applying for a preliminary order shall be liable for any costs and damages caused by the measure or the order to any party if the arbitral tribunal later determines that, in the circumstances, the measure or the order should not have been granted. The arbitral tribunal may award such costs and damages at any point during the proceedings.

Section 4 – Recognition and Enforcement of Interim Measures

Article 17H—Recognition and enforcement

(1) An interim measure issued by an arbitral tribunal shall be recognized as binding and, unless otherwise provided by the arbitral tribunal, enforced upon application to the competent court, irrespective of the country in which it was issued, subject to the provisions of Article 17-I.

(2) The party who is seeking or has obtained recognition or enforcement of an interim measure shall promptly inform the court of any termination, suspension or modification of that interim measure.

(3) The court of the State where recognition or enforcement is sought may, if it considers it proper, order the requesting party to provide appropriate security if the arbitral tribunal has not already made a determination with respect to security or where such a decision is necessary to protect the rights of third parties.

Article 17-I—Grounds for refusing recognition or enforcement

(1) Recognition or enforcement of an interim measure may be refused only:

(*a*) At the request of the party against whom it is invoked if the court is satisfied that;

(*i*) Such refusal is warranted on the grounds set forth in Article 36(1)(*a*)(*i*), (*ii*), (*iii*) or (*iv*); or

(*ii*) The arbitral tribunal's decision with respect to the provision of security in connection with the interim measure issued by the arbitral tribunal has not been complied with; or

(*iii*) The interim measure has been terminated or suspended by the arbitral tribunal or, where so empowered, by the court of the State in which the arbitration takes place or under the law of which that interim measure was granted; or (*b*) If the court finds that:

(*i*) The interim measure is incompatible with the powers conferred upon the court unless the court decides to reformulate the interim measure to the extent necessary to adapt it to its own powers and procedures for the purposes of enforcing that interim measure and without modifying its substance; or

(*ii*) Any of the grounds set forth in Article 36(1)(*b*)(*i*) or (*ii*), apply to the recognition and enforcement of the interim measure.

(2) Any determination made by the court on any ground in paragraph (1) of this Article shall be effective only for the purposes of the application to recognize and enforce the interim measure. The court where recognition or enforcement is sought shall not, in making that determination, undertake a review of the substance of the interim measure.

Section 5 – Court-ordered Interim Measures

Article 17J—Court-ordered interim measures

A court shall have the same power of issuing an interim measure in relation to arbitration proceedings, irrespective of whether their place is in the territory of this State, as it has in relation to proceedings in courts. The court shall exercise such power in accordance with its own procedures in considerations of the specific features of international arbitration.

CHAPTER V

Conduct of Arbitral Proceedings

Article 18—Equal treatment of parties

The parties shall be treated with equality and each party shall be given a full opportunity of presenting his case.

Article 19—Determination of rules of procedure

(1) Subject to the provisions of this Law, the parties are free to agree on the procedure to be followed by the arbitral tribunal in conducting the proceedings.

(2) Failing such agreement, the arbitral tribunal may, subject to the provisions of this Law, conduct the arbitration in such manner as it considers appropriate. The power conferred upon the arbitral tribunal includes the power to determine the admissibility, relevance, materiality and weight of any evidence.

Article 20—Place of arbitration

(1) The parties are free to agree on the place of arbitration. Failing such agreement, the place of arbitration shall be determined by the arbitral

tribunal having regard to the circumstances of the case, including the convenience of the parties.

(2) Notwithstanding the provisions of paragraph (1) of this Article, the arbitral tribunal may, unless otherwise agreed by the parties, meet at any place it considers appropriate for consultation among its members, for hearing witnesses, experts or the parties, or for inspection of goods, other property or documents.

Article 21—Commencement of arbitral proceedings

Unless otherwise agreed by the parties, the arbitral proceedings in respect of a particular dispute commence on the date on which a request for that dispute to be referred to arbitration is received by the respondent.

Article 22—Language

(1) The parties are free to agree on the language or languages to be used in the arbitral proceedings. Failing such agreement, the arbitral tribunal shall determine the language or languages to be used in the proceedings. This agreement or determination, unless otherwise specified therein, shall apply to any written statement by a party, any hearing and any award, decision or other communication by the arbitral tribunal.

(2) The arbitral tribunal may order that any documentary evidence shall be accompanied by a translation into the language or languages agreed upon by the parties or determined by the arbitral tribunal.

Article 23—Statements of claim and defence

(1) Within the period of time agreed by the parties or determined by the arbitral tribunal, the claimant shall state the facts supporting his claim, the points at issue and the relief or remedy sought, and the respondent shall state his defence in respect of these particulars, unless the parties have otherwise agreed as to the required elements of such statements. The parties may submit with their statements all documents they consider to be relevant or may add a reference to the documents or other evidence they will submit.

(2) Unless otherwise agreed by the parties, either party may amend or supplement his claim or defence during the course of the arbitral proceedings, unless the arbitral tribunal considers it inappropriate to allow such amendment having regard to the delay in making it.

Article 24—Hearings and written proceedings

(1) Subject to any contrary agreement by the parties, the arbitral tribunal shall decide whether to hold oral hearings for the presentation of evidence or for oral argument, or whether the proceedings shall be conducted on the basis of documents and other materials. However, unless the parties have agreed that no hearings shall be held, the arbitral tribunal shall hold

such hearings at an appropriate stage of the proceedings, if so requested by a party.

(2) The parties shall be given sufficient advance notice of any hearing and of any meeting of the arbitral tribunal for the purposes of inspection of goods, other property or documents.

(3) All statements, documents or other information supplied to the arbitral tribunal by one party shall be communicated to the other party. Also any expert report or evidentiary document on which the arbitral tribunal may rely in making its decision shall be communicated to the parties.

Article 25—Default of a party

Unless otherwise agreed by the parties, if, without showing sufficient cause.

(*a*) the claimant fails to communicate his statement of claim in accordance with Article 23(1), the arbitral tribunal shall terminate the proceedings;

(*b*) the respondent fails to communicate his statement of defence in accordance with Article 23(1), the arbitral tribunal shall continue the proceedings without treating such failure in itself as an admission of the claimant's allegations;

(*c*) any party fails to appear at a hearing or to produce documentary evidence, the arbitral tribunal may continue the proceedings and make the award on the evidence before it.

Article 26—Expert appointed by arbitral tribunal

(1) Unless otherwise agreed by the parties, the arbitral tribunal

(*a*) may appoint one or more experts to report to it on specific issues to be determined by the arbitral tribunal;

(*b*) may require a party to give the expert any relevant information or to produce, or to provide access to, any relevant documents, goods or other property for his inspection.

(2) Unless otherwise agreed by the parties, if a party so requests or if the arbitral tribunal considers it necessary, the expert shall, after delivery of his written or oral report, participate in a hearing where the parties have the opportunity to put questions to him and to present expert witnesses in order to testify on the points at issue.

Article 27—Court assistance in taking evidence

The arbitral tribunal or a party with the approval of the arbitral tribunal may request from a competent court of this State assistance in taking evidence. The court may execute the request within its competence and according to its rules on taking evidence.

CHAPTER VI

Making of Award and Termination of Proceedings

Article 28—Rules applicable to substance of dispute

(1) The arbitral tribunal shall decide the dispute in accordance with such rules of law as are chosen by the parties as applicable to the substance of the dispute. Any designation of the law or legal system of a given State shall be construed, unless otherwise expressed, as directly referring to the substantive law of that State and not to its conflict of laws rules.

(2) Failing any designation by the parties, the arbitral tribunal shall apply the law determined by the conflict of laws rules which it considers applicable.

(3) The arbitral tribunal shall decide *ex acquo et bono* or as *amiable compositeur* only if the parties have expressly authorised it to do so.

(4) In all cases, the arbitral tribunal shall decide in accordance with the terms of the contract and shall take into account the usages of the trade applicable to the transaction.

Article 29—Decision-making by panel of arbitrators

In arbitral proceedings with more than one arbitrator, any decision of the arbitral tribunal shall be made, unless otherwise agreed by the parties, by a majority of all its members. However, questions of procedure may be decided by a presiding arbitrator, if so authorised by the parties or all members of the arbitral tribunal.

Article 30—Settlement

(1) If, during arbitral proceedings, the parties settle the dispute, the arbitral tribunal shall terminate the proceedings and, if requested by the parties and not objected to by the arbitral tribunal, record the settlement in the form of an arbitral award on agreed terms.

(2) An award on agreed terms shall be made in accordance with provisions of Article 31 and shall state that it is an award. Such an award has the same status and effect as any other award on the merits of the case.

Article 31—Form and contents of award

(1) The award shall be made in writing and shall be signed by the arbitrator or arbitrators. In arbitral proceedings with more than one arbitrator, the signatures of the majority of all members of the arbitral tribunal shall suffice, provided that the reason for any omitted signature is stated.

(2) The award shall state the reasons upon which it is based, unless the parties have agreed that no reasons are to be given or the award is an award on agreed terms under Article 30.

(3) The award shall state its date and the place of arbitration as determined in accordance with Article 20(1). The award shall be deemed to have been made at that place.

(4) After the award is made, a copy signed by the arbitrators in accordance with paragraph (1) of this Article shall be delivered to each party.

Article 32—Termination of proceedings

(1) The arbitral proceedings are terminated by the final award or by an order of the arbitral tribunal in accordance with paragraph (2) of this Article.

(2) The arbitral tribunal shall issue an order for the termination of the arbitral proceedings when:

(*a*) the claimant withdraws his claim, unless the respondent objects thereto and the arbitral tribunal recognises a legitimate interest on his part in obtaining a final settlement of the dispute;

(*b*) the parties agree on the termination of the proceedings;

(*c*) the arbitral tribunal finds that the continuation of the proceedings has for any other reason become unnecessary or impossible.

(3) The mandate of the arbitral tribunal terminates with the termination of the arbitral proceedings, subject to the provisions of Articles 33 and 34(4).

Article 33—Correction and interpretation of award; additional award

(1) Within 30 days of receipt of the award, unless another period of time has been agreed upon by the parties;

(*a*) a party, with notice to the other party, may request the arbitral tribunal to correct in the award any errors in computation, any clerical or typographical errors or any errors of similar nature;

(*b*) if so agreed by the parties, a party, with notice to the other party, may request the arbitral tribunal to give an interpretation of a specific point or part of the award.

If the arbitral tribunal considers the request to be justified, it shall make the correction or give the interpretation within 30 days of receipt of the request. The interpretation shall form part of the award.

(2) The arbitral tribunal may correct any error of the type referred to in paragraph (1)(*a*) of this Article on its own initiative within 30 days of the date of the award.

(3) Unless otherwise agreed by the parties, a party, with notice to the other party, may request within 30 days of receipt of the award, the

arbitral tribunal to make an additional award as to claims presented in the arbitral proceedings but omitted from the award. If the arbitral tribunal considers the request to be justified, it shall make the additional award within 60 days.

(4) The arbitral tribunal may extend, if necessary, the period of time within which it shall make a correction, interpretation or an additional award under paragraph (1) or (3) of this Article.

(5) The provisions of Article 31 shall apply to a correction or interpretation of the award or to an additional award.

CHAPTER VII

Recourse Against Award

Article 34—Application for setting aside as exclusive recourse against arbitral award

(1) Recourse to a court against an arbitral award may be made only by an application for setting aside in accordance with paragraphs (2) and (3) of this Article.

(2) An arbitral award may be set aside by the court specified in Article 6 only if:

(*a*) the party making the application furnishes proof that:

(*i*) a party to the arbitration agreement referred to in Article 7 was under some incapacity; or the said agreement is not valid under the law to which the parties have subjected it or, failing any indication thereon, under the law of this State; or

(*ii*) the party making the application was not given proper notice of the appointment of an arbitrator or of the arbitral proceedings or was otherwise unable to present his case; or

(*iii*) the award deals with a dispute not contemplated by or not falling within the terms of the submission to arbitration, or contains decisions on matters beyond the scope of the submission to arbitration, provided that, if the decision on matters submitted to arbitration can be separated from those not so submitted, only that part of the award which contains decisions on matters not submitted to arbitration may be set aside; or

(*iv*) the composition of the arbitral tribunal or the arbitral procedure was not in accordance with the agreement of the parties, unless such agreement was in conflict with a provision of this Law, from which the parties cannot derogate, or failing such agreement, was not in accordance with this Law; or (*b*) the court finds that:

(*i*) the subject-matter of the dispute is not capable of settlement by arbitration under the law of this State; or

(*ii*) the award is in conflict with the public policy of this State.

(3) An application for setting aside may not be made after three months have elapsed from the date on which the party making that application had received the award or, if a request had been made under Article 33, from the date on which that request had been disposed of by the arbitral tribunal.

(4) The court, when asked to set aside an award, may, where appropriate and so requested by a party, suspend the setting aside proceedings for a period of time determined by it in order to give the arbitral tribunal an opportunity to resume the arbitral proceedings or to take such other action as in the arbitral tribunal's opinion will eliminate the grounds for setting aside.

Chapter VIII

Recognition and Enforcement of Awards

Article 35—Recognition and enforcement

(1) An arbitral award, irrespective of the country in which it was made, shall be recognised as binding and, upon application in writing to the competent court, shall be enforced subject to the provisions of this Article and of Article 36.

(2) The party relying on an award or applying for its enforcement shall supply the duly authenticated original award or a duly certified copy thereof and the original arbitration agreement referred to in Article 7 or a duly certified copy thereof. If the award or agreement is not made in an official language of this State, the party shall supply a duly certified translation thereof into such language.X

Article 36—Grounds for refusing recognition or enforcement

(1) Recognition or enforcement of an arbitral award, irrespective of the country in which it was made, may be refused only:

(*a*) at the request of the party against whom it is invoked, if that party furnishes to the competent court where recognition or enforcement is sought proof that:

(*i*) a party to the arbitration agreement referred to in Article 7 was under some incapacity; or the said agreement is not valid under the law to which the parties have subjected it or, failing any indication thereon, under the law of the country where the award was made; or (*ii*) the party against whom the award is invoked was not given proper notice of the appointment of an arbitrator or of the arbitral proceedings or was otherwise unable to present his case; or

(*iii*) the award deals with a dispute not contemplated by or not falling within the terms of the submission to arbitration, or it contains decisions on matters beyond the scope of the submission to arbitration, provided that, if the decisions on matters submitted to arbitration can be separated from those not so submitted, that part of the award which contains decisions on matters submitted to arbitration may be recognised and enforced; or

(*iv*) the composition of the arbitral tribunal or the arbitral procedure was not in accordance with the agreement of the parties or, failing such agreement, was not in accordance with the law of the country where the arbitration took place; or

(*v*) the award has not yet become binding on the parties or has been set aside or suspended by a court of the country in which, or under the law of which, that award was made; or

(*b*) if the court finds that:

(*i*) the subject-matter of the dispute is not capable of settlement by arbitration under the law of this State; or

(*ii*) the recognition or enforcement of the award would be contrary to the public policy of this State.

(2) If an application for setting aside or suspension of an award has been made to a court referred to in paragraph (1)(*a*)(*v*) of this Article, the court where recognition or enforcement is sought may, if it considers it proper, adjourn its decision and may also, on the application of the party claiming recognition or enforcement of the award, order the other party to provide appropriate security.

Appendix 3

UNCITRAL Conciliation Rules 1980

Application of the Rules

Article I

(1) These Rules apply to conciliation of disputes arising out of or relating to a contractual or other legal relationship where the parties seeking an amicable settlement of their dispute have agreed that the UNCITRAL Conciliation Rules apply.

(2) The parties may agree to exclude or vary any of these Rules at any time.

(3) Where any of these Rules is in conflict with a provision of law from which the parties cannot derogate, that provisions prevails.

Commencement of Conciliation Proceedings

Article 2

(1) The party initiating conciliation sends to the other party a written invitation to conciliate under these Rules, briefly identifying the subject of the dispute.

(2) Conciliation proceedings commence when the other party accepts the invitation to conciliate. If the acceptance is made orally, it is advisable that it be confirmed in writing.

(3) If the other party rejects the invitation, there will be no conciliation proceedings.

(4) If the party initiating conciliation does not receive a reply within thirty days from the date on which he sends the invitation, or within such other period of time as specified in the invitation, he may elect to treat this as a rejection of the invitation to conciliate. If he so elects, he informs the other party accordingly.

Number of Conciliators

Article 3

There shall be one conciliator unless the parties agree that there shall be two or three conciliators. Where there is more than one conciliator, they ought, as a general rule, to act jointly.

Appointment of conciliators

Article 4

(1)(*a*) In conciliation proceedings with one conciliator, the parties shall endeavour to reach agreement on the name of a sole conciliator;

(*b*) in conciliation proceedings with two conciliators, each party appoints one conciliator;

(*c*) in conciliation proceedings with three conciliators, each party appoints one conciliator. The parties shall endeavour to reach agreement on the name of the third conciliator.

(2) Parties may enlist the assistance of an appropriate institution or person in connexion with the appointment of conciliators. In particular,

(*a*) a party may request such an institution or person to recommend the names of suitable individuals to act as conciliator; or

(*b*) the parties may agree that the appointment of one or more conciliators be made directly by such an institution or person.

In recommending or appointing individuals to act as conciliator, the institution or person shall have regard to such considerations as are likely to secure the appointment of an independent and impartial conciliator and, with respect to a sole or third conciliator, shall take into account the advisability of appointing a conciliator of a nationality other than the nationalities of the parties.

Submission of Statements to Conciliator

Article 5

(1) The conciliator,* upon his appointment, requests each party to submit to him a brief written statement describing the general nature of the dispute and the points at issue. Each party sends a copy of his statement to the other party.

(2) The conciliator may request each party to submit to him a further written statement of his position and the facts and grounds in support thereof, supplemented by any documents and other evidence that such party deems appropriate. The party sends a copy of his statement to the other party.

---

* The term "conciliator" applies to a sole conciliator, two or three conciliators, as the case may be.

(3) At any stage of the conciliation proceedings the conciliator may request a party to submit to him such additional information as he deems appropriate.

Representation and Assistance

Article 6

The parties may be represented or assisted by persons of their choice. The names and addresses of such persons are to be communicated in writing to the other party and to the conciliator; such communication is to specify whether the appointment is made for purposes of representation or of assistance.

Role of Conciliator

Article 7

(1) The conciliator assists the parties in an independent and impartial manner in their attempt to reach an amicable settlement of their dispute.

(2) The conciliator will be guided by principles of objectivity, fairness and justice, giving consideration to, among other things, the rights and obligations of the parties, the usages of the trade concerned and the circumstances surrounding the dispute, including any previous business practices between the parties.

(3) The conciliator may conduct the conciliation proceedings in such a manner as he considers appropriate, taking into account the circumstances of the case, the wishes the parties may express, including any request by a party that the conciliator hear oral statements, and the need for a speedy settlement of the dispute.

(4) The conciliator may, at any stage of the conciliation proceedings, make proposals for a settlement of the dispute. Such proposals need not be in writing and need not be accompanied by a statement of the reasons therefor.

Administration Assistance

Article 8

In order to facilitate the conduct of the conciliation proceedings, the parties, or the conciliator with the consent of the parties, may arrange for administrative assistance by a suitable institution or person.

Communication between Conciliator and Parties

Article 9

(1) The conciliator may invite the parties to meet with him or may communicate with them orally or in writing. He may meet or communicate with the parties together or with each of them separately.

(2) Unless the parties have agreed upon the place where meetings with the conciliator are to be held, such place will be determined by the

conciliator, after consultation with the parties, having regard to the circumstances of the conciliation proceedings.

Disclosure of Information

Article 10

When the conciliator receives factual information concerning the dispute from a party, he discloses the substance of that information to the other party in order that the other party may have the opportunity to present any explanation which he considers appropriate. However, when a party gives any information to the conciliator subject to a specific condition that it be kept confidential, the conciliator does not disclose that information to the other party.

Co-operation of Parties with Conciliator

Article 11

The parties will in good faith co-operate with the conciliator and, in particular, will endeavour to comply with requests by the conciliator to submit written materials, provide evidence and attend meetings.

Suggestions by Parties before Settlement of Dispute

Article 12

Each party may, on his own initiative or at the invitation of the conciliator, submit to the conciliator suggestions for the settlement of the dispute.

Settlement Agreement

Article 13

(1) When it appears to the conciliator that there exist elements of a settlement which would be acceptable to the parties, he formulates the terms of a possible settlement and submits them to the parties for their observations. After receiving the observations of the parties, the conciliator may reformulate the terms of a possible settlement in the light of such observations.

(2) If the parties reach agreement on a settlement of the dispute, they draw up and sign a written settlement agreement.** If requested by the parties, the conciliator draws up, or assists the parties in drawing up, the settlement agreement.

(3) The parties by signing the settlement agreement put an end to the dispute and are bound by the agreement.

** The parties may wish to consider including in the settlement agreement a clause that any dispute arising out of or relating to the settlement agreement shall be submitted to arbitration.

Confidentiality

Article 14

The conciliator and the parties must keep confidential all matters relating to the conciliation proceedings. Confidentiality extends also the settlement agreement, except where its disclosure is necessary for purposes of implementation and enforcement.

Termination of Conciliation Proceedings

Article 15

The conciliation proceedings are terminated:

(*a*) by the signing of the settlement agreement by the parties, on the date of the agreement; or

(*b*) by a written declaration of the conciliator, after consultation with the parties, to the effect that further efforts at conciliation are no longer justified, on the date of the declaration; or

(*c*) by a written declaration of the parties addressed to the conciliator to the effect that the conciliation proceedings are terminated, on the date of the declaration; or

(*d*) by a written declaration of a party to the other party and the conciliator, if appointed, to the effect that the conciliation proceedings are terminated, on the date of the declaration.

Resort to Arbitral or Judicial Proceedings

Article 16

The parties undertake not to initiate, during the conciliation proceedings, any arbitral or judicial proceedings in respect of a dispute that is the subject of the conciliation proceedings, except that a party may initiate arbitral or judicial proceedings where, in his opinion, such proceedings are necessary for preserving his rights.

Costs

Article 17

(1) Upon termination of the conciliation proceedings, the conciliator fixes the costs of the conciliation and gives written notice thereof to the parties. The term "costs" includes only:

(*a*) the fee of the conciliator which shall be reasonable in amount;

(*b*) the travel and other expenses of the conciliator;

(*c*) the travel and other expenses of witnesses requested by the conciliator with the consent of the parties;

(*d*) the cost of any expert advice requested by the conciliator with the consent of the parties;

(*e*) The cost of any assistance provided pursuant to Article 4, paragraph (2)(*b*), and 8 of these Rules.

(2) The costs, as defined above, are borne equally by the parties unless the settlement agreement provides for a different apportionment. All other expenses incurred by a party are borne by that party.

Deposits

Article 18

(1) The conciliator, upon his appointment, may request each party to deposit an equal amount as an advance for the costs referred to in Article 17, paragraph (1) which he expects will be incurred.

(2) During the course of the conciliation proceedings the conciliator may request supplementary deposits in an equal amount from each party.

(3) If the required deposits under paragraphs (1) and (2) of this Article are not paid in full by both parties within thirty days, the conciliator may suspend the proceedings or may make a written declaration of termination to the parties, effective on the date of that declaration.

(4) Upon termination of the conciliation proceedings, the conciliator renders an accounting to the parties of the deposits received and returns any unexpended balance to the parties.

Role of Conciliator in Other Proceedings

Article 19

The parties and the conciliator undertake that the conciliator will not act as an arbitrator or as a representative or counsel of a party in any arbitral or judicial proceedings in respect of a dispute that is the subject of the conciliation proceedings. The parties also undertake that they will not present the conciliator as a witness in any such proceedings.

Admissibility of Evidence in Other Proceedings

Article 20

The parties undertake not to rely on or introduce as evidence in arbitral or judicial proceedings, whether or not such proceedings relate to the dispute that is the subject of the conciliation proceedings;

(*a*) views expressed or suggestions made by the other party in respect of a possible settlement of the dispute;

(*b*) admissions made by the other party in the course of the conciliation proceedings;

(*c*) proposals made by the conciliator;

(*d*) the fact that the other party had indicated his willingness to accept a proposal for settlement made by the conciliator.

Appendix 4

The ICADR Arbitration Rules 1996*

Preliminary

1. Short title and scope. (1) The rules may be called the ICADR Arbitration Rules, 1996.

(2) These rules shall apply where the parties have agreed in writing, that—

(*a*) a dispute which has arisen, or

(*b*) a dispute which may arise,

between them in respect of a defined legal relationship, whether contractual or not, shall be settled under the ICADR Arbitration Rules, 1996.

2. Definitions. In these rules, unless the context otherwise requires—

(*a*) "arbitral award" includes an interim award;

(*b*) "arbitral tribunal" means a sole arbitrator or a panel of arbitrators;

**[(*bb*) "Arbitration Act" means the Arbitration and Conciliation Act, 1996;]

(*c*) "Arbitration Rules" or "rules" means the ICADR Arbitration Rules, 1996;

(*d*) "arbitrator" means a person appointed as arbitrator and includes a presiding arbitrator;

(*e*) "Chairperson" means the Chairperson of the ICADR;

(*f*) "fast track arbitration" means arbitration in accordance with rule 38;

(*g*) "Governing Council" means the Governing Council of the ICADR;

---

* Source: ICADR, New Delhi.

** *Inserted* after approval by Governing Council/General Body of ICADR, w.e.f. 17.7.2016.

(*h*) "ICADR" means the International Centre for Alternative Dispute Resolution, New Delhi or, as the case may be, any of its Regional Offices;

(*i*) "international commercial arbitration" means an arbitration relating to disputes arising out of legal relationships, whether contractual or not, considered as commercial under the law in force in India and where at least one of the parties is—

(1) an individual which is a national of, or habitually resident in, any country other than India; or

(2) a body corporate which is incorporated in any country other than India; or

(3) *[..........] an association or a body of individuals whose central management and control is exercised in any country other than India; or

(4) the Government of a foreign country;

(*j*) "panel of arbitrators" means the panel of persons approved by the Governing Council to act as arbitrators;

(*k*) "party" means a party to an arbitration agreement;

(*l*) "Schedule" means a Schedule to these rules;

(*m*) "Secretary-General" means the Secretary-General of the ICADR.

PART I

Arbitration Proceedings in the ICADR

3. Notice of request for arbitration. (1) The claimant initiating the arbitration shall give a notice of request for arbitration to the respondent and to the ICADR.

(2) The arbitral proceedings commence on the date on which the notice of request for arbitration is received by the respondent.

(3) A notice of request for arbitration shall include the following:

(*a*) a request that the dispute be referred to arbitration;

(*b*) the names and addresses of the parties to the dispute;

(*c*) a reference to the contract out of or in relation to which the dispute has arisen;

(*d*) a reference to the arbitration clause or arbitration agreement relied upon;

(*e*) the general nature of the claim and where the claim is or can be quantified in terms of money, the amount of the claim;

---

* The words "a company or" *omitted* after approval by Governing Council/ General Body of ICADR, w.e.f. 17.7.2016.

(*f*) the relief or remedy sought;

(*g*) the preferred number of arbitrators, if not already agreed upon.

4. Number of arbitrators. (1) Unless otherwise agreed by the parties, the arbitral tribunal shall consist of a sole arbitrator.

(2) Where the arbitration agreement provides for an even number of arbitrators, the ICADR will appoint an additional arbitrator who shall be the presiding arbitrator.

5. Appointment of arbitrators. (1) Unless otherwise agreed by the parties, a person of any nationality may be an arbitrator.

(2) Where the arbitrator agreement provides that each party shall appoint one arbitrator, and the two appointed arbitrators shall appoint the presiding arbitrator, and—

(*a*) a party fails to appoint an arbitrator within thirty days from the receipt of a request to do so from the other party; or

(*b*) the appointed arbitrators fail to agree on the presiding arbitrator within thirty days from the date of their appointment,

the appointment shall be made, upon request of a party, by the ICADR.

(3) In an arbitration with a sole arbitrator, if the parties fail to agree on the arbitrator within thirty days from receipt of a request by one party from the other party to so agree, the appointment shall be made, upon request of a party, by the ICADR.

(4) A decision by the ICADR on a matter entrusted to it by sub-rule (2) or sub-rule (3) will be final and binding on the parties.

*[(5) Upon receipt of a request under sub-clause (a) of sub-rule (2) or sub-rule (3), the ICADR will follow the procedure specified in rule 35 and—

(*a*) make the appointment as promptly as possible,

(*b*) have regard to—

(*i*) any qualifications required of the arbitrator by the agreement of the parties;

(*ii*) such considerations as are likely to secure the appointment of an independent and impartial arbitrator; and

(*iii*) in the case of appointment of a sole or presiding arbitrator in an international commercial arbitration, the advisability of appointing a person of a nationality other than the nationalities of the parties];

---

* *Substituted* after approval by Governing Council/General Body of ICADR, w.e.f. 17.7.2016.

(6) A substitute arbitrator will be appointed in the same manner in which his predecessor had been appointed.

(7) *[The ICADR, before appointing a person as arbitrator or the presiding arbitrator, will obtain a declaration in writing, in the Form specified in Schedule III, from such person that—

(*i*) no circumstances exist in terms of sub-section (1) section 12 of the Arbitration Act read with Fifth Schedule thereof that give rise to justifiable doubts as to his independence or impartiality,

(*ii*) he does not have any relationship with any of the parties to the dispute or their counsel or the subject matter of the dispute as specified in the Seventh Schedule of the Arbitration Act, and

(*iii*) where any qualifications are required of an arbitrator by the agreement of the parties, he possesses those qualifications.]

6. Description of a proposed arbitrators. Where a party appoints an arbitrator, his full name, address and nationality and a description of his qualifications shall be given to the other party, or, where the appointment is made by the ICADR, it shall give such information to both parties.

7. Disclosure of grounds of challenge. An arbitrator, from the time of his appointment and throughout the arbitral proceedings, shall, without delay, disclose in writing to the parties and the ICADR any circumstances referred to in sub-rule (1) of rule 8 unless they have already been disclosed.

8. Grounds of challenge. *[(1) A party may challenge the appointment of an arbitrator or the presiding arbitrator only if—

(*a*) circumstances exist in terms of sub-section (1) of section 12 of the Arbitration Act, read with Fifth Schedule thereof that give rise to justifiable doubts as to his independence or impartiality, or

(*b*) he has any relationship with any of the parties to the dispute or their counsel or the subject matter of the dispute as specified in the Seventh Schedule of the Arbitration Act, or

(*c*) he does not possess the qualifications agreed to by the parties].

(2) A party may challenge an arbitrator appointed by him, or in whose appointment he has participated, only for reasons of which he becomes aware after the appointment has been made.

9. Challenge procedure. (1) A party who intends to challenge an arbitrator shall, within fifteen days after becoming aware of the constitution of the arbitral tribunal or of any ground referred to in sub-

---

* *Substituted* after approval by Governing Council/General Body of ICADR, w.e.f. 17.7.2016.

rule (1) of rule 8, send a written statement of the reasons for the challenge to the arbitral tribunal and to the ICADR.

(2) Unless the arbitrator challenged under sub-rule (1) withdraws from his office, or the other party agrees to the challenge, the arbitral tribunal shall decide on the challenge.

(3) If challenge under sub-rule (2) is not successful, the arbitral tribunal shall continue the arbitral proceedings and make an arbitral award.

10. Failure or impossibility to act. (1) The mandate of an arbitrator shall terminate if—

(*a*) he becomes *de jure* or *de facto* unable to perform his functions or for other reasons fails to act without undue delay; and

(*b*) he withdraws from his office or the parties agree to the termination of his mandate.

(2) If, under this rule or sub-rule (2) of rule 9, an arbitrator withdraws from his office or a party agrees to the termination of the mandate of an arbitrator, it shall not imply acceptance of the validity of any ground referred to in this rule or sub-rule (1) of rule 8.

11. Termination of mandate and substitution of arbitrator. (1) In addition to the circumstances referred to in rule 9 or rule 10, the mandate of an arbitrator shall terminate—

(*a*) where he withdraws from office for any reason; or

(*b*) by or pursuant to agreement of the parties.

(2) Where the mandate of an arbitrator terminates, a substitute arbitrator shall be appointed in the same manner in which his predecessor had been appointed.

(3) Where an arbitrator is replaced under sub-rule (2), any hearings previously held may be repeated at the discretion of the arbitral tribunal.

(4) An order or ruling of the arbitral tribunal made prior to the replacement of an arbitrator shall not be invalid solely because there has been a change in the composition of the arbitral tribunal.

12. Competence of arbitral tribunal to rule on its jurisdiction. (1) The arbitral tribunal may rule on its own jurisdiction, including ruling on any objections with respect to the existence or validity of the arbitration agreement, and for that purpose,—

(*a*) an arbitration clause which forms part of a contract shall be treated as an agreement independent of the other terms of the contract; and

(*b*) a decision by the arbitral tribunal that the contract is null and void shall not entail *ipso jure* the invalidity of the arbitration clause.

(2) A plea that the arbitral tribunal does not have jurisdiction shall be raised not later than the submission of the statement of defence; however, a party shall not be precluded from raising such plea merely because he has appointed, or participated in the appointment of, an arbitrator.

(3) A plea that the arbitral tribunal is exceeding the scope of its authority shall be raised as soon as the matter alleged to be beyond the scope of its authority is raised during the arbitral proceedings.

(4) The arbitral tribunal may, in either of the cases referred to in sub-rule (2) or sub-rule (3), admit a later plea if it considers the delay justified.

(5) The arbitral tribunal shall decide on the plea referred to in sub-rule (2) or sub-rule (3) and, where the arbitral tribunal takes a decision rejecting the plea, continue with the arbitral proceedings and make an arbitral award.

*[**13. Interim measures ordered by arbitral tribunal.** (1) The arbitral tribunal may, on an application made by a party to the dispute, make an order granting any interim measure of protection listed in sub-section (1) of section 17 of the Arbitration Act.

(2) The arbitral tribunal shall have the same power for making orders, as the Court has for the purpose of, and in relation to, any proceedings before it.

(3) An order made by the arbitral tribunal under this rule shall be enforceable under the Code of Civil Procedure, 1908 (5 of 1908) in the same manner as if it were an order of the Court].

14. Representation and assistance. Each party shall advise, in writing, the other party, the ICADR and the arbitral tribunal of—

(*a*) the names and addresses of persons who will represent or assist him, and

(*b*) the capacity in which those persons will act.

15. Equal treatment of parties. The parties shall be treated with equality and each party shall be given due opportunity to present his case.

16. Determination of rules of procedure. (1) Subject to these rules, the arbitral tribunal may conduct its proceedings in the manner it considers appropriate.

(2) The power of the arbitral tribunal under sub-rule (1) includes the power to determine the admissibility, relevance, materiality and weight of any evidence.

---

* *Substituted* after approval by Governing Council/General Body of ICADR, w.e.f. 17.7.2016.

17. Place of arbitration. *[(1) The place of arbitration shall be New Delhi or such other place where any of the Regional Offices of ICADR is situated as the parties may agree:

Provided that failing any agreement between the parties, the place of arbitration shall be determined by the arbitral tribunal having regard to the circumstances of the case, including convenience of the parties].

(2) The arbitral tribunal may, after consulting the ICADR, meet at any place it considers appropriate for consultation among its members, for hearing witnesses, experts or the parties, or for inspection of documents, goods or other property.

18. Language. (1) Where the arbitration agreement does not provide for the language to be used in the arbitral proceedings, the arbitral tribunal shall determine the language or languages to be used in the arbitral proceedings.

(2) The agreement or determination, unless otherwise specified, shall apply to any written statement by a party, any hearing and any arbitral award, decision or other communication by the arbitral tribunal.

(3) The arbitral tribunal may order that any documentary evidence shall be accompanied by a translation into the language agreed upon by the parties or determined by the arbitral tribunal.

19. Statements of claim and defence. (1) Within thirty days of the constitution of the arbitral tribunal, the claimant shall send to the arbitral tribunal and the respondent a statement of the facts supporting his claim, the points at issue and the relief or remedy sought, and the respondent shall, within thirty days after receipt of statement of claim, send to the arbitral tribunal and the claimant—

(*a*) his statement of defence in respect of these particulars;

*[(*b*) a statement of facts supporting his counter claim or a plea for set-off, if any, the points at issue and the relief or remedy sought];

(2) Within fifteen days of the receipt of statement of defence of the respondent and of the statement referred to in clause (b) of sub-rule (1), the claimant shall send to the arbitral tribunal and the respondent his rejoinder to the said statement of defence and his statement of defence to the counter claim **[or plea for set-off].

(3) Within fifteen days of the receipt of statement of defence to the counter-claim, the respondent shall send to the arbitral tribunal and the claimant his rejoinder to the said statement.

---

* *Substituted* after approval by Governing Council/General Body of ICADR, w.e.f. 17.7.2016.

** *Inserted* after approval by Governing Council/General Body of ICADR, w.e.f. 17.7.2016.

(4) The parties may submit with their statements all documents they consider to be relevant or may add a reference to the documents or other evidence they will submit.

(5) Either party may amend or supplement his claim or defence during the course of the arbitral proceedings, unless the arbitral tribunal considers it inappropriate to allow the amendment or supplement having regard to the delay in making it.

20. Hearings and written proceedings. (1) The arbitral tribunal may hold a pre-hearing proceeding—

(*a*) to discuss with the parties the procedure to be followed in the arbitration,

(*b*) to fix or determine any periods of time referred to in these rules,

(*c*) to discuss hearing dates, and

(*d*) to determine any other matter required or permitted under these rules to help to ensure the efficient progress of the arbitral proceedings.

(2) The arbitral tribunal will decide whether to hold oral hearing for the presentation of evidence or for oral argument, or whether the proceedings shall be conducted on the basis of documents and other materials:

Provided that the arbitral tribunal will hold oral hearing, at an appropriate stage of the proceedings, on a request by a party, unless the parties have agreed that no oral hearing shall be held.

*[Provided further that the arbitral tribunal shall, as far as possible, hold oral hearings for the presentation of evidence or for oral argument on day-to-day basis, and not grant any adjournments unless sufficient cause is made out, and may impose costs including exemplary costs on the party seeking adjournment without any sufficient cause].

(3) The parties shall be given sufficient advance notice of any hearing and of any meeting of the arbitral tribunal for the purposes of inspection of documents, goods or other property.

(4) All statements, documents or other information supplied to, or applications made to the arbitral tribunal by one party, shall be communicated to the other party, and any expert report or evidentiary document on which the arbitral tribunal may rely in making its decision shall be communicated to the parties.

(5) If a party intends to give evidence through a witness, he shall, within the time determined by the arbitral tribunal, communicate to the tribunal and to the other party—

---

* *Inserted* after approval by Governing Council/General Body of ICADR, w.e.f. 17.7.2016.

(*a*) the names and addresses of the witnesses he intends to present, and

(*b*) the subject upon which, and the language in which, those witnesses will give their testimony.

(6) The arbitral tribunal shall make arrangements for the translation of oral statements made at a hearing and for a record of the hearing if—

(*a*) either is deemed necessary by the tribunal under the circumstances of the case, or

(*b*) the parties have agreed to it and have communicated such agreement to the tribunal at least thirty days before the hearing.

21. Default of a party. Where, without showing sufficient cause,—

(*a*) the claimant fails to communicate his statement of claim in accordance with sub-rule (1) of rule 19, the arbitral tribunal shall terminate the proceedings;

(*b*) the respondent fails to communicate his statement of defence or the claimant fails to communicate his defence to the counter-claim in accordance with rule 19, the arbitral tribunal shall continue the proceedings without treating that failure in itself as an admission of the allegations made in the statement of claim or of counter-claim as the case may be *[and shall have the discretion to treat the right of the respondent or, as the case may be, of the claimant to file such statement of defence or counter-claim as having been forfeited].

(*c*) a party fails to appear at an oral hearing or to produce witness or documentary evidence, the arbitral tribunal may continue the proceedings and make the arbitral award on the evidence before it.

22. Appointment of expert by arbitral tribunal. (1) The arbitral tribunal may—

(*a*) appoint one or more experts to report to it on specific issues to be determined by the arbitral tribunal, and

(*b*) require a party to give the expert any relevant information or to produce, or to provide access to, any relevant documents, goods or other property for his inspection.

(2) If a party so requests or if the arbitral tribunal considers it necessary, the expert shall, after delivery of his written or oral report, participate in an oral hearing where the parties have the opportunity to put questions to him and to present expert witnesses in order to testify on the points at issue.

---

* *Inserted* after approval by Governing Council/General Body of ICADR, w.e.f. 17.7.2016.

(3) The expert shall, on the request of a party, make available to that party for examination all documents, goods or other property in the possession of the expert with which he was provided in order to prepare his report.

23. Rules applicable to substance of dispute. (1) Where the place of arbitration is situate in India,—

(*a*) in an arbitration other than an international commercial arbitration, the arbitral tribunal shall decide the dispute submitted to arbitration in accordance with the substantive law for the time being in force in India;

(*b*) in an international commercial arbitration,—

(*i*) the arbitral tribunal shall decide the dispute in accordance with the rules of law designated by the parties as applicable to the substance of the dispute;

(*ii*) any designation by the parties of the law or legal system of a given country shall be construed, unless otherwise expressed, as directly referring to the substantive law of that country and not to its conflict of laws rules;

(*iii*) failing any designation of the law under clause (*a*) by the parties, the arbitral tribunal shall apply the rules of law it considers to be appropriate given all the circumstances surrounding the dispute.

(2) The arbitral tribunal will decide *ex aequo et bono* or as *amiable compositeur* only if the parties have expressly authorized it to do so.

*[(3) The arbitral tribunal shall, in all cases, while deciding and making an award, take into account the terms of the contract and trade usages applicable to the transaction].

24. Decision making by arbitral tribunal. (1) In arbitral proceedings with more than one arbitrator, any decision of the arbitral tribunal shall be made by a majority of all its members.

(2) Notwithstanding sub-rule (1), if authorised by the parties or all the members of the arbitral tribunal, questions of procedure may be decided by the presiding arbitrator.

[24A. Time Limit for arbitral award.** (1) The arbitral award shall be made within a period of twelve months from the date the arbitral tribunal enters upon the reference.

Explanation. For the purposes of this rule, an arbitral tribunal shall be deemed to have entered upon the reference on the date on which the

---

* *Substituted* after approval by Governing Council/General Body of ICADR, w.e.f. 17.7.2016.

** *Inserted* after approval by Governing Council/General Body of ICADR, w.e.f. 17.7.2016.

arbitrator or all the arbitrators, as the case may be, have received notice, in writing, of their appointment.

(2) If the award is made within a period of six months from the date the arbitral tribunal enters upon the reference, the arbitral tribunal shall be entitled to receive such amount of additional fees as the parties may agree.

(3) The parties may, by consent, extend the period specified in sub-rule (1) for making award for a further period not exceeding six months.

(4) If the award is not made within the period specified in sub-rule (1) or the extended period specified under sub-rule (3), the mandate of the arbitrator(s) shall terminate unless the Court has, either prior to or after the expiry of the period so specified, extended the period under sub-section (4) of section 29A of the Arbitration Act:

Provided that while extending the period under that sub-section, if the Court finds that the proceedings have been delayed for the reasons attributable to the arbitral tribunal, then, it may order reduction of fees of arbitrator(s) by not exceeding five per cent. for each month of such delay.

(5) The extension of period referred to in the aforesaid sub-section (4) of section 29A may be on the application of any of the parties and may be granted only for sufficient cause and on such terms and conditions as may be imposed by the Court.

(6) While extending the period referred to in the aforesaid sub-section (4) of section 29A, it shall be open to the Court to substitute one or all of the arbitrators and if one or all of the arbitrators are substituted, the arbitral proceedings shall continue from the stage already reached and on the basis of the evidence and material already on record, and the arbitrator(s) appointed under the said section 29A shall be deemed to have received the said evidence and material.

(7) In the event of arbitrator(s) being appointed under the said section 29A, the arbitral tribunal thus reconstituted shall be deemed to be in continuation of the previously appointed arbitral tribunal.

(8) It shall be open to the Court to impose actual or exemplary costs upon any of the parties under the said section 29A.

(9) The provisions of sub-section (9) of section 29A of the Arbitration Act shall apply to an application filed under sub-rule (5).]

25. Settlement. (1) If, during arbitral proceedings, the parties settle the dispute, *[in terms of section 30 of the Arbitration Act] the arbitral tribunal shall terminate the proceedings and, if requested by the parties and not

---

* *Inserted* after approval by Governing Council/General Body of ICADR, w.e.f. 17.7.2016.

objected to by the arbitral tribunal, record the settlement in the form of an arbitral award on agreed terms.

(2) An arbitral award on agreed terms shall be made in accordance with rule 26 and shall state that it is an arbitral award.

(3) An arbitral award on agreed terms shall have the same status and effect as any other arbitral award.

26. Form and contents of arbitral award. (1) An arbitral award shall be made in writing and shall be signed by the members of the arbitral tribunal.

(2) For the purposes of sub-rule (1), in arbitral proceedings with more than one arbitrator, the signatures of the majority of all the members of the arbitral tribunal shall be sufficient so long as the reason for any omitted signature is stated.

(3) The arbitral award shall state the reasons upon which it is based, unless—

(*a*) the parties have agreed that no reasons are to be given, or

(*b*) the award is an arbitral award on agreed terms under rule 25.

(4) The arbitral award shall state its date and the place of arbitration referred to in r. 17 and the award shall be deemed to have been made at that place.

(5) After the arbitral award is made, a signed copy thereof shall be delivered to each party.

(6) The arbitral tribunal shall deposit the original award, together with record of the arbitration proceedings, with the ICADR authorising it to cause the award to be filed in the court of competent jurisdiction when required.

(7) Where so requested by a party, the arbitral tribunal may, at any time during the arbitral proceedings, make an interim arbitral award on any matter with respect to which it may make a final arbitral award.

27. Interest on sums awarded. (1) Where and in so far as an arbitral award is for the payment of money, the arbitral tribunal may include in the sum of which the award is made interest, at such rate as it deems reasonable, on the whole or any part of the money, for the whole or any part of the period between the date on which the cause of action arose and the date on which the award is made.

*[(2) A sum directed to be paid by an arbitral award shall, unless the award otherwise directs, carry interest at the rate of two percent higher than the current rate of interest prevalent on the date of award, from the date of award to the date of payment.

* *Substituted* after approval by Governing Council/General Body of ICADR, w.e.f. 17.7.2016.

Explanation. The expression "current rate of interest" shall have the same meaning as assigned to it under clause (*b*) of section 2 of the Interest Act, 1978 (14 of 1978).]

28. Costs (*a*) The costs of arbitration shall be fixed by the arbitral tribunal.

(*b*) The fees and charges to be included in the costs shall be as specified in Schedule-I.

(*c*) The arbitral tribunal shall determine which party shall bear the costs taking into account *[the provisions of sub-sections (2) to (5) of section 31A of the Arbitration Act] the circumstances of the case and may apportion the costs between the parties if it is reasonable to do so.

*[(*cc*) the arbitral tribunal may also determine whether costs are payable by one party to another party as provided in section 31A(1)(*a*) of the Arbitration Act];

Explanation. For the purpose of clause (*a*), "costs" **[means reasonable costs] relating to—

(*i*) the fees and expenses of the arbitrators and witnesses,

(*ii*) legal fees and expenses,

(*iii*) the administrative fees and charges of the ICADR, and

(*iv*) any other expenses incurred in connection with the arbitral proceedings and the arbitral award.

29. Termination of proceedings. (1) The arbitral proceedings shall stand terminated on making of the final arbitral award or by an order of the arbitral tribunal under sub-rule (2).

(2) The arbitral tribunal shall make an order for the termination of the arbitral proceedings where—

(*a*) the claimant withdraws his claim, unless the respondent objects to the order and the arbitral tribunal recognises a legitimate interest on his part in obtaining a final adjudication of the dispute.

(*b*) the parties agree on the termination of the proceedings, or

(*c*) the arbitral tribunal finds that the continuation of the proceedings has for any other reason become unnecessary or impossible.

(3) The arbitral tribunal shall send a copy of the order made under sub-rule (2) to each party.

---

* *Inserted* after approval by Governing Council/General Body of ICADR, w.e.f. 17.7.2016.

* *Substituted* after approval by Governing Council/General Body of ICADR, w.e.f. 17.7.2016.

(4) Upon termination of the arbitral proceedings, the arbitral tribunal shall send the file of the case containing the record of the arbitral proceedings and the arbitral award or the order made under sub-rule (2) to the ICADR.

(5) Subject to rule 30 and any order of court of competent jurisdiction in proceedings before it in respect of the award, the mandate of the arbitral tribunal shall terminate with the termination of the arbitral proceedings.

30. Correction and interpretation of award; additional award. (1) Within thirty days from the receipt of the arbitral award,—

(*a*) a party, with notice to the other party, may request the arbitral tribunal to correct any computation errors, any clerical or typographical errors or any other errors of a similar nature occurring in the award;

(*b*) if so agreed by the parties, a party, with notice to the other party, may request the arbitral tribunal to give an interpretation of a specific point or part of the award.

(2) If the arbitral tribunal considers the request made under sub-rule (1) to be justified it shall make the correction or give the interpretation within thirty days from the receipt of the request and the interpretation shall form part of the arbitral award.

(3) The arbitral tribunal may correct any error of the type referred to in clause (*a*) of sub-rule (1), on its own initiative, within thirty days from the date of the arbitral award.

(4) A party, with notice to the other party, may request, within thirty days from the receipt of the arbitral award, the arbitral tribunal to make an additional arbitral award as to claims presented in the arbitral proceedings but omitted from the arbitral award.

(5) If the arbitral tribunal considers the request made under sub-rule (4) to be justified, it shall make the additional arbitral award within sixty days from the receipt of such request.

(6) The arbitral tribunal may extend, if necessary, the period of time within which it shall make a correction, give an interpretation or make an additional arbitral award under sub-rule (2) or sub-rule (5).

(7) Rule 26 shall apply to a correction or interpretation of the arbitral award or to an additional arbitral award made under this rule.

31. Deposits. (1) The arbitral tribunal will, upon its constitution, in consultation with the ICADR, direct each party to deposit with the ICADR an equal amount as an advance for the costs referred to in rule 28, which it expects will be incurred:

Provided that where, apart from the claim, a counter-claim has been submitted to the arbitral tribunal, it may fix separate amount of deposit for the claim and counter-claim.

(2) During the arbitration proceedings, the arbitral tribunal may, in consultation with the ICADR, direct supplementary deposits with the ICADR in an equal amount from each party for the costs referred to in sub-rule (1).

(3) If the required deposits under sub-rules (1) and (2) are not made in full in respect of the claim or counter-claim within thirty days, the arbitral tribunal will inform the parties in order that one or the other party may make the required deposit and if the required deposit is not made, the arbitral tribunal may suspend the proceedings or may make a written declaration of termination of the proceedings to the parties, effective on the date of that declaration as regards the claim or counter-claim for which the deposit is not made.

(4) The ICADR shall hold any deposits required under this rule.

(5) The ICADR may, from time to time, pay to the arbitral tribunal from any deposit it holds under this rule any amount it considers reasonable and appropriate for fees earned or expenses incurred by the tribunal in the arbitral proceedings.

(6) Upon termination of the arbitral proceedings, the ICADR shall, in accordance with the final award, apply any deposits it holds to the costs of the proceedings, render an accounting to the parties of the deposits received and applied and return any unexpended balance to the parties.

32. Administrative assistance. The ICADR will arrange the administrative services specified in Part II if—

(*a*) the parties designate the ICADR for arranging such services, in the arbitration agreement;

(*b*) the parties, or the arbitral tribunal with the consent of the parties, request the ICADR to arrange such services.

Part II

Services for Procedures under the Arbitration Rules

33. Services for procedures under the rules. To facilitate the conduct of arbitral proceedings that the parties have agreed to conduct under the Arbitration Rules, the ICADR will—

(*a*) perform the functions of the appointing authority whenever—

(*i*) the ICADR has been so designated by the parties in the arbitration clause of their contract or in a separate agreement, or

(*ii*) the parties have agreed to submit a dispute to the ICADR under the Arbitration Rules without specifically designating it as the appointing authority; and (*b*) provide the administrative services herein specified when required by the agreement, or when requested by all parties, or by the arbitral tribunal with the consent of the parties.

34. Services as the registry. (1) On receiving a request in pursuance of rule 5(2) or 5(3), the ICADR will register the request and intimate in writing to the parties the registration number of the case which shall be quoted by the party while making any subsequent communication to the ICADR and the arbitral tribunal.

(2) The ICADR will scrutinise every request and the documents, make necessary entries in the register and prepare a file of the case.

35. Services as appointing authority. (1) On receipt of a request to appoint an arbitrator in pursuance of *[rule 5(2)(*a*) or 5(3)], the ICADR will follow the following procedure—

(*i*) the ICADR will communicate to each party a list containing the names, addresses, nationalities and a description of qualifications and experience of at least three individuals from the panel of arbitrators;

(*ii*) within thirty days following the receipt of the list, a party may delete any name to which he objects and after re-numbering the names in the order of his preference, return the list to the ICADR;

(*iii*) on receipt of the list returned by the party, the ICADR will appoint the arbitrator from the list taking into account the order of preference indicated by the parties;

(*iv*) if for any reason the appointment cannot be made according to the procedure specified in clauses (*i*) to (*iii*), the ICADR may appoint the arbitrator from the panel of arbitrators.

(2) In appointing an arbitrator the ICADR will have regard to the matters referred to in *[rule 5(5)(*b*)] and will carefully consider the nature of the dispute in order to include in the list, persons having appropriate professional or business experience, language ability and nationality.

(3) All appointments on behalf of the ICADR will be made by the Secretary-General and in his absence by such member of the Governing Council as is designated by the Chairperson:

Provided that where the Secretary-General is to be appointed as the arbitrator, the appointment will be made by the Chairperson.

---

* *Substituted* after approval by Governing Council/General Body of ICADR, w.e.f. 17.7.2016.

***[35A. Model Guidelines for expeditious conduct of arbitration proceedings.** An Arbitrator appointed under rule 35 and the parties to the dispute shall observe the Guidelines specified in Schedule IA for the purposes of expeditious conduct of arbitration proceedings under these rules.]

36. Administrative services. (1) The ICADR may provide the administrative services specified in this Part—

(*a*) upon the request of the parties;

(*b*) upon the request of the arbitral tribunal with the consent of the parties;

(*c*) if the parties designate the ICADR for providing such services.

(2) All oral or written communications from a party to the arbitral tribunal, except at the arbitral proceedings, may be directed to the ICADR which will transmit them to the arbitral tribunal and, where appropriate, to the other party.

(3) Agreement by the parties that the ICADR will provide the administrative services, constitutes consent by the parties that, for purposes of compliance with any time requirements of the rules, any written communications shall be deemed to have been received by the addressee when received by the ICADR. When transmitting communications to a party, the ICADR will do so to the addresses provided by each of them to the ICADR for this purpose.

(4) The ICADR will also assist in the exchange of information.

(5) The ICADR will assist the arbitral tribunal to establish the date, time and place of meetings and will give the parties advance notice of such meetings.

(6) The ICADR will provide a court room and retiring rooms for the arbitral tribunal and the parties or their counsel in the offices of the ICADR on the charges set out in Schedule I. These charges will be billed separately and are not included in the fee for administrative services. However, where these facilities are provided in any place other than the offices of the ICADR, the charges will be determined by the ICADR and billed separately in each case.

(7) Upon request, the ICADR will make arrangements for reporter transcripts of the arbitral proceedings or hearings. The cost of reporter transcripts will be determined by the ICADR and billed separately and is not included in the fee for administrative services.

* Inserted after approval by Governing Council/General Body of ICADR, w.e.f. 19.09.2009.

(8) Upon request, the ICADR will make arrangements for the services of interpreters or translators and the cost in respect thereof will be determined by the ICADR and billed separately and is not included in the fee for administrative services.

(9)(*a*) The ICADR will hold advance deposits to be made towards the cost of the arbitral proceedings.

(*b*) On termination of the arbitral proceedings, the ICADR will apply the proceeds of the advance deposits towards any of its unpaid administrative fees and charges and the costs of the arbitral proceedings and will render an accounting to the parties of the deposits received and applied and return any unexpended balance to the parties.

(10)(*a*) Upon request, the ICADR will provide other appropriate administrative services the costs of which will be determined by the ICADR and billed separately and are not included in the fee for administrative services.

(*b*) The kinds of services which can be provided are as follows:—

(*i*) secretarial support and clerical assistance;

(*ii*) long distance and local telephone access and telex and telecopier facilities;

(*iii*) photocopying and other usual office services.

(11)(*a*) The ICADR may require the party requesting one or more of the services referred to in sub-rules (6), (7), (8) or (10) to deposit an amount specified by it as advance towards the costs of such services;

(*b*) The ICADR may also require the parties to make supplementary deposits towards the costs of the services referred to in clause (*a*);

(*c*) If the required deposit under clause (*a*) or clause (*b*) is not made in full within the time specified by the ICADR, the ICADR may not provide the services requested for.

37. Administrative fees. (1) The fee of the ICADR for making appointment of arbitrators and for providing administrative services, other than those specified in sub-rules (6), (7), (8) and (10) of rule 36, is based upon the amount in dispute as disclosed when the statement of claim is submitted to the ICADR in pursuance of sub-rule (1) of rule 19. Items A.I.(1), B.I.(1) and C.I.(1) of Schedule I contains the ICADR's schedule of fees and charges.

(2) Where the ICADR is requested to act as appointing authority under rule 5(2) or 5(3), the requesting party shall pay the ICADR a non-

refundable fee at the time of the request. This fee is separately set out in Schedule I as item A.I.(2), B.I.(2) and C.I.(2).

(3) The Arbitration Rules provide that the costs of arbitration include the costs of the administrative fees or charges of the ICADR [rule 28(*a*)]. These costs are, borne equally by the parties unless the arbitral award provides for a different apportionment [rule 28(*b*)].

Part III

Fast Track Arbitration Proceedings in the ICADR

38. Fast track arbitration. Notwithstanding anything contained hereinbefore, the parties may agree, in writing, to fast track arbitration and thereupon these rules shall apply to such arbitration subject to the modifications specified in Schedule II.

*[Schedule I

A. Domestic Commercial Arbitration

I. Administrative fees:
referred to in rule 37(1) and 37(2)

(1) Fee referred to in rule 37(1)—
(ICADR acts as appointing authority and administrator)

	Amount in Dispute (in rupees)	**Amount of fee** (in rupees)
(*i*)	where the total amount in dispute does not exceed Rs. 5 lakh	Rs. 22,500.
(*ii*)	where the total amount in dispute exceeds Rs. 5 lakh but does not exceed Rs. 20 lakh	Rs. 22,500 plus 1.75 per cent. of the amount by which the total amount in dispute exceeds Rs. 5 lakh
(*iii*)	where the total amount in dispute exceeds Rs. 20 lakh but does not exceed Rs. 1 crore	Rs. 48,750 plus 1.5 per cent. of the amount by which the total amount in dispute exceeds Rs. 20 lakh
(*iv*)	where the total amount in dispute exceeds Rs. 1 crore but does not exceed Rs. 10 crore	Rs. 1,68,750 plus 0.75 per cent. of the amount by which the total amount in dispute exceeds Rs. 1 crore

* *Substituted* after approval by Governing Council/General Body of ICADR, w.e.f. 17.7.2016.

(*v*) where the total amount in dispute exceeds Rs. 10 crore but does not exceed Rs. 20 crore	Rs. 8,43,750 plus 0.5 per cent. of the amount by which the total amount in dispute exceeds Rs. 10 crore
(*vi*) where the total amount in dispute exceeds Rs. 20 crore	Rs. 13,43,750 plus 0.25 per cent. of the amount by which the total amount in dispute exceeds Rs. 20 crore with a ceiling limit of Rs. 15 lakhs

Note: Where dispute cannot be expressed in terms of money or the total amount in dispute is below Rs. 2 lakh, the Secretary-General shall determine the amount of administrative fees, in his discretion, in each case.

(2) Non-refundable fee referred to in rule 37(2)
(ICADR acts only as appointing authority)
Rs. 15,000

II. Arbitrator's fee:
referred to in rule 28

Amount of fee For one Arbitrator (in rupees)	**Amount in dispute** (in rupees)
(*i*) where the total amount in dispute does not exceed Rs. 5 lakh	Rs. 45,000
(*ii*) where the total amount in dispute exceeds Rs. 5 lakh but does not exceed Rs. 20 lakh	Rs. 45,000 plus 3.5 per cent. of the amount by which the total amount in dispute exceeds Rs. 5 lakh
(*iii*) where the total amount in dispute exceeds Rs. 20 lakh but does not exceed Rs. 1 crore	Rs. 97,500 plus 3 per cent. of the amount by which the total amount in dispute exceeds Rs. 20 lakh
(*iv*) where the total amount in dispute exceeds Rs. 1 crore but does not exceed Rs. 10 crore	Rs. 3,37,500 plus 1 per cent. of the amount by which the total amount in dispute exceeds Rs. 1 crore
(*v*) where the total amount in dispute exceeds Rs. 10 crore but does not exceed Rs. 20 crore	Rs. 12,37,500 plus 0.75 per cent. of the amount by which the total amount in dispute exceeds Rs. 10 crore
(*vi*) where the total amount in dispute exceeds Rs. 20 crore	Rs. 19,87,500 plus 0.5 per cent. of the amount by which the total amount in dispute exceeds Rs. 20 crore with a ceiling of Rs. 30 lakhs

Note 1: Where the arbitral tribunal consists of a Sole Arbitrator, he shall be entitled to an additional amount of 25% on the fee payable as mentioned above.

Note 2: Where the dispute cannot be expressed in terms of money or the total amount in dispute is below Rs. 2 lakh, the arbitral tribunal shall determine the amount of fee in each case.

III. Charges for facilities

referred to in rule 36(6)

Rs. 4,000 for one day or part thereof plus Rs. 500 Wi-fi charges for two hours (optional) plus Rs. 500 Documentation Camera charges for two hours (optional) plus Rs. 1,000 Stenographic service charges (optional)

Note: Where the facilities are provided in a place other than in ICADR's offices, the charges will be determined in each case and billed separately.

B. Domestic Non-Commercial Arbitration

I. Administrative fees:

referred to in rule 37(1) and 37(2).

(1) Fee referred to in rule 37(1)
(ICADR acts as appointing authority and administrator)

Where the dispute can be expressed in terms of money, the administrative fees will be the same as applicable for domestic commercial arbitration.

Note: Where the dispute cannot be expressed in terms of money or the total amount in dispute is below Rs. 2 lakh, the Secretary-General shall determine the amount of administrative fee, in his discretion in each case.

(2) Non-refundable fee referred to in rule 37(2).
(ICADR acts only as appointing authority)
Rs.15,000

II. Arbitrator's fee

referred to in rule 28

Where the dispute can be expressed in terms of money, the arbitrator's fees will be the same as applicable for domestic commercial arbitration.

Note: Where the dispute cannot be expressed in terms of money or the total amount in dispute is below Rs. 2 lakh, the arbitral tribunal shall determine the amount of fee in each case.

III. Charges for facilities

referred to in rule 36(6)

Rs. 4,000 for one day or part thereof plus Rs. 500 Wi-fi charges for two hours (optional) plus Rs. 500 Documentation Camera charges for two hours (optional) plus Rs. 1,000 Stenographic service charges (optional)

Note: Where the facilities are provided in a place other than in ICADR's offices, the charges will be determined in each case and billed separately.

C. International Commercial Arbitration

I. Administrative fee:

referred to in rule 37(1) and 37(2)

(1) Fee referred to in rule 37(1)—
(ICADR acts as appointing authority and administrator).

	Amount in dispute (in US dollars)	**Amount of fee** (in US dollars)
(*i*)	where the total amount in dispute does not exceed \$50,000	\$1,500
(*ii*)	where the total amount in dispute exceeds \$50,000 but does not exceed \$1,75,000	\$1,500 plus 3 per cent. of the amount by which the total amount in dispute exceeds \$50,000
(*iii*)	where the total amount in dispute exceeds \$1,75,000 but does not exceed \$5,00,000	\$5,250 plus 2 per cent. of the amount by which the total amount in dispute exceeds \$1,75,000
(*iv*)	where the total amount in dispute exceeds \$5,00,000 but does not exceed \$10,00,000	\$11,750 plus 1 per cent. of the amount by which the total amount in dispute exceeds \$5,00,000
(*v*)	where the total amount in dispute exceeds \$10,00,000 but does not exceed \$20,00,000	\$16,750 plus 0.5 per cent. of the amount by which the total amount in dispute exceeds \$10,00,000.
(*vi*)	where the total amount in dispute exceeds \$20,00,000 but does not exceed \$50,00,000	\$21,750 plus 0.25 per cent. of the amount by which the total amount in dispute exceeds \$20,00,000
(*vii*)	where the total amount in dispute exceeds \$50,00,000	\$29,250 plus 0.125 per cent. of the amount by which the total amount in dispute exceeds \$50,00,000 with a ceiling of \$35,000.

Note: Where dispute cannot be expressed in terms of money, the Secretary-General shall determine the amount of administrative fees, in his discretion, in each case.

(2) Non-refundable fee referred to in rule 37(2)
(ICADR acts only as appointing authority)
US $1000

II. Arbitrator's fee
referred to in rule 28

Amount in dispute (in US dollars)	Amount of fee for one arbitrator (in US dollars)
(*i*) where the total amount in dispute does not exceed $50,000	$3,000
(*ii*) where the total amount in dispute exceeds $50,000 but does not exceed $1,75,000	$3,000 plus 5 per cent. of the amount by which the total amount in dispute exceeds $50,000
(*iii*) where the total amount in dispute exceeds $ 1,75,000 but does not exceed $5,00,000	$9,250 plus 4 per cent. of the amount by which the total amount in dispute exceeds $1,75,000
(*iv*) where the total amount in dispute exceeds $ 5,00,000 but does not exceed $10,00,000	$22,250 plus 3 per cent. of the amount by which the total amount in dispute exceeds $5,00,000
(*v*) where the total amount in dispute exceeds $10,00,000 but does not exceed $20,00,000	$37,250 plus 2 per cent. of the amount by which the total amount in dispute exceeds $10,00,000
(*vi*) where the total amount in dispute exceeds $20,00,000 but does not exceed $50,00,000	$57,250 plus 1 per cent. of the amount by which the total amount in dispute exceeds $20,00,000
(*vii*) where the total amount in dispute exceeds $50,00,000	$87,250 plus 0.5 per cent. of the amount by which the total amount in dispute exceeds $50,00,000 with a ceiling of $ 1,00,000

Note: Where the dispute cannot be expressed in terms of money, the arbitral tribunal shall determine the amount of fee in each case.

III. Charges for facilities
referred to in rule 36(6)

US$ 350 for one day or part thereof plus $50 Wi-fi charges for two hours (optional), plus $50 Documentation Camera charges for two hours (optional) plus $100 Stenographic service charges (optional).

Note: Where the facilities are provided in a place other than in ICADR's offices, the charges will be determined in each case and billed separately.]

*[Schedule IA

Model Guidelines for the Arbitrators and the Parties for Expeditious Conduct of Arbitration Proceedings

1. The arbitrators and the parties to the dispute shall follow these guidelines to ensure economic and expeditious disposal of arbitration cases.

For Arbitrators

2. (1) The arbitrators must take up the arbitration expeditiously on receipt of the request from the ICADR and should also complete the same with reasonable despatch. Serious efforts should be made to settle arbitration cases expeditiously within a period of one year where the amount of claim exceeds 1 crore and within a period of 6 months where the amount of claim is less than Rs. 1 crore.

(2) The Arbitrator(s) shall send to the Arbitration Committee of ICADR a quarterly report of the progress of arbitration proceedings.

(3) The Arbitration Committee may, where necessary, give suggestions to the Arbitrator(s) concerned to expedite the proceedings.

3. When accepting his mandate, the arbitrator shall be able to perform his task with the necessary competence according to his professional qualifications.

**[4. When accepting his appointment, the arbitrator shall give a declaration in writing, in the Form specified in Schedule-III as under:

(*i*) no circumstances exist in terms of sub-section (1) of section 12 of the Arbitration Act read with Fifth Schedule thereof that give rise to justifiable doubts as to his independence or impartiality,

(*ii*) he does not have any relationship with any of the parties to the dispute or their counsel or the subject matter of the dispute as specified in the Seventh Schedule of the Arbitration Act, and

(*iii*) where any qualifications are required of an arbitrator by the agreement of the parties, he possesses those qualifications.

Where necessary due to supervening facts, this declaration shall be repeated in the course of the entire arbitral proceedings until the award is filed].

---

* *Inserted* after approval by Governing Council/General Body of ICADR, w.e.f. 19.09.2009.

** *Substituted* after approval by Governing Council/General Body of ICADR, w.e.f. 17.7.2016.

5. Where facts that should have been disclosed are subsequently discovered, the arbitrator may either withdraw or be challenged or the ICADR may refuse to appoint him in other arbitral proceedings on this ground.

6. The arbitrator may at all stages suggest the possibility of a settlement to the parties but may not influence their decision by indicating that he has already reached a decision on the dispute.

7. In the course of the arbitral proceedings, the arbitrator shall refrain from all unilateral contact with the parties or their counsel which is not notified to the ICADR so that the ICADR can inform the other parties and arbitrators.

8. The arbitrator shall refrain from giving the parties, either directly or through their counsel, notice of decisions in the evidence taking place or on the merits; notice of these decisions may be given exclusively by the ICADR.

9. The arbitrator shall neither request nor accept any direct arrangement on costs or fees with the party which has designated him. The arbitrator is entitled to reimbursement of expenses and a fee as exclusively determined by the ICADR according to its Schedule of Fees, which are deemed to have been agreed by the arbitrator when accepting his mandate.

10. The arbitrator shall encourage a serene and positive development of the arbitral proceedings. In particular, he shall decide on the date and manner of the hearings in such a way as to allow both parties to fully participate therein, in compliance with the principle of equal treatment and opportunity as specified in rule 15.

11. The first hearing of the arbitral tribunal should be convened within 15 days of the receipt of the complete reply of the respondent when the arbitral tribunal may issue necessary directions. Admission and denial of the documents may be got done expeditiously. Issues if any to be framed, may be done at the same or at the next hearing. The arbitrators should make efforts to hold arbitration hearings continuously on day-to-day basis during office hours.

12. The parties should be asked to furnish a list of their witnesses, if any, in advance and they should be asked to file affidavits of witnesses on the date fixed for evidence preferably within a week of the settlement of issues. Cross examination of such of the deponent's witnesses whose presence is demanded by the opposite party should be completed at a hearing to be fixed within 15 days.

13. Adjournments of duly fixed hearing should not be granted except for unavoidable reasons which should be spelt out in the adjournment order.

14. Arguments preferably should be heard within 15 days of the completion of evidence, to be followed by submission of written arguments, if any.

15. The Arbitrator should make the award expeditiously after the close of the hearings, preferably within 30 days.

16. The arbitrator who does not comply with the provisions of these guidelines may be replaced by the ICADR *[in consultation with the parties]. Where it is not appropriate to replace the arbitrator in order not to cause delay in the arbitral proceedings, the ICADR may also take such action after the conclusion of the arbitral proceedings, by refusing to appoint him in subsequent arbitral proceedings.

For Parties

17. The claimant should file the applications or demand for arbitration to the ICADR with all the information and papers as per Rules, full statement of claim and copies of documents relied upon, in 3 sets in case of a Sole Arbitrator and in 5 sets in case of three arbitrators.

18. The respondent should file his reply to the claim with complete information and documents relied upon, in 3 or 5 sets as above as early as possible within the prescribed time. Fresh documentation/ claims should not be entertained at a later stage of the proceedings unless the arbitral tribunal is satisfied about the reasons for granting such permission.

19. If any party to arbitration, particularly in cases where any arbitrator, advocate or any of the parties has to come from out station to participate in arbitration proceedings, desires to seek adjournment on any valid ground, it must submit a written request to the ICADR at least before 5 working days stating the grounds which compel it to request for postponement of the hearing so that the ICADR is in a position to take necessary steps to inform the Parties, Arbitrators and Advocates regarding postponement of the hearing. Parties seeking adjournment will have to pay cost to ICADR as may be determined by the arbitral tribunal.

20. Parties should deposit arbitration and administrative fees with the ICADR within the stipulated time, as per the Rules and no extension should be sought in this behalf except for compelling reasons.

21. To avoid excessive costs in arbitration proceedings, the parties are advised to choose their arbitrators from the Panel, as far as possible from the place where the arbitration hearings have to be held. In case, a party still chooses an arbitrator from a place other than the place of hearing, the concerned party will bear the entire extra cost to be incurred on stay TA/DA etc. of the arbitrator nominated by it.

---

* *Inserted* after approval by Governing Council/General Body of ICADR, w.e.f. 17.7.2016.

For Arbitration Committee of ICADR

22. The Arbitration Committee of ICADR may examine the arbitration case file, from time to time to evaluate the progress of the proceedings and to ascertain whether the arbitrators have granted adjournments only on reasonable grounds.

23. The Arbitration Committee of ICADR shall be sole judge of the grounds of violation of the guidelines and its decision shall be final and binding on the arbitral tribunal as well as the parties.

Schedule II

(See rule 38)

List of Modifications

Rule of the ICADR Arbitration Rules, 1996 requiring modification	Modification
19 and 20. **Statements of claim, counter-claim and defence.**	For rules 19 and 20, substitute- [19. (1) Within fifteen days of the constitution of the arbitral tribunal, the claimant shall send simultaneously to the arbitral tribunal and the respondent— (a) a statement of facts supporting his claim, the points at issue and the relief or remedy sought; (*b*) all documents he considers to be relevant; (*c*) where reliance is placed on the opinion of any expert, the particulars of that expert including his qualifications and experience, a copy of his opinion and a statement showing the relevance of such expert's opinion; (*d*) application for discovery or production of documents, if any; (*e*) full address, telephone and fax number, if any, for speedy communication; and (*f*) any other material considered relevant by the claimant. (2) The respondent shall, within fifteen days after the receipt of the documents referred to in sub-rule (1), send simultaneously to the arbitral tribunal and the claimant his statement of defence containing replies to the matters referred to in sub-rule (1) together with documentary evidence in support thereof, if any.

(3) Where the respondent has any counter-claim *[or a plea for set-off] against the claimant and wishes the same to be submitted to arbitration, the provisions of sub-rule (1) shall apply as if the respondent is a claimant.

(4) Where discovery or production of documents is allowed, the arbitral tribunal may allow the parties to submit, simultaneously their supplementary statements to the arbitral tribunal and direct them to simultaneously send copies thereof to each other.

Pre-hearing proceeding

20. (1) The arbitral tribunal may hold a pre-hearing proceeding to discuss with the parties the procedure to be followed for speedy arbitration, including day-to-day hearings, keeping in view the requirement of fair trial.

*[(1A) The arbitral tribunal shall make an award within a period of six months from the date the arbitral tribunal enters upon the fast tract arbitration reference].

(2) The decision of the arbitral tribunal on matters referred to in sub-rule (1) shall be final and binding on the parties.

21. In clause (*b*), for "or the claimant fails to communicate his defence to the counter-claim", substitute—

"or the counter-claim".

26. (a) for sub-rule (1), substitute—

[(1) An arbitral award shall be made in writing as early as possible but not later than ten days after the case is closed for making the award and it shall be signed by the members of the arbitral tribunal];

(b) sub-rule (7) shall be omitted.

30. (a) in sub-rules (1), (2), (3) and (4), for the words "thirty days", the words "fifteen days" shall be substituted;

(b) in sub-rule (5), for the words "sixty days", the words "thirty days" shall be substituted;

* *Inserted* after approval by Governing Council/General Body of ICADR, w.e.f. 17.7.2016.

	(c) in sub-rule (7), after "Rule 26 shall", insert "so far as may be,".
31.	In sub-rule (3), for the words "thirty days", the the words "fifteen days" shall be substituted.
35.	In sub-rule (1), in clause (ii), for the words "thirty days", the words "fifteen days" shall be substituted.

*[Schedule III

[See rule 5(7)]

NAME:

CONTACT DETAILS:

PRIOR EXPERIENCE (INCLUDING EXPERIENCE WITH ARBITRATIONS):

NUMBER OF ONGOING ARBITRATIONS:

CIRCUMSTANCES DISCLOSING ANY PAST OR PRESENT RELATIONSHIP WITH OR INTEREST IN ANY OF THE PARTIES OR IN RELATION TO THE SUBJECT-MATTER IN DISPUTE, WHETHER FINANCIAL, BUSINESS, PROFESSIONAL OR OTHER KIND, WHICH IS LIKELY TO GIVE RISE TO JUSTIFIABLE DOUBTS AS TO YOUR INDEPENDENCE OR IMPARTIALITY (LIST OUT):

CIRCUMSTANCES WHICH ARE LIKELY TO AFFECT YOUR ABILITY TO DEVOTE SUFFICIENT TIME TO THE ARBITRATION AND IN PARTICULAR YOUR ABILITY TO FINISH THE ENTIRE ARBITRATION WITHIN TWELVE MONTHS (LIST OUT):]

* *Inserted* after approval by Governing Council/General Body of ICADR, w.e.f. 17.7.2016.

APPENDICES

Appendix - A

Model Arbitration Clause

FOR ARBITRATION OF CONTRACTUAL DISPUTES

Parties to a contract who agree to resolve their contractual disputes in accordance with the ICADR Arbitration Rules, 1996 and to have the ICADR act as appointing authority and/or provide administrative services, may use the following clause:

> If a dispute arises out of or in connection with the contract, or in respect of any defined legal relationship associated therewith or derived therefrom, the parties agree to submit that dispute to arbitration under the ICADR Arbitration Rules, 1996.
>
> The Authority to appoint the arbitrator(s) shall be the International Centre for Alternative Dispute Resolution.
>
> The International Centre for Alternative Dispute Resolution will provide administrative services in accordance with the ICADR Arbitration Rules, 1996.

Note: Parties may consider to add the following:

(a) The number of arbitrator(s) shall be ....

(*b*) The language of the arbitration proceedings shall be ....

(*c*) Specific qualifications of the arbitrator(s) including (but not limited to) language, nationality, technical qualifications and experience.

(*d*) The place of arbitration proceedings shall be ....

Appendix - B

Model Arbitration Agreement

This agreement made this .... day of ....Two Thousand ....Between .... (full description and address of the Party to be given) of the ONE PART and ....

(full description and address of the Party to be given) of the OTHER PART.

WHEREAS certain disputes and differences have arisen and are .... subsisting between the aforesaid parties relating to .... (details of contract to be given),

AND WHEREAS the Parties agree to submit their dispute(s) in accordance with the ICADR Arbitration Rules, 1996.

Now the parties hereby agree as follows:

1. The parties agree to submit their dispute(s) to arbitration in accordance with the ICADR Arbitration Rules, 1996.
2. The authority to appoint the arbitrator or the arbitrators, as the case may be, shall be the International Centre for Alternative Dispute Resolution.*
3. The arbitration shall be administered by the International Centre for Alternative Dispute Resolution (ICADR) in accordance with the ICADR Arbitration Rules, 1996.
4. The place of arbitration shall be

* In case the ICADR is not required to appoint arbitrator(s), omit this clause.

In Witness Whereof, this Agreement has been signed this .... day of .... 20 ....

1. .... for and on behalf of ....
2. .... for and on behalf of ....

Note: The parties may:

(*a*) provide for qualification(s) of the arbitrator(s) including, but not limited to, language, technical experience, nationality and legal experience;

(*b*) specify the language for the conduct of arbitration.

Appendix 5

The ICADR Conciliation Rules 1996*

Preliminary

1. Short title and scope. (1) These rules may be called the ICADR Conciliation Rules, 1996.

(2) These rules shall apply where the parties have agreed in writing, that—

(*a*) a dispute which has arisen, or

(*b*) a dispute which may arise,

between them in respect of a defined legal relationship, whether contractual or not, should be resolved by amicable settlement under the ICADR Conciliation Rules, 1996.

**[(3) These rules shall, so far as may be, also apply to mediation proceedings as they apply to conciliation proceedings and all references to conciliation or conciliators hereinafter shall also be construed as references to mediation and mediators, respectively.

(4) These rules shall not apply to disputes which by virtue of any law for the time being in force may not be submitted to conciliation/mediation.]

2. Definitions. In these rules, unless the context otherwise requires,—

(*a*) "Chairperson" means the Chairperson of the ICADR;

(*b*) "Conciliation Rules" or "rules" means the ICADR Conciliation Rules, 1996;

(*c*) "Government Council" means the Governing Council of the ICADR;

* Source: ICADR, New Delhi.

** *Substituted* after approval by Governing Council/General Body of ICADR, w.e.f. 17.7.2016.

(*d*) "ICADR" means the International Centre for Alternative Dispute Resolution, New Delhi, or, as the case may be, any of its Regional offices;

(*e*) "panel of conciliators" means the panel of persons approved by the Governing Council to act as conciliators;

(*f*) "party" means a party to the agreement referred to in rule 1(2);

(*g*) "Schedule" means the Schedule to these rules;

(*h*) "Secretary-General" means the Secretary-General of the ICADR.

PART I

Procedures for Conciliation Proceedings in the ICADR

3. Commencement of conciliation proceedings. (1) The party initiating conciliation shall send to the other party a written invitation to conciliate under these rules, briefly identifying the subject of the dispute.

(2) Conciliation proceedings shall commence when the other party accepts in writing the invitation to conciliate.

(3) If the other party rejects the invitation, there will be no conciliation proceedings.

(4) If the party initiating conciliation does not receive a reply within thirty days from the date on which he sends the invitation, or within such other period of time as specified in the invitation, he may elect to treat this as a rejection of the invitation to conciliate and inform the other party accordingly.

4. Number and appointment of conciliators. (1) There shall be one conciliator unless the parties have agreed that there shall be two or three conciliators.

(2) The parties may agree to enlist the assistance of the ICADR in connection with the appointment of conciliator, and in particular,—

(*a*) a party may request the ICADR to recommend the names of suitable individuals to act as conciliator; or

(*b*) where the agreement between the parties provides for the appointment of conciliator by the ICADR, a party may request the ICADR in writing to appoint a conciliator.

(3) Where a request in pursuance of clause (*a*) or clause (*b*) of sub-rule (2) is made to the ICADR, the party making the request shall send to the ICADR,—

(*a*) a copy of the invitation to conciliate;

(*b*) a copy of the acceptance by the other party;

(*c*) a copy of the agreement, if any, between the parties providing for an amicable settlement of dispute between them by conciliation;

(*d*) any qualifications required of the conciliator;

(*e*) any additional information, if required, by the ICADR.

(4) In recommending or appointing an individual to act as conciliator, the ICADR will follow the procedure specified in rule 24 and will have regard to—

(*a*) any qualification required of the conciliator by the agreement of the parties;

(*b*) such considerations as are likely to secure the appointment of an independent and impartial conciliator; and

(*c*) where the parties are of different nationalities, the advisability of appointing a conciliator of a nationality other than the nationalities of the parties.

(5) A successor conciliator will be appointed in the manner in which his predecessor has been appointed.

5. Submission of statements to conciliator. (1) The conciliator may, upon his appointment, request each party to submit to him and the ICADR a brief statement in writing describing the general nature of the dispute, the points at issue and the amount, if any, of the claim. Each party shall send a copy of such statement to the other party.

(2) The conciliator may request each party to submit to him and the ICADR a further statement in writing of his position and the facts and grounds in support thereof, supplemented by any documents and other evidence that such party deems appropriate. The party shall send a copy of such statement, documents and other evidence to the other party.

(3) At any stage of the conciliation proceedings, the conciliator may request a party to submit to him and the ICADR such additional information as he deems appropriate.

6. Representation and assistance. Each party shall advise, in writing, the other party and the conciliator of—

(*a*) the name and address of any person who will represent or assist him, and

(*b*) the capacity in which the person will represent.

7. Role of conciliator. (1) The conciliator shall assist the parties in an independent and impartial manner in their attempt to reach an amicable settlement of their dispute.

(2) The conciliator shall be guided by principles of objectivity, fairness and justice, giving consideration to, among other things, the rights and

obligations of the parties, the usages of the trade concerned and the circumstances surrounding the dispute, including any previous business practices between the parties.

(3) The conciliator may conduct the conciliation proceedings in such manner as he considers appropriate, taking into account the circumstances of the case, the wishes the parties may express, including the request by a party that the conciliator hear oral statements, and the need for a speedy settlement of the dispute.

(4) The conciliator may, at any stage of the conciliation proceedings, make proposals for a settlement of the dispute. Such proposals need not be in writing and need not be accompanied by a statement of the reasons therefore.

8. Administrative services. The ICADR will arrange the administrative services specified in Part II if—

(*a*) the parties designate the ICADR for arranging such services, in the agreement to conciliate;

(*b*) the parties, or the conciliator, with the consent of the parties, request the ICADR to arrange such services.

9. Communication between conciliator and parties. (1) The conciliator may invite the parties to meet him or may communicate with them orally or in writing. He may meet or communicate with the parties together or with each of them separately.

(2) Unless the parties have agreed upon the place where meetings with the conciliator are to be held, such place shall be determined by the conciliator, taking into consideration the circumstances of the conciliation proceedings:

Provided that where administrative assistance by the ICADR is sought under rule 8, the place where meetings with conciliator are to be held shall be determined in consultation with the ICADR.

10. Disclosure of information. When the conciliator receives factual information concerning the dispute from a party, he shall disclose the substance of that information to the other party in order that the other party may have the opportunity to present any explanation which he considers appropriate:

Provided that when a party gives any information to the conciliator subject to a specific condition that it be kept confidential the conciliator shall not disclose that information to the other party.

11. Cooperation of parties with conciliator. The parties shall in good faith cooperate with the conciliator and, in particular, shall endeavour to comply with requests by the conciliator to submit written materials, provide evidence and attend meetings.

12. Suggestions by parties for settlement of dispute. Each party may, on his own initiative or at the invitation of the conciliator, submit to the conciliator suggestions for the settlement of the dispute.

13. Settlement agreement. (1) When it appears to the conciliator that there exist elements of a settlement which may be acceptable to the parties, he shall formulate the terms of a possible settlement and submit them to the parties for their observations. After receiving the observations of the parties, the conciliator may reformulate the terms of a possible settlement in the light of such observations.

(2) If the parties reach agreement on a settlement of the dispute, they may draw up and sign a written settlement agreement. If requested by the parties, the conciliator may draw up, or assist the parties in drawing up, the settlement agreement.

(3) When the parties sign the settlement agreement, it shall be final and binding on the parties and persons claiming under them respectively.

(4) The conciliator shall authenticate the settlement agreement, and furnish a copy thereof to each of the parties.

14. Confidentiality. The conciliator and the parties shall keep confidential all matters relating to the conciliation proceedings. Confidentiality shall extend also to the settlement agreement, except where its disclosure is necessary for purposes of its implementation and enforcement.

15. Termination of conciliation proceedings. (1) The conciliation proceedings shall be terminated—

(*a*) by the signing of the settlement agreement by the parties, on the date of agreement; or

(*b*) by a written declaration of the conciliator, after consultation with the parties, to the effect that further efforts at conciliation are no longer justified, on the date of the declaration; or

(*c*) by a written declaration of the parties addressed to the conciliator to the effect that the conciliation proceedings are terminated, on the date of the declaration; or

(*d*) by a written declaration of a party to the other party and the conciliator, if appointed, to the effect that the conciliation proceedings are terminated, on the date of the declaration.

(2) The conciliator shall, upon termination of the conciliation proceedings, send an intimation thereof in writing to the ICADR.

16. Resort to arbitral or judicial proceedings. The parties shall not initiate, during the conciliation proceedings, any arbitral or judicial proceedings in respect of a dispute that is the subject matter of the conciliation proceedings except that a party may initiate arbitral or judicial proceedings where, in his opinion, such proceedings are necessary for preserving his rights.

17. Costs. (1) Upon termination of the conciliation proceedings, the conciliator shall fix the costs of the conciliation and give written notice thereof to the parties. The fee of the conciliator and any assistance provided pursuant to rule 4(2)(*b*) and fees and charges for any administrative assistance pursuant to rule 8 shall be fixed by the conciliator in accordance with the Schedule:

Provided that the ICADR may, on request from the conciliator, fix the fee of the conciliator at a figure higher than that set out in the Schedule if, in exceptional circumstances of the case, this appears to be necessary.

(2) For the purpose of sub-rule (1), "costs" means costs relating to—

(*a*) the fee and expenses of the conciliator and witnesses requested by the conciliator with the consent of the parties;

(*b*) any expert advice requested by the conciliator with the consent of the parties;

(*c*) any assistance provided pursuant to rule 4(2) and rule 8;

(*d*) any other expenses incurred in connection with the conciliation proceedings and the settlement agreement.

(3) Where more than one conciliator is appointed, each conciliator shall be paid separately the fee set out in the Schedule.

(4) The costs shall be borne equally by the parties unless the settlement agreement provides for a different apportionment. All other expenses incurred by a party shall be borne by that party.

18. Deposits. (1) The conciliator will, upon his appointment, in consultation with the ICADR, direct each party to deposit with the ICADR an equal amount as an advance for the costs referred to in rule 17(2) which he expects will be incurred.

(2) During the course of the conciliation proceedings, the conciliator may, in consultation with the ICADR, direct supplementary deposits with the ICADR in an equal amount from each party for the costs referred to in sub-rule (1).

(3) If the required deposits under sub-rules (1) and (2) are not made in full within thirty days, the conciliator will inform the parties in order that one or the other party may make the required deposit and if the required deposit is not made, the conciliator may suspend the proceedings or may make a written declaration of termination of the proceedings to the parties, effective on the date of the declaration.

(4) Subject to any settlement agreement, upon termination of the conciliation proceedings, the ICADR shall apply the deposits to the costs of the proceedings, render an accounting to the parties of the deposits received and applied and return any unexpended balance to the parties.

19. Role of conciliator in other proceedings. Unless otherwise agreed by the parties,—

(*a*) the conciliator shall not act as an arbitrator or as a representative or counsel of a party in any arbitral or judicial proceeding in respect of a dispute that is the subject-matter of the conciliation proceedings;

(*b*) the conciliator shall not be presented by the parties as a witness in any arbitral or judicial proceedings.

20. Admissibility of evidence in other proceedings. The parties shall not rely on or introduce as evidence in arbitral or judicial proceedings, whether or not such proceedings relate to the dispute that is the subject-matter of the conciliation proceedings,—

(*a*) views expressed or suggestions made by the other party in respect of a possible settlement of the dispute;

(*b*) admissions made by the other party in the course of conciliation proceedings;

(*c*) proposals made by the conciliator;

(*d*) the fact that the other party had indicated his willingness to accept a proposal for settlement made by the conciliator.

21. Interpretation and application. If any question arises as to the interpretation or application of these rules or any procedural matter thereunder, the decision of the ICADR shall be final and binding on the parties.

PART II

Services for Procedures under the Conciliation Rules

22. Services for procedures under the rules. To facilitate the conduct of conciliation proceedings that the parties have agreed to conduct under the Conciliation Rules, the ICADR will—

(*a*) perform the function of the appointing authority whenever—

(*i*) the ICADR has been so designated by the parties in the conciliation clause of their contract or in a separate agreement, or

(*ii*) the parties have agreed to submit a dispute to the ICADR under the Conciliation Rules without specifically designating it as the appointing authority; and

(*b*) provide the administrative services herein specified when required by the agreement, or when requested by all the parties, or by the conciliator with the consent of the parties.

23. Services as the registry. (1) On receiving a request in pursuance of rule 4(2)(*a*) or 4(2)(*b*), the ICADR will register the request and intimate in writing to the parties the registration number of the case which shall be quoted by the party while making any subsequent communication to the ICADR.

(2) The ICADR will scrutinise every request and the documents, make necessary entries in the register and prepare a file of the case.

24. Services as recommending or appointing authority. (1) On receipt of a request in pursuance of rule 4(2)(*a*), the ICADR will communicate to the party making the request a list containing the names, addresses, nationalities and a description of qualifications and experience of at least three individuals from the panel of conciliators.

(2) On receipt of a request to appoint a conciliator in pursuance of rule 4(2)(*b*), the ICADR will follow the following procedure—

(*i*) the ICADR will communicate to each party a list containing the names, addresses, nationalities and a description of qualifications and experience of at least three individuals from the panel of conciliators;

(*ii*) within thirty days following the receipt of the list, a party may delete any name to which he objects and after renumbering the names in the order of his preference, return the list to the ICADR;

(*iii*) on receipt of the list returned by the parties, the ICADR will appoint the conciliator from the list taking into account the order of preference indicated by the parties;

(*iv*) if for any reason the appointment cannot be made according to the procedure specified in clauses (*i*) to (*iii*), the ICADR may, unless the parties recommend the name of the conciliator to be appointed by the ICADR, appoint the conciliator from the panel of conciliators.

(3) In recommending or appointing a conciliator the ICADR will have regard to the matters referred to in rule 4(4) and will carefully consider the nature of the dispute in order to include in the list, persons having appropriate professional or business experience language ability and nationality.

(4) All appointments on behalf of the ICADR will be made by the Secretary-General and in his absence by such member of the Governing Council as is designated by the Chairperson:

Provided that where the Secretary-General is to be appointed as the conciliator, the appointment will be made by the Chairperson.

25. Administrative services. (1) The ICADR may provide the administrative services specified in this Part—

(*a*) upon the request of the parties;

(*b*) upon the request of the conciliator with the consent of the parties; or

(*c*) if the parties designate the ICADR for providing such services.

(2) All oral or written communications from a party to the conciliator, except at meetings, may be directed to the ICADR which will transmit them to the conciliator and, where appropriate, to the other party.

(3) Agreement by the parties that the ICADR will provide the administrative services, constitutes consent by the parties that, for purposes of compliance with any time requirements of the rules, any written communications shall be deemed to have been received by the addressee when received by the ICADR. When transmitting communications to a party, the ICADR will do so to the addresses provided by each of them to the ICADR for this purpose.

(4) The ICADR will also assist in the exchange of information and of settlement proposals.

(5) The ICADR will assist the conciliator to establish the date, time and place of meetings and will give the parties advance notice of such meeting.

(6) The ICADR will provide a meeting room and retiring rooms for the conciliator and the parties or their counsel in the offices of the ICADR on the charges set out in the Schedule. These charges will be billed separately and are not included in the fee for administrative services. However, where these facilities are provided in any place other than the offices of the ICADR, the charges will be determined by the ICADR and billed separately in each case.

(7) Upon request, the ICADR will make arrangements for reporter transcripts of meetings or hearings. The cost of reporter transcripts will be determined by the ICADR and billed separately and is not included in the fee for administrative services.

(8) Upon request, the ICADR will make arrangements for the services of interpreters or translators. The cost of interpretation or translation will be determined by the ICADR and billed separately and is not included in the fee for administrative services.

(9) (*a*) The ICADR will hold advance deposits to be made for the costs of the conciliation proceedings.

(*b*) On termination of the conciliation proceedings, the ICADR will apply the proceeds of the advance deposits towards any of its unpaid administrative fees and charges and the costs of the conciliation proceedings and will render an accounting to the parties of the deposits received and applied and return any unexpended balance to the parties.

(10)(*a*) Upon request, the ICADR will provide other appropriate administrative services the costs of which will be determined by the ICADR and billed separately and are not included in the fee for administrative services.

(*b*) The kinds of services which can be provided are as follows:—

(*i*) secretarial support and clerical assistance;

(*ii*) long distance and local telephone access and telex and telecopier facilities;

(*iii*) photocopying and other usual office services.

(11)(*a*) The ICADR may require the party requesting one or more of the services referred to in sub-rules (6), (7), (8) or (10) to deposit an amount specified by it as advance towards the costs of such services.

(*b*) The ICADR may also require the parties to make supplementary deposits towards the costs of the services referred to in clause (*a*);

(*c*) If the required deposit under clause (*a*) or clause (*b*) is not made in full within the time specified by the ICADR, the ICADR may not provide the services requested for.

26. Administrative fees. (1) The fee of the ICADR for making appointment of conciliator and for providing administrative services, other than those specified in sub-rules (6), (7), (8) and (10) of rule 25, is based upon the amount in disputes as disclosed when the statement of dispute is submitted to the ICADR in pursuance of sub-rule (1) of rule 5. Items A.I.(1), B.I.(1) and C.I.(1) of the Schedule contains the ICADR's schedule of fees and charges.

(2) Where the ICADR is requested to act as appointing authority under rule 4(2), the requesting party shall pay the ICADR a non-refundable fee at the time of the request. This fee is separately set out in the Schedule as items A.I.(2), B.I.(2) and C.I.(2).

(3) The Conciliation Rules provide that the costs of conciliation include the costs of the administrative fee or charges of the ICADR [rule 17(2)]. These costs are, borne equally by the parties unless the settlement agreement provides for a different apportionment [rule 17(4)].

*[Schedule

A. Domestic Commercial Conciliation

I. Administrative fees:

referred to in rule 26(1) and 26(2)

(1) Fee referred to in rule 26(1)—
(ICADR acts as appointing authority and administrator).

	Amount in Dispute (in rupees)	Amount of fee (in rupees)
(*i*)	where the total amount in dispute does not exceed Rs. 5 lakh	Rs. 22,500
(*ii*)	where the total amount in dispute exceeds Rs. 5 lakh but does not exceed Rs. 20 lakh	Rs. 22,500 plus 1.75 per cent. of the amount by which the total amount in dispute exceeds Rs. 5 lakh
(*iii*)	where the total amount in dispute exceeds Rs. 20 lakh but does not exceed Rs. 1 crore	Rs. 48,750 plus 1.5 per cent. of the amount by which the total amount in dispute exceeds Rs. 20 lakh
(*iv*)	where the total amount in dispute exceeds Rs. 1 crore but does not exceed Rs. 10 crore	Rs. 1,68,750 plus 0.75 per cent. of the amount by which the total amount in dispute exceeds Rs. 1 crore
(*v*)	where the total amount in dispute exceeds Rs. 10 crore but does not exceed Rs. 20 crore	Rs. 8,43,750 plus 0.5 per cent. of the amount by which the total amount in dispute exceeds Rs. 10 crore
(*vi*)	where the total amount in dispute exceeds Rs. 20 crore	Rs. 13,43,750 plus 0.25 per cent. of the amount by which the total amount in dispute exceeds Rs. 20 crore with a ceiling limit of Rs. 15 lakhs

Note: Where dispute cannot be expressed in terms of money or the total amount in dispute is below Rs. 2 lakh, the Secretary-General shall determine the amount of administrative fees, in his discretion, in each case.

(2) Non-refundable fee referred to in rule 26(2)
(ICADR acts only as appointing authority)
Rs. 15,000

---

* *Substituted* after approval by Governing Council/General Body of ICADR, w.e.f. 17.7.2016.

II. Conciliator's fee
referred to in rule 17(1)

Amount in dispute (in rupees)	Amount of fee For one Conciliator (in rupees)
(*i*) where the total amount in dispute does not exceed Rs. 5 lakh	Rs. 45,000
(*ii*) where the total amount in dispute exceeds Rs. 5 lakh but does not exceed Rs. 20 lakh	Rs. 45,000 plus 3.5 per cent. of the amount by which the total amount in dispute exceeds Rs. 5 lakh
(*iii*) where the total amount in dispute exceeds Rs. 20 lakh but does not exceed Rs. 1 crore	Rs. 97,500 plus 3 per cent. of the amount by which the total amount in dispute exceeds Rs. 20 lakh
(*iv*) where the total amount in dispute exceeds Rs. 1 crore but does not exceed Rs. 10 crore	Rs. 3,37,500 plus 1 per cent. of the amount by which the total amount in dispute exceeds Rs. 1 crore
(*v*) where the total amount in dispute exceeds Rs. 10 crore but does not exceed Rs. 20 crore	Rs. 12,37,500 plus 0.75 per cent. of the amount by which the total amount in dispute exceeds Rs. 10 crore
(*vi*) where the total amount in dispute exceeds Rs. 20 crore	Rs. 19,87,500 plus 0.5 per cent. of the amount by which the total amount in dispute exceeds Rs. 20 crore with a ceiling of Rs. 30 lakhs

Note: Where dispute cannot be expressed in terms of money or the total amount in dispute is below Rs. 2 lakh, the Conciliator shall determine the amount of fee in each case.

III. Charges for facilities
referred to in rule 25(6)

Rs. 4,000 for one day or part thereof plus Rs. 500 Wi-fi charges for two hours (optional) plus Rs. 500 Documentation Camera charges for two hours (optional) plus Rs. 1,000 Stenographic service charges (optional)

Note: Where the facilities are provided in a place other than in ICADR's offices, the charges will be determined in each case and billed separately.

B. Domestic Non-commercial Conciliation

I. Administrative fees:

referred to in rule 26(1) and 26(2)

(1) Fee referred to in rule 26(1).
(ICADR acts as appointing authority and administrator)

Where the dispute can be expressed in terms of money, the administrative fees will be the same as applicable for domestic commercial conciliation.

Note: Where the dispute cannot be expressed in terms of money or the total amount in dispute is below Rs. 2 lakh, the Secretary-General shall determine the amount of administrative fee, in his discretion in each case.

(2) Non-refundable fee referred to in rule 26(2).
(ICADR acts only as appointing authority)
Rs. 15,000

II. Conciliator's fee

referred to in rule 17(1)

Where the dispute can be expressed in terms of money, the conciliator's fees will be the same as applicable for domestic commercial conciliation.

Note: Where the dispute cannot be expressed in terms of money or the total amount in dispute is below Rs. 2 lakh, the conciliator shall determine the amount of fee in each case.

III. Charges for facilities

referred to in rule 25(6)

Rs. 4,000 for one day or part thereof plus Rs. 500 Wi-fi charges for two hours (Optional) plus Rs. 500 Documentation Camera charges for two hours (optional) plus Rs. 1,000 Stenographic service charges (optional).

Note: Where the facilities are provided in a place other than in ICADR's offices, the charges will be determined in each case and billed separately.

C. International Commercial Conciliation

I. Administrative fees:

referred to in rule 26(1) and 26(2)

(1) Fee referred to in rule 26(1)
(ICADR acts as appointing authority and administrator).

	Amount in dispute (in US dollars)	**Amount of fee** (in US dollars)
(*i*)	where the total amount in dispute does not exceed $50,000	$1,500
(*ii*)	where the total amount in dispute exceeds $50,000 but does not exceed $1,75,000	$1,500 plus 3 per cent. of the amount by which the total amount in dispute exceeds $50,000
(*iii*)	where the total amount in dispute exceeds $1,75,000 but does not exceed $5,00,000	$5,250 plus 2 per cent. of the amount by which the total amount in dispute exceeds $1,75,000
(*iv*)	where the total amount in dispute exceeds $5,00,000 but does not exceed $10,00,000	$11,750 plus 1 per cent. of the amount by which the total amount in dispute exceeds $5,00,000
(*v*)	where the total amount in dispute exceeds $10,00,000 but does not exceed $20,00,000	$16,750 plus 0.5 per cent. of the amount by which the total amount in dispute exceeds $10,00,000.
(*vi*)	where the total amount in dispute exceeds $20,00,000 but does not exceed $50,00,000	$21,750 plus 0.25 per cent. of the amount by which the total amount in dispute exceeds $20,00,000
(*vii*)	where the total amount in dispute exceeds $50,00,000	$29,250 plus 0.125 per cent. of the amount by which the total amount in dispute exceeds $50,00,000 with a ceiling of $35,000.

Note: Where dispute cannot be expressed in terms of money, the Secretary-General shall determine the amount of administrative fees, in his discretion, in each case.

(2) Non-refundable fee referred to in rule 26(2)
(ICADR acts only as appointing authority)
US $1000

II. Conciliator's fee

referred to in rule 17(1)

Amount in dispute (in US dollars)	Amount of fee For one Conciliator (in US dollars)
(*i*) where the total amount in dispute does not exceed $50,000	$3,000
(*ii*) where the total amount in dispute exceeds $50,000 but does not exceed $1,75,000	$3,000 plus 5 per cent. of the amount by which the total amount in dispute exceeds $50,000
(*iii*) where the total amount in dispute exceeds $ 1,75,000 but does not exceed $5,00,000	$9,250 plus 4 per cent. of the amount by which the total amount in dispute exceeds $1,75,000
(*iv*) where the total amount in dispute exceeds $ 5,00,000 but does not exceed $10,00,000	$22,250 plus 3 per cent. of the amount by which the total amount in dispute exceeds $5,00,000
(*v*) where the total amount in dispute exceeds $10,00,000 but does not exceed $20,00,000	$37,250 plus 2 per cent. of the amount by which the total amount in dispute exceeds $10,00,000
(*vi*) where the total amount in dispute exceeds $20,00,000 but does not exceed $50,00,000	$57,250 plus 1 per cent. of the amount by which the total amount in dispute exceeds $20,00,000
(*vii*) where the total amount in dispute exceeds $50,00,000	$87,250 plus 0.5 per cent. of the amount by which the total amount in dispute exceeds $50,00,000 with a ceiling of $1,00,000

Note: Where the dispute cannot be expressed in terms of money, the conciliator shall determine the amount of fee in each case.

III. Charges for facilities

referred to in rule 25(6)

US $350 for one day or part thereof plus $50 Wi-fi charges for two hours (optional), plus $50 Documentation Camera charges for two hours (optional) plus $100 Stenographic service charges (optional).

Note: Where the facilities are provided in a place other than in ICADR's offices, the charges will be determined in each case and billed separately].

APPENDICES

Appendix - A

Model Conciliation/Mediation Clause for Conciliation/Mediation of Contractual Disputes

Parties to a contract who agree to resolve their contractual disputes in accordance with the ICADR Conciliation Rules, 1996 and to have the ICADR act as appointing authority and/or provide administrative services, may consider using the following clauses:

> If a dispute arises out of or in connection with this contract, or in respect of any defined legal relationship associated therewith or derived therefrom, the parties agree to seek an amicable settlement of that dispute by Conciliation/Mediation under the ICADR Conciliation Rules, 1996.
>
> The authority to appoint the Conciliator(s)/Mediators(s) shall be the International Centre for Alternative Dispute Resolution.
>
> The International Centre for Alternative Dispute Resolution will provide administrative services in accordance with the ICADR Conciliation Rules, 1996.

Note: Parties may consider to add the following:

(a) The number of Conciliator(s)/Mediators(s) shall be ....

(*b*) The language of the Conciliation/Mediation proceedings shall be ....

(*c*) Specific qualifications of the Conciliator(s)/Mediator(s) including, but not limited to, language, nationality, technical qualification and experience.

(*d*) The place of Conciliation/Mediation proceedings shall be ....

Appendix - B

Model Conciliation/Mediation Agreement

This agreement made this................................day of ....
Two Thousand .... BETWEEN ....

....

(Full description and address of the Party to be given) of the ONE PART and

....

(full description and address of the Party to be given) of the OTHER PART.

WHEREAS certain disputes and differences have arisen and are subsisting between the aforesaid parties relating to ....
.... (details of contract to be given).

AND WHEREAS the Parties agree to submit their dispute(s) for an amicable settlement in accordance with the ICADR Conciliation Rules, 1996;

Now the parties hereby agree as follows:

1. The Parties agree to resolve their dispute(s) by Conciliation/Mediation in accordance with the ICADR Conciliation Rules, 1996.
2. The authority to appoint the Conciliator/Mediator or the Conciliators/Mediators, as the case may be, shall be the International Centre for Alternative Dispute Resolution.*
3. The Conciliation/Meditation shall be administered by the International Centre for Alternative Dispute Resolution (ICADR) in accordance with the ICADR Conciliation Rules, 1996.
4. The place of Conciliation/Mediation shall be ....

* In case the ICADR is not required to appoint Conciliator(s)/Mediator(s), omit this clause.

In Witness Whereof, this Agreement has been signed this................day of .... 20 .... at .... by ....

1. .... for and on behalf of ....
2. .... for and on behalf of ....

Note: The parties may:

(a) provide for qualification(s) of the Conciliator(s)/Mediator(s) including, but not limited to language, technical experience, nationality and legal experience;

(*b*) specify the language for the conduct of Conciliation/Mediation.

Appendix 6

Rules & Procedures for Mini-Trial*

Preliminary

1. Short title and scope. (1) These rules may be called the ICADR Mini-trial Rules, 1996.

(2) These rules shall apply where the parties have agreed in writing that—

(*a*) a dispute which has arison, or

(*b*) a dispute which may arise,

between them in respect of a defined legal relationship, whether contractual or not, should be resolved by mini-trial under ICADR Mini-trial Rules, 1996.

(3) These rules shall not apply where by virtue of any law for the time being in force certain disputes may not be submitted to mini-trial.

2. Definitions. In these rules, unless the context otherwise requires—

(*a*) "Rules" means the ICADR Mini-trial Rules, 1996;

(*b*) "ICADR" means the International Centre for Alternative Dispute Resolution;

(*c*) "Neutral adviser" means the neutral adviser appointed under these rules;

(*d*) "Schedule" means a Schedule to these rules;

(*e*) "Secretary" means the Secretary of the ICADR;

(*f*) "Secretary-General" means the Secretary-General of the ICADR.

---

* Source: ICADR, New Delhi.

PART I

Mini-trial Proceedings

3. Commencement of mini-trial proceedings. (1) The party initiating mini-trial proceedings shall send to the other party a written invitation to participate in the mini-trial under these rules, briefly identifying the subject of the dispute.

(2) Mini-trial proceedings shall commence when the other party accepts in writing the invitation to mini-trial.

(3) If the other party rejects the invitation, there will be no mini-trial proceedings.

(4) The acceptance under sub-rule (2) shall be communicated in writing to the ICADR.

(5) If the party initiating mini-trial proceedings does not receive a reply within thirty days from the date on which he sends the invitation, or within such other period of time as specified in the invitation, he may elect to treat as a rejection of the invitation to mini-trial and inform the other party accordingly.

4. Appointment of neutral adviser. (1) Where the parties agree to mini-trial under these rules, they shall, if no written agreement exists to that effect, sign an agreement in the Form contained in Schedule "A" with such modification, if any, as they agree.

(2) Where the parties do not wish to appoint their own neutral adviser(s), they may enlist the assistance of the ICADR in connection with the appointment of the neutral adviser, and in particular, a party may request the ICADR to recommend the name of a suitable individual to act as neutral adviser or to appoint a neutral adviser from its panel of ADR neutrals.

(3) Where a request under sub-rule (2) is made to the ICADR, the party making the request shall send to the ICADR—

(*a*) a copy of the invitation to hold mini-trial;

(*b*) a copy of the acceptance by the other party or parties;

(*c*) a copy of the agreement between the parties providing for resolution of dispute between them by mini-trial;

(*d*) any additional information, if required, by the ICADR.

(4) In recommending or appointing an individual to act as neutral adviser, the ICADR shall have regard to—

(*a*) any qualifications required of the neutral adviser by the agreement of the parties; and

(*b*) such considerations as are likely to secure the appointment of an independent and impartial neutral adviser.

(*c*) Where the parties are of different nationalities, the advisability of appointing a neutral adviser of a nationality other than the nationalities of the parties.

5. Submission of statements by parties. (1) The neutral adviser upon his appointment, shall call upon the initiating party (claimant) to submit a statement of case containing:–

(*a*) the nature of the dispute.

(*b*) the facts and circumstances giving rise to the dispute and legal issues involved;

(*c*) the points at issue between the parties and the nature and extent of claim;

(*d*) the copies or the details of the documents in support of his case;

(*e*) where reliance is sought on the testimony of any witness, a brief summary of the statement of the witness;

(*f*) the time sought for presentation of his case;

(*g*) where reliance is placed on the opinion of any expert, the particulars of that expert including his qualifications and a brief statement justifying the relevance of the expert evidence; and

(*h*) such other particulars as the neutral adviser deems necessary.

(2) The claimant shall simultaneously send a copy of the statement submitted under sub-rule (1) to the other party and the ICADR.

(3) Upon receipt of copy of the statement from the claimant under sub-rule (2), the other party shall within thirty days submit his reply containing the details in respect of items (*a*) to (*h*) of sub-rule (1) to the neutral adviser and send a copy thereof to the claimant and the ICADR.

(4) Where the party submitting the reply in pursuance of sub-rule (3) has his own claims against the claimant, he shall also submit, together with the reply, a statement of his counter-claim, in the manner required under sub-rule (1).

(5) The neutral adviser may request each party to submit to him and to the ICADR a further statement of his position and the facts and grounds in support thereof, supplemented by any document or other evidence that such party deems appropriate.

(6) At any stage of the mini-trial, the neutral adviser may call upon a party to submit to him such additional information as he may require.

(7) The party submitting the reply under sub-rule (3) or the statement of claim under sub-rule (4) and further statement under sub-rule (5) and additional information under sub-rule (6) shall simultaneously send copies thereof to the other party and the ICADR.

(8) Where counter-claim is made under sub-rule (4), the claimant shall within thirty days submit his reply containing the details in respect of items (*a*) to (*h*) in the manner required under sub-rule (1).

(9) Where any particulars are required by the neutral adviser from a party he shall make compliance with the same within thirty days of receipt of such requisition.

6. Representation at mini-trial. Each party shall advise the other party, the ICADR and the neutral adviser, in writing, of—

(*a*) the names and addresses of the persons including experts, if any, who will make presentation on his behalf and the capacity in which they will act.

(*b*) the name and address of the Senior Executive, having the authority to participate and take decisions on behalf of that party at the mini-trial.

7. Schedule of mini-trial. The neutral adviser shall, as promptly as possible after the receipt of the documents referred to in rules 5 and 6, in consultation with the ICADR, inform the parties in writing, of—

(*a*) the venue and date for the mini-trial;

(*b*) the time allowed to each of the parties to present the case and to make responding and winding up statement.

8. Request for additional time by parties. Where the representative of a party requires time in addition to the time allowed under rule 7, he shall intimate in writing the neutral adviser and simultaneously send a copy to the ICADR along with additional deposit as required under these rules.

9. Conduct of mini-trial. (1) In order to facilitate conduct of mini-trial, the parties or the neutral adviser with the consent of the parties, may arrange for administrative assistance by the ICADR.

(2) The parties shall be represented at the mini-trial by their Senior Executives authorised to take decisions which shall be binding on the respective parties.

(3) At the commencement of the mini-trial, the neutral adviser shall inform the parties about the process and the procedure that are to be followed and of the confidential, privileged, non-biased and non-binding nature of the process.

(4) The claimant shall thereafter present his case summarising the evidence and making legal submissions. Use may be made of photographs, films, charts or other devices in making the presentation. The presentation shall be concluded within the permitted period.

(5) The other party will thereafter present his case, using any of the devices referred to in sub-rule (4) within the permitted period. Where

the claim is against more than one party, the neutral adviser will determine the order in which they will make their respective presentations.

(6) A party may address, with the permission of the neutral adviser, any question to the other party for seeking clarification of any point made during the presentation.

(7) The neutral adviser may put questions to the parties for clarification of any point made during the presentation. In so doing, the neutral adviser shall ensure that the questions put by him do not have the effect of damaging or supplementing the case of a party.

(8) Where the parties so request, their experts may have mutual dialogue with each other so as to assist the neutral adviser and the Senior Executive to make their assessment of the points made by the experts during presentation.

(9) The claimants, and thereafter the other party, shall have opportunity to make a winding up statement, within the period allowed to them.

10. Post-trial discussion. (1) At the end of the presentation of their case by the parties, the neutral adviser will proceed to discuss with the Senior Executives of parties the presentation made on behalf of the parties.

(2) During discussions with the Senior Executives the neutral adviser shall indicate his view of the respective strengths and weaknesses of each side, the aspects of the case which were reasonably clear and those which were uncertain.

(3) During discussion, the neutral adviser will answer questions put to him by the Senior Executives and give any information and the views that may help the parties to gain a better understanding of the issues and the merits of the case.

(4) The Senior Executives will thereafter enter into mutual, discussions with a view to arriving at a settlement. The neutral adviser if so required by the Senior Executives, shall assist them in such discussion, as a facilitator, but not as a judge of the dispute.

11. Obligations of the parties. (1) The parties shall in good faith cooperate with the neutral adviser at all stages of the proceedings.

(2) The neutral adviser and the parties shall keep confidential all matters relating to the mini-trial. Confidentiality shall also extend to the settlement, except where its disclosure is necessary for purposes of its implementation and enforcement.

12. Conclusion of mini-trial. (1) If the matter is settled, the terms of settlement shall be reduced to writing and signed by the Senior Executives on behalf of the parties. The neutral adviser, if so asked, will counter-sign the settlement as a witness.

(2) Where the mini-trial has not resulted in settlement, the parties shall be at liberty to resort to the remedies available under the law. Each party shall, unless agreed otherwise, be barred from relying on admission made by the other party in the course of mini-trial.

13. Termination of mini-trial. The mini-trial shall terminate—

(*a*) by the signing of settlement in terms of sub-rule (1) of rule 12 on the date of signing of the agreement;

(*b*) on a written declaration by the neutral adviser to the effect that further efforts at settlement are no longer justified, on the date of the declaration.

14. Bar to resort to arbitral or judicial proceedings. A party shall not initiate during the mini-trial any arbitral or judicial proceedings in respect of the subject-matter of the mini-trial except that a party may initiate arbitral or judicial proceedings where in his opinion, such proceedings are necessary for preserving his rights.

15. Costs. (1) Upon termination of the mini-trial proceedings, the neutral adviser shall fix the cost of the proceedings and give written notice thereof to the parties. The fee of the neutral adviser and the fee and charges for assistance provided by the ICADR shall be fixed by the neutral adviser in accordance with Schedule "B". Provided that the ICADR may fix the fees of the neutral adviser at a figure higher than that which would result from the application of the fee set out in Schedule "B". If, in exceptional circumstances of the case, this appears to be necessary.

(2) For the purpose of sub-rule (1), "costs" means reasonable costs relating to—

(*a*) fee and expenses of the neutral adviser;

(*b*) any direct or incidental expenses for the services provided by the ICADR: and

(*c*) any other expenses incurred in connection with the mini-trial and the settlement.

(3) Unless directed otherwise by the neutral adviser, the parties shall bear their own cost and share equally the cost of the neutral adviser and of the services provided by the ICADR.

16. Role of neutral adviser in other proceedings. Unless otherwise agreed by the parties—

(*a*) the neutral adviser shall not act as an arbitrator or as a representative or counsel of a party in any arbitral or judicial proceedings in respect of the subject-matter of the mini-trial in which he may have acted as neutral adviser.

(*b*) the neutral adviser shall not be presented by the parties as a witness in any arbitral or judicial proceedings.

17. Exclusion in other proceedings. The parties shall not rely on or introduce as evidence in arbitral or judicial proceedings, whether or not such proceedings relate to the dispute that is the subject-matter of the mini-trial proceedings—

(*a*) views expressed or suggestions made by the other party or the neutral adviser in respect of the merits of the case of a party or in respect of possible settlement of the dispute;

(*b*) admission made by the other party in the course of the mini-trial;

(*c*) views indicated by the neutral adviser or proposals made by the party or his Senior Executive during proceedings for settlement agreement; and

(*d*) the fact that the other party has indented his willingness to accept a proposal for settlement.

PART II

Services Provided by ICADR in Mini-Trial Proceedings

18. Functions of ICADR. To facilitate the conduct of mini-trial that the parties have agreed to conduct under these rules, the ICADR will—

(*a*) perform the functions of the authority for appointment of neutral adviser whenever—

(*i*) the ICADR has been so designated by the parties in the relevant clause of the contract (Model Clause contained in Schedule "C") or in a separate agreement, or

(*ii*) the parties have agreed to submit a dispute to the ICADR under these rules without specifically designating it as the authority for appointment of neutral adviser; and

(*b*) provide the administrative services herein specified when required by a contract or when requested by all parties or by the neutral adviser, with the consent of the parties.

19. Procedure for appointment of neutral adviser. (1) On receipt of a request to appoint a neutral adviser, the ICADR will communicate a list of at least three persons as the panel of neutral advisers to both the parties. Within fifteen days each party may return the list to the ICADR after having deleted any name to which he objects, and numbering the remaining names in order of preference.

(2) In appointing a neutral adviser, the ICADR will take into account the matters referred to in these rules and will carefully consider the nature of the dispute in order to include in the list, persons having appropriate professional or business expertise, language ability and nationality.

(3) All appointments on behalf of the ICADR shall be made by the Secretary-General or in his absence by a member of the Governing Council of ICADR nominated by the Chairperson, as far as possible from the panel of the neutral advisers, maintained by the ICADR, provided where the parties request that the Secretary-General to be the neutral adviser, the appointment shall be made by the Chairperson.

20. Administrative Services. (1) Upon the request of the parties or the neutral adviser with the consent of all the parties, the ICADR may arrange the administrative services outlined hereunder.

(*a*) Where the parties use the Model Clause or agreement naming the ICADR to provide the administrative services for the mini-trial in accordance with its rules, the neutral adviser may, in exercise of his authority under the rules, request the ICADR to provide the administrative services outlined hereunder. All oral and written communications from a party, to neutral adviser, except at mini-trial, may be directed to the ICADR which will transmit the same to the neutral adviser, and where appropriate, to the other party.

(*b*) Agreement by the parties that the ICADR will administer a case constitutes consent by the parties that, for the purpose of compliance with any time requirements of the rules, any written communication shall be deemed to have been received by the addressee when received by the ICADR. When transmitting communication to a party, the ICADR will do so to the addresses provided by each of them to the ICADR for this purpose.

(*c*) The ICADR will also assist with the exchange of information.

(*d*) The ICADR will assist the neutral adviser to establish the date, time and place of the mini-trial and discussion and will give parties advance notice of such meetings.

(*e*) The ICADR will provide, wherever possible, a meeting room and retiring room for the neutral adviser, the parties, senior Executives and their representatives, whenever so requested. Where the facilities are provided at a place other than the office of the ICADR, the charges will be determined and billed separately for each case.

(*f*) Upon request of a party, the ICADR will make arrangements for transmitting transcript of meetings or hearings. The cost of these transcripts will be billed separately to the party requesting such facility and not included in the fee for administrative services.

(*g*) Upon request by either party the ICADR will make arrangements for the services of interpreters or translators.

The cost of interpretation or translation will be billed separately and not included in the fee for administrative services.

(*h*) The fee of the neutral adviser and the ICADR will generally be borne equally if there are two parties to the dispute and in such other ratio as the neutral adviser may direct if there are more than two parties:

Provided that whenever a party asks for more time than the time allotted by the neutral adviser for presentation of his case or for winding-up statement, the party so asking for additional time will be required to pay the entire cost payable to the neutral adviser. ICADR and for other facilities for such additional time.

(*i*) The parties moving the ICADR for mini-trial shall make deposit of the advance provided in sub-rule (2) of rule 21.

The neutral adviser may, in consultation with ICADR, direct each party to deposit with the ICADR such further advance as he may deem proper to cover the expenses which he expects to be incurred during mini-trial.

(*j*) The ICADR will hold advance deposits to be made on account of the fee of the neutral adviser and the cost of the mini-trial proceedings.

(*k*) After the termination of the mini-trial, the ICADR will apply the proceeds of the advance deposits towards any of its unpaid administrative fees and charges and the cost of the mini-trial and render an account to the parties of the deposits received and applied and return the balance to the parties in accordance with the settlement agreement or order of termination proceedings.

(2) Upon request, the ICADR will, wherever possible, provide other appropriate administrative services which will not be included in its fee for administrative services. The kind of such services details of which may be obtained from the Secretary, the ICADR, include—

(*i*) secretarial support and clerical assistance,

(*ii*) long distance and local telephone access and telex and telecopier facilities,

(*iii*) photocopy and other usual office services, and

(*iv*) provision and reservation for lodging, local conveyance and travel facilities.

21. Fees and administrative charges. (1) The fees of the neutral adviser and administrative fees of the ICADR, unless fixed otherwise, shall be computed in accordance with Schedule "B".

(2) Each party to the dispute shall deposit fifty per cent of the fee set out in Schedule "B" with the ICADR immediately on commencement of the mini-trial and not later than submission of their written statement as provided in Rule 5. The mini-trial shall not proceed until such an advance is deposited with the ICADR. If one party fails to pay the required fee the other party may deposit the total fee required. In case there are more than two parties to the dispute, the ICADR or the neutral adviser in consultation with the ICADR, will apportion the amount to be deposited.

(3) A portion of the advance fee deposited by the parties pursuant to sub-rule (2) will be towards non-refundable fee and will be contributed equally. The non-refundable portion of the advance fee is separately set out in Schedule "B" as non-refundable fee.

SCHEDULE "B"

SCHEDULE OF FEES

PART I

Mini-Trial (Domestic-Commercial)

(a) Administrative fees of the ICADR:

(referred to in rule 21)

(Where the ICADR acts as an appointing authority and administrator)

	Amount in dispute (In Rupees)	**Amount of Fee** (In Rupees)
(*i*)	where the total amount is dispute does not exceed Rs. 5,00,000	Rs. 5,000
(*ii*)	where the total amount in dispute exceeds Rs. 5,00,000 but does not exceed Rs. 10,00,000	Rs. 5,000 plus 1 per cent of the amount by which the total amount in dispute exceeds Rs. 5,00,000
(*iii*)	where the total amount in dispute the exceeds Rs. 10,00,000 but does not exceed Rs. 25,00,000	Rs. 10,000 plus 0.5 per cent of amount by which the total amount in dispute exceeds 10,00,000
(*iv*)	where the total amount in dispute exceeds Rs. 25,00,000 but does not exceed Rs. 50,00,000	Rs. 17,500 plus 0.25 per cent of the amount by which the total amount in dispute exceeds Rs. 25,00,000
(*v*)	where the total amount in dispute exceeds Rs. 50,00,000	Rs. 23,750 plus 0.125 per cent of the amount by which the total amount in dispute exceeds Rs. 50,00,000 subject to the maximum of Rs. 35,000*

---

* Where the dispute cannot be expressed in terms of money, the Secretary-General shall determine the amount of administrative fees, in his discretion, in each case.

(b) Non-refundable fee referred to in rule 21:

Rs. 5,000

(Where the ICADR acts only as an appointing authority)

(c) Fee of the Neutral Adviser

(referred to in rule 21)

	Amount in dispute (In Rupees)	**Amount of Fee** (In Rupees) For one Neutral Adviser
(*i*)	where the total amount in dispute does not exceed Rs. 5,00,000	Rs. 10,000
(*ii*)	where the total amount in dispute exceeds Rs. 5,00,000 but does not exceed Rs. 10,00,000	Rs. 10,000 plus 1 percent of the amount by which the total amount in dispute exceeds Rs. 5,00,000
(*iii*)	where the total amount in dispute exceeds Rs. 10,00,000 but does not exceed Rs. 25,00,000	Rs. 15,000 plus 0.5 percent of the amount by which the total amount in dispute exceeds Rs. 10,00,000
(*iv*)	where the total amount in dispute exceeds Rs. 25,00,000 but does not exceed Rs. 50,00,000	Rs. 22,500 plus 0.25 percent of the amount by which the total amount in dispute exceeds Rs. 25,00,000
(*v*)	where the total amount in dispute exceeds Rs. 50,00,000	Rs. 28,750 plus 0.125 percent of the amount by which the total amount in dispute exceeds Rs. 50,00,000 subject to the maximum of Rs. 1,00,000.*

(d) Charges for facilities: Rs. 1500 for one day or part thereof

(referred to in rule 21)**

PART II

Domestic Non-Commercial Mini-Trial

(a) Administrative fees of the ICADR:

(referred to in rule 21)

---

* Where the dispute cannot be expressed in terms of money, the Neutral Adviser shall determine the amount of fee in each case in consultation with the ICADR.

** Where the facilities are provided in a place other than in the ICADR's offices, the charges will be determined in each case and billed separately.

(Where the ICADR acts as an appointing authority and administrator)*

(b) Non-refundable fee (referred to in rule 21):

(Where the ICADR acts as an appointing authority)	Rs. 5,000

(c) Fee of the Neutral Adviser:

(referred to in rule 21)

The amount as determined by the Neutral Adviser in each case in consultation with the ICADR.

(d) Charges for facilities: (referred to in rule 21)	Rs. 1500 for one day or part thereof.**

PART III

International Commercial Mini-Trial

(a) Administrative fees of the ICADR:

(referred to in rule 21)

(Where the ICADR acts as an appointing authority and administrator)

Amount in dispute (In US $)	**Amount of Fee** (In US $)
(*i*) where the total amount is dispute does not exceed $50,000	$1,000
(*ii*) where the total amount in dispute exceeds $50,000 but does not exceed $1,00,000	$1,000 plus 1 percent of the amount by which the total amount in dispute exceeds $50,000
(*iii*) where the total amount in dispute exceeds $1,00,000 but does not exceed $2,50,000	$1,500 plus 0.5 percent of the amount by which the total amount in dispute exceeds $1,00,000
(*iv*) where the total amount in dispute exceeds $2,50,000 but does not exceed $5,00,000	$2,250 plus 0.25 percent of the amount by which the total amount in dispute exceeds $2,50,000

---

* Where the dispute can be expressed in terms of money, the fee will be the same as applicable for domestic commercial arbitration.

Where the dispute cannot be expressed in terms of money, the Secretary-General shall determine the amount of administrative fees, in his discretion, in each case.

** Where the facilities are provided in a place other than in the ICADR's office, the charges will be determined in each and billed separately.

(*v*) where the total amount in dispute exceeds $5,00,000	$2,875 plus 0.125 percent of the amount by which the total amount in dispute exceeds $5,00,000 subject to the maximum of $10,000*

(b) Non-refundable fee

(referred to in rule 21):	US $500
(Where the ICADR acts only as an appointing authority)	

Fee of the Neutral Adviser:

(referred to in rule 21)

Amount in dispute (In US $)	Amount of Fee (In US $)
	For one Neutral Adviser
(*i*) where the total amount is dispute does not exceed $50,000	$2,000
(*ii*) where the total amount in dispute exceeds $50,000 but does not exceed $1,00,000	$2,000 plus 1 percent of the amount by which the total amount in dispute exceeds $50,000
(*iii*) where the total amount in dispute exceeds $1,00,000 but does not exceed $2,50,000	$2,500 plus 0.5 percent of the amount by which the total amount in dispute exceeds $1,00,000
(*iv*) where the total amount in dispute exceeds $2,50,000 but does not exceed $5,00,000	$3,250 plus 0.25 percent of the amount by which the total amount in dispute exceeds $2,50,000
(*v*) where the total amount in dispute exceeds $5,00,000	$3,875 plus 0.125 percent of the amount by which the total amount in dispute exceeds $5,00,000 subject to the maximum of $50,000**

(c) Charges for facilities: (referred to in rule 21)	US $250 for one day or part thereof.***

---

* Where the dispute cannot be expressed in terms of money, the Secretary-General shall determine the amount of administrative fees, in his discretion, in each case.

** Where the dispute cannot be expressed in terms of money, the Neutral Adviser shall determine the amount of fee in each case in consultation with the ICADR.

*** Where the facilities are provided in a place other than in the ICADR's office, the charges will be determined in each case and billed separately.

SCHEDULE "C"

The Model Clause

To be used in the Agreement for providing for Mini-Trial

"The parties will attempt in good faith to resolve any dispute or claim arising out of or relating to this Agreement/Contract promptly through negotiations between the parties.

If the matter is not resolved through negotiation, the parties will attempt in good faith to resolve dispute or claim by holding mini-trial in accordance with the ICADR Mini-Trial Rules, 1996.

If the matter has not been resolved by mini-trial procedure within 90 days of the initiation of such procedure, or if either party will not participate in such procedure, the dispute shall be referred to arbitration in accordance with the ICADR Arbitration Rules, 1996.

The construction, performance and validity of this Agreement shall in all respects be governed by Indian Law.

The proceedings for mini-trial and/or arbitration will be conducted at New Delhi and in the English language."

Appendix 7

Civil Procedure Alternative Dispute Resolution and Mediation Rules 2006*

In exercise of the rule-making power under Part X of the Code of Civil Procedure, 1908 (5 of 1908) and clause (*d*) of sub-section (2) of section 89 of the said Code, the High Court at Calcutta is hereby framing the following Rules:

PART I

Alternative Dispute Resolution Rules

1. Title. These rules in Part I shall be called the 'Civil Procedure Alternative Dispute Resolution Rules, 2006'.

2. Procedure for directing parties to opt for alternative modes of settlement. (*a*) The Court shall, after recording admissions and denials at the first hearing of the suit under Rule I, Order X and where it appears to the Court that there exist elements of a settlement which may be acceptable to the parties, formulate the terms of settlement and, give them to the parties for their observations under sub-section (1) of section 89, and the parties shall submit to the Court their responses within thirty days of the first hearing:

Provided that the response may include settlement by the parties on terms other than those formulated by the court and unless unlawful, the court may act upon such settlement.

(*b*) At the next hearing, which shall be not later than thirty days of the receipt of responses, the Court may reformulate the terms of a possible settlement and shall direct the parties to opt for one of the modes of settlement of disputes outside the court as specified in clauses (*a*) to (*d*)

* *Vide* Notification No. 4679G dated 6th December 2006.

of sub-section (1) of section 89 read with Rule I-A of Order X in the manner stated hereunder:

Provided that the court, in the exercise of such power, shall not refer any dispute to arbitration or to judicial settlement by a person or institution without the written consent of all the parties to the suit.

3. Persons authorized to take decision for the Union of India, State Governments and others. (1) For the purpose of Rule 2, the Union of India or the Government of a State of Union Territory, all local authorities, all Public Sector Undertakings, all statutory corporations and all public authorities shall nominate a person or persons on group of persons who are authorized to take a final decision as to the mode of alternative dispute resolution in which it proposes to opt in the event of direction by the Court under section 89 and such nomination shall be communicated to the High Court within the period of three months from the date of commencement of these Rules and the High Court shall notify all the subordinate courts in this behalf as soon as such nomination is received from such Government authorities.

(2) Where such person or persons or group of persons have not been nominated as aforesaid, such party as referred to in clause (1) shall, if it is a plaintiff, file along with the plaint or if it is a defendant, file along with or before the filing of the written statement, a memo into the Court, nominating a person or persons or group of persons who is or are authorized to take a final decision as to the mode of alternative dispute resolution, which the party refers to adopt in the event of the Court directing the party to opt for one or other mode of alternative dispute resolution.

4. Court to give guidance to parties while giving direction to opt. (*a*) Before directing the parties to exercise option under clause (*b*) of Rule 2, the Court shall give such guidance as it deems fit to the parties, by drawing their attention to the relevant factors which parties will have to take into account, before they exercise their option as to the particular mode of settlement, namely:

(*i*) that it will be to the advantage of the parties, so far as time and expense are concerned, to opt for one or other of these modes of settlement referred to in section 89 rather than seek a trial on the disputes arising in the suit;

(*ii*) that, where there is no relationship between the parties which requires to be preserved, it may be in the interest of the parties to seek reference of the matter of arbitration as envisaged in clause (*a*) of sub-section (1) of section 89;

(*iii*) that, where there is a relationship between the parties which requires to be preserved, it may be in the interest of parties to seek reference of the matter to conciliation or mediation, as envisaged in clause (*b*) or (*d*) of sub-section (1) of section 89;

Explanation. Disputes arising out of matrimonial, maintenance and child-custody matters shall, among others, be treated as the cases where a relationship between the parties has to be preserved.

(*iv*) that, where parties are interested in a final settlement which may lead to a compromise, it will be in the interests of the parties to seek reference of the matter to the Lok Adalat or to judicial settlement as envisaged in clause (*c*) of sub-section (1) of section 89;

(*v*) the difference between the different modes of settlement, namely, arbitration, conciliation, mediation and judicial settlement is explained below:

Settlement by *'arbitration'* means the process by which an arbitrator appointed by the parties or by the Court, as the case may be, adjudicates the disputes between the parties to the suit and passes an award by the application of the provisions of the Arbitration and Conciliation Act 1996 (26 of 1996), insofar as they refer to arbitration.

Settlement by *'conciliation'* means the process by which a conciliator who is appointed by the parties or by the Court, as the case may be, conciliates the disputes between the parties to the suit by the application of the provisions of the Arbitration and Conciliation Act, 1996 (26 of 1996) insofar as they relate to conciliation, and in particular, in exercise of his powers under sections 67 and 73 of that Act, by making proposals for a settlement of the dispute and by formulating or reformulating the terms of a possible settlement and has a greater role than that of a mediator.

Settlement by *'mediation'* means the process by which a mediator appointed by the parties or by the Court, as the case may be, mediates the dispute between the parties to the suit by the application of the provisions of the Mediation Rules, 2006 in Part II, and in particular, by facilitating discussion between parties directly or by communicating with each other through the mediator, by assisting parties in identifying issues, reducing misunderstandings, clarifying priorities, exploring areas of compromise, generating options in an attempt to solve the dispute and emphasizing that it is the parties' own responsibility for making decisions which affect them.

Settlement in the *Lok Adalat* means settlement by the Lok Adalat as contemplated by the Legal Services Authorities Act, 1987.

'Judicial settlement' means a final settlement by way of compromise entered into before a suitable institution or person to which the Court has referred the dispute and such institution or person is deemed to be the Lok Adalats under the provisions of the Legal Services Authorities Act, 1987 (39 of 1987) and where after such reference, the provisions

of the said Act apply as if the dispute was referred to a Lok Adalat under the provisions of that Act.

5. Procedure for reference by the Court to the different modes of settlement. (*a*) Where all the parties to the suit decide to exercise their option and to agree for settlement by arbitration, they shall apply to the Court, within thirty days of the direction of the Court under clause (*b*) of Rule 2 and the Court shall, within thirty days of the said application, refer the matter to arbitration and thereafter the provisions of the Arbitration and Conciliation Act 1996 (26 of 1996) which are applicable after the stage of making of the reference to arbitration under the Act, shall apply as if the proceedings were referred for settlement by way of arbitration under the provisions of that Act.

(*b*) Where all the parties to the suit decide to exercise their option and to agree for settlement by the Lok Adalat or where one of the parties applies for reference to the Lok Adalat, the procedure envisaged under the Legal Services Authorities Act, 1987 and in particular, by section 20 of that Act shall apply.

(*c*) Where all the parties to the suit decide to exercise their option and to agree on a judicial settlement, they shall apply to the Court within thirty days of the direction under clause (*b*) of Rule 2 and then, the Court shall, within thirty days of the application, refer the matter to a suitable institution or person and such institution or person shall be deemed to be a Lok Adalat and thereafter, the provisions of the Legal Services Authorities Act 1987 (39 of 1987) which are applicable after the stage of making of the reference to the Lok Adalat under that Act, shall apply as if the proceedings were referred for settlement under the provisions of that Act.

(*d*) Where none of the parties are willing to agree to opt or agree to refer the dispute to arbitration, or the Lok Adalat, or to a judicial settlement, within thirty days of the direction of the Court under clause (*b*) of Rule 2, they shall consider if they could agree for a reference to conciliation or mediation, within the same period.

(*e*) (*i*) Where all the parties opt and agree for conciliation, they shall apply to the Court, within thirty days of the direction under clause (*b*) of Rule 2 and the Court shall, within thirty days of the application refer the matter to conciliation and thereafter the provisions of the Arbitration and Conciliation Act, 1996 (26 of 1996) which are applicable after the stage of making of the reference to conciliation under the Act, shall apply, as if the proceedings were referred for settlement by way of conciliation under the provisions of that Act.

(*ii*) Where all the parties opt and agree for mediation, they shall apply to the Court, within thirty days of the direction under clause (*b*) of Rule 2 and the Court shall, within thirty days of the application, refer the matter to mediation and then, the Mediation Rules 2003 in Part II shall apply.

(*f*) Where under clause (*d*), all the parties are not able to opt and agree for conciliation or mediation, one or more of the parties may apply to the Court within thirty days of the direction under clause (*b*) of Rule 2, seeking settlement through conciliation or mediation, as the case may be, and in that event, the Court shall within a further period of thirty days, issue notice to the other parties to respond to the application, and

(*i*) In case all the parties agree for conciliation, the Court shall refer the matter to conciliation and thereafter, the provisions of the Arbitration and Conciliation Act 1996 which are applicable after the stage of making of the reference to conciliation under that Act, shall apply.

(*ii*) In case all the parties agree for mediation, the Court shall refer the matter to mediation in accordance with the Civil Procedure Mediation Rules, 2003 in Part II shall apply.

(*iii*) In case all the parties do not agree and where it appears to the Court that there exist elements of a settlement which may be acceptable to the parties and that there is a relationship between the parties which has to be reserved, the Court shall refer the matter to conciliation or mediation, as the case may be. In case the dispute is referred to conciliation, the provisions of the Arbitration and Conciliation Act, 1996 which are applicable after the stage of making of the reference to conciliation under that Act and in case the dispute is referred to mediation, the provisions of the Civil Procedure Mediation Rules, 2003, shall apply.

(*g*) (*i*) Where none of the parties apply for reference either to arbitration or the Lok Adalat, or judicial settlement, or for conciliation or mediation, within thirty days of the direction under clause (*b*) of Rule 2, the court shall, within a further period of thirty days, issue notices to the parties or their representatives fixing the matter for hearing on the question of making a reference either to conciliation or mediation.

(*ii*) After hearing the parties or their representative on the day so fixed, the court shall, if there exist elements of a settlement which may be acceptable to the parties and there is a relationship between the parties which has to be preserved, refer the matter to conciliation or mediation. In case the dispute is referred to conciliation, the provisions of the Arbitration and Conciliation Act, 1996 which are applicable after the stage of making of the reference to conciliation under the Act shall apply and in case the dispute is referred to mediation, the provisions of the Civil Procedure Mediation Rules, 2006 shall apply.

(*h*) (*i*) No next friend or guardian for the suit shall, without the leave of the court expressly recorded in the proceedings of the court, opt for any one of the modes of alternative dispute resolution nor shall he enter into any settlement on behalf of a minor or person under disability with reference to the suit in which he acts as mere next friend or guardian.

(*ii*) Where an application is made to the court for leave to enter into a settlement through the alternative dispute resolution proceedings on behalf of a minor or other person under legal disability and such minor or other person under disability is represented by a counsel or a pleader, the counsel or the pleader shall file a certificate along with the said application to the effect that the settlement is, in his opinion, for the benefit of the minor or other person under disability. The decree of the court based on the settlement to which the minor or other person under legal disability is a party, shall refer to the sanction of the court thereto and shall set out the terms of the settlement.

6. Referral to the court and appearance before the Court upon failure of attempts to settle disputes by conciliation or judicial settlement or mediation. (1) Where a suit has been referred for settlement for conciliation, mediation or judicial settlement and has not been settled or where it is felt that it would not be proper in the interest of justice to proceed further with the matter, the suit shall be referred back again to the Court with a direction to the parties to appear before the Court on a specific date.

(2) Upon the reference of the matter back to the Court under sub-rule (1) or under sub-section (5) of section 20 of the Legal Services Authorities Act, 1987, the Court shall proceed with the suit in accordance with law.

7. Training in alternative methods of resolution of disputes, and preparation of manual. (*a*) The High Court shall take steps to have training courses conducted in places where the High Court and the District Courts or Courts of equal status are located, by requesting any institution recognised by the High Court or the universities imparting legal education or retired faculty members thereof or other persons who, according to the High Court, are well versed in the techniques of alternative methods of resolution of disputes, to conduct training courses for the lawyers and the judicial officers.

(*b*) (*i*) The High Court shall nominate a committee of judges, faculty members including retired persons belonging to the above categories, senior members of the Bar, other members of the Bar specially qualified in the techniques of alternative dispute resolution, for the purpose referred to in clause (*a*) and for the purpose of preparing a detailed manual of procedure for alternative dispute resolution to be used by the Courts in the State as well as by the arbitrators, or authority or person in the case of judicial settlement or the conciliators or the mediators.

(*ii*) The said manual shall describe the various methods of alternative dispute resolution, the manner in which any one of the said methods is to be opted for, the suitability of any particular method for any particular type of dispute and shall specifically deal with the role of the above persons in the disputes which are commercial or domestic in nature or which relate to matrimonial, maintenance and child-custody matters.

(*c*) The High Court and the District Courts shall periodically conduct seminars and workshops on the subject of alternative dispute resolution procedures throughout the State or States over which the High Court has jurisdiction with a view to bring awareness of such procedures and to impart training to the lawyers and the judicial officers.

(*d*) Persons who have experience in the matter of alternative dispute resolution procedures, and in particular, in regard to conciliation and mediation, shall be given preference in the matter of empanelment for the purposes of conciliation or mediation.

8. Applicability to other proceedings. The provisions of these Rules may be applied to the proceedings before the Courts, including the Family Courts constituted under the Family Courts Act (66 of 1984), while dealing with the matrimonial, maintenance and child-custody-disputes, wherever necessary, in addition to the rules framed under the Family Courts Act (66 of 1984).

9. Until the manual referred to in Rule 7 is prepared by the High Court, the Courts mentioned in Rule 2, may nominate the person indicated in Rule 5 hereof of its choice provided such person has the requisite qualification and is otherwise suitable.

PART II

Civil Procedure Mediation Rules

1. Title. These Rules in Part II shall be called the Civil Procedure Mediation Rules, 2006.

2. Appointment of mediator. (*a*) Parties to a suit may all agree on the name of the sole mediator for mediating between them.

(*b*) Where, there are two sets of parties and are unable to agree on a sole mediator, each set of parties shall nominate a mediator.

(*c*) Where parties agree on a sole mediator under clause (*a*) or where parties nominate more than one mediator under clause (*b*), the mediator need not necessarily be from the panel of the mediators referred to in

Rule 3 nor should he possess the qualifications referred to in Rule 4 but he should not be a person who suffers from the disqualifications referred to in Rule 5.

(*d*) Where there are more than two sets of parties having diverse interests, each set shall nominate a person on its behalf and the said nominees shall select the sole mediator and failing unanimity in that behalf, the Court shall appoint a sole mediator.

3. Panel of mediators. (*a*) The High Court shall, for the purpose of appointing mediators between the parties in suits filed on its original side, prepare a panel of mediators and publish the same on its notice board, within thirty days of the coming into force of these Rules, with a copy to the Bar Association, Bar Library Club and The Incorporated Law Society.

(*b*) (*i*) The Courts of the Principal District and Sessions Judge in each district or the Courts of the Principal Judge of the City Civil Court or the courts of equal status shall, for the purposes of appointing mediators to mediate between parties in suits filed on their original side, prepare a panel of mediators, within a period of sixty days of the commencement of these Rules. After obtaining the approval of the High Court to the names included in the panel, the same shall be published on the respective notice boards.

(*c*) The consent of the persons whose names are included in the panel shall be obtained before empanelling them.

(*d*) The panel of names shall contain a detailed annexure giving details of the qualifications of the mediators and their professional or technical experience in different fields.

4. Qualifications of persons to be empanelled under Rule 3. The following persons shall be treated as qualified and eligible for being enlisted in the panel of mediators under Rule 3, namely:

(*a*) (*i*) Retired Judges of the Supreme Court of India;

(*ii*) Retired Judges of the High Court;

(*iii*) Retired District and Sessions Judges or retired Judges of the City Civil Court or courts of equivalent status.

(*b*) Legal practitioners with at least fifteen years' standing at the Bar at the level of the Supreme Court or the High Court or the District Courts or the courts of equivalent status.

(*c*) Experts or other professionals with at least fifteen years' standing;

(*d*) Institutions which are themselves experts in mediation and have been recognized as such by the High Court, provided the names of its members are approved by the High Court initially or whenever there is change in membership.

5. Disqualifications of persons. The following persons shall be deemed to be disqualified for being empanelled as mediators:

(*i*) any person who has been adjudged as insolvent or is declared of unsound mind, or

(*ii*) any person against whom criminal charges involving moral turpitude are framed by a criminal court and are pending, or

(*iii*) any person who has been convicted by a criminal court for any offence involving moral turpitude,

(*iv*) any person against whom disciplinary proceedings or charges relating to moral turpitude have been initiated by the appropriate disciplinary authority which are pending or have resulted in a punishment,

(*v*) any person who is interested or connected with the subject-matter of dispute or is related to any one of the parties or to those who represent them, unless such objection is waived by all the parties in writing,

(*vi*) any legal practitioner who has or is appearing for any of the parties in the suit or in any other suit or proceedings,

(*vii*) such other categories of persons as may be notified by the High Court.

6. Venue for conducting mediation. The mediator shall conduct the mediation at one or other of the following places:

(*i*) Venue of the Lok Adalat or permanent Lok Adalat.

(*ii*) Any place specified by the District Judge within the court precincts for the purpose of conducting mediation.

(*iii*) Any place specified by the Bar Association or State Bar Council for the purpose of mediation, within the premises of the Bar Association or State Bar Council, as the case may be.

(*iv*) Any other place as may be agreed upon by the parties subject to the approval of the court.

7. Preference. The Court shall, while nominating any person from the panel of mediators referred to in Rule 3, consider his suitability for resolving the particular class of dispute involved in the suit and shall give preference to those who have proven-record of successful mediation or who have special qualification or experience in mediation.

8. Duty of mediator to disclose certain facts. (*a*) When a person is approached in connection with his possible appointment as a mediator, the person shall disclose in writing to the parties any circumstances likely to give rise to a justifiable doubt as to his independence or impartiality.

(*b*) Every mediator shall, from the time of his appointment and throughout the continuance of the mediation proceedings, without delay, disclose to the parties in writing about the existence of any of the circumstances referred to in clause (*a*).

9. Cancellation of appointment. Upon information furnished by the mediator under Rule 8 or upon any other information received from the parties or other persons, if the Court, in which the suit is filed, is satisfied after conducting such inquiry, as it deems fit, and after giving a hearing to the mediator, that the said information has raised a justifiable doubt as to the mediator's independence or impartiality, it shall cancel the appointment by a reasoned order and replace him by another mediator.

10. Removal or deletion from panel. A person, whose name is placed in the panel referred to in Rule 3, may be removed or his name may be deleted from the said panel, by the Court which empanelled him, if:

(*i*) he resigns or withdraws his name from the panel for any reason; or

(*ii*) he is declared insolvent or is declared of unsound mind; or

(*iii*) he is a person against whom criminal charges involving moral turpitude are framed by a criminal court and are pending; or

(*iv*) he is a person who has been convicted by a criminal court for any offence involving moral turpitude; or

(*v*) he is a person against whom disciplinary proceedings on charges relating to moral turpitude have been initiated by the appropriate disciplinary authority which are pending or have resulted in a punishment; or

(*vi*) he exhibits or displays conduct, during the continuance of the mediation proceedings, which is unbecoming of a mediator; or

(*vii*) the Court which empanelled, upon receipt of information, if it is satisfied, after conducting such inquiry as it deems fit, is of the view that it is not possible or desirable to continue the name of that person in the panel:

Provided that, before removing or deleting his name, under clauses (*vi*) and (*vii*), the Court shall hear the mediator whose name is proposed to be removed or deleted from the panel and shall pass a reasoned order.

11. Procedure of mediation. (*a*) The parties may agree on the procedure to be followed by the mediator in the conduct of the mediation proceedings.

(*b*) Where the parties do not agree on any particular procedure to be followed by the mediator, the mediator shall follow the procedure hereinafter mentioned, namely:

(*i*) he shall fix, in consultation with the parties, a time-schedule, the dates and the time of each mediation-session, where all parties have to be present;

(*ii*) he shall hold the mediation-conference in accordance with the provisions of Rule 6;

(*iii*) he may conduct joint or separate meetings with the parties;

(*iv*) each party shall, ten days before a session, provide to the mediator a brief note setting forth the issues, which according to it, need to be resolved, and its position in respect to those issues and all information reasonably required for the mediator to understand the issue; such memoranda shall also be mutually exchanged between the parties;

(*v*) each party shall furnish to the mediator, *copies of pleadings or documents* or such other information as may be required by him in connection with the issues to be resolved:

Provided that where the mediator is of the opinion that he should look into any original document, the Court may permit him to look into the original document before such officer of the Court and on such date or time as the Court may fix;

(*vi*) Each party shall furnish to the mediator such other information as may be required by him in connection with the issues to be resolved.

(*c*) Where there is more than one mediator, the mediator nominated by each party shall first confer with the party that nominated him and shall thereafter interact with the other mediators, with a view to resolving the disputes.

12. Mediator not bound by the Evidence Act, 1872 or the Code of Civil Procedure, 1908. The mediator shall not be bound by the Code of Civil Procedure, 1908 or the Evidence Act, 1872, but shall be guided by the principles of fairness and justice, having regard to the rights and obligations of the parties, usages of trade, if any, and the nature of the dispute.

13. Non-attendance of parties at sessions or meetings on due dates. (*a*) The parties shall be present personally or may be represented by their counsel or power-of-attorney holders at the meetings or sessions notified by the mediator.

(*b*) If a party fails to attend a session or a meeting notified by the mediator, other parties or the mediator can apply to the court in which the suit is filed, to issue appropriate directions to that party to attend before the mediator and if the court finds that a party is absenting himself before the mediator without sufficient reason, the court may take action against the said party by imposition of costs.

(*c*) The parties not resident in India may be represented by their counsel or power-of-attorney-holders at the sessions or meetings.

14. Administrative assistance. In order to facilitate the conduct of mediation proceedings, the parties, or the mediator with the consent of the parties, may arrange for administrative assistance by a suitable institution or person.

15. Offer of settlement by parties. Any party to the suit may, "without prejudice", offer a settlement to the other party at any stage of the proceedings, with notice to the mediator.

16. Role of the mediator. The mediator shall attempt to facilitate voluntary resolution of the dispute by the parties, and communicate the view of each party to the other, assist them in identifying issues, reducing misunderstandings, clarifying priorities, exploring areas of compromise and generating options in an attempt to solve the dispute, emphasizing that it is the responsibility of the parties to take decisions which affect them; he shall not impose any terms of settlement on the parties.

17. Parties alone responsible for taking decision. The parties must understand that the mediator only facilitates in arriving at a decision to resolve disputes and that he will not and cannot impose any settlement nor does the mediator give any warranty that the mediation will result in a settlement. The mediator shall not impose any decision on the parties.

18. Time-limit for completion of mediation. On the expiry of sixty days from the date fixed for the first appearance of the parties before the mediator, the mediation shall stand terminated, unless the court, which referred the matter, either *suo motu*, or upon request by the mediator or any of the parties, and upon hearing all the parties, is of the view that extension of time is necessary or may be useful; but such extension shall not be beyond a further period of thirty days.

19. Parties to act in good faith. While no one can be compelled to commit to settle his case in advance of mediation, all parties shall commit to participate in the proceedings in good faith with the intention to settle the dispute, if possible.

20. Confidentiality, disclosure and inadmissibility of information. (1) When a mediator receives confidential information concerning the dispute from any party, he shall disclose the substance of that information to the other party, if permitted in writing by the first party.

(2) When a party gives information to the mediator subject to a specifie condition that it should be kept confidential, the mediator shall not disclose that information to the other party, nor shall the mediator

voluntarily divulge any information regarding any document or what is conveyed to him orally or as to what transpired during the mediation.

(3) Receipts or perusal, or preparation of records, reports or other documents by the mediator, or receipt of information orally by the mediator while serving in that capacity, shall be confidential and the mediator shall not be compelled to divulge any information regarding the documents nor in regard to the oral information nor as to what transpired during the mediation.

(4) Parties shall maintain confidentiality in respect of the events that transpired during mediation and shall not rely on or introduce the said information in any other proceedings as to:

(*a*) views expressed by a party in the course of the mediation proceedings;

(*b*) documents obtained during the mediation which were expressly required to be treated as confidential or other notes, drafts or information given by the parties or the mediators;

(*c*) proposals made or views expressed by the mediator;

(*d*) admission made by a party in course of the mediation proceedings;

(*e*) the fact that a party had or had not indicated willingness to accept a proposal;

(5) There shall be no stenographic or audio or video recording of the mediation proceedings.

21. Privacy. Mediation sessions and meetings are private; only the parties or their counsel or power-of-attorney-holders concerned can attend. Other persons may attend only with the permission of the parties and with the consent of the mediator.

22. Immunity. No mediator shall be held liable for anything *bona fide* done or omitted to be done by him during the mediation proceedings for civil or criminal action nor shall he be summoned by any party to the suit to appear in a court of law to testify in regard to any information received by him or action taken by him or in respect of drafts or records prepared by him or shown to him during the mediation proceedings.

23. Communication between mediator and the court. (*a*) In order to preserve the confidence of parties in the Court and the neutrality of the mediator, there should be no communication between the mediator and the court, except as stated in clauses (*b*) and (*c*) of this Rule.

(*b*) If any communication between the mediator and the court is necessary, it shall be in writing and the copies of the same shall be given to the parties or their counsel or the constituted attorney representing such party.

(*c*) Communication between the mediator and the court shall be restricted to the following matters:

(*i*) about the failure of the party to attend;

(*ii*) regarding the assessment of the mediator that the case is not suited for settlement through mediation;

(*iii*) the information that the parties have settled the dispute or disputes;

(*iv*) such other matters as the parties may agree in writing as provided in clause (*b*) above.

24. Settlement agreement. (1) Where an agreement is reached between the parties in regard to all the issues in the suit or some of the issues, the same shall be reduced to writing and signed by the parties or their constituted attorney representing them. If any counsel have represented the parties, they shall attest the signature of their respective clients.

(2) The agreement of the parties so signed and attested shall be submitted to the mediator who shall, with a covering letter signed by him, forward the same to the court in which the suit is pending.

(3) Where no agreement is arrived at between the parties before the time-limit stated in Rule 18 or where, the mediator is of the view that no settlement is possible, he shall report the same to the said court in writing.

25. Court to fix a date for recording settlement and passing decree. (1) Within seven days of the receipt of any settlement, the Court shall issue notice to the parties fixing a day for recording the settlement, such date not being beyond a further period of fourteen days from the date of receipt of settlement, and the Court shall record the settlement, if it is not illegal or opposed to Public Policy or collusive.

(2) The Court shall then pass a decree in accordance with the settlement so recorded, if the settlement disposes of all the issues in the suit.

(3) If the settlement disposes of only certain issues arising in the suit, the Court shall record the settlement on the date fixed for recording the settlement and

(*i*) If the issues are severable from the other issues and if a decree could be passed to the extent of the settlement covered by those issues, the Court may pass a decree straight away in accordance with the settlement on those issues without waiting for a decision of the court on the other issues which are not settled.

(*ii*) If the issues are not severable, the Court shall wait for a decision of the Court on the other issues which are not settled.

26. Fees of the mediator and costs. (1) At the time of referring the disputes to mediation, the Court shall, after consulting the mediator and the parties, fix the fees of the mediator.

(2) As far as possible a consolidated sum may be fixed rather than for each session or meeting.

(3) Where there are two mediators as in clause (*b*) of Rule 2, the Court shall fix the fees payable to the mediators which shall be shared equally by the two sets of parties.

(4) The expenses of the mediation including the fees of the mediator, costs of administrative assistance, and other ancillary expenses concerned, shall be borne equally by the various contesting parties or as may be otherwise directed by the Court.

(5) Each party shall bear the costs for production of witnesses on his side including that of experts, or for production of documents.

(6) The mediator may, before the commencement of the mediation, direct the parties to deposit equal sums, tentatively, to the extent of 30% of the probable costs of the mediation, as referred to in clauses (1), (3) and (4). The remaining 70% shall be deposited with the mediator, after the conclusion of mediation. For the amount of costs paid to the mediator, he shall issue the necessary receipts and a statement of account shall be filed by the mediator in the Court.

(7) In the event the expenses of the mediation including the fees are not paid by the parties, the Court shall, on the application of the mediator or the parties, direct the parties concerned to pay, and if they do not pay, the Court shall recover the said amount as if there was a decree for the said amount.

(8) Where a party is entitled to the legal aid under section 12 of the Legal Services Authorities Act, 1987, the amount of the fees payable to the mediator and costs shall be paid by the Legal Services Authority concerned under that Act.

27. Ethics to be followed by the mediator. The mediator shall:

(1) follow and observe these Rules strictly and with the due diligence;

(2) not carry on any activity or conduct which could reasonably be considered as conduct unbecoming of a mediator;

(3) uphold the integrity and fairness of the mediation process;

(4) ensure that the parties involved in the mediation are fairly informed and have an adequate understanding of the procedural aspects of the process;

(5) satisfy himself/herself that he/she is qualified to undertake and complete the assignment in a professional manner;

(6) disclose any interest or relationship likely to affect impartiality or which might seek an appearance of partiality or bias;

(7) avoid, while communicating with the parties, any impropriety or appearance of impropriety;

(8) be faithful to the relationship of trust and confidentiality reposed in the office of the mediator;

(9) conduct all proceedings related to the resolutions of a dispute in accordance with the applicable law;

(10) recognize that the mediation is based on the principle of self-determination by the parties and that the mediation process relies upon the ability of the parties to reach a voluntary, undisclosed agreement;

(11) maintain the reasonable expectations of the parties as to confidentiality;

(12) refrain from promises or guarantees of results.

28. Transitory provisions. Until a panel of the mediators is prepared by the High Court and the District Court, the courts referred to in Rule 3, may nominate a mediator of their choice if the mediator belongs to the various classes of persons referred to in Rule 4 and is duly qualified and is not disqualified, taking into account the suitability of the mediator for resolving the particular dispute.

Appendix 8

The Commercial Courts Act 2015

Chapter IIIA

PRE-INSTITUTION MEDIATION AND SETTLEMENT

12A. Pre-institution Mediation and Settlement. (1) A suit, which does not contemplate any urgent interim relief under this Act, shall not be instituted unless the plaintiff exhausts the remedy of pre-institution mediation in accordance with such manner and procedure as may be prescribed by rules made by the Central Government.

(2) The Central Government may, by notification, authorise the Authorities constituted under the Legal Services Authorities Act, 1987 (39 of 1987), for the purposes of pre-institution mediation.

(3) Notwithstanding anything contained in the Legal Services Authorities Act, 1987 (39 of 1987), the Authority authorised by the Central Government under sub-section (2) shall complete the process of mediation within a period of three months from the date of application made by the plaintiff under sub-section (1):

Provided that the period of mediation may be extended for a further period of two months with the consent of the parties:

Provided further that, the period during which the parties remained occupied with the pre-institution mediation, such period shall not be computed for the purpose of limitation under the Limitation Act, 1963 (36 of 1963).

(4) If the parties to the commercial dispute arrive at a settlement, the same shall be reduced into writing and shall be signed by the parties to the dispute and the mediator.

(5) The settlement arrived at under this section shall have the same status and effect as if it is an arbitral award on agreed terms under sub-section (4) of section 30 of the Arbitration and Conciliation Act, 1996 (26 of 1996).

Comments

Section 12A of the Commercial Courts Act 2015 provides that a suit, where no urgent relief is sought for under the Act, shall not be instituted without the plaintiff exhausting the remedy of pre-institution mediation according to the procedure prescribed by the rules made by the Central Government. The Central Government may by way of notification authorise the Authorities constituted under the Legal Services Authorities Act 1987 for the purposes of pre-institution mediation, and such authority authorised by the Central Government under the Legal Services Authorities Act 1987 shall complete the process of mediation within a period of three months from the date of application made by the plaintiff under sub-section (1). It must be noted that the provisions contained under the Legal Services Authorities Act 1987 shall not a bar to such authority to act under sub-section (3). However, such period may be extended to a further period of two months with the consent of the parties. Moreover, the duration of time taken by the parties to get occupied in pre-institution mediation shall not be computed for the purpose of limitation under the Limitation Act 1963. As a result of such pre-institution mediation, if the parties to the commercial dispute arrive at a settlement, the settlement shall be reduced into writing and signed by the parties to the dispute and the mediator. The settlement shall be treated as an arbitral award on agreed terms under section 30(4) of the Arbitration and Conciliations Act 1996.

Appendix 9

The Commercial Courts (Pre-Institution Mediation and Settlement) Rules 2018*

In exercise of the powers conferred by sub-section (2) of section 21-A read with sub-section (1) of section 12-A of the Commercial Courts Act, 2015 (4 of 2016), the Central Government hereby makes the following rules, namely:—

1. **Short title and commencement.** (1) These rules may be called the Commercial Courts (Pre-Institution Mediation and Settlement) Rules, 2018.

(2) They shall come into force on the date of their publication in the Official Gazette.

2. Definitions. (1) In these rules unless the context otherwise requires,—

(a) "Act" means the Commercial Courts Act, 2015 (4 of 2016);

(*b*) "applicant" means a person who approaches the Authority under rule 3 for the initiation of mediation process;

(*c*) "Authority" means the Authority notified by the Central Government under sub-section (2) of section 12-A of the Act;

(*d*) "commercial dispute" means the commercial dispute as defined in clause (*c*) of sub-section (1) of section 2 of the Act;

(*d*) "Form" means the Form specified in the Schedule to these rules;

---

* *Vide* G.S.R. 606(E), dated 3-7-2018, published in the Gazette of India, Ext., Pt. II, section 3(*i*), dated 3-7-2018.

(*e*) "mediation" means a process undertaken by a Mediator to resolve, reconcile and settle a commercial dispute between the parties thereto;

(*f*) "Mediator" means a person empanelled by the Authority for conducting the mediation;

(*g*) "opposite party" means a party against whom relief is sought in a commercial dispute;

(*h*) "Schedule" means the Schedule appended to these rules; and

(*i*) "settlement" means the settlement of commercial dispute arrived at by the parties to the mediation.

(2) The words and expressions used and not defined in these rules, shall have the same meanings respectively as assigned to them in the Act or the Legal Services Authorities Act, 1987 (39 of 1987) or in any other law for the time being in force.

3. Initiation of mediation process. (1) A party to a commercial dispute may make an application to the Authority as per Form 1 specified in Schedule I, either online or by post or by hand, for initiation of mediation process under the Act along with a fee of one thousand rupees payable to the Authority either by way of demand draft or through online;

(2) The Authority shall, having regard to the territorial and pecuniary jurisdiction and the nature of commercial dispute, issue a notice, as per Form 2 specified in Schedule I through a registered or speed post and electronic means including e-mail and the like to the opposite party to appear and give consent to participate in the mediation process on such date not beyond a period of ten days from the date of issue of the said notice.

(3) Where no response is received from the opposite party either by post or by e-mail, the Authority shall issue a final notice to it in the manner as specified in sub-rule (2).

(4) Where the notice issued under sub-rule (3) remains unacknowledged or where the opposite party refuses to participate in the mediation process, the Authority shall treat the mediation process to be a non-starter and make a report as per Form 3 specified in the Schedule I and endorse the same to the applicant and the opposite party.

(5) Where the opposite party, after receiving the notice under sub-rule (2) or (3) seeks further time for his appearance, the Authority may, if it thinks fit, fix an alternate date not later than ten days from the date of receipt of such request from the opposite party.

(6) Where the opposite party fails to appear on the date fixed under sub-rule (5), the Authority shall treat the mediation process to be a non-starter and make a report in this behalf as per Form 3 specified in Schedule I and endorse the same to the applicant and the opposite party.

(7) Where both the parties to the commercial dispute appear before the Authority and give consent to participate in the mediation process, the Authority shall assign the commercial dispute to a Mediator and fix a date for their appearance before the said Mediator.

(8) The Authority shall ensure that the mediation process is completed within a period of three months from the date of receipt of application for pre-institution mediation unless the period is extended for further two months with the consent of the applicant and the opposite party.

4. Venue for conducting mediation. The venue for conducting of the mediation shall be the premises of the Authority.

5. Role of Mediator. The Mediator shall, on receipt of the assignment under sub-rule (7) of rule 3, facilitate the voluntary resolution of the commercial dispute between the parties and assist them in reaching a settlement.

6. Representation of parties. A party to a commercial dispute shall appear before the Authority or Mediator, as the case may be, either personally or through his duly authorised representative or Counsel.

7. Procedure of mediation. (1) The mediation shall be conducted as per the following procedure—

(i) At the commencement of mediation, the Mediator shall explain to the parties the mediation process;

(ii) The date and time of each mediation sitting shall be fixed by the Mediator in consultation with the parties to the commercial dispute.

(iii) The Mediator may, during the course of mediation, hold meetings with the parties jointly or separately, as he thinks fit;

(iv) The applicant or opposite party may share their settlement proposals with the Mediator in separate sittings with specific instruction as to what part thereof can be shared with the other party;

(v) The parties to the mediation can exchange settlement proposals with each other during mediation sitting either orally or in writing;

(*vi*) During the process of mediation, the Mediator shall maintain confidentiality of discussions made in the separate sittings with each party and only those facts which a party permits can be shared with the other party;

(*vii*) Once both the parties reach to a mutually agreed settlement, the same shall be reduced in writing by the Mediator and shall be signed by the parties to the commercial dispute and the Mediator as per Form 4 specified in the Schedule I;

(*viii*) The Mediator shall provide the settlement agreement, in original, to all the parties to a commercial dispute and shall also forward a signed copy of the same to the Authority; and

(*ix*) Where no settlement is arrived at between the parties within the time specified in the sub-section (3) of section 12-A of the Act or where the Mediator is of the opinion that the settlement is not possible, the Mediator shall submit a report to the Authority, with reasons in writing, as per Form 5 specified in Schedule I.

(2) The Authority or the Mediator, as the case may be, shall not retain the hard or soft copies of the documents exchanged between the parties or submitted to the Mediator or notes prepared by the Mediator beyond a period of six months other than the application for mediation under sub-rule (1) of rule 3, notice issued under sub-rule (2) or (3) of rule 3, settlement agreement under clause (*vii*) of sub-rule (1) of rule 7 and the Failure report under clause (*ix*) of sub-rule (1) of rule 7.

8. Parties to act in good faith. All the parties to a commercial dispute shall participate in the mediation process in good faith with an intention to settle the dispute.

9. Confidentiality of mediation. The Mediator, parties or their authorized representatives or Counsel shall maintain confidentiality about the mediation and the Mediator shall not allow stenographic or audio or video recording of the mediation sittings.

10. Maintenance and publication of mediation data. (1) The District Legal Services Authority shall forward the detailed data of the mediation dealt by it under the Act to the State Legal Services Authority.

(2) The State Legal Services Authority shall, maintain the data of all mediations carried out by it or under its jurisdiction and publish the same, on quarterly basis, on its website as per Form 6 specified in the Schedule I.

11. Mediation Fee. Before the commencement of the mediation, the parties to the commercial dispute shall pay to the Authority a one-time mediation fee, to be shared equally, as per the quantum of claim as specified in Schedule II.

12. Ethics to be followed by Mediator. The Mediator shall—

(*i*) uphold the integrity and fairness of the mediation process;

(*ii*) ensure that the parties involved in the mediation are fairly informed and have an adequate understanding of the procedural aspects of the mediation process;

(*iii*) disclose any financial interest or other interest in the subject-matter of the commercial dispute;

(*iv*) avoid any impropriety, while communicating with the parties to the commercial dispute;

(*v*) be faithful to the relationship of trust and confidentiality reposed in him;

(*vi*) conduct mediation related to the resolution of a commercial dispute, in accordance with the applicable laws for the time being in force;

(*vii*) recognise that the mediation is based on the principles of self-determination by the parties and that mediation process relies upon the ability of parties to reach a voluntary agreement;

(*viii*) refrain from promises or guarantees of results;

(*ix*) not meet the parties, their representatives, or their counsels or communicate with them, privately except during the mediation sittings in the premises of the Authority;

(*x*) not interact with the media or make public the details of commercial dispute case, being mediated by him or any other allied activity carried out by him as a Mediator, which may prejudice the interests of the parties to the commercial dispute.

SCHEDULE I

FORM 1

Mediation Application Form

[*See* rule 3(1)]

Name of the Authority and address

DETAILS OF THE PARTIES:

1. Name of applicant:
2. Address and contact details of applicant:
   Address: —
   Telephone No. .... Mobile .... E-mail ID: ....
3. Name of opposite party:
4. Address and contact details of opposite party:
   Address: —
   Telephone No. .... Mobile .... E-mail ID: ....

DETAILS OF THE DISPUTE:

1. Nature of dispute as per section 2(1)*(c)* of the Commercial Courts Act 2015 (4 of 2016):
2. Quantum of claim:
3. Territorial jurisdiction of the competent Court:
4. Brief synopsis of commercial dispute (not to exceed 5000 words):
5. Additional points of relevance:

DETAILS OF FEE PAID:

Fee paid by DD No. .... dated .... Name of Bank and branch ....

Online transaction No. .... dated ....

Date: Name and Signature of Applicant

Note.—Form shall be submitted to the Authority with a fee of one thousand rupees.

FOR OFFICE USE
Form received on:
File No. allotted:
Mode of sending notice to the opposite party:
Notice to opposite party sent on:
Whether Notice acknowledged by opposite party or not:
Date of Non-starter report/Assignment of commercial dispute to Mediator:

Form 2

Notice/Final Notice to the Opposite Party for Pre-Institution Mediation

[*See* rule 3(2) and rule 3(3)]

Name of the Authority and address

1. Whereas a commercial dispute has been submitted to *(name of Authority)* by *(name of applicant)* against *(name of opposite party)* requesting for pre-institution mediation in terms of section 12-A of Chapter III-A of Commercial Courts Act, 2015. A copy of the mediation application Form is attached herewith.

2. The opposite party is hereby directed to appear in person or through his duly authorised representative or Counsel on .... (Date) .... (Time) at the *(Authority address)* and convey his consent to participate in mediation process.

3. Failure to appear before the Authority by opposite party would be deemed as his refusal to participate in mediation process initiated by the applicant.

4. In case, the date and time mentioned in para 2 is sought to be rescheduled the same can be done by the opposite party either on its own or through its authorised representative or counsel by making a request in writing at-least two days prior to the scheduled date of appearance.

Date: Signature of the Authority

Form 3

Non-Starter Report

[*See* rule 3(4) and (6)]

Name of the Authority and address

1. Name of the applicant:
2. Date of application for Pre-Institution mediation:
3. Name of the opposite party:
4. Date scheduled for appearance of opposite party:
5. Report made under rule 3(4) or 3(6):
6. Non-Starter Report reason: ....
   ....
   ....

Signature of the Authority

Date:

Copy to:

Applicant.

Opposite Party.

FORM 4

Settlement

[*See* rule 7(1)(*vii*)]

Name of the Authority and address

1. Name of the Mediator:
2. Name of the applicant:
3. Name of the opposite party:
4. Date of application for Pre-Institution mediation:
5. Venue of mediation:
6. Date(s) of mediation:
7. No. of sittings and duration of sittings:
8. Terms of settlement:

Date:

Signature of Applicant Signature of Opposite Party

Signature of Mediator

FORM 5

Failure Report

[*See* rule 7(1)(*ix*)]

Name of the Authority and address

1. Name of the Mediator:
2. Name of the applicant:
3. Name of the opposite party:
4. Date of application for Pre-Institution mediation:
5. Venue of mediation:
6. Date(s) of mediation:
7. No. of sittings and duration of sittings:
8. Reasons for failure:

Date:

Signature of Applicant Signature of Opposite Party

Signature of Mediator

FORM 6

Mediation Data

[*See* rule 10(2)]

Sl. No.	Name of the Authority	No. of application received by Authority	Nature of Applicant Party		Nature of Opposite Party		No. of applications slabwise as per Schedule II					No. of application disposed off as per Rule 3(4) and 3(6)	No. of application referred for mediation	No. of application where no settlement arrived at as per Rule 7(1)(*ix*)	No. of application where parties reached a settlement as per Rule 7(1)(*vii*)
			Individual	Corporate	Individual	Corporate	I	II	III	IV	V				

*SCHEDULE II

Mediation Fee

[*See* rule 11]

Sl. No.	Quantum of Claim	Mediation Fee Payable to Authority (in Indian rupees)
1.	From Rs. 3,00,000 to Rs.10,00,000	Rs. 15,000
2.	Above Rs. 10,00,000 and upto Rs. 50,00,000	Rs. 30,000
3.	Above Rs. 50,00,000 and upto Rs. 1,00,00,000	Rs. 40,000
4.	Above from Rs. 1,00,00,000 and upto Rs. 3,00,00,000	Rs. 50,000
5.	Above Rs. 3,00,00,000	Rs. 75,000

* Corrigendum by G.S.R. 880(E), dated 14-9-2018.

Index